Stefan C. Reif

Jews, Bible and Prayer

Beihefte zur Zeitschrift für die alttestamentliche Wissenschaft

Edited by
John Barton, Reinhard G. Kratz, Nathan MacDonald,
Carol A. Newsom and Markus Witte

Volume 498

Stefan C. Reif

Jews, Bible and Prayer

Essays on Jewish Biblical Exegesis and Liturgical Notions

DE GRUYTER

ISBN 978-3-11-063676-5
e-ISBN (PDF) 978-3-11-048670-4
e-ISBN (EPUB) 978-3-11-048585-1
ISSN 0934-2575

Library of Congress Cataloging-in-Publication Data
A CIP catalog record for this book has been applied for at the Library of Congress.

Bibliographic information published by the Deutsche Nationalbibliothek
The Deutsche Nationalbibliothek lists this publication in the Deutsche Nationalbibliografie; detailed bibliographic data are available on the Internet at http://dnb.dnb.de.

This volume is text- and page-identical with the hardback published in 2017.
Printing and binding: CPI books GmbH, Leck

♾ Printed on acid-free paper
Printed in Germany

www.degruyter.com

For Renate
...she and I both know why

Contents

Introduction —— 1

1 The Damascus Document from the Cairo Genizah: Its Discovery, Early Study and Historical Significance —— 10

2 Aspects of the Jewish Contribution to Biblical Interpretation —— 34

3 Early Rabbinic Exegesis of Genesis 38 —— 50

4 The Classical Jewish Commentators on Exodus 2 —— 73

5 Medieval Jewish Commentators on Numbers 13 —— 108

6 Psalm 93: An Historical and Comparative Survey of its Jewish Interpretations —— 144

7 Some Comments on the Connotations of the Stem גער in Early Rabbinic Texts —— 165

8 On some Connotations of the Word *Ma'aseh* —— 180

9 How did Early Judaism Understand the Concept of *'Avodah?* —— 196

10 Wisdom Traditions in Some Early Rabbinic Prayers? —— 210

11 The Figure of David in Early Jewish Prayer —— 231

12 The Function of History in Early Rabbinic Liturgy —— 260

13 Peace in Early Jewish Prayer —— 278

14 The *'Amidah* Benediction on Forgiveness: Links between its Theology and its Textual Evolution —— 297

15 The Fathership of God in Early Rabbinic Liturgy —— 314

16 Some Divine Metaphors in Early Rabbinic Liturgy —— 334

Introduction

In the course of the past two decades, most of the articles that I have contributed to anthologies, to conference proceedings and to *Festschriften* have centred on the themes of the Cairo Genizah, the rabbinic exegesis of the Hebrew Bible, and the development of Jewish liturgy. It is in the nature of such contributions that they are rarely provided with the opportunity of being compared with each other, or of attracting the attention of readers who are neither contributors nor honorands. As a consequence, the scholarly suppositions that underlie their composition, and the conclusions that derive from the analysis of the sources that they contain, are often neither carefully assessed nor evaluated more broadly. Such assessment and evaluation might raise new issues, tackle old ones in a fresh way, and even stimulate specialists and readers with wider interests to examine topics not previously part of their intellectual agenda.

I therefore warmly welcome the kind invitation extended to me by the editors of the *Beihefte zur Zeitschrift für die alttestamentliche Wissenschaft* (*BZAW*), and their publishers, Walter de Gruyter, to compile a volume containing a selection of my recent articles, as well as one lengthy new one. It not only allows me to make some minor revisions and updates in these items but also to offer some introductory remarks about my motivations and conclusions. Bringing them together and prefacing them in this way may help to ensure that they are rescued from what otherwise might become a dusty fate on the dark and rarely consulted shelves of a few distinguished research libraries. Given current trends in some circles towards reducing, moving or even abandoning hard copies of these kinds of publications, such a fate might not be the worst prospect to be faced by scholarly materials of this sort. Let me therefore suggest why I believe that the essays included here may repay a close read on the part of specialists, as well as those with a more general interest in these topics.

I commence with the more personal and less clinical of my concerns. Whether or not this is indicative of the aging process, I have in recent years extended my enthusiasm for the study of medieval manuscripts, commentaries and liturgies to include a more intense appreciation of those personalities who have preceded me in such recondite pursuits. It has often proved intriguing – at least to me – to uncover the motivations for their involvement in specific aspects of research, the manner in which they undertook their projects, and the nature of the relationships that they enjoyed (if that is the correct word) with their colleagues and competitors. For the purist proponents of the *Wissenschaft des Judentums*, some of whom were among my most inspiring teachers, such a preoccupation with the purveyors of scholarship, rather than, or even in addition to, the

DOI 10.1515/9783110486704-001

scientific materials that they delivered, was nothing short of anathema. They held strongly to the view that their findings were to be judged on academic merit alone, without reference to the background, education and personal traits of those presenting them.

Perhaps it was the human story, or collections of human stories, that lay behind the discovery, exploitation and publication of the literary and documentary treasures from the Cairo Genizah, that set me on this path. Be that as it may, I found myself progressively less able to deal with detailed aspects of research topics without relating, at least in some degree, to the individuals who had, in one way or another, undertaken the pioneering work that had inspired their emergence. I tried to trace the efforts of such individuals in my studies of the Cambridge Genizah Collections, as well as in articles concerning the early examination of such items as the Ben Sira fragments and the Damascus Document. Readers of the current volume will find that I commence the first chapter with a quotation from the late and lamented doyen of Jewish historians, Jacob Katz, as to how he viewed such personalization of higher learning. Despite his horror at what he termed such a 'chutzpa', I proceeded to examine how Schechter and his contemporaries dealt with one of the most exciting Genizah finds of their day and with the contentious relationships that existed between those who were involved – or were denied involvement – in its description and analysis.

There are also some personal elements in the next seven essays presented here. These latter deal primarily with the Jewish interpretation of the Hebrew Bible in a broad *überblick*; offer examples of such exegesis as it occurs in the case of four specific biblical chapters; and finally examine the wide-ranging and evolving senses of three Biblical Hebrew expressions. I shall shortly have more to say about the approach that characterizes these essays. Meanwhile, it seems appropriate to point out why I have not omitted here the remarks I originally made in some of them about the individuals in whose honour the contributions were originally made.

Demonstrating again my recent interest in the role of human stories within the larger scholarly context, I have prefaced essays written in the *Festschriften* offered to the late Shelomo Morag and John Emerton, and in honour of my contemporaries, Andrew Macintosh and Robert Gordon, by recalling at least some of the ways in which we connected during our lengthy academic careers. Such reminiscences are often included in the original oral presentation of a paper but omitted at the published stage. I think this is a pity, since they may well then be lost forever. When, many decades from now, what we have written on a scholarly topic might have been superseded by more fashionable and alternatively researched work, it is possible that what we have had to say about fellow scholars may remain of value. In the case of what I have had to say about my colleagues, it is perhaps not immodest to hope that it will be relevant for those historians who ultimately come to write the history (*Wissenschaftsgeschichte*) of Hebrew and Jewish scholarship at the University of Cambridge in the second half of the twentieth century and in the first two decades of the twenty-first.

What then were the motivations for my essays on the Jewish interpretation of some chapters of the Hebrew Bible? It seemed to me that the nineteenth-century study of the Hebrew Bible had been dominated by some distinguished Christian scholars who had made an outstanding contribution to the field but had often suffered from two shortcomings. Firstly, they seemed unaware of the theological *tendenz* that sometimes affected (or infected?) their analysis and conclusions. It is perhaps inevitable that religious commitments should have an impact on one's work on sacred texts but a genuine scholar is surely duty-bound to be aware of these and to make a maximum effort to minimize them. Such an effort was lacking on the part of a number of Christian hebraists who made a mark on the subject but also therefore left an imprint of their religious bias. Secondly, there was in that classical period of biblical criticism a hesitation about the use of rabbinic sources for the clarification of biblical topics. There were perhaps a number of reasons for this. They may well have lacked the competence to deal with such sources or lacked sympathy for their contents. In addition, they often subscribed to the notion that valuable culture was to be found in the Greek and Roman worlds, and then again after the Renaissance and Reformation. The period between was that of the 'dark ages' and anything medieval came to be regarded as outdated, irrelevant, even primitive. I should add that the Christian scholars who adopted such an approach were sometimes no more enthusiastic about pre-modern Christian scholasticism than they were about its Islamic and Jewish counterparts. It has to be acknowledged that there were Christian scholars such as S. R. Driver who were innocent of such trends but there is no doubt that 'Old Testament' studies of the twentieth and twenty-first centuries did not wholly free themselves from the shortcomings just described.

It therefore seemed to me to be a valuable exercise to look closely at a number of chapters in the Hebrew Bible and to summarize what the talmudic-midrashic literature has to say about them, and how they were interpreted by the classical Jewish commentators of Franco-Germany, Spain, Provence and Italy in the Middle Ages. I was not arguing that such pre-modern sources somehow anticipated modern critical theory, but rather suggesting that the same questions were being asked and that the linguistic and exegetical responses were at times not greatly at variance with each other. Once this is acknowledged, the door is open to a greater appreciation of such rabbinic material for the current exegesis of the Hebrew Bible. With this in mind, I have not shirked from comparing modern exegetes with their medieval counterparts. There are instances in which this can be of no more than historical interest but in other cases I feel that a genuine contribution may thereby be made to the better understanding of scripture, generally in the spheres of literary appreciation and theology, but more especially in the areas of Hebrew language and grammar.

It is indeed philology that has a central role in my three essays dealing with גער, מעשה and עבודה (*ga'ar*, *ma'aseh* and *'avodah*). In dealing with the occurrences of such terms in the Hebrew Bible, I developed the impression that the evidence of the Second Temple period, the age of the early Rabbis and emergent Christianity, and the world of the medieval Jewish exegetes and linguists should be taken into account. My assumption was that this would not only help to appreciate the sense of the biblical words but also lead to a better understanding of their linguistic evolution over the centuries. Hebrew may have ceased as a serious vernacular in the third or fourth century but, contrary to popular reports, it did not die. It continued as a vibrant and dynamic literary medium in the talmudic and medieval periods and took on the new challenges involved in the emergence of Jewish philosophy, theology, exegesis, liturgy, poetry and lexicography, as well as in the growing use of personal correspondence. If the sense attributed to a word or phrase by the standard modern dictionaries seems not to include a nuance that appears possible to the attentive reader of a text, it is often productive to refer back to earlier Jewish sources and to examine closely the manner in which they used the Hebrew being assessed. The consultation of such sources should not be limited to the comments of biblical commentators and philologists but may also extend into such genres as midrash and *piyyuṭ*. The intensive and wide-ranging use of the Hebrew language that was common to the authors of both such genres is a rich source of nuances and linguistic insights. This may have been missed by the lexicographers who were basing themselves on what may be defined as the more standard literature of the Hebrew Bible and the Mishnah. Insufficient account may also have been taken of them by the translators for whom it was more convenient to use the same rendering in different contexts than to dig deeper into the soil surrounding Hebrew roots and identify surprising sets of offshoots.

Nor should it be forgotten that the close study of the Hebrew used in personal letters found in the Cairo Genizah is still in its scientific infancy and will no doubt reveal to us many previously unidentified linguistic usages that will sometimes prove to be coinages but on other occasions testify to a long-term evolution of meaning. Going back into the Second Temple period, a comparison of the Hebrew of the Bible with the Greek of the Septuagint is also likely to shed light on linguistic understanding and development and how they relate to Jewish religious ideology. Now that we have so many Hebrew texts from the Dead Sea

Scrolls, we may also check the use of a Hebrew stem in that rich cache of documents and ascertain how it relates to its earlier and later equivalents. A good example to back up such a claim is to be found in the case of the word *'avodah* where the evidence is not only of linguistic significance but is also important for our understanding of Jewish liturgical history. The texts discussed appear to testify to the manner in which the *weltanschauung* of the Jews of the homeland – whether of Jerusalem or of Qumran – did not necessarily match that of their coreligionists in the Jewish diaspora.

This brings us to the liturgical studies contained in the remaining part of this volume. I have long felt, and indeed argued, that the scientific analysis of Jewish liturgy may bring the scholar rewards that go far beyond the discovery of which community adopted whose rite, and why and when this took place. The prayerbook is a work that prefers not to reveal clearly its historical evolution but to present itself as a quasi-canonical *fait accompli.* It is the task of the researcher to uncover what is being subtly adopted, or adapted, within the inner dynamic of these collections of prayers, as well as to contemplate matters that are not only exclusively liturgical but also relate to broader realms. Such realms may include language and literature, theology, mysticism, eschatology, the use of biblical lectionaries, intellectual as well as social and political history, and the ordering of society, in addition to a variety of responses to the non-Jewish world. Of course, not every liturgical text has something to tell us about each of these areas but it may confidently be stated that such areas are jointly and severally enriched by the fertile materials derived from the field of rabbinic worship.

I believe that this assessment is exemplified by the seven essays dealing with liturgical topics that constitute the second half of this collection. What emerges from these studies is that the composers of early rabbinic liturgy may in some respects be seen as transmitters of elements of the wisdom traditions of the ancient near east. They saw Torah as a great deal more than an intellectual exercise but they chose to include within its liturgical manifestations considerations of, and speculations on, educational, cosmological and eschatological themes. In this respect, they were not unlike other sets of thinkers in the Classical world around them. It would, however, be erroneous to suggest that they had a similarly Greek or Roman notion of history. The early rabbis avoided any sort of genuine historical content or allusion when creating their liturgical compositions and it was not until the post-talmudic period, inspired perhaps by the Jewish scholars of the Holy Land, that the writers of prayers began to increase the number and significance of historical elements to be included within their approved liturgy.

The treatment of the figure of David is a useful yardstick against which to measure the manner in which rabbinic liturgy inherited biblical subjects and subjected them over the centuries to a variety of adjustments in the light of their contemporary ways of thinking. While the figure of David is in no way central to the earliest forms of rabbinic liturgy, that situation changes in the post-talmudic period when the expanded use of Psalms in the prayers gives the rabbis the opportunity of including blessings, in connection with the recitation of such Psalms, that make acknowledgement to David as their composer. The liturgy also come to associate him more closely with spiritual and political redemption, while also idealizing him as a true penitent, and there are texts that take on board the historical figure much more noticeably than heretofore. The late medieval and early modern periods accord him an increased mystical and cosmological role.

The themes of peace (*shalom*) and of forgiveness (*seliḥah*), particularly as they are included in the *'amidah*, also provide evidence of broadening treatments within the prayers. In the case of the former, the basic sense that occurs in the Hebrew Bible is that of a comfortable and ideal existence, one that is free from troubles of various sorts. The context is a worldly one but the later books of the Hebrew Bible demonstrate a growing concern with the cosmic and celestial aspects of such a peace. The early rabbis extend the concept to apply to the family, the community and the world, seeing ethical behaviour and a correct ordering of society as essential elements in the achievement of *shalom*. The cosmic and celestial aspects are applied to angels, to creation and to God's relations with the Jewish people. Although the rabbinic prayers reflect these nuances, and retain the original biblical concept of total well-being with safety and security, there are texts that imply more than a rescue from worldly tribulations. They appear to make entreaty for an idealized relationship between God and his people, his heavenly retinue and his world, as well as between the heaven and earth, thus reflecting what might be regarded as more purely spiritual notions. It should also be noted that the *shalom* benediction of the *'amidah* incorporated the priestly benediction and all that is understood and promised within that text.

With regard to the achievement of divine forgiveness, the matter has remained a complex theological one for Jews from the biblical until the modern period, and this situation is reflected in the rabbinic liturgy. The issue revolves around the damage done by sinfulness and the manner of, as it were, wiping the slate clean; the expectation that spiritual crime should not pay and that repentance is required; and the concern that a merciful God should not be taken for granted but should be entreated to activate his propensity towards the granting of pardon. Interestingly, while evidence of such complexity is to be found in the Jewish theologies of the Hebrew Bible, the Second Temple period and the talmudic rabbis, the earliest version of the forgiveness prayer in the *'amidah* is no more than a simple request that God, who has the power to do so, should pardon our sins. The textual variations, the commentaries of the medieval era, and the development of a whole genre of specific litanies acknowledging wrongdoing and requesting forgiveness, again testify to the Jewish worshippers' awareness of what is religiously at stake here. It should also, however, be admitted that some liturgical commentators of the modern period seem more concerned with the grammar and the language than with the theological content. That said, I have tried to demonstrate that there was also an alternative, and religiously broader, approach, especially in the context of nineteenth-century German Orthodoxy.

It is often claimed that the Paternoster of Christianity, as attributed to Jesus and reported in two of the Gospels, is the kind of prayer that would have been familiar to the Jews of the first century and that addressing God as 'our Father who is in heaven' was already an established liturgical phrase within Jewish communities of the period. Although God is undoubtedly a 'father figure' in the Hebrew Bible and the Second Temple period, a close examination of the relevant sources raises a number of intriguing questions about which circles among the Jews and Jewish Christians chose directly to address him as such in their prayers, and when such a development took place. There was some ambivalence among the talmudic rabbis about whether prayer should be to the paternal God or to the royal one, and a novel solution was proposed and widely adopted. The matter was further complicated when the Jewish communities of the Islamic world were formulating their prayers. The abhorrence felt by the Muslims for what they saw as the anthropomorphic nature of addressing God as one's father may even have had an impact on the manner in which some Jews expressed themselves liturgically.

The final essay in this volume deals more broadly with the issue of metaphors for God in early rabbinic liturgy. The midrashim and the *piyyuṭim* (liturgical poems), taking their cue from some biblical texts, employ a welter of terms to refer to the divine object of their prayers and seem unembarrassed about describing God is what are effectively human terms. The Jewish philosophers of the Middle Ages, led magisterially by Moses Maimonides, were theoretically appalled by this tendency and would, if only they could, have opted for silence, or for terminology of a purer, theological nature. Alas, even they admitted the reality that simple worshippers can rarely achieve such a Jewish nirvana and have to be permitted to use language that relates more closely to how they actually feel in their hearts rather than what they should ideally think in their minds. Compromises therefore had to be made. The formulation of the statutory prayers was undoubtedly influenced by the colourful language of the poets and the aggadists but was at the same time subject to more theological control. As is the nature of such developments, some metaphors were incorporated, and others removed, by the watchful halakhic authorities. The essays offered here focus more on the earlier periods of rabbinic prayer but it should not go unstated that many kabbalists ultimately went their own way and opted for a highly personalized relationship between God and the people approaching him in prayer.

With the exception of chapter 5, which appears here for the first time, earlier versions of the essays were published in various volumes and I am deeply grateful to the publishers for kindly granting their permission for them to be included in this volume. I am also grateful to the Herbert D. Katz Center for Advanced Jewish Studies at the University of Pennsylvania, Philadelphia, USA, where I was a visiting fellow in 2001–2, and where I prepared the first version of the essay that is here included as chapter 5. The bibliographical details are as follows, with the first number indicating the chapter in which it here appears, followed by the title and other data relating to the original volume:

1. *The Damascus Document: A Centennial of Discovery*, eds. J. M. Baumgarten, E. Chazon and A. Pinnick (Leiden: Brill, 2000), pp. 109–31;
2. *Cambridge Companion to Biblical Interpretation*, ed. J. Barton (Cambridge: Cambridge University Press, 1998), pp. 143–59;
3. *The Exegetical Encounter between Christians and Jews in Late Antiquity*, eds. E. Grypeou and H. Spurling (Leiden: Brill, 2009), pp. 221–44;
4. *Studies in Hebrew and Jewish Languages presented to Shelomo Morag*, ed. M. Bar-Asher (Jerusalem: Bialik Institute and Center for Jewish Languages and Literatures, Hebrew University of Jerusalem, 1996), pp. *73-*112;
5. New chapter
6. *Genesis, Isaiah and Psalms: A Festschrift to Honour Professor John Emerton for his Eightieth Birthday*, eds. K. Dell, G. Davies and Y. V. Koh (Leiden, Brill, 2010), pp. 193–214;
7. *Leshon Limmudim. Essays on the Language and Literature of the Hebrew Bible in Honour of A. A. Macintosh*, eds. D. A. Baer and R. P. Gordon (London: Bloomsbury T&T Clark, an imprint of Bloomsbury Publishing Plc, 2013), pp. 253–67;
8. *Studies on the Text and Versions of the Hebrew Bible in Honour of Robert Gordon*, eds. G. Khan and D. Lipton (Leiden: Brill, 2012), pp. 337–51;
9. *Deuterocanonical and Cognate Literature, Yearbook 2015–16: Various Aspects of Worship in Deuterocanonical and Cognate Literature*, eds. I. Balla, G. Xeravits and J. Zsengellér (Berlin: de Gruyter, 2017), pp. 1–15;
10. *Wisdom for Life: Festschrift for Friedrich V. Reiterer*, eds. R. Egger-Wenzel, K. Schöpflin and J. F. Diehl (Berlin: de Gruyter, 2013), pp. 223–45;
11. *Deuterocanonical and Cognate Literature, Yearbook 2008: Biblical Figures in Deuterocanonical and Cognate Literature*, eds. H. Lichtenberger and U. Mittmann-Richert (Berlin: de Gruyter, 2009), pp. 509–46;

12. *Deuterocanonical and Cognate Literature, Yearbook 2005: How Israel's Later Authors Viewed Its Earlier History*, eds. N. Calduch-Benages and J. Liesen (Berlin: de Gruyter, 2006), pp. 321–39;
13. *Deuterocanonical and Cognate Literature, Yearbook 2010: Visions of Peace and Tales of War in Deuterocanonical and Cognate Literature*, eds. J. Liesen and P. C. Beentjes (Berlin: de Gruyter, 2010), pp. 377–99;
14. *Seeking the Favor of God: Volume 3: The Impact of Penitential Prayer beyond Second Temple Judaism*, eds. M. J. Boda, D. K. Falk and R. A. Werline (Atlanta: Scholars Press, 2008), pp. 85–98;
15. *Deuterocanonical and Cognate Literature, Yearbook 2012/13. Family and Kinship in the Deuterocanonical and Cognate Literature*, ed. A. Passaro (Berlin: de Gruyter, 2013), pp. 505–25;
16. *Deuterocanonical and Cognate Literature, Yearbook 2014/2015: The Metaphorical Use of Language in Deuterocanonical and Cognate Literature*, eds. M. Witte and S. Behnke (Berlin: de Gruyter, 2015), pp. 487–507.

In bringing all these studies together, I have tried to create a reasonably coherent whole and to avoid too many inconsistencies and repetitions. There are instances, however, where it seemed more sensible neither to attempt to fit one chapter into the straitjacket of some of the others nor to omit relevant material because it occurs in another context within the volume. Each essay therefore retains some of the conventions that were employed in its original context. I had originally planned to create one list of publications cited and to place this at the end but it proved to be somewhat unwieldy and I decided that it would be more comfortable for readers if they could find the sources cited in abbreviated form within the footnotes of a particular chapter immediately at the end of that chapter itself. This has inevitably meant repetitions of the same bibliographical details in a number of the lists of works cited, for which I crave the reader's indulgence. It remains for me only to thank, once again, the editors and publishers for their important part in the creation of this volume, and those numerous institutions and individuals who assisted my research in various ways and whose kindness I have acknowledged in the relevant footnotes within the studies that follow. I should add how grateful I always am to St John's College, in the University of Cambridge, not only for electing me to a Fellowship almost twenty years ago but also for the many generous facilities it has afforded me since then. These privileges have, to no small degree, made it possible for me to continue to be a productive scholar into my retirement years.

Cambridge, UK/Bet Shemesh, Israel; December, 2016 — Stefan C. Reif

1 The Damascus Document from the Cairo Genizah: Its Discovery, Early Study and Historical Significance

What is history?

'Such a view', declares one of the doyens of modern Jewish historiography, 'effectively negates any question of objectivity from even the most capable of historians. [It is] a view I cannot but regard as cynical, if not downright impudent, or, to use the more vigorous Yiddish expression, a *chuzpa*.' This is how Jacob Katz responds to the critical advice of one scholar who suggests that, before examining any historical work, one should take a good look at the life, times and outlook of the writer. Such an examination, according to that scholar, will constitute a better guide to the work than the academic theories of the writer himself. At the same time, however, Katz unequivocally acknowledges the importance of the debate about whether any historian is capable of adopting a totally impersonal position with regard to the events of the past. Indeed, having noted the impudence of the extreme version of such a scholarly scepticism, he backtracks more than somewhat and states his own belief that an acquaintance with the life of a writer will assist the reader in assessing the degree to which that writer's views may be regarded as objective. Since, in his opinion, historians would never claim absolute detachment for any of their statements or judgements, they are aware that their personal stories will interest those who are acquainted with their publications. In this way, Katz justifies his decision to compose his own autobiography.[1]

A few more words require to be said about the importance of personal and even ephemeral data in the study of scholarly views and theories, and about the differences in this connection between nineteenth- and twentieth-century methods of historical research. Until well into the past century, it was believed, in common with the Victorian teachers, that the true student of the past was capable of standing outside his own chronology and locality and could, by an enthusiastic and judicious marshalling of progressively more intricate data from chosen sources, replace the folktales of tradition with the scientific analysis of the present, producing a picture of the past precisely as it was. In the amusing and perceptive words of E. H. Carr, 'three generations of German, British and

1 Katz, *My Own Eyes*, p. x. These introductory remarks do not appear in the original Hebrew edition.

DOI 10.1515/9783110486704-002

even French historians marched into battle intoning the magic words '*wie es eigentlich gewesen ist*' ['as it really happened'] like an incantation – designed, like most incantations, to save them from the tiresome obligation to think for themselves.' More recent historians are no less committed to the pursuit of reliable information and fresh sources; but they recognize that neither the historian nor his source can ever be regarded as dispassionate and that academic history is a matter of placing everyone and everything in their contexts and interpreting their significance accordingly and with as little subjectivity as one can manage.[2]

Current scholars are more at home with the humanity of history than with its grander sweeps. Testimonies to the petty incident, details of the underprivileged group and remnants of the unconventional text are given a status once denied them and there is an almost voyeuristic obsession with individuals, their lives and their motivations. Today's intense interest in both the most obscure contents of the Genizah Collection itself and in the people associated over the years with its discovery and exploitation is to a considerable degree due to such changes in scholarly outlook. What Schechter and his colleagues set aside in their day as unimportant attracts fresh attention today, whether it is economic data, printed matter or magical charms. *Wissenschaftsgeschichte* ('the history of scholarship') is now a flourishing science and it is widely felt that enthusiasm for an academic subject must also entail a fascination with those who have promoted it. Here too, it has become as important to know about the personal involvement as it is to be *au fait* with the technical data.[3]

Ben Sira case

I recently applied this approach, I believe with some success, to a close study of Schechter's involvement with the textual history of the book of Ben Sira. An examination of his earlier scholarly work and the way it related to that of his colleagues in Oxford revealed theological as well as historical and literary reasons for his deep interest in finding an authentic Hebrew version of the work. These undercurrents explained the almost paroxysmal excitement generated in him in

---

2 Some of the relevant issues are touched on in the entry 'History' in *NEB*, pp. 572–74, and much of the debate was fired by the controversial study of the subject by E. H. Carr, *What is History?*; the German quotation is from p. 3.

3 Such an interest in mundane details and in personalities is exemplified in two exhibitions that were mounted at the Israel Museum, Jerusalem, and at Cambridge University Library, to mark the centenary of Solomon Schechter's famous and successful visit to Cairo early in 1897; see the exhibition catalogues *The Cairo Genizah* and *History in Fragments*.

May, 1896, when he identified a manuscript folio brought to him by Mrs Agnes Lewis and Mrs Margaret Gibson as a tenth-century fragment of just such a version.[4] When later, as a widow, Mrs Mathilde Schechter reminisced about the years that she had spent with her husband in Cambridge, she recalled how very keen he had been to locate the original Hebrew of Ben Sira. 'The subject interested him very much', she wrote, 'and occupied his mind intensely, for the great savant who lived 200...years before Christ had been the subject of argument among biblical critics and Christian theologians throughout the century.' After he had made his identification of the Lewis-Gibson fragment, Dr Schechter, would, according to his wife's testimony, often say 'If only I had leave of absence and sufficient money, I would go in search of that lost Hebrew original.'[5]

In my article, I pointed out that Schechter's trip to Cairo was privately financed by Charles Taylor, the Master of St John's College, and not institutionally by the University of Cambridge, for fear that any formal announcement would lead to alternative bids to uncover the manuscript source. This, in Mathilde Schechter's frankly expressed statement, 'would have brought Oxford University and probably other places into competition, and might have spoiled any chance of Dr Schechter's success.' She also cited her husband's conviction that 'if the original Hebrew of Jesus Ben Sira was in existence, it could be found only in the Genizah of old Cairo, as Sa'adya Gaon, the last person to quote Jesus Ben Sira, hailed from Cairo, and his manuscripts would naturally be hidden there, as it was the old Jewish custom never to destroy but to hide or bury Hebrew writings, mostly in synagogues.' According to my analysis, the subsequent jockeying for scholarly prominence in the subject was the inspiration for many discoveries and publications and it was not difficult to identify the human motivations, some more honourable than others, that lay behind the academic enterprises.[6]

Searching for a background

When kindly invited by the organisers of an Orion symposium held in Jerusalem in 1998 to make a novel contribution to the current discussions about the Damascus Document (=CD), particularly in connection with Schechter's discovery of the Genizah manuscripts, it occurred to me that it could be interesting for me, as

4 Reif, 'Discovery'.

5 These and the following quotations from Mrs Schechter are to be found in her memoirs, located in the Schechter Papers at the Library of the Jewish Theological Seminary of America in New York. I am grateful to the Library for permission to use and cite this and similar material.

6 Reif, 'Discovery', pp. 3–11.

well as for my listeners and, ultimately, my readers, if I could subject this topic to an analysis that was in essence similar to that earlier undertaken in the case of the Ben Sira Genizah fragments.[7] One could then once again uncover the personal feelings and controversies that inspired the discovery, locate earlier treatments of the subject, and place Schechter's work in the context of earlier historical research. Alas, as the Scots poet, Robert Burns, wisely concluded, no doubt at the end of an especially abortive effort at one literary composition or another, 'the best-laid schemes o' mice an' men gang aft a-gley [=often go awry].'[8] Had he been born in Galicia rather than Ayrshire, he would no doubt have expressed it in Yiddish as 'a mensch tracht und Gott lacht.' None of Schechter's pre-Genizah publications reveals any particular interest in Jewish sectarian literature. He was not at the time of his discovery of CD engaged in any controversy about the existence of Hebrew literature that appeared to originate in non-rabbinic circles. There was no reason – at least none that I could identify – why he might have a burning ambition to locate the theological and exegetical ideas of a previously unknown sect. In sum, I was unable to place the discovery of the CD Document in the kind of human context that I had successfully found for the explosion of Ben Sira research at the same period.

But today's scholars also have motivations for their studies. If one is scheduled to give a paper at a conference, a topic has to be developed. If one's expenses are to be paid, they have to be justified by the treatment of a fresh theme. If a *curriculum vitae* is to be updated for a research assessment exercise, it had better include some additional items. The questions might have to be different for CD than they were for Ben Sira but a closer look at personal and institutional archives, at the interpretations offered by Schechter and his supporters and critics, and at the results of broader studies relating to the scholarly interaction with Genizah materials, would undoubtedly produce some worthwhile findings. When did Schechter discover the manuscripts of CD and why did it take him so long to publish them? Was there any development in his theories about CD and, if so, under whose influence? Are there any obviously personal elements in the scholarly controversies? Does current research about the earliest Genizah discoveries contribute anything to the discussions about CD? How do Schechter's views, and those of his contemporaries, compare with post-Qumranic interpretations? A fresh treatment of these questions will make it possible to assess the degree to which George Margoliouth of the British Museum is justified when he

7 I welcome the opportunity of recording my gratitude to Professor Michael Stone and Dr Esther Chazon for organizing the symposium and for their kind invitation to me to participate in it.
8 The line occurs in his poem *To a Mouse*, the first line of which reads: 'Wee, sleeket, cowrin, timrous beastie'.

claims in 1910 that Schechter 'has added glory to his name by bringing to light a document which will, in the opinion of many, take an even higher rank than the Hebrew text of Ecclesiasticus, which owes its identification to the same ingenious and practised scholar.'[9]

Gradual revelations

Although Schechter published CD in the first volume of his *Documents of Jewish Sectaries* that made its appearance in Cambridge in 1910, he obviously discovered and identified it many years earlier.[10] When he left Cambridge for New York in 1902, he arranged to borrow both manuscripts of CD and he had obviously therefore made his exciting find during the years of his intensive Genizah research in Cambridge. The personal excitement and the human progress of these five years, from 1897, when he returned from Cairo with his famous 'hoard of Hebrew manuscripts', until 1902, when he sailed for the United States to take over the leadership of the Jewish Theological Seminary, are well documented in his archives and those of his academic colleagues, as well as in more formal University documents. The team of enthusiastic specialists that Schechter gathered around him are seen to be busy making all manner of discoveries and sharing the details of these with each other. A picture emerges of industrious activity relating to the study, transcription, conservation and publication of the fragments presented by Schechter and Taylor, and to the possible purchase and acquisition of other Genizah material. Scholarly and popular articles appear in considerable number and there are times when Schechter makes a positive nuisance of himself by bombarding his colleagues with information about his latest revelations.[11]

Given such a situation, it is more than a little surprising that his first encounters with CD are not trumpeted from the ramparts of the records. Not only is there no major publicity about his revelations; there seems to be a positive reticence about reporting and explaining them, and it is only with some difficulty that one can ascertain when they occurred. The first hint that he had identified such items is offered in an article that he published in *The Jewish Chronicle* of London on 1 April, 1898. Continuing the general report on the Genizah Collection's broad contents that he had commenced in *The Times* of London on 3 Au-

9 Margoliouth, 'Sadducean Christians', p. 659.

10 Schechter, *Documents*. The classmarks of the two CD manuscripts at Cambridge University Library are T-S 10K6 and T-S 16.311.

11 Details are given in Reif, 'Jenkinson'. See also the first paragraph of the article 'Facts and fictions'.

gust, 1897, he promises the historian a wealth of new material relating to forgotten groups and their religious writings:

> And what raptures of delight are there in store for the student when sifting and reducing to order the historical documents which the Genizah has furnished in abundance, *including even the remains of the sacred writings of strange Jewish sects that have long since vanished* [emphasis mine – SCR]. Considerations of space, however, forbid me to enter into detailed descriptions; these would require a whole series of essays.[12]

Clearly Schechter is aware that has uncovered texts that are of major significance for Jewish sectarian history but he is loath to describe them in detail. Nor is any mention made of them either in the report prepared by the University Library's Cairo Subsyndicate in 1899 or, perhaps even more strangely, in the summary of the Collection drawn up in 1900 by Herman Leonard Pass, the young convert from Judaism to Christianity employed by Schechter to identify and describe a broad range of biblical and apocryphal items.[13] It is of course possible that Schechter is anxious to keep the discovery to himself but, given that he had publicized so much else that he was researching or planned to research, such a motivation is by itself insufficient to explain his behaviour. It is also known that Schechter held things back for publication in America in order to bring prestige to his new institution,[14] but in this case the edition of CD did not appear until 1910, eight years after he arrived at the Seminary. Taken together, however, with a hesitation on his part to commit himself to a definitive identification of historical provenance, theological context and literary importance, these motivations become more convincing. Schechter undoubtedly had the imagination, the flair and the enthusiasm to locate manuscripts of outstanding significance for Hebrew and Jewish studies, but it was sometimes left to others to complete the detailed scholarly process. As his student and friend Norman Bentwich, in his famous biography of the master, put it: 'After his first editions he was outstanding rather as the discoverer than the commentator, a master of intuition rather than erudition. He was the explorer reporting his travels in the land of manuscripts as he went.'[15]

---

12 Schechter, 'Work'.

13 Papers prepared for the Cambridge University Library Syndicate and presented to them at their meetings of 24 October, 1900 (minute 10; data prepared by Pass) and 14 November, 1900 (minute 7; data prepared by Norman McLean and A. T. Chapman); and *Cambridge University Reporter*, no. 1360 (12 June, 1901), pp. 1088 and 1107–8.

14 Sarna, 'Two traditions', p. 62. His comments are based on Ben-Horin, 'Solomon Schechter', p. 285, and Jacobs, 'Solomon Schechter', *Students Annual* 3 (1916), p. 99.

15 Bentwich, *Solomon Schechter*, p. 263.

Early interpretation

This theory about his overall hesitation is borne out by the fact that Schechter begins to allude to CD in slightly more detail in his own reports on the Taylor-Schechter Collection as University Reader in Talmudic, and as Curator in Oriental Literature at the University Library, published as appendices to the Library Syndicate's reports between 1900 and 1902. In his statement of 6 May, 1900, he is more explicit than he had been in a letter to Cyrus Adler of two weeks earlier, [16] this time not only noting CD's borrowings from the Book of Jubilees but also favouring a Samaritan origin, via the Dosithean sect. He knew that he was looking for a sect that had survived from Second Temple times into the Middle Ages and the one that was referred to by rabbinic, early Christian and medieval Islamic sources, and linked with the personal name Dosa, Dostai, Dusis or Dustan (Dositheos in Greek), seemed to be an obvious candidate:

> We have now fragments of the original Hebrew of Ben Sira representing three different manuscripts, which have been edited by the Master of St John's and Dr Schechter. The Megillath Antiochus is represented in many copies. Mr Pass has lately discovered an Aramaic fragment, similar in character to a Targum, which probably formed the original of the Testament of the Twelve Patriarchs. *In this connection may be mentioned a larger fragment of Samaritan origin (probably emanating from the sect of the Dostaim) which gives many quotations from the Book of Jubilees and which on further study should help to solve the problem of this Apocryphon* [emphasis mine – SCR].[17]

By the time that he is about to leave Cambridge for Seminary pastures, he has clear-cut plans to publish his various fragments relating to Jewish sects and he reports on 25 February, 1902, that 'the fragments of Anan's book will form part of a volume on Jewish Sectaries which is being printed by the Cambridge University Press.'[18] At that time, however, the link he has made is still primarily with the Samaritans, as is made clear by the notes prepared in the University Library at that time, no doubt with Schechter's involvement, and relating to the loan being made to him of those items required for the preparation of his volume:

16 Adler, 'Solomon Schechter', p. 53.

17 Appendix II of Library Syndicate's report for 1899, entitled 'Report of the Reader in Talmudic on the Taylor-Schechter Collection', dated 6 May, 1900, published in the *Cambridge University Reporter*, no. 1308 (15 June, 1900), pp. 1082–83.

18 Appendix II of Library Syndicate's report for 1900, entitled 'Report of the Curator in Oriental Literature on the Taylor-Schechter Collection', dated 18 March, 1901, published in the *Cambridge University Reporter*, no. 1360 (12 June, 1901), pp. 1107–8.

> Dr Schechter took with him from Cambridge March 14/02 (Returned by Dr Schechter 1910):
> T-S 16.311 Samaritan paper
> T-S 10K6 Samaritan paper 8 leaves
> Anan (Karaites Polemics) Vellum T-S 16.359–367 (returned by Dr Schechter 1910 July 13)[19]

Apparently, soon after he had settled in the United States, he had a discussion about the CD fragments with the distinguished scholar and leader of Reform Judaism, who presided over the Hebrew Union College from 1903, Kaufmann Kohler. From that discussion, Kohler concluded that the Samaritan and Dosithean connections were still central to Schechter's theories, as he reported when he wrote a review of *Documents of Jewish Sectaries* in 1911 and complained about the author's alteration of these:

> Indeed, eight years ago, Professor Schechter was far nearer the truth, when, in conversation with the writer, he spoke of the Dosithean character and origin of the manuscript he had brought from Cambridge. The very opening words of the document show it to have been the messianic *pronunciamento* of the Samaritan heresiarch...[20]

Not only Kohler's report but also an account of a lecture given by Schechter to a well attended meeting of the Society of Biblical Literature and Exegesis at Columbia University in New York City on 30–31 December 1902 attest to an evolution in the lecturer's thoughts about CD. The Samaritan connection is replaced by a Karaite link and, perhaps even more importantly, Schechter acknowledges the tentative nature of his hypothesis:

> Prof. Solomon Schechter of the Jewish Theological Seminary of America then spoke on 'A Newly-Discovered Document of an Old Jewish Sect.' From the Cairo Genizah he had brought several MSS., *whose meaning he was at a loss to explain.* As he is publishing the text, he believed that some scholar to whose attention the subject might be brought would be able to solve the mystery. The MS. contains references to a Samaritan city. It speaks of the three cardinal sins and of polygamy, against which it makes a novel argument. *Professor Schechter claims that this MS. must be the laws of some Jewish sect, like the Karaites, perhaps, surely midway between the Jews and the Samaritans. The sect is not like the Samaritans, for it acknowledges certain prophets as authorities; besides, it lives in Damascus at the period of the destruction of the second temple, and not in Gerizim* [emphasis mine – SCR].[21]

---

19 These details appear on the copy of a typed sheet relating to the Loan Collection that Schechter took to New York and bound together with the fragments in binder T-S Misc. 35.1–57.
20 Kohler, 'Dositheus', p. 406.
21 *Jewish Comment* xvi, no. 12, Baltimore, 2 January 1903, p. 11. I am grateful to Dr Michael Grunberger of the Library of Congress for kindly providing me with a copy of this page. For the intellectual background to some of Schechter's work on the Zadokites, see Grossman, 'Schechter's Zadokites'.

It may hardly be doubted that Schechter was a very busy man at the Seminary during the next few years with many administrative burdens, a heavy teaching load, and a demanding agenda in the wider Jewish and non-Jewish communities. This took its toll of the time available for research and inevitably led to a delay in the appearance of the volumes devoted to CD and Anan the Karaite. At the same time, I believe that there may have been other factors that also contributed to that delay. If, as has been suggested, Schechter was slowly adjusting his views, or reaching the conclusion that only a tentative hypothesis was possible, this would have created a hesitancy on his part to commit himself to print. His earlier work had been of a considerably different character, more concerned with establishing critical texts on the basis of manuscript comparisons, and less demanding of historical and theological theorizing.[22] His other Genizah work was in fields with which he was thoroughly familiar and where he could feel confident about his interpretations. CD represented a singularly different challenge and it is possible that the team of distinguished scholars of Judaica that now surrounded him in New York, and that he had indeed newly added to the Seminary's faculty, had both a favourable and less favourable effect on his project.

Collegial influences

In his preface to *Fragments of a Zadokite Work*, Schechter makes acknowledgement to three of his colleagues, Israel Friedlaender and Alexander Marx at the Seminary, and Henry Malter at Dropsie College, for assistance with Arabic texts and with manuscript readings.[23] Although no more details are given about Friedlaender's contribution to Schechter's research, it seems likely that he made more than a minor impact on its direction. A graduate of the Hildesheimer Rabbinical Seminary in Berlin and an expert Semitist who had studied with Theodor Nöldeke in Strasbourg, Friedlaender functioned as the Seminary's professor of Bible.[24] He had little enthusiasm for this role and preferred to concentrate his efforts on medieval Jewish and Islamic sects, with the focus, as his biographer puts it, on 'popular movements, not élitist philosophies, religious enthusiasm rather than conventional piety, heterodoxy more than orthodoxy.'[25] His published studies of medieval sectarianism and his views on the religious interchange between Islam and Judaism have left their mark on scholarship and he

22 Compare his *Aboth de Rabbi Nathan*; *Agadath Shir Hashirim*; and *Talmudical Fragments.*
23 Schechter, *Documents*, preface.
24 For biographical details, see Shargel, *Practical Dreamer.*
25 Shargel, *Practical Dreamer*, p. 68.

presupposed, without being able to identify the route, a movement of religious ideas from the ancient world to the philosophies of medieval sects. I find it hard to believe that he provided Schechter only with translations of Arabic texts but am not yet in a position to cite documentary evidence for my suspicions. Both Marx and Malter, encouraged by Schechter's example and assistance, specialized in various aspects of Genizah research and it is hardly surprising to find their names mentioned in Schechter's CD volume.[26]

A name that is, however, conspicuous by its absence from that study is that of the scholar who was undoubtedly the most distinguished among the group of Judaic experts that Schechter had brought to the Seminary, namely, Louis Ginzberg. Some further attention should therefore be given to the relationship enjoyed by these two outstanding teachers and researchers during Schechter's presidency of the Seminary. Ginzberg's son, Eli, has described that relationship as mutually warm and supportive. They admired each other's scholarship to such a degree that Schechter entrusted to Ginzberg whole areas of Genizah research that he could not himself find the time to undertake, and Ginzberg was genuinely distraught when faced with a Seminary without Schechter on the latter's untimely death in 1915. At the same time, there were clearly some tensions between them. Eli Ginzberg must have had some specific discussions and situations in mind when he claimed that 'Schechter could not have escaped moments of disquietude when he realized that my father's single-handed devotion to scholarship was propelling him into a position of international renown.'[27] One such tense situation was undoubtedly created when Schechter asked Ginzberg whether the fragments of the Talmud Yerushalmi that he had found in the Genizah had any special value. His younger colleague's less than modest reply was 'Yes, when I have added my notes and commentary.'[28]

In my view, such tensions are also manifest in the matter of CD and help to explain the differences between Schechter and Ginzberg with regard to its interpretation. Schechter had already passed enough Genizah material to Ginzberg to ensure that he would overtake his chief in the matter of the quantity of his Genizah publications and was anxious to retain exclusive control of CD. Perhaps the acknowledgements in his preface imply that Ginzberg's views were receiving little or no attention. Schechter saw the work as decidedly non-Pharisaic and in opposition to the talmudic Judaism in which Ginzberg was so expert. Ginzberg

26 On various aspects of Schechter's Genizah initiatives with his Seminary colleagues, see Reif, 'Cambridge Genizah'.

27 Ginzberg, *Louis Ginzberg*, pp. 90 and 95–96.

28 Ginzberg, *Louis Ginzberg*, p. 119.

was convinced that Schechter's identification of the sect was mistaken and that the sect represented by CD was essentially Pharisaic, and he published a lengthy set of German articles, in many instalments, saying precisely why.[29] The impression given by his corrections to Schechter's readings and interpretations, and presumably intended by the author, is that he is the greater talmudist and more brilliant expounder of manuscripts. For his part, Schechter declared that he had 'an inveterate objection to reading scientific matter in instalments.' This situation created hurt feelings on both sides, with remorse about the clash subsequently being felt by the two academics. Schechter was loath to produce his second edition and to take on the task of refuting Ginzberg, while Ginzberg stalled for the rest of his life in the matter of the publication of an English edition of his work. He was willing to disagree with his senior colleague during the latter's lifetime but reticent about carrying on the battle after the Seminary President's death.[30]

Schechter's hypothesis

The views that Schechter finally adopted were therefore in a number of ways a reflection of ten years' discussion and human interplay, as well as the result of strictly scientific inquiry and deep personal contemplation. He concluded that his work would prove to be a valuable contribution to the history of early Jewish sects, revealing as it did the religious law and theology of a sect long extinct, that once enjoyed its own sacred literature, its own calendar and its own interpretation of the Hebrew Bible, and that fathered later traditions at variance with Rabbinic Judaism. He saw the special loyalty to the Prophets and the close connections with apocryphal and pseudepigraphical books in general, and with Jubilees, Testaments of the Twelve Patriarchs and Enoch in particular, as indicative of adherence to a form of Jewish faith and practice at variance with 'official' pharisaic and Rabbinic Judaism and, indeed, distinctly hostile to it. Important parallels could be drawn with aspects of Samaritanism and Karaism, and with the religious traditions of the Falashas, but he had to admit that 'the annals of Jewish history contain no record of a Sect agreeing in all points with the one depicted in the preceding pages.' He was aware that the state of knowledge in his day was such that only a workable hypothesis was possible and he claim-

29 Ginzberg's response to Schechter's publication appeared as *Eine unbekannte jüdische Sekte* as a series of article and then in one volume, and later as *An Unknown Jewish Sect*.
30 Schechter, 'Reply', p. 474; Adler, 'Schechter', pp. 50–51; Eli Ginzberg, foreword, *Unknown Jewish Sect*, p. x.

ed that he would be delighted if future discoveries would further elucidate the history of the sect, and even upset his own theories.[31] Cyrus Adler, who was close to him while he was working on CD, was able to testify soon after his death that Schechter 'went about this edition with the greatest caution, as was his custom, and wrote his introduction, and stated his theory with the full realization of the fact that it was an hypothesis and that his conclusions might be attacked, but he deemed it cowardly to simply issue a text with philological notes and not be courageous enough to endeavor to present it in its proper historical and literary setting.'[32]

Schechter's workable hypothesis was that the limited available evidence indicated that CD constituted extracts from the writings of the Zadokites whose existence is noted in Karaite writings, notably those of Qirqisani. The origins of such a sect were likely to be among the Sadducees, not the Pharisees, and the various reports about the Dositheans justified the conclusion that it amalgamated with the Zadokite group and made more proselytes among the Samaritans than among the Jews. The characteristic features of such groups were not, however, wholly clear or consistent and the versions of earlier works presupposed in CD often did not tally with the texts known to us from elsewhere.[33] In addition, the readings and interpretations offered for the manuscripts were in no way definitive. Schechter's own words summarize the situation neatly, modestly and cautiously:

> The defective state of the MS. and the corrupt condition of the text in so many places make it impossible to draw a complete picture of the Sect. Yet what remains offers us a few distinct features and salient points enabling us to catch a few glimpses of the history of the sect, its claims and its relation to the rest of the nation.[34]

Responses to the publication

When Schechter had formally arranged with the University of Cambridge to borrow a set of Genizah manuscripts on which he was working and to remove them to New York, the intention had been, according to his fellow donor, Charles Taylor, to return

31 Schechter, *Documents*, especially pp. xii, xvi, xviii, xxi–xxii, xxv–xxix.
32 Adler, 'Schechter', p. 51.
33 Schechter, *Documents*, pp. xxi–xxii, xxv–xxix.
34 Schechter, *Documents*, p. xii.

these within two or three years.[35] It was, however, not until July, 1910 that the CD and Anan manuscripts were returned to the University Library by Schechter, during an extended visit to Europe, and, indeed, a further fifteen years were to pass before the remaining items found their way back to Cambridge. When he handed the CD fragments over to the University Librarian, Francis Jenkinson, he stipulated – one wonders precisely by what authority, since no special conditions had earlier been attached to CD – that they should not be made available to any other scholar for another five years. Jenkinson did as he was bade but five years to the day later he swiftly had the CD codex bound up, re-attached the two manuscripts to the remainder of the Genizah collection, and made them fully available.[36] It seems reasonable to suggest that Schechter's motivation was again to do with his doubts and hesitations. Once he had received the comments and criticisms of his peers, he would be in a position to respond to them, and then he could afford to allow them full access. Not that he was not proud of what he had achieved; he was delighted when Jenkinson expressed interest in reading his two volumes on Jewish sectarians and quickly regaled him with copies of the work. The Librarian dutifully read them but confided to his diary that they were rather out of his depth. When the Jewish philanthropist, musician and bibliophile, Mr James Loeb (founder of the Loeb Classical Library), was in Cambridge, during Schechter's visit to his old academic hunting ground, he welcomed the opportunity of viewing the CD fragments in their editor's presence.[37]

Schechter's edition was, as Cyrus Adler succinctly put it, 'followed by a trail of admiration, criticism, and discussion.'[38] A host of alternative identifications were made of the sect and the whole subject preoccupied what would today be called the field of Jewish studies, particularly for the remaining five years of Schechter's life. Ginzberg at the Jewish Theological Seminary in New York insisted that CD represented an earlier and purer form of Pharisaism than that familiar to the Rabbis and offered a host of alternative readings and interpretations

---

35 One of the conditions of the gift of the Genizah collection made by Taylor and Schechter was that the donors should have exclusive access to the fragments of Ben Sira and the Greek palimpsests until they had completed their editions of them but Taylor had indicated that this would be done within two or three years; see *Cambridge University Reporter*, no. 1215, 14 June, 1898, pp. 968–69. For the whole story of the Loan Collection, see Reif, 'Cambridge Genizah'.
36 See the bound volumes catalogue in the Manuscripts Reading Room at Cambridge University Library under T-S 10K6 and the personal diary of Jenkinson for 20 July, 1910 (Add. 7433), p. 201.
37 See the personal diary of Jenkinson for 19–20 and 31 December, 1910 (Add. 7433), pp. 353–54 and 365, and for 16 January, 1911 (Add. 7434), p. 16; also Schechter's letters to Jenkinson from the Kingsley Hotel in London dated 27 December, 1910, and 11 January, 1911 (Add. 6463.7061 and 7072).
38 Adler, 'Schechter', p. 51.

of the texts.[39] For Kaufmann Kohler at the Hebrew Union College, the fragments were a remnant of that religious system of the Zadokites, Sadducees, Samaritans and Karaites which preserved ancient and élitist traditions and practices in contrast to the progressive and populist notions of the Pharisees and had been reliably transmitted by the Dositheans.[40] The CD fragments were seen by Adolph Büchler, Principal of Jews' College, the Orthodox Rabbinical Seminary in London, as containing the fabricated history of a sect living in Damascus in the seventh or eighth century and as belonging not to any earlier period but to the period of the religious upheavals that preceded the emergence of the Karaite movement.[41] It was the link with early Christianity that appealed to George Margoliouth of the British Museum and he dated CD around the time of the destruction of the Second Temple, the work of the 'Sadducean Christians of Damascus'.[42] George Foot Moore, the Presbyterian but ecumenical professor of religious studies at Harvard, found himself substantially in agreement with Schechter, equally hesitant about a precise identification but tending to the view that earlier ideas championed by Samaritans and Sadducees had survived long enough 'to be gathered...into the capacious bosom of Karaism' and consigned to the Genizah by way of 'some Rabbanite controversialist in Egypt'.[43] The Jewish hebraist, Moses Hirsch Segal, then in England but later at the Hebrew University of Jerusalem, added his notes to the text but felt that Schechter's overall interpretation still left scholars in the dark about the sect's origins, relationships with other groups, and place in Jewish history.[44]

Since part of our remit in this treatment of the subject is to uncover the human angle on the scholarly developments, it is relevant to draw attention to the possibility that a number of those who responded to Schechter's theory had, even if perhaps only subconsciously, their own religious or personal agendas. Was Ginzberg at least partially motivated by a desire to associate CD with proto-Rabbinic Judaism so that his own impressive competence in the talmudic field would become more directly relevant to the topic and provide him with the opportunity of bettering Schechter in finding parallels to CD? Given that Kohler was engaged in religious polemics about the validity of Reform Judaism, did he not welcome the opportunity of demonstrating that talmudic Judaism was the reforming element in its day and that the more ancient and authentic voice

39 Ginzberg, *Unknown Jewish Sect*, p. xviii.
40 Kohler, 'Dositheus', pp. 404–35.
41 Büchler, 'Jewish Sectaries'.
42 Margoliouth, 'Sadducean Christians', *Athenaeum* and *Expositor.*
43 Moore, 'Covenanters', especially p. 377.
44 Segal, 'Additional notes'.

was to be found among those groups who took the Scriptures more literally? Did Margoliouth, from a Jewish family who had converted from Judaism and become leading Anglicans, have a special interest in finding kindred spirits who were both Jewish and Christian as long ago as the first century C.E.? Could there be some substance in the suggestion that Moore's favourable response to Schechter's theories was part of his friendly approach to Rabbinic Judaism as a whole, arising out of the liberal nature of his modern Christian convictions?[45] I wonder also if Büchler harboured a grudge against Schechter for having stolen the Genizah limelight from himself and his uncle, Adolf Neubauer, given that the two of them had actually published fragments from that source earlier than their Cambridge colleague and competitor?[46]

Angry reactions

What surely cannot be gainsaid is that the two Oxford scholars, Robert Charles[47] and Samuel David Margoliouth,[48] were angry with Schechter and barely hid their feelings in their publications. Distinguished rabbinic scholars such as Schechter and Ginzberg were never slow in demonstrating their contempt for the Christian professors who tackled the history of the Jews and Judaism in the Second Temple period without what these two Jewish scholars regarded as the necessary mastery of post-biblical Hebrew and the earliest rabbinic sources. In this case too, they had scant respect for Charles's work. He for his part, occupied as he was with preparing the classic English edition of the Apocrypha and Pseudepigrapha, bitterly resented the exclusive access to the Genizah manuscripts of CD that Schechter had arranged for himself and the restriction of facsimiles to only one folio. According to the Oxford biblical scholar and Christian cleric,

---

45 In addition to the biographical details about Ginzberg contained in his son Eli's volume *Louis Gimzberg*, see also. Kohler 'Sketch' and D. Philipson 'Reformer' and the reprint of Kohler's *Jewish Theology*; the entry for George Margoliouth in *Who Was Who*, with general information on the Margoliouth family to be found in Gidney, *London Society* pp. 16–17, 216, 247, 281, 399, 534–35 and 626 and Katz, *Jews*, pp. 379–80; and Morton Smith, 'George Foot Moore'.

46 For an account of the degree to which they pre-empted Schechter, see Reif, 'Fragments'. Biographical details of Büchler by Isidore Epstein appear in his posthumously published *Studies*, pp. xiii–xxii.

47 In his 'Obituary of Charles', the Cambridge palaeographer who had worked with Schechter on the Genizah fragments, Francis Burkitt, referred to the fact that Charles 'was not very patient of adverse criticism.'

48 On D. S. Margoliouth, see the appreciation by G. Murray; see also n. 45 above regarding the Margoliouth family.

Schechter deserved the reprobation of scholars for his selfishness and their criticism for his careless editing and dubious translations.[49] Margoliouth was of course Schechter's sparring partner in the whole matter of the Hebrew of Ben Sira[50] and the rabbinic specialist's new publishing venture called forth the bitterest invective from the Laudian Professor of Arabic at the University of Oxford. CD was no more than the remains of a Karaite essay dating from no earlier than the eighth century that should have been permitted to remain in its obscurity and the whole Genizah was virtually without value. He expressed himself in the following forthright fashion:

> About a score of years ago the University of Cambridge was presented with the contents of a huge waste-paper basket, imported from Egypt, where such stores abound. The material contained in these repositories is almost always valueless, like the gods of the Gentiles unable to do good or harm, and so neither worth preserving nor worth destroying; and the first great product of the *Genizah* [the Hebrew of Ben Sira] corresponded with this description...
>
> In 1910 Dr. Schechter produced another of these treasures – 'Fragments of a Zadokite Work,' being some twenty pages of Hebrew text...the ignorance of Hebrew and of the Bible which is displayed by these documents is intolerable... this document also might have slept in its obscurity without serious loss, except perhaps to specialists in the controversy between Rabbanites and Karaites.[51]

Despite a controversy that Norman Bentwich called 'fiercer and more voluminous than that about Ben Sira'[52], what virtually all the experts were nevertheless agreed about was that Schechter had laid all scholars of Judaism under his debt by his discovery and publication of CD, had inspired his colleagues to apply themselves afresh to Jewish life and thought from the axial period to the rise of Karaism, and had added even more glory to his name by this work than by his famous contributions to Ben Sira studies. As is well known, Schechter expressed the intention of publishing a second edition, with corrections and additions, with a full facsimile and with a detailed response to all his critics.[53] Alas, he failed to do so before he was prematurely summoned to the heavenly academy and scholars had to wait until the Qumran discoveries before the subject was again extensively covered.

---

49 Charles, *Fragments*, especially the preface and the introduction, pp. xvi–xvii.
50 Reif, 'Discovery', pp. 4–8.
51 Margoliouth, 'Zadokites', pp. 157–64, especially pp. 157, 159 and 164.
52 Bentwich, *Schechter* (n. 15 above), p. 159.
53 Schechter, 'Reply' (n. 30 above), p. 474; Adler, *Schechter* (n. 16 above), p. 51.

Dating of Genizah manuscripts

In the final part of this paper, it will be appropriate to offer some remarks about how some of the issues raised and the theories offered by Schechter, as well as a number of the responses that they attracted from his contemporaries, compare with the conclusions being reached about CD by a consensus of specialists who have been able to benefit from the discoveries made in the Judean desert since 1947, precisely fifty years ago, and fifty years after Schechter's own forays in the Cairo Genizah. The first question to be asked in this connection is whether the recent developments in Hebrew palaeography provide any indication of the accuracy or otherwise of Schechter's dating of the Genizah manuscripts of CD. The problem that immediately confronts us in this connection is that we are here dealing with a literary and not a documentary text. At the same time, it is neither biblical nor rabbinic. There is therefore a distinct lack of parallels that might assist us in dating and we shall have to wait for further studies to be completed before a more definitive assessment can be made. A few points are, however, worth stressing in the meantime. There are close similarities between our CD manuscripts and texts written in the square oriental style and dated from the eighth to the tenth centuries. There are no more than a few scribal characteristics that would point to a sophisticated and developed system of transcription.[54] On the other hand, there are a more standard number of lines and a larger number of folios than are common for many codices of the period. There is the occasional indication (as has been suggested recently by Pancratius Beentjes with regard to the Genizah manuscripts of Ben Sira) that the transcription may have been done on the basis of an oral recitation, or one recalled from memory, rather than copies from an exemplar.[55] Comparison with a biblical text from 933 C.E. and with an Egyptian square script from a similar period indicates that Schechter's estimate of the tenth century for the fuller manuscript is fairly accurate and that, if any adjustment is to be made, it should be towards the ninth rather than the eleventh century. The situation with regard to the other manuscript is clearer, parallels being found among numerous Genizah texts and indicating that a twelfth-, or possibly thirteenth-century oriental provenance is highly likely.[56]

---

54 For an excellent facsimile, see Broshi, *The Damascus Document*.

55 Many commentators have drawn attention to what they regard as the poor transmission, either oral or textual, of the Genizah CD versions. See also P. C. Beentjes, 'Reading'.

56 Birnbaum, *Hebrew Scripts*, plates 91*–93 and 185–86; Beit-Arié, *Codicology:* plate 21; and the general treatment of the subject by Richler, *Hebrew Manuscripts*.

Issue of canonicity

Schechter did not clearly indicate whether he thought that the appearance of the CD manuscripts in the Genizah pointed to their canonicity in rabbinic, or indeed in any other circles, although he did seem to place them in the context of apocryphal and pseudepigraphical literature, rather than in that of what he referred to as 'official Judaism'. The difficulty of using the Genizah provenance to support an assumption of rabbinic canonicity is categorically and even somewhat mischievously highlighted by Louis Ginzberg:

> A famous historian of religion has declared in the chief organ of German Oriental studies that the fragments should not be attributed to a particular sect in as much as their discovery in the Genizah of the community of Cairo shows that they were there regarded as canonical. Following out this line of reasoning, the begging letters, the prescriptions for gout and anaemia, the invoices of merchandise and the exercises of schoolboys learning their ABC's, which are all abundantly represented in the Genizah, must have enjoyed canonical status in the community. All that now remains is for the genizah of a community in Lithuania to come to light, and our historians of religion will make the happy discovery that Karl Marx's *Das Kapital* and Eugene Suë's novel *The Mysteries of Paris* enjoyed a canonical dignity among the Lithuanian Jews of the nineteenth century. Fragments of these works will inevitably be found in the genizot, which are the ultimate repositories of everything that is written or printed in Hebrew characters; in the eleventh century it may be a sectarian book, and in the nineteenth a novel translated from the French.[57]

More modern awareness of the problem of drawing conclusions about the rabbinic canonicity of Genizah texts is to be found in recent suggestions made by Menahem Ben-Sasson and Mark Cohen. The Polish Karaite leader, Abraham Firkovich, who was an enthusiastic collector of manuscripts, appeared on the Egyptian scene in 1864–65 and a substantial proportion of his extensive collection undoubtedly came from the Karaite synagogue in Cairo. Firkovich was neither explicit about the provenances of his finds nor averse to doctoring what he found to support an early date for the emergence of Karaism. It therefore remains unclear, even after much recent investigation of the matter by Ben-Sasson, whether or not some of his haul, including many choice historical items, came from the Ben Ezra synagogue. What is clear is that he knew of the importance of its *genizah* and that, if his financial situation had permitted it, he might have persevered longer in Cairo and pre-empted Schechter's extensive

57 Ginzberg, *Unknown Jewish Sect*, preface, p. xvii.

discoveries of more than thirty years later.[58] In a paper co-authored with Yedida Stillman, Mark Cohen has pointed out that what is referred to as Genizah material may not all have originated in one depository or in the same synagogue. The nature and location of the *genizah* in the Ben Ezra synagogue changed from time to time and there were various communal centres in Cairo, Karaite as well as Rabbanite, where such material was stored. Use was also made of the Bassatin cemetery and some items were acquired from local dealers in antiquities, with no information being provided about their previous provenance. Perhaps even more significantly, during the renovations carried out in the Ben Ezra in 1890, manuscripts from its *genizah* were buried in the synagogal grounds and what was later returned to the inside of the building may have come from various sources.[59] Who can therefore be certain about where a particular text was stored, let alone how it was regarded by the community that consigned it to such storage?

Interestingly, the same serious doubts about the definition and extent of canonicity are entertained by contemporary scholars with regard to the manuscripts found at the Dead Sea. It is now widely recognized that some of that precious collection may reflect wider Jewish beliefs and practices and not only those of the groups that settled in and around Qumran. What is being uncovered may consequently testify to a lack of consistency in the matter of the sacred or authoritative status of particular pieces of literature. It is likely that CD enjoyed a greater theological respect among some Jews than it did among others. Indeed, the later evidence of talmudic literature is again somewhat ambivalent. Does the citation of verses from Ben Sira indicate a canonical status, a tolerance of the text as readable but not formally in the synagogue, or the remnant of an earlier approach that preceded its classification as heretical? What also remains open to question is whether one is entitled to draw parallels between the function occupied by texts of Ben Sira and the Testament of Levi on the one hand and those of CD and the apocryphal psalms on other. It is possible that only those more closely concerned with what Haran has called 'the biblical vision' could have been transmitted by rabbinic circles. Alternatively, the rabbinic tradition was less central than it later imagined itself to have been and found room at that stage for a

58 The origins of the Firkovich collection and its relationship to Genizah collections in general are analysed by Ben-Sasson, 'Firkovich's Second Collection', and by Elkin and Ben-Sasson, 'Abraham Firkovich'.

59 Cohen and Stillman, 'The Cairo Geniza'.

wider variety of theological expression. The matter remains almost as open now as it did in Schechter's day.[60]

Historical links

As far as the establishment of direct historical links between CD and known sects is concerned, it will be recalled that Schechter drew the obvious Samaritan, Karaite and Falasha parallels but was hesitant about precise dates and identifications. He opted for a faith and practice at variance with Pharisaic and Rabbinic Judaism and originating in some form of Sadducean and Zadokite Judaism, albeit transmitted by a Dosithean sect. He saw the literary context as that of the apocryphal and pseudepigraphical writings and looked forward to further discoveries that would elucidate the history of those who wrote and transmitted. Somewhat remarkably, if one examines the latest scholarly views on such matters, they are not so much at variance with what Schechter proposed and with the cautious approach he advised. Some see the Nestorian Patriarch Timotheus's report of around 800 C.E. as the clue to the adoption by the Karaites of earlier views, as found in the caves,[61] while others argue that alternative historical and theological factors must have been more dominant. There are scholars who trace the ideas to be found in Second Temple sects and literature and among the Manicheans, through aspects of Rabbinic Judaism and early Muslim groups in Iraq as well as in the Holy Land, to their successful incorporation, not necessarily with consistency or theological intent, into Karaism. There is also opposition to such an interpretation on the part of those who prefer to see the novelty of some Karaite traditions and a direct debt to Islam in the case of others, and point to the fact that Karaites themselves did not claim a Sadducean origin and expressed themselves in all manner of ways.[62]

If one carefully reads the conclusions of those who have recently summarized the content and significance of the Dead Sea Scrolls, one can hear echoes of some of Schechter's remarks of almost a century ago. Such a comprehensive, careful and balanced treatment as that offered by Larry Schiffman talks of the leading role of the Zadokite priests and the major impact of the Sadducean approach. He refers to the presence of Samaritan traditions, to the common herit-

60 Haran, *The Biblical Collection*, especially chs. 3 and 5, pp. 141–200 and 276–303; Reif, 'Cairo Genizah'.
61 Kahle, *Cairo Geniza*, p. 16.
62 For a useful summary of the issues and arguments, see the exchanges, in Hebrew, between Y. Erder and H. Ben-Shammai, *Cathedra* 42 (1987), pp. 54–86; see also Reif, 'Reviewing'.

age of apocryphal literature, and to the presence among the Judean scrolls of works originating among a number of Jewish groups. Although he argues that sectarian groups such as the Essenes and the Sadducees disappeared as independent entities after the destruction of the Second Temple, he acknowledges that some of their traditions remained in circulation long enough to influence the Karaites and that some of the texts found at Qumran circulated in different versions among the Jews of the early Middle Ages.[63] Specifically about CD, Schiffman writes:

> From the very first discovery of what we now know to be a Qumran text – the *Zadokite Fragments* found in the Cairo *genizah* – it was clear that the new material would be of great importance for our understanding of the history and development of Jewish law. When the Qumran library itself was discovered, the presence of multiple copies of that text, as well as other halakhic material, made clear that the new texts had much to teach us in this area of research... The nine copies of the *Zadokite Fragments* found at Qumran confirm the general reliability of the medieval copies of this text. At the same time, the Qumran texts have doubled the size of the preserved text known to us.[64]

Given that achievement, and the additional realization that his interpretations have retained more than a little value, we can, in conclusion, express wholehearted agreement with the evaluation of his CD edition offered by Büchler who unabashedly opted for the medieval Karaite hypothesis but nevertheless noted, as have a number of today's specialists in the field,[65] scholarship's debt to Schechter:

> Let us be grateful to Professor Schechter for his discovery and for the thoroughness with which he has elucidated many of the most difficult points; and especially for the many-sided commentary and the learned introduction in which he has drawn our attention to the numerous problems awaiting solution. Even if his find should not prove to be an early Zadokite book...it has drawn the attention of the literary world to a chapter of Jewish history which has rightly invited the collaboration of many great minds and will long continue in attracting and captivating our best scholars.[66]

---

63 Schiffman, *Reclaiming*, especially pp. 76, 89, 101, 113, 130, 167, 178, 185–86, 192, 195, 198, 253, 274, 403, and 408–9.
64 Schiffman, *Reclaiming*, pp. 245 and 273–74.
65 See, for example, Davies, *Damascus Covenant*, introduction, pp. 5–7, where he favourably assesses Schechter's work and argues that the Dosithean theory is 'one of the few elements... that has not borne fruit in subsequent research.'
66 Büchler, 'Jewish Sectaries', p. 485.

Works cited

Adler, C., 'Solomon Schechter: a biographical sketch', *American Jewish Year Book* 5677 [1916 – 17], pp. 25 – 67.

Beentjes, P. C., 'Reading the Hebrew Ben Sira manuscripts synoptically: a new hypothesis', in *The Book of Ben Sira in Modern Research*, ed. P. C. Beentjes (Berlin: de Gruyter, 1997), pp. 95 – 111.

Beit-Arié, M., *Hebrew Codicology: Tentative Typology of Technical Practices Employed in Hebrew Dated Medieval Manuscripts* (Paris: CNRS, 1977; Jerusalem: Israel Academy, 1981).

M. Ben-Horin, 'Solomon Schechter to Judge Mayer Sulzberger', *Jewish Social Studies* 25 (1963), pp. 249 – 86.

Ben-Sasson, M., 'Firkovich's Second Collection: remarks on historical and halakhic material', *Jewish Studies* 31 (1991), pp. 47 – 67.

Bentwich, N., *Solomon Schechter. A Biography* (Philadelphia: Jewish Publication Society of America, 1938).

Birnbaum, S. A., *The Hebrew Scripts*, 2 parts (London: Palaeographia / Leiden: Brill, 1954 – 57, 1971).

Broshi, M., *The Damascus Document Reconsidered* (Jerusalem: Israel Exploration Society, Shrine of the Book, Israel Museum, 1992).

Büchler, A., 'Schechter's 'Jewish Sectaries'', *Jewish Quarterly Review* NS 3 (1912 – 13), pp. 429 – 85.

Büchler, A., *Studies in Jewish History*, eds. I. Brodie and J. Rabbinowitz (London: Oxford University Press, 1956).

Burkitt, F. C., 'Robert Henry Charles 1855 – 1931', *Proceedings of the British Academy* 17 (1931), pp. 437 – 45.

Burns, Robert, *To a Mouse. On turning her up in her nest with the plough, November, 1785* (Kilmarnock edition, 1786).

Carr, E. H., *What is History? The George Macaulay Trevelyan Lectures delivered in the University of Cambridge January–March 1961* (London: Vintage, 1961; second edition, ed. R. W. Davies, London: Macmillan 1986), especially pp. 1 – 24.

Charles, R. H., *Fragments of a Zadokite Work Translated from the Cambridge Hebrew Text and Edited with Introduction, Notes and Indexes* (Oxford: Clarendon, 1912).

Cohen, M. and Stillman, Y., 'The Cairo Geniza and the custom of Geniza among Oriental Jewry. An historical and ethnographical study', *Pe'amim* 24 (1985), pp. 3 – 35.

Davies, P. R., *The Damascus Covenant: An Interpretation of the 'Damascus Document'* (JSOTSup 25; Sheffield: Journal for the Study of the Old Testament, 1983).

Elkin, Z. and Ben-Sasson, M., 'Abraham Firkovich and the Cairo Genizas in the light of his personal archive', *Pe'amim* 90 (2002), pp. 50 – 95.

'Facts and fictions about Aquila', by an occasional correspondent, *Jewish Chronicle*, 15 October, 1897, p. 21.

Gidney, W. T., *The History of the London Society for Promoting Christianity among the Jews, from 1809 to 1908* (London: London Society for Promoting Christianity among the Jews, 1908).

Ginzberg, E., *Louis Ginzberg: Keeper of the Law. A Personal Memoir* (reprint of 1966 edition with 'afterword' by EG; Philadelphia: Jewish Publication Society, 1996).

Ginzberg, L., '*Eine unbekannte jüdische Sekte*', *Monatsschrift für Geschichte und Wissenschaft des Judentums*, vol. 55 (1911), pp. 666–98, vol. 56 (1912), pp. 33–48, 285–307, 417–48, 546–66, 664–89, vol. 57 (1913), pp. 153–76, 284–308, 394–418, 666–96, and vol. 58 (1914), pp. 16–48, 143–77, and 395–429. Published in one volume as *Eine unbekannte jüdische Sekte* (New York: privately published, 1922) and in a posthumous English edition entitled *An Unknown Jewish Sect* (New York: Olms, 1976), with a foreword by Eli Ginzberg.

Grossman, M., 'Schechter's Zadokites. Ancient Jewish authority in nineteenth-century perspective', in *Jewish Antiquity and the Nineteenth-Century Imagination*, eds. H. Lapin and D. B. Martin (Bethesda, MD: University Press of Maryland, 2003, pp 123–40.

Haran, M., *The Biblical Collection: Its Consolidation to the End of the Second Temple Times and Changes of Form to the End of the Middle Ages* (Hebrew; Jerusalem: Magnes, 1996).

Jacobs, J., 'Solomon Schechter as scholar and as man' and 'Some Aspects of Schechter', *Jewish Theological Seminary Students Annual* 3 (1916), pp. 93–109 (pagination kindly provided by Dr Jay Rovner, Manuscript Bibliographer at the Library of the Jewish Theological Seminary, New York).

Kahle, P., *The Cairo Geniza* (Oxford; Blackwell, 1959, 2nd edn.).

Katz, D. S., *The Jews in the History of England* (Oxford: Clarendon, 1994).

Katz, J. *With My Own Eyes. The Autobiography of an Historian*, Eng. trans. A. Brenner and Z. Brody (Hanover: University Press of New England, 1995; original Hebrew *Bemo 'Enay*, Jerusalem: Keter, 1989).

Kohler, K., 'Dositheus, the Samaritan Heresiarch, and his relations to Jewish and Christian doctrines and sects', *American Journal of Theology* 15 (1911), pp. 404–35.

Kohler, K., *Jewish Theology Systematically and Theologically Considered*, reprint with a new introduction by J. L. Blau (New York: Ktav, 1968).

Kohler, M. J., 'Biographical sketch', in *Studies in Jewish Literature Issued in Honor of Professor Kaufmann Kohler*, eds. J. Morgenstern, D. Philipson and D. Neumark (Berlin: Reimer, 1913), pp. 1–10.

Margoliouth, D. S., 'The Zadokites', *The Expositor* 6 (1913), pp. 157–64.

Margoliouth, G., entry for him in *Who Was Who 1916–1928* (London: A. & C. Black, 1929), p. 540.

Margoliouth, G., 'The Sadducean Christians of Damascus', *The Athenaeum* no. 4335, 26 November, 1910, pp. 657–659.

Margoliouth, G., 'The Sadducean Christians of Damascus', *The Expositor* 2 (1911), pp. 499–517.

Moore, G. F., 'The Covenanters of Damascus: a hitherto unknown Jewish sect', *Harvard Theological Review* 4 (1911), pp. 331–77.

Murray, G., 'David Samuel Margoliouth 1858–1940', *Proceedings of the British Academy* 26 (1940), pp. 389–97.

NEB =*The New Encyclopaedia Britannica*, vol. 20 (Chicago: Encyclopaedia Britannica, 1991).

Philipson, D., 'Kaufmann Kohler as reformer', in *Studies in Jewish Literature Issued in Honor of Professor Kaufmann Kohler*, eds. J. Morgenstern, D. Philipson and D. Neumark (Berlin: Reimer, 1913), pp. 11–29.

Raccah-Djivre, D. (ed.), *The Cairo Genizah: A Mosaic of Life* (Jerusalem: Israel Museum, 1997).

Reif, S. C. and S.(eds.), *History in Fragments: A Genizah Centenary Exhibition* (Cambridge: Cambridge University Library, 1998).

Reif, S. C., 'Cairo Genizah', in the *Encyclopedia of the Dead Sea Scrolls*, eds. L. H. Schiffman and J. C. VanderKam (New York, 1998), pp. 105–8.
Reif, S. C., 'The Cambridge Genizah story: some unfamiliar aspects' (Hebrew), in *Te'uda* 15, ed. M. A. Friedman (Tel Aviv: Tel Aviv University Press, 1999), pp. 413–28.
Reif, S. C., 'The discovery of the Cambridge Genizah fragments of Ben Sira: scholars and texts', in *The Book of Ben Sira in Modern Research*, ed. P. C. Beentjes (Berlin: de Gruyter, 1997), pp. 1–22.
Reif, S. C., 'Fragments of Anglo-Jewry', *The Jewish Year Book 1998*, pp. lviii–lxvii.
Reif, S. C., 'Jenkinson and Schechter at Cambridge. An expanded and updated assessment', *Transactions of the Jewish Historical Society of England* 32 (1993), pp. 279–316.
Reif, S. C., 'Reviewing the links between Qumran and the Cairo Genizah', in *The Oxford Handbook of the Dead Sea Scrolls*, eds. T. H. Lim and J. J. Collins (Oxford, 2010), pp. 652–79.
Richler, B., *Hebrew Manuscripts: A Treasured Legacy* (Cleveland: Ofek Institute, 1990).
Sarna, J. D., 'Two traditions of Seminary scholarship', in *Tradition Renewed: A History of the Jewish Theological Seminary of America*, ed. J. Wertheimer (New York: Jewish Theological Seminary, 1997), vol. 2: *Beyond the Academy*, pp. 53–80.
Schechter, S. (ed.), *Aboth de Rabbi Nathan* (Vienna: Ch. D. Lippe, 1887).
Schechter, S. (ed.), *Agadath Shir Hashirim* (Cambridge: Deighton Bell, 1896).
Schechter, S., *Documents of Jewish Sectaries*, vol. I, *Fragments of a Zadokite Work* (Cambridge: Cambridge University Press, 1910).
Schechter, S., 'Reply to Dr. Büchler's review of Schechter's 'Jewish Sectaries'', *Jewish Quarterly Review* NS 4 (1913–14), pp. 449–74.
Schechter, S. (with S. Singer), *Talmudical Fragments in the Bodleian Library* (Cambridge: Cambridge University Press, 1896).
Schechter, S., 'Work in the Cambridge-Cairo Genizah', *Jewish Chronicle*, 1 April, 1898, p. 26.
Schiffman, L. H., *Reclaiming the Dead Sea Scrolls. The History of Judaism, the Background of Christianity, the Lost Library of Qumran* (Philadelphia: Jewish Publication Society, 1994).
Segal, M. H., 'Additional notes on 'Fragments of a Zadokite Work'', *Jewish Quarterly Review* 3 (1912–13), pp. 301–11.
Shargel, B. R.. *Practical Dreamer: Israel Friedlander and the Shaping of American Judaism* (New York: Jewish Theological Seminary, 1985).
Smith, M., 'The Work of George Foot Moore', *Harvard Library Bulletin* 15 (1967), pp. 169–79.

2 Aspects of the Jewish Contribution to Biblical Interpretation

Introduction

As is often the case with such invitations, editor John Barton's request to me for a contribution to his volume *A Cambridge Companion to Biblical Interpretation* represented a challenge to think seriously about how each of us was viewing the topic, and about how best to tackle it in the envisaged context. In the original letter inviting me to submit an article, the editor explained that the volume would attempt to cover the principal approaches to the Bible in the modern 'critical' era. Conscious as he was of the continuation of older methods and approaches, 'whether naive in the sense of simply untouched by criticism, or anti-critical and conscientiously opposed to criticism', he was anxious that Jewish and Christian conservatism, including fundamentalist interpretations, should receive attention. Given that Christian conservatism was likely to be discussed in other chapters, he thought it would be good if the chapter I was being invited to write could be 'preponderantly Jewish in its concerns'. He was hoping for an article that not only covered the field but represented personal opinions, not just 'bland consensus'.

As I indicated to Professor Barton in my reply, there were a number of presuppositions and definitions in his overture that made me feel uneasy and that were in themselves at the heart of the differences between Jewish and Christian approaches to the interpretation of the Bible. If I were to take on the assignment, I should wish to deal with these and to offer some comments that challenged their validity, as well as attempting to say something general about Jewish interpretation of the Bible. I immediately received a kind and encouraging response, accepting my proposal and welcoming the challenges it might offer to the assumptions underlying the volume.[1] What this essay will therefore try to do is to formulate this one Jewish scholar's personal analysis of the kind of biblical studies that currently dominate the field in what, for want of a better term, may be called 'the cultured western world'; his brief survey of Jewish approaches to the subject in the past and the present; and, throughout the paper, his assessment of how the one relates to the other.

1 Correspondence between John Barton and Stefan Reif, dated 28 September, 3 October and 8 October, 1995.

DOI 10.1515/9783110486704-003

Christian presuppositions

What then are the 'presuppositions and definitions' that underlie the creation of Barton's volume and much similar literature being produced in departments of biblical study at many academic institutions, and what is the wider context in which they should be placed and understood? The Bible is of course defined as the Old Testament *and* the New Testament. This specific terminology is retained in all cases and takes it as axiomatic that the former's validity can continue only in the context of its fulfilment in the latter. The two are integral parts of the biblical whole and are to be globally understood and interpreted. Such theological foundations notwithstanding, the study of the Bible in academic contexts is seen as critical and scientific while the traditional interpretations that predate the modern period are regarded as naive and unhistorical. Such interpretations are often fundamentalist in nature and, it is assumed, are similarly represented in both the Christian and Jewish traditions. They are of interest to *bona fide* scholars, not for any serious contribution they make to modern study but as examples of views that were once widely held. They are probably now representative of a conservative minority.[2]

Not all of such presuppositions are by any means held by every scholar of Christian background, nor are some restricted to Christian interpreters of the Bible. There is indeed a considerable tension between those who subscribe to them and refuse to take seriously much post-modernist interpretation and those who are aware of the biased nature of the standard approach and seek to disassociate themselves from it.[3] There are also Jewish Bible critics who are content to accept some of the results of the presuppositions, without allying themselves theologically with those who take them for granted.[4] Since, however, the majority of those teaching and researching the Old Testament at the higher educational level in Europe and North America are practising Christians, some comments will be in order about the background to their assumptions concerning scriptural texts.

---

2 I recall that in a series of open lectures given in the spring of 1996 in the Faculty of Divinity at the University of Cambridge, on the theme of the future of biblical theology, all the speakers (Professor R. Clements, Dr [now Professsor] G. Davies, Professor M. Hooker and Professor D. Ford) appeared to subscribe to most or all of these presuppositions.

3 An excellent example of the tension may be found in the articles of I. W. Provan and P. R. Davies in 1995. See also the Hebrew essays in *The Controversy over the Historicity of the Bible*, eds. L. I. Levine and A. Mazar (Hebrew; Jerusalem: Yad Ben-Zvi, 2001).

4 M. Haran denies the serious critical value of pre-modern exegesis in 'Midrashic and literal exegesis' but his case is overstated.

As is well known, it was the Protestant Reformation that placed the Bible, divorced from ecclesiastical traditions, at the centre of its theology and challenged the individual believers to strengthen their understanding of the faith and their commitment to it by creating a personal as well as an institutional relationship with the words of God. To that end, a knowledge of Hebrew and Greek became more widely regarded as a prerequisite, and every encouragement was given to the development of related theological studies at the universities. Jewish exegetical traditions and linguistic prowess could be employed in the interpretation of the Old Testament but the overall approach had to remain a predominantly Pauline-Lutheran one. Those parts of the Old Testament that stressed faith, morals, spirituality and universal values (at least in Christian eyes) were of continuous significance, while details of laws, rituals and particularly Israelite concerns could be subsumed under 'works' rather than 'faith'. They therefore had a limited importance, overtaken as they had been, by greater theological events and ideas centred on the figure of the messianic Jesus. The early leaders of the Reformation gave expression to their theological ideas very much by way of biblical exegesis, and when converted Jews with hebraic insights could be joined to the cause, so much the better. If Jews remained loyal to their own rabbinic traditions, they might still be permitted to function as 'language teachers' in limited contexts but their understanding of the Old Testament was severely flawed, particularly since they rejected an essential tool for its valid interpretation, namely, the New Testament.[5]

Modern O.T. views

Surely, then, such Christian theological notions were a part of the scholastic philosophy only in the pre-modern period and were widely replaced by critical and scientific propositions when the historical approach became dominant in the nineteenth century? The remarkable fact is that only in a very limited sense can this be said to be true. There are faculties in which biblical civilization is today taught in a truly open and liberal fashion, usually in the context of religious studies, by scholars whose own religious commitments are to a large extent irrelevant to their professional activities. This is, however, a recent phenomenon and the truth is that the rise of modern biblical criticism has, over the past century and a half, failed to have any major impact on the theological presuppositions and religious prejudices of many of those who teach the Old Testament.

5 See the relevant articles in *The Cambridge History of the Bible*, ed. Greenslade.

Far from seeing the historical approach as a replacement of the theological one, generations of Christian scholars have insisted on achieving a harmonization of the two.

Beginning with Wellhausen, the leading figures have adopted an approach that has permitted them to retain all the Protestant principles of exegesis, while claiming to have absorbed the best of modern literary and historical analysis. As Edward Greenstein has put it, 'so many categories in the study of Biblical literature, and its religion in particular, derive from patently Christian doctrines.'[6] Students of the Old Testament have speculatively reconstructed pristine forms of biblical religion, of Hebrew text, and of Israelite identity that may comfortably be associated with the 'true Israel' and have traced the continuation of those authentic forms into Christianity. All those elements of the Old Testament tradition that do not fit in with this reconstruction – the best example is of course legal material – are downgraded and regarded as a corrupted version of the religion. They are not linked with Christianity but with the ideology that made no further spiritual progress but ended in what is seen as the sterile religion of the rabbis. The rabbinic tradition may generally be ignored, if not debunked, unless it is needed for completing the historical or linguistic picture, while the continuation of the greatest biblical ideas may be traced in the ongoing Christian tradition. The systematic description of these religious ideas is a central part of Old Testament studies and cannot be achieved without the adoption of a coherent integration of the Old and New Testaments. An essential element in academic Hebrew studies is a close acquaintance with, if not a commitment to such an understanding of the Old Testament. A recent book on the methodology of Old Testament exegesis openly explains that a particular chapter 'would teach the Christian to understand Christ as the holy place... as a person... as the release of meaning... as the guide...'.[7]

This has undoubtedly had an impact on the attitudes of modern Christian Bible scholars to Jews as such. Some have welcomed Jewish scholars as colleagues and have even struggled to have them accepted in traditional faculties, not generally as valid interpreters of the Old Testament, which activity remains a Christian prerogative and commitment, but as teachers of Hebrew grammar, post-biblical texts, medieval and modern Hebrew language and literature, Jewish history, and the like.[8] There have been those, at the other extreme, who have allied themselves with political and social anti-Semitism and have been party to

---

6 On the whole topic, see Levenson, *Hebrew Bible* and Greenstein, *Essays*.

7 Steck, *Exegesis*, p. 207.

8 The situation at Cambridge over the years may serve to illustrate the point; see Reif, 'Hebrew', pp. 1–35.

the exclusion of Jews not only from universities but also from civilized society as a whole.[9] The majority have eschewed any policy of discrimination in the wider context while, often unaware of the consequences of their educational philosophy, have maintained positions that permit them to indulge in various aspects of cultural anti-Judaism, and to call it scientific scholarship. Raphael Loewe has pointed out that for a century before the discovery of the Dead Sea Scrolls forced a rethink, many Christian scholars ignored rabbinics even as a tool for New Testament studies.[10] Overall, it is important to distinguish between those who are aware of the bias in at least part of their O.T. work and those who make a virtue out of it. This has been clearly expressed by J. D. Levenson: 'Even if we do not subscribe to the naive positivism that claims the historian simply tells what really happened (*wie es eigentlich gewesen ist*), we can still differentiate scholars who strive after a not fully realisable objectivity from those who openly acknowledge their transcendent commitments and approach their work in the vivid hope of deepening and advancing them.'[11] It has to be admitted that the former are thinner on the ground in Europe's traditional centres of learning than they are in the more pluralistic educational institutions of North America.

Jewish positions

It may of course immediately be countered that much Jewish interpretation of the Bible is open to a similar accusation of theological *tendenz*. It arises out of the talmudic and midrashic traditions, takes for granted the existence of an integral link between the written and oral versions of the Torah, and makes central use of the Hebrew Bible, particularly of the Pentateuch, for the validation of halakhic (religio-legal) norms. Jewish exegesis also emphasizes the people, the land and the language more than it does any systematic theology and sees the continuity of the covenant between God and Israel in terms of the history of the Jews from ancient to contemporary times. It has repeatedly returned to the Torah, not only as the foundation for its development of the legal and more generally religious ideologies of *halakhah* (religious law) and *aggadah* (religious

9 One of best known anti-Semitic semitists was Paul de Lagarde who was an outstanding student of the ancient versions but also regarded the Jews as 'a repulsive burden with no historical use', as noted in the entry for him in the *Encyclopaedia Judaica*. For an expanded presentation of anti-Jewish bias in 'Old Testament' scholarship, see Reif, 'Jews'.

10 R. Loewe, 'Christian Hebraists', col. 19.

11 Levenson, *Hebrew Bible*, pp. 37–38; see also Sperling, *Students*.

lore) but also as a source for the novel ideas of each generation. The Hebrew Bible has also been extensively used in the liturgical and educational activities of both synagogue and academy and the distinction between religious practice and scholarly analysis may consequently be said to have become blurred to such a degree that the Jewish interpretation is no more capable of being disinterested than its Christian counterpart.[12] If, therefore, it is claimed that much of current biblical scholarship is insufficiently unbiased to be regarded as seriously scientific, it must surely be admitted at the same time that two thousand years of Jewish biblical exegesis has little to contribute to current understanding of the Hebrew Bible in a serious academic context.

While the latter admission would indeed be made by some contemporary Jewish scholars, I myself believe that a brief overview of certain parts of what has been achieved by Jewish commentators on the Bible over the centuries will point out to today's students of the Old Testament the need to be more inclusive of older traditions than they might otherwise be, as well as stressing the ways in which the relationship of Jews to the Bible differs in its basic nature from that of Protestant Christians. Before proceeding to such an *überblick*, another point requires to be made in response to the suggestion that the correct scholarly response must be 'a plague on both your houses.' It is that among Jewish academic institutions it is only in the traditional *yeshivot* (rabbinical academies) that one would find a strong and exclusive ideological commitment to the kind of tendentious interpretations noted above. In most other contexts, there is a greater degree of open-mindedness, even a conviction that 'there are seventy different ways of interpreting the Torah',[13] and certainly no confident assertion that one's own form of exegesis is the only truly scientific one. It is not Christian exegesis to which many Jewish scholars take exception but the apparent inability of many Old Testament scholars to recognize that what to them appears as critical and scientific Hebrew study may be anything but that to those who feel unable to share their theological convictions.

12 On the general history of Jewish biblical interpretation, see M. Soloweitschik and S. Rubascheff; Casper, *Introduction*; Segal, *Parshanut*; Rosenthal, *Studia*, pp. 165–85 and 244–71; Jacobs, *Exegesis*; and Greenberg, *Jewish Bible*.
13 Midrash Rabbah, Num 15:13.

Earliest exegesis

As far as the origin of Jewish exegesis of the Hebrew Bible is concerned, a strong argument could and indeed has been made for locating this in the expansions, variations and alternatives that are found for some earlier texts in their later occurrences in the *Tenakh* (Hebrew Bible) itself. There is even specific mention in Nehemiah (8:8) of the public exposition of the 'divine Torah'.[14] One might also look upon the Septuagint as an early commentary on biblical Hebrew texts, as they were understood in the hellenistic world of Egyptian Jewry. That world produced its own interpretation of the Bible, most commonly known from the work of Philo and Josephus but undoubtedly more variegated and extensive.[15] Certainly the *pesher* method recorded among the Judean scrolls testifies to a Jewish belief in the eternal message of the Bible and a need to find guidance for today in the divine message of yesterday.[16] If we define all such exegetical activity as 'Jewish', we enter into the controversial area of how, and to what degree, that sense of 'Jewish' differs from the later Jewish approach to Scripture and, indeed, from the early Christian understanding of sacred texts. It therefore seems sensible to leave such matters unresolved in this context and to proceed to the earliest forms of the rabbinic exegetical tradition.

The forms that I here have in mind are those to be found in the rabbinic literature of the period between the rise of Christianity and the emergence of Islam. For our purposes, it is essential to note the manner in which such literature looks upon the Hebrew Bible. It is regarded without question as the word of God but there is no one dogmatic and systematic function for it in the tradition, nor one true meaning for it in parts or as a whole, which the individual, rather than the Jewish community, has to search out and absorb. Since the central element in Rabbinic Judaism is the commitment to Jewish religious law (*halakhah)* and the performance of the 'precepts' (*miṣvot),* the Hebrew Bible, particularly the Pentateuch, is regarded as the authoritative source (the Written Torah), linked to the practice (the Oral Torah) by the interpretation of the relevant verses. The authority is, however, to be found in the *halakhah* and not in the process of interpretation, for which there exist various types.[17]

These types of interpretation may be legal in nature and tied to laws specifically mandated in the Pentateuch, or they may be more generally associated

14 Soloweitschik and Rubascheff, *History*, pp. 9–11; Segal, *Parshanut*, pp. 5–7; and Haran, 'Midrashic', pp. 19–20. See also, in general, Fishbane, *Biblical Interpretation.*

15 For the whole background, see Stone, *Jewish Writings.*

16 Stone, *Jewish Writings*, pp. 503–13.

17 Safrai, *Literature.*

with the fields of ethics, behaviour and current problems, known broadly as *aggadah*. Sometimes the exegetical treatment of the text has the aim of offering a running commentary, while in other cases a specific difficulty is addressed, or a homiletical idea is pursued in various verses. Linguistic and literary points may be made, as well as theological and historical ones, with some exegetes indicating a preference for paying attention to minute details of the text while others opt for understanding the particular passage of Scripture as a piece of literature. Literal, expansive and fanciful interpretations are to be found and are even compared but no clearly defined distinction is made in the early rabbinic literature between what later commentators saw as the opposing systems of simple meaning (*peshaṭ*) and applied exegesis (*derash*).[18] There is an obvious tendency to react to understandings of the Hebrew Bible and its message that are based on allegorical, typological and rhetorical treatments favoured by Christians, on the intellectual and mystical approaches of the Gnostics, or on the unsympathetic attitudes of pagan thinkers. This leads to changes of stress, particularly with regard to such matters as the identity and reputation of Israel, the nature of deity, the messianic period, the value of ritual, and the character and activities of major pentateuchal figures.[19]

The sources of such rabbinic treatments of Scripture are the Babylonian and Palestinian Talmudim, where the exegesis occurs incidentally, and the various early midrashim, where the coverage is more systematic. It would seem to be the case that interest in commenting on biblical verses was more pronounced in the Holy Land than in Babylon, and that both Origen and Jerome were influenced by such an interest. It is difficult to date the targumic traditions but there can be little doubt that they existed and were developed side by side with the talmudic and midrashic traditions, influencing and being influenced in their turn.[20] How precisely the synagogal, academic and literary contexts for these various works emerged and interrelated is too large a question even to be touched on here, but what may be said with confidence is that the Hebrew Bible had an important place in each. The devotional and liturgical use of the pentateuchal, prophetic and hagiographical books took the form of lectionaries for sabbaths, festivals and fasts; public expositions and homilies; and psalms readings.[21] It must be acknowledged that as the talmudic tradition grew and dominated, so did the tendency in at least some Jewish circles, perhaps particularly

---

18 Stemberger, *Introduction*; Porton, *Rabbinic Midrash*; Jacobs, *Midrashic Process*; and Loewe, 'Plain meaning'. See also chapter 3 below, n. 1.

19 Hirshman, *Rivalry*; Stemberger, 'Exegetical contacts'.

20 Greenberg, *Exegesis*, pp. 11–13; Mulder, *Mikra*.

21 Reif, *Jewish Archive*, pp. 98–120.

in Babylon, where the major talmudic academies flourished, to concentrate on the applied religious senses of the Hebrew Bible, rather than on any more literal meaning.

Islamic world

An approach that remained closer to the Hebrew Bible did not, however, lack its Jewish protagonists in the centuries between the Islamic conquest of the Near East and the end of the Babylonian talmudic hegemony in the eleventh century. Perhaps inspired by earlier Palestinian trends, and by the concerns of the Samaritans, Christians and Muslims to establish what they saw as pure and authentic versions of scriptural text and tradition, the Karaite Jews took up the cudgels on behalf of the Bible and wielded them powerfully in the early period of their existence. Their interpretation of Judaism came to the fore in the eighth century and their Bible scholars made remarkable progress in ensuring the accurate transmission of the text, its literal translation, and its didactic clarification. Suspicious as they were of the rabbinic traditions, they produced their own word-for-word translations, alternate renderings and interpretations, amounting to what has been defined by Meira Polliack as a kind of scientific literalism, and were at the forefront of the important Masoretic developments of the period.[22]

The Karaites were not the only group to force Rabbinic Judaism to reconsider the degree of attention that it was paying to the *Tenakh*. In vindication of their own qur'anic version of the monotheistic revelation, the Muslims not only argued that the Jews had falsified Scripture but also made every effort to protect and promote their own sacred texts. They entered into polemical discussions with both Christians and Jews about the validity of the accounts and ideas contained in the Hebrew and Greek Bibles.[23] Jews, too, were among those who repeated and expanded what had already been said in the Classical world about the questionable content of the Jewish Scriptures. A ninth-century Persian Bible critic, Ḥiwi al-Balkhi, raised 200 objections, arguing that there were clear-cut instances of divine injustice, anthropomorphism, contradictions and irrationalities.[24]

Naṭronai ben Hilai, head (*ga'on*) of the Sura academy in the ninth century, expressed criticism of the relative neglect of the Hebrew Bible in his circles

22 Polliack, *Karaite Tradition*, pp. 278–81.
23 Lazarus-Yafeh, *Intertwined Worlds*.
24 Rosenthal, *Ḥiwi*; and on a poetic version (discovered in the Cambridge Genizah Collection), see Fleischer, 'A fragment'.

and the trend to correct this alleged imbalance may be traced among his successors.[25] Perhaps the most famous of all the geonic scholars, Sa'adya ben Joseph (882–942), set out to respond to all the challenges facing Rabbinic Judaism on various fronts and some of his most important scholarly activities were concentrated in the biblical field. He produced new, authoritative translations and interpretations of the biblical books, in which his linguistic and rational approach predominated, and his grammatical and lexicographical works made a major contribution to the better understanding of biblical Hebrew. He preferred the literal rendering, except when he regarded it as irrational, unnatural, contradictory, or untraditional.[26] Similarly, another *ga'on* of Sura, Samuel ben Ḥofni (d. 1013), wrote a commentary that demonstrated how one could remain faithful to the biblical source, provide rational responses to the problems raised by the texts, and offer sound linguistic explanations of difficult words and passages.[27] There can be little doubt that such scholars laid the foundations on which were built the considerable exegetical achievements of the Jewish exegetes of medieval Spain, France and Provence.

Medieval Europe

Very much underpinning such foundations was the Islamic-Jewish cultural symbiosis and the linguistic interchange between Hebrew, Aramaic and Arabic. This led to the development of a primitive form of comparative Semitic linguistics and the creation of new and extensive dictionaries and grammars, thus considerably influencing and expanding the field of Jewish biblical exegesis.[28] The earliest manifestations of such progress were still very much tied to the Arabic language and Islamic trends but as they moved from Spain, where they first flourished, into Provence and France, they also acquired a Hebrew garb, thus bringing the results of the latest linguistic research deeper into non-Mediterranean Europe. The overall theme of that research is that one can distinguish clearly between literal and applied meanings, some exegetes going further than others in rejecting anything that is not pure *peshaṭ*, or simple sense. Although the period under discussion ranges from the eleventh to the thirteenth centuries and is replete with names, works and scholarly variety, all that is possible in

---

25 Baron, *History*, 6. 235–36.

26 Greenberg, *Exegesis*, pp. 16–19; Rosenthal, *Studia*, pp. 8–125; Zucker, *Saadya's Translation* and *Saadya's Commentary*.

27 Greenbaum, *Biblical Commentary*.

28 Téné, 'Comparative linguistics'.

the present limited context is a brief survey, with a few examples, of each geographical sphere.

Inheriting as he did the finest linguistic scholarship of the Jews in Islamic Spain, and best representing as he does its application to biblical interpretation, Abraham Ibn Ezra (1089 – 1164) deserves special mention at the outset. His commentaries reflect an itinerant and unsettled life but also one that is open to many influences and ideas. He rarely misses an opportunity of introducing technical matters of grammar, philosophy and the physical sciences and he often challenges traditional rabbinic views, more often by implication than directly. His preference is for the rational and the literal but his cryptic and elliptic style ensures that only the scholar will understand the significance of many of his comments. By the time that Moses ben Naḥman, or Naḥmanides (1194 – 1270), was active in Bible commentary, there was a move in Spain towards the mystical and the pietistic, and he challenged many of Ibn Ezra's comments, often preferring more traditional rabbinic interpretations. Nevertheless, he still paid attention to linguistic, contextual, medical and chronological points and is not averse to criticizing biblical heroes for what he regards as their moral shortcomings.[29]

It is not yet clear how much of the approach of Solomon ben Isaac, or Rashi (1040 – 1105), was due to the influence of his teachers and the wider environment but what is without doubt is that he became the leading commentator of Franco-German circles and ultimately the most popular Jewish exegete of all time. He tried to answer the basic questions the reader might ask and produced a remarkable blend of the literal, the linguistic and the fanciful that informed and edified many generations. His attempt to distinguish contextual from applied interpretation and in this way to distinguish between *peshaṭ* and *derash* was taken much further by a number of his pupils, especially by his grandson, Samuel ben Meir, or Rashbam (1080 – 1160), who reports that he directly and successfully confronted his grandfather with the need for change. He committed himself to pursuing the 'absolutely literal meaning of the text' and concerned himself with words, context and style rather than the rabbinic message, often finding himself seriously at variance with traditional interpretations. There is undoubtedly a mutual influence between his exegesis and that of some of the Christian mendicant orders of his time, apparently the result of personal exchanges.[30]

The Jewish scholarship of twelfth- and thirteenth-century Provence is a remarkable blend of the latest developments with the best of rabbinic learning, the field of biblical exegesis being best represented by the Qimḥi family, the fa-

29 Greenberg. *Exegesis*, p. 47 – 68; and chapter 4 below.
30 Greenberg, *Exegesis*, pp. 68 – 85; and chapter 4 below, p. 78.

ther Joseph and the sons, Moses and David. Though only David's work is extensively preserved, it is clear that they were all devoted to literal interpretation, to careful linguistic analysis, and to the kind of exegesis that could challenge the dominant Christian use of the Hebrew Bible in their day. David ('Redaq') produced a sound synthesis of various types of treatment, including science and philosophy as well as concentrating on grammatical and Masoretic matters.[31]

Before concluding with the medieval achievements, a word about the late Italian contribution is in order. Don Isaac Abrabanel (1437–1508) was reared in the Iberian peninsula but spent his adult life as a diplomat in Italy and very much reflects the early Renaissance world. He demonstrates knowledge of, and even sometimes sympathy for non-Jewish explanations of Scripture and is able to apply his practical knowledge of politics to the better understanding of such matters as court intrigue. He deals with literary structure and matters of authorship, as well as attempting to explain the intent of the biblical writer. Another link between the medieval and modern worlds is Obadiah Sforno (1470–1550), a broadly educated North Italian doctor of medicine who is concerned with conveying the various humanistic and universalistic aspects of the text. He is interested in the literary as well as the literal and is keen to analyse structure and content. As a teacher of Johannes Reuchlin (1455–1522), he, together with many of his Jewish predecessors, contributed in no small degree to the flowering of early modern Christian hebraism, and consequently to the creation of such literary masterpieces as the King James Version.[32]

Modern world

The attitudes of Jewish scholars in the modern world to the study of the Hebrew Bible are closely bound up with issues of intellectual enlightenment and socio-political emancipation. The process of transition from the more established and traditional sources and outlooks to 'purely' secular or religiously disinterested positions began in Germany with the work of Moses Mendelssohn (1729–1786) and his team of collaborators. Their idea was to combine the best of older Jewish scholarship with the latest linguistic expertise and religious thinking and to produce an aesthetic translation of the Bible (*Bi'ur*) that could serve to educate Jews not only in Scripture but also in modernity. Such notions were also attractive to

31 Greenberg, *Exegesis*, pp. 86–91; and Talmage, *Kimhi*.
32 Greenberg, *Exegesis*, pp. 96–100; Rosenthal, *Studia*, pp. 21–54, 56–85 and 127–64; and chapter 4 below, p. 80.

those who developed the scientific study of Judaism (*Wissenschaft des Judentums*) in Germany and the Austro-Hungarian Empire in the nineteenth century but there was still a caution about approaching the biblical text, particularly that of the Pentateuch, in any sort of iconoclastic fashion, and radical criticism was preferably applied to rabbinic texts and ideology.[33]

Further steps in the transition were taken by the Italian scholar, Samuel David Luzzatto (1800 – 1865) who succeeded in widening the *wissenschaftliche* approach to include at least the books of the Prophets and Hagiographa. Although observant and traditional in his lifestyle, he was capable of sharp and novel analysis and applied this to various aspects of biblical study. He acknowledged the importance of acquainting oneself with Christian scholarship and set out principles of exegesis that included consideration not only of rabbinic and linguistic matters but also of literary, text-critical and chronological interpretation. So scientific was his approach that it damaged his relations with Orthodox contemporaries; so Jewish that it was rejected by his Christian correspondents. Arnold Ehrlich (1848 – 1919) went further along the critical path, basing himself on the conviction that linguistic meaning was as important as language itself, while Benno Jacob (1862 – 1945) challenged many of the ideas of the Christian Bible critics with a blend of philology and lexicography and with a commitment to internal Jewish interpretation and the Torah's own sense of its message.

Although the traditional rabbinic commentators, particularly of Eastern Europe, were averse to such developments because of their possibly negative influence on traditional philosophy and practice, they were sufficiently moved by their existence to pay greater attention to the study of the Hebrew Bible, even if still part of the combined revelation of Written and Oral Torah. Such leading rabbinic figures as Elijah ben Solomon of Vilna (1720 – 1797), Naphtali Ṣevi Yehudah Berlin (1817 – 1893), Meir Leibush ben Yeḥiel Michal (Malbim) (1809 – 1879) and Samson Raphael Hirsch (1808 – 1888) succeeded in winning afresh for the *Tenakh* itself the attention and affection of many observant Jews. What is more, their return to *peshaṭ*, their inclusion of wider cultural material, and their desire to respond to the questions being raised outside their circles, combined to ensure that they produced important insights into the biblical texts.[34]

In the twentieth century, Jews were represented in all manner of modern and traditional approaches to the Hebrew Bible and it becomes more difficult to trace any special tendency. What can, however, be stated is that in addition to the

---

33 Greenberg, *Exegesis*, pp. 113 – 22; B. A. Levine, 'The European background' in Sperling, *Students*, pp. 15 – 32.

34 Greenberg, *Exegesis*, pp. 122 – 36; B. A. Levine, 'The European background' in Sperling, *Students*, pp. 15 – 32; see also Di Giulio, 'Luzzatto'.

purely secular stance and, at the other end of the spectrum, the strongly traditional angle on exegesis, one must acknowledge the existence of trends that are not wholly consistent with those of the 'Protestant' world of scholarship, earlier described. Particularly in such 'Jewish' institutions as the Israeli universities and the theological seminaries of the United States and Europe, and indeed among many individual specialists elsewhere, there still continues to be less concern with intensive source criticism and the search for a systematic theology, and greater interest in textual criticism, history and archaeology, and the Semitic background to Hebrew language and literature. On the other hand, there remains a hesitancy about tackling head-on some of the textual, literary and historical problems highlighted by pentateuchal criticism.[35]

Conclusions

A number of brief, concluding remarks need to be made. At most points in the history of exegesis, Christians and Jews have, of course, confidently believed in the rightness of their own positions but have also been aware of each other's treatment of the texts. In response, they have either absorbed the best of the 'devil's tunes' or made a conscious effort to deny any euphony in their sound. They have recognized the value of earlier achievements and have often used these as foundations for their own exegetical structures. The quest for the literal sense is represented in both traditions but has always been particularly strong among the Jews, for whom language rather than theology has dominated. What is needed today is a genuine attempt at unbiased scholarship and a willingness to question one's own position by asking, in all honesty, whether a degree of tendentiousness is so inbuilt as to have become virtually unrecognisable to those whom it surrounds; whether all that is modern is necessarily more scholarly than the learning that precedes it; and whether approaches associated with one religious group need be rejected by another.[36]

---

35 Sperling, *Students*. Challenges to Jewish exegetes to deal with the source-critical approach, particularly as it relates to the Pentateuch, are now made from time to time, as at various points in the publications of M. Haran and J. D. Levenson (as listed below)) and in the essay by B. B. Levy, 'On the Periphery' in Sperling, *Students*, pp. 159–204. See also Greenstein, *Essays*.

36 See the wise and balanced remarks of Segal, *Parshanut* (n. 12 above), pp. 128–31. This article was written while I was a professorial fellow in the Institute for Advanced Studies at the Hebrew University of Jerusalem and I welcome the opportunity of thanking the Institute for its facilities and many kindnesses.

Works cited

Baron, S. W., *A Social and Religious History of the Jews*, vol. 6 (New York, London and Philadelphia: Columbia University Press and the Jewish Theological Seminary of America, 1958).

Casper, B. M., *An Introduction to Jewish Bible Commentary* (New York and London: Thomas Yoseloff, 1960).

Davies, P. R., 'Method and madness. Some remarks on doing history with the Bible', *Journal of Biblical Literature* 114 (1995), pp. 699–705.

Di Giulio, M., 'S. D. Luzzatto's program for restoring Jewish leadership in Hebrew studies', *Jewish Quarterly Review* 105 (2015), pp. 340–66.

Fishbane, M., *Biblical Interpretation in Ancient Israel* (Oxford: Oxford University Press, 1985).

Fleischer, E., 'A fragment from Ḥiwi al-Balkhi's criticism of the Bible', *Tarbiz* 51 (1981), pp. 49–57.

Greenbaum, A., (ed.), *The Biblical Commentary of Rav Samuel ben Hofni Gaon according to Geniza Manuscripts* (Hebrew; Jerusalem: Rav Kook Institute, 1979).

Greenberg, M., (ed.), *Jewish Bible Exegesis. An Introduction* (Hebrew; Jerusalem: Bialik Institute, 1983), dealing himself with the talmudic-midrashic, targumic (pp. 1–13) and French contributions (pp. 68–86), and with essays by A. S. Halkin on the Arabic commentaries outside Spain (pp. 15–28), U. Simon on Spain (pp. 29–60), J. S. Licht on Naḥmanides (pp. 60–68), F. Talmage on Provence (pp. 86–91), and on the interchange with Christian exegesis (pp. 101–12), S. Z. Leiman on Spain, Provenace and Italy (pp. 91–98), Abraham Grossman on Sforno (98–100), and Y. Horowitz (pp. 113–36) on the modern period.

Greenslade, S. D. (ed.), *The Cambridge History of the Bible. The West from the Reformation to the Present Day* (Cambridge: Cambridge University Press, 1963).

Greenstein, E. L., *Essays on Biblical Method and Translation* (Brown Judaica Series 92; Atlanta, Georgia: Scholars Press, 1989), pp. 24–26.

Haran, M., 'Midrashic and literal exegesis and the critical method in biblical research', in *Studies in Bible*, ed. S. Japhet (Scripta Hierosolymitana 31; Jerusalem: Magnes Press, 1986), pp. 19–48.

Hirshman, M., *A Rivalry of Genius. Jewish and Christian Biblical Interpretation in Late Antiquity*, Eng. trans. B. Stein (SUNY Series in Judaica; Albany, N. Y.: State University of New York Press, 1996).

Jacobs, I., *The Midrashic Process. Tradition and Interpretation in Rabbinic Judaism* (Cambridge: Cambridge University Press, 1995).

Jacobs, L., *Jewish Biblical Exegesis* (New York: Behrman House, 1973).

Lagarde, Paul: Editorial entry on him in *Encyclopaedia Judaica* 10 (Jerusalem: Keter Publishing House, 1971), col. 1356.

Lazarus-Yafeh, H., *Intertwined Worlds. Medieval Islam and Biblical Criticism* (Princeton: Princeton University Press, 1992).

Levenson, J. D., *The Hebrew Bible, the Old Testament and Historical Criticism* (Louisville, Kentucky: Westminster/John Knox Press, 1993), especially chapters 1, 2 and 4.

Loewe, R., 'Christian Hebraists', *Encyclopaedia Judaica* 8 (Jerusalem: Keter Publishing House, 1971), cols. 9–71.

Loewe, R., 'The 'plain' meaning of Scripture in early Jewish exegesis', *Papers of the Institute of Jewish Studies London* 1 (1964), pp. 140–85.

Mulder, M. J., (ed.), *Mikra. Text, Translation, Reading and Interpretation of the Hebrew Bible in Ancient Judaism and Early Christianity*, (Compendia Rerum Judaicorum ad Novum Testamentum 2/1; Assen: Van Gorcum, 1988).

Polliack, M., *The Karaite Tradition of Arabic Bible Translation. A Linguistic and Exegetical Study of Karaite Translations of the Pentateuch in the Tenth and Eleventh Centuries CE* (Études sur le Judaïsme Médiéval 17; Leiden: Brill, 1997).

Porton, G. G., *Understanding Rabbinic Midrash. Texts and Commentary* (Hoboken, N. J.: Ktav Publishing House, 1985).

Provan, I. W., 'Ideologies literary and critical: reflections of recent writing on the history of Israel', *Journal of Biblical Literature* 114 (1995), pp. 585–606.

Reif, S. C., 'Hebrew and hebraists at Cambridge. An historical introduction', *Hebrew Manuscripts at Cambridge University Library. A Description and Introduction* (Cambridge: Cambridge University Press, 1996).

Reif, S. C., *A Jewish Archive from Old Cairo: The History of Cambridge University's Genizah Collection*, (Curzon Press, 2000).

Reif, S. C., 'Jews, hebraists and 'Old Testament' studies', in *Sense and Sensitivity: Essays on Biblical Prophecy, Ideology and Reception in Tribute to Robert Carroll*, eds. A. G. Hunter and P. R. Davies (Sheffield: Sheffield Academic Press, 2002), pp. 224–45.

Rosenthal, E. I. J., *Studia Semitica. 1. Jewish Themes* (Cambridge: Cambridge University Press, 1971), pp. 165–85 and 244–71.

Rosenthal, Judah, *Ḥiwi Al-Balki. A Comparative Study* (Philadelphia: Dropsie College, 1949).

Safrai, S., (ed.) *Literature of the Sages*, (Compendia Rerum Judaicorum ad Novum Testamentum 2/3a; Assen: Van Gorcum, 1987).

Segal, M. H., *Parshanut Ha-Miqra* (Jerusalem: Kiryat Sepher, second edn., 1952)

Soloweitschik, M., and Rubascheff, S., *The History of the Bible Criticism* (Hebrew; Berlin: Dewir-Mikra, 1925).

Sperling, S. D., *Students of the Covenant. A History of Jewish Biblical Scholarship in North America*, written and edited by S. D. S., with contributions by Baruch A. Levine and B. Barry Levy (Confessional Perspectives Series; Atlanta, Georgia: Scholars Press, 1992).

Steck, O. H., *Old Testament Exegesis. A Guide to the Methodology*, Eng. trans. J. D. Nogalski (SBL Sources for Biblical Study 33; Atlanta, Georgia: Scholars Press, 1995).

Stemberger, G., 'Exegetical contacts between Christians and Jews in the Roman empire', in *Hebrew Bible/Old Testament. The History of its Interpretation*, ed. M. Sæbø, vol. 1, part 1 (Göttingen: Vandenhoeck & Ruprecht, 1996), pp. 569–86.

Stemberger, G., *Introduction to the Talmud and Midrash*, Eng. trans. M. Bockmuehl (Edinburgh: T. & T. Clark, 1996, 2nd edn.).

Stone, M. E. (ed.), *Jewish Writings of the Second Temple Period. Apocrypha, Pseudepigrapha, Qumran, Sectarian Writings, Philo, Josephus*, (Compendia Rerum Judaicorum ad Novum Testamentum 2/2; Assen: Van Gorcum, 1984), pp. 1–481.

Talmage, F., *David Kimhi. The Man and the Commentaries* (Cambridge, Mass.: Harvard University Press, 1975).

Téné, D., 'Comparative linguistics and the knowledge of Hebrew' (Hebrew), in *Hebrew Language Studies presented to Professor Zeev Ben-Hayyim*, eds. M. Bar-Asher, A. Dotan, G. B. Sarfati and D. Téné (Jerusalem: Magnes Press, 1983), pp. 237–87.

Zucker, M., *Rav Saadya Gaon's Translation of the Torah* (New York: Feldheim, 1959).

Zucker, M., *Saadya's Commentary on Genesis* (Hebrew; New York: Jewish Theological Seminary of America, 1984).

3 Early Rabbinic Exegesis of Genesis 38

Foreword

I wrote the original form of this essay for a conference sponsored by the Centre for the Study of Jewish-Christian Relations (now the Woolf Institute), headed by Dr Edward Kessler, and the Faculty of Divinity, and held in in the University of Cambridge in June, 2007. It was published two years later in a volume entitled *The Exegetical Encounter between Jews and Christians in Late Antiquity.* Details of that publication are given in the introduction to this volume. At that time, I was unaware of the DHL dissertation written in 2003 by Esther Blachman at the Hebrew Union College-Jewish Institute of religion in Los Angeles. A revised version of that dissertation appeared in 2013 under the title *The Transformation of Tamar (Genesis 38) in the History of Jewish Interpretation* (Contributions to Biblical Exegesis & Theology 71; Leuven: Peeters, 2013). Dr Blachman has provided a comprehensive anthology of comments and interpretations relating to the figure of Tamar in Jewish literature, ranging from the late Second Temple period, through rabbinic texts medieval commentaries, and into the early modern period. There are some parallels and overlaps with what I have written in my essay but the impetus for my brief and modest treatment was not the same as hers and I therefore approached it in a different manner. I have therefore thought it useful to include the essay here and to refer readers to Dr Blachman's much more extensive study for greater detail and wider coverage. I hope, nevertheless, that my coverage might still provide a few alternative angles on various aspects of the overall topic.

Methodology

Any attempt at explaining how the exegetical encounter between Jews and Christians is exemplified in their respective approaches to a particular passage in the Hebrew Bible must (to my mind, self-evidently) begin by eschewing any comparative study of these spiritual competitors and opting to analyse closely the relevant sources within one or other of the two sets of traditions. Such an analysis should ideally characterize, date and contextualize each block of material, compare and contrast the diverse approaches and explain how they, each in its own way, represent specific elements of the religious practice and the theology of their composers. As far as Jewish literature is concerned, such an exercise may fairly successfully be undertaken in the case of the earliest biblical versions, the apocryphal and pseudepigraphical works, the hellenistic literature and the texts from Qumran. Such

DOI 10.1515/9783110486704-004

Second Temple contexts are, after all, not too difficult to define geographically, historically and even – though perhaps to a lesser extent – theologically. Similarly, in the case of the more literal and systematic exegetes, who can be traced from as early as the tenth century but who do not deprive the process of midrash of its central role until at least two hundred years later, enough is known about their background, education and outlook to permit some reasonably accurate definitions of their work. A more serious problem arises when the researcher attempts to exploit the midrashic corpora which range over a period of almost a thousand years and cover almost every aspect of Jewish religious thought.[1]

Although the situation with regard to midrashic texts is well known, a brief rehearsal of the major problems will no doubt help to explain and justify the necessary methodology. Imagine, if you will, making a circuit of all one's favourite places of worship in a large metropolis on December 31 in any year and collecting one paragraph from each of the sermons delivered in the course of the previous twelve months by diverse preachers on a wealth of topics and with various homiletical styles. Place these in a box, in no particular order, and without any reference to their date, provenance or overall theme and leave them for at least a century before attempting to explain them. Serious students of midrash face a somewhat analogous set of circumstances. What has been fortuitously preserved is generally incomplete; the original context can rarely be identified; and the underlying intent may remain obscure. Indeed, the preachers or teachers may have been anxious to present their messages not as *ad hoc* responses to external sets of circumstances but as authoritative pieces of exegesis with eternal value. Add to this mêlée of problems the fact that representatives of the midrashic genre may be expositional, homiletical, halakhic, folkloristic or, simply, entertaining, and you swiftly become aware of the challenge facing those who wish to use them in any sort of historical examination. It is true that by and large it is the Jewish homeland – whether as Eretz Yisrael, Judaea, Syria Palestina or Es-Sham – that constitutes the crucible in which these midrashim are moulded and refined but its cultural and political milieu begins by being Jewish, then becomes Roman, is subsequently Byzantine, and finally reflects Islamic and Crusader conquests, all before these collections of biblical exegesis acquire a fairly stable form and content.[2]

---

1 There is a vast body of recent scholarly literature on midrashic exegesis. Among some of the published work that provides sound guidance are the volumes and articles of Vermes, Bloch, Porton, Kasher, 'Interpretation', Stern, Weiss Halivni, Jacobs, *Impact* and *Process*, Hirshman, Fishbane, Kessler, and Kugel, *Ladder* and *Studies*.

2 On the dating, provenance and study of the whole range of midrashim, see Stemberger, *Introduction*, pp. 233–359.

If, then, to be more specific, I wish to compare and contrast early Jewish and Christian treatments of the story of Judah and Tamar as told in chapter 38 of Genesis, I have to summarize what we know from the raw text itself, allude to the evidence from the Second Temple and early Christian periods, and explain what the issues were for those haggadists or midrashists expounding the text and for the students and/or congregants whom they were addressing. I should attempt to itemize the numerous themes that occur in the various midrashim, to explain briefly how they relate to the original biblical text, as well as to each other, and to indicate how this might convey to us what overall religious messages were being transmitted. It may also then be possible to touch on, at least cautiously and possibly chronologically, some adjustments in overall method as well as in specific exegesis on the part of Jewish commentators through the ages. I would then require my colleague with specialization in the area of Christian biblical interpretation to do something similar so that we could then compare notes on the broader sweeps of historical and theological development. In this connection, it should be borne in mind that treating the encounter between Jewish biblical exegesis and its Christian (and, indeed, pagan) counterparts during the first few Christian centuries is at least as challenging as attempting to explain the cultural interplay of English, French, German and Italian ideas and ideologies between the eleventh and sixteenth centuries. Fortunately, as Sebastian Brock points out in his contribution to this volume, the Syriac Fathers have geographical and linguistic affinities with the midrashic rabbis which makes it a little less difficult to identify similar themes and treatments but this is only one section of a complicated historical and theological jigsaw puzzle.[3]

Summary of Genesis 38

Judah moves away from his brothers and takes up with Hira the Adullamite, as a result of which he marries the daughter of the Canaanite, Shua (or the Canaanite woman, Bat-shua), who bears him three sons, Er, Onan and Shelah, the last at Keziv. Judah arranges a marriage for Er with a certain Tamar but his firstborn displeases God and forfeits his life. In order to ensure Er's dynastic continuity, Judah instructs his second son, Onan, to conduct a levirate marriage with Tamar. Unenthused with this idea, Onan consistently practises *coitus interruptus*, which further displeases God and also leads to his premature departure from this life. Since Shelah is still too young to conduct a levirate marriage (and Judah is

3 Brock, 'Women's voices'.

apprehensive about his fate), Tamar follows Judah's advice to remain a widow in her father's home, ostensibly until he matures enough to fulfil this function.

Although the necessary years pass, Judah apparently forgets (or chooses not to implement) his plan for Tamar and Shelah and, following the death of his Canaanite wife, takes consolation in renewing his friendship with Hira the Adullamite with whom he sets out to attend the sheep-shearing in Timna. Tamar is told of his presence in that neighbourhood and decides to wait no longer for something to be done. Having removed her widow's clothing, she wraps herself in a veil and sits down by a crossroads on the highway to Timna and is thought by Judah to be a prostitute. Unaware of who she really is, he turns to her and asks for her sexual favours. As the price, Tamar elicits from him the promise of a young goat and, as surety until it is delivered, takes from him his seal, cord and cane. He has relations with her and she, having abandoned the disguise and immediately returned to her widowhood, becomes pregnant. Judah entrusts his friend Hira with the promised young goat and the task of retrieving his personal belongings from her but the Adullamite fails to find her. When he enquires of the locals about the prostitute that was at the crossroads, they assure him that there was never any prostitute there. He duly reports this to Judah who decides that discretion is the better part of valour and abandons hope of retrieving his property.

Some three months later Judah is informed that his daughter-in-law is pregnant as a result of illicit relations and he gives a ruling that she should be publicly put to the stake. As she is being led to her execution, she sends a message to Judah indicating that she is pregnant by the man who owns these three items and invites him to identify who that might be. Judah makes the identification and declares her to be more sinned against than sinning and himself to have failed to have arranged her marriage to Shelah. He chooses not have any further sexual relationship with her and she duly gives birth to twins. During the delivery, one of the babies stretches out his hand and the midwife ties a red thread on it to mark him as the first-born. No sooner has he withdrawn his hand when the other baby makes his appearance in the world, leading the midwife to exclaim that he had burst on to the scene and to his being given the appropriate name of Peretz. His brother, of red thread fame, then arrives and is dubbed Zerah. Given the nature of this intriguing tale, it is hardly surprising that it has formed the basis for a number of dramatic reconstructions and historical novels.[4]

4 For an alternative summary from the viewpoint of modern biblical studies, see Barton and Muddiman, *Oxford*, p. 61. Examples of literature based on the story are by Goller and Cooper. See also the summary in Kugel, *Ladder*, pp. 169–70. On Goller, see Sivan, 'Izak Goller'.

Findings of Esther Marie Menn

Before attention is given to the overall midrashic picture and how it relates to medieval exegesis, it will be useful to cite an impressive work by Esther Marie Menn that was published in 1997 as a thoroughly revised version of a doctoral dissertation written under the supervision of Michael Fishbane. Menn provides a background for ancient Jewish exegesis of Genesis 38 by analysing the content of the chapter and pointing out the problems that face the exegete. She chooses the treatments of the subject provided by the Testament of Judah, the Targum Neofiti and Bereshit Rabbah and demonstrates that all three sources are well aware that the relationship between Judah and Tamar leads to the creation of the davidic dynasty, the Hebrew royalty and, ultimately, the messianic king. In the Testament of Judah, the Hebrew hero represents a warrior king with an impressive military record who, like Heracles in Greek literature, is tragically undone by his passion for the morally offensive in the shape of wine, women and wealth. The tale is transformed from a biblical to a hellenistic milieu, there are some unflattering portrayals of women, and the object seems to be to teach the reader the value of abstemious behaviour.[5] In Targum Neofiti the emphasis is on *qiddush ha-shem*, the sanctification of the Divine Name by offering oneself to martyrdom, and a central role is consequently given to Hananiah, Mishael and Azariah, the descendants of Tamar. Judah is repentant and is presented as an idealized proto-rabbinic teacher while God's presence and plan are integral to the human story. The Targum concentrates on the climax of the story and de-emphasizes its royal and messianic implications. God's pervasive presence is also central to the midrashic teachings of Bereshit Rabbah which attempts to resolve the moral problems in the story by stressing the impressive religious standards of Judah and Tamar and how these are bequeathed to the future Hebrew monarchy, spiritual leadership and messianic redeemers. Such a message, especially as it related to the anticipated developments of the future, undoubtedly provided some comfort for those undergoing religious, political and social persecution. Menn's detailed and careful analysis provides an excellent starting point for the further study of other (and very extensive) midrashic material.[6]

5 In addition to Menn's study, see also Kugel, *Ladder*, pp. 174–85.

6 Menn, *Judah and Tamar.*

Issues

For those Jews reading this story during the first Christian millennium, what were the issues that would obviously confront them? First of all, they might wish to know why this story is placed here in the overall Joseph narrative and especially how it relates to earlier and later events in the tales of Jacob's family. They would certainly be aware that Judah was, according to the Hebrew Bible, the ancestor of the Israelite monarchs and would therefore be interested in dwelling on this connection in a variety of ways and in expanding on any other genealogical issues arising out of the relationship of Judah and Tamar. In addition, they might be troubled by the behaviour of Judah who was, after all, a Jewish patriarchal figure and would prefer to see him in the best possible light rather than as one who apparently engaged in intermarriage, fornication and hypocrisy. Were his troubles in this context, they might muse, perhaps the result of his actions in an earlier context? At the same time they would be aware of the tensions between the non-Hebrew origins of Tamar and her behaviour on the one hand, and her role as a matriarchal figure for the Jewish people on the other. They would wonder precisely why Judah's sons met their deaths so young and why Judah's Canaanite wife also appears to have died prematurely. It is perfectly plausible that they were intrigued (or troubled?) by the apparently peremptory manner in which Tamar was sentenced to death, by the proposed method of execution, and by Judah's failure to resume a physical relationship with her after her innocence had been proved. Also, they would wish to understand what precisely lay behind some of the unspecific or problematic language and content, the Hebrew names and the apparently redundant phrases that occur in the chapter, and whether any of these might be alluding to any of the grander notions that they might expect from the divinely revealed message. They would undoubtedly be attracted to the idea of fate, or rather heaven, taking a hand in somewhat mundane matters to ensure the correct historical outcome for their own ancestors.[7] It should be added that there were some Jewish commentators, such as Josephus and the compiler of the Pirqei de Rabbi Eliezer, who apparently felt so uncomfortable with the chapter on Judah and Tamar that they declined to offer it any attention.

---

7 The total midrashic picture is of course included in the classic work of Ginzberg, *Legends*, 2.32–37, 142–43, 198–201; 5.332–37 and 367–68. While Ginzberg incorporates the midrashim into one combined narrative, I have opted rather to treat them thematically.

Midrashic themes

As with most pentateuchal narratives, the rabbis of the early Christian centuries found in our chapter some halakhic guidance concerning the legal definitions to be drawn up in the cases of levirate marriage and the birth process.[8] Since this may, however, be regarded as essentially an internal rabbinic matter and of limited relevance to the topic of the exegetical encounter between Jews and Christians, as it is played out from verse to verse or chapter to chapter, it need not receive further attention here. What should, on the other hand, be noted is the rabbinic decision about the suitability of the chapter for inclusion in the regular synagogal lectionary, not only in its original Hebrew form but also in its Aramaic translation. There are biblical phrases and passages that the tannaitic rabbis found offensive for one reason or another, and that were adjusted or, in the case of the Aramaic translation, actually omitted. It might consequently have been argued that a chapter such as Genesis 38 that records so many religiously questionable activities on the part of an eponymous and centrally significant ancestor of the Jews should not be translated in the synagogue. The mishnaic decision is that the whole chapter is permissible for synagogal use, in Hebrew and Aramaic, and the Babylonian Talmud attributes this to Judah's exemplary behaviour in the final part of the story, which restores his reputation.[9] This tension between the acknowledgement that Judah sinned and the national desire or theological need to exonerate him is one that will be encountered in a number of instances throughout this analysis.

Judah criticized

Such acknowledgement of Judah's inadequate behaviour is given expression in a number of midrashic comments. Lying behind most of these comments is the awareness of the genealogy in the book of Ruth which traces the ancestry of King David, the Hebrew monarchy and the Messiah of the future through Ruth and Boaz back to Peretz, the son of Judah and Tamar. What is more, rabbinic tradition – possibly in response to a view that distinguishes between royal and prophetic authority – also identifies the father of the prophet Isaiah with King Amaziah and therefore sees Judah as the progenitor not only of the royalty but also of

8 See, for example, *b. Yebam.* 59a and *b. Nid.* 28a.
9 *m. Meg.* 4.10 and *b. Meg.* 25b. See Menn, pp. 284–85.

the prophetic leadership.[10] An assessment of Judah's activities was therefore very relevant to understanding the history and religion of the Jewish people from its earliest days. BR cites Mic 1:15 as a criticism of Judah, suggesting that 'the Glory of Israel has come to Adullam' עד עדלם יבוא כבוד ישראל is an exclamatory reference to Judah's friendship with Hira the Adullamite and marriage to a Canaanite. T spells this out more forcefully, stating that Judah the most senior member of Jacob's household married a Canaanite woman and that the prophet Micah had harangued him for this stating that the glorious progeny of Jacob, who was destined to be the ancestor of Israel's monarchy, descended to the level of Adullam and the local Canaanite women.[11] MHG goes even further and uses a parable to describe Judah's behaviour. Sometimes a lion will consume what has been rejected by a dog. Even Esau rejected the Canaanite women as evil, while Judah, the lion of Judah, opted to marry one. Are we encountering here something of a polemic against those who would prefer a more universalist, or less ethnic, stance?[12] For MT, this estimate of Judah's behaviour explains why the high priesthood was denied to his descendants, although T, while linking the monarchy with Peretz, associates a priesthood with Zerah. Treating Tamar as a prostitute was an act of calumny and having relations with her demonstrated his sexual appetite and self-indulgence, as the verse in Ps 101:5 puts it מלושני בסתר רעהו אותו אצמית גבה עינים ורחב לבב, midrashically expounded as 'I have to eliminate from consideration for the high priesthood one who slanders another person and abuses them proudly and voraciously'.[13] What is more, as will become clear below when word-plays are considered, BR links the very unworthy activities of Achan with his ancestor Judah.

There is yet more criticism of Judah in BR which notes that Judah was undone in this story in the matter of a goat as a punishment for his having deceived his father about the fate of Joseph when he brought him his coat that he had dipped in goat's blood.[14] Recorded in the BT and in T is the view that Judah's descent (ירידה) describes his banishment by his brothers for not having completed his rescue of his brother Joseph. Once he had persuaded them not to kill him, he should then have attempted to persuade them to restore him to his father. Had he done so, they claimed, they would again have listened to him.[15] The matter of Judah's questionable honesty also exercises Rashi in the eleventh century. He

---

10 *b. Soṭah* 10b and *b. Meg.* 10b.
11 BR 85.1 (2.1029) and T *Va-Yeshev* 10 (p. 91b).
12 MHG, pp. 643–44.
13 MT, p. 214a and T *Va-Yeshev* 21 (p. 94b).
14 BR 85.9 (2.1043); see also the section entitled 'Allusions' below.
15 *b. Soṭah* 10b; T *Va-Yeshev* 8 (p. 91a) and 13 (p. 92b).

explains v. 11 as indicating that, given the fate of the elder two brothers, Judah had, despite what he said, no intention whatsoever of marrying her off to Shela. Although more explicitly expressed, Rashi's explanation is effectively an expansion of comments in BR and BT that had alluded to this many centuries earlier.[16]

T claims that other events described in the chapter also represent Judah's punishment for such a failure to set the example.[17] In a passage that occurs a number of times in BT, it is suggested that doubt hung over the head of Judah until Moses finally persuaded God to exonerate him fully by arguing that it was Judah's repentance and honesty that had set the example for Reuben to follow in connection with the latter's illicit relations with his father's concubine. Only after Moses had successfully made his representations to God was Judah finally admitted to full membership of the celestial academy.[18] What the aggadist is perhaps doing here is placing the ultimate power in the hands of the teacher *par excellence*, that is משה רבינו ('our teacher Moses'), rather than with the monarchy. Interestingly, Jacob of Serugh also involves Moses in this story by suggesting that Tamar's behaviour had not only invited no reproach from him but had impressed him through its spirituality.[19] A hesitation about Judah's own ability to achieve forgiveness may also be detected in the claim that he was ultimately forgiven by angelic prayer. In a late midrash there is an attempt to stress the divine love for Judah in spite of everything. 'Even when you misbehave', says God, 'I am still with you, indicating just how much I love you.' The stress in this case is on the special relationship forever assured by God for Judah and his people, Israel, perhaps in response to those who would deny its eternal nature.[20]

Judah defended

Other midrashic sources offer defence and praise of Judah's actions in spite of his apparent immorality, or in response to accusations of improper behaviour. The background to this is the assumption that he was imbued with enough divine inspiration for him to be aware that his descendants would be among Israel's leaders. A rich passage in the Babylonian Talmud ascribes credit to him for that fact that he did not have intercourse with Tamar until he had, alleg-

16 On Rashi, see below the section entitled 'Medieval exegesis'; *b. Yebam.* 64b; BR 85.5 (2.1039).
17 T *Va-Yeshev* 10 (p. 91b).
18 *b. Soṭah* 7b, *b. B. Qam.* 92a and *b. Mak.* 11b.
19 See Brock, 'Women's voices'.
20 'Aggadat Tefillat Shemoneh 'Esreh' cited in Jellinek, pp. xxiv and 54; AB, p. 54b. On the role of angels in such midrashic exegesis, see Grypeou and Spurling, 'Abraham's angels'.

edly, checked that she was religiously converted, maritally available and ritually pure. It also approves of the fact that he admitted her honesty publicly.[21] There is also a view recorded there that Judah (perhaps to his credit?) did not abandon her but continued to have relations with her, although other early sources claim that it was the Holy Spirit that made a declaration about Judah's ceasing to have relations with her and that he desisted because she was his daughter-in-law.[22] A somewhat more historical analysis is offered in MHG according to which Judah lived in pre-Torah times when it was perfectly legitimate to have such a physical relationship.[23]

PT notes that Timna is mentioned in the stories of both Judah and Samson and explains that Judah's visit there was for religious purposes while Samson's was not, as indicated by the use of descent (וירד) in one case and ascent (ויעל) in the other![24] One of the problems, namely, his marriage to a Canaanite, is neatly eliminated in the BT by a claim that the word is here used in its meaning of 'merchant' as in Hos 12:8.[25] In common with earlier biblical characters such as Adam, Abraham and Jacob, Judah is said in BR and ShR to have observed some aspect of the Torah (in this case levirate marriage) before it was given to the Jewish people at Sinai, to have married off his son at the right time, and to have bequeathed to his royal descendants through Tamar his religious and physical power.[26] Judah is rewarded for his honesty in admitting his error and, exculpating Tamar, by the rewards of royalty, the lives of Hananiah, Mishael and Azariah in the fiery furnace and David's progeny in the face of Saul, Absalom and Avishai.[27] If the davidic dynasty is allegedly continued in the Jewish leadership of the talmudic and post-talmudic periods, it would be natural for the aggadist to defend Judah's behaviour to a considerable degree. The alleged continuation of such authority would also constitute a challenge to those who might seek David's dynasty elsewhere.

---

21 *b. Soṭah* 10ab.

22 *t. Soṭah* 9.3 (ed. Zuckermandel, p. 312); *y. Soṭah* 9.6 (23d); *Siphre*,§ 88, 87.

23 MHG, p. 648.

24 y. *Soṭah* 1.8 (17a).

25 *b. Pesaḥ*. 50a; see also the Targumim Onqelos and Pseudo-Jonathan.

26 BR 85.5 (2.1038); ShR 1.2.5 (p. 5a); 'Midrash Ha-Bi'ur' of Sa'adya b. David in MS cited by Kasher, *Torah*, p. 1449, no. 29; BR 85.9 (2.1043).

27 *Mekilta*, ed. Lauterbach, 1.236; *Mechilta*, ed. Horovitz and Rabin, p. 106; *Shemot Rabbah*, 16.4 pp. (32b–33a); *b. Soṭah* 10b; 'Midrash Ha-Ḥefeṣ' of Zechariah Ha-Rofeh cited by Kasher, *Torah*, p. 1476, no. 117.

Tamar praised

The midrashim of the talmudic period are united in their interpretation of Tamar's behaviour in the best possible light. Passages in BT and PT comment at length on the whole story and have a fair amount to say about her actions. When in the home of her father-in-law, Judah, during her marriages to his elder two sons, she had consistently demonstrated her modesty by covering her hair in such a way that it was impossible for Judah to recognize her when he was attracted to her on the road to Timna.[28] The place that she chose in order to carry out her ruse was outside the tent of Abraham where everyone could see her (so understanding פתח עינים).[29] Contrary to what one might understand from the biblical text itself, her sexual impropriety was totally different from that of Zimri (Num 25:1–15) since her actions led to dynasties of kings and prophets while his led to the deaths of thousands of Israelites.[30] Before undertaking her project she looked heavenwards and prayed for success (so understanding פתח עינים) and it was she, and apparently not Judah, who raised the matter of her marital availability and ritual purity.[31] A number of passages draw attention to the fact that she set an admirable moral example in not publicly accusing Judah by drawing direct attention to his sexual involvement with her, choosing rather to be burnt to death than treat a fellow human in such an embarrassing fashion.[32]

The midrashim recorded outside the talmudic sources appear to be even more direct about her origins, motivations and religious status. As is allegedly indicated by the imposition of the death penalty by burning, she was the daughter of Shem who is regarded by the aggadah as a priest and her name indicates that she was as straight as a palm tree, that is to say that, as well as being physically beautiful, she demonstrated a faultless integrity.[33] In addition to other examples of this integrity already included in the talmudic passages cited above, BR cites the fact that she may be compared to Rebecca since both modestly donned veils, although it also records the view that while only one of Rebecca's twins, namely Jacob (and not Esau), was righteous, both of Tamar's twins dis-

28 *b. Soṭah* 10b and *b. Meg.* 10b.
29 b. *Soṭah* 10b; see also Targum Pseudo-Jonathan (as well as the rendering by Targum Onqelos) and Kugel, *Ladder*, 178–79.
30 *b. Nazir* 23b and *Hor.* 10b.
31 *y. Soṭah* 1.4 (16d) with parallel in *Ketub.* 13.1 (35c); so BR 85.7 (2.1041).
32 *b. Soṭah* 10b, *b. Meṣ.* 59a, *b. Ketub.* 67b, and *b. Ber.* 43b.
33 BR 85.10 (2.1044), LT on Gen 38:24 (p. 98a); MHG, p. 644; on the relationship with Shem, see also Targum Pseudo-Jonathan.

played high levels of piety.[34] LT refers approvingly to her reluctance to leave Judah's household after the death of her first two husbands who were his sons.[35] This is taken even further by MHG which appears to credit her with at least a degree of prophetic inspiration. Although the classic talmudic passage that lists seven women prophets does not include Tamar in the list of Sarah, Miriam, Deborah, Hannah, Abigail, Hulda and Esther, MHG explain that she was informed by the Holy Spirit of Judah's plans to travel to Timna and that her dangerous plan was motivated by her hope to produce royal progeny that would ultimately include the Messiah. [36] It is noteworthy that the Syriac Fathers, Ephrem and Jacob of Serugh, in the fourth and fifth centuries, also refer to her pious motivations and her special spiritual status.[37] There is, however, perhaps a hint of criticism in T which explains v. 24 as an indication that she told her female friends in the bath-house that they should make way for her because she was pregnant with royalty.[38] The action she took to ensure that she would become pregnant from her only sexual act with Judah is noted in the next section below. The overall impression is of an idealized woman of righteousness who is worthy of initiating a dynasty that is to become central for Jewish leadership to the end of time. Any tendency to regard this righteous woman as a proto-Christian might be countered by such a stress on the link with eternal Jewish leadership.

Wicked characters

It is not an uncommon phenomenon for midrashim to dwell and expand on the disreputable activities of those biblical characters who are in some way defined in the biblical text as of questionable morality, especially if there is no reason to number them among the recognized heroes of the Jewish people.[39] Given Scripture's attribution of the premature deaths of Er and Onan to direct divine activity, the aggadists were anxious to establish that such a fate was richly deserved and vied with each to suggest the precise nature of the salacious behaviour that precipitated it. It is widely presupposed that Er was guilty of the same sexual

34 BR 85.7 (2.1040) and 85.13 (2.1048).
35 LT on Gen 38:6 (p. 96b).
36 *B. Meg.* 14a; MHG, p. 646.
37 See Brock, 'Women's voices' and Frishman, 'Abraham'.
38 T *Va-Yeshev* 17 (p. 94a); compare BR 85.10 (p. 1044).
39 See Salvesen, 'Keeping it'.

immorality as his brother, Onan, and this is defined broadly as forbidden sexual relationships, as well as more precisely as masturbation, *coitus interruptus* and anal intercourse.[40] Interestingly, the notion that they were reluctant for Tamar to become pregnant because that would spoil her outstanding beauty is already found in early rabbinic sources, undoubtedly reflecting a problematic attitude, as the midrashists saw it, on the part of the Jews of their own day.[41] Even more interesting is the assumption that Judah was the first man to have standard intercourse with Tamar. This leads to the question of how she could become pregnant from this act since it was regarded as axiomatic that pregnancies do not occur as a result of the first intercourse. The reply is offered that this is true when the first intercourse has to break the virginal hymen but Tamar arranged matters cleverly by piercing that membrane herself before performing the act with Judah.[42] This appears not to have elicited any unfavourable comment among these exegetes, perhaps because they regarded it as another example of her determination to be the female ancestor of the Hebrew royalty and the davidic dynasty. The sexual immorality presupposed in the story is described in detail as characteristic of non-Hebrews in order to support the rabbinic notion that Jews have to maintain higher standards of self-control than other sects, religions and peoples in the broader world around them.

Meaning in names

Another aggadic principle is that the names of people and places that might perfectly well have been omitted from Scripture without damaging the narrative in any way are included in order to convey a special religious message. The names of Er and Onan, the two sons of Judah and his Canaanite consort, are therefore provided since they indicate that the elder was wicked (רע as the metathesis of ער) and died childless, the name ער being associated with ערירי, and that his younger brother caused much grief (אנינות) by dying so young. The birth of Shela is associated with the name כזיב because the Hebrew root of that name alludes to 'failure', in this case the failure of Judah's Canaanite wife to produce any more offspring. [43] Hira, the Adullamite friend of Judah, is, somewhat anachronistically, identified with Hiram,

40 'Midrash Ha- Ḥefeṣ' cited by Kasher, *Torah*, p. 1450, no. 36; *b. Nid.* 13a; *Kallah* 17–19; *b. Yebam.* 34b; BR 85.4 (2.1037).

41 *b. Yebam.* 34b; BR 85.4 (2.1037).

42 *b. Yebam.* 34b; compare also the lengthy discussion of this topic by Kasher, *Torah*, pp. 1453–54.

43 LT on Gen 38:6 (p. 96b); BR 85.4 (2.1037); all incorporated in Targum Pseudo-Jonathan. Fragmentary Targum makes use of the play on the word כזיב.

king of Tyre in David's day, although it is acknowledged that he must therefore have been many centuries old by that time.[44] Peretz's name is linked with his messianic descendant by way of Mic 2:13 and Zerah's with the bright (Hebrew root זרח, 'to shine') red thread that the midwife tied to his hand.[45] Aggadic explanations of the names Timna (contrasting Judah and Samson) and of the words פתח עינים (v. 14) have already been cited above.

Allusions

Similarly, the use of the same expression in different biblical accounts may indicate a link between them while a specific number of uses of the same word in a limited context may also suggest a connection with another biblical passage where that number is significant. This is part of an overall midrashic tendency to lessen the number of personalities and events mentioned in the Hebrew Bible. For example, the expression הכר נא occurs both here in v. 25 and also in Gen 37:32 where Judah invites his father Jacob to identify Joseph's bloody coat, implying that this was part of Judah's punishment for that deception.[46] A red thread is part of this story and also recurs in the tale of the conquest of Jericho in which the Israelite spies invite the hospitable Rahab to save her life during the conquest by the use of a red thread. The spies must therefore be Peretz and Zerah.[47] In vv 28–30 of the Judah story, the word יד occurs four times and this constitutes an allusion to Achan's four thefts of forbidden property (Josh 7), an appropriate reference since he was a descendant of Zerah.[48] Jacob received his blessing from Isaac through the goatskins that he and Rebecca attached to his hands and neck, and Judah arranged monarchy among his descendants through a young goat.[49]

If we may now return briefly to the actions of Judah that have not yet received attention, the matter of why he chose to offer his seal, cord and cane provides a splendid opportunity for some midrashic expositions. In BR they are said to allude to the monarchy, the Sanhedrin and the Messiah while in an Oxford manuscript of T they are interpreted as pointing to the basic requirements of

---

44 BR 85.4 (2.1035–36).
45 BR 85.13 (2.1049); AB, p. 54b: LT on Gen 38:30 (p. 98b).
46 *b. Soṭah* 10b.
47 MHG, p. 371.
48 BR 85.13 (2.1050).
49 LT on Gen 38:17 (p. 97b).

the female from the male, namely, food, clothing and sex.[50] According to an unspecified midrash cited by Joshua Ibn Shuaib, they symbolize the First Temple, Second Temple and Messianic Temple, while a midrash cited as ילמדנו lays the emphasis on the cane which it identified as the same item used by Moses for striking the rock in order to obtain water (Num 20:8) and by Jacob when he crossed the Jordan river (Gen 32:10).[51] Inevitably, Christian commentators also sought to symbolize these three items and for Jacob of Serugh they represented faith, baptism and the cross.[52] Do the midrashic comments represent an attempt to forestall any impact likely to be made by non-Jewish symbolism or typology? Judah's ruling that Tamar should be sent to the stake inspires T to explain that we are of course dealing here with a properly constituted court of Shem on which Judah sat with his father Jacob and his grandfather Isaac and leads the PT to cite a difference of opinion between R. Johanan and Resh Laqish about why in that case Judah spoke first. If the practice in non-Jewish courts (i. e. courts that do not follow the Torah given at Sinai) is the same as Jewish courts then the pre-Sinaitic Judah was speaking first as the most junior member. If, on the other hand, this is not their practice, one is forced to explain that Judah spoke last but since he convinced the others of his view the verdict is recorded in his name.[53]

Divine role

An unassailable response to all aggressive challenges to actions recorded in the Hebrew Bible is of course that this was all part of the divine plan and was consequently inevitable. This kind of response is found in a number of instances in connection with the story of Judah and Tamar. The unfortunate events that now take place in Judah's life represent the punishment that has been assigned to him.[54] When Judah uses the word צדקה to announce that Tamar is innocent (v. 26), the doubt remains that he may be wrong and that someone else may be the father of her child. This leads God to intervene through a heavenly voice

---

50 BR 85.9 (pp. 1042–43); T, introduction, p. 69b, referring to Bodleian, Oxford, MS Opp. 187, as described in Neubauer, no. 156, col. 26, and Beit-Arié and May, col. 21.

51 Ibn Shuaib is cited by Kasher, *Torah*, p. 1464, no. 82, the original comment occurring in his *Derashot 'al Ha-Torah*, Constantinople 1523, the folio marked as 10b but actually 17b, as kindly confirmed for me by Dr Dan Davies; Yalquṭ Shim'oni on Num 20:8, section 763, pp. 433–34. Contrast the interpretation in the Testament of Judah which relates the items to Judah's own royal status, as explained in Menn, p. 360.

52 Brock, 'Women's voices'.

53 T *Va-Yeshev* 17 (p. 94a); *y. Sanh.* 4.8[7] (22b); see also Kugel, *Ladder*, p. 171.

54 *b. Sanh.* 102a.

(בת קול) and add the word ממני, meaning that 'it is decreed so by me', that is, by God'.[55] Her evidence in the form of Judah's three personal belongings had gone missing at the time of the trial and was divinely restored to her just in time.[56] Being the righteous person he was, Judah would have ignored Tamar waiting for him on the road and not succumbed to the temptation but God arranged for an angel to arouse his sexual desire and to challenge him on the need for future progeny to rule Israel and to provide the Messiah.[57] Thus it came about that the ancestor of the Messiah destined to redeem Israel was born before the ruler (apparently Pharaoh) who would attempt to enslave them forever.[58] It is not out of the question that such a reference to a non-Jewish ruler is obliquely alluding to more contemporary non-Jewish power. Judah's attraction to the Canaanite woman, the marriage of his sons to Tamar, the death of his sons, and the loss of his wife were all directly planned by God in order to bring Tamar and Judah together, and at the birth of the twins God prevented Zerah being born first because the Messiah was to be a descendant of Peretz, as prophesied in Mic 2:13. Similar comments note that the inclusion of the word היא in v. 16 alludes to God's part in the proceedings; that when the angel Samael tried to prevent Tamar's acquittal while his colleague Gabriel acted on her behalf, God indicated to Gabriel that he should emerge the victor; and that God killed off her first two husbands so that Tamar could carry Judah's child, the ancestor of the Messiah. [59]

Medieval exegesis

As is well known, many of the Jewish commentators between the tenth and sixteenth centuries gradually moved away from the midrashic approach (*derash*) towards more linguistic, contextual, literary and historical approaches that may broadly be defined as *peshaṭ* ('literal sense').[60] Given its more restrictive nature and its greater tendency towards the objective, *peshaṭ* will inevitably be less inclined than *derash* to reveal the polemical and the tendentious but the choices

---

55 *b. Mak.* 23b; compare Menn, p. 356, and Kugel, *Ladder*, p. 171. See also Pseudo-Jonathan and Fragmentary Targum.

56 *b. Soṭah* 10b; T *Va-Yeshev* 17 (p. 94a); MHG, pp. 653–54. See also Pseudo-Jonathan and Fragmentary Targum at considerable length.

57 BR 85.8 (pp. 1041–42); compare T *Va-Yeshev* 17 (p. 94a) which stresses that Tamar prayed for such divine intervention and does not spell out the matter of the royal and messianic progeny.

58 BR 85:1 (1030), expounding Isa 66:7.

59 BR 85.1 (1030); AB, p. 54b; LT, p. 97b; *b. Soṭah* 10b; LT, p. 96b; and see n. 56 above.

60 See chapter 2 above and the list of works cited at its end.

made by the various commentators will still be of interest to this discussion. It should also not be forgotten that midrashim sometimes included what the later commentators would have defined as *peshaṭ*. Identification of those cases in which such commentators still opted for midrashic renderings will assist the researcher in assessing the degree to which they remained committed to the particular message that such renderings were attempting to convey.

Of all the commentators, Rashi is obviously the one who, despite his move towards the literal, continued to cite numerous midrashim in his pentateuchal commentary. Among midrashic comments cited above that are retained in his commentary, virtually as they were in the original works, are those relating to the reduction of Judah's status among his brothers, the translation of כנעני as a merchant, the retention of female beauty by the avoidance of pregnancy, Tamar as the daughter of Shem, the name Timna, Judah's religious and mighty descendants, God's interjection with the word ממני, Tamar's reluctance to embarrass Judah in public, the piety of Tamar's twins, and the reference to Achan's disobedience. Rashi cites both midrashic and literal explanations in his comments on the word כזיב, on the expression פתח עינים, on the phrase כי כסתה פניה ('for she covered her face') in v. 15, and on Judah's relations with Tamar after her acquittal. He also explains Judah's suggestion to Tamar in v. 11 as specifically indicating that he had no intention whatsoever of marrying her off to Shela because of the fate of the elder two brothers, expanding on comments in BR and BT *Yevamot* that allude to this.[61] Given his rigid and consistent preference for the *peshaṭ*, it is only to be expected that Rashbam would specifically reject a number of the midrashic interpretations (some of them recorded by his grandfather, Rashi), and he has alternative, and more literal explanations of כזיב, פתח עינים, Tamar's face covering, Judah's personal belongings, ממני and the death penalty passed on Tamar. Somewhat surprisingly, however, we find that Rashbam also explains כנעני as a merchant, as well as including a reference to the avoidance of pregnancy for cosmetic reasons.[62] Ibn Ezra also rejects outright the midrashic interpretations of כזיב and Judah's 'descent' but remains undecided about the word כנעני and about referring the phrase כי כסתה פניה ('for she covered her face') in v. 15 to Tamar's days in the marital home and not to the incident on the road to Timna.[63]

For his part, Ḥizzequni cites the reduction of Judah's status while adding a chronological note; notes the midrashic explanation of כזיב, while adding a linguistic comment; refers to the avoidance of pregnancy while spelling out that

61 Ed. Berliner, pp. 77–79; ed. Chavel, *Rashi*, pp. 137–39; eds. Rosenbaum and Silbermann, 1.185–90.

62 Ed. Rosin, pp. 53–55; trans. Lockshin, pp. 261–69.

63 Ed. Weiser, 1.109–111. For a useful English translation of Ibn Ezra, see Strickman and Silver.

Judah therefore married Tamar as a virgin; expands further on Rashi's explicit rendering of the midrashic comments on Judah's instructions to Tamar; spells out the Timna midrash a little more clearly; accepts the idea that Judah, Isaac and Jacob judged Tamar, while explaining that he spoke first as the junior member; notes identification of Tamar as the daughter of Shem and explains the ramifications of this, including a note to the effect that priesthood was removed from Shem and given to Abraham and his descendants; explains more fully the two contrasting interpretations of the phrase ולא יסף עוד לדעתה in v. 26, namely, either that he no longer had relations with her or that he did not refrain from having further relations with her; and that Peretz anticipated his brother because his progeny was destined to be royalty.[64] The claim that the priesthood was transferred from Shem to Abraham may have been made in response to claims that the Christian priesthood has earlier antecedents than the Jewish one.

Naḥmanides explains כנעני as a merchant and has a long comment on why marriage with Canaanite women must have been a rare phenomenon among the Hebrews. He is clearly not entirely happy with the various midrashic explanations of names and offers some alternative reasons for their adoption. Rashi's explanation of v. 11 is also unsatisfactory for him because Judah, given his anger at her alleged immorality, must originally have wanted her to remain in the family, having accepted that she was guiltless in the matter of his sons' misbehaviour. Naḥmanides also questions the midrashic interpretation of Tamar's modesty in her marital home, arguing that in that case even if she had not covered her face, he would not have recognized her. Judah's sentence that Tamar be burnt, even if she was the daughter of Shem, has no biblical or rabbinic basis, according to Naḥmanides, and must therefore be explained as an *ad hoc* decision on his part. He also provides his own clarifications of the two contrasting expositions of v. 26.[65]

Sforno only once refers directly to a midrash and that is in his comment on v. 25 where he praises Tamar for not shaming Judah in public. But elsewhere he incorporates the teaching of the aggadists. It was part of the divine plan that Tamar should have offspring from Judah since he was a more appropriate ancestor of the Messiah than Shelah might have been. The items that Tamar chose as her surety were all indicative of Judah's stature and what she had in mind was to have children of similar stature. Judah's exoneration of Tamar amounted to a recognition that her apparently immoral behaviour was not for her own benefit but for a higher and religiously admirable purpose, that is to say, to have children from Judah.[66]

64 Ed. Chavel, *Ḥizzequni*, pp. 144–47.
65 Ed. Chavel, *Perushey*, pp. 212–19; trans. Chavel, *Ramban*, pp. 463–79.
66 Eds. Gottlieb and Darom, pp. 91–95; trans. Pelkovitz, pp. 184–88.

Exegetical questions and responses

Earlier in this essay it was suggested that certain questions, doubts and anxieties may well have occurred in the minds of those who were reading the Hebrew scripture, or listening to its translation and interpretation. It was to such thoughts that the aggadists addressed themselves when they formulated and transmitted their exegetical comments on Scripture. In addition to points of detail, such preachers and teachers were dealing with broader questions and it is possible on the basis of a close reading of the variety of comments recorded earlier to draft a list of such questions and of the answers that they appear to be proposing. Such questions and answers may of course have changed from generation to generation but the occurrence of many themes that are common to various midrashim originating in different ages do permit us to identify a fair number which consistently remained at the centre of exegetical consideration.

1. Are there items that should be excluded from the synagogal readings, thus reflecting a view that a choice must be made about suitability and relevance?
   - One can achieve a compromise by including all pentateuchal passages but exercising choice regarding prophets and hagiographa, as well as regarding targumic renderings.
2. Do the pentateuchal texts and the biblical characters provide guidance for contemporary Jews with regard to intermarriage, conversion, sexuality?
   - Those assumed to be fine examples of proto-Jews either sinned and repented, or never actually sinned because their motives were pure, or did sin and were punished, or achieved forgiveness only through special mediation on their behalf at a later time.
3. Do the promises, genealogies and personal characteristics that are encountered is scripture relate to the present and future as well as to the past?
   - Some Jewish institutions and individuals of the present are the successors of their biblical precedents and others will enjoy such a status in the future time.
4. Does God adjust his relationship with the Jewish people and their heroes in the light of their unsatisfactory behaviour?
   - There is a permanently close relationship between God and his people Israel.
5. Were the pre-Sinaitic leaders observers of the Torah or of a different set of religious traditions?
   - Either they adhered to the Torah or to parts of it before it was given to Israel as a whole or they followed the Noahite laws which constitute what is required of non-Jewish peoples.

6. Did priesthood already exist in pre-Sinaitic times and was the office held by non-Hebrews?
   - There were priests such as Melchizedek, who is to be identified with Shem or one of his progeny, but their priesthood was transferred to Abraham and then later to the tribe of Levi.
7. To what extent was Tamar a religiously inspired woman, with special qualities?
   - Tamar, who was a virgin when she had sexual relations with Judah, did not have prophetic stature but did receive divine guidance about how to proceed in connection with the creation of the divinely approved dynasty of Judah and David and is broadly viewed as having been well motivated in her actions.
8. Are there specific kinds of sexual relations that are more characteristic of pagans rather than Jewish people?
   - According to some aggadists, any departure from normative intercourse which may lead to pregnancy is to be regarded as a disreputable act, unworthy of pious Jews.
9. Do names and utensils carry any significance beyond their simple nomenclature?
   - Some aggadists use them as allusions to events or activities not specifically recorded in the biblical text, or to other parts of scripture, or see them as pointers to future developments, while others are more comfortable with their more literal sense and usage.
10. How can we be sure that what is related in the text of the Hebrew Bible is not merely the story of ancient people, with their foibles and vicissitudes, which might have moved in all manner of haphazard directions?
   - The biblical narrative always reflects the overall divine plan and God, as it were, takes a hand in ensuring that matters move in the right direction to ensure the future viability and loyalty of the Jewish people up to and including the messianic age.

It seems to me that one does not require a great deal of imagination to suggest how such questions might have related to the broader topic of the Jewish-Christian exegetical encounter. What undoubtedly emerges from much of the exegesis cited above is a clear endorsement of the views that intermarriage is not something to be condoned and that unqualified disapproval has to be expressed of aspects of life in the gentile world. The status of the Jewish people has not changed from ancient to current times and God still has a special relationship with the Jews. There is distinct tendency to forestall attempts at finding proto-Christians in the pentateuchal narrative or at proposing that royalty, prophecy and priesthood have moved away from those who once held them in the Jewish world. If typologies are to be employed, they had better be Jewish ones. It seems to me that all these notions are capable of being understood in the context of the Jewish-Christian exegetical encounter. But, as I indicated early in this brief study, what must be undertaken before we can properly assess that encounter is the sound definition of what constituted broad Jewish and Christian understandings of the chapter before us. I hope that I have made some contribution to the Jewish side and that, when an equivalent essay has been completed on the Christian approaches, we may then make some further progress towards at least a degree of comparative analysis.

Works cited

Aggadat Bereshit (= AB), ed. S. Buber (Cracow: Fischer, 1903).

Barton, J. and Muddiman, J. (eds.), *The Oxford Bible Commentary* (Oxford: Oxford University Press, 2001).

Bereschit Rabba (= BR), eds. J. Theodor and Ch. Albeck (Jerusalem: Wahrmann 1965, 2nd edn.).

Berliner, A. (ed.), *Raschi: Der Kommentar des Salomo b. Isak über den Pentateuch* (Frankfurt-am-Main: Kauffman, 1905).

Bloch, R., 'Midrash', in *Approaches to Ancient Judaism: Theory and Practice*, ed. W. S. Green (Brown Judaic Studies 1, Missoula: Scholars Press, 1978), pp. 29–50.

Brock, S. P., 'Creating women's voices: Sarah and Tamar in Syriac narrative poems', in *The Exegetical Encounter between Jews and Christians in Late Antiquity*, eds. E. Grypeou and H. Spurling (Jewish and Christian Perspectives Series 18, Leiden: Brill, 2009), pp. 125–41.

BT = Babylonian Talmud.

Chavel, C. B. (ed.), *Ḥizzequni. Perushey Ha-Torah Le-Rabbenu Ḥizqiyah b. Manoaḥ* (Jerusalem: Rav Kook, 1981).

Chavel, C. B. (ed.), *Perushey Rashi 'al Ha-Torah* (Jerusalem: Rav Kook, 1983, 3rd edn.).

Chavel, C. B. (ed.), *Perushey Ha-Torah Le-Rabbenu Mosheh ben Naḥman*, 2 vols. (Jerusalem: Rav Kook, 1969, 5th edn.).

Chavel, C. B. (Eng. trans.), *Ramban (Nachmanides): Commentary on the Torah*, 5 vols. (New York: Shilo, 1971–76).

Cooper, B., *Genesis 38* (London: Heinemann, 1964).

Fishbane, M., *The Exegetical Imagination: On Jewish Thought and Theology* (Cambridge, Mass.: Harvard University Press, 1998).

Frishman, J., 'And Abraham had faith. But in what? Ephrem and the Rabbis on Abraham and God's blessing', in *The Exegetical Encounter between Jews and Christians in Late Antiquity*, eds. E. Grypeou and H. Spurling (Jewish and Christian Perspectives Series 18, Leiden: Brill, 2009), pp. 163–79.

Ginsburger, M. (ed.), *Das Fragmententhargum (Thargum jeruschalmi zum Pentateuch)* (Berlin: Calvary, 1899).

Ginsburger, M. (ed.), *Pseudo-Jonathan (Thargum Jonathan ben Usiël zum Pentateuch)* (Berlin: Calvary, 1903).
Ginzberg, L., *The Legends of the Jews*, 7 vols. (Philadelphia: Jewish Publication Society of America, 1909–38).
Goller, I., *Judah and Tamar: A Novel in Drama, reconstructing Genesis 38:11–26* (London: Ghetto Press, 1931).
Gottlieb, Z. (W.) and Darom, A. (eds.), *Bi'ur Ha-Torah Le-Rabbi 'Ovadyah Seforno* (Jerusalem: Rav Kook, 1980).
Grypeou, E., and Spurling, H., 'Abraham's angels. Jewish and Christian exegesis of Genesis 18–19', in *The Exegetical Encounter between Jews and Christians in Late Antiquity*, eds. E. Grypeou and H. Spurling (Jewish and Christian Perspectives Series 18, Leiden: Brill, 2009), pp. 181–203.
Hirshman, M., *A Rivalry of Genius: Jewish and Christian Biblical Interpretation*, Eng. trans. B. Stein (SUNY Series in Judaica; Albany, N. Y.: State University of New York Press, 1996).
Jacobs, I., *The Impact of Midrash* (JSSSup., Oxford: Oxford University Press, 2006).
Jacobs, I., *The Midrashic Process: Tradition and Interpretation in Rabbinic Judaism* (Cambridge: Cambridge University Press, 1995).
Jellinek, A., (ed.), *Bet ha-Midrasch* (Leipzig: Nies, 1853–57).
Kasher, M. (ed.), *Torah Shelemah* (New York and Jerusalem: American Biblical Encyclopedia Society, 1927–).
Kasher, R., 'The interpretation of Scripture in rabbinic literature', in: M. J. Mulder (ed.), *Mikra: Text, Translation, Reading and Interpretation of the Hebrew Bible in Ancient Judaism and Early Christianity* (Assen, Maastricht and Philadelphia: Van Gorcum, Fortress Press, 1988), pp. 547–94.
Kessler, E., *Bound by the Bible: Jews, Christians and the Sacrifice of Isaac* (Cambridge: Cambridge University Press, 2004).
Klein, M. L., (ed.), *The Fragment Targums of the Pentateuch according to their Extant Sources*, 2 vols. (Rome: Biblical Institute Press, 1980).
Kugel, J. L., *The Ladder of Jacob: Ancient Interpretations of the Biblical Story of Jacob and his Children* (Princeton: Princeton University Press, 2006).
Kugel, J. L. (ed.), *Studies in Ancient Midrash* (Cambridge, Mass.: Harvard University Center for Jewish Studies, 2001).
Lekach-Tob (=LT), ed. S. Buber (Vilna: Romm, 1880).
Lockshin, M. I., *Rabbi Samuel ben Meir's Commentary on Genesis: An Annotated Translation* (Lewiston: Edwin Mellen Press, 1989).
Mechilta D'Rabbi Ismael, ed. H. S. Horovitz and I. A. Rabin (Frankfurt-am-Main: Kauffman, 1931).
Mekilta de-Rabbi Ishmael, ed. J. Z. Lauterbach, 3 vols. (Philadelphia: Jewish Publication Society of America, 1933–35).
Menn, E. M., *Judah and Tamar (Genesis 38) in Ancient Jewish Exegesis: Studies in Literary Form and Hermeneutics* (Leiden: Brill, 1997).
Midrasch Tanchuma (=T), ed. S. Buber, 2 vols. (Vilna: Romm, 1885).
Midrasch Tehillim (Schocher Tob) (=MT), ed. S. Buber (Vilna: Romm, 1891).
Midrash Ha-Gadol (=MHG), ed. M. Margulies (Jerusalem: Rav Kook, 1947–72).
Neubauer, A., *Catalogue of the Hebrew Manuscripts in the Bodleian Library* (Oxford: Clarendon Press, 1886), with *Supplement* by M. Beit-Arié and R. A. May (Oxford: Oxford University Press, 1994).

Perles, J. (ed.), *Biure Onkelos: Scholien zum Targum Onkelos von Simon Baruch Schefftel,* (Munich: Akermann, 1888).
Porton, G. G., *Understanding Rabbinic Midrash : Texts and Commentary* (Hoboken, N. J.: Ktav, 1985).
PT = Palestinian or Yerushalmi Talmud.
Rosenbaum, M., and Silbermann, A. M., *Pentateuch with Rashi's Commentary translated into English* (London: Shapiro, Vallentine, 1929–34).
Rosin, D. (ed.), *Perush Ha-Torah 'asher katav Rashbam* (Breslau: Schottlender, 1881).
Salvesen, A., 'Keeping it in the family: Jacob and his Aramean heritage according to Jewish and Christian sources', in *The Exegetical Encounter between Jews and Christians in Late Antiquity*, eds. E. Grypeou and H. Spurling (Jewish and Christian Perspectives Series 18, Leiden: Brill, 2009), pp. 205–220.
Shemot Rabbah (Vilna: Romm, 1878).
Shir Ha-Shirim Rabbah (=ShR) (Vilna: Romm, 1878).
Siphre D'Be Rab, ed. H. S. Horovitz (Leipzig: Gustav Fock, 1917).
Sivan, G., 'Izak Goller (1891–1939): Zionist poet, playwright and teacher', *Jewish Historical Studies: Transactions of the Jewish Historical Society of England* 41 (2007), pp. 145–71.
Stemberger, G., *Introduction to the Talmud and Midrash* (Eng. trans. M. Bockmuehl, Edinburgh: T. & T. Clark, 1996, 2nd edn.).
Stern, D., *Parables in Midrash: Narrative and Exegesis in Rabbinic Literature* (Cambridge, Mass.: Harvard University Press, 1991).
Strickman, H. N., and Silver, A. M., *Ibn Ezra's Commentary on the Pentateuch. Genesis (Bereshit)* (New York: Menorah, 1988).
Vermes, G., *Scripture and Tradition in Judaism: Haggadic Studies* (Leiden: Brill, 1973, 2nd edn.).
Weiser, A. (ed.), *Perushey Ha-Torah Le-Rabbenu Avraham Ibn 'Ezra*, 3 vols. (Jerusalem: Rav Kook, 1977).
Weiss Halivni, D., *Peshat and Derash: Plain and Applied Meaning in Rabbinic Exegesis* (Oxford: Oxford University Press, 1991).
Yalquṭ Shim'oni, eds. D. [=A. B.] Hyman and Y. Shiloni, *Bemidbar* (Jerusalem: Rav Kook, 1986).

4 The Classical Jewish Commentators on Exodus 2

Introduction

In choosing a topic suitable for inclusion in a volume of essays compiled in honour of an outstanding scholar whose work I had admired and whose friendship I had cherished for over a quarter of a century, I was naturally motivated in the first instance by what would be of special interest to him, given his academic philosophy and subject preferences. I believe that it was as a graduate student that I first encountered the view that not all aspects of what is presented as the scholarly study of the Hebrew Bible may truly be regarded as genuinely scientific and, if I am not greatly mistaken, it was from the lips of Shelomo Morag that I heard it. The close linguistic study of the biblical Hebrew text and its traditional recitation were always an essential accompaniment of his intensive research into the Hebrew language and its history and one of his presuppositions was that the medieval Hebrew grammarians and commentators might profitably be consulted in our efforts to master the analysis and exegesis of the Hebrew Bible.[1] As an accomplished teacher and lecturer he knew the value of returning to basic sources and ensuring that we fully appreciate their import and intent rather than indulging ourselves in imaginative literary speculation that may be more of an intellectual exercise than a productive means of study. As a dedicated pedagogue he also knew the importance of providing students with easy access to the sources and data that are basic for the understanding of the subject.

It therefore seemed fitting to utilize that context for an ambition that I had entertained for a number of years but had never been able fully to realize. The aim of this paper is to offer an analysis of the Hebrew comments of a number of medieval Jewish Bible commentators that should serve as a useful introduction to those who are not specialists in the field and even perhaps inspire further thoughts on the part of those who are. My hope is that such an undertaking will exemplify the contribution they made to biblical exegesis and Hebrew language study (as undertaken by both Christians and Jews), and demonstrate the degree to which their comments are still useful in various ways to contemporary scholarship. It seems to me that this tallies with the recent tendencies of both scholarship and publication. An instructive example of the former may be found in the

1 Examples of the kind of research I have in mind are his *Vocalization Systems*; *Hebrew Language Traditions;* 'Some Notes' and *Vocalised Talmudic Manuscripts.*

DOI 10.1515/9783110486704-005

programme of lectures for the Eleventh World Congress of Jewish Studies held in Jerusalem in 1993. One of the themes treated there was the contribution of traditional biblical exegesis to its modern counterpart and various lecturers identified a renewed interest in the medieval commentators and a greater awareness of their contemporary relevance.[2] While Christian and Jewish scholars of previous generations in the modern period had turned a blind eye to such sources and characterized them as insufficiently neutral and scientific, more recent researchers had come to different conclusions. They had acknowledged that the philosophy and methodology underlying the works of the Middle Ages did not tally with current academic approaches but had come to the realization that linguistic and literary analysis had now broadened to such a degree that it could usefully incorporate aspects of the medieval heritage. The acceptance of multiple interpretations gave midrashic views a new relevance; the search for fresh information and insights led to a re-evaluation of the literary and aesthetic sensitivities of pre-modern commentators; and the recognition that early Hebrew language traditions could have been preserved in the Middle Ages inspired a healthier respect for the first Hebrew grammarians.[3]

Problems and texts

Recent publication projects have also made a major and practical impact on the scholarly use of medieval Jewish Bible commentaries. Formerly, anyone wishing to consult these texts in a conveniently available anthology was forced to make reference to the standard Rabbinic Bible or *Miqra'ot Gedolot*. In such volumes the commentaries were inevitably printed in small letters, often of the so-called 'Rashi' type and generations of printers had left the marks of their ignorance in the manner in which punctuation, introductory wording, comment division

2 The lectures of particular relevance to this discussion were by Adele Berlin, 'Traditional Jewish exegesis'; by Uriel Simon on literary-aesthetic interpretation; and by Richard Steiner on linguistic aspects. For various contributions to the topic by Simon, see his collected articles, *The Ear Discerns*. See also Greenspahn, 'How modern', Sarna, *Exodus*, pp. 8–13, and chapter 2, n. 3 above.

3 The issue remains a controversial one among 'Old Testament' scholars. A. A. Macintosh, who made extensive use of the medieval Jewish commentators in preparing his ICC commentary on Hosea, alluded to their importance for contemporary scholarship in a paper to the Society for Old Testament Study at its conference in Exeter in the summer of 1993 ('Towards an I.C.C. on Hosea: the prophet's language') but his view was challenged by David Clines who claimed that they had only historical interest.

and verse citation were arranged, and difficult readings were often corrupted.[4] Now two new series, *Torat Ḥayyim* and *Mikra'ot Gedolot Haketer*, have appeared, which aim to replace such unsatisfactory editions with more readable, reliable and attractively produced texts of the Hebrew Bible, the Targum and the most distinguished of the medieval Jewish commentators, making extensive use of much of the manuscript research and exegetical study of recent years.[5]

Neither series will provide comprehensively scientific editions of all the texts but they have already demonstrated that a vast improvement can be made in the production of such reference works and will inevitably encourage future generations of scholars to approach the material they contain with a good deal less trepidation than hitherto.[6]

In spite of the existence of such admirable publications, a number of serious problems remain before students of the Hebrew Bible can extend their competence to the comments of their medieval Jewish predecessors. The language of these texts is medieval Rabbinic Hebrew (where it is not Judaeo-Arabic or glosses in Romance languages) with its allusive and elliptic style, its dialectical argumentation, and its confident assumptions of the reader's prior and extensive knowledge of a host of other sources. It is no simple matter to place each comment in the context in which it was originally made and all too easy to impose one's own understanding of a biblical text on the medieval commentary. It is also easy to forget that no exegete can ever be properly understood unless one is aware of the questions and problems that were troubling him when he confronted the scriptural verse. Furthermore, there is the backdrop of a long and complicated history of Jewish Bible commentary against which each exegete requires to be set, and a host of discussions and arguments, without a knowledge of which it is well-nigh impossible to evaluate his contribution.[7] Given that reasonable texts are now available and that biographical details are to be found in works of general reference, an urgent priority is to choose a suitable biblical passage; to introduce each of the chosen commentators and briefly estimate his contribution; to summarize the questions that the passage posed for the medieval commentator; to offer a précis of the answers suggested by each exegete; to focus on a number of verses and attempt a comparison of how they are treated

4 The best known editions are those published by Daniel Bomberg in sixteenth-century Venice and those of Warsaw and Vienna in the nineteenth century.

5 Both published in Israel, in Jerusalem and Ramat-Gan respectively.

6 See the review of the Cohen edition, Ofer, 'New edition'.

7 On the general history and style of medieval Jewish Bible commentary, see Segal, *Parshanut;* Casper, *Introduction*; Jacobs, *Exegesis*; Melamed, *Bible Commentators*; Greenberg, *Exegesis*; and A. Grabois, *Commentaires*.

by the various glossators; and to make at least passing reference to similar interpretations and contemporary treatments.

Before proceeding to the body of the task, a few remarks are in order about the choice of biblical text and particular medieval commentators. As any pentateuchal text, Exodus 2 has obviously attracted major attention from generations of Jewish readers as well as being of interest to critical scholars of the modern period. Its narrative nature calls for literary and linguistic comment rather than legal, philosophical or mystical exploitation and therefore eases the burden of understanding placed on the contemporary analyst. Unusually, the story is self-contained and there are no digressions, the theme being the birth and early life of Moses, with a concluding section reminding the reader of the situation of his kinsmen in Egypt. There is also ample midrashic and talmudic comment that provides the opportunity of gauging the degree to which the medieval rabbis had departed from the methodology established by their forerunners.[8] As far as the choice of commentators is concerned, this has effectively been conditioned by their presence in the various editions of the rabbinic Bible, particularly in the *Torat Ḥayyim* series to which reference has already been made, and permits an overview taking in a fairly wide range of periods and places. The tenth-century Babylonian tradition is represented by Sa'adya Gaon;[9] the French schools of the eleventh, twelfth and thirteenth centuries by Rashi, Rashbam and Ḥizzequni;[10] the Spanish approach of the twelfth and thirteenth centuries by Ibn Ezra (both the short and long commentaries) and Naḥmanides;[11] and the sixteenth-century Italian world by Obadiah Sforno.[12] Before proceeding to examine the text as they saw it, it will be appropriate to recall briefly their places in Jewish literary history by noting a few elementary facts about them and their work.

Commentators

All Jewish scholarship received a massive impetus from the founding and spread of Islam in the seventh, eighth and ninth centuries and the most outstanding representative of this academic symbiosis was Sa'adya Gaon (882–942) who headed

---

8 These are listed in n. 24 below.
9 See Segal, pp. 37–41; Casper, pp. 42–49; and Greenberg, pp. 15–19.
10 See Segal, pp. 63–72; Casper, pp. 59–65; Jacobs, pp. 1–7, 22–30 and 69–75; Melamed, pp. 353–513; and Greenberg, pp. 70–79 and 85–86.
11 See Segal, pp. 78–86 and 96–102; Casper, pp. 66–72 and 81–89; Jacobs, pp. 8–21 and 46–60; Melamed, pp. 519–714 and 933–1021; and Greenberg, pp. 47–68.
12 Jacobs, pp. 134–43; and Greenberg, pp. 98–100.

the rabbinical school in Sura, Babylonia. Characterized by Ibn Ezra as the 'chief spokesman on all matters' of Jewish learning,[13] Sa'adya excelled in philosophy, poetry and *halakhah* but underlying all his studies were a passion for the Hebrew Bible and the Hebrew language and a desire to polemicize against non-rabbinic interpretations and philosophies, especially those of the Karaite sect. Fearless controversialist that he was, he set himself the tasks of translating and explaining the Hebrew Bible in Arabic for the Jewish and non-Jewish populace and of producing a detailed commentary for a more scholarly clientele. His simpler version became standard for all subsequent generations of oriental Jewish communities but the more intensive treatment of the text survived only in parts. He prefaces his comments with introductions to individual books, makes major and innovative use of grammar and syntax, offers clear definitions of vocabulary, and tackles theological problems. He is conscious of the need to impress the reader with his Arabic literary style and prefers the literal rendering except when it is irrational, unnatural, contradictory or untraditional. Anthropomorphisms are eliminated so that no accusation may be made that the rabbinic notion of God is a purely human one, and translation is so important that even place-names are given suitable renderings. In a word, Sa'adya attempted to enhance the status of the Bible among the intellectuals of his day and his influence was felt for centuries, particularly among the Jews of North Africa and Spain.[14]

So great was its popularity that an acquaintance with 'Ḥumash-Rashi', that is, the commentary of Rabbi Solomon ben Isaac on the Pentateuch, was once a minimum requirement for any Jew claiming to be hebraically literate. Born in the Champagne district of France in 1040 and educated in the Franco-German centres of rabbinic learning, Rashi invariably taught and wrote with the average student in mind so that by the time of his death in 1105 his work was highly regarded and widely known. The intention of his commentary is not only to provide answers to all the basic questions that the reader might ask but also to offer a blend of literal explanation, linguistic guidance and the more fanciful comments of some midrashim. With his broad approach and his modestly expressed views, he succeeded in producing a commentary that was informative as well as religiously edifying and capable of retaining the attention of many generations. So popular did his interpretations become that they formed the basis of much of the English translation in the King James (Authorised) Version of 1611, and

---

13 In the introduction to his *Moznayim* when introducing his list of grammarians, f. 1b.

14 Zucker, *Saadya's Translation* and *Saadya's Commentary*; Qafiḥ, *Sa'adyah Ga'on*. The most comprehensive, if somewhat dated, guide to his life remains that of Malter, *Saadia*. See also Brody's excellent survey, *Geonim*, pp. 235–332.

the cursive script employed by printers to differentiate between text and commentary came to be known as the 'Rashi script'.[15]

Rashi had no sons but his daughters were reputed to be scholars in their own right and the eldest, Yokheved, married one of her father's most prominent students, Meir ben Samuel. From their union came some of the leading teachers of twelfth-century France and Germany, among them Rabbi Samuel ben Meir (=Rashbam), born about 1080. Rashbam abandoned the blend of the literal and the midrashic that his grandfather had championed and concerned himself exclusively with text, context, style and, above all, with what he adamantly referred to as the 'absolutely literal sense of the text'. This sometimes led him to explain verses in a manner so at variance with established interpretations that he was afraid of disseminating these comments in easily read texts and couched them in coded form to discourage the less avid reader from studying them.[16] He obviously had discussions and disagreements with his grandfather on the subject and even convinced him that the time had come to change the nature of Jewish Bible interpretation. In his comments on Gen 37:1–2, Rashbam reports such discussions and Rashi's remark that if he had had the time he would have rewritten his commentary in the light of the novel findings of contemporary scholarship.[17]

While Rashbam was fighting for the adoption of the literal meaning in France, Rabbi Abraham ben Meir Ibn Ezra was waging a similar campaign for a more rational approach among the Sefardi Jews in the south. Born in Tudela in Spain in 1089, he lived the seventy-five years of his life as an itinerant scholar, first in Spain and North Africa and later in Italy, France and England. His lack of a settled life and his poor circumstances may account for the brevity and various versions of his commentaries, his breadth of general knowledge and the sharpness and cynicism of some of his comments. Ibn Ezra it was who claimed that if he dealt in candles the sun would never set and if he took up the manufacture of shrouds nobody would ever die.[18] Although he systematically expounds his methodology in the in-

---

15 The literature on Rashi as pentateuchal commentator is vast but the most recent and important works and editions are Gelles, *Peshat*; Lehmann, *Commentary*; Chavel, *Perushey Rashi*; Banitt, *Rashi*; Kamin, *Exegetical Categorization*. The best guides to his life and work is Grossman, *Rashi*; see also Shereshevsky, *Rashi*. For a scholarly translation of the pentateuchal commentary, see Rosenbaum and Silbermann.

16 See his comments on the meaning of the divine name in Exod 3:14 and Rosin, *Samuel b. Meir*, pp. 83, 100–1 and 148, n. 10.

17 Rosin, *Samuel b. Meir and Perush Ha-Torah* and various articles by E. Touitou on Rashbam and his contemporaries beginning with 'Concerning the methodology' and collected in *Exegesis*, and by Sara Japhet, conveniently available in her *Collected Studies*. For an excellent translation and commentary, see Lockshin, *Rashbam's Commentary*. See also n. 61 below.

18 Carmi, *Hebrew Verse*, p. 353.

troduction to his commentary on the Pentateuch, his cryptic and elliptic style presents a daunting challenge to those who would understand him. He rarely misses an opportunity of introducing technical matters of grammar, philosophy and the physical sciences into his commentary and often challenges traditional rabbinic views by implication rather than directly. If Rashi is the lay people's commentator, Ibn Ezra is most assuredly the scholar's scholar.[19]

'Openly critical if secretly devoted' is how Rabbi Moses ben Naḥman (=Ramban) describes his own feelings about the commentary of Ibn Ezra.[20] Though also a native of Spain, Naḥmanides was born one hundred and five years after Ibn Ezra and in the course of that century the deterioration of the Jewish situation in what had once been a great centre was such that rational and scientific interests had given way to more mystical and pietistic tendencies. In spite, however, of his propensity to defend the traditional interpretations of the Talmud and the midrashim against rationalists such as Ibn Ezra and Maimonides, and to offer what he regarded as the deeper, kabbalistic interpretations of key verses, Naḥmanides could not quite bring himself to abandon the literal approach to the Torah. His lengthy comments still pay attention to linguistic, contextual, medical and chronological points and he is by no means averse to criticizing biblical heroes for moral shortcomings. Having made valiant attempts to defend Judaism against the theological onslaughts of Spanish Christians, he put his Zionist ideals into practice and spent the last few years of his life in Jerusalem. In spite of the political and military upheavals of the period, he succeeded in establishing a centre for Jewish learning there before his death in 1270.[21]

Another representative of the thirteenth century included here is Rabbi Hezekiah ben Manoaḥ (Ḥizzequni) whose activities as a pentateuchal commentator may be classified as among the final products of the great Franco-Jewish school that had flourished since the days of Rashi. The members of that school had, incidentally, enjoyed some contact (perhaps extending to mutual influence) with their non-Jewish equivalents in the monasteries. If Rashi's careful fusion of *peshaṭ* and *derash*, as he understood them, produced an insufficiently sharp

---

19 Weiser, *Perushey Ha-Torah*; Prijs, *Kommentar*; Levin, *Abraham Ibn Ezra*; Díaz Esteban, *Abraham Ibn Ezra*. The most important studies of his non-pentateuchal commentaries have recently been published by U. Simon; see especially his *Four Approaches*. For English translations of his pentateuchal commentary, see Strickman and Silver, *Commentary* and Shachter, *Commentary*. See also Twersky and Harris, *Studies* and Lancaster, *Deconstructing*.

20 The description is to be found towards the end of the poetic introduction to his pentateuchal commentary.

21 Chavel, *Perushey Ha-Torah*; *Kitvey Rabbenu Mosheh*; *Ramban. His Life*; *Ramban (Nachmanides). Commentary*.

scalpel for the surgically precise anatomy of the text favoured by his grandson, Rashbam, there were others such as Ḥizzequni who preferred such a dualistic style and extended the application of each of its elements. Ḥizzequni did not hesitate to incorporate both *halakahah* and grammar into his comments but his main intention was to synthesize the best of both the midrashic tradition and the literal approach. While demonstrating a fine literary sense, a rationalist bent, and a keen awareness of the realities of everyday life, he adhered firmly to his aggadic inheritance and even preserved some midrashic material virtually unknown elsewhere. But he did use the midrashic interpretations in a fairly sophisticated fashion, harmonizing them when they appear to contradict each other and shaping them to fit snugly into the other exegetical items on offer. His solutions to historical problems may not be impressive to the modern historian but he does at least demonstrate an awareness of their troublesome nature. He enjoyed word-plays and allusions but was at the same time conscious of the need to translate into French and to incorporate, albeit anonymously, many comments of his Jewish compatriots.[22]

The final stop in this journey through the commentaries may be made in the period of the Italian Renaissance. Flourishing as he did in the late fifteenth and early sixteenth centuries, Rabbi Obadiah Sforno is one of the links between those medieval exegetes and their modern counterparts. Like a number of his predecessors, Sforno changed his domicile a number of times, moving from his birthplace of Cesena in the papal state of north central Italy, first to Rome and later to Bologna. As one would expect from a qualified physician with the characteristically broad general education of his day, he seems more concerned with conveying the various humanistic and universalistic aspects of the text than engaging in religious polemics. Where his approach is theological, it serves to provide practical religious guidance for his fellow Jews. He is clearly devoted to the literary as well as the literal sense of the biblical text and often presents his analysis of its structure and general context. It is a fitting tribute to the balanced nature of his contribution that he was, at one and the same time, the teacher of the famous Christian hebraist, Johannes Reuchlin (1455–1522), who influenced so much later scholarship and encouraged a more enlightened attitude to Jews, and a mentor to his own co-religionists in matters of both Jewish law and communal activity.[23]

---

22 Chavel, *Ḥizzequni*; Japhet, 'Ḥizkuni's commentary'.
23 Gottlieb and Darom, *Bi'ur 'al Ha-Torah*; Pelcovitz, *Sforno.*

Exegetical issues

No exegetical comments are likely to make sense to a student who is unaware of the concerns that prompted them. Such concerns will of course differ in part from generation to generation but may nevertheless include an interest in responding to basic questions that commonly occur to anyone reading the scriptural text. It may therefore be useful here to summarize the problems as the medieval exegetes saw them, before proceeding to an examination of some of their responses (the numbers referring to the verses in Exodus 2):

1. Who were the couple, what is meant by the statement that the man 'went', and, given that Moses was the youngest of three children, why does his birth follow immediately upon the reference to his parents' marriage?
2. What special features in Moses encouraged his mother to hide him and why was it possible to hide him for the specific period of three months?
3. Is there any special reason why she could no longer hide him and what were her reasons for using clay and pitch, and placing the container among the reeds in the Nile?
4. Was there any realistic prospect of Moses being found?
5. Where precisely did Pharaoh's daughter and her servants go and why, and how was the baby fetched?
6. What is the sense of the anticipatory suffix in the second verb, why are two words used to describe the boy, and which phrases are the causes and which the effects?
7. Why was it not possible for an Egyptian woman to nurse him?
8. Is the use of an unusual word to describe Moses's sister significant?
9. How are the two imperative forms to be grammatically explained?
10. Is the name Moses Hebrew or Egyptian, who gave it to him, and how does the name relate to the fate of Moses?
11. What kind of maturity is here being described and what were the emotions that inspired Moses to act the way he did?
12. Was Moses's intention to kill and, if so, by what right?
13. How can argument be justly described as wickedness and why did Moses interfere?
14. Why was there an objection to Moses acting as a judge, what is the parallel here being drawn between this and the earlier incident, which 'thing' is known and of what is Moses afraid?
15. Who told Pharaoh, how was it that he failed to kill Moses, why did Moses flee to Midian and how do the last two statements in the verse relate to each other?
16. Who was the girls' father and what was his religious and social status?

17. Why did the shepherds drive away the shepherdesses and what motivated Moses to come to their rescue?
18. Who was Reuel? (See also vv. 16 and 20)?
19. What sense is conveyed by the emphatic use of the verb דלה (*dlh*)?
20. What motivated Reuel to offer hospitality to Moses?
21. How long is the time-span here presupposed, how was it spent by Moses, and what conclusions may be reached about Zipporah's identification and the meaning of her name?
22. Is there significance in the absence of any reference to conception and how do the names of Moses's children relate to the events of his life?
23. When did these events take place and in what way did they precipitate Israelite sorrow and the return of Moses to Egypt?
24. How does the word used here to describe the Israelites' cries differ in definition from that used in the previous verse and what is implied by the reference to God's memory?
25. What are meant here by God's sight and his knowledge?

Focus on the commentaries will proceed chronologically, with initial attention being given to Sa'adya Gaon, and references to relevant comments in midrashic[24] and modern[25] treatments of the chapter will be made in the footnotes.

Sa'adya

The relatively simple narrative exercises Sa'adya purely as a linguist, and his comments, brief and few as they are, are mainly geared to helpful guidance in the definition of Hebrew words and prepositions. He identifies *ye'or* as the Nile and translates the Hebrew terms *gome'* and *suf* into the Arabic *bardi* and *dis* (v. 3).[26] He suggests (to Ibn Ezra's subsequent chagrin) that the unusual form *heylikhi* should be understood as the equivalent of *hinneh lakh* meaning

24 The midrashic material is to be found in *b. Soṭah* 12ab =BT; Tanḥuma, ff. 64a–66a =T; Shemot Rabbah (ff. 5b–8b =SR; Leqaḥ Ṭov, ff. 4a–8a =LT; and Yalquṭ Shim'oni, ff. 53b–56a and ed. Hyman/Shiloni, pp. 17–46 =YS. See also the English translation of Midrash Rabbah.

25 A selection of modern commentaries of various kinds has been consulted and consists of Driver, Jacob, Noth, Cassuto, *The Broadman Bible Commentary*, Hyatt, Childs, Leibowitz, and *The Expositor's Bible Commentary*.

26 See Lane, *Lexicon*, p. 185 ('papyrus') and Wehr, *Dictionary*, p. 352 ('ampelodesma tenax'). Zohary, *Plants*, pp. 136–37 identifies the plants in the verse as papyrus and cattail (Typha).

'this child is now yours' (v. 9)[27] and points out that the root *'/m/r/* in v. 14 connotes volition rather than speech[28] and that *'akhen* in the same verse stresses Moses's certainty about the matter being public knowledge. In v. 19 he apparently takes the occurrence of the infinitive absolute *daloh* as the object of the verb rather than its qualification, equating it here with 'water', possibly to forestall a midrashic rendering,[29] while in v. 24 he explains that the root *n/'/q/* conveys the sense of repeated weeping. Sa'adya overcomes the problem of the precise sense of the root *y/'/l/* in v. 21 by paraphrasing it to mean that Moses enjoyed a long stay with his host.[30] The vagueness of the double use of the expression *koh* (v. 12) is replaced by a precise 'right and left' and the commentator makes clear that *rasha'* in v. 13 is not a moral judgement but a judicial assessment of their respective cases.[31]

As far as prepositions are concerned, he demonstrates an admirable awareness that these have often to be translated *ad sensum* rather than by standard equivalents, explaining that *le-ven* indicates that she treated him 'as a son' (v. 10),[32] and noting that *'al he-ye'or* means 'in the Nile' while *'al yad ha-ye'or* should be understood as 'on the bank of the Nile' (v. 5).[33] Given that, according to Sa'adya, the princess was in the water and her servants on the bank, there is no sense in her sending one of them to find the box; he consequently translates *wa-tishlaḥ 'et 'amatah* as 'she stretched out her hand'. Since the princess was already in the water, there is no need for the well-known midrashic miracle to explain how she reached her goal (v. 5).[34] While *'et* usually signifies the accusative, as in its first two occurrences in v. 24, its third occurrence there, with reference to Abraham, is as a preposition meaning 'with'.[35]

---

27 See the Syriac Bible, BT, Rashi, SR, LT, YS, Childs (p. 6) and EBC (p. 310) for a similar rendering.

28 See Jacob (p. 258), using the translation '*Wilt* thou kill me as thou hast slain the Egyptian?'

29 E.g. SR, LT, YS and Cassuto (p. 25) where different explanations are offered of the use of the infinitive absolute.

30 Various aspects of commitment are suggested by T, SR and YS; see also Driver (p. 16), Cassuto (pp. 25–26) and BBC (p. 326).

31 A similar view is expressed in LT and Childs (pp. 28 and 30) but Cassuto (p. 23) argues that the assault on his neighbour was an immoral act.

32 Jacob (pp. 249–51) objects to the view that a formal adoption is here implied, such as suggested by Driver (p. 12), Noth (p. 26), Cassuto (pp. 21–22), Leibowitz (p. 39) and EBC (p. 309). Sa'adya (as also SR and LT) prefers to speak of his being treated *as* a son.

33 Driver (p. 10), Hyatt (p. 64) and EBC (p. 309) argue that the first phrase may *also* mean 'by the Nile'.

34 BT, SR, LT and YS record the two possible translations of *'amatah* as 'her arm' and 'her maidservant'.

35 As generally reflected in the translation 'with Abraham, with Isaac and with Jacob'.

Sa'adya also draws attention to syntactical matters. The phrase beginning *wa-tere'* in v. 2 is not a principal clause but a subordinate clause indicating the reason why his mother hid Moses.[36] Similarly, the description of Moses as having grown (v. 10) is not a statement of fact in its own right but an indication of when he was brought to the princess. As a theologian and a philosopher, he clearly felt that there are certain points in the text that cry out for comment. Righteous prophet as he is traditionally portrayed in other ancient Jewish sources, Moses could not possibly have set out to murder the Egyptian and what occurred in v. 12 is clearly a case of manslaughter. As the word *wa-yakh* indicates, Moses merely struck the Egyptian – the fact that he died was an unintended consequence.[37] Sa'adya is equally unhappy with the idea that God somehow came to know something unknown to him previously, as a simple translation of the words at the end of v. 25 might imply. He prefers to postulate another sense for the root *y/d/'/*, one not included in the list of its various meanings that he gives in his commentary on Psalms namely, 'took pity (on the Israelites)'.[38]

Rashi

Whatever the scholarly merits of his work, Rashi deserves major attention because his commentary certainly outclassed those of his predecessors and successors in the quest for popularity. Clearly aware of the need to entertain his readers, both in order to retain their attention for more weighty matters and to allay fears they might have about any attempt to displace the well-established midrashic traditions, he recites a number of *'aggadot* based on the verses of this chapter, albeit in his own systematic and consistent manner. The marriage of

---

36 As Cassuto (p. 18) puts it, the clause . . . is to be understood as giving the reason for the statement that follows'.

37 The victim's alleged misdemeanours are cited by the midrashim as the justification for the imposition of a death penalty (so T, SR, LT and YS). As Leibowitz (p. 41) and Childs (pp. 40–42) point out, commentators through the ages have expressed favourable and unfavourable evaluations of Moses's act. Cassuto (p. 22), BBC (p. 325) and Hyatt (p. 66) see it as reflecting a passion for justice while Jacob (pp. 255–58) takes a similar line to that of Sa'adya and refers to it as 'manslaughter'.

38 *Tehillim. . . Sa'adyah*, pp. 39–40. Theological concerns about the meaning of God's knowledge may already underlie the Septuagint's preference for a passive sense here ('made himself known to them') and those midrashic explanations that refer to a knowledge of future developments (e.g. SR). The idea that empathy is what the narrator has in mind is repeated by LT, Driver (p. 17), Cassuto (p. 29), BBC (p. 327), Leibowitz (p. 49) and EBC (p. 313).

Moses's parents (vv. 1–2) must have been a remarriage after a period of estrangement, or the births of Miriam and Aaron would have been reported before that of Moses.[39] The heroic stature of Moses is amplified by reference to the following factors: the use of clay inside his ark to spare the righteous child the odour of tar (v. 3);[40] his refusal to be breastfed by Egyptian women (based on v. 7);[41] his enunciation of the Tetragrammaton to eliminate the Egyptian taskmaster (based on v. 14);[42] his survival of an attempted execution by Pharaoh (based on v. 15);[43] and his magical powers in drawing a vast volume of water (based on v. 20).[44] Unnamed personalities occurring in the story, such as the quarrelling and calumnious Israelites in v. 13 and the Egyptian taskmaster in v. 11, are respectively identified as Dathan and Abiram[45] and the seducer of Shelomit, daughter of Divri (with accompanying details of the seduction),[46] and the use of the unusual form *heylikhi* in v. 9 provides the opportunity of translating it as two Aramaic words meaning 'she is yours', thereby making the daughter of Pharaoh an unwitting prophetess.[47] The Israelites are given a press bad enough to justify God's imposition of exile and slavery upon them (v. 14);[48] Pharaoh does not die but gorily bathes in Jewish blood to cure the deathly disease of leprosy (v. 23);[49] and Jethro is 'whitewashed' as a Midianite priest who had abandoned the idolatrous faith of his fathers (v. 16).[50]

In a number of other instances Rashi offers his readers both the meaning immediately derivable from the text *and* the midrashic interpretation, thereby easing them gently away from an exclusive preoccupation with the traditional rabbinic treatments of the text. The word *'amah* (v. 5) is understood by the Rabbis to refer to a miraculous lengthening of Pharaoh's daughter's arm but Rashi offers the more literal rendering of 'slave-girl', not, one may add, through any apparent objection to the assumed miracle, but for sound grammatical reasons![51] The pronominal accusative in 'she saw him, the boy' (v. 6) may be a case of an anticipatory suffix,

---

39 See BT, SR, LT and YS.
40 See BT, SR, LT and YS.
41 See BT, T, SR, LT and YS.
42 See T, SR and LT.
43 See T, SR, LT and YS.
44 See T, SR and YS.
45 See T, SR, LT and YS.
46 See SR, T and LT.
47 See BT, SR, LT, YS and n. 27 above.
48 See T, SR and YS.
49 See SR and LT.
50 See T, SR and (differently) YS.
51 See n. 34 above.

but is also the basis for a midrashic reference to the Shekhinah.[52] The fear ascribed to Moses in v. 14 after his encounter with the two quarrelling Israelites may be taken literally but there may also have been an allusion to his doubts about Israel's worthiness of redemption.[53] The verb *wayyo'el* in v. 21, which is an indication of Moses's pleasure (from the root *y/'/l/*), may also indicate that he swore an oath (from the root *'/l/h/*) not to leave Midian without Jethro's permission.[54] In his linguistic and grammatical comments and definitions, Rashi moves more clearly towards what we should define as the literal, equating *'al* with *'al yad* in v. 5, and *n'r* with *yld* in v. 6;[55] paraphrasing *n'q* as *ṣ'q* in v. 24; pointing out the two functions of *'et* (meaning 'with' and marking the accusative) in the same verse in v. 24;[56] and rejecting Menaḥem Ibn Saruq's lack of distinction between the verbs *m/w/sh/* and *m/sh/h/* on v. 10.[57] Perhaps the most fascinating of Rashi's comments are those about which insufficient attention has been given to their possible value for the literal interpretation of the text. Is the word *'lmh* used in v. 8 to indicate the enthusiasm and energy exhibited by the girl?[58] Does v. 17 betray a local animosity towards Jethro and his family?[59] May the 'eating of bread' mentioned in v. 20 be taken as a metaphorical expression for a sexual relationship?[60]

Rashbam

About Rashi's grandson's preference for *peshaṭ* over what we may for convenience summarize as *derash*, there is no ambiguity whatsoever. In his famous comments on Genesis 37:1–2 he argues forcefully against traditional rabbinic in-

52 The midrashic rendering occurs in BT, SR, LT and YS; Cassuto (p. 19) justifies the construction as good Semitic usage.
53 While the other midrashim refer to Israel's unworthiness (see n. 48 above and Acts 7:25), LT presupposes a literal fear; see also Jacob (p. 257), BBC (p. 325), Hyatt (p. 66) and Childs (p. 31).
54 See n. 30 above.
55 Interestingly, the moderns here agree with Rashi rather than Sa'adya; see n. 33 above.
56 See n. 35 above.
57 *Maḥberet*, p. 246*; Filipowski, *Lexicon*, p. 120.
58 See BT (and Rashi's comment there), SR, LT (with a long explanation of why it cannot exclusively mean 'virgin'!) and YS. Driver (p. 11) and Hyatt (p. 64) also understand the word to refer to a mature young woman while Cassuto (p. 20) finds the 'celerity' in the verb rather than in its subject and EBC (p. 310) opts for 'the term is the same as 'the virgin' of Isaiah 7:14'.
59 See T and SR where the shepherds' behaviour is explained against the background of Jethro's rejection of their religious commitments.
60 See T and SR; but Cassuto (p. 25) stresses that 'bread here signifies food in general'; see Reif, 'Bread'.

terpretations and claims that his grandfather would have modified his comments in the direction of the more modern and literal if he had had the leisure to do so.[61] No doubt this conviction made it less traumatic for Rashbam often to reject the interpretations adopted by his grandfather as still too fanciful, albeit rarely by direct reference to his forbear's commentary. As against Rashi's suggestions, the parents of Moses were married only once and there is a gap of many years between the events described in vv. 1 and 2;[62] the use of the clay as well as the tar in v. 3 was to perfect the waterproofing;[63] and *'amah* in v. 5 can mean only a slave-girl.[64] Rashbam also pursues the *peshaṭ* when there is no midrashic comment by Rashi against which he wishes to polemicize and he often demonstrates a keen and independent sense of the literal. Apparently conscious that the root *n/k/h/* is used in v. 13 to describe physical violence and the change made to *h/r/g/* in v. 14 to indicate murder, he forestalls the question why this distinction is not made in vv. 11 and 12 by pointing out on v. 11 that the root *n/k/h/* may carry either sense.[65] He offers the two possibilities that Reuel might be Jethro's father with Hobab an alternative name for the latter, and that Reuel might be Jethro and Hobab the latter's son, expressing preference for the latter on the basis of the verse in Judg 4:11 that explicitly identifies Hobab as *ḥoten mosheh*, a phrase used elsewhere exclusively of Jethro.[66] Unlike the other commentators, he takes the trouble to explain the link between the name given to Gershom and the reference to Moses's period as a stranger in a foreign land (v. 22) by translating the sense of the name as 'a stranger over there in a distant land'.[67]

---

61 See also his comments on Exod 21:1, 40:35 and Lev 1:1. On the relationship between the two methodologies, see Greenberg, '*Ha-yaḥas*'.

62 In the *Chronicles of Moses*, ed. Shinan, p. 107; ed. Jellinek, p. 2; and Eng. trans. in Rankin, p. 28, the births of Miriam and Aaron are here inserted into the story (so YS). The omission of these events here may be imprecise (Driver, p. 8), a concern for only the primarily relevant (Cassuto, p. 17 and EBC, p. 310), or a literary device (Childs, p. 18).

63 See Cassuto (p. 18) and EBC (p. 308).

64 See n. 34 above and Rashi's comment at n. 51 above.

65 Some of the moderns point out that the different nuances of the verb are of special interest for the exegesis of the story; see Jacob (p. 256), Noth (pp. 35–36), Cassuto (p. 22), Hyatt (p. 66), Childs (p. 28) and Leibowitz (pp. 41–43).

66 The various names given to the father-in-law of Moses have preoccupied commentators both ancient (see Septuagint) and modern; see e.g. among the moderns, Driver (p. 15), Noth (p. 37), Cassuto (p. 39), BBC (p. 326), Hyatt (p. 67), Childs (pp. 318–29 and 332–36) and EBC (p. 313). See also Ibn Ezra and Naḥmanides.

67 Driver (p. 16), Hyatt (p. 68) and EBC (p. 313) make precisely the same point. See also SR: 'and God rescued him *from there*'.

Perhaps the best example of Rashbam's perspicacity is his treatment of the four statements in v. 6:

a. 'she saw that he was a male'
b. 'he was crying'
c. 'she had pity on him'
d. 'she said that he was one of the Hebrew boys'.

He argues that the order of the sense, as against that assumed by the Masoretes, is not **a b c d** but **b c a d**, that is to say, 'when she saw him crying, she took pity on him, and when she saw that he was a male, she said that he was one of the Hebrew boys.' He cites a similar example from I Sam 1:4–5 where he adjusts the order of the verses to yield the sense 'he gave Hannah one choice portion because he loved her, but only one because the Lord had made her barren, while he gave Peninah and her sons and daughters many portions, because she had many children.' Rashbam takes his grandfather's dissatisfaction with the biliteral theory of Menaḥem Ibn Saruq a step further by pointing out that the root of *wa-tĕniqehu* in v. 9 is not *n/q/* but *y/n/q/* and the word is an abbreviated form of *watēniqehu*; that *we-teniq* in v. 7 is *hiph'il* while the *qal* would be *we-tinaq*; and that *meshitihu* in v. 10 follows the paradigm of the root *q/n/h/*.[68] Most interestingly, one encounters here, as elsewhere, comments of Rashbam that do not appreciably expand on Rashi's own notes (as in vv. 5, 6 and 10), leading to the question whether elements of Rashbam's commentary were incorporated into that of Rashi at a stage when it was being orally transmitted in the academies of Franco-Germany as work emanating from the great teacher's household.

Ibn Ezra

Immediately noticeable about the commentary, or two versions of commentary, produced by Ibn Ezra is that it is altogether broader in its nature, but at the same time may be seen to pay major attention to the rational and the literary on the one hand, as well as to the grammatical and linguistic on the other. Examples of the former variety include his claim (v. 10) that *mosheh* is a Hebrew version of what must have originally been an Egyptian name,[69] his definition of the word *rsh'* in v. 13 as a relative term, that is, the 'aggressor' rather than the 'wicked

---

68 See his grammatical theories as explained by Rosin, *Samuel b. Meir*, p. 138 and n. 57 above.
69 Driver (p. 11), Noth (p. 26), Cassuto (pp. 20–21), Hyatt (p. 65), Childs (p. 7) and EBC (p. 309) all relate the name to an Egyptian word meaning 'born' as in Ptahmose, Thutmose, Ahmose and Ramose, but Jacob (p. 252) argues for an exclusively Hebrew etymology.

one',[70] and his explanation of the change of gender from 'she gave birth' to 'he called' in v. 22 on the grounds that it was Moses who gave Gershom his name, apparently as an allusion to his own experiences.[71] While these three comments are common to both the shorter and longer commentaries, Ibn Ezra's explanation in v. 19 of Jethro's daughters' claim that Moses had drawn water for them when they had done so themselves is either that they were exaggerating or that they later required more, and this is unique to the longer commentary.[72] Another unique comment is found in v. 12 in the shorter version and suggests that Moses killed the Egyptian with a stone or a spear, clearly militating against the midrash about the enunciation of the Tetragrammaton.[73] In one instance, Ibn Ezra argues against the application of rationalism to a pentateuchal verse. On the basis of his identification of Moses's mother as the paternal aunt of his father, he argues, in his longer commentary on v. 1, the mistaken nature of the theory that explains the later Sinaitic prohibitions against sexual relationships between such close relatives on the basis of the greater fecundity of exogamy. The reason for such regulations is not rational but to encourage a greater degree of holiness through abstention. This effectively prevents the Karaites from arguing the more rational nature of their own stricter marriage laws.[74] On a similar theme, Ibn Ezra on v. 2 explains the variations in the length of the human gestation period in his longer version and simply notes in the shorter one that nobody could have known the precise date of Moses's conception.[75]

The majority of comments in both the longer and shorter versions contain some linguistic or grammatical element that often touches on the explanation of an unusual verbal form (such as vv. 3, 4, 6 and 9 (against Sa'adya),[76] 13 and 20) or

---

70 See n. 31 above.

71 The change of gender is explained by SR as reflecting the custom of righteous men to give names to their children that allude to the miraculous events of their lives.

72 SR credits Moses with having watered *all* the flocks while Cassuto (p. 25) offers three possible reasons why the original efforts of Jethro's daughters had to be supplemented.

73 Alternatives to the use of the Tetragrammaton (see n. 42 above) are his fist and a building trowel (so T and SR).

74 Such stricter laws had been the norm in the period of Anan but had to be relaxed by Jeshuah ben Judah in the eleventh century; see Nemoy, *Anthology*, pp. 18 and 126–27. I owe this reference to my sometime colleague, Meira Polliack.

75 He thus militates against the midrashic views concerning the Egyptians' suspicions about when the child was due, as in SR, LT and YS.

76 Concerning the division of the word *heylikhi* into two; see n. 27 above. It is somewhat surprising that Ibn Ezra makes so many basic grammatical points at the beginning of his commentary on Exodus; if this text is wholly genuine he is perhaps using an oblique opportunity of presenting a grammatical text-book to his readers.

such unexpected occurrences as the suffixed pronominal *mem* twice used in v. 17 for the usual feminine *nun*.[77] The definition of the basic meaning of nouns is also popular with Ibn Ezra, as when he explains in his longer commentary that *ben* may mean son or foster-son (v. 10)[78] and *'av* father or grandfather (v. 20);[79] that 'brothers' may be environmental or ethnic, as the two examples in v. 11; and that the basic sense of *k/h/n/* is 'to serve' (v. 16).[80] But Ibn Ezra is also fond of demonstrating less technical and more general knowledge. He explains the 'descent' of v. 5 as necessitated by the height of the palace,[81] in his longer version, and by the universal rule that waterways are lower than ground level, in the shorter version. He assumes in the longer commentary on v. 15 that Moses had to live the secluded life of a shepherd even in Midian, because that country was under the domination of Egypt,[82] and refers in v. 10 to Greek and Arabic sources for his view that the original Egyptian name of Moses was Monios.[83] Sources of which he approves much less are the pseudepigraphical works that provide details about biblical figures that he classifies as inaccurate and misguided, such as the Chronicles of Moses, The Book of Zerubbabel and The Book of Eldad the Danite (v. 22 in the longer commentary).[84] Moving from the polemical to the more philosophical, he expresses the view that Moses's young life as an Egyptian prince was perhaps planned by God so that he could acquire high degrees of education and moral behaviour and thus be able to undertake

77 Ibn Ezra explains the first occurrence as occasioned by the need to avoid the supposition that a paragogic *nun* is intended (so Cassuto, p. 24) and the second as an antipathy to the double use of a *nun*. The midrashic explanation (as in T, SR, L and YS) refers to an attempted rape by the shepherds which was thwarted by Moses (driving them away?) while EBC (p. 312) postulates the presence of male servants with Jethro's daughters.

78 Perhaps he has in mind a formal adoption such as that proposed by later commentators; see n. 32 above.

79 For the possibility that Reuel was actually the grandfather, see YS, BBC (p. 326), Hyatt (pp. 67–68) and EBC (p. 313).

80 LT defines *kohen* here (as in 2 Sam 8:18) as a political rather than religious functionary, namely, *sar ha-'ir*; see also Hyatt (p. 67: 'may have occupied some position of authority other than that of a priest') and EBC (p. 312, referring to the fact that the word *kohanim* in 2 Sam 8:18 becomes *rishonim* in 1 Chr 18:17).

81 Driver (p. 10) also presupposes a 'descent' from the palace.

82 Driver, however, assumes Midian to have been 'beyond Egyptian jurisdiction', as against Sayce's view that the Sinai Peninsula was 'an Egyptian province' (p. 14).

83 Josephus (Antiquities II.ix.6) offers an etymology from a professedly Egyptian *moû esês* (see also Philo, *De Vita Mosis* I.iv.17) but Ibn Ezra's source is, as John Ray and Colin Baker kindly inform me, probably an Arabic translation of one of the Coptic versions of a hellenistic work included among those generally characterized as 'geoponica'.

84 See Strack/Stemberger, *Introduction*, pp. 361–63.

the successful leadership of his people (his longer commentary on v. 3).[85] As far as God's knowledge is concerned, this must refer to a prophetic type of knowledge rather than a knowledge of facts or, alternatively, the expression could simply be anthropomorphic (shorter commentary on v. 25).[86]

Ramban

Although he rarely couches his comments in the neat and concise manner of his predecessor, Ramban is also capable of demonstrating a rational approach and a sensibility to the wider context of a simple narrative. Not totally convinced by Rashi's transposition of the first part of v. 5 to yield the sense that Pharaoh's daughter went down to the river to bathe, he suggests that the descent was from the royal palace to the steps just by the river, and not actually into the full river itself, thus justifying the word order as it stands and the use of the preposition *'al*.[87] Behind the simple description of Moses going out to his brothers in v. 11 lies a more moving scenario. Moses was apparently told that he was a Jew and became interested in seeing how his brothers were faring. He was so incensed by what he saw that he expressed his rage by killing the Egyptian who was maltreating one of his newly found brothers.[88] Ramban explains the absence of Jethro from the narrative by suggesting that he was, in his capacity of 'priest of Midian' (v. 16), serving in the local temple.[89] He suggests a reason for the apparent contradiction between the statement that his daughters drew water and their later report that Moses had done so for them. They had, contrary to the usual practice, drawn some water before their male counterparts and then been driven off so that Moses had to finish the task for them. These changes in their routine had so expedited the completion of their chores that they

---

85 There is an old Jewish tradition about Moses's Egyptian education reflected in hellenistic literature and in the New Testament (Acts 7:22) and noted by Noth (p. 35), BBC (p. 325) and Leibowitz (p. 40). Jacob (pp. 249–55) polemicizes against such a theory arguing that even if Moses had received it 'he would have thoroughly repudiated that wisdom' (p. 251); see n. 32 above.

86 See n. 38 above.

87 See nn. 33 and 55 above.

88 Underlying the statement about his exit from the palace to see his kinsfolk is the presupposition that he strongly wished to identify with them; so Heb 11:24–26, T, SR, LT, Driver (p. 13), Jacob (p. 255), Noth (p. 35), Cassuto (p. 22), BBC (p. 325), Hyatt (p. 66), Childs (p. 30) and Leibowitz (pp. 39–40).

89 Naḥmanides thus refects the midrashic 'whitewash' of Jethro (see the sources listed in n. 50 above).

reached home earlier than usual, inviting the obvious inquiry from Reuel about their swift return (vv. 16–18).[90]

Naḥmanides (Ramban) generally reacts rather than innovates and one of his main aims is to harmonize the earlier interpretations with the rational exegesis more popular in his own day, or to offer them as equally valid alternatives. The marriage of Moses's parents (v. 1) may literally be taken as a first marriage and its place immediately before the report of Moses's birth is not significant, the births of Miriam and Aaron having simply been ignored in the present context. Alternatively, Moses's parents had separated because of Pharaoh's decree and were now re-united on the advice of Miriam who prophesied the birth of a deliverer from their reunion.[91] Aaron could have been only about two years old and the midrashic reference to his participation in the festivities is to be explained either by the fact that Miriam taught him, or that God inspired him.[92] Rashi's explanation of the phrase 'by the river' in v. 5 as 'into the river' may be justified (in spite of Ramban's own preference, as reported above) by reference to I Sam 2:11 and Jer 23:35, in both of which verses the word *'al* has the same meaning as *'el*. The midrashic comment that the double report of Moses having grown up (vv. 10 and 11) indicates a physical followed by a political maturity may be regarded as the literal sense. The first expression means that Moses matured from a baby into a child while the second indicates the move from childhood to manhood.[93] Less troubled than Ibn Ezra by the biblical interchange of names for the same personality, Ramban on v. 16 points to various examples of conversions to Judaism being accompanied by changes of names and argues that Hobab is simply Jethro's Jewish name.[94] Of the commentators here being treated, Ramban is by far the most theologically and mystically orientated and it is rare to encounter a chapter of the Pentateuch in which he does not offer what might be regarded by some as more spiritual comments. Here on v. 25 he interprets the reference to God's sight of the Israelites as indicating a change from Divine displeasure to sympathy and predicates this change on the fact

---

90 See n. 72 above.

91 For the midrashic explanations, see n. 39 above; another later midrash and the modern commentators' views are cited in n. 62 above.

92 See BT, SR, LT and YS, who report that Miriam and Aaron danced at their parents' remarriage.

93 T and SR refer only to an extraordinary degree of growth while Ramban's reference to two kinds of growth is found in Tanḥuma, ed. Buber, p. 16b, Eng. trans. Townsend, 2.45. A similar distinction between the two occurrences of the same word *wa-yigdal* is made by Driver (pp. 11 and 13), Jacob (pp. 254–55), Cassuto (pp. 20–21), Hyatt (pp. 64 and 66) and Childs (p. 28).

94 YS: 'He was called Hobab because for God he was as beloved as a child.' EBC (p. 313) makes the point that 'dual names for the same person are well known from South Arabian sources.' See n. 66 above.

that they cried to him in prayer.[95] He also there refers to mystical teachings to explain how such redemption is dependent upon a unification of God's two (*shenayim*) attributes of justice and mercy and to an interpretation of the word *shanim* in Hab 3:2 that alludes to such a unification.[96]

Ḥizzequni

Although steeped in the rabbinic tradition and anxious to make use of it in his commentary (as will shortly be noted), Ḥizzequni was no less anxious to point out to his readers correct grammar (vv. 5 and 9),[97] the realistic background to the text, and the logic of its narrative. Moses's mother made the basket of reeds because it would therefore be invisible among the rushes and, hoping as she did to remove him later, she strengthened it internally with clay and externally, against the water, with tar (v. 3).[98] Pharaoh's daughter had to hire a Hebrew nurse because no Egyptian woman would suckle a Hebrew child (v. 7).[99] Moses was able to bury the murdered Egyptian in the sand because that material was available there in quantity because of the building works (! v. 12),[100] while no mention is made of Zipporah's conception (v. 22) before her birth because she was young enough for it not to be noticed.[101] Pharaoh's daughter saw Moses because she was in the water while the others were on the bank (v. 3);[102] Moses put the Egyptian to death after finding him guilty of raping the Hebrew's wife (v.

95 In spite of their lack of general piety (so T and SR), their prayer (Leibowitz, p. 49 and EBC, p. 313) and God's empathy with them (see n. 38 above) are enough to move God to action. LT refers to the sight of their slavery and YS to the divine foresight of their sanctuary in the wilderness.

96 Such kabbalistic notions are already found in the writings of Abraham b. David of Posquières (c. 1125–1198); see Scholem, *Kabbalah*, pp. 216–18.

97 In the cases of the words *heylikhi* and *'amatah*, implicitly rejecting the midrashic renderings (see nn. 27, 34 and 64 above).

98 See n. 63 above.

99 While the midrashim (see n. 41 above) stress the child's refusal, Ḥizzequni points with logic to the fact that it was more likely to have been the Egyptian women who declined to nurse such a child; so Driver (p. 10).

100 As far as the building works are concerned, the midrashim mention only the possibility that the murder weapon was a building trowel (see n. 73 above), while understanding the word *ḥol* figuratively. Childs (p. 30): 'he buried him quickly because the ground was sandy.'

101 So LT which is not averse to the inclusion of more literal exegesis.

102 Thus agreeing with the views of Sa'adya, earlier recorded, and Rashbam, both of whom suggest that Pharaoh's daughter was in the water while her servants were on the bank.

12);[103] the judicial process was resented by his fellow Hebrew because he was regarded as too young to sit in judgement (v. 14).[104] The reason why Jethro, though chief prince of Midian, found himself with no shepherds and only his daughters to do his work was because he had abandoned idolatry and had therefore been excommunicated by his compatriots (v. 16).[105] God finally took note of the Israelites' private and public sorrows and of the weeping precipitated by the pain of persecution because the time was ripe for their rescue (vv. 24–25).[106] While Ḥizzequni is concerned to explain, in rational terms, that Moses received a name with a Hebrew etymology via his mother and that the active form was chosen by her to point to his future rescue of his people (v. 10),[107] he is content with the more allusive interpretations of *'almah*_(v. 8) as the one who hid the fact that she was his sister[108] and of Zipporah (v. 21) as a woman as attractive as the song of a bird (*ṣippor*) or as beautiful and bright as the morning (*safra'*).[109]

This tendency to marry midrashic with more literal exegesis is characteristic of both Hezekiah ben Manoaḥ and his environment. He does offer pure midrashim, as when he explains the reference to the servant girls 'going' as meaning 'going to their deaths for not rescuing Moses' (v. 5)[110] and the use of the word *na'ar* (v. 6) as meaning either Aaron or the bridegroom's canopy *(ḥuppat ne'arim)*.[111] On the other hand, there are occasions when he contrasts the literal and midrashic renderings or attempts to harmonize different midrashim. In v. 1 he cites the midrashic interpretation that the marriage of Moses' parents is reported immediately before the birth of Moses because, after divorcing in the wake of Pharaoh's decree, they had now remarried at Miriam's bidding. He then offers as an alternative the literal interpretation (*peshaṭ*) which explains that the mar-

103 He thus opts for a briefer and more rational explanation of the killing than that offered by the midrashim (see n. 37 above).
104 The point about Moses's age is raised in T, SR and YS.
105 Once again he offers a slightly more rational twist to the midrashic 'whitewash' suggested by Rashi and the midrashim (see n. 50 above).
106 See n. 95 above for a variety of comments that tally with this one.
107 Among the moderns, only Jacob expresses a similar view about the Hebrew etymology (see n. 69 above) while the explanation of the active form as 'one who draws out' or 'rescuer' is to be found in LT, Sforno (below), Driver (p. 11), Noth (p. 26), Cassuto (p. 20), Hyatt (p. 64) and EBC (p. 310).
108 Cited in the name of R. Samuel b. Naḥman in SR, LT and YS; see also n. 58 above.
109 Plays on the name are made in SR, LT and YS while the literal meaning is annotated by Noth (p. 37), Hyatt (p. 68) and EBC (p. 313: 'Lady Bird'!).
110 See BT, SR, LT and YS.
111 See the cited Midrash Avkir for the first suggestion and BT, SR, LT and YS for the second.

riage noted in v. 1 took place before Pharaoh's decree and that the narrative briefly alludes to it before taking up the later story.[112]

Although he does not classify his two interpretations of v. 23 as midrashic and literal, they may certainly be understood as such. In the first, he comments that the Israelites were impatient and distressed with their slavery because they misunderstood the reference to four hundred years (Gen 15:13) as commencing from Abraham's covenant with God rather than from the birth of Isaac. Hence the precipitate action of the tribe of Ephraim in leaving Egypt thirty years before the exodus was ordained and suffering massacre at the hands of the Philistines. Ḥizzequni then offers the alternative exegesis that during the previous Pharaoh's reign they always hoped for his death and an improvement in the situation with the enthronement of a new ruler. When this did not happen they were distressed.[113] In one instance (vv. 3–4) he cites a rather ingenious if somewhat forced harmonization of two rabbinic interpretations. According to the first, described by him as *peshaṭ*, Moses was born three months prematurely and this presented his mother with the opportunity of hiding him for that length of time and then claiming that the pregnancy had aborted, while according to the second (and presumably with the same outcome) the first three months of her pregnancy had occurred (miraculously?) prior to her remarriage to Amram.[114] If the notion of prematurity is also applied to the second scenario and the Egyptians checked the situation at term, that would have been nine months after the marriage and given her six months' grace, and not as scripture has it. Ḥizzequni's solution to the problem is to suggest that the Egyptians were aware of premature births and therefore checked six months after her remarriage, that is, three months after the premature baby was born. According to the second interpretation too, then, she had three months' leeway before further questions were asked.

Sforno

In the commentary of Obadiah Sforno we already find tendencies that are more characteristic of the modern than the medieval world. This is not to say that the traditional style and issues are wholly absent. He offers definitions of such roots

---

112 See nn. 39 and 62 for examples of the literal and midrashic interpretations.
113 On the supposed action of Ephraim, see Ginzberg, *Legends*, 3.8–9, 4.332 and 6.2–3; and on the disappointed expectation of an improvement in the situation with the death of the king, compare Childs (p. 32): 'Nothing has improved . . . Israel continues to groan under its burden.'
114 See BT, SR, LT and YS as well as *b. Meg.* 13a and *b. Qidd.* 38a. The midrashim also refer to the problem of a baby's loud crying, a point made by Noth (p. 25) and Cassuto (p. 18).

as *z/'/q/* (v. 23) and *n/'/q/* (v. 24)[115] and explains that the name of Moses in its active participial form (משה) not only describes him as one who will rescue (=draw away) others from their troubles but also alludes to the fact that he himself was drawn from the water by heavenly decree for precisely such a purpose.[116] This concept of the overall divine plan is also used to explain Moses's physique (v. 2), the fateful activities of the princess's entourage (v. 5), and the recall of the promise to Abraham, Isaac and Jacob (v. 24);[117] and God is said not (anthropomorphically) to hear, see and know (vv. 23–25) but to champion fairness, reliability and sincerity.[118] The 'many days' of v. 23 allude to the fact that Moses was eighty when he argued his people's case before Pharaoh (Exod 7:7)[119] and the description of Midian as *nokhriyyah* has to do with Moses being a foreigner there and, presumably, is not intended to judge its religious status.[120]

Where the commentary conveys a fresher flavour is in the areas relating to the nature of humanity, as regards both its physical and behavioural characteristics. Not surprisingly for one professionally involved in medicine, Sforno makes use of his specialized, though obviously now outmoded, knowledge to explain the use of the terms *yeled* and *na'ar* in v. 6. Though not yet physically developed (*yeled*), his movements (*n'r*) were prematurely advanced enough to excite special interest.[121] His mother too had previously noted his unusually fine physique, an indication, according to Sforno, that he was a specially gifted individual in other respects and destined to exhibit powers of leadership (v. 2).[122] The point is taken further in v. 7 where the need for a Hebrew woman to nurse him is explained by reference to the greater suitability of her milk to the baby's constitution and the

115 As is done, to various degrees, in SR, Driver (p. 17) and Cassuto (pp. 28–29); see also Sa'adya and Rashi.

116 See n. 107 above for explanations of the active form.

117 The moderns also note the overall divine plan, e.g. Driver (p. 8), Jacob (p. 248), Cassuto (p. 17), BBC (p. 325), Hyatt (p. 63), Childs (pp. 24–26), Leibowitz (p. 40) and EBC (pp. 309 and 313).

118 See n. 38 above.

119 See Driver (p. 17) and Hyatt (p. 69) who point out that the 'long period' here matches the chronology presupposed in Exod 7:7, according to which Moses was eighty when he addressed Pharaoh.

120 What Sforno apparently has in mind is that the root is used in Rabbinic Hebrew to refer to heathens/gentiles. See also n. 67 above.

121 See the Samaritan Pentateuch on 2:19 which reads *na'ar* for *yeled*. According to BT, T, SR, LT and YS, the voice of the child was like that of a youth and according to the cited Midrash Avkir it was Aaron's voice (see n. 111 above).

122 One of the midrashic interpretations of the word *ṭov* is 'suitable for prophecy'; so BT, SR, LT and YS, as well as Heb 11:23. The fine physical aspect is noted by Driver (p. 8), Cassuto (p. 18) and Childs (p. 18) while EBC (p. 308) mentions both this and the 'qualities of his heart'.

reason for his upbringing in the palace by reference to his overall aristocratic qualities.[123]

Sforno's awareness of what would in more recent times be called class distinctions also comes through from his comment on the behaviour of the princess in v. 5. Public bathing would not have been possible for such royalty and the meaning must consequently be that she was relaxing in a 'bathing-hut' near the river.[124] The attendant who fetched the child was the most junior maid left to attend to her needs when the more distinguished 'ladies-in-waiting' went for their stroll and this was again by divine design since the latter would have been more likely to apply with strictness Pharaoh's decree about male Hebrew children whatever the preferences of the princess.[125]

There are also insights into the minds of the heroes of the story. Moses's mother chose the rushes because he was less likely to be detected there but also because illegitimate children were abandoned there and, if found, he stood a good chance of being rescued as one of those (v. 4).[126] Another reason for the choice was to defy the decree calling for him to be thrown into the Nile by doing no more than consigning him to the rushes at the edge of the Nile (v. 3).[127] The response of Moses himself to the three situations described in vv. 11, 13 and 17 are explained by the assumption of a different motivation at work in each case. The attack on the Hebrew by the Egyptian aroused brotherly feelings of revenge; the clash between two Hebrews inspired him to offer moral guidance to his people; the misbehaviour of the shepherds was of no moral consequence to him and he therefore restricted himself to coming to the assistance of those being persecuted.[128] As far as Jethro's invitation to Moses

123 Sforno rejects both the alternative explanations noted in nn. 41 and 99 above.

124 The moderns are similarly sceptical about public bathing in the Nile by a princess; see Driver (p. 10), Hyatt (p. 64) and EBC (p. 309).

125 BT, SR and YS mention that such a woman of rank could not have been left alone at any time. The one she sent was therefore her own private 'lady-in-waiting'; see Driver (p. 10).

126 That Moses's mother had in mind the possible rescue of her child is also suggested by Jacob (pp. 246–47), Noth (pp. 25–26), BBC (p. 325), Childs (p. 18) and EBC (p. 309).

127 SR points out that the Egyptian astrologers were misled by the fact that the child was indeed consigned to the Nile, as Pharaoh had commanded, while Jacob (p. 249) notes that if reproached for being a party to the thwarting of Pharaoh's decree his daughter could argue that this had not technically been disobeyed!

128 The three acts of Moses are linked by Driver (pp. 12 and 15) who defines them as chivalry; Jacob (pp. 255–58) who stresses how they complement each other; Childs (pp. 29–30) who notes how they testify to a whole range of emotions; and Leibowitz (p. 40) who identifies an aristocratic courage as underlying them. Childs (p. 43), however, describes them as only 'accidentally connected with each other.'

(v. 20) is concerned, he had no hidden motive for this but simply wished to repay the kindness of a stranger by offering him the favour of hospitality.[129]

Select verses

The next section of this chapter is devoted to a comparative analysis of our commentators on a few selected verses. It will cite some remaining comments, provide overviews of the treatment of each verse, and demonstrate the gradually changing face of medieval Jewish Bible commentary.

According to v. 2, when Moses's mother saw that he was *ṭov*, she hid him for three months, and the two questions that lie behind the comments to be examined are what precisely *ṭov* means, and why this led to a concealment of the baby for precisely that length of time. Rashi follows two talmudic statements that claim that at his birth the house became suffused with light, and that this took place prematurely after only six months, thus allowing his mother a leeway of three months before the Egyptians made the expected enquiries.[130] Rashbam does not quarrel with his grandfather's acceptance of the tradition about Moses's premature birth but is happy neither with the miraculous light nor with the assumption that a mother would save a baby from murder only if he were something special.[131] He prefers to understand the word *ṭov* as meaning a fully formed baby and explains that once Moses's mother saw that he was not, in spite of his early birth, an aborted foetus, she realized that she had to hide him and was able to do so for three months.[132] The miraculous nature of the birth is again stressed by Ḥizzequni who mentions its premature nature and the claim that Moses was born circumcised while arguing, more rationally, that Moses's mother was able to claim that she had thrown him into the Nile when challenged to report on the birth.[133] For his part, Ibn Ezra's detailed knowledge of the obstetrics of his day leads him to question the assumption of premature birth here. He points out that the Egyptians could not have known the date of conception, nor whether it would be a longer or shorter pregnancy, only noted the fact that she was

---

129 Bedouin hospitality rather than an interest in marrying off a daughter (see Rashi at n. 60 above) is the theme; see Driver (p. 16) and EBC (p. 312).

130 BT, and also recorded in SR, LT and YS.

131 See Cassuto (p. 18): 'Even if the child had been weak and sickly, his death would have caused his mother much grief.'

132 See n. 122 above.

133 For the occurrences of the midrash about his being born circumcised, see n. 130 above. The point about consigning him to the Nile, as instructed, is also made by Jacob (see n. 127 above).

pregnant, and that this gave Moses's mother a leeway of three months before they would ask questions. He is less troubled by a mother making distinctions between who is to be saved and who not, suggesting that *ṭov* in the present context means an exceptionally good-looking child and therefore, it would seem, worthy of special attention. Ramban follows Rashbam in arguing that all mothers love their children, regardless of their physical appearance, and suggests that she made special efforts for him because she saw something unique about him that encouraged her to believe that he was fated to survive. Such a spiritual uniqueness is linked by Sforno to an impressive physical appearance and explains why Moses's mother was aware of his potential from the outset.[134]

The description in v. 6 of the same baby as a *yeled* and then, almost immediately afterwards as a *na'ar*, troubles all the exegetes and leads Rashbam to find a verse in Judg 13:8 in which a newly-born child is also called *na'ar* and Ibn Ezra to suggest that the baby's limbs were large enough for him to be described as a *na'ar*. Rashi cites the talmudic explanation that his voice was that of an older child, a view that is forcefully rejected by Ramban not only because it attributes an unnatural voice to Moses but because a report on the quality of his voice would be totally pointless here. Ramban also rejects Ibn Ezra's remark about the child's mature body and records the suggestion that the baby's voice may have been as determined as that of an older child and the alternative that he may have been as self-controlled as an older child until the angel Gabriel slapped him and forced him to cry and draw attention to himself. His own preference is for the equation of *yeled* and *na'ar* and he cites Judg 13:8, 2 Sam 12:16, Gen 21:16–17 and I Sam 1:23–24 in support. Sforno defines the physical and psychological developments that mark the change from *yeled* to *na'ar* and again stresses what a fine specimen Moses was.[135]

As far as v. 10 is concerned, it was apparently the root, grammatical form and sense of the word *meshitihu* that concerned Rashi and his grandson. In the text before us, Rashi explains that the meaning is 'remove' and that the root is, according to Menaḥem Ibn Saruq, *m/w/sh/*. He then offers the alternative view that it means 'drawing out' from the root *m/sh/h/* and argues grammatically at length for this second alternative. Since this is previously the position taken by Rashbam with the minor addition of the parallel root *q/n/h/*, it seems likely that the second view reflects either a change of heart on the part of Rashi, or the views of his pupil(s) incorporated into the comment. Ibn Ezra argues that the

134 See nn. 122 and 131 above. On the relationship between the pentateuchal commentaries of Rashbam and Ibn Ezra, see Margaliot, '*Ha-Yaḥas*', pp. 357–69.
135 See nn. 111 and 121 above.

Hebrew name of Moses is a translation of the original Egyptian, and that his name was given to him by the princess, his foster-mother, who either learnt Hebrew or asked for the equivalent. Names are not to be understood as seriously as grammatical paradigms. He polemicizes against the midrashic tendency to relate many different names to a few famous personalities, pointing out that when a personality enjoys more than one name the Hebrew Bible usually informs us. Ḥizzequni cites the midrashic view that the princess converted and learned Hebrew and offers the alternative that it was his mother who gave Moses his name and that the princess then approved the choice. Both Ḥizzequni and Sforno stress that the name is in an active form and refers as much to his future activities on behalf of Israel as to his removal from the waters of the Nile.[136]

Two of the problems facing the interpreter of v. 14 are the sense of the word *'omēr* and the significance of the phrase 'as you killed the Egyptian'. Rashi cites the midrash that Moses used the enunciation of the Tetragrammaton to kill the Egyptian, so that the Israelite is understood to be asking Moses whether he will enunciate the Divine name in order to kill him, as he did in the case of the Egyptian. For Rashbam there is no enunciation of God's name here but the verb *'omēr* simply means 'intend' (equivalent, according to Sa'adya, to the word *roṣeh*), and the Israelite is asking whether Moses intends to kill him for striking his fellow, just as he already killed the Egyptian for striking a Hebrew. For Ḥizzequni, the phrase accuses Moses of deliberately stirring up strife to justify another homicide on his part. Ibn Ezra is clearly of a similar mind but he stresses the linguistic validity of taking the verb *'mr* in the sense of 'speaking to oneself' or 'thinking' by referring to Ecclesiastes 2:1. For Ḥizzequni, it is the contrast between his youthful years and his personal ambition to lead that is being stressed by his antagonist. Somewhat surprisingly, Naḥmanides points out that the root *'/m/r/* here may have its usual sense of 'saying' and the Hebrew is asking Moses whether he is saying his piece, i.e. preaching his sermon about violence in order to find a pretext to kill him, precisely as he did in the case of the Egyptian. He also offers a possible reconstruction of the event on the assumption that the idea of death by the enunciation of the Tetragrammaton is a possible one. The Hebrew either knew about this because he had seen Moses placing his hands on the Egyptian and cursing him in the name of God, or knew only that Moses had killed the Egyptian and, perhaps, that he had buried him, without being sure how this had been done. In the first case *'omēr* might be a reference to enunciation

---

136 See nn. 57, 68, 83, 94 and 107 above, and see BT, T, SR, LT and YS for the notion of the conversion of Pharaoh's daughter from idolatry.

while in the second it could mean either 'thinking', 'intending' or 'saying his piece', as already explained.[137]

The new section of the narrative beginning in v. 23 is set 'in those many days' and reports that Pharaoh died and that the Israelites cried to God in their anguish. Subsequently God notes their distress and his appearance to Moses the shepherd is introduced in the next chapter. What precisely is the chronology here? How could Pharaoh's death lead to more anguish for the Israelites? In what way does this little section of vv. 23–25 link the two chapters? Rashi answers by placing these incidents during Moses's stay in Midian and following the midrashic interpretation that Pharaoh did not actually die but was stricken with leprosy. The situation became worse for the Israelites when he killed Israelite children and bathed in their blood in an attempt to cure the disease, and Israel cried to God for urgent assistance.[138] The next chapter of the biblical narrative indicates how that assistance was provided.

Rashbam dwells on the word 'many' in the phrase 'those many days' and sets the scene many years after Moses's flight from Egypt, when he was eighty years old. Israel had suffered all the time but God could only now appeal to Moses to help them because Pharaoh had died and Moses had no reason to be afraid of him, as he had previously been, and could therefore return to Egypt. The report of the death of Pharaoh triggers, as it were, the account of God's appearance to Moses and his assurance to him in 4:19 that he may safely return to Egypt since all those who had sought to kill him were now dead. Ibn Ezra agrees that the death of Pharaoh is reported in order to explain why it was safe for Moses to return but suggests that Israel's cries were increased by this event because the new king was harsher than his predecessor. All their suffering had been brought upon them because they adopted the idolatrous Egyptian cults, as indicated in Ezek 20:5–10, but they now repented and God therefore heeded their cries. Having miscalculated the expected date of their delivery from Egyptian enslavement, the Israelites, according to Ḥizzequni, thought that relief was imminent or that the rule of a new king would bring an improvement and were subsequently disappointed in their expectations. But matters were still brought to a head by Pharaoh's death because this encouraged the return of Moses to Egypt.

In spite of the word *rabbim*, Ramban argues that the events here described took place soon after Moses's arrival in Midian and marriage there. He records

137 See nn. 28, 42 and 104 above.

138 See n. 49 above and Childs (p. 33): 'The old king of Egypt whose reign first marked the beginning of Israel's trouble (1:8) has died. What will the future bring?'

the suggestions that the reference to 'many days' is an allusion to the fact that Israel's suffering made all periods of time seem long and the alternative proposal that by this time their tribulations had continued for a substantial length of time. He himself prefers to understand the word as an indication of the long period during which Moses was a fugitive. Having fled Egypt as a young man, he remained in remote areas rather than in areas of settlement, always concealing his identity, until he finally arrived in Midian where he settled down in marriage. Immediately after this last event, and at the end of the whole long period of exile, Pharaoh died and the Israelites cried to God for fear of an even more cruel successor and God's attributes are such that he responded to their prayers. Sforno proves that Moses was in Midian 'for many days' by referring to his age of eighty when he appeared before Pharaoh and stresses that it was not Israelite repentance or prayer that brought divine assistance but the unfairness of their persecution.[139]

Conclusions

It remains for me to express a brief view on the value of the medieval Jewish Bible commentators for modern Hebrew Bible scholarship. It must be said at the outset that there is a clear distinction between the pious presuppositions of the Middle Ages and the critical assumptions of contemporary scholars and it would be foolish to expect either set of ideas to step out of its historical context and be judged by the criteria applied by the other. That having been acknowledged, there is clearly value in these medieval commentaries from the historical, exegetical and theological viewpoints. As historians of Jewish, Christian and modern study of the Hebrew Bible, we may use their comments to acquire a deeper understanding of how translations were composed, how *peshaṭ* and *derash* and their exegetical forerunners were understood in each generation, and how various exegetes opted for only one, while others (perhaps more than was once thought) preferred an amalgam of the two. Similarly, they may provide us with a historical guide to the development of grammatical and philological studies of the Hebrew language and its place in the Semitic family, a better understanding of how later generations carefully incorporated or cautiously rejected the interpretations of their esteemed ancestors, and a clearer idea of when so-called modern interpretations have little genuine claim to novelty.

139 See nn. 113 and 119 above. Both Cassuto (p. 29) and EBC (p. 313) link the death of Pharaoh with the end of an Egyptian vendetta against Moses.

Exegetically too, however, there is a fair amount to be gleaned from their comments. Not only do they often provide a wider perspective and novel ideas, or the inspiration for such ideas, but they also serve as transmitters of otherwise lost traditions from a great variety of sources. Indeed, it is not outside the realms of possibility that *'aggadot* related by them to the text were originally part of a wider body of ancient traditions from which the final canonized text was culled. The questions that underlie their proposed solutions are always worth pondering even if the solutions themselves do not always find sympathy with us, while their literary analysis is capable of uncovering layers of hidden meaning. In an age when we are constantly being informed that texts have all manner of meanings rather than one literal sense, such a capability is not to be underestimated. One hesitates to include theology in their contribution to exegesis but the truth is that both those who wrote the texts, and those who read them generation after generation, saw them as theological text-books, and that we are duty-bound to understand what they had in mind. If we are aware that some of the commentators sometimes allowed the theological tail to wag the literary dog, this may succeed in making us more cautious about the dangers of doing so ourselves.[140]

Post scriptum

At precisely the time when I was completing my revision of this chapter for the current volume, I noticed that a new book had just been published by Keith Bodner under the title of *Ark on the Nile: Beginning of the Book of Exodus* (Oxford: Oxford University Press, 2016). I quickly acquainted myself with its contents, particularly chapters 4–7, which deal with Exodus 2. His approach is that of the contemporary literary critic assessing the events and personalities rather than that of the traditional commentator systematically explaining words, phrases and verses. There are a few parallels to the issues discussed above, as when Bodner connects the significance of the waters of the Nile for the overall story (pp. 94–100); discusses the etymology of the name of Moses (pp. 113–16); and offers reasons for the double occurrence of ויגדל in vv. 10–11 (pp. 120–21). What is more, the author has a high regard for the power and the artistry of the appealing story told here. There is, however, almost no interest in the medieval Jewish commentators, with only Rashi obtaining a brief note

140 This chapter originated in a brief communication given at the congress of the International Organisation for the Study of the Old Testament held in Jerusalem in the summer of 1986. For related treatments of Gen 38 and Num 13, see chapters 3 above and 5 below.

(p. 123), courtesy of another commentator, William Propp. That said, those reading the chapter just concluded will benefit from Bodner's comprehensive and up-to-date bibliography and may find it useful to compare his approach with those of the other scholars, medieval and modern, noted here.

Works cited

Banitt, M., *Rashi. Interpreter of the Biblical Letter* (Tel Aviv: Tel Aviv University, 1985).
BBC = *The Broadman Bible Commentary*, vol. 1 (London: Marshall, Morgan & Scott, 1970).
Berlin, A., 'On the use of traditional Jewish exegesis in the modern literary study of the Bible', in *Tehillah Le-Moshe: Biblical and Judaic Studies in Honor of Moshe Greenberg*, eds. Mordechai Cogan, Barry L. Eichler, Jeffrey H. Tigay (Winona Lake, Ind.: Eisenbrauns, 1997), pp. 173–83.
Brody, R., *The Geonim of Babylonia and the Shaping of Medieval Jewish Culture* (New Haven: Yale University Press, 1998).
BT = Babylonian Talmud
Carmi, T. (ed.), *The Penguin Book of Hebrew Verse* (Harmondsworth: Penguin, 1981).
Casper, B., *An Introduction to Jewish Bible Commentary* (New York: Yoseloff, 1960).
Cassuto, U., *A Commentary on the Book of Exodus*, Eng. trans. I. Abrahams (Jerusalem: Magnes, 1967).
Chavel, C. B., *Ḥizzequni. Perushey Ha-Torah Le-Rabbenu Ḥizqiyah b. Manoaḥ* (Jerusalem: Rav Kook, 1981).
Chavel, C. B., *Kitvey Rabbenu Mosheh ben Naḥman*, 2 vols. (Jerusalem: Rav Kook, 1963).
Chavel, C. B., *Perushey Ha-Torah le-Rabbenu Mosheh ben Naḥman*, 2 vols. (Jerusalem: Rav Kook, 1969, 5th edn.).
Chavel, C. B., *Perushey Rashi 'al Ha-Torah* (Jerusalem: Rav Kook, 1982).
Chavel, C. B., *Ramban. His Life and Teachings* (New York: Feldheim, 1960).
Chavel, C. B., *Ramban (Nachmanides). Commentary on the Torah*, 5 vols. (New York: Shilo, 1971–76).
Childs, B. S., *Exodus. A Commentary* (London: SCM, 1974).
Chronicles of Moses, ed. A. Shinan, *Ha-Sifrut* 24 (1977), pp. 110–16; ed. A. Jellinek, *Bet Ha-Midrasch* (Leipzig: Nies, 1853–78), vol. 2, pp. 1–13; Eng. trans. in O. S. Rankin, *Jewish Religious Polemic* (Edinburgh: Edinburgh University Press, 1956), pp. 26–46.
Díaz Esteban, F., *Abraham Ibn Ezra and his Age* (Madrid: Asociación Española de Orientalistas, 1990).
Driver, S. R., *The Book of Exodus* (Cambridge: Cambridge University Press, 1911).
EBC = *The Expositor's Bible Commentary*, vol. 2 (Grand Rapids, MI.: Zondervan, 1990).
Filipowski, H. (ed.), *The First Hebrew and Chaldaic Lexicon to the Old Testament* (London, Edinburgh and Leipzig: *Ḥevrat me'orerey yeshenim*, 1854).
Gelles, B. J., *Peshat and Derash in the Exegesis of Rashi* (Leiden: Brill, 1981).
Ginzberg, L., *The Legends of the Jews*, 7 vols. (Philadelphia: Jewish Publication Society, 1909–38).
Gottlieb, Z. (W.) and A. Darom, A., *Bi'ur 'al Ha-Torah Le-Rabbi 'Ovadyah Sforno* (Jerusalem: Rav Kook, 1980).

Grabois, A., *Les Sources Hébraïques Médiévales. II. Les Commentaires Exégétiques* (Turnhout: Brepols, 1993)
Greenberg, M., '*Ha-yaḥas beyn perush Rashi le-ferush Rashbam la-Torah*', in the *Isaac Leo Seeligmann Volume*, eds. Y. Zakovitch and A. Rofe (Hebrew; Jerusalem: Rubenstein, 1983), pp. 559–67.
Greenberg, M. (ed.), *Jewish Bible Exegesis* (Hebrew; Jerusalem: Bialik, 1983).
Greenspahn, F. E., 'How modern are modern biblical studies?', in *Minḥah Le-Naḥum. Biblical and Other Studies presented to Nahum M. Sarna in honour of his 70th Birthday*, eds. M. Brettler and M. Fishbane (Sheffield: JSOT Press, 1993), pp. 164–82.
Grossman, A., *Rashi* (Oxford: Littman, 2012).
Hyatt, J. P., *New Century Bible. Commentary on Exodus* (London: Oliphants, 1971).
Hyman, D., and Shiloni, Y. (eds.), *Yalquṭ Shim'oni* =YS (Jerusalem: Rav Kook, 1977–).
Ibn Ezra, Abraham, *Sefer Moznayim* (Altona, 1770 and Offenbach 1791).
Jacob, B., 'The childhood and youth of Moses, the messenger of God', in *Essays in honour of . . . J. H. Hertz*, eds. I. Epstein, E. Levine and C. Roth (London: Edward Goldston, 1942), pp. 245–59.
Jacobs, L., *Jewish Biblical Exegesis* (New York: Behrman House, 1973).
Japhet, S., *Collected Studies in Biblical Exegesis* (Jerusalem: Bialik Institute, 2008), pp. 135–309.
Japhet, S., 'Ḥizkuni's commentary on the Pentateuch: its genre and purpose' (Hebrew), in *Rabbi Mordechai Breuer Festschrift: Collected Papers in Jewish Studies*, 2 vols. (Jerusalem: Academon, 1992).
Kamin, S., *Rashi's Exegetical Categorization in Respect to the Distinction between Peshat and Derash* (Hebrew; Jerusalem: Magnes, 1986).
Lancaster, I., *Deconstructing the Bible. Abraham ibn Ezra's Introduction to the Torah* (London: Routledge Curzon, 2003).
Lane, E. W., *An Arabic-English Lexicon*, vol. 1 (London: Williams and Norgate, 1863).
Lehmann, M. R., *The Commentary of Rashi on the Pentateuch* (Hebrew; New York: Lehmann, 1981).
Leibowitz, N., *Studies in Shemot*, Eng. trans. A. Newman (Jerusalem: World Zionist Organization, 1976).
Leqaḥ Ṭov = LT, ed. S. Buber (Vilna: Romm, 1880–84).
Levin, I., *Abraham Ibn Ezra. His Life and his Poetry* (Tel Aviv: Hakibbutz Hameuchad, 1976, 2nd edn.).
Lockshin, M. I., *Rashbam's Commentary on Exodus. An Annotated Translation* (Atlanta, Ga.: Scholars, 1997).
Macintosh, A. A., *A Critical and Exegetical Commentary on Hosea* (ICC series, Edinburgh: T. & T. Clark, 1997).
Malter, H., *Saadia Gaon. His Life and Works* (Philadelphia: Jewish Publication Society, 1921).
Margaliot, E., '*Ha-yaḥas she-beyn perush ha-Rashbam le-perush ha-AbE 'al ha-torah*', in *Sefer Assaf*, eds. M. D. Cassuto, J. Klausner and J. Guttmann (Jerusalem: Rav Kook, 1953), pp. 357–69.
Melamed, E. Z., *Bible Commentators*, 2 vols. (Hebrew; Jerusalem: Magnes, 1975).
Menaḥem ben Saruq, *Maḥberet*, ed. A. Sáenz-Badillos (Granada: Universidad de Granada, 1986).
Midrash Rabbah Translated into English, 10 vols. (London: Soncino, 1939).

Mikra'ot Gedolot, Second Rabbinic Bible, edited by Jacob ben Ḥayyim (Venice: Daniel Bomberg, 1524–25). See also ed. Warsaw, 1860–66, and ed. S. Netter (Vienna: Zamarski & Dittmarsch, 1859).
Mikra'ot Gedolot Haketer, ed. M. Cohen (Ramat-Gan: Bar-Ilan University Press, 1992–)
Morag, S., *The Hebrew Language Tradition of the Baghdadi Community* (Hebrew; Jerusalem: Hebrew University, 1977).
Morag, S., *The Hebrew Language Tradition of the Yemenite Jews* (Hebrew; Jerusalem: Hebrew University, 1963).
Morag, S., 'Some notes on Šelomo Almoli's contributions to the linguistic science of Hebrew', in *Interpreting the Hebrew Bible. Essays in Honour of E. I. J. Rosenthal*, eds. J. A. Emerton and S. C. Reif (Cambridge: Cambridge University Press, 1982), pp. 157–77.
Morag, S., *The Vocalization Systems of Arabic, Hebrew and Aramaic. Their Phonetic and Phonemic Principles* (The Hague: Mouton, 1962).
Morag, S., *Vocalised Talmudic Manuscripts in the Cambridge Genizah Collections* (Cambridge: Cambridge University Press, 1988).
Nemoy, L. (ed.), *Karaite Anthology* (New Haven: Yale University Press, 1952).
Noth, M., *Exodus*, Eng. trans. J. S. Bowden (London: SCM, 1962).
Ofer, J., 'A new edition of miqraot gedolot', *Tarbiz* 61 (1991), pp. 163–71.
Pelcovitz, R., *Sforno. Commentary on the Torah. Translation and Explanatory Notes*, 2 vols. (Brooklyn, NY: Mesorah, 1987–89).
Prijs, L., *Abraham Ibn Esra's Kommentar zu Genesis. Kapitel 1. Einleitung, Edition und Superkommentar* (Wiesbaden: Steiner, 1973).
Qafiḥ, J. (ed.), *Perushey Rabbenu Sa'adyah Ga'on 'al Ha-Torah* (Jerusalem: Rav Kook, 1963).
Qafiḥ, J. (ed.), *Tehillim 'im Targum U-Ferush . . . Sa'adyah* (Jerusalem: Rav Kook, 1966).
Reif, S. C., 'Bread with another meaning?', in *From Forbidden Fruit to Milk and Honey: A Commentary on Food in the Torah*, ed. D. Lipton (forthcoming, Jerusalem: Ktav).
Rosenbaum, M., and Silbermann, A. M., *Pentateuch with Rashi's Commentary translated into English* (London: Shapiro, Vallentine, 1929–34).
Rosin, D., *R. Samuel b. Meir als Schrifterklärer* (Jahresbericht des jüdisch-theologischen Seminars, Breslau: Jungfer, 1880).
Rosin, D., *Perush Ha-Torah 'asher katav Rashbam* (Breslau: Schottlender, 1881).
Sarna, N. M., *The JPS Torah Commentary. Exodus* (Philadelphia: Jewish Publication Society, 1991).
Scholem, G., *Origins of the Kabbalah*, Eng. trans. A. Arkush (Philadelphia and Princeton: Jewish Publication Society and Princeton University Press, 1987).
Shachter, J. F., *The Commentary of Abraham ibn Ezra on the Pentateuch. Volume 3. Leviticus* (Hoboken, NJ: Ktav, 1986).
Segal, M. H., *Parshanut Ha-Miqra'* (Jerusalem: Hebrew University, 1944, 1952, 2nd edn.).
Shemot Rabbah = SR (Vilna: Romm, 1878).
Shereshevsky, E., *Rashi. The Man and his World* (New York: Sepher-Hermon, 1982).
Simon, U., *The Ear Discerns Words: Studies In Ibn Ezra's Exegetical Methodology* (Hebrew; Ramat-Gan: Bar-Ilan University Press, 2013).
Simon, U., *Four Approaches to the Book of Psalms. From Saadiah Gaon to Abraham Ibn Ezra*, Eng. trans. L. J. Schramm (Albany: State University of New York Press, 1991).
Strack H. L. and G. Stemberger, G., *Introduction to the Talmud and Midrash*, Eng. trans. M. Bockmuehl (Edinburgh: T. & T. Clark, 1991).

Strickman, H. N., and Silver, A. M., *Ibn Ezra's Commentary on the Pentateuch. Exodus (Shemot)* (New York: Menorah, 1988).
Tanḥuma = T, 2 vols. in 1 (Warsaw: J. Munk, 1879); ed. S. Buber (Vilna: Romm, 1885), Eng. trans. J. T. Townsend, *Midrash Tanḥuma* (Hoboken, N. J.: Ktav, 1989 – 2003).
Torat Ḥayyim. Ḥamishah Ḥumshey Torah, Genesis–Deuteronomy in 7 vols., ed. M. L. Katzenellenbogen (Jerusalem: Rav Kook, 1986 – 93).
Touitou, E., 'Concerning the methodology of R. Samuel b. Meir in his commentary to the Pentateuch', *Tarbiz* 48 (1979), pp. 248 – 73.
Touitou, E., *Exegesis in Perpetual Motion. Studies in the Pentateuchal Commentary of Rabbi Samuel Ben Meir* (Hebrew; Ramat Gan: Bar-Ilan University Press, 2003).
Twersky, I. and Harris, J. M. (eds.), *Rabbi Abraham Ibn Ezra. Studies in the Writings of a Twelfth-Century Jewish Polymath* (Cambridge, Mass.: Harvard University Press, 1993).
Wehr, H., *A Dictionary of Modern Written Arabic* (Wiesbaden: Harrassowitz, 1979, 4th edn.).
Weiser, A., *Perushey Ha-Torah Le-Rabbenu 'Avraham Ibn 'Ezra*, 3 vols. (Jerusalem: Rav Kook, 1977).
Yalquṭ Shim'oni = YS (Vilna: Romm, 1898).
Zohary, M., *Plants of the Bible* (Cambridge: Cambridge University Press, 1982).
Zucker, M., *Rav Saadya Gaon's Translation of the Torah* (Hebrew; New York: Feldheim, 1959).
Zucker, M., *Saadya's Commentary on Genesis* (New York: Jewish Theological Seminary, 1984).

5 Medieval Jewish Commentators on Numbers 13

Introduction

This purpose of this essay is to analyse and explain the exegesis offered of Numbers 13 by a number of leading Jewish commentators of the Middle Ages, and to relate their comments to earlier interpretations of the text and to the worlds in which they lived. It also sets out to compare, at least in some respects that do not blur the distinction between a medieval and a modern approach to the Hebrew Bible, their treatment of the chapter with those of more recent times. In order to do this, the content of the Hebrew text will be cited and summarized in English. The medieval comments will then be offered in my own translations, and some of the remarks of a selection of modern exegetes – especially when they relate closely to what their predecessors had written – will then be noted.

Part of my intention is to draw the attention of scholars of the Hebrew Bible to the work done by the classical Jewish commentators of the Middle Ages, since many have little or no acquaintance with such work. The aim is not argue the superiority or inferiority of the two sets of interpretation but to suggest that there may be various advantages to be had by contemporary scholars if they examine the work of their Jewish predecessors in detail. Such advantage is of course more likely to be in the areas of linguistic and literary analysis than in the realm of historical criticism but should not therefore be underestimated. Each generation has its contribution to make and the dating of the contribution need not always be the central factor in assessing the totality of its value. It may also of interest for the historian of exegesis to note the degree to which ideas recorded in the Middle Ages make their re-appearance in the modern period and to speculate on the reason for this.

Masoretic text

א וַיְדַבֵּר יְהוָה אֶל-מֹשֶׁה לֵּאמֹר. ב שְׁלַח-לְךָ אֲנָשִׁים וְיָתֻרוּ אֶת-אֶרֶץ כְּנַעַן אֲשֶׁר-אֲנִי נֹתֵן לִבְנֵי יִשְׂרָאֵל
אִישׁ אֶחָד אִישׁ אֶחָד לְמַטֵּה אֲבֹתָיו תִּשְׁלָחוּ כֹּל נָשִׂיא בָהֶם. ג וַיִּשְׁלַח אֹתָם מֹשֶׁה מִמִּדְבַּר פָּארָן עַל-פִּי
יְהוָה כֻּלָּם אֲנָשִׁים רָאשֵׁי בְנֵי-יִשְׂרָאֵל הֵמָּה. ד וְאֵלֶּה שְׁמוֹתָם לְמַטֵּה רְאוּבֵן שַׁמּוּעַ בֶּן-זַכּוּר. ה לְמַטֵּה
שִׁמְעוֹן שָׁפָט בֶּן-חוֹרִי. ו לְמַטֵּה יְהוּדָה כָּלֵב בֶּן-יְפֻנֶּה. ז לְמַטֵּה יִשָּׂשכָר יִגְאָל בֶּן-יוֹסֵף. ח לְמַטֵּה
אֶפְרָיִם הוֹשֵׁעַ בִּן-נוּן. ט לְמַטֵּה בִנְיָמִן פַּלְטִי בֶּן-רָפוּא. י לְמַטֵּה זְבוּלֻן גַּדִּיאֵל בֶּן-סוֹדִי. יא לְמַטֵּה
יוֹסֵף לְמַטֵּה מְנַשֶּׁה גַּדִּי בֶּן-סוּסִי. יב לְמַטֵּה דָן עַמִּיאֵל בֶּן-גְּמַלִּי. יג לְמַטֵּה אָשֵׁר סְתוּר בֶּן-מִיכָאֵל. יד
לְמַטֵּה נַפְתָּלִי נַחְבִּי בֶּן-וָפְסִי. טו לְמַטֵּה גָד גְּאוּאֵל בֶּן-מָכִי. טז אֵלֶּה שְׁמוֹת הָאֲנָשִׁים אֲשֶׁר-שָׁלַח
מֹשֶׁה לָתוּר אֶת-הָאָרֶץ וַיִּקְרָא מֹשֶׁה לְהוֹשֵׁעַ בִּן-נוּן יְהוֹשֻׁעַ. יז וַיִּשְׁלַח אֹתָם מֹשֶׁה לָתוּר אֶת-אֶרֶץ

DOI 10.1515/9783110486704-006

כְּנָעַן וַיֹּאמֶר אֲלֵהֶם עֲלוּ זֶה בַּנֶּגֶב וַעֲלִיתֶם אֶת-הָהָר. יח וּרְאִיתֶם אֶת-הָאָרֶץ מַה-הִוא וְאֶת-הָעָם הַיֹּשֵׁב
עָלֶיהָ הֶחָזָק הוּא הֲרָפֶה הַמְעַט הוּא אִם-רָב. יט וּמָה הָאָרֶץ אֲשֶׁר-הוּא יֹשֵׁב בָּהּ הֲטוֹבָה הִוא אִם-רָעָה
וּמָה הֶעָרִים אֲשֶׁר-הוּא יוֹשֵׁב בָּהֵנָּה הַבְּמַחֲנִים אִם בְּמִבְצָרִים. כ וּמָה הָאָרֶץ הַשְּׁמֵנָה הִוא אִם-רָזָה
הֲיֵשׁ-בָּהּ עֵץ אִם-אַיִן וְהִתְחַזַּקְתֶּם וּלְקַחְתֶּם מִפְּרִי הָאָרֶץ וְהַיָּמִים יְמֵי בִּכּוּרֵי עֲנָבִים. כא וַיַּעֲלוּ וַיָּתֻרוּ
אֶת-הָאָרֶץ מִמִּדְבַּר-צִן עַד-רְחֹב לְבֹא חֲמָת. כב וַיַּעֲלוּ בַנֶּגֶב וַיָּבֹא עַד-חֶבְרוֹן וְשָׁם אֲחִימַן שֵׁשַׁי
וְתַלְמַי יְלִידֵי הָעֲנָק וְחֶבְרוֹן שֶׁבַע שָׁנִים נִבְנְתָה לִפְנֵי צֹעַן מִצְרָיִם. כג וַיָּבֹאוּ עַד-נַחַל אֶשְׁכֹּל וַיִּכְרְתוּ
מִשָּׁם זְמוֹרָה וְאֶשְׁכּוֹל עֲנָבִים אֶחָד וַיִּשָּׂאֻהוּ בַמּוֹט בִּשְׁנָיִם וּמִן-הָרִמֹּנִים וּמִן-הַתְּאֵנִים. כד לַמָּקוֹם
הַהוּא קָרָא נַחַל אֶשְׁכּוֹל עַל אֹדוֹת הָאֶשְׁכּוֹל אֲשֶׁר-כָּרְתוּ מִשָּׁם בְּנֵי יִשְׂרָאֵל. כה וַיָּשֻׁבוּ מִתּוּר הָאָרֶץ
מִקֵּץ אַרְבָּעִים יוֹם. כו וַיֵּלְכוּ וַיָּבֹאוּ אֶל-מֹשֶׁה וְאֶל-אַהֲרֹן וְאֶל-כָּל-עֲדַת בְּנֵי-יִשְׂרָאֵל אֶל-מִדְבַּר פָּארָן
קָדֵשָׁה וַיָּשִׁיבוּ אֹתָם דָּבָר וְאֶת-כָּל-הָעֵדָה וַיַּרְאוּם אֶת-פְּרִי הָאָרֶץ. כז וַיְסַפְּרוּ-לוֹ וַיֹּאמְרוּ בָּאנוּ אֶל-
הָאָרֶץ אֲשֶׁר שְׁלַחְתָּנוּ וְגַם זָבַת חָלָב וּדְבַשׁ הִוא וְזֶה-פִּרְיָהּ. כח אֶפֶס כִּי-עַז הָעָם הַיֹּשֵׁב בָּאָרֶץ
וְהֶעָרִים בְּצֻרוֹת גְּדֹלֹת מְאֹד וְגַם-יְלִדֵי הָעֲנָק רָאִינוּ שָׁם. כט עֲמָלֵק יוֹשֵׁב בְּאֶרֶץ הַנֶּגֶב וְהַחִתִּי
וְהַיְבוּסִי וְהָאֱמֹרִי יוֹשֵׁב בָּהָר וְהַכְּנַעֲנִי יוֹשֵׁב עַל-הַיָּם וְעַל יַד הַיַּרְדֵּן. ל וַיַּהַס כָּלֵב אֶת-הָעָם אֶל-מֹשֶׁה
וַיֹּאמֶר עָלֹה נַעֲלֶה וְיָרַשְׁנוּ אֹתָהּ כִּי-יָכוֹל נוּכַל לָהּ. לא וְהָאֲנָשִׁים אֲשֶׁר-עָלוּ עִמּוֹ אָמְרוּ לֹא נוּכַל
לַעֲלוֹת אֶל-הָעָם כִּי-חָזָק הוּא מִמֶּנּוּ. לב וַיֹּצִיאוּ דִּבַּת הָאָרֶץ אֲשֶׁר תָּרוּ אֹתָהּ אֶל-בְּנֵי יִשְׂרָאֵל לֵאמֹר
הָאָרֶץ אֲשֶׁר עָבַרְנוּ בָהּ לָתוּר אֹתָהּ אֶרֶץ אֹכֶלֶת יוֹשְׁבֶיהָ הִוא וְכָל-הָעָם אֲשֶׁר-רָאִינוּ בְתוֹכָהּ אַנְשֵׁי
מִדּוֹת. לג וְשָׁם רָאִינוּ אֶת-הַנְּפִילִים בְּנֵי עֲנָק מִן-הַנְּפִלִים; וַנְּהִי בְעֵינֵינוּ כַּחֲגָבִים וְכֵן הָיִינוּ בְּעֵינֵיהֶם.

Summary

A charmingly constructed narrative in thirty-three verses reports that God instructs the Israelites to send a team of leaders to spy out the land of Canaan. Each of the twelve tribes provides one spy, who is named in each case, and Moses sets them on their way from the Paran desert, having changed the name of the representative of the tribe of Ephraim from Hoshea to Joshua. His instructions are that they should enter the country from the south and ascend the hill country. Their objective is to ascertain the strength of the local people, the quality and fertility of the land, and the layout of the cities. They are to bring back some of the local fruit and the text notes that it was the grape season.

The journey of the spies is plotted and they are said to have reached Hebron, built seven years before Zoan in Egypt, and to have seen Anakites there. At Wadi Eshkol they cut a bunch (Hebrew: *'eshkol*) of grapes that needed to be carried on a pole between two of them, as well as taking with them some pomegranates and some figs. Hence, the place acquired the Hebrew name Wadi Eshkol. After a journey of forty days, they returned to Moses, Aaron and the whole Israelite community at Qadesh, in the Paran desert, and presented their report, together with their samples of fruit. They agreed that the land was a fertile one, as shown by the fruit they had brought back, but were also concerned that the inhabitants were strong, and the cities well-fortified.

They had seen the Anakites and they listed the names of the various peoples of Canaan and which parts of the country they occupied. Caleb hushed the people and assured them that they had the ability to enter and conquer the country but the others denied this, citing the strength of the locals. They offered a troubling report of the land that they had transversed, describing it as one that consumed its inhabitants, all of whom were of great stature. They had seen the Nefilim, of the Anakite people, and had felt themselves as small as grasshoppers compared to them, and indeed that is how they were viewed by them.

Underlying questions

In order to understand how some of the best-known and appreciated medieval Jewish exegetes understood this chapter, it is necessary to appreciate the questions that occurred to them when they read its content. I suggest that the following were uppermost in their minds and dictated the nature of their responses:

Vv. 1–2: Did God and/or Moses command the Israelites to send spies? Did the Israelites sin in this connection? What was the status of the spies who were chosen and why were they described as נשיאים (*nesi'im*)?

V. 3: What are the senses of the words אנשים (*'anašim*) and ראשי (*rašey*) here?

Vv. 4–15: Is there any significance in the order of the names and their tribal association, and in Caleb's patronymic?

V. 16: When and why did Moses change Joshua's name?

V. 17: How exactly were the Israelites to enter the land of Canaan?

V. 18: What exactly are they to find out about the land and the people, and to what purpose?

V. 19: Why is the land mentioned here again and what is the significance of knowing the form of the settlements?

V. 20: What is the significance of 'fat' or 'lean' land and why are trees specifically mentioned? In what way had they to be strong and what is conveyed by the mention of the season?

V. 21: How did they in fact travel across the land?

V. 22: Why does the verb suddenly change to the singular and what is the sense of the comparison between Hebron and Zoan? What is the purpose of mentioning the Anakites here?

Vv. 23–24: What precisely was carried, and by whom, and how did Wadi Eshkol get its name?

V. 25: When and how long was the journey of the spies?

V. 26: Why are there two verbs at the beginning of the verse, where is 'Paran Qadesh', and to whom do the pronominal accusatives in 26b and the dative in v. 27a refer?

V. 27: Why did the spies begin by praising the land?

V. 28: What precisely did the spies have to say about the people and the cities?

V. 29: Is there any significance in the geographical distribution recorded here?

V. 30: Exactly how did Caleb behave here (especially vis-à-vis Moses) and what was meant by his comment?

V. 31: How are we to understand the spies' response to Caleb's confident assertions?

V. 32: What precisely is meant by the words דבה (*dibbah*) and מדות (*middoth*) and in what way did the land 'consume its inhabitants'?

V. 33: Who are the Nefilim and what is the significance of the names they are given and how are we to understand the grasshopper simile?

Medieval comments

Since the dates, provenances and styles of the commentators to be cited here have already been described earlier in this volume, it will not be necessary to repeat that information in the present context.[1] We may therefore proceed directly to a list of their comments on particular verses, under each of their names.[2] I have summarized the comments to be found in the various editions and added a few footnotes for clarification:

Verse 2

Rashi[3]

1. The command is given at this point so that the spies could have the opportunity of appreciating the evil of calumny from the incident in which Aaron and

1 See chapters 2–4, pp. 34–107.

2 The commentaries are conveniently available in the *Bemidbar* volume of the *Torat Ḥayyim* series, pp. 104–12.

3 For all his comments on this chapter, see ed. Berliner, pp. 304–6; ed. Chavel, *Perushey Rashi*, pp. 444–7; ed. Lehmann, pp. 140–43; trans. Rosenbaum/Silberman, pp. 61–65.

Miriam spoke against Moses. They did not, however, learn the lesson but chose to commit a similar sin.[4]

2. He follows Tanḥuma in attempting to resolve the contradiction between this verse, which reports the episode of the spies as undertaken at God's command, and Deut 1:22, which reports that the Israelites undertook the initiative in this matter; see also Exod 3:17 where God describes the land as flowing with milk and honey.[5]

Rashbam[6]

1. The word נשיא (*nasi'*) does not here carry its usual meaning of 'prince' or 'leader'. It is rather related to the meaning of the expression נשא לב with the sense of 'volunteering'. Moses is required to announce the task and to seek volunteers and to choose twelve from among them, since those who offer themselves will by definition be those brave enough to undertake the task of entering a foreign land and taking some of its produce. This is distinct from Num 1:5–17 and 34:16–29 where the names are laid down by God at the outset.

2. The pointing of the word כל (*kol*) indicates that the meaning is not 'every' but 'all of these' (i.e. absolute and not construct) and supports the interpretation just offered; see Ps 8:7.

Ibn Ezra[7]

1. Deut 1:22 is a fuller version of how God responded to Israel's request by suggesting that they send spies; here only God's response is recorded.

2. The word איש (*'iš*) here carries the special sense of 'recognized warrior' as in Num 13:3, I Kgs 2:2 (which would otherwise be meaningless since he was of course already a man!).

3. The word means תור (*twr*) 'to search', as in Num 15:39, ולא תתורו אחרי לבבכם ואחרי עיניכם.

4. The word כל (*kol*) is equivalent to כל אחד (*kol 'eḥad*), the word אחד being carried forward from its previous occurrence in the verse. There are many examples

4 Tanḥuma, Warsaw, p. 67a; ed. Buber, pp. 64–65.

5 Tanḥuma, Warsaw, p. 67b; ed. Buber, p. 64.

6 For all his comments on this chapter, see ed. Rosin, pp. 180–82; Eng. trans. Lockshin, pp. 205–13.

7 For all his comments on this chapter, see ed. Weiser, pp. 150–51; Eng. trans. Strickman/Silver, pp. 101–6.

of this phenomenon, as in 2 Sam 4:2 where ושני אנשים שרי גדודים היו בן שאול means היו [שרי] בן שאול.

Ḥizzequni[8]

1. The phrase כל נשיא (*kol nasi'*) is in apposition to the verb תשלחו (*tišlehu*). Each נשיא will have the responsibility of sending one man from his tribe. He is therefore taking the absolute כל as the equivalent of the construct כל and the word בהם (*bahem*) as meaning 'among the Israelites'.

Ramban[9]

1. If, as Rashi, following Tanḥuma, suggests (see above), Israel sinned in asking for spies to be sent, then surely Moses did so too by asking the spies to bring back details? And how did they sin if they only carried out his instructions and replied to all his questions? In any case, what they reported back was little different from what Moses had earlier warned them about. No, the incident is rather to be explained as follows. Israel followed normal military procedure in doing a reconnaissance of the land before the projected conquest and not relying on miracles. Being as close as Egypt, they knew about the land, but they had to send spies to find the best way of conquering it. Their espionage would also reveal the best qualities of the land and therefore encourage the people. So Moses discussed it with God and then gave them authority to do this.[10] My view is that they decided to send spies and God advised them how best to choose the right people. It was the people's initiative, and not that of God or Moses, but then Moses backed them and was supported by God.[11]
2. The Deuteronomy passage expands on the story that is only briefly told here. According to the Rabbis, their sin was in asking for spies at all and not trusting God on the basis of their previous experience with him, and Moses just went along with this.
3. God did not choose the actual men as in Num 1:5–16 and 34:17–28, or else no harm would have come to the project.[12] He merely instructed that they should be

8 For all his comments on this chapter, see ed. Chavel, *Ḥizzequni*, pp. 458–61.
9 For all his comments on this chapter, see ed. Chavel, *Perushey Ha-Torah*, pp. 240–46 and Eng. trans., *Ramban*, pp. 118–32.
10 Bemidbar Rabbah 16:5: ואף משה לא רצה לשלחם מדעת עצמו עד שנמלך בהקב'ה על כל אחד ואחד; see also Tanḥuma, ed. Warsaw, p. 67b; ed. Buber, p. 65.
11 See *b. Soṭah* 34b: אמר ריש לקיש וייטב הדבר בעיני [דברים א:טו] בעיני ולא בעיניו שלמקום
12 See Rashbam above and Tanḥuma, ed. Warsaw, p. 67b; ed. Buber, pp. 64–65.

נשיאים (*nesi'im*) and Moses chose them on that basis, and the spies themselves brought about the bad results.

Sforno[13]

1. God could not allow them to send whomever they wished since they might choose a group unqualified to appreciate the quality of the land, leading Israel to think that God had misled them and not to be willing to do repentance. The group that Moses chose did mislead the people because of their lack of faith but they also told the truth about the land even if they felt they were unable to conquer it. When Israel appreciated their sin, they repented and asked for forgiveness but this public profanation of God could only be atoned for with their deaths.[14]
2. The word נשיא (*nasi'*) means a person superior enough to the rest of his tribe to recognize the nature of the land of Israel.

Verse 3

Rashi

1. The phrase על פי (*'al pi*) does not indicate God's instruction but his acquiescence.[15]
2. The word איש (*'iš*) here carries an honorific sense; at that point the spies still retained their integrity.[16]

Ḥizzequni

1. Rashi's comment here has to be harmonized with his comment on v. 26, based on *b. Soṭah* 35a, namely, that they were corrupt as soon as they set out. What is meant here is that they were men of integrity when they were chosen.[17]

---

13 For all his comments on this chapter, see ed. Gottlieb/Darom, pp. 276–79; Eng. trans. Pelcovitz, pp. 626–30.

14 Compare *b. Soṭah* 35a in which various teachers describe their deaths by plague (Num 14:37), elongated tongues, worms, and diphtheria.

15 Thus matching the interpretation offered in v. 2.

16 The words כל אנשים שבמקרא are absent from the *editio princeps* of Rashi; Tanḥuma, ed. Warsaw, p. 67a has: וכל מקום שנאמר בו אנשים בני אדם צדיקים הן; ed. Buber, p. 64, has: בכל מקום שנאמר אנשים צדיקים הם.

17 So Bemidbar Rabbah 16:5.

2. As Bekhor Shor suggests,[18] the word ראש here is to be defined as a commander of a thousand men.[19]

Sforno

The word איש here means 'warrior' as in 1 Sam 26:15 and 1 Kgs 2:2.

Verse 4

Ramban

The order used here follows neither the tribal seniority nor the order of marching but is in accordance with their personal qualities since they are variously described as ראשים (*rašim*) and נשיאים (*nesi'im*), which implies a variety of levels. The Torah is thus giving preference to those who were wiser or more honoured than their fellows, according to personal and not tribal qualifications. This is also done when the princes receive their land allocation, namely, according to their qualities and not their genealogy.[20]

Sforno

All of these named individuals were equally distinguished and the Torah lists them according to their personal ages, and not according to the tribal seniority or marching order, since at that point they were all equal in the task allotted to them.

Verse 6

Ḥizzequni

This Caleb is the same as the one usually referred to as 'Caleb, son of Hezron', and the patronymic יפונה is used here to allude to the fact that he departed (פנה) from the views of the other spies.[21]

---

18 Bekhor Shor, *Perush*, p. 261.

19 See Ḥizzequni's comments on Deut. 1:23; ed. Chavel, *Ḥizzequni*, p. 524.

20 But according to R. Isaac in *b. Soṭah* 34b, the names revealed their actions: אמר ר' יצחק דבר זה מסורת בידינו מאבותינו מרגלים על שם מעשיהם נקראו 'they were called *meraglim* because they were guilty of slander' (*rekhiluth*).

21 So *b. Soṭah* 11b.

Verse 11

Ḥizzequni

Although Joseph is elsewhere represented by the tribe of Ephraim,[22] he is here included in the tribe of Menasseh because both Joseph and this representative from Menasseh were guilty of calumny, the former about his brothers (Gen 37:2) and the latter about the land of Israel (in this chapter). The same explanation holds for Num 34:23 and Josh 17:1 since these verses also deal with the allocation of the land which was the object of the calumny. Ephraim is distinguished from Menasseh here because its representative, Joshua, was not guilty of that calumny.

Verse 16

Rashi

The significance of the change of name and the introduction of the *yod* is to allude to God's name which was mentioned by Moses in a prayer to the effect that God would save Joshua from the views of the other spies.[23]

Rashbam

It was not at this point that Moses changed Hoshea's household name to Joshua[24] (see Exod. 24:13, 32:17 and 33:11, and Num. 11:28) but rather when he appointed him as his assistant and *major domo*. That was the contemporary custom, as when Pharaoh called Joseph 'Ṣaphenath Pa'neaḥ' (Gen 41:45) and Nebuchadnezzar called Daniel 'Belshazzar' after the name of his god.[25]

Ibn Ezra

The phrase אלה שמות האנשים ('these are the names of the men') in v. 16 is not simply a repeat of what was stated in v. 4. It stresses that, unlike Joshua, these spies had only the names given here and no others.

---

22 As in Ezek 37:16.
23 See *b. Soṭah* 34b.
24 See Exod 24:13, 32:17 and 33:11, and Num 11:28.
25 Dan 1:7.

Ḥizzequni

1. No representative was appointed from the tribe of Levi because they were not allocated any portion of the land of Israel.

2. Joshua's name at home was Hoshea but Moses changed it to Joshua when he appointed him as his assistant. This custom is also found in the case of Abraham, Sarah, Jacob, [Joseph,] David, Hananel, Mishael and Azariah, Zedekiah whose name was Matanya, and Nehemiah whose name was Hatirshata.[26] [Some say that Moses changed Hoshea's name prophylactically because he was to be among the spies and to pass through Amalek.][27]

Sforno

Although he was known in his tribe as Hoshea, Moses first called him Joshua (as in 11:28) as an honorific title and now did so as an act of prayer that he would be saved and would save others.

Verse 17

Sa'adya

First go southwards in the land and then ascend the mountainous area.

Rashi

The Negev is the least impressive part of the land of Israel. This is how merchants behave, first showing the worst of their goods and then later the best of them.[28]

Ibn Ezra

They were told to enter the land by way of its southern part. Egypt is of course to the south of Israel as IE has himself pointed out in his commentary on Daniel 11:5. Scientifically, Egypt is 30° from the equator and Jerusalem 33°. The desert of Paran is in the south of the land of Canaan.[29] The word נגב here refers not

---

26 Gen 17:5, 15; Gen 32:28; Gen 41:45; Dan 1:7; 2 Kgs 24:17; Neh 8:9. So Bekhor Shor, *Perush*, p. 261.

27 Chavel, *Ḥizzequni*, p. 459n, notes the absence of manuscript support for this reading. It may perhaps represent a pious scribal gloss.

28 This comment is from Tanḥuma, ed. Warsaw, p. 68a, ed. Buber, pp. 66–67, and is absent from some printed and manuscript versions of Rashi.

29 Correcting the reading מצרים.

to the Israelite encampment but to the southern area of the land of Israel. The proof is from Hebron which belongs to the tribe of Judah and the verse in Josh 18:5 states that Judah should stand on his border at the south.

Ḥizzequni

Go the south of the land of Israel and once you know how to conquer the mountainous territory it will be easy for you to conquer the plains.[30]

Sforno

Enter the land from the side where we are now encamped which is much easier to do than making a detour and entering from another area.

Verse 18

Rashi (on vv. 18–19)

1. What kind of land is it? Some lands produce strong inhabitants, others weak ones; some have large populations, others smaller ones.[31]

2. Moses advised them how to estimate the strength of the inhabitants. If they lived in open rather than fortified cities, they were confident about their strength.[32] The meaning of the word במחנים is indicated by the TO's rendering into בפצחין i.e. 'open cities without walls'.

Rashbam

1. They were told to establish whether the border-land was afforested or smooth or marshland (מטוננת) and thereby to prepare the necessary weapons for cutting down the forests and preparing paths for their troops. They were confident about God's gift of the land but aware that it could not be achieved without military preparations.
2. All the instructions were in order to establish how best to conduct the necessary war.

---

30 Adapted from Bekhor Shor, *Perush*, p. 261.

31 See Tanḥuma, ed. Warsaw, p. 68a; ed. Buber, p. 67.

32 Tanḥuma, ed. Warsaw, p. 68a, ed. Buber, p. 67, has: מנין אתם יודעים כחם, הבמחנים אם במבצרים, while Rashi has: סימן מסר להם, אם בפרזים יושבין חזקים הם שסומכין על גבורתם ואם בערים בצורות הם יושבין חלשים הם אם במחנים הם שרוים הם גבורים ובוטחים על כחם, אם מבצרים חלשים הם ולבם רך

Ibn Ezra

1. The expression ואת העם (*we-'eth ha'am*) is to be understood as ומה העם (*u-mah ha'am*) like the preceding and subsequent phrases.
2. Establishing whether they are strong means ascertaining their military strength.

Sforno

They had to find out whether the land was well inhabited, with many cities and settlements. They also had to know the state of health enjoyed by the population. This is like medical advice to check the health and number of a place's inhabitants in order to ascertain its quality. Large and healthy populations indicate that the air and the produce are of a high standard and the reverse is also true.

Verse 19

Sa'adya

The word במחנים (*be-maḥanim*) refers to camps of tent-dwellers.

Rashi

A good land is one with wells and a good supply of healthy underground aquafers.

Rashbam

1. The first reference to הארץ (*ha-'areṣ*) in v. 18 is to the uninhabited edge of the kingdom while the current reference is to inhabited land.
2. The words טובה (*ṭovah*) and רעה (*ra'ah*) refer to the question of whether it has lots of produce, thus obviating the necessity of provisioning one's troops beforehand.
3. A knowledge of the type of settlements will indicate whether it is necessary to prepare towers and mounds[33] in order to conquer them.

---

33 Ezek 4:2.

Ibn Ezra

The questions about the land refer to the quality of its air and water. The word במחנים refers to tent-dwellers like the Arab bedouin.

Ḥizzequni

A land is 'bad' when its inhabitants perish, as in 2 Kgs 2:19. The subsequent answer to that question was that the land consumed its inhabitants (Num 13:32).

Ramban (vv. 19 – 20)

Ibn Ezra equates the quality of a land with that of its air, water and produce. The truth is, however, that the words טובה and רעה have a much broader definition and the words שמנה (*šemenah*) and רזה (*razah*) qualify this. You can have a good land with lots of rich produce and fruit or another that is good but not so rich in that it needs irrigation and cultivation. It produces drier and less rich items such as nuts, apples, carobs and forest fruits. So what is included in the question is whether the land is rich like plains, or leaner like hilly territory. Targum Onqelos renders the latter two words עתירא and מסכנא i.e. 'rich' and 'poor', because some countries are so rich in produce that they can export while others are needy and dependent on their neighbours, even if they may still be described as 'good' rather than 'bad'.

Sforno

1. A 'good' land is one that has an abundant and healthy water supply, as in Deut 8:7.
2. Do they live in open settlements with no fear of attack or are they in fortified cities because of such a fear (Judg 5:7)?

Verse 20

Sa'adya

1. What is the quality of the soil?
2. The word עץ ('*eṣ*) refers to cultivated trees.[34]

34 Not natural forests.

Rashi

1. The word עץ is a metaphor for a fine person whose merits might be able to protect the people of the land.[35]
2. The expression בכורי ענבים (*bikkurey ʻanavim*) refers to the time of the year when the early grapes ripen. The singular of the word, i.e. בכור, is therefore a gerundive form.

Rashbam

1. The invitation to check the richness of the land was a way of insuring that they discovered that the land was indeed 'flowing with milk and honey', as God had promised.
2. The verb והתחזקתם (*we-hithḥazaqtem*) conveys the sense that they were to be like fearless warriors and take whatever they wished.
3. The Torah refers to the season in order to set the background for the comment in v. 23 about the heavy branch of grapes that they had to carry.

Ibn Ezra

The word שמנה (*šemenah*) refers to the land's capability of producing wheat.

Ḥizzequni

They needed to be encouraged (והתחזקתם) to take the produce because it was harvest time when there were guards in the fields.

Ramban

They were to be brave enough not to be afraid of being discovered as spies.

Sforno

1. The fatness of the land (שמנה) refers to riches and goods, using a metaphor similar to that in Deut 8:9.[36]
2. The reference to trees alludes to the produce for which Israel is famous, i.e. wine, figs, pomegranates, olives and honey.

---

35 An abbreviated version of *b. B. Bat.* 15a.

36 Where poverty is described in terms of eating.

3. Do not be afraid (והתחזקתם) that they will suspect you of espionage.
4. Although it was not yet time for the other items to be fully ripe, Moses was nevertheless confident that the size and quality of the produce even at that time would be sufficient to indicate to them that the land was deeply impressive.

Verse 21

Rashi

The references to Ṣin and Reḥov are intended to convey the fact that they travelled the length and breadth of the country, in the shape of a *gamma*. They traversed the southern border from east to west (as instructed in v. 17) as far as the Mediterranean, and then followed the coastline as far as the north western limit, as described in Num 34:7.

Ḥizzequni

Their travel was in a diagonal line from south-east to north-west, as Num 34 indicates.

Verse 22

Sa'adya

The phrase ילידי הענק (*yelidey ha-'anaq*) refers to a group [descendants?] of mighty warriors.

Rashi

1. The use of the singular in the verb ויבא (*wa-yavo'*) indicates that only Caleb went to Hebron where he prayed at the patriarchal tombs that he should not be seduced by the views of the other spies. This is why Deut 1:36 refers to his sole travel and why he was granted Hebron according to Judg 1:20.[37]
2. Since it is impossible to conceive that Ham would build Hebron for Canaan, his younger son, before he built Zoan for Miṣrayim, his elder one, the 'seven years' are not to be taken literally but mean that the land of Hebron was

37 As in *b. Soṭah* 34b.

seven times better endowed than Zoan, in spite of the fact that Hebron was the most stony in Israel and Zoan the finest in Egypt.[38]

Rashbam

1. The aggadic midrash about Caleb [cited in Rashi] may carry a literal sense, given the verses in Deut 1:36 and 14:24, and in Josh 21:12. The truly literal meaning is, however, that the singular here refers to each one of them since vv. 28 and 33 presuppose that they had all been שם [=at Hebron] and seen the Anakites.
2. The 'seven years' are to be taken literally and the point being made about Hebron is that it was older and more distinguished even than the famous Zoan, so well known to the Israelites, and this was a way of adding to the prestige of the Israelite cities. It was also because it was so ancient that the Anakites of the early generations still lived there.

Ibn Ezra

1. According to the talmudic interpretation the singular verb ויבא used here refers to Caleb, son of Yefuneh, since each one of the spies went his own way at this point.
2. The attachment of מצרים to the name צוען indicates that it was the one near Egypt, a usage also found in the phrase מבית לחם יהודה in Ruth 1:1. The interpretation of those that link the name צוען with the root צען (*ṣʻn*) that occurs in Isa 33:20 with the meaning of 'uproot' is far-fetched.
3. Hebron is mentioned to stress its great antiquity.

Ḥizzequni

1. The reason why Caleb went, as Rashi tells us, to pray at Hebron, was that Moses had not prayed for him as he had done for Joshua.[39] Alternatively, the singular refers to each one of them as in Josh 8:19.
2. The names of the Anakites are mentioned here in order to make it clear what is meant later by the comments of the spies about seeing them (v. 28).[40]

---

38 Here Rashi follows *b. Soṭah* 34b more closely than he does Tanḥuma, ed. Warsaw, p. 68ab, ed. Buber, p. 67.
39 So *b. Soṭah* 34b.
40 So Bekhor Shor, *Perush*, p. 262.

3. The reference to the antiquity of Hebron explains that it still had some of the Nefilim of the early generations, thus disproving the statement of the spies about the land consuming its inhabitants (v. 32).[41]
4. It also shows the importance of the land of Israel, compared with Egypt, from where the Israelites had come and about whose distinction they were well acquainted.

Ramban

1. Rashi explains the 'seven years' metaphorically. My own view is that Hebron's other name is Qiryath 'Arba' after the powerful man called 'Arba' who built it (so Josh 14:15) and whose son Anak was the father of the later Anakites, three of whom are mentioned here. It is reported that Hebron was built seven years before the very ancient Egyptian city of Zoan to show the amazing achievements of that family whose members were also much larger and longer-living than normal.
2. The question about the 'fatness' of the land also perhaps alludes to Hebron. If this ancient land could still produce such wonderful fruit as that described in v. 23, how much more could be produced by newer land?
3. It is also possible that *'anaq* is an epithet meaning 'huge' and not a proper name and that those three mentioned here were the children of 'Arba'. This would account for the definite article on the word in Josh 15:13–15.
4. The passive form נבנתה (*nivnethah*) is used without reference to the name of the builder because it was well known who built it by virtue of its alternative name. Or the point being made is that the three mentioned here were still alive so long after their father had built the city for them.

Verse 23

Sa'adya

The preposition *bet* in the word בשנים (*bišenayim*) here has the sense of בין = 'between', i.e. carried between two.

Rashi

1. The word זמורה (*zemorah*) means a vine-branch with a cluster of grapes on it.

41 So Bekhor Shor, *Perush*, p. 262.

2. If one pole was involved then so obviously were two people and the word בשנים 'between two' is necessarily redundant. It rather refers to two poles, each carried by two men at each end, that is, eight men for the vine branch. One spy carried a huge fig and one a huge pomegranate. Caleb and Joshua opted out of this since they knew that the aim was to slander the land as weird. To calculate the whole weight, reckon that a man can lift forty seahs and three times that amount if he is assisted.[42]

Ibn Ezra

Since the name Wadi Eshkol was given to the place only afterwards on account of the huge cluster of grapes, it is anachronistic to call it Wadi Eshkol here, and it was therefore Moses who wrote this later into the Torah. Alternatively, it always had two names (see Gen 14:14 re Dan) and this one became more popular after the event with the spies.[43]

Ḥizzequni

The words זמורה and אשכול describe two different items and the word בשנים refers to two other poles they used, and not to the spies. Hence, they carried the cluster of grapes by placing it on a large branch as one pole, supported below by two others at right angles.[44]

Verse 24

Ibn Ezra

The subject of the verb קרא (*qr'*) is understood, as with the verb ילדה (*yaledah*) in Num 26:59.

42 Rashi has carefully abbreviated and translated the passages in *b. Soṭah* 34a and *y. Soṭah* 7:5 (21d); see also Tanḥuma, ed. Warsaw, p. 68b; ed. Buber, pp. 67–68.

43 IE is attempting to refute the idea, recorded in Tanḥuma, ed. Warsaw, p. 68b, ed. Buber, p. 68, that it already had such a name from earliest times, given in a prophetic way.

44 This would appear to account for four of the spies, leaving the others to deal with the pomegranates and figs.

Sforno

It was the Canaanites who gave the name Wadi Eshkol to this place to mark their astonishment at the fuss made by the Israelites over this cluster of grapes. Far from being something rare and marvellous for them, such growth was standard or even less than standard.

Verse 25

Rashi

They were able to travel so far in such a short time (twice the normal distance) because of miraculous Divine intervention.[45]

Ibn Ezra

The word מקץ (*mi-qeṣ*) may mean the beginning of a period of time, as in Deut. 14:28, 15:1 and 31:10, as well as the end of one, and ארבעים יום (*'arb'aim yom*) may mean 'on the fortieth day', and not 'after forty days'.[46]

Ḥizzequni

As explained in *b. Ta'anith* 29a, they began on 29 Sivan and finished on 8 Av, Tammuz being a full month (30, and not 29 days) that year.

Verse 26

Rashi

1. The word וילכו (*wa-yelekhu*) is not redundant but indicates that they set out with the same evil intent as they demonstrated when they returned.[47]
2. The word אתם (*'otham*) refers to Moses and Aaron, to whom they reported.

---

45 See Tanḥuma, ed. Warsaw, p. 68b; ed. Buber, p. 68.
46 See the next comment, by Ḥizzequni, which accounts differently for the extra day.
47 So *b. Soṭah* 35a.

Ibn Ezra

1. The word וילכו indicates that they went straight to Moses and Aaron to give their report, rather than returning to their tents.
2. The word אתם (*'otham*) refers to Moses and Aaron, to whom they reported [as in Rashi].

Ḥizzequni

It is obvious from [their apparent interchange in] 12:16, 33:18, 33:36 and 32:8 that Paran, Ṣin, Ḥaṣeroth, Qadesh Barne'a and Rithma are all close to each other.[48]

Sforno

The use of both names, viz. Paran and Qadesh, means that they came to that part of the Paran Desert opposite Qadesh Barne'a.

Verse 27

Rashi

As explained in *b. Soṭah* 35a, lies are not convincing unless some element of truth in them; hence their need to praise the land at the outset. A comparison of four texts clarifies how Rashi has adapted his sources:

> Munich MS: כל לשון הרע שאין אמת בתחלתו אין אמת בסופו
> Bavli Vilna: כל [עין יעקב: + דבר] לשון הרע שאין בו דבר אמת בתחילתו אין מתקיים בסופו
> Tanḥuma: כך דרכם של מספרי לשון הרע, פותחין בטובה ומשלימין ברעה
> Rashi ed.: כל דבר שקר שאין אומרים בו קצת [נ'א: דבר] אמת בתחילתו אין מתקיים בסופו [נ'א: אין מקיימין אותו]

Ibn Ezra

The singular pronoun לו (*lo*) is used to indicate they addressed themselves (ויספרו) primarily to Moses who was the real leader.[49]

---

48 Similar to *b. Šabb.* 89a; so Bekhor Shor, *Perush*, p. 262.
49 Compare Leqaḥ Ṭov's comment (p. 212): הם העיקר וכל העדה טפלה לה

Ramban

With the exception of one matter [see on v. 29 below], they truthfully answered the questions they had been asked about the fertility of the land and its produce.

Sforno

Describing it as 'flowing with milk and honey' was a way of saying that it was not only a good land but one that could effortlessly produce an abundance of cattle, milk, honey and the most luxurious items.

Verse 28

Sa'adya

The word עז here means harsh.[50]

Rashi

The word בצרות (*beṣuroth*) carries the sense of 'strong'. Targum Onqelos's rendering כריכן means 'circular fortresses' since the root כרך in Aramaic has the basic sense of 'round'.

Ḥizzequni

They mentioned both the strength of the people and the fortifications of their cities to forestall the possible argument that they were only one and not the other. They also mentioned the Anakites who were renowned for being invincible (as in Deut 9:2).[51]

Ramban

They did not report, in reply to the question about the people and their cities, the simple facts but prefaced them with the totally negative word אפס and appended them with a reference to the Anakites.

---

50 Does he mean to rule out the other senses of עז (*'az*) such as 'protective' or 'defiant'?
51 So Bekhor Shor, *Perush*, p. 262.

Sforno (vv. 28–29)
Despite the richness of the land, we cannot conquer it because the people and their cities are strong and the inhabitants are our enemies and include the Amalekites who will not even allow us to penetrate the border.

Verse 29

Rashi
1. The spies mentioned the Amalekites because they had already suffered at their hands.[52]
2. The word יד (*yad*) before the reference to the Jordan has the sense of 'by the side of', meaning that they literally live right next to the Jordan and it will therefore be impossible to cross.

Ḥizzequni
Don't just ask about the seven nations that inhabit the land but also about their allies and those who occupy their borders, leaving us no way of entering the land.

Ramban
They mentioned the Amalekites, in the south, and the Amorites in the hills, to indicate the impossibility of conquest. This was done obliquely not to annoy Moses and Aaron but they nevertheless succeeded in getting their negative message through to the people. They did not here respond to the question of the number of the inhabitants but left that until later [v. 32] when they were being only negative.

Verse 30

Sa'adya
1. The meaning of the word ויהס (*wa-yahas*) is that Caleb silenced the people in order to let Moses speak [since they knew the views of Moses and would not have been willing to listen to him].

52 Compare Rashi's comment לפי שנכוו בעמלק כבר, הזכירוהו מרגלים כדי ליראם with that to be found in Bemidbar Rabbah משל לתינוק שסרח ולקה ברצועה וכשמבקשין להפחידו מזכירין לו את הרצועה שלקה בו

2. Although the pronominal suffix in the word לה (*lah*) is singular, the meaning is ‘we shall overcome them’, i.e. it refers to the enemy and not the land.

Rashi

1. Caleb silenced them all so that Moses could be heard. He began by saying ‘And is that all that the son of Amram has done…’ and, being incensed against Moses by what the spies had said, they quietly waited to hear more insults. But Caleb of course went on to praise Moses for what he had done regarding the Red Sea, the Manna and the quails.[53]
2. ‘We shall certainly ascend’ even as far as heaven, should Moses ask it of us, and we shall do so successfully.[54]
3. The root of the word ויהס means ‘to silence’ as in Zech 2:17 and Amos 6:10 and is onomatopoeic. When it is necessary to silence a group of people, one says ‘*št*’ to them.

Rashbam

The word ויהס means that he obtained their silence by using wise means.[55]

Ibn Ezra

According to Ibn Janaḥ, ויהס means that he said הסו to them, i.e. ‘he hushed them’. The word has an onomatopoeic origin.[56]

Ḥizzequni

You can read between the lines here and understand how Moses responded to the spies, while in Deut 1:29 it specifically states that he told the people not to be afraid.[57]

---

53 See *b. Soṭah* 34b.
54 See *b. Soṭah* 34b.
55 Compare *b. Soṭah* 35a: אמר רבה שהסיתן בדברים...וכי זו בלבד עשה לנו בן עמרם...
56 Ibn Janaḥ, p. 122: ופרוש ויהס כלב וצהצה כלב כלומר גער בם והשתיקם באמרו להם הס ואין ויהס כלב פועל משתמש אבל ענינו שאמר להם הס או הסו כמו שצהצה בל' ערב אינו פועל אלא ענינו אמר צה. Tanḥuma, ed. Warsaw, p. 69a: עמד לו על הספסל והיה משתקן ואומר הסו הסו והם שותקין לשמוע ממנו; the text varies slightly in ed. Buber, pp. 63 and 68.
57 Similarly, Bekhor Shor, *Perush*, p. 262.

Ramban

When the people became agitated and vociferous, Caleb silenced them and told them that, in spite of the Canaanites' strength, the Israelites would prove more powerful than them and their cities.

Sforno

1. The people began to shout, as it is reported that they did later (14:1), and Caleb silenced them so that they could hear Moses's reply. Perhaps he specifically said what is reported in Deut 1:29 and Caleb supported him with his statement, justifying an ascent into the land and claiming that the enemy would be unable to attack them and prevent this.
2. The further reference to inheriting the land means that the Canaanites were already fearful of the Israelites and it only needed an invasion for them to flee and leave the land to the invaders.

Verse 31

Rashi

The words חזק ממנו (*ḥazaq mi-mennu*) may be taken to be blasphemous, recording their statement that the people of Canaan were more powerful than the Israelite God.[58]

Ramban

The spies' reply to Caleb was 'Not only will we be unable to conquer their cities, but even if they leave them in order to engage us on the battlefield, we shall be unequal to the fight.' The terms 'going up' and 'going down' refer to engagement in battle, as in 1 Sam 17:8.

Sforno

They will rise against us and prevent us from progressing, as indeed did happen after their sinful response when 'the Amalekites and Canaanites descended' (Num 14:45).

---

58 See *b. Soṭah* 35a.

Verse 32

Sa'adya

The word דבה (*dibbah*) means a bad report here and is used in the construct case in the sense of 'concerning the land'.

Rashi

1. The spies saw that the inhabitants were always busy with burials and thought the land was consuming its inhabitants. They did not appreciate that God was arranging this in order to divert their attention away from the spies. The following comparison will illustrate how Rashi adapts his source:

> Rashi: בכל מקום שעברנו מצאנום קוברי מתים, והקב'ה עשה לטובה [כדי] לטרדם באבלם ולא יתנו לב לאלו
> Bavli: דרש רבא אמר הקב'ה אני חשבתיה לטובה והם חשבו לרעה אני חשבתיה לטובה דכל היכא דמטו מת חשיבא דידהו [קטע גניזה: הווה שכיב חשיבא דמתא] כי היכי דניטרדו ולא לשאלו אבתרייהו...הם חשבו לרעה ארץ אוכלת יושביה היא

2. They were so strong and tall that people felt obliged to give their measurements, as in 1 Sam 17:4 regarding Goliath and in 2 Sam. 21:20 and 1 Chon. 11:23.

Ibn Ezra

1. As I have explained elsewhere (Song 7:10), the word דבה is from the root דבב and means 'speech' or 'report'. When used with the *hiph'il* of the verb יצא, it means 'to invent a report', but when attached to the *hiph'il* of the verb בוא, the meaning is 'to pass on a report', as in Gen 37:2 about Joseph and his brothers.
2. A land that 'consumes its inhabitants' is one with bad air.
3. Although the basic meaning of the word מדה (*middah*) is 'measure', it is used here in the sense of 'abnormally large measure'. A similar usage is אנשי לבב in Job 34:34 which means 'people of great intelligence' and there are many more examples in the Hebrew Bible.

Ramban

1. Initially, the spies had exchanges with Moses, Aaron and Caleb and left the Israelites undecided, some depending only on their own strength while others had faith in God. But now they were so terrified that the opposing view would prevail, and that they would have to face these awful giants, that they went around the camp promoting their own view (see Num 14:36) by the use of false-

hoods, terrifying their fellow Israelites and dissuading them from mounting the invasion. When דבה is used with the *hiph'il* of the verb יצא, it means 'to invent a dishonest report', as in Prov 10:18, but when attached to the *hiph'il* of the verb בוא, the meaning is 'to pass on an honest report', which may be an evil thing, as in Gen 37:2 about Joseph and his brothers. For this sin of calumny, the spies perished in a plague, as reported in Num 14:37.
2. Lands that are poor in soil and water produce weak people but the spies reported that the land's qualities were of such a high standard that it permitted the survival only of unnaturally powerful people and killed off all those with normal constitutions, as does food that is too rich. This brought the spies back to the subject of the Anakites who had survived in the land and who were descended from the ancient and notorious Nefilim, in the time of Noah. This reference, and the point now added by the spies about feeling like grasshoppers, were calculated to terrify the Israelites.

Sforno

The spies argued that the inhabitants were not strong because of the land's qualities but because only the strong, with their excellent constitutions, had been able to survive the bad air which had killed off all the others.

Verse 33

Sa'adya

The word נפילים (*nefilim*) means 'terrifyingly mighty warriors'.

Rashi

1. These נפילים were Anakites, the children of Shamḥazai and 'Aza'el who had fallen from heaven in the generation of Enosh (*b. Niddah* 61a and *b. Yoma* 67b).
2. We knew that we were like grasshoppers to them because we heard them say that they had seen ants resembling humans in the vineyards. Note how Rashi adapts his talmudic source:

> Rashi: שמענו [שהיו] אומרים זה לזה נמלים [יש] בכרמ[ים] כאנשים
> *b. Soṭah:* שמעי דקאמרי קחזינן אינשי דדמו לקמצי באילני
> Genizah text: שמעינהו דקאמרי חד לחבריה חזינא אינשי דיתבין בארזי דדמו לקמצי

3. They are called ענקים (*‘anaqim*) because they are large enough to give the impression that they could ‘necklace the sun’.[59]

Rashbam

1. The second occurrence of the נפילים is a reference to those mentioned in Gen 6:4.
2. The grasshopper simile is used for describing the difference felt between those who are huge and those who are much smaller. This is clear from the verse in Isa 40:22 which talks of God sitting on the rim of the earth and of its inhabitants as grasshoppers.[60]

Ibn Ezra

1. As I have explained in Gen. 6:4, they are called נפילים because they cause a sinking (נפל) in the hearts of those who see their huge stature.[61]
2. The second occurrence of the word נפילים in this verse refers to those of the species who are predicted in Gen 6:4 and existed after the Flood; the origin of these giants was among the בני האלהים that are the subject of that passage.

Ḥizzequni

1. Some explain the word נפילים as meaning ‘huge’. A similar use of the root occurs in Job 14:18 where the participle נופל means ‘huge’.
2. Rashi [based on b. *Soṭah* 34b] says that they were so huge they could ‘necklace the sun’. What this means is that they were so huge that it seemed that the links in their necklaces were large enough for the sun to go through, as Rashi himself explains in his comments on the talmudic passage.
3. The use of ‘grasshoppers’ in the simile is not critical but means simply that the spies were extremely small compared to these giants. This is the figurative way that the Hebrew Bible expresses itself, as in Isa 40:22.[62]

---

59 Compare *b. Soṭah* 34b which has: שמעניקין חמה בקומתן and Tanḥuma, ed. Warsaw, p. 68a, which has:שהיה עונק את החמה . The text in ed. Buber, p. 66, varies slightly. See also see Ḥizzequni below on v. 33.
60 Compare *b. Soṭah* 35a: אמר רב משרשיא מרגלי[ם] שקרי הוו.
61 Compare comment in Leqaḥ Ṭov, p. 213: שכל הרואה אותם נופל מאימתם, which stresses a physical and not a psychological ‘fall’. On the overall topic of the giants of the Hebrew Bible, see Doak, *Rephaim*.
62 So Bekhor Shor, *Perush*, p. 263. Compare Rashbam above, on this verse.

Sforno

1. The two expressions בני ענק and נפילים are used to indicate that they were the former on their paternal side and the latter on their maternal side[63] [referring to the passage in Gen 6:4 and interpreting נפילים as early and unusual births because of the interbreeding].
2. We were like grasshoppers, or even something less than that, to them, so they made no move against us. They took no account of us at all and would have regarded it as demeaning to trouble themselves with harming us.

Modern comments

A. B. Ehrlich

The choice of the spies (v. 2), given their unsatisfactory behaviour, could not have been that of God; see Ramban.
The word הארץ (*ha-'areṣ*) in vv. 18–19 in one case refers to the air and the climate and in another to the soil; see Ibn Ezra, Ramban and Sforno.
The seasonal reference in v. 20 is a way of setting the background for the story of the huge cluster of grapes in v. 23; see Rashbam.
The reference to Hebron in v. 22 is intended to equate antiquity with importance and to make a link with the Anakites; see Rashbam, Ibn Ezra, Ḥizzequni and Ramban.
Caleb silenced the people (v. 30) to enable Moses to speak; see Sa'adya, Rashi and Sforno.
The word דבה (*dibbah*) in v. 32 carries both a good and a bad sense; see Ibn Ezra and Ramban.

A. H. McNeile

The basic sense of the Hebrew word נגב (*ngv*) in v. 17 means 'parched land' but was applied specifically to the south of Canaan and thereby came to have the sense of 'south'; see Sa'adya 's various translations of the word.
The 'grasshopper' simile in v. 33 means 'very small and helpless'; see Ḥizzequni and Sforno.

---

63 Following Abrabanel, he is referring to the passage in Gen 6:4 and interpreting נפילים as early and unusual births because of the interbreeding. See Pelkovitz, p. 630.

G. B. Gray

The word כל (*kol*) in v. 2 is a collective subject, distributed by the singular predicate, i.e. 'all severally a prince'; see Rashbam.
The word נשיא (*nasi'*) in v. 2 does not mean 'prince' but 'eminent person'; see Sforno.
The date signified by the period of the early grape harvest (v. 20) is mid-July; see the dating suggested in *b. Ta'anit* 29a and cited by Ḥizzequni on v. 25.
The expression ילידי הענק (*yelidey ha-'anaq*) in v. 22 is not a proper name but means 'long-necked people'; see Ramban.
The *waw* attached to the word אשכול (*'eshkol*) v. 23) is a '*waw* of association', not a conjunctive; see Rashi.
The dative pronoun לו (lo) in v. 27 refers to Moses; see Ibn Ezra.
The expression על יד (*'al yad*) here (v. 29) means 'on the banks of the Jordan'; see Rashi.
The calumny (v. 32) was spread among the people; see Ramban.

M. Noth

What is envisaged in v. 23 is a 'kind of wooden bier' (not just a pole); see Ḥizzequni.

Broadman Bible Commentary

The use of the word אפס (*'efes*) at the beginning of v. 28 indicates the spies' view that there was no hope of conquering the people of Canaan; see Ramban.

N. Leibowitz

Leibowitz expands on the views of Ramban on vv. 27–29, Rashi on v. 31, and Sforno on v. 32.

P. J. Budd

There is a possible link between the name נפילים (*nefilim*) and the root נפל 'to fall'; see Ibn Ezra.

Expositor's Bible Commentary

The act of espionage called for men (v. 3) who, though younger and more robust, were no less respected by their peers than the tribal leaders listed elsewhere; see Rashbam and Ramban.
Joseph is represented (vv. 8 and 11) by Manasseh, not Ephraim, and Levi is omitted; see Ḥizzequni.
Moses changes Joshua's name (v. 16) as a fatherly action, marking his aide for greatness; see Rashbam and Ḥizzequni.
The word והתחזקתם (*we-hithḥazaqtem*) in v. 20 means 'brace yourselves for thievery since the land is to be yours'; see Rashbam, Ḥizzequni and Ramban.
The first part of the spies' report (v. 27) was truthful; see Rashi and Ramban.

J. Milgrom

He specifically cites the views of the medieval commentators, as on vv. 2, 3, 17, 19, 22, 27, 30 and 32. In addition (sometimes cited in end-notes):
The initiative to arrange the espionage (v. 1), given its unfavourable outcome, cannot be that of God; see Ramban.
The word אנשים (*'anašim*) in v. 3 refers to important and brave men; see Ibn Ezra on v. 2 and Sforno on v. 3.
The names mentioned in v. 26, and their alternatives elsewhere, refer to a group of places that were close to each other; see Ḥizzequni and Sforno.
The spies' report included answers to the specific questions they were asked to address; see Ramban on v. 27.
The word ויהס (*wa-yahas*) used in v. 30 to convey the sense that Caleb silenced the people is from a verb formed from the interjection meaning 'hush'; see Rashi and Ibn Ezra.
The verb לעלות (*la-'alot*) in v. 31 has a military sense; see Ramban.

B. A. Levine

The adjectives טובה (*ṭovah*) and רעה (*ra'ah*) in v. 19 refer to greater or lesser productivity; see Rashbam and Ramban.
The overall effect of v. 29 is to indicate the existence of hostile and powerful peoples on all sides; see Ramban.
The word מדות (*middot*) in v. 32 means 'large measurements'; see Ibn Ezra.

Conclusions

The comments just cited allow us to form some impression of what each of the medieval Jewish commentators wished to achieve by his exegetical efforts.

Sa'adya is a linguist and a grammarian and uses his talents to clarify problematic terms and the precises sense of phrases and verses. Some of his remarks betray an impatience with the more imaginative type of rabbinic exegesis and a commitment to presupposing that the Torah is referring to a set of circumstances that characterize normal life. He also indicates when the meaning that immediately occurs to the reader may not be an accurate reflection of the intent of the verse and he opts for a more innovative interpretation.

In setting out to resolve some of the obvious questions that might occur to his students, Rashi is undoubtedly functioning as a pedagogue. At the same time, he chooses solutions that will not only educate his students about the meaning – or, perhaps more accurately, *a* meaning – of the text but will also illustrate religious lessons and provide spiritual guidance. With those ends in mind, he utilizes the talmudic and midrashic passages that best service his purpose and he often adapts their wording to make the lesson or the message clearer. Convinced as he is of the total consistency of the rabbinic outlook, he sets out to harmonize biblical and talmudic-midrashic texts that appear to contradict each other. He makes use of parables on numerous occasions, proving that he is not only catering for talmudic students but also for members of the wider, and less knowledgeable Jewish community. Rashi is unafraid of citing rabbinic texts that reflect the culture of the Greek and Roman worlds, even if they are no longer contemporary phenomena for him. That said, he has no hesitation in bringing miracles into the picture, even if they are not directly reported in the biblical text, and in citing aggadic folklore which has little relevance for the strict understanding of the biblical text. When such comments are followed by precisely such an understanding of the text, he may be catering to different tastes, or the text has been tampered with by later transmitters, intent on stressing the more literal sense and placing it in the mouth of their authoritative predecessor. He enjoys quoting passages that praise the land of Israel, even if he lives thousands of miles from the Jewish homeland. Where the narrative does not spell out exactly what has happened, he takes up the story and makes good what might appear to the uninitiated as gaps in the sense, often thereby enlivening the tale being told. He defines the meanings of individual Hebrew words and phrases, often with a homiletical intent, but sometimes utilizing targumic renderings, or his grammatical expertise, in order to convey what some of his successors would be happy to regard as the literal sense. For this reason, his comments left an impact on the Christian translators of the Hebrew Bible in the Reformation period.

Unlike his grandfather, Rashbam pursues a more unilateral, and indeed literal, method. He anxious to uncover the real senses of the words and phrase of each verse and does not hesitate to strike out on his own in this respect. He argues that the order in which events are written in the Torah may sometimes be at variance with their chronological occurrence and on occasion refers to the cultures of other peoples to illustrate the background to Hebrew practice. He does not attempt to spiritualize the Israelites' spying campaign but describes the chapter in terms of a military expedition undertaken with all the necessary preparations. There is a need to ensure supplies for one's troops and to plan how best to achieve one's objectives. The psychological training of the soldiers is also an important factor in arranging the conquest. Rashbam indicates that facts mentioned earlier in a narrative are intended to provide the background for the development and understanding of later events. Unusual grammatical structures are not to be used as a springboard for fanciful expansions of the content but are to be explained within the genuine setting of the overall narrative. Where the content needs to be expanded to clarify the sense, the expansion should be one that takes account of the reality of human relations, rather than indulging in flights of fancy. Similes that refer to human feelings are to be understood in that context and need not be explained as reports on what was said by those involved but not included in the text.

Ibn Ezra is also devoted to the more literal sense of the biblical text but his exegetical methodology is less single-minded than that of Rashbam. Broader literary and linguistic considerations are of interest to him. The explanation for apparent contradictions between two biblical texts may lie in the possibility that one is simply more detailed than the other. The meaning of a word or phrase is sometimes to be ascertained because of its immediate context. There are, however, instances in which the sense of a term may be illuminated by its occurrence elsewhere and one context may help clarify another. The recognition that there are examples of ellipsis in Biblical Hebrew can be an important tool for exegesis and there is a need for the reader to fill in the gaps. Phrases that occur more than once in the same passage may serve different purposes in each case. Some expressions become clearer if one recognizes that the preposition in Hebrew may carry a variety of senses or that a Hebrew root has an onomatopoeic origin. Names may also have their origins in some aspect of the characteristics of those to whom they are attached. The meaning of a noun may change in accordance with the auxiliary verb used with it, or it may at times have a superlative meaning without changing its form. Ibn Ezra makes use of his geographical and astronomical knowledge, and he demonstrates his awareness of environmental, agricultural and social elements in Torah narratives. Although there are instances when he cites talmudic-midrashic views as a matter of information, there are others in which he wishes to question their validity. In these latter cases, he opts for literary, logical or chronological explanations rather than the traditional rabbinic ones.

Ḥizzequni is the master of harmonization. In order to avoid a possible duplication of meaning, he is willing to offer an innovative structuring of syntax and the unusual definition of a noun. Anxious as he is to avoid any suggestion that Rashi contradicts himself in his interpretation of two verses in this chapter, he finds a novel way of solving this. If the patronym is different in two biblical texts, that is because one is his name and the other a description of his behaviour. He also finds a justification for Joseph here being included in the tribe of Menasseh and not Ephraim, to which he is attached elsewhere. He offers explanations for the absence of Levi from the list of tribes and for Joshua's change of name. The use of different names for the same area is because they were so close to each other. Ḥizzequni also favours rational treatments of the text and in this respect is often dependent on the earlier comments of Joseph Bekhor Shor. The route to be taken by the spies was logical, given that it involved the difficult territory before the easier one and another Numbers passage suggests that it was diagonal and not as suggested by Rashi. A metaphor or a name used here may be understood by reference to a similar usage in another biblical book, and what is only implied here may be categorically stated elsewhere. Metaphors and hyperboles are not to be taken literally but are figures of speech. The spies had to be encouraged because the security conducted by the locals was stricter during harvest time. Favourable comparisons are made with Egypt because that is the place with which they had been most familiar. He offers an explanation of how exactly the fruit was carried and by how many spies and of how the ten spies attempted to strengthen the force of their arguments. At times, he ingeniously offers comments that incorporate both logical and traditional interpretations.

Less comments but lengthier, even prolix, ones are the style of Ramban. He often takes his lead from the comments of Rashi, at times defending them and at others expanding them or making alternative suggestions. Such suggestions are almost always in line with earlier rabbinic exegesis, even if adjusted somewhat. He is anxious to defend the notion that divine behaviour is consistently impeccable. The order of names in the biblical text is not indicative of their genealogy but of their personal qualities. He notes Ibn Ezra's idea that the quality of the land refers to environmental matters but suggests a broader definition that includes the agricultural element and the degree of the land's fertility, citing the rendering of Targum Onqelos as supportive of his suggestion. As with earlier exegetes, he stresses the importance of bravery and the required military strategy on the part of those on spying missions. Taking issue with Rashi, Ramban argues that it was a family with rare physical power and longevity that built and developed Hebron, its alternative name of Qiryath 'Arba' alluding to its founder. If such an ancient land could be productive, how much more so the newer land that was about to be settled and cultivated? Although the spies lied only once with regard to the land of Canaan, they prefaced and laced their remarks with negative expressions and comments and gradually presented the kind of picture that would discourage the people from undertaking the conquest. Caleb's response is not simply a matter of silencing the people but rather of assuring them that the Canaanite strength would be no match for that of the Israelites. The people's response was that it was not only in the fortified cities that the Canaanites would be strong but also in the battlefield outside. Ramban reconstructs the propaganda battle conducted by the spies among the people, describing how their strategy moved from discouragement to downright calumny. They countered the argument that the richness of the soil might be an advantage by suggesting that the products of such soil were suitable only for unnaturally powerful people but fatal to ordinary members of society.

Sforno reflects a later style that stands between the medieval and the modern. He sets out to explain the relations between God and Israel, the importance of repentance and the qualities required for leadership. He sometimes explains individual words and does not hesitate to explain names and terminology in what we would call theological terms. In other instances, he sees the use of alternative names as motivated by the proximity of the places concerned, or as pointing to paternal and maternal origins. He understands the need to avoid lengthy detours on military expeditions. As a doctor, he appreciates the significance of checking the health of people in a location in order to assess the quality of the environment, including the water supply. He also notes the importance of establishing the quantity of food supplies and the local produce. The Canaanites knew the high standards and the luxuries they enjoyed and it was only the Israelite spies who marvelled at the quality of the local fruits. Those who shelter behind well protected cities are afraid of aggressors so the spies should be brave in their mission and the conquest could then be successfully completed. That said, ten spies felt that there were too many potential enemies in the total area for the Israelites to conquer it and that they might not even make it across the border. Like Ramban, Sforno reconstructs the discussion between those in favour of advancing and those against such a move. He suggests that the latter group saw the strength of some powerful individuals not as the result of the land's produce but as indicative that only the strongest could survive the poor quality of the air. The metaphor about grasshoppers means that the inhabitants considered it beneath their dignity to take any account whatsoever of the presence of these foreign spies.

It is interesting that so many of the comments of the moderns have parallels in the exegesis of their medieval predecessors but perhaps even more significant that these parallels range over a wide variety of comment. What we encounter in both sets of exegetes are topics such as the relationship of God and Israel, the qualities of the spies and the significance of name-changing. They are all concerned with definitions of Hebrew words, phrases, grammar and syntax and with the setting the seasonal and agricultural scene of the narrative. Military strategy and the explanation of metaphors need to be addressed in all commentaries. They also expand on the nature and the development of the arguments between the 'pros' and 'cons' of conquest.

Milgrom acknowledges his debt to the classical medieval exegetes while other moderns are less inclined to do so. This does not mean that they had not seen or inherited some of the earlier treatments; perhaps only that they did not wish to exhibit a respect for such 'outdated' sources. When I lectured on the medieval commentaries on this chapter in Philadelphia and in Oxford, there were those who adopted a similar pose. Their argument was that medieval and modern sources should not be considered together, nor compared, since the latter are truly scientific and the former too early to be so inclined.[64] I believe that such an approach is not a desideratum for modern research and that much may still be learnt from just such comparisons, while not shying away from the notion that the thinking of the modern ad medieval worlds are each to be recognized as *sui generis*. Why there is such an intense animosity on the part of some scholars to the use of the Jewish works of the Middle Ages is a topic that I have touched upon elsewhere and need not concern us any further in the present context.[65] Perhaps the treatment offered in the chapter just concluded may contribute usefully to the debate.

Works Cited

Bekhor Shor, Joseph ben Isaac, *Perush Yosef Shor Bor 'al ...Ha-Torah*, vol. 3 (Jerusalem: Rav Kook, 1978).

Berliner, A. (ed.), *Raschi: Der Kommentar des Salomo b. Isak über den Pentateuch* (Frankfurt-am-Main: Kauffman, 1905).

Broadman Bible Commentary (London: Marshall, Morgan & Scott, 1970).

Budd. P. J., *Numbers* (Waco, Tx.: Word Books, 1984).

Chavel, C. B., *Ḥizzequni. Perushey Ha-Torah Le-Rabbenu Ḥizqiyah b. Manoaḥ* (Jerusalem: Rav Kook, 1981).

Chavel, C. B., *Perushey Ha-Torah le-Rabbenu Mosheh ben Naḥman*, 2 vols. (Jerusalem: Rav Kook, 1969, 5th edn.).

64 See also chapter 4 above, n. 3, p. 74.

65 Reif, 'Jews, Hebraists'.

Chavel, C. B., *Perushey Rashi 'al Ha-Torah* (Jerusalem: Rav Kook, 1982).
Chavel, C. B., *Ramban (Nachmanides). Commentary on the Torah*, 5 vols. (New York: Shilo, 1971–76).
Doak, B. R., *The Last of the Rephaim: Conquest and Cataclysm in the Heroic Ages of Ancient Israel* (Ilex Foundation series 7. Cambridge: Harvard University Press, 2012).
Ehrlich, A. B., *Mikrâ ki-Pheschutô*, vol. 1 (Berlin: Poppelauer, 1899).
Expositor's Bible Commentary, vol. 2, Genesis-Numbers (Regency Reference Library, Grand Rapids, Mich.:, Zondervan, 1990).
Gottlieb, Z. (W.) and A. Darom, A., *Bi'ur 'al Ha-Torah Le-Rabbi 'Ovadyah Sforno* (Jerusalem: Rav Kook, 1980).
Gray, G. B., *The Fourth Book of Moses Called Numbers* (London: Dent, 1902).
Ibn Janaḥ, Jonah, *Sepher Haschoraschim. Würzelwörterbuch der hebräischen Sprache*, ed. W. Bacher (Berlin: Itzkowski, 1896).
Lehmann, M. R. (ed.), *The Commentary of Rashi on the Pentateuch* (Hebrew; New York: Lehmann, 1981).
Leibowitz, N. *Studies in Bamidbar (Numbers)*, Eng. trans. A. Newman (Jerusalem: World Zionist Organization, 1980).
Leqaḥ Ṭov, ed. S. Buber (Vilna: Romm, 1880–84).
Levine, B. A., *Numbers 1–20. A New Translation with Introduction and Commentary* (New York: Doubleday, 1993).
Lockshin, M. I., *Rashbam's Commentary on Leviticus and Numbers: an Annotated Translation* (Brown Judaic Studies 330, Providence, RI.: Brown University, 2001).
McNeile, A. H., *The Book of Numbers in the Revised Version, with Introduction and Notes* (Cambridge: Cambridge University Press, 1911).
Midrash Rabba: Bemidbar (Vilna: Romm, 1878).
Milgrom, J., *The JPS Torah Commentary. Numbers במדבר* (Philadelphia: Jewish Publication Society, 1990).
Noth, Martin, *Numbers. A Commentary*, Eng. trans. J. D. Martin (London: SCM, 1968).
Pelcovitz, R., *Sforno. Commentary on the Torah. Translation and Explanatory Notes*, vol. 2 (Brooklyn, NY: Mesorah, 1989).
Reif, S. C., 'Jews, hebraists and 'Old Testament' studies', in *Sense and Sensitivity: Essays on Biblical Prophecy, Ideology and Reception in Tribute to Robert Carroll*, eds. A. G. Hunter and P. R. Davies (Sheffield: Sheffield Academic Press, 2002), pp. 224–45.
Rosenbaum, M., and Silbermann, A. M., *Pentateuch with Rashi's Commentary Translated into English*, 5 vols. (London: Shapiro, Vallentine, 1929–34).
Rosin, D., *Perush Ha-Torah 'asher katav Rashbam* (Breslau: Schottlender, 1881).
Strickman, H. N., and Silver, A. M., *Ibn Ezra's Commentary on the Pentateuch. Numbers (Ba-midbar)* (New York: Menorah, 1999).
Tanḥuma, 2 vols. in 1 (Warsaw: J. Munk, 1879); ed. S. Buber (Vilna: Romm, 1885), Eng. trans. J. T. Townsend, *Midrash Tanḥuma*, 3 vols. (Hoboken, N. J.: Ktav, 1989–2003).
Torat Ḥayyim. Ḥamishah Ḥumshey Torah (Genesis–Deuteronomy in 7 volumes), ed. M. L. Katzenellenbogen (Jerusalem: Rav Kook, 1986–93).
Weiser, A., *Perushey Ha-Torah Le-Rabbenu 'Avraham Ibn 'Ezra*, vol. 3, *Bemidbar–Devarim* (Jerusalem: Rav Kook, 1977).

6 Psalm 93: An Historical and Comparative Survey of its Jewish Interpretations

Introduction

One of the particular pleasures of functioning as an academic colleague of John Emerton over a period of some thirty-five years was the opportunity that this occasionally provided of assessing the importance of the medieval commentators for various cruces in the Hebrew Bible that were being closely studied by him, and in the interpretation of which he was anxious not to neglect the pre-modern Jewish exegetical tradition. The resulting discussions with him on the views expressed in these commentaries, and on the manner in which they related to the relevant treatments offered by contemporary biblical scholarship, often clarified for me the sense of both, and consequently contributed to the advancement of my own research in the field.

When honoured by an invitation to add a paper to the distinguished offerings being made in his honour by leading scholars of the Old Testament, it occurred to me that it would be appropriate to engage on a topic that would be pertinent to the many scholarly discussions that I had had with John. It would be especially suitable if I could find a subject that again made a link between the medieval Jewish and the modern critical analysis of some verses from the Hebrew Bible. No sooner had this thought occurred when I found myself reciting Ps 93 in the synagogue and asking myself, in an unconscionable departure from liturgical concentration, what Jewish exegetes had made of this short but undoubtedly challenging collection of five verses. A quick glance at some of the medieval commentators revealed such a singular lack of consensus that further serious inquiry became a highly desirable option. This was followed soon afterwards by a note from one of the editors of the proposed volume suggesting that Psalms might be one of the books that would best feature in the collection of essays being planned. And so was born the present brief study which I offered to John in gratitude for the generous support he had always offered to my plans for the promotion of Genizah research.

Recent critical studies

A useful starting point for this survey are the conclusions reached in a number of modern scholarly commentaries, by both Jews and Christians, on the book of Psalms. Obviously it would take us greatly beyond the present remit to survey any more than a small sample of the relevant literature. I have therefore chosen

DOI 10.1515/9783110486704-007

two works from around the beginning of the twentieth century and two from its end, in the hope that this will provide a reasonable guide to the manner in which contemporary scholars have understood the literal meaning and religious message of Ps 93. Against the background of such a guide, it will be possible to exemplify, summarize and assess earlier Jewish interpretations of the same chapter, and to offer a comparative evaluation of the various approaches.

The production of 'The Cambridge Bible for Schools and Colleges', published by Cambridge University Press, stands singular testimony to the degree to which Biblical Hebrew was regarded in many circles as part of a classical education in the late Victorian and early Edwardian years. The series was edited by A. F. Kirkpatrick (1849–1940) who served as Regius Professor of Hebrew (1882–1903), Master of Selwyn College (1898–1907) and Lady Margaret's Professor of Divinity (1903–1907), all in the University of Cambridge, and the contributors included the finest scholars of the Hebrew Bible in the United Kingdom of his day. It was the editor himself who wrote the commentary on Psalms, the three volumes of which appeared between 1891 and 1901.[1]

Kirkpatrick describes Ps 93 as a 'prelude to the remarkable group of theocratic psalms 95–100' and argues that the stress on kingship is not part of a prophetic vision of the messianic period but a response to the sixth-century BCE restoration after the Babylonian exile which represented proof to the psalmist of the divine sovereignty. He accepts as liturgically authentic the LXX's superscription, which notes its recitation on the sixth day, refers to its talmudic parallels, and suggests that the LXX's phrase about the peopling of the land may just as well refer to the restoration as to the creation. God's firmly established throne is a contrast to the 'tottering order of the world' and the waters are a figure for the heathen nations who menace the kingdom of God, but to no avail. He interprets the testimonies of v. 5a as the revealed Torah rather than the prophetic promises, and v. 5b as an undertaking that the Temple will never again 'be defiled by Israel' or 'desecrated by foreign invaders'.[2]

Another series that has left a major mark on the scholarship of the Hebrew Bible until the present day is 'The International Critical Commentary on the Holy Scriptures of the Old and New Testaments', edited by S. R. Driver of Oxford, A. Plummer of Durham and C. A. Briggs of New York, and published by T. & T. Clark. Charles Augustus Briggs, perhaps most famous for his part in helping S. R. Driver and Francis Brown to produce *A Hebrew and English Lexicon of the Old Testament* (Oxford, 1907), taught at the Union Theological Seminary in New York for most

1 Kirkpatrick, *The Book of Psalms.*
2 *Books IV and V: Psalms XC–CL*, pp. 563–65.

of his career. Influenced as he was by the findings of German historical and literary scholarship, Briggs was committed to a critical view as to the textual reliability, authorship and historical fulfilment of Scripture. There was some doubt within the Presbyterian Church at that time about the acceptability of such views on the part of an ordained minister and this led to a trial for heresy from which he emerged bruised but not beaten. Briggs, with the assistance of his daughter, Emilie Grace, wrote the commentary on Psalms for the 'ICC' in 1906–07.[3]

The Briggs family team place Ps 93 in the group of royal psalms represented by Pss 96–100 but 'separated from them for liturgical reasons.' Their view of the LXX's superscription matches that of Kirkpatrick regarding liturgical use and the matter of repopulation, but they see this psalm, and the others in the group, as dependent on Deutero-Isaiah and in accord with parts of its Servant Songs, comparing v. 1 with Isa 51:9 and 52:7, and v. 2 with Isa 44:8, 45:21 and 48:3, 5, 7–8. God has now 'shown Himself to be king by a royal advent' and from his eternal throne has set aright the 'whole order of the habitable world'. The powerful waters of vv. 3–4 are not symbolic of mighty foes but are 'a graphic description of the majesty of the sea in a great storm', the magnificence of which is surpassed by that of God who can reduce it to order. They regard v. 5 as a liturgical addition, constituting a prosaic gloss that introduces 'corresponding thoughts of the Law and the Temple.'[4]

Nahum Sarna's primary contributions to biblical Hebrew studies in the second half of the twentieth century lay in the major impact he had on generations of students at Brandeis University, the contribution he made to Jewish understanding of modern scholarship, and the part he played in the creation of the Jewish Publication Society of America's new translation of the Hebrew Bible.[5] Educated at Jews' College, London, and in the University of London, as well as at Dropsie College in Philadelphia, he attempted to synthesize the best in scientific learning with the most valuable in Jewish traditional study, as especially exemplified in his commentaries on Genesis and Exodus.[6] His study of the book of Psalms appeared in 1993 and was republished as a paperback in 1995.[7]

Sarna cites the liturgical usage noted by LXX and Talmud and also makes reference to the talmudic view (*b. Roš. Haš.* 31a) that the completion of creation through the formation of man on the sixth day established God's overall sovereignty. He does not regard the concept of God as king as emanating from the surrounding cultures of the ancient Near East but as an internal Israelite de-

3 Briggs, *Psalms*.
4 Briggs, *Psalms*, 2.299, 301–3 and 311.
5 *Tanakh*, 1985.
6 Sarna, *Genesis*; Sarna, *Exodus*.
7 Sarna, *Songs of the Heart*.

velopment that occurred after the establishment of the Israelite monarchy. He is sceptical about aspects of Sigmund Mowinckel's theory of enthronement psalms as the liturgy of an annual festival borrowed from Mesopotamia that celebrated God's victory over chaos and the establishment of his sovereignty.[8] He does, however, accept that the Jewish New Year festival's stress on God's kingship may owe something to an ancient pre-exilic holy day. This psalm celebrates the eternal, indisputable fact of God's kingship and uses the image of royal apparel to emphasize God's eternal omnipotence and invulnerability, and the manner in which he ensures the stability of the world. Later verses mention the chaos of the primordial waters and how God brought it to order, before concluding with a recognition of the eternity of God's reliability, holiness and celestial shrine.[9]

The tendency of the more traditional wings of Judaism and Christianity is to approach each of the biblical books in a more holistic fashion. This can of course be done without sacrificing academically acceptable levels of scientific understanding, as has been amply demonstrated by David M. Howard Jr in his various studies of the historical and poetic books of the Hebrew Bible. Howard, who teaches Old Testament at Bethel Theological Seminary and is active in the Evangelical Church, completed a doctoral dissertation under the supervision of David Noel Freedmen at the University of Michigan in 1986. His extensive revision of that dissertation appeared in 1997 as *The Structure of Psalms 93–100* and offers a thorough, synchronic and structural analysis of these chapters which identifies their similarities of theme and language, and dates them all as pre-exilic.[10]

Howard sees Ps 93 as a burst of praise for the eternally present and enthroned God as the sovereign king and proud creator. The psalm expresses total confidence in him and highlights the contrast between him and those who rebel against him, and whom he crushes. Like the whole section of Pss 93–100, it is concerned with the divine kingship and functions as an introduction to the theme, and as an appropriate transition between the more detailed and specific texts of Pss 90–92 and 94. The psalmist affirms that God is sovereign even over the rebellious waters (of myth and cosmology) and stresses the ongoing importance of God's covenant and decrees (= Torah) and of his shrine. Primarily on linguistic grounds, and in view of the links with Ugaritic literature, Howard dates the Psalm to the earliest stages of Hebrew poetic writing, no later than the tenth century BCE and perhaps even two centuries earlier.[11]

---

8 Mowinckel, *Psalms*.
9 Sarna, *On the Book of Psalms*, pp. 177–88.
10 Howard, *Structure of Psalms*.
11 Howard, *The Structure of Psalms*, pp. 34–43, 105–19, 171 and 184–89.

Issues

These sample studies clearly identify at least some of the major issues that have confronted the modern exegete approaching Ps 93.

1. Does it have any liturgical function and, if so, from which period or periods?
2. What is the background to its stress on the kingship of God and what is the nature of this latter divine quality?
3. Is the psalm centred on the past, the present or the future?
4. How does it relate to the other chapters in this part of the book and to others parts of the Hebrew Bible?
5. Is the creation of the world one of the themes and are the references to the waters metaphorical or cosmological?
6. In which way are God and the world here related and what precisely is conveyed by the allusions to the divine testimonies and God's house?
7. With those questions in mind, it will be interesting to survey the earliest history of Jewish interpretation as it relates to these five tantalizing verses and their internal and external relationships.

Ancient Versions

The tradition of associating Ps 93 with Friday is clearly an ancient one. The texts of the Septuagint and the Vulgate include a heading that describes it as a psalm of David 'for the day before the sabbath when the earth was inhabited'.[12] This same association with Friday is made in the Mishnah (*m. Tamid* 7.4) which lists the specific psalms said to have been recited in the Temple on each day of the week. The explanation for the connection with Friday by reference to the particular act of creation completed on that day is also to be found in the Babylonian Talmud (*b. Roš. Haš.* 31a) which notes that Friday was the day on which God completed his work (by creating man) and was therefore able to assume his kingship. This piece of exegesis goes beyond the mishnaic text and links v. 1 with the divine act of creation. Interestingly, 4QPs[b] reads נוה and not נאוה in v. 5, seeing here a noun yielding the sense of 'habitation', rather than an epithet with the sense of 'pleasant', and thus effecting a parallel with 'your house' (ביתך).

12 LXX: Εἰς τὴν ἡμέραν τοῦ προσαββάτου, ὅτε κατῴκισται ἡ γῆ· αἶνος ᾠδῆς τῷ Δαυιδ. Vulgate: laus cantici David in die ante sabbatum quando inhabitata est terra.

Talmud

Five passages, in addition to the two noted in the previous paragraph, also deserve attention in the present context. The first of these concerns the word וישרנה that describes an action on the part of the cows when they were bringing back the ark of the covenant to Bet Shemesh (1 Sam 6:12). The word is linked in *b. 'Abod. Zar.* 24b with the Hebrew for a 'song' and what the cows sang as they walked is variously identified by a number of tannaitic teachers as Exod 15, Isa 12:4, an anonymous (unidentified?) psalm, Ps 98:1, Ps 99:1, Ps 93:1, and a *piyyuṭ*, possibly relating to Num 10:35. The identification with Ps 93 is made by R. Samuel b. Naḥman, an accomplished preacher in late third-century Lod, and appears to indicate his awareness of the liturgical importance of Ps 93. Equally important is a tannaitic tradition (*b. Ned.* 39b) that lists seven items that existed before the creation of the world, namely, Torah, repentance, heaven and hell (= 'garden of Eden and Gehinnom'), God's throne of glory, the Temple and the name of the messiah. The source for the primordial existence of the throne of glory is given as Ps 93:2, indicating that the phrase נכון כסאך מאז and perhaps other parts of the psalm were given a cosmological interpretation.[13]

Three other talmudic texts are of no more than homiletical significance but should be cited for the sake of completeness. The later talmudic commentators are led a somewhat sorry dance (by a playful piece of exegesis from the third-century teacher R. Yoḥanan cited in *b. Beṣa* 15b) which associates the tree with God's celestial power because of the use of the same stem (אדר) in both cases.[14] Secondly, the epithet אדיר is reported (*b. Menaḥ* 53a) to have been the subject of a homiletical discourse by the (third century?) rabbinic teacher, Ezra, grandson of R. Avtolos, which linked Ps 93:4 with Ps 16:3 and Exod 15:10. Finally, the link made by a young pupil between Ps 90:1 (תפלה למשה) and Ps 93:5 (ה' לארך ימים) helped the fourth-century Babylonian talmudic scholar R. Ḥagga to understand that Moses had to pray intensely before he succeeded in seeing divine patience restored. This midrash relates to the broader rabbinic view (Midrash Tehillim 90.3) that Pss 90–100 represent eleven prayers of Moses. But precisely how this story (*b. Sanh.* 111b) relates to the one told in Midrash Tehillim (cited below), and what we are to make of the textual variants, are not immediately clear and requires closer attention in an independent context.[15] What, at

13 תניא שבעה דברים נבראו קודם שנברא העולם ואלו הן: תורה, ותשובה, גן עדן, וגיהנם, כסא הכבוד, ובית המקדש, ושמו של משיח... כסא כבוד דכתיב 'נכון כסאך מאז' [תהלים צג:ב]

14 See the summary of their attempted explanations in ed. Steinsalz, at the foot of p. 67.

15 ר' חגא הוה סליק ואזיל בדרגא דבי רבה בר שילה שמעיה לההוא ינוקא דאמר עדותיך נאמנו מאד לביתך נאוה קדש ה' לאורך ימים וסמיך ליה תפלה למשה וגו' אמר ש"מ ארך אפים ראה

least, is demonstrated by these three homilies is that Ps 93 was not an unpopular choice of text for the preachers of the early talmudic period. There appear to be no parallel homilies cited in the Talmud Yerushalmi.

Minor tractates

Those smaller post-talmudic tractates that are generally dated to the geonic period (covering the seventh to the eleventh centuries) also contain some passages that are of interest to this discussion. Although there are some instances in which the traditions recorded there may have earlier origins, these particular passages appear to reflect developments that are post-talmudic. In the first of them, in Avoth de-Rabbi Nathan, the tradition about the use of Ps 93 in the Temple, already encountered above, appears to have been slightly expanded. Although the Hebrew text (מהו אומר) is ambiguous, it is possible to explain it as reporting that Adam recited the same psalms that were recited in the Temple on each of the days of the week.[16] The attribution to Adam may reflect an interest in promoting the recitation of these daily psalms by adding to the custom's historical prestige.

Three liturgical instructions recorded in the tractate Soferim testify to a growing use, within the statutory rabbinic liturgy, of biblical verses in general and of verses from the book of Psalms in particular. In the first of these, mention is again made of the psalms said to have been recited by the Levites in the Temple but it is then categorically explained that use of biblical verses in the appropriate liturgical context is equivalent to rebuilding the altar and making an offering on it (שכל המזכיר פסוק בעונתו מעלה עליו כאילו בנה מזבח חדש והקריב עליו קרבן). The second passage lists various verses to be recited on removing the Torah scroll from the ark, including an amalgam of Ps 10:16, Ps 93:1 and Exod 15:18, stressing God's eternity. In the third, reference is made to the use (in whole or in part) of Ps 93 among the selection of chapters from the book of Psalms used as introductory material to inspire the correct, spiritual frame of mind before the recitation of the prayers proper.[17]

Two comments in Kallah Rabbathi are based, respectively, on the opening and concluding verses of Ps 93. The verse about God's royal clothing inspires

Genizah fragment, Cambridge University Library, T-S F2(1).122), reads: צער גדול היה למשה רבינו עד שהחזירו ארך אפים למקומו

16 Recension A, ed. S. Schechter /Kister, p. 5. In his English translation, Cashdan takes it as a reference to what Adam said each day while in his version Judah Goldin (p. 11) refers it to the Levites in the Temple, as in the talmudic passage.

17 Soferim, 18.2 (p. 312), 14.4 (p. 256), 18.1 (p. 308); E. T. 18.1 (p. 300), 14.8 (p. 278), 17.11 (p. 298).

the explanation, in Aramaic, that the exercise of God's great power and glory includes being eternally exalted in his heights and robed in excellency as in a cloak. This may be seen as part of the attempt being made in this post-talmudic anthology to offer various forms of ethical and spiritual edification, in this case by expatiating on the nature of God's power. The phrase ה' לאורך ימים is expounded in the context of a commendation of the Torah for its manifold qualities. It is said to indicate that one of the Torah's many attributes is that its protective power is everlasting, providing reward in both this and the next world. What is here being demonstrated is an interest in using appropriate biblical verses to develop theological notions concerning the divine nature.[18]

Midrashim

This theological tendency is also to be found in Midrash Tehillim which, again, may include some earlier material but reflects, on the whole, post-talmudic thinking. It constitutes an anthology of comments on each Psalm which probably represents an edited version dating from the late geonic period in the land of Israel, at least as far as the first section, including our chapter, is concerned. On the word מלך in v. 1, it argues, by reference to Jer 10:6 – 7 and 1:5, that God's sovereignty, as Jeremiah's prophecy, is directed not only to Israel but to the whole world, thereby stressing the universal aspect of the Psalmist's message. In his comment on לבש in v. 1, the homilist cites seven scriptural instances in which God is described as being clothed. In five of these (Exod 15, Isa 59, Jer 51, Esth 8, Isa 63), he is clothed as a warrior who defeats the Egyptians, Babylonians, Medes, Greeks and Edomites, while the remaining two relate to the messianic age (Dan 7:9) and to the revelation at Sinai (Pss 93:1).[19] The phrase עז התאזר describes how Israel received the benefit of the divine strength during that revelation.[20]

The word כסא in v. 2 elicits the comment that God's throne of glory was one of the six (not seven) things already in existence before the creation of the world. While this list follows the passage in *b. Ned.* 39b in including – as well as the throne – the Torah, the Temple, the messiah and repentance, it adds Israel but omits the Garden of Eden and Gehinnom. The notion of God's throne is therefore seen as standing outside the normal worlds of nature and history. The

18 52b and 54b, E. T. (London: Soncino, 1965), 3.4 (p. 449) and 8 (p. 507). On Kallah Rabbathi, see Lerner, 'External tractates', pp. 393 – 97.
19 *Midrasch Tehillim*, ed. Buber, p. 413; Braude, *Midrash on Psalms*, pp. 124 – 25, 498.
20 The Buber text refers to Ps 29:11 but, as Braude suggests, following Reifmann, a more appropriate reference would be to Ps 93:1, then followed by the phrase: כנגד עוז שנתן לעמו בסיני.

references to water in vv. 2–4 indicate that primordial waters praised God. During the process of creation, the mighty waters had threatened to overpower the whole universe but God set controls on them so that they were limited to seas and lakes, as well as to the depths of the oceans. The waters are also said to represent the arrogant Philistines who captured the ark and were punished by God, in addition to those who destroyed the Temple and the nations who carried Israel off into exile, who will ultimately be wiped out by waters sent by God against them. The aggadic interpretation therefore wavers between the waters associated with the act of creation and waters as a metaphor for the enemies of Israel.[21]

The homilist takes the word עדתיך in v. 5 to mean that Moses advises God that what He does to the Jewish people accurately testifies to his evaluation of Israel and her adversaries. The success of the Temple and the Torah silences the wicked nations, while the humiliation of these two Jewish institutions strengthens the voice of Israel's enemies.[22] God is asked to restore the holiness of the Temple, but on this occasion on a permanent basis. The phrase ה' לארך ימים is understood to allude to God's patience, that is, his ארך אפים (Exod 34:6). In the context of a discussion of some of God's attributes, the issue is raised of this great, divine quality. The story is told that R. Ḥaggai was once walking through a double colonnade in Tiberias when he heard the youngsters in the synagogue class reciting Ps 93:5 (ה' לארך ימים), followed immediately by Ps 94:1 (אל נקמות ה'). From this he derived that God takes his time in taking revenge on the wicked but punishes the righteous immediately. The midrashic lesson is apparently that the Jews have paid the price of their wrongdoing while the wicked nations have their punishment awaiting them in the future, evidently intended as some sort of consolation to the long-suffering Jewish listener.[23]

This reference would appear to be to the third-century *amora* R. Ḥaggai and the question arises as to how this can be harmonized with the similar story told in *b. Sanh.* 111b and cited above. It is unclear whether there were two such teachers with this name, one in third-century Palestine and the other in fourth-century Babylonia, or only one, who spent time in both centres. The talmudic text, as already indicated above, is in any event problematic so it would not be surprising to find that errors have crept into one or both of the transmissions.

21 Buber, pp. 414–16; Braude, pp. 125–29, 499.
22 אמר משה לפני הקב'ה רבש'ע השפלת קולה של תורה וקולו של בית המקדש והגבהת קולן של רשעים
23 Buber, pp. 416–17; Braude, pp. 129–30, 499.

Summary of rabbinic interpretations

What emerges, unsurprisingly, from these talmudic, post-talmudic and midrashic sources is that Ps 93 was from the earliest times regarded as of liturgical importance – at least potential if not actual – and that this importance grew during the geonic period. It was also seen as belonging to the group Pss 90 – 100, comprising the prayers of Moses. Parts of Ps 93 were associated by the exegetes with the creation of the world and with their notions of cosmology while others were regarded as conveying central teachings about the power, sovereignty and patience of God and the special qualities of the Torah, as well as the universalism of God's message. The references to water were understood as a metaphor for the enemies of Israel and various words and expressions were fairly popular with the Jewish homilists.

Liturgy

As is now widely recognized, the process of standardizing the rabbinic liturgy made considerable progress between the geonic period and the high Middle Ages.[24] It will now therefore be of value to this study to examine the manner in which the liturgical use of Ps 92 developed during those centuries, and what we may conclude therefrom with regard to the history of its interpretation. Although the Mishnah already makes reference to the recitation of Ps 93 in the Temple on Fridays, there is no clear-cut evidence that a similar custom was practised in the talmudic synagogue. The references to Ps 93:1 in *b. Roš. Haš.* 31*a* and. *'Abod. Zar.* 24b indicate that there was a special interest in, and consciousness of, its liturgical possibilities, but one cannot be sure that this expressed itself in a formal inclusion in the Friday morning liturgy of the day. The praise accorded to the use of biblical verses on appropriate occasions, together with a specific note about the psalms for Friday and Saturday (as recorded in the post-talmudic tractate Soferim and cited above), would appear to indicate at least a limited liturgical use of Pss 92–93 by the late geonic period. One such use is widely recorded among Genizah manuscript fragments reflecting the rite of the land of Israel, before or just after the Crusader period. It relates not to a daily recitation of an appropriate psalm but to the use of Pss 92–93 on the sabbath.

The two psalms were recited together not only in the evening but also on Saturday morning. Although it is essentially the first one of these that is strictly

---

24 Reif, *Hebrew Prayer*, pp. 122–52.

relevant to the sabbath, they were regarded virtually as inseparable so that Ps 93 was often recited immediately after Ps 92. This also had an impact on the liturgical poems (*piyyuṭim*) for the sabbath in which verses from both psalms were incorporated. What is more, Ps 93 also came to be widely used as an introduction to the other blocks of psalms being recited on a festival, even when that festival did not coincide with the sabbath. Although much of the rite of the land of Israel disappeared after the early thirteenth century, there are remnants of the earlier use of Pss 92–93 on Friday evenings in the Romaniote and Persian liturgies. According to Fleischer, there may even be a hint of the use of a daily psalm, other than on the sabbath, in some Genizah manuscripts, although this is by no means unequivocal, since many others do not appear to attest to such a custom. The rites of some late medieval oriental, North African, Provençal and Sefardi communities included the recitation of Pss 92–93 before the statutory prayers on Friday evening, but this was not widely adopted by the Ashkenazi and other prayer-books until after the sixteenth century.[25]

The Babylonian rite and the prayer-books that follow it reflect a different situation. With regard to the daily recitation of an appropriate psalm, there is no mention of the custom in the early liturgical manuscripts of Naṭronai Gaon (9th century) or Sa'adya Gaon (10th century), while the text in *Seder Rav 'Amram* may simply be a repetition of the Mishnah in *Tamid* 7.4 as a whole, rather than a text of which a different part had to be read each day. There are indeed some manuscripts of Sa'adya Gaon's prayer-book that record the use of Pss 92–93 on sabbath morning, but it is possible that these represent examples of Palestinian influence on the authentic Babylonian ritual.[26] The mishnaic passage from *Tamid* also occurs in the *Maḥzor Vitry*, emanating from Simḥah of Vitry of the Franco-German school of Rashi, but there the custom is attached to the sabbath prayers, and not those of the weekdays. In any event, the unreliability of the texts of prayer-book of Amram Gaon prevent us from assuming that he himself included it, in whatever form, in the ninth century. But *Seder Rav 'Amram* often reflects the customs of the post-geonic period, typically of about the twelfth century, and such a dating for the introduction of the daily recitation of Ps 93, with the other psalms listed in Mishnah *Tamid*, would match other evidence.[27]

Maimonides, for instance, records such a liturgical usage as that of 'some folk', although it is unclear whether he is referring to those in his place of domicile in twelfth-century Egypt, those who emigrated there from the land of Israel,

25 Fleischer, *Eretz-Israel*, pp. 38, 164, 167–78, 190, 192, 213; Ta-Shma, *Ashkenazic Prayer*, p. 151.
26 Ginzberg, *Geonica* 2.114–17; Davidson/Assaf/Joel, *Siddur RSG*, pp. 118–19; *Seder Rav 'Amram Ga'on*, ed. E. D. Goldschmidt (Jerusalem: Harav Kook, 1971), p. 40; Fleischer, *Eretz-Israel*, p. 197.
27 *Maḥzor Vitry*, 1.176; Brody, 'Liturgical uses', pp. 63–64.

or the custom of Muslim Spain whence he hailed. Nevertheless, it appears not to have become widespread as early as that century since Abraham ben Nathan of Lunel in his *Sefer Ha-Manhig* in the early thirteenth century draws attention to a 'fine custom' that he has observed in the city of Toledo and its environs to recite towards the end of the prayers a psalm suitable for each day. Interestingly, the British Museum manuscript of *Seder Rav 'Amram*, which dates from about the fourteenth century, expands each of the brief Psalm references in that mishnaic passage into the whole psalm text, giving the distinct impression that in the time of its scribe they were being recited individually on the specific day.[28] By that time, too, it has become widespread to include Pss 92–93 among those added to the morning psalms on sabbaths.

Although the detailed liturgical history of the use of Pss 92–93 remains unclear and more concentrated research remains to be done, it is possible to offer some tentative conclusions that will contribute to the present analysis. It appears to be safe to presuppose that Ps 93 had a significant liturgical history among the Jews of the land of Israel as part of the collections of psalms for sabbaths and festivals that preceded the statutory prayers, while there was a more limited use in the Babylonian rite. In the course of the high Middle Ages, it eventually won a place at the end of the daily prayers on Fridays. It also became customary in that era to add Pss 92–93 to the sabbath morning psalms. Moreover, it appears likely that the ultimately widespread custom of reciting both Ps 92 and Ps 93 before the formal commencement of the sabbath evening prayers is a remnant of the Jewish liturgy of pre-Crusader Palestine. It was not until the late medieval and early modern period that the custom of reciting the whole of m. *Tamid* 7.4 on a daily basis became widespread.

Especially important in the present context is the reason why Psalm 93 stubbornly remained attached to so many liturgical contexts where it might have given way to an exclusive use of Ps 92, and why it even functioned as an introductory liturgical passage. Here, Wieder makes an important point about its theological content. Having earlier cited numerous examples of texts being used in the liturgy because they stress the eternity of God, he draws attention to the phrases נכון כסאך מאז מעולם אתה (v. 2) and ה' לאורך ימים (v. 5) and points out that they refer to the two dimensions of eternity, the first alluding to the past and the second to the future.[29] He notes that Ibn Ezra also stresses the Psalm's message about eternity. What may be added on the basis of the above findings is that other aspects of its theological

28 'Maimonides' Book of Prayer', ed. Goldschmidt, p. 205; *Hamanhig*, ed. Raphael, 1.107; *SRAmram*, ed. Goldschmidt, p. 40.
29 Wieder, *Formation*, 1.125.

messages also became sufficiently attractive to the worshippers to warrant its more extensive use in the regular liturgy.

Medieval commentaries

In the high Middle Ages, the Jewish exegetes' concern with making greater use of biblical texts for the application of Jewish religious law, theology and liturgy, than for achieving deeper literary and linguistic understanding, was reversed in a number of intellectual circles. Although earlier interpretations had not been without their interest in the basic sense of a biblical word, phrase or story, a significant change took place in the climate of Jewish thought. The change was precipitated on the one hand by the influence of Islamic (and some Christian) rationalists, philosophers and linguists, and on the other by a Jewish desire to demonstrate to Christians that the latter's illumination of the Old Testament by way of the New Testament did not represent an accurate explanation of the original sense of the relevant texts. Particularly in France, Spain, and Provence between the eleventh and fourteenth centuries, there developed a kind of exegesis that was at first not wholly satisfied with anything that was *derash* (applied sense) rather than *peshaṭ* (literal sense) and ultimately grew into an almost obsessive tendency to reject out of hand any explanation of the text that did not analyse it as a piece of literature.[30] The novel nature of this exegesis, as well indeed as the manner in which it so often speaks in a certain degree to the modern scientific mind, makes it a potentially attractive component in any current treatment of texts from the Hebrew Bible. The problem is that few of those who occupy themselves with such treatment are competent in, and familiar enough with, the genre to allow them to exploit it in any accurate, or even adequate fashion. It may therefore broadly be found useful if some of the comments made in such circles about Ps 93 are now summarized.[31]

30 For a brief summary of this part of Jewish exegetical history, see chapter 2 above, pp. 43–45.
31 For the Hebrew texts, I have employed the excellent editions reproduced in *Mikra'ot Gedolot Haketer*, pp. 80–81.

Rashi

R. Solomon b. Isaac ('Rashi', 1040–1105) was the outstanding exegete of eleventh-century Franco-Germany who made great efforts to provide his students with a mixed diet so that they could taste and enjoy contextual as well as applied interpretations. He succeeded so well that he became for the Jews (and for some Christians) one of the best known and most widely used of the biblical commentators.[32] For Rashi, the psalmist is looking forward to a time when the world will be glad at the acknowledgement of God's sovereignty. Meanwhile, he complains about the arrogance of the nations towards God but expresses confidence that God's power will ultimately prove greater than theirs. He regards as thoroughly authentic the prophetic comments about God's holy habitation and is convinced that they will be fulfilled even if this takes a long time. Rashi also offers unadorned linguistic comments on the word דכים and נאוה. In sum, he sees the Psalm as a reference to the messianic age when God's authority and power will be established and welcomed, when the conceit of the nations will be shown to be vacuous, and when the words of Scripture will finally be implemented. The references to God's clothing are apparently taken as metaphors for his power, and mighty waters as literary figures for the nations. The divine throne will in the future be as well established as it was in the past. A good example of his approach is to be found in his comment on v. 3:

> נשאו נהרות יי : God is here being addressed by way of appeal and complaint. The sense is 'God, these nations who stream out like flowing rivers, noisily raise their voices and always increase the level of their low growling, in order to behave arrogantly towards you.' The root דכא always has the sense of 'low and debased'.[33]

Ibn Ezra

R. Abraham b. Meir Ibn Ezra (1089–1164), who was born in Spain but travelled widely in western Europe, was an enthusiast for the rational and the literal and sometimes used these, often in a cryptic or elliptic style, to challenge long-estab-

---

32 From among the extensive literature on Rashi, see Kamin, *Rashi's Exegetical Categorization*; Sed-Rajna (ed.), *Rashi 1040–1990.*); Grossman, *Rashi*; Gruber, *Rashi's Commentary on Psalms*, pp. 589–91 and 846 where the text differs slightly from the one used here (see n. 31 above).

33 לשון צעקה וקובלן זה. אתה יי הנה האומות השוטפים כנהרות נשאו קולם ויהמיון ואת דוך עמקי נבכיהם ישאו ויגביהו תמיד להתגאות נגדך. כל לשון דכא לשון עומק ושפלות

lished rabbinic traditions. He also made wide use of the physical sciences of his day, addressing himself primarily to the intellectuals rather than the more common Jewish folk targeted by Rashi.[34] For Ibn Ezra, the psalmist uses regal and military metaphors to describe God's power and the manner in which it ensures the continuing existence of the earth. That power is represented in the higher spheres by the throne of glory which has been occupied by God from eternity. Further indications of God's power may be identified in the movements of rivers and seas and in the winds that transform gentle waves into vigorous tides. The sounds emanating from the celestial spheres are even more powerful than these natural phenomena, but only those with the required spiritual faculties can hear them. God's revealed message is even more reliable than those phenomena because of the eternity of his presence. The concluding reference to 'length of days' may allude to this eternity or represent the psalmist's prayer that God's Temple will last for a long time. Ibn Ezra has created links between what appear to be disparate elements in the psalm, essentially seeing it a description of God's power in nature and revelation, and an affirmation of his eternity. He employs Neoplatonic cosmology to make the association between the lower and higher spheres and appears to polemicize against those who are incapable of receiving the divine message. Ibn Ezra's comment on v. 4 demonstrates how he links the apparently disparate parts of Ps 93:

> v. 4: מקולות: One thing that is even greater than the noise of many waters that are themselves powerful, such as the waves of the sea, is the power of God on high. This proves that sounds do emanate from the celestial spheres, as is reported in Ezekiel's vision (1:24), כקול מים רבים. But these sounds cannot be heard by those who are deaf to them, just as the awesome acts of God cannot be seen by those who are blind to them (Isa 42:18).[35]

Qimḥi

R. David b. Joseph ('Redaq', 1160 – 1235) came from a Provençal family of linguists and exegetes and the object of his commentaries was to synthesize what he regarded as all the best and varied parts of the Jewish exegetical tradition. His comments are clearly expressed and wide-ranging and it is not uncom-

34 See, for example, Díaz Esteban (ed.), *Abraham Ibn Ezra*; Simon, *Four Approaches*; Lancaster, *Deconstructing*; Silver, 'Ibn Ezra'. Silver's text differs slightly but not significantly from the one used here.

35 יותר מקולות מים רבים שהם אדירים שהם משברי ים יותר אדיר השם במרום. וזה לאות כי לגלגלים קולות וכן כתוב ביחזקאל (א:כד) כקול מים רבים. ואלה הקולות לא ישמעו החרשים כאשר לא יביטו העורים (יש' מב:יח) מעשה השם הנוראים.

mon for him to make use of them in order to challenge Christian interpretations.[36] For Qimḥi, Psalms 93–101 refer to the messianic age. They begin by asserting that at that future time God will be acknowledged not only as equitable (as at the conclusion of Ps 92) but also as the universal ruler, the only one 'clothed in majesty' and 'dressed as a warrior'. Given that degree of acknowledgement, national leaders will no longer follow the example of Nebuchadnezzar, Pharaoh and the kings of Assyria and Tyre but will leave the earth secure and untroubled by war. God's eternal occupation of his throne of glory will also receive wide recognition. The rivers and seas of the Psalm are metaphors for the armies of evil that will attack Jerusalem at the end of time since they are as noisy, as destructive and as troublesome as torrents of water. However noisy and powerful these hordes, God in his greater might will lay them low. The 'reliable testimonies' refer to the prophetic oracles about the end of time which will then be truly fulfilled and seen by all to have been wholly authentic. The Temple will never again be destroyed but will, in its great beauty, be the object of widespread pleasure and the site of universal pilgrimage. Qimḥi consistently supports his interpretations by reference to other prophetic verses and includes grammatical and lexicographical comments on the words תמוט/תכון, דכים, and נאוה. He relates the whole Psalm to the novel circumstances of the messianic period, explains the roles of the various participants in these future events, and points to similar thoughts about universal recognition, the messianic age, and the role of the Temple as expressed by the Hebrew prophets. His comment on the first part of v. 5 relates to the reliability of the prophetic message:[37]

> עדותיך נאמנו מאד : These testimonies are the scriptural words of your prophets that bear witness to your kingship and will then be truly fulfilled. The use of the word מאד indicates that no one at that time will have any doubt whatsoever about this. לביתך נאוה קדש : In this case the *alef* has a *ḥaṭef pataḥ* while in the other instances of this word in the Hebrew Bible (Ps 33:1, Isa 52:7 and Song 1:10) it is unvocalized.

Me'iri

Menaḥem b. Solomon Me'iri (1249–1316), also from a Provençal family, spent his whole life in Perpignan and established a reputation as a lucid expounder of Talmud and Bible. Another synthesiser, with a relatively open mind towards

36 Baker and Nicholson, *The Commentary of Rabbi David Kimḥi*; Talmage, *David Kimhi.*

37 והם דבריך הכתובים על ידי נביאיך המעידים על מלכותך, יתקיימו אז מאד, כלומר שלא יהיה לשום אדם ספק בלבו אז בזה. לביתך נאוה קדש האל'ף מונעת בחטף פתח והשאר נחה בהם האל'ף

Christianity, philosophy and contemporary science, Me'iri includes in his commentary on Psalms both the literal sense and traditional religious teachings.[38] He sees here a creation Psalm, the phrases about the powerful waters in verses 3–4 constituting a reference to the events described in Gen 1:9 and to the defined areas of the earth as laid out by God. The phrases about the divine throne and the earth are also to be understood cosmologically, alluding to the various parts of the universe. God's majesty, unlike its human equivalent, is constructive rather than destructive and is relevant here because it is seen by all as a powerful and miraculous ability to exist eternally and to create a universe *ex nihilo*, with everything in its required form and totally perfect. The final verse makes an association between all the matters of religious faith known from Jewish tradition and belief in God's creation of the world. Such a faith, in order to be perfect, must go beyond what can be understood by the logical minds of humanity. The psalmist is expressing the view that only those with such a level of faith are worthy of sanctifying and beautifying God's shrine and praying for the survival of the Temple, when it is still standing, and, later, for its restoration and permanence in the messianic age. In this preferred exegesis, Me'iri is clearly anxious for the message of the Psalm to be seen as theological, cosmological and doctrinal. He sets out for the reader of the Psalm the relative and related roles of God, the universe, monotheistic humanity and pious Jewry. The act of creation is seen to lead on to God's universal recognition and Jewish religious faith is with the historical and eschatological fate of the Jerusalem shrine. Having first expressed himself in these somewhat unique terms, Me'iri then goes on to cite the alternative interpretation according to which Ps 93 refers to the messianic age. Although often expressed in his own language, his comments here align to a great extent with those of Qimḥi. There are, however, some variations. He defines the word מלך as what would in modern times be called a prophetic perfect. The phrase לארך ימים is regarded by him as an allusion to the messianic age. He rejects the derivation of נאוה from the stem אוה and the consequent rendering that links it to the pleasure to be taken by humanity in the restored Temple. Me'iri's introductory comment on Ps 93 is a fine combination of cosmology and theology:

> ה׳ מלך גאות לבש: It seems to me that this psalm also alludes to the creation of the world, particularly to the exposure of the land when 'the waters were gathered to one place' (Gen 1:9). These four words convey the sense that the celestial and earthly beings will both recognize some of God's powerful and miraculous ability and that he girded himself with strength (התאזר עז) and with might when he created the world *ex nihilo* and when he

38 *Commentarius*, ed. Cohn.

permanently fixed the earth in the middle of the world בל תמוט so that it can never move off in another direction.[39]

Themes

A broad assessment of the themes that are of interest to these medieval Jewish commentators will obviously be instructive. They wish to establish a context for the psalm and to relate it to the power and eternity of God, as well as to his revealed message. They contrast worldly and divine rulership, as well as Israel and the nations. Some elements of doctrine are noted but not expanded or significantly promoted while there is little interest in practical *halakhah* or synagogal liturgy. Expressions are explained metaphorically for the sake of arriving at a literal meaning and there is a concern with cosmology as well as with the ultimate future and the status of the Temple at that time.

Conclusions

One must of course be wary of drawing any wide-ranging conclusions on the basis of such a limited range of sample material as that cited above. It does, however, draw one's attention to the fact that sources that are historically, religiously and methodologically distant from each other may have a number of strikingly similar or even parallel statements to make or approaches to champion. This does not by any means imply that we may expect modern critical viewpoints among the ancient or medieval sources or that any interpretation of religious ideology offered within such viewpoints is to be judged in the same way as its earlier counterparts. What may nonetheless be stated with confidence is that a thematic analysis is as important and as revealing as a historical one. As Adele Berlin wisely expressed it, there are 'crucial differences in the purposes of traditional exegetes and modern literary scholars but major similarities in the ways that they work with the biblical text.' Not only can modern interpreters of the Hebrew Bible find value in the traditional Jewish 'treasure of lexical and grammatical observations' but they may also benefit from an 'unlimited supply of raw material' throughout the rabbinic corpora.[40]

---

39 גם זה המזמור נראה לי שרומז על חדוש העולם ובפרט על הגלות הארץ בהקוות המים אל מקום אחד. ואמ' ה' מלך גאות לבש כלומ' עליונים ותחתונים יכירו כיצד מעלתו העצומה ובו התאזר עוז וגבורה בחדשו העולם יש מאין ובהכינו תבל באמצע העולם בל תמוט ותנוע לשום צד

40 Berlin, 'Traditional Jewish Exegesis'. See also Viezel, 'Medieval Bible Commentators'.

The summaries of the modern, ancient, early rabbinic and medieval exegesis of Ps 93 offered above uncover as many common factors as divergent ones and illuminate the degree to which an early generation's contribution, whatever the variations of methodology, may well remain in certain senses valuable to those interpreters who are tackling the same biblical text many centuries later. Sometimes it merely assists with a philological point or the explanation of a figure of speech; at others it may clarify the broader context or stress the centrality of a particular religious message. There are undoubtedly also occasions on which it simply inspires a knowing smile. In whatever way it aids the process of current exegesis, it will almost always, as John Emerton consistently understood, prove itself worthy of the close attention that it demands in order for its own sense to become apparent to the contemporary reader. Consequently, I like to think that the discussions I had with him over the years played some role in advancing knowledge of some of the many scriptural texts that were challenging to our two intellects, as well as close to both his heart and mine.

Works cited

'Avoth de-Rabbi Nathan, Recension A, ed. S. Schechter (Vienna, London and Frankfurt-am-Main: Lippe, Nutt, Kauffmann, 1887); reprinted with a prolegomenon by Menahem Kister (New York and Jerusalem: Jewish Theological Seminary of America, 1997; Eng. trans. E. Cashdan, *Minor Tractates* (London: Soncino, 1965); ed. J. Goldin (New Haven: Yale University Press, 1955).

Baker, J. and Nicholson, E. W., eds. and Eng. trans., *The Commentary of Rabbi David Kimḥi on Psalms CXX–CL* (Cambridge: Cambridge University Press, 1973).

Berlin, A., 'On the use of traditional Jewish exegesis in the modern literary study of the Bible', in *Tehillah le-Moshe: Biblical and Judaic Studies in Honor of Moshe Greenberg*, eds. M. Cogan, B. L. Eichler and J. H. Tigay (Winona Lake, Ind.: Eisenbrauns, 1997), pp. 173–83.

Briggs, C. A. and Briggs, E. G., *A Critical and Exegetical Commentary on the Book of Psalms*, vol. 2 (Edinburgh: T. & T. Clark, 1907).

Brody, R., 'Liturgical uses of the Book of Psalms in the Geonic period', in *Prayers that Cite Scripture*, ed. J. L. Kugel (Cambridge, London: Harvard University Press, 2006).

Davidson, I., Assaf, S., and Joel, B. I. (eds.), *Siddur R. Sa'adya Gaon. Kitāb Ǵāmi' Aṣ Ṣalawāt Wat-Tasābīh* (Jerusalem: Mekize Nirdamim, 1963, 2nd edn.).

Díaz Esteban, F. (ed.), *Abraham Ibn Ezra Y Su Tiempo. Abraham Ibn Ezra and his Age* (Madrid: Asociatiōn Española de Orientalistas, 1990).

Fleischer, E., *Eretz-Israel Prayer and Prayer-Rituals as Portrayed in the Geniza Documents* (Hebrew; Jerusalem: Magnes, 1988).

Ginzberg, L., *Geonica*, 2 vols. (New York: Jewish Theological Seminary, 1909), pp. 114–17.

Goldschmidt, E. D. (ed.), 'The Oxford Ms. of Maimonides' Book of Prayer', in his collected articles entitled *On Jewish Liturgy: Essays on Prayer and Religious Poetry* (Hebrew; Jerusalem: Magnes 1978), pp. 187–216.

Grossman, A., *Rashi* (Oxford: Littman, 2012).
Gruber, M. I., *Rashi's Commentary on Psalms* (Leiden: Brill, 2004).
Howard, D. M., *The Structure of Psalms 93–100* (Biblical and Judaic Studies from the University of California, San Diego, 5; Winona Lake, Ind.: Eisenbrauns, 1997).
Kamin, S., *Rashi's Exegetical Categorization in Respect to the Distinction between Peshat and Derash* (Hebrew; Jerusalem: Magnes, 1986).
Kirkpatrick, A. F. (ed.), *The Book of Psalms: Book I: Psalms I–XLI* (Cambridge: Cambridge University Press, 1891); *The Book of Psalms: Books II and III: Psalms XLII–LXXXIX* (Cambridge: University Press, 1895); *Books IV and V: Psalms XC–CL* (Cambridge: Cambridge University Press, 1901).
Lancaster, I., *Deconstructing the Bible. Abraham ibn Ezra's Introduction to the Torah* (London: Routledge Curzon, 2003).
Lerner, M. B., 'The external tractates', in *The Literature of the Sages, First Part: Oral Tora, Halakha, Mishna, Tosefta, Talmud, External Tractates*, eds. S. Safrai and P. J. Tomson (Assen/Maastricht, Philadelphia: Van Gorcum, Fortress, 1987).
Maḥzor Vitry, ed. S. Hurwitz, 2 vols. (Nuremburg: Mekize Nirdamim, 1923, 2nd edn.).
Massekheth Soferim, ed. M. Higger (New York: Debe Rabbanan, 1937); Eng. trans. I. W. Slotki (London: Soncino, 1965).
Menaḥem b. Solomon Me'iri, *Commentarius Libri Psalmorum: פירוש לספר תהלים*, ed. J. Cohn (Jerusalem: Mekize Nirdamim, 1936, 1970, 2nd edn.).
Midrasch Tehillim (Schocher Tob), ed. S. Buber (Vilna: Romm, 1891); *The Midrash on Psalms*, Eng. trans. W. G. Braude (New Haven: Yale University Press, 1959).
Mikra'ot Gedolot Haketer, Psalms, part II, ed. M. Cohen (Ramat-Gan, Bar-Ilan University Press, 2003).
Mowinckel, S., *The Psalms in Israel's Worship*, a revised text of the original Norwegian *Offersang og Sangoffer* (Oslo: Aschehoug, 1951), Eng. trans. D. Ap-Thomas (Oxford: Blackwell, 1962).
Reif. S. C., *Judaism and Hebrew Prayer. New Perspectives on Jewish Liturgical History* (Cambridge: Cambridge University Press, 1993).
Sarna, N. M., *The JPS Torah Commentary: Genesis. בראשית. The Traditional Hebrew Text with the New JPS Translation. Commentary* (Philadelphia: Jewish Publication Society, New York, Jerusalem, 1989).
Sarna, N. M., *The JPS Torah Commentary: Exodus. שמות. The Traditional Hebrew Text with the New JPS Translation. Commentary* (Philadelphia: Jewish Publication Society, New York, 1991).
Sarna, N. M., *Songs of the Heart: An Introduction to the Book of Psalms* (New York: Schocken, 1993); republished in paperback as *On the Book of Psalms: Exploring the Prayers of Ancient Israel* (New York: Schocken, 1995).
Seder Rav 'Amram Ga'on, ed. E. D. Goldschmidt (Jerusalem: Harav Kook, 1971).
Sed-Rajna, G. (ed.), *Rashi 1040–1990. Hommage à Ephraïm E. Urbach* (Paris: Les Éditions du Cerf, 1993).
Sefer Hamanhig: Rulings and Customs ed. Y. Raphael, 2 vols (Hebrew; Jerusalem: Harav Kook, 1978).
Silver, E., 'Ibn Ezra and his commentary on Psalms', in the companion volume to *The Parma Psalter. A Thirteenth Century Illuminated Hebrew Book of Psalms with a Commentary by Abraham Ibn Ezra. A Facsimile Edition* (London: Falter, 1996), pp. 149–275.

Simon, U., *Four Approaches to the Book of Psalms from Saadiah Gaon to Abraham Ibn Ezra*, Eng. trans. by L. J. Schramm of the Hebrew edition of 1982 (Albany, New York: State University of New York Press, 1991).

Steinsalz, A., *Talmud Bavli. Beṣah* (Jerusalem: Israel Institute for Talmudic Publications, 1982).

Talmage, F. E., *David Kimhi. The Man and the Commentaries* (Cambridge, Mass.: Harvard University Press, 1975).

Tanakh = The Holy Scriptures. The New JPS Translation according to the Traditional Hebrew Text (Philadelphia: Jewish Publication Society, 1985).

Ta-Shma, I. M., *The Early Ashkenazic Prayer: Literary and Historical Aspects* (Hebrew; Jerusalem: Magnes, 2003).

Viezel, E., 'Medieval Bible commentators on the question of the composition of the Bible: research and methodological aspects', *Tarbiz* 84 (2015–16), pp. 103–58.

Wieder, N., *The Formation of Jewish Liturgy in the East and the West: A Collection of Essays*, 2 vols. (Hebrew; Jerusalem: Ben Zvi, 1998).

7 Some Comments on the Connotations of the Stem גער in Early Rabbinic Texts

Andrew and I

How very appropriate that Andrew Macintosh and I, both of whose professional lives have been devoted to academic pursuits, should first have made contact some forty years ago in the pages of a scholarly periodical and, consequently, have seen our names together enter the dictionaries of Biblical Hebrew.[1] In 1969, Andrew was promoted from chaplain to the combined posts of Tutor and Assistant Dean at St John's College in the University of Cambridge. It was clear to him that in such a role he was expected to research and publish, and the passion he had developed for Biblical Hebrew, under the tutelage of David Winton Thomas, Regius Professor of Hebrew in the Faculty of Oriental Studies (as it then was), and Henry Hart, Reader in Hebrew and Intertestamental Studies in the Faculty of Divinity, was such that what was almost his first venture into print was on a linguistic topic in the Hebrew Bible.[2] Analysing carefully the occurrences in the Hebrew Bible of the root גער, he convincingly demonstrated the inadequacy of the English translation 'rebuke' and concluded that the root basically denotes passionate anger and its physical expression ('snorting fury'). When used with God as subject, Andrew pointed out, גער conveys the further sense of the effective working out of his anger. So far so good. But then Andrew went on to make another claim. He suggested that the translation of גער with words signifying moral rebuke 'may be held to be a reflection of the intense moral and legal nature of post-exilic Judaism and affords evidence that, at least from the third century B.C. onwards, the Jews understood the word גער primarily in these terms'.[3]

That was a red rag to a bullish young Jewish scholar by the name of Stefan Reif, then teaching in the Department of Hebrew and Semitic Languages at the University of Glasgow. On the sharp lookout as I somewhat zealously was for anything published that was insufficiently appreciative or inaccurately descriptive of post-biblical Jewish learning, and ambitiously anxious as I had become to make progress with my scholarly publications, I examined the topic closely to see whether indeed Jewish scholars of later generations understood the root גערprimarily in terms of moral rebuke. Unsurprisingly, of course, given the vast

1 See, for example, Caquot on the root גער.
2 Macintosh, 'Consideration'.
3 Macintosh, 'Consideration', p. 478.

DOI 10.1515/9783110486704-008

range of post-biblical Judaica, I found adequate evidence that the mediaeval Jewish commentators on the Hebrew Bible had located within the root various other facets of meaning and had therefore to some degree anticipated the findings that Andrew had presented in his article.[4] When my short response drawing attention to such evidence appeared in print, I had a most gracious letter from Andrew, welcoming its appearance, defending his overall treatment but acknowledging that by using the phrase 'from the third century B.C. onwards' he had laid himself open to the 'just criticism' that I had advanced. More significantly, he reported that while he was conscious that the views of mediaeval Jewish exegetes were at times rejected by modern scholarship, he now saw the need to consult them.[5]

In fact, Andrew has since then done a great deal more than consult them. He has consistently subjected them to close examination, both in Arabic and in Hebrew, and has taken great pleasure in fathoming their sometimes obscure exegetical depths. Since my arrival in Cambridge in 1973, he has often invited me to discuss these sources with him, and I believe that they have, as a result, become clearer and more accessible to both of us. Andrew's important scholarly work has regularly made reference to the lexicographical skills and exegetical insights demonstrated by such scholars as Jonah ibn Janaḥ and Abraham ibn Ezra, and I believe that his admiration for their deep understanding of the Hebrew language has grown over the years.[6] In a more recent message to me, he generously noted that my short response to his article had been 'a formative moment in my particular pilgrimage for it jolted me (a gentile parson!) into understanding that your Rabbis *must* be consulted on all such topics.'[7] It has been my privilege not only to have co-operated with him in his research into such mediaeval texts but also to have benefited from his kind patronage at St John's, to have joined and to have enjoyed the fellowship there with his active support, and to have developed a warm friendship with him that has brought me added joy in happy times and personal comfort in sadder circumstances.

Close examination

Having been invited to contribute to a much deserved tribute to a meticulous scholar, an inspiring teacher and a fine individual, I glanced back at what he

4 Reif, 'Note'.
5 Typewritten letter from Macintosh to Reif, 13 April, 1971.
6 See, for example, his *Isaiah xxi* and his *Hosea*.
7 Electronic mail, Macintosh to Reif, 29 July, 2010.

and I wrote four decades ago, and focused a more mature eye on the topic. What was still needed was a close examination of the talmudic-midrashic sources that straddled the period from the early Christian centuries until the classical Jewish Bible commentators of the high Middle Ages. Does such literature contribute anything to our knowledge of how the Hebrew root גער was employed and does it take us any further than the conclusions reached by Andrew and myself, as each of us took his first faltering steps as a scholar in print, כאשר ימשש העור באפלה (Deut 28:29)? I have tried to identify the different nuances associated with the root in the midrashim and to place these under separate headings. There is inevitably a degree of overlap and I am not convinced that every single instance may be so categorically and tightly defined. But that is the inevitable nature of lexicographical research. I believe that there are enough instances in each case, and that I have in general cited a large enough proportion of existing passages, to give an accurate overall impression and to permit some tentative conclusions.[8]

1 Moral rebuke or reprimand

Midrashic texts regularly testify to such a sense of the root in late talmudic and early mediaeval times. The Tanḥuma-Yelammedenu midrashim—which exist in two versions, namely, the common printed edition and the manuscript-based Buber edition—probably originated in the land of Israel in the late talmudic period and underwent a process of redaction in Babylon in the subsequent two centuries. In his treatment of the opening two words of the book of Exodus, the aggadist stresses the importance of disciplining one's children. By way of an exegesis of Pss 2:1 and 3:2, he forges a link between the lack of such parental activity, and its consequences, and two verses describing the war of Gog and Magog at the end of time. While in the earlier eschatological verse, as the rabbinic preacher sees it, it is only the nations that are stirred up against Israel, the latter verse has David bewailing the deep enmity of his own children towards him. All this because he had failed to provide them with appropriate parental guidance. With regard to Adonijah, the Hebrew expression is ולא גער בו, and this could well be rendered as 'he failed to issue the necessary moral rebuke due from a father to a child'. The midrashic text further notes that, although Adonijah engaged in disreputable behaviour, his father did not call him to

8 For the dating of midrashic compilations, I have used Stemberger, *Introduction*. For identifying sources that include the root גער, I am gratefully indebted to the Bar-Ilan University's Responsa Project and the Ma'agarim Project of the Hebrew Language Academy in Jerusalem.

task over this (ולא רידהו אביו), providing further evidence of the point being made.[9] The text is paralleled in the later midrash Shemot Rabbah without significant variation.[10]

Eli, the priest at the Shiloh sanctuary, judge in Israel, and the mentor of the prophet Samuel, also denied adequate discipline to his children, in this case of course the source being the biblical verse itself. According to Midrash Shemuel (edited in the mediaeval period but containing much earlier material), the meaning of the expression ולא כהה בהם in 1 Sam 3:13 is that לא גער בהון, that is to say, he offered no moral rebuke.[11] The family context and the rebuke delivered to a child by a parent is again the theme in a midrash about King Solomon that apparently belongs to a late collection of tales that stress his piety rather than his shortcomings. When wandering the world as a beggar, he is given menial tasks in the kitchen of the king of Ammon whose daughter Naamah falls in love with him. Her mother chides her for this (ואמה גערה בה) suggesting more appropriate alliances but the daughter has her way and, not only do they live happily ever after, but Naamah is also accorded a high religious status by the talmudic-midrashic literature.[12]

This general and expected sense of 'moral rebuke' for the root גער is found in many other midrashic contexts, in collections from different periods, with particular reference to the activities of various biblical characters. According to Pirqei de-Rabbi Eliezer (8th–9th centuries?), Zimri, son of Salu (Num 25:1–15), did not follow the example of his ancestor Simeon who, with his brother Levi, made an aggressive stand against the sexual immorality of the Shechemites vis-à-vis their sister Dinah (Gen 31), but chose not to condemn the Israelites' whoring with the Midianite women (ולא גער בבחורי ישראל). What is more, he himself indulged in such behaviour and was consequently dispatched by the more zealous Phinehas.[13] The verse in Ecc 7:5 that refers to גערת חכם is explained by Qohelet Rabbah and Yalquṭ Shim'oni as alluding to the admonitions delivered by Moses to Israel, by Pesiqta Rabbati as God's unsuccessful warnings to Israel, and by

---

9 *Midrash Tanḥuma*, ed. Warsaw, pp. 62a–62b.

10 *Shemot Rabbah*, p. 2a. For English edition, see *Midrash Rabbah: Exodus*, p. 3.

11 *Midrash Shemuel*, 10.1, p. 76. The use of the Aramaic word בהון appears to indicate that the aggadist may here be citing a targumic version of the verse. Sperber, *Bible in Aramaic*, 2.101, records the variant נזף for כהה in Codex Reuchlinianus but makes no mention of a variant גער that would be parallel to the midrashic rendering here cited.

12 *Ozar Midrashim*, 2.530.

13 *Pirqei RE*, p. 43a; ed. Higger, p. 235; English edition, *Pirḳê*, p. 369.

Leqaḥ Ṭov as the moral advice given by Solomon himself in the book of Qohelet.[14]

A remarkable exegesis relating to the same verse in Qohelet is found in Qohelet Rabbah and Midrash Zuṭa and contrasts the phrases גערת חכם and שיר כסילים.[15] The former is taken as a reference to those (דרשנים) who offer moral or halakhic guidance (גערה) by way of addresses in the synagogue while the latter is explained as an allusion to those who expand on the biblical text by way of a targumic method (מתורגמנין). This could refer to those who deliver loudly to the people what the teacher has quietly communicated to them, or to those who translate and expand the biblical verses in Aramaic. Given that the word שיר is being interpreted, however, it seems likely that the criticism here is of the *payyeṭanim* who expanded on the biblical verses by way of their poems, often providing linguistic and literary entertainment rather than moral guidance[16]

These examples – and various others – indicate that midrashic Hebrew of the talmudic and early mediaeval period continued to use the root for descriptions of 'moral rebuke' but usually with a favourable, exemplary and welcome sense.

2 Authoritative aspect

A common feature of some talmudic and midrashic texts is the use of the root to describe a serious censure, at times involving unceremonious or even dishonourable dismissal. In such instances the Hebrew is a little more complex and takes the form of a sentence such as גער בו והוציאו בנזיפה. This is not easily rendered in English but conveys something like 'he censured him severely and discharged him' or, more popularly, 'he ticked him off and sent him packing'. Some examples will undoubtedly clarify the overall sense intended. When, as detailed in the tannaitic midrash Sifre and in the post-talmudic tractate Avot de-Rabbi Nathan, the angel of death approached Moses and demanded that he give up his soul, Moses claimed superiority of rank and dismissed the angel. It was God himself

14 *Qohelet Rabbah*, p. 19a; English edition, *Midrash Rabbah: Ecclesiastes*, p. 179; *Yalquṭ Shim'oni*, no. 973; *Pesiqta Rabbati*, p. 132b; *Pesiqta Rabbati*, ed. Ulmer, 2.667; English edition, *Pesikta Rabbati*, 2.543; *Lekach-Tob* on Deuteronomy, p. 1a.

15 *Qohelet Rabbah*, p. 19a; English edition, p. 179; *Midrasch Suta*, p. 109; *Kohelet Zuta*, p. 134. But compare the significant textual variation in Feinberg, *Tobia*, p. 32.

16 Opposition to *piyyuṭim* is a well-recognized phenomenon in rabbinic literature from as early as the middle of the geonic period in the eighth century; see Petuchowski, *Theology*, pp. 16–19.

who then arranged for Moses a special place in the celestial world and who consigned his soul to that fate.[17] The same four-word idiom occurs in the well-known story of the would-be proselyte who approached Shammai with some difficult and provocative questions about the rabbinic notion of Torah and some demands about his future status as a Jew. While Shammai dismissed him angrily, Hillel treated him with greater patience, engaged him in religious dialogue and won him over to Judaism. The tale is told in Hebrew in numerous texts, including the Babylonian Talmud and Avot de-Rabbi Nathan, but occurs in a different form in Qohelet Rabbah where the two rabbinic characters are Rav and Samuel, the inquirer is a Persian and the language is Aramaic. More correctly, the language of the pericope is Aramaic with the exception of our phrase גער בו והוציאו בנזיפה![18]

Rabbi Eliezer ben Hyrcanus was a leading second-century scholar and teacher of Rabbi Akiva. Banished by his colleagues from their society for refusing to abide by majority decision, Eliezer seems to have led a lonely life, and his teachings were deliberately ignored. The talmudic story has it that, when he lay dying, he was visited by Akiva and other rabbis who sat at a distance, unsure of whether they ought to come closer. It was Friday afternoon and Eliezer's son, Hyrcanus, following a rabbinic ruling about not wearing *tefillin* on the sabbath, attempted to remove his father's set because of the approaching dusk, but was summarily dismissed by Eliezer (גער בו והוציאו בנזיפה). Hyrcanus's comment that his father had lost his senses elicited from the old man the remark that he was the sane one in the family. 'How can you abandon a pentateuchal law, the neglect of which is punishable by death because of a rabbinic prohibition?' The visiting rabbis drew closer to hear more, but maintained the distance of 'four amot' because of the ban.[19] Our expression occurs again in the tale of another unexpectedly favourable assessment of a character normally subject to severe criticism. The question is asked in Seder Eliyahu Rabbah (from the geonic period?) why some credit accrues to the arch idolater Jeroboam II (ben Joash) and the reply is given that he refused to countenance the scandalous remarks made about the prophet Amos by the priest Amaziah but sent him on his way 'with a flea in his ear' (גער בו והוציאו בנזיפה).[20] In addition, when Avot de-Rabbi

17 *Sifre on Deuteronomy*, ed. Finkelstein, pp. 326 – 27; English edition, *Sifre*, pp. 296 – 97; *Avoth de-Rabbi Nathan*, ed. Kister, pp. 25a–25b; English edition, *Fathers*, pp. 65 – 66. See also *Yalquṭ Shim'oni*, no. 940.

18 *b. Šabb* 31a; *Avoth de-Rabbi Nathan*, pp. 31a–31b; English edition, pp. 80 – 82; *Qohelet Rabbah*, 19b; English edition, p. 187.

19 *b. San.* 68a.

20 *Seder Eliahu Rabba and Seder Eliahu Zuta*, pp. 88 and 184, citing 2 Kgs 14:23 – 29 and Amos 7:10 – 17. See also *Yalquṭ Shim'oni*, no. 232.

Nathan criticizes those who refuse hospitality to a poor beggar it utilizes our expression to describe how the door is slammed in his face (וגוערין בו והוציאו בנזיפה).[21]

Another way of describing such a serious censure involves the use of the alternative phrase גער בו גערה גדולה...נזף בו. Avot de-Rabbi Nathan explains how Satan challenged God in the matter of the genuineness of Job's piety. Once this had been proved, God censured Satan severely and banished him from the celestial sphere (והשליכו מן השמים).[22] In a number of other midrashim, the word גער is used more simply but it is in each case obvious from the context that a severe reprimand is intended. When Moses ascends to heaven at God's invitation in order to take delivery of the divine Torah, various angels meet him and object strongly to his presence among them. Each one challenges him in an offensive manner (גער בו במשה) asking him 'What are you, Amram's mortal son, doing here among such holy company?'[23] In some instances there are interesting variations in the different treatments of the theme of God and his confrontations with the angels.[24] In other cases a more aggressive act on the part of God appears to be presupposed and they are therefore included in section 7 below.[25]

In all these passages there is a clash between two characters, with the more powerful of the two censuring the other for some unacceptable behaviour and dismissing, or attempting to dismiss, him from the environment under his control.

3 Rejection

A weaker sense of the root גער connoting 'dismissal', more akin to 'rejection' than to 'rebuke' or 'reprimand', is to be found in a talmudic *baraita* reporting a question by a woman who had experienced sexual intercourse at the age of three. She asked whether she was permitted to a priest in marriage, presumably aware that such an act might define her as a זונה, who is forbidden to a priest (Lev 21:7). Rabbi Akiva replied in the affirmative, presumably on the grounds that this, at such an age, had not been a voluntary act. She then put her case in a different light by way of a simile. Her case is like that of an infant whose finger is dipped into honey. The child angrily pushes it away twice but on the third occasion

21 *Avoth de-Rabbi Nathan*, p. 17b; English edition, p. 48.

22 *Avoth de-Rabbi Nathan*, addendum 2, to Recension A, p. 82b.

23 *Pesiqta Rabbati*, p. 96b; ed. Ulmer, 1.422–23; English edition, 1.405–6; *Ozar* (ed. Eisenstein), 2.306.

24 *Pesiqta Rabbati*, p. 203a; *Tanḥuma* (ed. Warsaw), pp. 124ab.

25 See n. 43 below.

sucks it with pleasure. Akiva appreciated her point and revised his ruling, albeit inviting objections from his students. The word describing the infant's initial rejection of the honey is גוער.[26]

Here the root is being used to denote no more than a gentle refusal. There are no moral implications, no degree of censure, no question of authority and no hint of anger.

4 Reprimand

Another use of the root גער belongs to a similar semantic context but with a somewhat weaker application, perhaps best rendered 'reprimand' rather than 'moral rebuke'. It is found in a midrashic parable that occurs in a large number of compilations, as early as Pesiqta de-Rabbi Kahana in the talmudic period and Tanḥuma and Pitron Torah in the geonic, and as late as Yalquṭ Shim'oni, perhaps in the thirteenth century.[27] In promoting the tithing of one's produce (Deut 14:22), the aggadist tells of a householder who built up large stores of wine and oil but paid no tithes. Divine punishment was meted out to him in what reads as a somewhat amusing fashion. His mind was taken over by a mischievous sprite that induced him to take a stick and set about smashing all the jars that he himself had stored. When one of his domestic staff took issue with him (גער בו בן ביתו), the householder beat him on the head for his pains and complained: 'Instead of helping me, you lecture me (תחות מסייעת יתי את גער בי).' Quick to learn, his servant followed his master's example and smashed twice as many jars.

The Babylonian Talmud makes use of the verb when reporting Rabbi Joshua's response to one of the miracles said to have occurred in apparent support of the individual views of R. Eliezer ben Hyrcanus against the majority views of his colleagues. R. Eliezer calls on the walls of the rabbinical school to demonstrate that his view is correct and they do so by threatening to collapse. At which point, R. Joshua chides them (גער בהם רבי יהושע) for interfering in a matter that concerns only the halakhic experts.[28] In a liturgical context, the Palestinian Talmud reports that when a precentor bowed too low when reciting his prayers, one of the talmudic teachers (whose identity is uncertain) removed him. A different version of the story is then offered according to which he was not removed but

26 *b. Nid.* 45a.

27 *Pesikta de Rav Kahana*, 1.164; English edition, *Pesikta*, p. 189; *Midrasch Tanchuma*, ed. Buber, vol. 2, on Deuteronomy, p. 12a; English edition, *Midrash Tanḥuma*, 3.312; *Tanḥuma*, ed. Warsaw, p. 108b; *Sefer Pitron Torah*, pp. 259–60; *Yalquṭ Shim'oni*, nos. 892 and 932.

28 *b. B. Meṣ.* 59b.

was subject to גערה.[29] If this constitutes less of a stricture than removal, it must bear a fairly mild sense, perhaps akin to 'rebuke' or, more likely, 'reprimand'.

These examples, then, testify to a reprimand that is no more than what we would colloquially call a 'ticking off'.

5 Dissolution

An awareness that the root גער may in midrashic literature carry a sense that goes significantly beyond that of reprimand, moral rebuke and authoritative censure is found in the twelfth-century midrash Sekhel Ṭov. The author, Menaḥem ben Solomon, comments on the phrase ויגער בו אביו (Gen 37:10) that describes Jacob's response to Joseph's reports of the dreams he had experienced. The aggadist explains that there are two meanings of the root גער. The first describes the frank reprimand that is given to a junior, to a child or to a pupil by way of censure, and examples occur in this Genesis verse as well as in Ecc 7:5 and Jer 29:27. The second refers to a call for dissolution (גערת מאמר השמר), as in Pss 68:31, 9:6 and 80:17.[30] In this respect, the compiler of Sekhel Ṭov is more of a linguist and has more in common with the mediaeval rational exegetes, such as Ibn Ezra and Qimḥi,[31] than with other midrashim of assorted dates, such as Bereshit Rabbah, Midrash Aggadah and Yalquṭ Shim'oni, that comment on the same Genesis verse. They simply cite the first of the two meanings and make a link between the reprimand recorded here and that noted in Jer 29:27.[32] The idea of גערה as dissolution is taken further in a talmudic passage that explains the substantive גערה as one of the various descriptions of death. Death in a day is a swift death; in two days a delayed death; in three, the result of גערה; in four, the result of נזיפה; and in five, a normal death. Interesting for our purposes here is the notion that גערה is the kind of curse that results in injury or death.[33]

---

29 *y. Ber.* 1.5(4) (3d); for English translations, see *Talmud*, ed. Schwab, pp. 24–25, and *Talmud*, ed. Guggenheimer, p. 138.

30 *Sechel Tob*, 1.216. It is contextually clear that this phrase is intended to mean 'dissolution' but less obvious how this is to be explained from the final word, unless it has the sense of 'threat' or 'warning'. The text should perhaps be emended to השמד and, given that this could mean 'apostasy' to a censor (rather than the intended 'destruction'), it is not difficult to imagine why it was changed. I am grateful to my friend and colleague Dr Avi Shivtiel for helping me to clarify.

31 See Reif, 'Note', pp. 242–43.

32 *Bereschit Rabba*, 2.1014; English edition, *Midrash Rabbah: Genesis*, pp. 777–78; *Midrash Aggadah*, p. 89; *Yalquṭ Shim'oni*, no. 141.

33 *b. Mo'ed Qaṭ.* 28a.

6 Fatal curse

This latter sense, which extends to controlling, overpowering, execrating and eliminating, is also recorded in numerous midrashim. The giant Og, king of Bashan, is a popular figure in midrashic literature which enjoys expanding on the huge dimensions already presupposed for him in the Pentateuch. In one post-talmudic tractate, he is identified with Abraham's loyal servant, Eliezer, and it is said that Abraham so execrated him (גער בו) that one of his teeth fell out. Not passing up on a chance to benefit from such a mishap, Abraham promptly used the tooth to build himself an ivory bed where he always subsequently slept, or, according to another view, an ivory chair in which he regularly sat.[34] Two midrashic passages cited by Eisenstein refer to a scream so terrifying (גערה גדולה) that the one against whom this is directed instantly takes flight.[35]

An extensive and assorted list of aggadic passages, early and late, use the root גער to describe the destruction of Israel's enemies at the end of time. Utilizing one of numerous phrases in Psalm 68 that are virtually impossible to translate and therefore a great gift to the rabbinic homilist, the exegesis recorded in one talmudic and three midrashic passages centres on the words גער חית קנה in verse 31. It sees there a reference to the ultimate destruction (גער) of the people who are associated with the reed and it sometimes spells this out as Edom/Esau/Rome, possibly meaning Christianity.[36] Already in Dan 7, the various empires from which the Jews suffered were designated as beasts, so that it is not altogether surprising to find the word חיה similarly used by the aggadist. The underlying reasons for associating the word קנה with Rome relate, variously, to that city's alleged origin in a reed planted in the sea by the angel Gabriel when Solomon married Pharaoh's daughter, to the quill it used to sign its anti-Jewish decrees, and to its living among the reeds (an unclear allusion). There may also be some connection here with the root קנה and its meaning of taking possession and, possibly, with the wood of the cross.

The theme of God's ultimate destruction of Israel's enemies, who are constantly devising evil against her, and the use of the word גער to describe this, are common to a number of other midrashim from various dates and provenances, but in this case by way of their interpretation of Ps 9:6 where the root גער occurs in parallel with the root אבד (גערת גוים אבדת רשע). In five midrashic

34 *Massekhet Soferim*, addendum 1, section 2, pp. 366–67.

35 *Ozar*, 1.73 and 2.382.

36 *b. Pesaḥ.* 118b;. *Shemot Rabbah*, p. 63b; English edition, p. 434; *Midrasch Tehillim*, p. 160b; English edition, 1. 548; *Aggadat Bereshit*, pp. 50a and 57b.

texts, the wicked individuals and nations are identified as Esau/Edom and Amalek/Haman, and these midrashim carefully note that Jacob/Israel is excluded from this ultimate elimination from the scene.[37] In other pieces of aggada, the Hebrew of Ps 119:21 (גערת זדים ארורים השגים ממצותיך) is understood as a reference to the ultimate and serious punishment of those who transgress some of the most essential requirements for civilized behaviour. Their misdemeanours include idolatry, adultery, incest, murder and slander and these are often the result of drunkenness.[38] The root that we are discussing obviously carries in these passages a fearful and destructive sense.

7 Powerful control

We already encountered how Satan and the angels were severely censured. There are other midrashic tales that use the root גער to describe an act of control or the exercise of power. They usually relate to what may be remnants of ancient Israelite myths about creation, celestial beings, fire and water, and the major figures and events in early Israelite history. It is not an unusual phenomenon for midrashic literature to preserve ancient Israelite myths that tended to be curtailed or totally suppressed when the battle with idolatry was still such an ongoing one in the biblical period.[39]

During the creation, according to two midrashim, the angel of darkness objected to God's plan to create light. God therefore exercised his power over that angel and over all the other angels (גער בהם) and, according to some versions, threatened them with destruction (אני גוער בך ומאבדך מן העולם), so that they scattered.[40] In other collections, it is explained that the primeval waters had the intention of spreading wherever they wished but God prevented this. He exercised control over them (גער בהם or גער בים), set their limits and restricted them to

---

37 *Pesikta de Rav Kahana*, p. 43. *Pesiqta Rabbati*, pp. 48b–51a; ed. Ulmer, 1.179; English edition, 1.225–31; *Midrasch Tanchuma*, ed. Buber, on Deuteronomy, 2.20a; English edition, 3.342; *Midrasch Tehillim*, p. 42a; English edition, 1.137; *Yalquṭ Shim'oni*, no. 938.

38 *Bemidbar Rabbah*, 2.35b; English edition, *Midrash Rabbah: Numbers*, p. 348; *Midrash Tanḥuma* ed. Warsaw, 2.13b; *Pitron Torah*, p. 30.

39 On various aspects of the midrashic genre, see Hirshman, *Rivalry*; Jacobs, *Midrashic Process* and *Impact*; Kasher, 'Interpretation', pp. 547–94; Porton, *Rabbinic Midrash*.

40 *Midraš Berešit Rabbati*, p. 10; and *Pesiqta Rabbati*, pp. 95a and 203a; ed. Ulmer, 1.414; English edition, 1.400.

certain areas.[41] Tanḥuma (Warsaw edition) cites Ps 104:7 and provides an explanation of how the root גערis being understood in this context by paraphrasing it with the use of the root בעט meaning 'kick' or, less literally, 'militate against'.[42]

One aggadic tale, repeated in various collections, describes God's powerful intervention when an attempt was made to prevent the *'aqedah.* When Abraham and Isaac were in danger of drowning in the river that Satan placed in their path as they proceeded to Mount Moriah, God took control of the waters and dried them up, or, in another version, overpowered Satan.[43] Similarly, another attempt to prevent a historical miracle was thwarted by God. When the Israelites wished to cross the Red Sea during their escape from Egypt, the waters tried to resist but God overpowered them and they parted.[44] The Israelites complained so much in the desert that God began to consume them with fire (Num 11:2). The biblical verse reports that Moses prayed to God, but a midrash makes the remarkable claim that Moses overpowered the divine fire (משה גער באש).[45] Qohelet Rabbah expands on the wickedness of Titus who not only destroyed the Jerusalem Temple but also performed acts of violence, blasphemy and fornication in its precincts. Experiencing a storm at sea during his return to Rome, he then claimed that Israel's God had power only in the sea. God immediately decided to take his revenge by other means and imposed calm on the sea (מיד גער הקב"ה לים). He later dispatched the Roman general by means of one of nature's tiniest creatures, the mosquito.[46] What these latter midrashim have in common is their compilers' conviction that the miraculous, as against the natural, was enthusiastically employed by God, or permitted by him through Moses, in the overwhelming divine desire to support the promotion, survival and vindication of Israel. Forms of the root גער constituted appropriate expressions to describe how power was miraculously employed to that purpose.

---

41 *b. Ḥag.* 12a; *Bereschit Rabba*, 1.31–35; English edition, pp. 34–36; *Shemot Rabbah*, pp. 30a–30b; English edition, pp. 190–91; *Tanḥuma*, ed. Warsaw, pp. 32a-32b; *Batei Midrashot*, 1.25; 2.422; *Yalquṭ Shim'oni*, nos. 560 and 913; *Oṣar*, 2.314.

42 *Tanḥuma*, ed. Warsaw, p. 32b.

43 *Tanḥuma*, ed. Warsaw, p. 30b; *Midrash Aggadah*, p. 51; *Yalquṭ Shim'oni*, no. 99; *Midraš Berešit Rabbati*, p. 89. *Ozar*, 1.147.

44 *Midrasch Tehillim*, p. 238a; English edition, vol. 2, p. 221; *Yalquṭ Shim'oni*, no. 873.

45 Mann, *Bible*, 1, Hebrew section, p. 80; *Yalquṭ Shim'oni*, no. 406.

46 *Qohelet Rabbah*, p. 15a; English edition, p. 140.

Conclusions

Clearly, גער was widely used over a long period to signify moral rebuke, but there are also numerous examples through the whole midrashic era of its occurrence with a sharper connotation, as when it conveys the sense of a serious censure by someone with a degree of authority over an inferior. In this latter sense, the narrative often employs a stereotyped, literary expression. There are also weaker meanings for the verb and these range from the talmudic to the late midrashic periods, that is, until the high Middle Ages. Such meanings include the kinds of refusal or reprimand that are more akin to questions or appeals and that imply no more than a negative preference or a gentle chiding. But, as in the Hebrew Bible, there is a usage that hints at a much stronger act than that of moral rebuke. There the result is damage, death or dissolution and these are brought about by way of an oath or curse loudly uttered by the perpetrator. The tales about such acts may have early origins in Hebrew mythology, since the topic is often the divine control over the powers of nature. There are, however, also cases where the deserving victims may be the enemies of Israel at various points in her history or where the perpetrator is Moses. Once again, it is well-nigh impossible to associate the linguistic usage with one particular period since it is documented in various midrashim dating from different times. On the other hand, it is well recognized that the midrashic genre is such that the date of the tale or the idea may be singularly at odds with the date of the compilation, and one's expectations in this respect cannot be high. Having also briefly glanced at some of the *piyyuṭim* in which the root גער occurs, it seems to me that much of what has been said above about the midrashic texts applies also to the poetic ones which, after all, date from the same period and often use similar themes. But there may be additional nuances that can be detected among the *piyyuṭim* and it might therefore be worthwhile for researchers to examine this in detail at some future date.

In sum, Andrew Macintosh was correct in identifying moral rebuke and passionate anger as two sides of the same linguistic coin in the case of the root גער, and I was justified in pointing out that these two meanings had been discussed by the mediaeval Jewish exegetes. Neither of us was then fully aware of the wider nuances that were to be found in the rabbinic texts and that have been located in the passages cited above. It is good not only to be able to pay tribute to Andrew in this essay but also to be in a position to compliment him on the valuable linguistic assessment he made at such an early stage of his academic career. I hope that we may be blessed with many more years of active academic co-operation and close friendship.

Works cited

Aggadat Bereshit, ed. S. Buber (Vilna: Romm, 1925).

Avoth de-Rabbi Nathan: Solomon Schechter Edition, ed. M. Kister (New York and Jerusalem; Jewish Theological Seminary of America, 1997), Recension A. For English editions, see J. Goldin, *The Fathers according to Rabbi Nathan* (Yale Judaica Series, 10; New Haven: Yale University Press, 1955), and E. Cashdan in *Minor Tractates of the Talmud* (London: Soncino, 1965).

Batei Midrashot, eds. S. A. Wertheimer and A. Wertheimer, 2 vols. (Jerusalem: Rav Kook, 2nd edn, 1953).

Bemidbar Rabbah in *Midrash Rabbah*; 3 vols. in 2 (Vilna: Romm, 1878); for English edition, see *Midrash Rabbah:* Numbers, Eng. trans. J. J. Slotki (London: Soncino, 3rd edn., 1961).

Bereschit Rabba, eds. J. Theodor and Ch. Albeck, 3 vols. (Jerusalem: Wahrmann, 2nd edn, 1965); for English edition, see *Midrash Rabbah: Genesis*, Eng. trans. H. Freedman (London: Soncino, 3rd edn, 1961).

Caquot A., entry גער in *Theological Dictionary of the Old Testament*, 3, Eng. trans. J. T. Willis and G. W. Bromiley (Grand Rapids, Mich.: Eeerdmans, 1978), pp. 49–53.

Feinberg, G. (ed.), *Tobia ben Elieser's Commentar zu Koheleth (Lekach Tob) samt Einleitung und Commentar* (Berlin: Itzkowski, 1904).

Hirshman, M., *A Rivalry of Genius: Jewish and Christian Biblical Interpretation*, Eng. trans. B. Stein (Albany: State University of New York Press, 1996).

Jacobs, I., *The Midrashic Process:Tradition and Interpretation in Rabbinic Judaism* (Cambridge: Cambridge University Press, 1995).

Jacobs, I., *The Impact of Midrash* (JSSSup, 19; Oxford: Oxford University Press, 2006).

Kasher, R., 'The interpretation of Scripture in rabbinic literature', in M. J. Mulder (ed.), *Mikra: Text, Translation, Reading and Interpretation of the Hebrew Bible in Ancient Judaism and Early Christianity* (Assen: Van Gorcum, Maastricht and Philadelphia: Fortress, 1988).

Kohelet Zuta, ed. S. Buber (Vilna: Romm, 1925).

Lekach-Tob, ed. S. Buber (Vilna: Romm, 1894).

Macintosh, A. A., 'A consideration of Hebrew גער', *Vetus Testamentum* 19 (1969), pp. 471–79.

Macintosh, A. A., *A Critical and Exegetical Commentary on Hosea* (ICC; Edinburgh: T. & T. Clark, 1997).

Macintosh, A. A., *Isaiah xxi: a Palimpsest* (Cambridge: Cambridge University Press, 1980).

Mann, J., *The Bible as Read and Preached in the Old Synagogue*, 2 vols. (New York: Ktav, 2nd edn., with prolegomenon by B. Z. Wacholder, 1971).

Massekhet Soferim, ed. M. Higger (New York: Debe Rabbanan, 1937).

Midraš Berešit Rabbati ex libro Mosis Haddaršan collectus, ed. Ch. Albeck (Jerusalem: Mekize Nirdamim, 1940).

Midrasch Suta, ed. S. Buber (Berlin: Itzkowski, 1894).

Midrasch Tanchuma, ed. S. Buber, 2 vols. (Vilna: Romm, 1885); Eng. trans. J. T. Townsend; 3 vols. (Hoboken, N. J.: Ktav, 1989–2003).

Midrasch Tehillim: Schocher Tob, ed. S. Buber (Vilna: Romm, 1891; Eng. trans. W. G. Braude, *The Midrash on Psalms*, 2 vols. (Yale Judaica Series, 13; Yale University Press, 1959).

Midrash Aggadah: Agadischer Commentar zum Pentateuch, ed. S. Buber (Vienna: A. Fanto, 1894).

Midrash Rabbah: Exodus, Eng. trans. S. M. Lehrman (London: Soncino Press, 3rd edn, 1961).

Midrash Shemuel, ed. S. Buber (Cracow: J. Fischer, 1893).

Midrash Tanḥuma, 2 vols. in 1 (Warsaw: J. Munk, 1879).
Ozar Midrashim, ed. J. D. Eisenstein, 2 vols. (New York: Eisenstein, 1915).
Pesikta de Rav Kahana, ed. B. Mandelbaum, 2 vols. (New York: Jewish Theological Seminary of America, 1962); Eng. trans. W. G. Braude and I. J. Kapstein (Philadelphia: Jewish Publication Society of America, 2nd edn, 1978).
Pesiqta Rabbati, ed. M. Friedmann (Vienna: J. Kaiser, 1880); ed. R. Ulmer, *Pesiqta Rabbati: A Synoptic Edition of Pesiqta Rabbati Based Upon All Extant Manuscripts and the Editio Princeps* 2 vols. (South Florida Studies in the History of Judaism, 155; Atlanta: Scholars Press, 1997–99); Eng. trans. W. G. Braude, 2 vols. (Yale Judaica Series, 18, New Haven: Yale University Press, 1968).
Petuchowski, J. J., *Theology and Poetry: Studies in the Medieval Piyyut* (Littman Library of Jewish Civilization; London: Routledge and Kegal Paul, 1978).
Pirqei de-Rabbi Eliezer, ed. C. M. Horowitz (Jerusalem: Makor, 1972); ed. M. Higger in *Horeb* 10 (1948); Eng. trans. G. Friedlander, *Pirḳê de Rabbi Eliezer (The Chapters of Rabbi Eliezer the Great) according to the text of the manuscript belonging to Abraham Epstein of Vienna* (London: Kegan Paul, Trench, Trubner, 1916).
Porton, G. G., *Understanding Rabbinic Midrash: Texts and Commentary* (Hoboken, N. J.: Ktav, 1985).
Qohelet Rabbah, in *Midrash Rabbah*; 3 vols. in 2 (Vilna: Romm, 1878); Eng. trans. A. Cohen (London: Soncino Press, 3rd edn, 1961).
Reif, S. C., 'A note on גער', *Vetus Testamentum* 21 (1971), pp. 241–44.
Sechel Tob, ed. S. Buber, 2 vols. (Berlin: Mekize Nirdamim, 1900).
Seder Eliahu Rabba and Seder Eliahu Zuta, ed. M. Friedmann (Jerusalem: Bamberger and Wahrman, 1960, 2nd edn.).
Sefer Pitron Torah, ed. E. E. Urbach (Jerusalem: Magnes, 1978).
Shemot Rabbah in *Midrash Rabbah*, 3 vols. in 2 (Vilna: Romm, 1878).
Sifre on Deuteronomy, ed. L. Finkelstein (New York: Jewish Theological Seminary of America, re-publication of the Berlin edition of 1939, repr., 1969). For English edition, see R. Hammer, *Sifre: a Tannaitic Commentary on the Book of Deuteronomy* (Yale Judaica Series, 24; New Haven: Yale University Press, 1986).
Sperber, A., *The Bible in Aramaic*, vol. 2, *The Former Prophets according to Targum Jonathan* (Leiden: E. J. Brill, 1959).
Stemberger, G., *Introduction to the Talmud and Midrash*, Eng. trans. M. Bockmuehl (Edinburgh: T. & T. Clark, 2nd edn, 1996).
The Talmud of Jerusalem: Vol. I. Berakhoth, trans. M. Schwab (London: Williams and Norgate, 1886); and *The Jerusalem Talmud: First Order: Zera'im: Berakhot*, trans. H. W. Guggenheimer (Berlin: de Gruyter, 2000).
Yalquṭ Shim'oni, eds. D. Hyman and Y. Shiloni (Jerusalem: Rav Kook, 1973–).

8 On some Connotations of the Word *Ma'aseh*

Robert and I

Some forty years ago, Robert Gordon and I – academic novices both – shared an office at the University of Glasgow. The building in which it was situated was occupied by the staff of the closely associated departments of Hebrew and Semitic Languages and Old Testament Language and Literature. I had been appointed to a lectureship in the former and he joined me when taking up a similar post in the latter. Alas, by the necessary order of such things, many of those who were our colleagues in that building have gone to their eternal rest while, equally sadly but by a somewhat less necessary order laid down in the name of academic progress (*so genannt*), such university departments have long been consigned to the *genizah* of educational history. I soon appreciated that Robert loved all manner of scholarly fare but always sought to season it with generous sprinklings of humour and even a soupçon of irreverence. Teaching for him essentially meant giving of himself and on many occasions assigning priority to students over his own ambitions and interests. While deeply committed to the critical study and sound analysis of primary sources, he never felt that this precluded him from personal commitment and institutional involvement in the religious sphere. I found myself in awe of his deep, emotional attachment not only to the Hebrew Bible but also to the land of Israel. And so it was that from our first meeting we discovered that we shared not only a professional place of work but a definition of what kind of scholarly *esprit de corps* we wished to adopt and encourage. To our minds, the maintenance of honesty and integrity was much to be desired and promoted in scholarly circles. Since those early days in our academic careers until the present time in Cambridge, when we somehow appear to have acquired a seniority at least of years, we have enjoyed being friends, exchanging confidences, supporting some fairly harmless forms of iconoclasm, and even, I daresay, indulging in a degree of mutual admiration. There is no scholar in the realm of Biblical Hebrew studies more worthy of recognition, admiration and respect and I was delighted to offer this modest contribution to the volume that was intended to bring him at least part of the honour that he richly deserved.

Variety of meaning

A problem that often confronts teachers and students of Hebrew, especially in its Biblical and early post-Biblical forms, is the tendency of the language to use a

DOI 10.1515/9783110486704-009

limited number of verbs and nouns for a great variety of meanings, rather than to develop a more extensive vocabulary[1]. Whether this is an innate characteristic of a language with a simple triliteral root system that inevitably has its limitations, or a phenomenon that should not be unexpected in its earlier, and therefore more primitive, forms, will not here concern us. What has often intrigued me is the degree to which the verb עשה and the noun מעשה exemplify the problem and consequently present a challenge to translators and exegetes alike. The topic I specifically propose to address is whether, in the case of the word מעשה, the lexicographers have provided adequate guidance as to its semantic range and variety of nuances, and whether the translations and comments provided for its occurrences in a wide range of Biblical Hebrew verses do adequate justice to the meaning being conveyed in each instance. Given the average size of each essay in this collection, I shall obviously not be able to deal with every relevant verse but I hope to provide enough examples to be able to illustrate the problem and to suggest that there may be some cases in which renderings and annotations might be improved.

Lexicographers

Firstly, then, what is noted by the lexicographers about any special senses of the word מעשה? Given the major contribution he made to the development of Hebrew grammatical studies in the Middle Ages, it is not inappropriate to begin with the views of one of the most distinguished and insightful Jewish scholars of Hebrew in eleventh-century Spain, Jonah (Abu'l-Walid Merwan) Ibn Janaḥ. In his comments on the stem עשה, he points to the sense of 'property' sometimes carried by the word מעשה and goes on to champion an explanation that this derives from the basic agricultural sense of 'collecting and storing up produce'.[2] He cites Ezek 28:4 for the verbal use but, more pertinently to the current analysis, makes reference to Jer 48:7, in which Moab is accused of trusting in במעשיך ובאוצרותיך, and to the rendering by Targum Jonathan which finds precisely such a sense in the word במעשיך, translating it as באוצרך ('your riches') and the subsequent word as בבית גנזך ('your treasure house'). David Qimḥi of twelfth-century Provence, and therefore still very much under the Spanish influence, follows Ibn Janaḥ in his definition of the basic sense of מעשה but he himself offers a slight expansion, suggesting that the word means 'acquisition,

1 Sáenz-Badillos, *History*, pp. 74–75.
2 Ibn Janaḥ, *Haschoraschim*, p. 388.

collection and treatment' (הקנין האסיפה והתיקון).[3] He cites with approval the view of Judah Ḥayyuj that the various meanings of the stem עשה represent essentially one overall sense and notes that the context dictates precisely which nuance is to be preferred.[4] Both Ibn Janaḥ and Qimḥi cite numerous verses where slightly varying senses pertain but their overall definitions cover all these.

The modern dictionaries provide lists of meanings for the stem עשה and then move on to treat the noun מעשה. Ben Yehuda lists thirteen usages for the verb: 'make', 'create/produce', 'prepare food', 'celebrate a festival', 'appoint', 'act justly', 'take action', 'busy oneself', 'deal with', 'conducted/appropriate/suitable' [in the passive mood], 'tarry', 'amount to', 'add up to', noting, in addition, the abbreviated עש for עשה in medieval Hebrew poetry.[5] Nine sense are listed for the noun: 'work', 'act/action', 'occupation', 'character', 'creation by a human', 'story/event', 'activity', 'achievement/behaviour', 'performance'.[6] It would therefore seem that BY is slightly at variance with Ibn Janaḥ and Qimḥi, opting rather for a basis sense of 'doing', 'making', with variations on this theme, but not stressing any agricultural origin for the various usages, or any central sense of 'collection'.

For its part, BDB divides the stem into two general headings covering the two senses of 'do' and 'make'. Under the first of these headings are listed subdivisions that detail who is doing, making or dealing what to, with or for whom. The emphasis here is on the remainder of the phrase or expression and how it qualifies and clarifies the basic meaning. Under the second heading, examples are provided of the stem when it bears the senses of 'making', 'producing', 'preparing', 'offering', 'arranging', 'celebrating', 'appointing', 'bringing about' and 'passing time'.[7] Here the lexicographers are stressing that the stem occurs as more than an auxiliary and are suggesting that these noted instances demonstrate extensions of its semantic range. BDB lists the senses of the nominal form מעשה under the two main headings of 'deed' and 'work'. The first list is sub-divided into: 'work', 'labour', 'business', 'pursuit', 'undertaking', 'enterprise', 'achievement', 'deeds', 'works'; while the second list notes the three senses of 'work': 'thing made by man', 'work done by God', 'product'.[8] Effectively, then, BDB adheres closely to the meaning of 'activity' in defining the word

---

3 Qimḥi, *Radicum Liber*, p. 281.
4 Ḥayyuj, *Treatises*, ed. Nutt, p. 90.
5 Ben Yehuda, *Dictionary*, pp. 4765–72.
6 Ben Yehuda, *Dictionary*, pp. 3202–08.
7 BDB, pp. 793–95.
8 BDB, pp. 795–96.

מעשה and is again interested in defining who is carrying out the action in each case, especially whether human beings or God, and in what circumstances.

The comprehensive and extensive dictionary of the Israeli educator and writer, Avraham Even-Shoshan, identifies six basic senses of the stem עשה, namely (in my translations): 'make'/'carry out work'/'actively engage in preparing something', 'produce'/'yield', 'behave'/'bring about', 'appoint', 'spend time', 'complete'/'achieve'. When used as an auxiliary, it yields the meanings 'execute', 'arrange' and 'perform'.[9] For the noun מעשה, Even-Shoshan offers three headings. The first covers the senses of 'activity', 'work', 'business' and 'execution'. The definition given under the second is 'the manner in which something is made, constructed or formed', while the third lists instances of the word bearing the sense of 'occurrence', 'happening' or 'fact'.[10] Here, the basic sense is 'performing', 'creating' and 'effecting'.

Fifteen basic meanings are given for the verb in the revised English edition of KBL: 'make/ manufacture', 'attach', 'make for/with', 'create', 'give effect to/ do', 'acquire', 'prepare', 'make', 'carry out/perform', 'perform' (in a forensic context), 'perform labour', 'act/behave', 'behave' (in various ways), 'do/treat', 'enjoy oneself'.[11] The substantive מעשה is translated as 'work', 'labour', 'accomplishment', 'works and deeds of God', 'human achievement', and 'deal with someone'.[12] The general stress is on 'activity'.

The Dictionary of Classical Hebrew, edited by David Clines, treats the verb under the nineteen headings of 'work/perform', 'be active', 'create', 'produce/ yield/ procreate', 'bring about', 'make/proclaim a decree/conclude an agreement', 'appoint', 'acquire', 'achieve', 'prepare', 'offer sacrifice', 'attend to', 'use for', 'cultivate', 'make a journey', 'spend time', 'comprise', 'violate (sexually)', 'be carried out'[13]. As regards the noun, the two main senses are given as 'work' and 'making' and these are followed by the five standard meanings of 'deed'/'action', 'deeds'/'activity'/'behaviour', 'product'/''produce'/'work'/'manufacture', 'labour'/'occupation'/'trade'/'business', and 'creation'/'creature'/'created being'. Three other meanings, which occur in later Hebrew, especially in the language of the Dead Sea Scrolls, cover 'object of mockery'/'substance'/'cultic apparatus', 'sexual intercourse', and 'event'/'episode'/'story'.[14] These latter senses, as well as the inclusion of a variety of renderings in the earlier list appear

9 Even-Shoshan, *Millon*, pp. 2012.
10 Even-Shoshan, *Millon*, pp. 1451–52.
11 KBL, 2.890–92.
12 KBL, 2.616–17.
13 Clines, *Dictionary*, 6.569.
14 Clines, *Dictionary*, 6.416.

to indicate an awareness of some connotations that are less than obvious and may easily be missed.

Helmer Ringgren aims for a greater degree of precision, listing, in the case of the verb, twelve broadly described and discussed senses, among which there are some overlaps. For our purposes, these may be summarized as: 'make'/'hold (a feast)'/'prepare' or 'offer (a sacrifice)', 'make (gods and idols)' which are then described as מעשה ידי־ם, 'make' (specifically to describe creative activity by God), 'produce' and 'yield' (that is, food and drink), 'create/acquire (wealth/reputation)', 'bring about' – as with God's bringing about great deeds/wonders/justice/revenge and punishment, 'practise (justice, mercy and kindness)', 'do good or evil, 'carry out (an instruction)', 'bring about (war, peace)' and 'commit (evil, wickedness or sin)', 'do (something for someone else)' or 'make into'/'cause to become', 'act (on the part of God in bringing about his wishes in the process of history)'. He also notes various locutions making use of עשה, such as with מה, or with כה.[15] For the noun, Ringgren lists 'work of human hands' (approved or disapproved), 'idols'/'wealth', 'fruit'/'produce', 'pattern'/'design', 'God's work', 'deed', 'conduct', 'continuing action/behaviour', 'deeds of mortals', 'labour'/'occupation/'business', 'general activity including achieving great things', 'God's activity in history', and 'divine providence'. Ringgren claims that Qumran has little new to offer and identifies the primary renderings in the Septuagint as ποιεῖν for the verb (with eight other, less common translations) and ἔργον for the noun. In the case of the latter there is also the occasional employment of ποιήμα, ποιήσις, and εργασίς. Interestingly, then, Ringgren includes with the usual 'creation' and 'activity' such notions as 'wealth', 'produce' and 'behaviour'.[16]

Commentators on two verses

The question now to be addressed is how some of the major medieval and modern commentators relate to the meaning of the word מעשה in a number of contexts where it may be less than obvious. While lexicographers are generally constrained by the extensive nature of their commitment to provide a brief definition and translation of all vocabulary, exegetes have the opportunity of expanding on the contextual meaning of a single word or expression. They may therefore be in a better position to detect and note a nuance – especially a less than usual one – that may have escaped the writer of a dictionary. Contexts and phraseology often pro-

15 Ringgren, *TDOT*, 11.389–98.
16 Ringgren, *TDOT*, 11.399–403.

vide the clues to such ranges of meaning. 'Acts' in English may, among other things, be parliamentary, divine or theatrical but no English speaker would for a moment expect such epithets to apply if the phrase in question were 'indecent acts'.

When the pentateuchal legislation demands of the Israelites that they do not do according to the מעשים of the surrounding peoples, what precisely is its intent? There are two verses that might usefully be consulted in this context, Lev 18:3 and Exod 23:24.

Lev 18:3: כמעשה ארץ-מצרים אשר ישבתם-בה לא תעשו וכמעשה ארץ-כנען אשר אני מביא אתכם שמה לא תעשו ובחקתיהם לא תלכו

The Spanish Jewish exegete, Abraham ben Meir ibn Ezra (1089–1164), expresses the view that the activities of the Egyptians and the Canaanites, to which this pentateuchal passage is most opposed, are those of idolatry and sexual immorality, which are in any event often closely associated. By way of introduction to this passage, he refers to his comments on other verses in order to establish the nature of the current context.[17] In his interpretation of Lev 17:7, he indicates that the reference to the שעירים ('demons' or 'satyrs') was motivated by Egyptian practices pursued by the Hebrews during their slavery. It is a call to avoid being disloyal to God and to true belief in Him.[18] The reference to abominable activities in Lev 18:26 refers back to all the forbidden sexual relationships just listed which were practised by the Canaanites and defiled the land of Israel.[19]

In his comments on Lev 18:3 itself, Ibn Ezra appears to use the word משפטים to mean the whole Egyptian way of life, including their legal and religious customs.[20] In his published translation of Ibn Ezra's commentary on Leviticus, which is a highly commendable piece of work, Jay F. Shachter translates the word as 'Egyptian legal system'.[21] Given, however, Ibn Ezra's references to these other contexts of idolatry and sexual immorality, it would be appear to me that he is here using משפטים to mean the religious *and* legal systems, that is to say, their total behaviour. In his comments on Lev 18:3, he draws a parallel with Exod 22–23, which certainly includes all manner of practices, not only legal, and in Lev 18:26 he links the legal aspect with the punishment for transgressing the sexual restrictions just listed.

---

17 *Torat Ḥayyim*, p. 159.
18 *Torat Ḥayyim*, pp. 155–56.
19 *Torat Ḥayyim*, p. 169.
20 *Torat Ḥayyim*, p. 160.
21 Shachter, *Commentary*, p. 90.

On Hag 2:12, in the standard Rabbinic Bible, Ibn Ezra refers to the term קדיש (ה), as in Deut 23:18, and defines it in a remarkable way, thus shedding further light on his understanding of ancient Egyptian practice. He explains that the humidity of the Nile weakens the Egyptians so much that by the age of forty they are themselves physically unable to penetrate a virgin. They therefore engage younger Egyptians to commence penetration and take over themselves once the hymen is breached. Such a youngster is known as a קדיש.

Moses Naḥmanides (1194–1270) of Gerona, and later of Jerusalem, greatly admired Ibn Ezra but often took the opportunity of criticizing his work. In this case, he cites Ibn Ezra's interpretation in support but himself expands on it. He too makes a link between all the forbidden practices associated with idolatry and immorality, indicating that the Egyptians were not simply guilty of the former but also of the latter.[22] In support, he makes reference to a halakhic midrash of the early Rabbinic period, where it is alleged that the Egyptians of the day were steeped in serious, sexual misconduct of various sorts.[23] Naḥmanides also points to the biblical verses in 1 Kgs 14:24 and Ezek 16:26, the sexual import of which is linguistically clarified by Ezek 23:20, Lev 15:2 and 15:19, where בשר ('flesh') is clearly a euphemism for the sexual organ. It may be added that this is another example of a word that carries a special, contextual nuance.

An adjacent *Sifra* passage is most interesting for the present discussion. It comments on the word מעשה:

> יכול לא יבנו בנינים ולא יטעו נטיעות כמותם ת׳ל ובחקותיהם לא תלכו. לא אמרתי אלא בחוקים החקוקים להם ולאבותיהם ולאבות אבותיהם. ומה היו עושים? האיש נושא לאיש והאשה לאשה. האיש נושא אשה ובתה והאישה ניסת לשנים לכך נאמר ובחקותיהם לא תלכו.
>
> [In my English translation:] Looking at the word מעשה on its own, I might have concluded that Israel is here being prohibited from following Egyptian and Canaanite practices in the spheres of construction and agriculture. The context is, however, clarified by the subsequent phrase ובחקותיהם לא תלכו. What is meant is that Israel should not follow practices that have been ingrained in ancient Egyptian and Canaanite culture for countless generations. What then are the acts they performed that are here prohibited by the word מעשה? Single sex marriages, both male and female; a man marrying a woman and her daughter; and a woman functioning as a wife with [consorting with?] two men.'[24]

For this early rabbinic midrash, then, the emphasis in the current prohibition is on the sexual aspects of the Egyptian and Canaanite practices, rather than on their more mundane pursuits, the word מעשה carrying a sexual nuance. For

22 *Torat Ḥayyim*, p. 160.
23 *Sifra* 9.3 and 13.8; pp. 85b–86a.
24 *Sifra*, 9.8; p. 85b.

two of the leading medieval Jewish exegetes, the word may best be translated as 'lifestyle', since its semantic range goes well beyond the sexual. These alternative renderings of מעשה as 'lifestyle' and 'sexual misdemeanour' are reflected in the ancient versions and in the modern translations and commentaries. The Septuagint renders מעשה as επιτηδεύματα meaning 'habits, customs, way of life',[25] while the Targum Onqelos remains neutral and uses the Aramaic עובדין which tells us no more than the original Hebrew.[26] Pseudo-Jonathan, on the other hand, adds an adjective, offering עובדין בישין, thereby understanding the prohibition to be aimed at 'bad behaviour'.[27] E. S. Hartom is a little more specific, using the Modern Hebrew phrase מנהגים מתועבים ('foul habits') and associating this with idolatrous customs, thus adopting the link made by the medieval commentators between idolatry and immorality.[28] J. Milgrom refers broadly to 'practices, mores',[29] while B. Levine argues that the term implies incest, bestiality and homosexuality.[30] The NEB ('as they do in Egypt') and JPS ('the practices of the land of Egypt') evidently regard the term מעשה as non-specific. In sum, a fair number of interpreters see here an allusion to idolatry and sexual immorality, which is a nuance that does not figure prominently in the dictionaries.

Another passage in the Hebrew Bible in which מעשים occurs, and where there are clear allusions to both idolatry and sexual immorality, is Ps 106:33–40. There, in a powerful summary of their history, the Israelites are accused of having followed the practices of other nations, serving their idols, even at times by way of sacrificing their children, polluting thereby the land of Israel, and antagonizing God. Three phrases occur in vv. 35–36. The first, ויתערבו בגוים, refers to non-Israelite influences, and the third, ויעבדו את-עצביהם, to idolatry. The middle phrase, וילמדו מעשיהם, could, in another context, have the general sense of 'following their practices' but, given the phrases which precede and follow it, it seems reasonable to conclude that the reference is to sexual immorality. The Psalmist's criticism of his people is that, having integrated with the Canaanites, they adopted their indecent behaviour and worshipped their gods. Such an understanding of the passage matches well with the overall theme. The word מעשיהם occurs again in v. 39 (ויטמאו במעשיהם ויזנו במעלליהם) where the complaint is that the Israelites have defiled with their מעשים and whored with their מעללים. If these two nouns are parallel, they could both be understood as idolatry or as sexual immorality;

25 Rahlfs, 1.190.
26 *Torat Ḥayyim*, p. 160.
27 Ginsburger, *Pseudo-Jonathan*, p. 204.
28 Hartom, *Ha-Miqra*, p. 58.
29 Milgrom, *Numbers*, p. 1518.
30 Levine, *Leviticus*, p. 118.

alternatively, they may each refer to only one of these religious misdemeanours. Either way, מעשים is to be understood as something undoubtedly more precise and nuanced than 'deeds', 'ways' or 'customs'. This appears to have been the way the text was understood by Briggs, Hartom and *Da'at Miqra*.[31]

Idolatry

There are a number of other verses in which מעשה may conceivably, even if not convincingly, allude to idolatry, and should therefore be noted at this point in the discussion. In the sixth chapter of his prophecies, Micah rails against the people of Israel for their nefarious activities, and in v. 16 he accuses them of maintaining the practices of Omri, and in a parallel expression, of following the מעשה of the house of Ahab. Which kinds of behaviour are implied by the word מעשה? Most of the translations and commentaries opt for a general sense of misbehaviour but Hartom finds a reference here to idolatry and T. K. Cheyne to the worship of Baal.[32] Ringgren specifically rejects such a meaning here, while Smith, Ward and Bewer in the ICC regard the word מעשה as an allusion to the criminal act of murdering Naboth in order to steal his vineyard.[33] The question in Isa 66:18 is whether the activities and thoughts being noted are those of the idolaters described in the previous verse. This is the interpretation favoured by *Da'at Miqra* and Hartom,[34] while J. Skinner and J. Blenkinsopp, following Bernhard Duhm, remove the doubt by relocating the first phrase of this verse in the idolatrous context of the previous verse.[35] King Jehoshaphat receives praise in 2 Chr 17:4 for not having subscribed to Baal worship and in the subsequent verse it is stated that he followed the religious traditions of his davidic ancestor, and not מעשה ישראל ('Israelite practice'). *Da'at Miqra* and Hartom see such practice as idolatry[36] and this is the view taken by E. L. Curtis and A. A. Madsen in the ICC, with a supporting reference from 2 Chr 11:15, and by W. A. L. Elmslie, with a supporting reference from 2 Chr 13:8–9.[37]

Exod 23:24: לא תשתחוה לאלהיהם ולא תעבדם ולא תעשה כמעשיהם כי הרס תהרסם ושבר תשבר מצבתיהם

31 Briggs, *Psalms* 2.353; Hartom, *Ha-Miqra*, p. 235; *Da'at Miqra*, pp. 290–91.
32 Hartom, *Ha-Miqra*, p. 102; Cheyne, *Micah*, p. 54.
33 Ringgren, *TDOT*, 11.400; *ICC*, p. 135.
34 *Da'at Miqra*, p. 695; Hartom, *Ha-Miqra*, p. 193.
35 Skinner, *Isaiah*, p. 229; Blenkinsopp, *Isaiah*, p. 310; Duhm, *Jesaia*, p. 455.
36 *Da'at Miqra*, p. 687; Hartom, *Ha-Miqra*, pp. 120–21.
37 *ICC*, p. 392; Elmslie, *Chronicles*, p. 236.

This verse carries a similar message to the one from Lev 18:3 that has just been discussed. The Canaanite gods are not be worshipped but they and their altars are to be eliminated in favour of the service of God. Between these two instructions is the prohibition not to practise their 'מעשים'. But to which practices is the verse alluding?

Ibn Ezra explains that the intention of all the laws in the Book of the Covenant is to prohibit idolatry.[38] The collection of such laws begins, for him, in Exod 20:20, where it is forbidden to make silver images even in God's honour, and ends in Exod 23:33, where the instruction is given to rid the Holy Land of all idolaters since they will only lead the Israelites astray. Even if they perform every positive precept of the Torah, their idolatry makes them guilty of every negative precept and damns them in this world and the next. The context for Ibn Ezra is therefore definitely that of idolatry but in the case of this verse he does not define precisely what kind of idolatry is meant by the word כמעשיהם.

Naḥmanides raises the possibility that the allusion made by the word כמעשיהם in this verse may be to magical and superstitious activities, such as are forbidden by the talmudic rabbis unless they are known to have sound, therapeutic efficacy.[39] The sense here would therefore be similar to that carried by the phrase ובחקתיהם לא תלכו in Lev 18:3, which is specifically identified by R. Meir as a reference to such magical and superstitious activities.[40] He then expresses his preference for an interpretation of the phrase as a prohibition against idolatry that includes an additional aspect. This constitutes a warning not to follow idolatrous practices, even if they are to be carried out in a manner that might be construed by the Israelites as an insult to the gods being worshipped. Naḥmanides cites a midrashic interpretation of Deut 12:3 which sees it as categorically prohibiting just such a kind of practice, even if it may be argued that by engaging in it the Jew feels that he is offending the idol.[41] Here, therefore, the word מעשה is to be construed as a direct reference to idolatry.

An even more precise definition of the word in this context is offered by Levi ben Gershom (Gersonides, 'Ralbag', 1288 – 1344), philosopher and Bible exegete from the south of France. He claims that the notion is the same as that mentioned in Deut 12:30 and conveys the idea that the Israelites should not follow the liturgical practices of other nations when they worship God.[42] Such a liturgical sense is also reflected, in different ways, in some modern treatments of the

38 *Torat Ḥayyim*, pp. 63 – 64.
39 *Torat Ḥayyim*, pp. 63 – 64; *b. Šabb.* 67a.
40 *Sifra* 13.9; p. 86a.
41 *b. San.* 61b and 64a.
42 Levi b. Gershom, *Commentary*, f. 99v.

verse. Nahum Sarna appears to suggest that תעשה כמעשיהם refers to the 'adoption of their cultic practices' while the New English Bible renders 'nor observe their rites', assuming a different sense from that occurring in Lev 18:3.[43] Arnold Ehrlich innovatively understands the word to refer to the items worshipped and not the worshippers, that is, 'do not construct idols like those of the Canaanites'.[44] This is also the view of August Dillmann.[45] W. C. Propp cites the possibility that sacrifices are what the verse prohibits, but rejects the rendering 'idols', claiming that nowhere else does מעשים have such a sense.[46] In truth, the rendering 'idols' is usually employed for the longer Hebrew compound מעשה יד, but מעשה could be an abbreviated form of such a usage, as supported by the phrase ונמחו מעשיכם in Ezek 6:6. This is how the latter verse is understood by A. B. Davidson and *Da'at Miqra*, while Greenberg sees here 'illicit forms of worship'.[47]

Liturgical sense

Further support for a liturgical sense of מעשה may be adduced from two other verses in Chronicles. The first, in 1 Chr 23:28, describes part of the service performed by the Levites in the Jerusalem Temple as ומעשה עבדת בית האלהים, with the first word arguably having the sense of performing or carrying out the cultic procedure. Interestingly, there is a talmudic passage in which the word appears to have a related sense. In *b. Hor.* 13a it is ruled that שיהא ראשון קודם לפר העדה בכל מעשיו, that is to say, that the high priest's bullock should be offered first, preceding that of the assembly in all its procedures, the word מעשיו being used in the sense of 'cultic procedures'. The problem in the Chronicles verse may be sidestepped by emending the text (as Curtis and Madsen in the ICC), or by adopting a literal and unilluminating rendering such as 'work of the service' (as Elmslie) or 'general service' (NEB).[48] Other modern treatments do, however, nod in the liturgical direction. *Da'at Miqra* and J. M. Myers see here a reference to the necessary preparation that precedes the sacrifice itself, with JPS rendering 'and the performance of the service of the house of God'.[49] The second verse is in 2 Chr 4:6 and describes a rinsing procedure that was followed by the priests in the Jerusa-

---

43 Sarna, *Exodus*, p. 148.
44 Ehrlich, *Mikrâ*, 1.185–86.
45 Dillmann, *Exodus und Leviticus*, p. 282.
46 Propp, *Exodus*, pp. 288–89.
47 Davidson, *Ezekiel*, p. 42; *Da'at Miqra*, p. 38; Greenberg, *Ezekiel*, pp. 129, 133.
48 *ICC*, p. 268; Elmslie, *Chronicles*, p. 141.
49 *Da'at Miqra*, p. 412; Myers, *Chronicles*, p. 158.

lem Temple in the case of מעשה העולה. Rashi, in the Rabbinic Bible, addresses the problem of what precisely is meant by the words מעשה העולה by paraphrasing as קרבי העולה, 'the body parts of the animal being used as a burnt offering'. Hartom sees the phrase as a description of the meat being offered (קרבנות) בשר העולה, so that מעשה is conveying the sense of קרבן ('offering').[50] To conclude this aspect of the discussion, such liturgical senses are again not of significance to the lexicographers and Ringgren (400) specifically rejects such a sense in the case of the Exodus verse.[51]

Power

Dt. 3:24: אשר יעשה כמעשיך וכגבורתך
Deut. 11:3: ואת אתתיו ואת מעשיו אשר עשה בתוך מצרים

Both these verses refer to the divine power, the first declaring that there can be no equivalent in heaven or on earth, and the second describing its historical manifestations in Egypt. In the first instance the word מעשים is being employed as a parallel to גבורות, just as the phrase ידך החזקה is parallel to גדלך, earlier in the same verse. In that case it bears the sense of 'great, powerful or impressive acts'. Abraham Ibn Ezra and the thirteenth-century French exegete, Hezekiah ben Manoaḥ, recognize that both these acts are remarkable but distinguish מעשים from גבורות as acts performed with wisdom rather than with power.[52] JPS prefers to treat the phrase כמעשיך וכגבורתך as a hendiadys, rendering 'powerful deeds' but the NEB opts for a parallelism and offers 'thy works and mighty deeds'. Neither appears to take account of the powerful syntactical case for a parallelism here.

The parallelism in the second verse cited (Deut 11:3) is between מעשים and אותות so that one is again justified in understanding the word מעשים as 'great, powerful or impressive acts'. This is further supported by the fact that the subsequent verses list the miracles performed for Israel in Egypt and in Sinai. In addition, a similar parallel again occurs here, in the previous verse. The Septuagint renders καὶ τὰ σημεῖα αὐτοῦ καὶ τὰ τέρατα αὐτοῦ, raising the question whether it read מופתים rather than מעשים since the word τέρατα is used for מופתים elsewhere, as in Deut 6:22 and 7:19.[53] But the verb that occurs with מופת, when

---

50 Hartom, *Miqra*, p. 91.
51 Ringgren, *TDOT*, 11.400.
52 Ibn Ezra, *Torat Ḥayyim*, p. 33; Hezekiah ben Manoaḥ, *Torat Ḥayyim*, p. 32.
53 Rahlfs, 1.306.

God is the subject, is usually שים, נתן or שלח, as in Exod 4:21, with the verb עשה referring to human activity, as in Exod 11:10.[54] Perhaps, then, the Greek translators also had the notion that the word מעשים here carries the nuance being suggested. Ibn Ezra and Naḥmanides differ in the significance they attach to each of these parallel expressions, the former relating each of the phrases to a specific event while the latter argues that they are general messages about the power of God to punish evil. Ibn Ezra explains the first part of v. 3 as especially referring to the miracles that God did at Pharaoh's expense, so for him מעשיו apparently means 'wondrous deeds'.[55]

There are four other instances in which a good case may be made for identifying in the word מעשים a sense of 'great, powerful or impressive acts'. In Num 16:28, Moses is arguing his case against Koraḥ and his followers and declares that God has sent him to do כל המעשים האלה and they are not his own initiatives. Rashi, his grandson Samuel ben Meir, Ibn Ezra and Hezekiah ben Manoaḥ, and, similarly, Milgrom among modern exegetes – all see in this phrase a reference to specific actions, such as taking the priesthood away from the firstborn and giving it to the Levites, and/or testing Koraḥ and his supporters with the incense, that constitute unexpected and innovative acts of leadership on the part of Moses.[56] Naḥmanides goes further and regards the phrase as relevant to all his distinguished acts of leadership throughout his career, and not to these events alone.[57] Either way – and regardless of whether one refers the phrase to past events or to the judgement on Koraḥ and his followers that is about to be witnessed by the Israelites – a plausible sense is 'impressive acts'. Three verses in Psalms also testify to such a sense. Ps 106:13, in the course of describing the powerful acts that God had performed for his people in their journey through the Sinai desert, notes that they soon forgot מעשיו. In a section of his poem that discusses God's power as a healer of the sick, the poet in Ps 107:21–22 invites those who have derived benefit from this power to praise God for his wonders and to thank him by joyfully relating מעשיו. These can only be precisely such powerful acts as have just been noted. Qimḥi, in the Rabbinic Bible, describes them as 'acts of generosity' while *Da'at Miqra* and Briggs – rightly in my view – go further and refer, respectively, to 'God's miraculous deeds' and 'divine works of deliverance'.[58] The phrase הגיד לעמו כח מעשיו in Ps 111:6 was sufficiently

---

54 BDB, p. 69.

55 Ibn Ezra, *Torat Ḥayyim*, p. 93; Naḥmanides, *Torat Ḥayyim*, pp. 92–93.

56 *Torat Ḥayyim*, p. 146; Milgrom, *Numbers*, p. 137.

57 *Torat Ḥayyim*, p. 146.

58 *Da'at Miqra*, p. 302; Briggs, *Psalms*, p. 361.

unusual to invite the attention of some of the medieval commentators, as recorded in the new edition of the Rabbinic Bible.[59]

Rashi quotes a midrash that explains that God, who can give his property to whomsoever he wishes, wrote for Israel the story of the world's creation to strengthen its claim to the land. The paraphrase used by Qimḥi was נפלאותיו ומעשיו הגדולים, 'his wonders and his great deeds', while Menaḥem b. Solomon Me'iri (1249–1316), from a Provençal family, added the word נפלאותיו to the phrase כח מעשיו. *Da'at Miqra* explains the phrase as an allusion to God's miraculous conquest of the land of Canaan.[60]

It will be recalled that among all the lexicographers, it was only Ringgren who paid some attention to the nuance here being suggested for מעשים but, on the basis of the evidence presented above, it seems fair to say that it appears to be an important enough usage to merit more than a passing attention. I do not believe that in this short study I have exhausted all the possibilities with regard to the semantic range of the word מעשים in Biblical Hebrew, nor do I believe that a close study of its occurrences in later Hebrew would prove exegetically uninteresting or devoid of value for the linguist. Perhaps I, or a scholar with similar such interests, will return to the topic at a future date. Meanwhile, Robert Gordon exemplifies well Rabbi Simeon ben Gamaliel's claim that לא המדרש עיקר אלא המעשה. It is after all not just study (המדרש) that is at the centre of all that we do, but also – dare I? – impressive behaviour (המעשה).[61]

Works cited

Ben Yehuda, E. E., *A Complete Dictionary of Ancient and Modern Hebrew* (Hebrew; Jerusalem, New York: Yoseloff, 1908–1959, 1960).

Blenkinsopp, J., *Isaiah 56–66: A New Translation with Introduction and Commentary* (New York: Doubleday 2003).

Briggs, C. A. and E. G., *A Critical and Exegetical Commentary on the Book of Psalms*, vol. 2 (Edinburgh: T. & T. Clark, 1907).

Brown, F., Driver, S. R. and Briggs, C. A., *A Hebrew and English Lexicon of the Old Testament* (Oxford, Clarendon, 1906).

Cheyne, T. K., *Micah* (Cambridge: Cambridge University Press, 1921).

Cohen, M. (ed.), *Mikra'ot Gedolot Haketer, Psalms*, part II (Ramat-Gan: Bar-Ilan University Press, 2003).

Clines, D. J. A. (ed.), *The Dictionary of Classical Hebrew*, vols. 5–6 (Sheffield: Sheffield Academic Press, 2001–07).

59 Cohen, *Mikra'ot Gedolot Haketer*, pp. 142–43.
60 *Da'at Miqra*, p. 331.
61 *m. Avot* 1.17.

Curtis, E. L., and Madsen, A. A., *The Books of Chronicles* (Edinburgh: T. & T. Clark, 1910).
Da'at Miqra (Hebrew), *Isaiah*, com. A. Hakham (Jerusalem: Rav Kook, 1984); *Ezekiel*, com. Y. Z. Moshcovitz (Jerusalem: Rav Kook, 1985); *Psalms*, vol. 2, com. A. Hakham (Jerusalem: Rav Kook, 1987); *Chronicles*, 2 vols, com. Y. Qil (Jerusalem: Rav Kook, 1986).
Davidson, A. B., *The Book of the Prophet Ezekiel* (Cambridge: Cambridge University Press, 1892).
Dillmann, A., *Die Bücher Exodus und Leviticus: kurzgefasstes exegetisches Handbuch zum Alten Testament* (Leipzig: Hirzel, 1897).
Duhm, B., *Das Buch Jesaia übersetzt und erklärt* (Gottingen: Vandenhoeck & Ruprecht, 1892).
Ehrlich, A. B., *Mikrâ ki-Pheschutô*, vol. 1 (Berlin: Poppelauer, 1899).
Elmslie, W. A. L., *The Books of Chronicles* (Cambridge: Cambridge University Press, 1899).
Even-Shoshan, A., *Ha-Millon He-Ḥadash*, 7 vols. (Jerusalem: Kiryath Sepher, 1980).
Ginsburger, M. (ed.), *Pseudo-Jonathan (Thargum Jonathan ben Usiël zum Pentateuch)* (Berlin: Calvary, 1903).
Greenberg, M., *Ezekiel 1–20: A New Translation with Introduction and Commentary* (Garden City, NY: Doubleday, 1983).
Hartom, E. S., *Sifrey Ha-Miqra*, 16 vols. (Tel-Aviv: Yavneh, 1964).
Ibn Janaḥ, Jonah (Abulwalîd Merwân Ibn Ganâh), *Sepher Haschoraschim*, ed. W. Bacher (Berlin: Itzkowski, 1896).
JPS = *The Torah* (Philadelphia: Jewish Publication Society of America, 1967, 2nd edn.); *The Prophets* (1978); *The Writings* (1982).
Ḥayyuj, Judah, *Two treatises on Verbs Containing Feeble and Double Letters*, ed. J. W. Nutt (London: Asher & Co., 1870).
Koehler, L., and Baumgartner, W., *The Hebrew and Aramaic Lexicon of the Old Testament*, ed. J. J. Stamm, vol. II, English translation (Leiden: Brill, 1995).
Levine, B., *The JPS Torah Commentary: Leviticus* (Philadelphia: Jewish Publication Society, 1989).
Levi ben Gershom, *Commentary on the Torah* (פירוש על התורה) (Venice: Bomberg, 1547).
Milgrom, J., *The JPS Torah Commentary: Numbers* (Philadelphia: Jewish Publication Society, 1990).
Myers, J. M., *Chronicles: A New Translation with Introduction and Commentary* (Garden City, NY: Doubleday, 1965).
NEB = *The New English Bible: The Old Testament* (Oxford and Cambridge: Oxford University Press and Cambridge University Press, 1970).
Propp, W. H. C., *Exodus 1–18: A New Translation with Introduction and Commentary* (New York: Doubleday, 1998).
Qimḥi, David, *Rabbi Davidis Kimchi Radicum Liber*, eds. J. H. R. Biesenthal and F. Lebrecht (Berlin: Bethge, 1847).
Rahlfs, A. (ed.), *Septuaginta: Id Est Vetus Testamentum Graece Iuxta LXX Interpretes* (New York: American Bible Society, 1952, 5th edn.).
Ringgren, Helmer, entry עשה in *Theological Dictionary of the Old Testament*, eds. G. J. Botterweck, H. Ringgren and H.-J. Fabry, vol. XI, Eng. trans. D. E. Green, (Grand Rapids, Mich: Eerdmans Publishing Company, 2001), pp. 387–403.
Sáenz-Badillos, A., *A History of the Hebrew Language*, Eng. trans. J. Elwolde (Cambridge: Cambridge University Press, 1993).
Sarna, N. M., *The JPS Torah Commentary: Exodus* (Philadelphia: Jewish Publication Society, 1991).

Shachter, J. F., *The Commentary of Abraham Ibn Ezra on the Pentateuch. Volume 3: Leviticus* (Hoboken, NJ: Ktav, 1986).
Sifra. Commentar zu Leviticus, ed. I. H. Weiss (Vienna: Schlossberg, 1862).
Skinner, J., *The Book of the Prophet Isaiah, XL-LXVI* (Cambridge: Cambridge University Press, 1898).
Smith, J. M. P., Ward, W. H. and Bewer, J. A., *Micah, Zephaniah, Nahum, Habakkuk, Obadiah and Joel* (Edinburgh: T. & T. Clark, 1911).
Torat Ḥayyim (Hebrew), *Ḥamishah Ḥumshey Torah*, ed. M. L. Katzenellenbogen, 7 vols. (Jerusalem: Rav Kook, 2004).

9 How did Early Judaism Understand the Concept of *'Avodah?*

Introduction

In order to tackle the topic in hand it will be necessary to examine the Hebrew and Greek sources that reflect the manner in which the Jews of the Second Temple period used their languages to give expression to the relevant religious ideas, whether these represented inherited traditions, or their own innovative notions. To that end, the standard dictionaries of the Hebrew Bible will be closely examined for indications of what was conveyed by the term *'avodah* and their conclusions will be critically compared with the linguistic evidence available from the Dead Sea Scrolls. This comparison will be followed by a close analysis, by way of numerous biblical verses, of how the Jews who translated the Hebrew Bible into Greek rendered the word *'avodah*, and an examination of what some of the apocryphal texts have to offer in this connection. What should then become apparent is the degree to which linguistic usage and religious ideology impacted on each other within the dynamic cultural developments that characterized Jewish history in the centuries being discussed. If the question is raised as to why the linguistic evolution is so important to our proper understanding of a theological notion, my reply would be that without the use of accurate linguistic and literary tools, the reconstruction of a cultural edifice amounts to no more than imaginative speculation. It may sound interesting but it is not interestingly sound. As the German classicist and antiquarian, August Böckh, noted some two centuries ago, 'philology is the historical construction of the collective life of a people in its practical and spiritual tendencies, therefore of its entire culture and all its products.'[1]

Where, however, should one begin such a complex, scholarly procedure? One could quote the grave comment of the King to the White Rabbit in Lewis Carroll's *Alice in Wonderland:* 'Begin at the beginning...and go on till you come to the end: then stop', but what would serve in this context as a useful beginning? As a student of rabbinic literature, I have a personal penchant for combing the rich deposits of variegated material that were amassed by the early rabbis and attempting to relate these to the Jewish religious ideas that preceded and followed them. What I propose to do here, therefore, is to start with two such texts and ask whether what is presupposed in those traditions about the mean-

1 See the review by Peter N. Miller of *Philology* by James Turner, in *Times Literary Supplement*, March 27, 2015, p. 27.

DOI 10.1515/9783110486704-010

ing of the word *'avodah* is a reliable witness to what had been understood by earlier Jews, or constitutes no more than a figment of rabbinic imagination. This will provide us with yardstick of some sort against which to measure the earlier Hebrew and Greek texts mentioned above. Once we have established how these two sets of Jewish sources relate to each other, it will be useful at the end of the article to return to the rabbinic corpus and ascertain whether additional traditions cited therein can teach us anything more about linguistic and theological interaction.

Early rabbinica

It is notoriously difficult to date the mishnaic tractate *'Abot* which is often known as 'the chapters of the father' or 'the ethics of the fathers' but may just as well mean 'the main teachings', given that *'av* is not uncommonly used in that sense in early rabbinic texts.[2] Be that as it may, at least some of the contents of that tractate may reflect pre-mishnaic teaching and/or vocabulary, especially when there are linguistic parallels to be cited from other material that appears to record traditions presupposing the existence of the Jerusalem Temple and therefore dating to the first half of the first century C.E. On such example occurs in *m. 'Abot* 1.2:

> שמעון הצדיק היה משיירי אנשי כנסת הגדולה. הוא היה אומר, על שלושה דברים העולם עומד: על התורה, על העבודה, ועל גמילות חסדים
>
> Simeon the Righteous was one of the last members of the Great Assembly. He used to say: The world stands on three things, namely, on Torah, **Temple worship** and charitable behaviour

The attribution to 'Simeon the Righteous' is not one that can be historically authenticated and, as the recent research of Amram Tropper has demonstrated, may represent only a rabbinic awareness of the early nature of this teaching and a desire to link it with a personality already known from the book of Ben Sira and much admired in that source.[3] That said, the parallel use of the expression על העבודה in *m. Yoma* 7.1, as well as the nature of the content here, supports the proposal that we are encountering a use of the word עבודה that refers directly to the Temple ritual. That is indeed how the logion is understood in all the early rabbinic interpretations. Was this then the only meaning in the wider Jewish circles of the axial period?

---

2 See, e.g., the expression אבות נזיקין in *m. B. Qam.* 1.1.

3 Tropper, *Simeon*, pp. 213–16.

There is rabbinic evidence that points to an awareness of a wider semantic range for the word under discussion. One of the earliest midrashic collections, and one that perhaps contains interpretations from as early as the second or third Christian centuries, is the exegetical treatment of parts of Deuteronomy that is known as Sifre, which takes its name from the Aramaic term for books, that is, some of the Pentateuchal books. The aggadist is concerned to explain what is meant in Deut 11:13 by the command not only to love God but also ולעבדו, usually translated 'and to serve him'. What kind of עבודה ('service') is required? The midrash opens by suggesting that it refers to Torah study but rejects that suggestion in favour of the more literal meaning of 'labour' on the basis of Gen 2:16. That verse describes how God placed Adam in the Garden of Eden לעבדה ולשמרה, 'to work it and look after it'. Such a rendering is also set aside by the aggadist on the grounds that Adam was required to undertake such labour only later as a punishment for his disobedience and *'avodah* is therefore again explained as Torah study and *shemirah* as the observance of the precepts. The midrashic interpretation does not end there but adds another possibility. It is suggested that that *'avoda* refers to prayer, on the grounds that the service of God demanded by the verse is to be with all one's heart and soul and that can only be by prayer.[4] What we have then observed is a range of interpretations for the word עבודה within early rabbinic exegesis. It may mean 'temple ritual', 'Torah study', 'work' and 'prayer'. What must next be established is whether such meanings are also to be found in earlier Jewish texts.

Dictionaries of Biblical Hebrew

It is instructive that the dictionaries record a range of meanings for the root עבד. The following are examples of what they record:

BDB: 1. labour, work; 2. labour of a servant or a slave; 3. labour, service of captives or subjects; 4. service of God [relating primarily to sanctuary, temple and cult].[5]

KBL: 1. Arbeit (work); 2. Dienst (service which is rendered); 3. Gottesdienst (service of worship) – a. Kult (ceremonially); b. Kultbrauch (cultic custom).[6]

Ben Yehuda: 1. labour; 2. work; 3. service.[7]

---

4 *Sifre*, ed Finkelstein, pp. 87–88.
5 BDB, *Lexicon*, p. 715.
6 KBL, *Lexicon*, p. 733.
7 Ben Yehuda, *Dictionary*, p. 4259.

DCH: 1. work, labour, servitude; 2. deed, activity, function, task, duty; 3. service; 4. sacred service.[8]

The entry in **TDOT**, mainly the work of Helmer Ringgren, is also worthy of citation.[9] There it is noted that there is a widespread occurrence of the root עבד in the Semitic languages in the basic sense of 'work, 'do' or 'make' but also in the specialized sense of serving a superior such as a king or a god. It has the sense of performing a cultic act, making a sacrificial offering, celebrating a rite for God or idols, approved or illicit worship. The noun עבודה never refers to the worship of idols. There is, however, no indication in those dictionaries of a wider semantic range that might cover such topics as prayer and good deeds, noted by early rabbis. Have the Dead Sea Scrolls anything to offer in this regard?

Dead Sea Scrolls

Obviously it is not possible to cite all the instances in which the noun עבודה occurs in the Scrolls but a varied selection of texts provides important clues about the range of meanings covered in those texts. There are of course numerous examples of the usages listed in the dictionaries just cited but, in addition, the following examples document the existence of other meanings:

a. Carrying out activities of various sorts, including menial tasks and daily activities:
CD 14.16:ולנער[א]שר אין לו דורש כל **עבודת** החבר
CD 20.7: אל...יאות איש עמו בהון ובעבודה
4Q511 63 iii.3 (Song of the Sage):תמימי דרךְ ומשפטים לכוֹל **עבודת** מעשיהם

b. Performance of a task or a duty
1QH 9.18:פלגתה **עבודתם** בכול דוריהם
CD 10.19:אל ידבר בדברי המלאכה **והעבודה** לעשות למשכים

c. Army service and community involvement
1QM 2.9:בחמש ושלושים שני **העבודה** תערך המלחמה שש שנים ועורכיה כול העדה יחד
1QSa [=1Q28a, Appendix to Rule] 1.19:וברובות שני איש לפי כוחו יתנו משאו ב[עבו]דת העדה

d. Behaviour of a righteous or irreligious nature
1QS 4.9: ולרוח עולה רחוב נפש ושפול ידים **בעבודת** צדק
4Q511 63 – 64.ii.4: שפתי צדק ובהנכון לכול **עבודת** אמת
1QM 13.5: רשעם וזעומים המה בכול **עבודת** נדת טמאתם
1QpHab 10.11: בעבור כבודה לוגיע רבים **בעבודת** שוו
4Q511(Song of the Sage) 18:ii.6: ורוח בינתי ו ה **עבודת** רשעה

8 *DCH*, ed. Clines, 6.226 – 28.
9 *TDOT*, 10.403 – 5.

e. Religious commitment (in its totality)
1QH 10.38:לעזוב **עבודתכה** מפחד הוות רשעים
4Q521(Messianic Apocalpyse) 2 ii. 3:התאמצו מבקשי אדני **בעבדתו**

f. Correct behaviour
4Q215 (Testament of Naphtali) 2 ii.8:פעולתם בטרם הבראם ועבודת הצדק פלג גבולותם

g. Divine service, maybe also prayer
4Q408 3/3a 9 (Sapiential Work, Apocalypse of Moses, 2c BCE?):**לעבדתם** לברך את שמ קדשך

In sum, the evidence from the Scrolls testifies to a broader semantic range than that noted in the dictionaries. It includes numerous kinds of daily tasks, whether menial, military or communal; various types of approved or disapproved behaviour; as well as divine worship. It should be noted that DCH, as cited above, did come nearer to this kind of definition than the other dictionaries, presumably because it took account of the evidence from the Scrolls.

Greek sources

There are various terms that are used for the translation of the word **עבודה** in the Greek Jewish sources of the Second Temple period and these will now be cited from the original texts under the heading of each term:

a. **λειτουργία, -ας** public, religious or liturgical service; service, ministry (of priest).

i. Num 4:26: וְאֶת-כָּל-כְּלֵי **עֲבֹדָתָם;** וְאֵת כָּל-אֲשֶׁר יֵעָשֶׂה לָהֶם, וְעָבָדוּ

καὶ πάντα τὰ σκεύη **τὰ λειτουργικά** ὅσα λειτουργοῦσιν ἐν αὐτοῖς ποιήσουσιν

and all the vessels of service that they minister with they shall attend to

Meaning: 'relating to liturgy'.

ii. Num 7:5: וְהָיוּ, לַעֲבֹד **אֶת-עֲבֹדַת** אֹהֶל מוֹעֵד

καὶ ἔσονται πρὸς **τὰ ἔργα τὰ λειτουργικὰ** τῆς σκηνῆς τοῦ μαρτυρίου

*And they shall be **for the works of the services** of the tabernacle of the witness*

Meaning: 'for the liturgical functioning'.

Note here the use of two words (ἔργα and λειτουργικὰ) in Greek for the identical Hebrew root.

iii. 2 Sam 19:19: **וְעָבְרָה הָעֲבָרָה לַעֲבִיר** אֶת-בֵּית הַמֶּלֶךְ וְלַעֲשׂוֹת הַטּוֹב בְּעֵינָו

καὶ ἐλειτούργησαν **τὴν λειτουργίαν** τοῦ διαβιβάσαι τὸν βασιλέα καὶ διέβη ἡ διάβασις ἐξεγεῖραι τὸν οἶκον τοῦ βασιλέως καὶ τοῦ ποιῆσαι τὸ εὐθὲς ἐν ὀφθαλμοῖς αὐτοῦ

*And they performed **the service of bringing the king over**; and there went over a ferry-boat to remove the household of the king and to do that which was right in his eyes*

The LXX has here offered a duplicated rendering, once reading עבר and once עבד, testifying to an awareness on the part of one translator that the root could have a broader meaning than that of liturgy, together with an uneasiness on the part of another translator about applying such a secular sense to עבד.

iv. 1 Chr 26:30: מֵעֵבֶר לַיַּרְדֵּן מַעְרָבָה **לְכֹל מְלֶאכֶת יְהוָה וְלַעֲבֹדַת הַמֶּלֶךְ**

πέραν τοῦ Ιορδάνου πρὸς δυσμαῖς **εἰς πᾶσαν λειτουργίαν κυρίου καὶ ἐργασίαν τοῦ βασιλέως**

*beyond Jordan westward, **for all the service of the Lord and work of the king***

The LXX prefers to attach the word **עבודה** only to the service of God and to use the word מלאכה for the work of the king; unless of course the Hebrew version has been amended to express the opposite preference, but that seems less convincing.

v. 1 Chr 28:21: וְהִנֵּה מַחְלְקוֹת הַכֹּהֲנִים וְהַלְוִיִּם לְכָל-עֲבוֹדַת בֵּית הָאֱלֹהִים וְעִמְּךָ בְכָל-מְלָאכָה לְכָל-נָדִיב בַּחָכְמָה **לְכָל-עֲבוֹדָה** וְהַשָּׂרִים וְכָל-הָעָם לְכָל-דְּבָרֶיךָ

καὶ ἰδοὺ αἱ ἐφημερίαι τῶν ἱερέων καὶ τῶν Λευιτῶν εἰς πᾶσαν λειτουργίαν οἴκου τοῦ θεοῦ καὶ μετὰ σοῦ ἐν πάσῃ πραγματείᾳ καὶ πᾶς πρόθυμος ἐν σοφίᾳ **κατὰ πᾶσαν τέχνην** καὶ οἱ ἄρχοντες καὶ πᾶς ὁ λαὸς εἰς πάντας τοὺς λόγους σου

*And see, here are the courses of the priests and Levites for all the service of the house of the Lord, and there shall be with thee men for every workmanship, **and every one of ready skill in every art**; and also the chief men and all the people, ready for all thy commands*

Here again the Greek translator uses what seems to him to be a more secular word by rendering עבודה not with λειτουργία but with τέχνη (L&S: art, craft, cunning).

vi. Ezra 7:19: וּמָאנַיָּא דִּי-מִתְיַהֲבִין לָךְ **לְפָלְחָן בֵּית אֱלָהָךְ** הַשְׁלֵם קֳדָם אֱלָהּ יְרוּשְׁלֶם

καὶ τὰ σκεύη τὰ διδόμενά σοι **εἰς λειτουργίαν οἴκου θεοῦ** παράδος ἐνώπιον τοῦ θεοῦ ἐν Ιερουσαλημ

*And deliver the vessels that are given thee **for the service of the house of God**, before God in Jerusalem*

Note that the LXX regards the Aramaic פלחן as exactly equivalent to the Hebrew עבודה.

vii. Sir 50:28/19: עד כלותו **לשרת** מזבח

καὶ τὴν λειτουργίαν αὐτοῦ ἐτελείωσαν

*[the high priest] completed **the service** at the altar*

Young Ben Sira sensed that the use of the word שרת here was obviously a cultic one and therefore used the Greek normally employed for עבודה. Segal's comment about the looseness of the Greek rendering is not therefore wholly justified.[10]

b. **ἐργασία, -ας** from **ἔργ**ον meaning work, business, deed, industry. Then with the further developed meanings of work, business, trade, productive labour. Used to translate עבודה/מלאכה/מעשה פעולה/עשק/חסד/ with the meanings of labour, production, work, workmanship, ministration, service, business, [kind] acts.

i. Gen 29:27: מַלֵּא שְׁבֻעַ זֹאת וְנִתְּנָה לְךָ גַּם-אֶת-זֹאת **בַּעֲבֹדָה** אֲשֶׁר תַּעֲבֹד עִמָּדִי עוֹד שֶׁבַע-שָׁנִים אֲחֵרוֹת

συντέλεσον οὖν τὰ ἕβδομα ταύτης καὶ δώσω σοι καὶ ταύτην **ἀντὶ τῆς ἐργασίας ἧς ἐργᾷ** παρ' ἐμοὶ ἔτι ἑπτὰ ἔτη ἕτερα

*for your **labour** done*

The LXX translator rightly uses a word with the sense of **work** since no ritual is involved.

ii. 1 Chr 6:33: וַאֲחֵיהֶם הַלְוִיִּם נְתוּנִים **לְכָל-עֲבוֹדַת** מִשְׁכַּן בֵּית הָאֱלֹהִים

καὶ ἀδελφοὶ αὐτῶν κατ' οἴκους πατριῶν αὐτῶν οἱ Λευῖται δεδομένοι **εἰς πᾶσαν ἐργασίαν λειτουργίας** σκηνῆς οἴκου τοῦ θεοῦ

all the ministration of the cult

Since the Levites were not responsible for the actual cultic acts but merely the accompanying ministrations, the translator inserts the word ἐργασίαν before λειτουργίας. See also 1 Chr 9:13 where he uses the same translation for the priests because the Hebrew itself has מלאכת עבודה.

iii. Ps 103 (Heb:104):23: יֵצֵא אָדָם לְפָעֳלוֹ **וְלַעֲבֹדָתוֹ** עֲדֵי-עָרֶב

ἐξελεύσεται ἄνθρωπος ἐπὶ τὸ ἔργον αὐτοῦ **καὶ ἐπὶ τὴν ἐργασίαν αὐτοῦ** ἕως ἑσπέρας

Man shall go forth to his work **and to his labour** till evening

10 Segal, *Ben Sira*, p. 246.

The LXX translator needs to stress that such an ordinary man has nothing to do with the cultic עבודה as he himself defines it.

iv. Sir 6:19: **ἐν γὰρ τῇ ἐργασίᾳ** αὐτῆς ὀλίγον κοπιάσεις

כי בעבודתה מעט תעבוד

For in cultivating her *you will labour but little*

While Ben Sira himself was happy to use this very prosaic sense of the root **עבד**, his grandson translated this mundane activity with a word without any cultic overtones.

v. Sir 7:15: ἔμβαλε αὐτὸν **εἰς ἐργασίαν**

אל תאיץ בצבא מלאכת עבודה

Hate not [the routine of] ***laborious work***

Again the grandson is careful about rendering the root **עבד** in a mundane sense.

In sum, the LXX translations of the Hebrew root עבד make it clear which sense applies in each verse, and that only the priests are involved in the central ritual. Ben Sira himself employs the root in the mundane sense but his grandson makes distinctions whenever necessary in his renderings.

c. **δουλεία, -ας** defined by L&S as meaning slavery, bondage, service, labour, toil.
Used to translate עבדה/עבדות/ עבדים/משל with meanings such as labour, toil, agriculture, military activity, service, yoke, burden, bondage, servitude, slavery.

i. Gen 30:26: כִּי אַתָּה יָדַעְתָּ, אֶת-עֲבֹדָתִי אֲשֶׁר עֲבַדְתִּיךָ

γὰρ γινώσκεις **τὴν δουλείαν ἣν δεδούλευκά σοι**

but you know ***the toil that I have toiled for you***

Understood by the LXX translator in its most basis sense of physical labour

ii. Exod 13:3: זָכוֹר אֶת-הַיּוֹם הַזֶּה אֲשֶׁר יְצָאתֶם מִמִּצְרַיִם **מִבֵּית עֲבָדִים**

μνημονεύετε τὴν ἡμέραν ταύτην ἐν ᾗ ἐξήλθατε ἐκ γῆς Αἰγύπτου **ἐξ οἴκου δουλείας**

Remember this day in which ye came forth out of the land of Egypt, ***out of the house of bondage***

Perhaps the LXX translator does not wish to describe the Israelites as slaves and therefore refers not to the house of slaves but to the house of slavery, bondage. The calumny (as, for instance, by Manetho) that the Jews were a tribe of lepers and brought plagues upon themselves may lie behind this hesitation.[11]

iii. 1 Kgs 9:9: וַיַּחֲזִקוּ בֵּאלֹהִים אֲחֵרִים וַיִּשְׁתַּחֲוּ לָהֶם **וַיַּעַבְדֻם**

καὶ ἀντελάβοντο θεῶν ἀλλοτρίων καὶ προσεκύνησαν αὐτοῖς καὶ **ἐδούλευσαν** αὐτοῖς

and they attached themselves to strange gods, and ***worshipped*** *them, and served them*

The LXX translator uses his translation to indicate that this was a 'service' to other gods and is not comparable to the Hebrews' legitimate temple or tabernacle worship.

iv. Ezra 6:18: וַהֲקִימוּ כָהֲנַיָּא בִּפְלֻגָּתְהוֹן וְלֵוָיֵא בְּמַחְלְקָתְהוֹן **עַל-עֲבִידַת אֱלָהָא** דִּי בִירוּשְׁלֶם

καὶ ἔστησαν τοὺς ἱερεῖς ἐν διαιρέσεσιν αὐτῶν καὶ τοὺς Λευίτας ἐν μερισμοῖς **αὐτῶν ἐπὶ δουλείᾳ θεοῦ** τοῦ ἐν Ιερουσαλημ

And they set the priests in the divisions, and the Levites in their separate orders, ***for the service of God*** *in Jerusalem*

Although the priests are mentioned earlier, the later part refers to the Levites, and the LXX translator does not wish to refer to the work of the Levites as λειτουργία but as δουλεία.

v. Ezra 8:20: וּמִן-הַנְּתִינִים שֶׁנָּתַן דָּוִיד וְהַשָּׂרִים **לַעֲבֹדַת הַלְוִיִּם**

καὶ ἀπὸ τῶν ναθινιμ ὧν ἔδωκεν Δαυιδ καὶ οἱ ἄρχοντες **εἰς δουλείαν τῶν Λευιτῶν**

And of the Nathinim, whom David and the princes had appointed ***for the service of the Levites***

The word δουλεία is even more appropriate here since the reference is not to the work of the Levites but to that of the Nethinim, a lower class of functionaries.

11 See Stern, *Authors*, 1.63.

They were identified as the Gibeonites who surrendered in the time of Joshua and whose descendants became menial servants in the Temple.[12]

In sum, the LXX translator uses a word that is usually used for tasks that are more mundane than those that are decribed by λειτουργία or ἐργασία and again makes a distinction between the real worship and other more menial forms of service.

d. **λατρεία, -ας** defined in L&S as service, religious rite, worship, servitude

i. Exod 13:5: וְהָיָה כִי-יְבִיאֲךָ יְהוָה אֶל-אֶרֶץ הַכְּנַעֲנִי וְהַחִתִּי וְהָאֱמֹרִי וְהַחִוִּי וְהַיְבוּסִי אֲשֶׁר נִשְׁבַּע לַאֲבֹתֶיךָ לָתֶת לָךְ אֶרֶץ זָבַת חָלָב וּדְבָשׁ **וְעָבַדְתָּ אֶת-הָעֲבֹדָה** הַזֹּאת בַּחֹדֶשׁ הַזֶּה

καὶ ποιήσεις τὴν λατρείαν ταύτην ἐν τῷ μηνὶ τούτῳ

thou shalt perform this service *in this month*

The LXX translator does not use λειτουργία but opts for a slightly less cultic term in spite of the fact that this is an instruction about the paschal lamb. Perhaps he has in mind that the ceremony also has a domestic aspect when the paschal lamb is consumed *en famille* and that this is an extra-temple activity.

ii. Josh 22:27: כִּי עֵד הוּא בֵּינֵינוּ וּבֵינֵיכֶם וּבֵין דֹּרוֹתֵינוּ אַחֲרֵינוּ **לַעֲבֹד אֶת-עֲבֹדַת** יְהוָה לְפָנָיו בְּעֹלוֹתֵינוּ וּבִזְבָחֵינוּ וּבִשְׁלָמֵינוּ

ἀλλ᾽ ἵνα ᾖ τοῦτο μαρτύριον ἀνὰ μέσον ἡμῶν καὶ ὑμῶν καὶ ἀνὰ μέσον τῶν γενεῶν ἡμῶν μεθ᾽ ἡμᾶς **τοῦ λατρεύειν λατρείαν κυρίῳ** ἐναντίον αὐτοῦ ἐν τοῖς καρπώμασιν ἡμῶν καὶ ἐν ταῖς θυσίαις ἡμῶν καὶ ἐν ταῖς θυσίαις τῶν σωτηρίων ἡμῶν

that this may be a witness between you and us, and between our posterity after us, that we may do ***service to the Lord*** *before him, with our burnt-offerings, and our meat-offerings and our peace-offerings*

Here, given the references to Temple sacrifices, cultic activity is the obvious subject. The LXX translator uses the phrase λατρεύειν λατρείαν to describe the commitment to serve the Lord, which in this case consists of making the necessary sacrifices in the Temple.

iii. 3 Macc 4:14: ἀπογραφῆναι δὲ πᾶν τὸ φῦλον ἐξ ὀνόματος οὐκ εἰς τὴν ἔμπροσθεν βραχεῖ προδεδηλωμένην τῶν ἔργων κατάπονον **λατρείαν**

12 *TDOT*, 10.105–7; Ben Yehuda, *Dictionary*, p. 3870.

> *the whole race should be registered by name, not for the wearisome service of* ***labour*** *which was briefly described before*

In this instance, the author of 3 Maccabees clearly uses the word λατρεία for labour, and not for any divine service.

In sum, the word λατρεία is used to denote a broad notion of religious service but also in its simpler sense of labour.

Summary of Greek evidence

What emerges is that for the Greek-speaking Jewish translators and authors, the notion of עבודה refers exclusively to divine service, formal worship and, at times, to para-liturgical activity. Other usages of the Hebrew word are to be rendered by alternative Greek expressions that do not carry any liturgical nuances. Ben Sira, for his part, uses the Hebrew word in the mundane senses of agriculture and labour but his grandson seeks to translate these instances with Greek that cannot be confused with any cultic activity. It is therefore clear from a comparison of the Hebrew evidence of the Dead Sea Scrolls with the Greek evidence of the LXX and contemporary Jewish literature in Greek that the former reflects a broader semantic range for the word עבודה and that this is not transferred to the Greek. Does this broader semantic range manifest itself also in rabbinic texts other than those cited at the beginning of this article?

Other rabbinic traditions

a. Although עבודה (temple service) was said by the talmudic teachers, as noted earlier, to have been replaced by תפלה (prayer), the former term was still used in the statutory prayers of post-talmudic times to refer to the Jerusalem cult.
In the *'amidah*, according to the Babylonian rite, for example, the benediction third from the end is still entitled ברכת העבודה (the benediction concerning the temple service) and includes the phrases: והשב את העבודה לדביר ביתך 'restore the Temple service to your shrine of your dwelling place' and ותהי לרצון עבודת ישראל עמך 'may the Temple service of Israel your people be found pleasing'.
In the *'amidah*, according to the rite of Eretz Yisrael, that same benediction contains the sentence: ושכון בציון יעבדוך עבדיך בירושלים 'dwell in Zion and may your servants perform your service in Jerusalem.' It is clear from the references to Zion and Jeru-

salem that the root עבד must here refer to the Temple ritual.[13] Similarly, the grace after meals, as preserved in Sefardi rites, includes at the conclusion of the third benediction the entreaty תבנה ציון ברנה ותכון עבודת ה׳ בירושלים 'rebuild Zion with joy and re-establish the service in Jerusalem', which again is clearly an allusion to the system of worship that was practised in the Jerusalem Temple.[14]

b. *m. Sanh.* 7.6: העובד עבודה זרה–אחד העובד, ואחד המזבח, ואחד המקטר, ואחד המנסך, ואחד המשתחווה, והמקבלו עליו באלוה, והאומר לו אלי אתה
*With regard to the definition of **serving idolatry**, it is all the same if one serves, sacrifices, offers incense, pours a libation, prostrates oneself, accepts the idol as a god or says 'you are my god'.*

c. *m. Šeb.* 2.5: מקום שנהגו לסוך אינן סכין מפני שהיא עבודה
Where there is a custom to oil unripe fruits, this should not be done in the seventh year because it constitutes **labour.**

d. *m. Ḥul.* 9.2: וכולן שעיבדן, או שהילך בהן כדי עבדה–טהורים, חוץ מעור האדם
*When the hides of all of these have been trodden on as part of their **treatment**, they are ritually pure, but not human skin*
Whether the text is pointed as *'abada* or *'avoda*, the meaning is that the skin has undergone a **process of tanning.**

e. Mek. Rab. Yishma'el, *Shabbat* 1 (ed. Lauterbach, 3.205): וביום השביעי שבת וינפש (Exod 31:16):ממחשבת עבודה
The sense here is **planning one's work.**

f. Sifre *Bemidbar* 75, ed. Horovitz, p. 70:א׳ל [ר׳ טרפון לר׳ עקיבא] העבודה שלא בדיתה: אשריך אברהם...
The word העבודה is here a reference to **Temple worship** but used as an oath, equivalent to: **By Heaven!**

g. *b. B. Qam.* 109b:ומנין שעבודתה ועורה שלו ת׳ל ואיש את קדשיו לו יהיו
The meaning here is the **meat of the sacrifice** that is not offered on the altar. By metonymy or synecdoche, the meat offered as part of the **Temple worship** is given the name of that worship.

---

13 See Finkelstein, 'Amidah', pp. 162–63; Ehrlich, *Amidah*, p. 221.
14 See Finkelstein, 'Birkat Ha-Mazon', p. 258; Jacobson, *Nethiv Binah*, 3.61.

Conclusions

The data examined through this article allow us to draw some conclusions in reply to the question raised about how early Judaism understood the concept of *'avodah*. Although the dictionaries of Biblical/Classical Hebrew record various senses of the word that range from work and labour to service and ritual, it is clear that the Dead Sea Scrolls and early rabbinic texts testify to broader semantic usage. The LXX translators prefer to represent such a broader usage by employing a number of Greek expressions and to restrict the translation λειτουργία to those instances in which reference is being made to the formal service of God. A comparison of the Hebrew of Ben Sira with the Greek translation by his grandson confirms such a distinction between the approaches of those writing in these two languages. There are numerous texts in the early rabbinic corpora that also demonstrate that the broader semantic range was retained in the Hebrew of the first few centuries of the Christian era.

These conclusions have ramifications for our critical understanding not only of the development of Hebrew language but also of the evolution of Jewish theology. While one may detect an increasing tendency within the books of the Hebrew Bible towards the religious centrality of *'avodah*, it would appear, perhaps unsurprisingly, that the literature represented among the Dead Sea Scrolls exchanges that centrality for a broader notion of 'service'. The Jews in the Hellenistic environment are anxious to preserve the unique nature of formal worship while the early rabbis record all manner of meanings of *'avodah* but are undoubtedly committed to a re-evaluation of how such a concept is to be played out in the practical and everyday expression of Judaism.

Works cited

Ben Yehuda, E. E., *A Complete Dictionary of Ancient and Modern Hebrew* (Hebrew; Jerusalem, New York: Yoseloff, 1908–1959, 1960).

Brown, F., Driver, S. R. and Briggs, C. A., *A Hebrew and English Lexicon of the Old Testament* (Oxford: Clarendon, 1906).

Clines, D. J. A., *The Dictionary of Classical Hebrew*, 8 vols. (Sheffield: Sheffield Phoenix (Academic) Press, 1993–2011).

Ehrlich, U., *The Weekday Amidah in Geniza Prayer Books: Origins and Transmission* (Hebrew; Jerusalem: Yad Ben-Zvi Press, 2013).

Finkelstein, L., 'Birkat Ha-Mazon', *Jewish Quarterly Review* NS 19 (1928–29), pp. 211–62.

Finkelstein, L., 'The development of the Amidah', *Jewish Quarterly Review* NS 16 (1925), pp. 1–43, 127–70.

Jacobson, B. S., *Nethiv Binah*, 5 vols. (Hebrew; Tel Aviv: Sinai, 1968–83).

Koehler, L., and Baumgartner, W., *The Hebrew and Aramaic Lexicon of the Old Testament*, Eng. trans. (Leiden: Brill, 1995).
Segal, M. H. (ed.), *Sefer Ben Sira Ha-Shalem* (Jerusalem: Mosad Bialik, 1972, 2nd edn.).
Sifre on Deuteronomy, ed. L. Finkelstein (New York: Jewish Theological Seminary of America, re-publication of the Berlin edition of 1939, 1969).
Stern, M., *Greek and Latin Authors on Jews and Judaism, with Introductions, Translations, and Commentary*, 3 vols. (Jerusalem: Israel Academy of Sciences and Humanities, 1974).
Theological Dictionary of the Old Testament, eds. G. J. Botterweck, H. Ringgren and H.-J. Fabry, vol. 10, Eng. trans. D. W. Stott (Grand Rapids Mich.: Eerdmans, 1999).
Tropper, A., *Simeon the Righteous in Rabbinic Literature: A Legend Reinvented* (Leiden: Brill, 2013).

10 Wisdom Traditions in Some Early Rabbinic Prayers?

Higher education

Before I attempt to identify the nature of any wisdom traditions that might be recognizable in early rabbinic liturgy, I should like to offer a few remarks on the nature of wisdom as it was understood by teachers of higher education who taught in central Europe, or originated in central Europe, and taught elsewhere, a few decades ago, when Friedrich Reiterer and I were students. As will shortly be appreciated, these introductory comments have more than minor significance for the topic in hand. Those who taught us were experts in Semitic languages, in the literary appreciation of the biblical books, in the history of the religious ideas of Judaism, Christianity and Islam, and they demanded of their pupils that they should master these subjects, and acquire expertise in handling primary source material, before the new generation (as we were then) could in any way win recognition even as budding scholars, let alone serious colleagues.[1] I can do no better than quote Friedrich's description of Ben Sira 6:24–29: 'the acquiring of wisdom is difficult; it requires effort and presumes a great deal of self-control and focus of one's will. A pupil has to deal with significant problems ... the subordination to the rules of wisdom ... lays chains and ropes on someone, one must bend one's neck under her yoke, and great exertion is required for profit from her.'[2] That was certainly the approach of our masters in the 1960s. Not for them broad cultural studies, multi-disciplinary courses, inter-denominational seminars or, indeed, a quick informative fix from Wikipedia. Such, and similar activities, in so far as they were pursued, were not regarded as the stuff of scholarship.

And there was much to commend their approach. It ensured that we acquired the necessary languages, tackled the most difficult of texts, and developed sound research abilities and techniques that would stand us in good stead for the academic careers that awaited us. But there was a negative side too. It meant that scholarly wisdom as it was transmitted to us was somewhat shackled by the preconceived notions of nineteenth-century *Wissenschaft* and we had to teach ourselves to venture into broader pastures in pursuit of our

---

1 His professors were Ludger Bernhard and Notker Füglister, and mine Naphtali Wieder and Sigfried Stein. Some of the higher educational background is discussed in Ringer, *Decline*, esp. pp. 20–21.

2 Reiterer, 'Significance', p. 226.

DOI 10.1515/9783110486704-011

Elysian fields of advanced scholarship. So it was that scholars such as Friedrich and I, and our whole generation, were able to benefit greatly from our teachers' high standards but at the same time we had to find for ourselves new ways of extending our learning, teaching and researching so that we could also promote ancillary academic activities such as learned societies, series of publications, and the better understanding of our disciplines outside the ivory towers. We taught ourselves to extrapolate from the precise detail of the text to the overall significance of its content in human history. Friedrich has contributed so much to such important developments with regard to the language, literature and theology of Second Temple Judaism that it gives me inordinate pleasure to be able to dedicate this brief study to him on the occasion of his retirement. Like all those for whom idleness is never an option, he will undoubtedly be busier than ever once he joins us in the ranks of the senior citizens and we look forward to seeing, on many future occasions, the results of his scholarly efforts.

Task

I promised that some of these introductory remarks would be pertinent to the subject of this study. What I had in mind was that, probably as a result of the purist notions of earlier scholars about what constituted scientific learning, expertise in wisdom literature and specialization in rabbinic liturgy have not generally been brought together for the sake of clarifying how some wisdom ideas might have penetrated or infiltrated into the prayers composed and transmitted in rabbinic circles in the first few centuries of the Christian era. It would seem sensible for anyone anxious to ascertain the degree of such penetration or infiltration to check the obvious reference works in the justifiable expectation of finding some existing analysis. What would the major encyclopedias have to say about it and how did the major figures in the critical analysis of Jewish liturgical developments deal with it? Alas, although the works of Elbogen, Finkelstein, Idelsohn, Petuchowski and Fleischer all make important contributions, in their own generations, to different aspects of the critical history of Jewish prayer, they have little or nothing to offer in this area[3]; and the *Encyclopaedia Judaica* (1974) offers no guidance. In an honest fit of self-criticism, I should add that a certain Reif is equally guilty, to date, of ignoring the topic.

---

3 Elbogen, *Gottesdienst*, *Tefillah*, *Liturgy*; Finkelstein, 'Amidah', 'Birkat Ha-Mazon'; Idelsohn, *Liturgy*; Petuchowski, *Prayer*; Fleischer, *Eretz Israel*; Wieder, *Formation*.

As might have been expected, given his broad theological interests, Kaufmann Kohler had an inkling that it might be profitable to seek out wisdom influences in post-biblical Jewish literature. He touched upon the topic in the *Jewish Encyclopedia* but the rabbinic prayer-book received no mention by him in this connection.[4] Stemberger has recently tackled sages, scribes and seers in Rabbinic Judaism (of which more anon) but the *siddur* is not one of the subjects that figures in his article. Are we then to assume that there is nothing that may be related to the wisdom theme in that famous Jewish liturgical work? What I shall attempt to do in this chapter is to rehearse in a few sentences how wisdom literature is generally perceived, and to define briefly what wisdom meant for the generations of Jews that preceded the earliest rabbis, and for the circles in which their religious ideas flourished and were championed. I shall then focus on the elements of wisdom literature that have been identified in rabbinic literature and will then be in a position to comb the early rabbinic prayers for any hint of such and similar elements, whatever they may turn out to be.

Ancient wisdom

As is well known, and clarified by Crenshaw, Boadt, and Declaissé-Walford, wisdom literature in the Near East goes back some three millennia before the Second Temple and in areas and cultures much at distance from the land of Israel, even if the latter centre ultimately became subject to their influences. It concerns itself with knowledge about the world, the way it is ordered and how it works. This includes everything that is experienced by human beings and much that is subject to their intellectual speculation. Wisdom literature is interested not only in people but also in the broader animal, vegetable and mineral worlds. Gods, or a god, may be part of this set-up and there is the assumption of a harmony in the cosmos that sometimes suffers disturbance, leading to unpleasant consequences for all involved. The problems of life, death and suffering concern the intelligent and thoughtful individual, and various explanations are sought and offered for what humanity finds difficult to understand. Wisdom not only deals with such complex intellectual challenges but also provides the means for tackling such topics as medicine, magic, astronomy and dreams. Wise individuals have to study in order to perform efficiently in various areas of life, especially if they have prominent positions, and they are entrusted with the task of passing on this wisdom to coming generations. The ideal for such individuals is

4 Kohler, 'Wisdom', pp. 537–38.

to cultivate the kind of prudent and judicious behaviour that benefits home, work and society in general, and that contributes to harmony with fellow beings, as well as within the cosmic order. Wisdom is often identified with a god or goddess and sought among special individuals. It is sometimes expressed in a higher register of language that may include maxims, poems, proverbs, numerical sayings and disputations.[5]

As has often been pointed out, and is clearly explained by the scholars just mentioned, as well as by Dell, wisdom material acquires a slightly different hue in ancient Israel. Although there appears at times to be a less intensive and technical interest in national history, revelation and religious laws, there is no doubt that connections are being made between what wisdom has to say about life and what the Israelite traditions impart about God, theodicy and justice. Good and wise people fear God, behave uprightly and observe the religious practices inherited from their family and their teachers. Learning and teaching play a major role in encouraging such behaviour at home, at court and in the dispensation of law. The outstanding wisdom books of the Hebrew Bible are Job, Proverbs and Ecclesiastes. These books, respectively, confront human inability to understand the ways of God, provide guidance in the cultivation of an admirable lifestyle, and blend a peppery cynicism about life with some pious statements designed to dilute the sharpness of its taste on the religious palate. The *ḥakhamim* (the 'wise') function in all manner of ways for society and they are at times perhaps in competition with other leading groups such as kings, courtiers, prophets and priests for the allegiance and the ear of the populace. Practical aspects of wisdom are especially cultivated by the priestly class, and wisdom makes an impact on literacy.[6]

After Persia

During the Second Temple period, as we learn in detail from Gilbert and Reiterer, as well as more generally from Crenshaw, such notions are more widely and sharply developed, at least partly due to the impact made on the Jews by the cultures of Persia and Greece. It is not relevant here to argue whether these cultures owed anything in their turn to the ancient wisdom of the Near East, merely to acknowledge that they constitute a fresh ideological current in the stream of Jewish thinking in the Second Temple era. Many texts from that period, in the

5 Crenshaw, *Wisdom*, pp. 251–72; Boadt, 'Wisdom literature', p. 1381; Declaissé-Walford, 'Wisdom', pp. 862–65.

6 Crenshaw, *Wisdom*, pp. 61–153; Boadt, 'Wisdom literature', pp. 1380–82; Dell, 'Wisdom', pp. 869–75.

Hebrew Bible as well as in the Greek Jewish texts of the apocryphal/pseudepigraphical/deutero-canonical works, contain wisdom content, but the two books that are undoubtedly the most prominent in this respect are Ben Sira and the Wisdom of Solomon. Although they are manifestly influenced by Greek notions of wisdom, they also reflect Jewish religious attempts to offer an alternative viewpoint and lifestyle to those of Hellenism. Wisdom is hypostasized and comes to be identified with Torah, which is regarded as having existed at the Creation. It is also bound up with many aspects of Jewish religious observance, ethics, prayer, the fear of God and the desire to win His favour. The cult, Temple and priesthood are all parts of this indivisible religious entity. Learning and teaching occupy a central role and there appear to be specific places where such educational processes are undertaken. There is a doctrine of an afterlife for the soul, and wisdom, which is the pledge of immortality, is a gift of God. Unlike Proverbs, the wisdom texts of Ben Sira include prayers on behalf of the Jewish people, with 36:6–22 recording pleas to God for deliverance from enemies, for the ingathering of the exiles, for mercy towards Israel, Jerusalem and the Temple, for the fulfilment of the prophetic visions in the Hebrew Bible, and for the success of all such prayers. The Creation and the Exodus are of central significance and the latter is the subject of extensive interpretation not only as recital of the biblical events but also for its relevance to contemporary religious thought.[7]

Qumran

The new availability, in recent years, of texts from Qumran and its environs has made it possible to trace the manner in which wisdom ideas made their appearance among the Jewish literary works of the Second Temple period that were preserved in the Dead Sea scrolls. These were not necessarily represented among other Jewish corpora known to us from biblical, hellenistic and rabbinic sources. There is no particular value in the present context in arguing whether or not these texts may be defined as 'sectarian'; the fact is that they reflect Jewish religious ideology in pre-rabbinic times and as such are important for the current discussion. What emerges from a recent translation and analysis of twenty-nine items by Kampen is a confirmation of the use of proverbs, instructions, speeches, poetry, and other sapiential texts that are too fragmentary to define

7 Crenshaw, *Wisdom*, pp. 155–187; Gilbert, 'Wisdom literature', pp. 283–324; Reiterer, 'Significance', pp. 218–38.

more precisely. In these texts, strong links are made between wisdom, Torah and the correct way of life and there is a conviction that human existence is transient and that there is danger in any failure to obtain wisdom. Eschatology and apocalypse are integrated with wisdom and there is a close concern with creation, history, the struggle against evil, and the future, as well as reflections of dualistic notions such as the two ways to go. The wise are represented by the *maskilim* who are responsible for 'admission, instruction and advancement', possess important Torah knowledge, and head the religious hierarchy. It is these wise individuals who, as recipients of divine knowledge, teach about the mysteries of existence, possess an understanding of end-time and are especially expert in matters of angelology. Included in the texts are macarisms, that is, lists of those who are declared especially happy or blessed (אשרי).[8]

Rabbinic literature

And so to rabbinic literature. What are the relevant ideas that occur in the talmudic-midrashic sources, at least in the first few Christian centuries, and that may assist us in our quest for some wisdom material in the rabbinic prayers? Urbach takes a holistic approach and makes little distinction between what was edited in the talmudic period and what underwent compilation a number of centuries later, on the basis of the conviction that there are early traditions that are committed only at later dates to the textual format. With a little caution, we may make use of his summaries of the situation with regard to the *ḥakhamim* ('wise men'), a term that becomes synonymous in rabbinic literature with rabbis. Their wisdom is of course identical with Torah and with the debates and controversies associated with its study, but they also have other attributes. They may serve as judges, administrators and communal leaders, although there is a ubiquitous tension in their ranks between those who see Torah as a full-time occupation and those who prefer to make their living from more mundane occupations, with some strong statements being made in the context of this controversy, such as 'whoever occupies himself exclusively with Torah is like an atheist'![9] For some, the pursuit of their rabbinic wisdom took precedence over their prayers and they saw themselves as an élite, while, for others, their wisdom had to include the guidance of pupils, the performance of charitable

8 Kampen, *Commentaries*, pp. 1–35, 310–13, and in his introductory remarks to each of the subsequent translations.
9 *b.'Abod. Zar.*, 17b.

deeds, and the activation of the kind of social conscience that elicited compassion for the under-privileged.[10]

There is one noteworthy passage of aggadah that was probably not written down before the tenth century but that contains a most remarkable, and for us an eminently relevant, expression of opinion about wisdom. I believe that the homily is worthy of citation and translation in its entirety, particularly since Urbach uses (and Abrahams translates from Modern Hebrew into English)[11] only parts of it, and appears to omit some of the more obscure sentences:[12]

> It has been said by Jeremiah [9.22] 'Let not the wise man glory in his wisdom'. If he does not acknowledge who created him, in what way is he wise? Indeed there are among the gentiles[13] those who are wise in their own eyes. There are folk who understand the sun, the moon and the planets and who can work out how the solar year is longer than the lunar one and how the lunar months may very precisely be calculated, without error, and related to the solar year. They are wise enough to make such major calculations and to understand the nature of God's heavens but they fail to acknowledge who created them and the world at large. They can build countries, provinces and houses, and construct weapons of war. They can also use magical formulas[14] to control waters and hover in the wind over them where there is no road or path. But they are not wise enough to know who created them and who makes the wind blow. They are wise enough to calculate things for other people but they have insufficient sense to sort themselves out. Wise in everything else, they are foolish in one thing. But through that one deficiency, that inability to acknowledge God, they destroy all their wisdom. [As Jeremiah says in 10:8] 'But they are dull and foolish; their doctrine is but delusion. It is a piece of wood[15] [emend from עין to עץ]', and if they are burning in Gehinnom, what advantage is their wisdom to them?

A more cautious approach would restrict the use of rabbinic evidence in the talmudic-midrashic literature to those traditions that more obviously emanate from the worlds of early Christianity and late antiquity. Such an approach is preferred by Hezser who sees the rabbinic wisdom as practised by a relatively small number within the Jewish community (not as the norm in the way that the later

10 Urbach, *Sages*, pp. 593 – 648.

11 Urbach, *Sages*, p. 620.

12 Schechter (ed.), *Agadath Shir*, p. 19.

13 I have little doubt (given that there are hundreds of such examples in rabbinic literature) that the original text read גוים ('gentiles') here and, because of the censor, was replaced by the word רשעים ('wicked'), which appears in the Schechter edition.

14 The Hebrew word בלפדנים is difficult and I suspect that the reference may be to פדניםwhich is a word used in the practice of magic, as is attested in the Maagarim (Historical Hebrew Dictionary) Project of the Academy of the Hebrew Language, Jerusalem, to which I am indebted for this and other important data.

15 I have emended from עין to עץ to match the Jeremiah verse.

rabbis portrayed it) and as generally transmitted by the oral method and not by means of texts. This commitment to orality may owe as much to Greek philosophy as to rabbinic notions concerning the alleged Sinaitic origin of the 'Oral Torah'. The teaching was done in communal contexts such as synagogues (בתי כנסת) and learning centres (בתי מדרש), and elementary education probably consisted of no more than competence in reading or reciting scripture and some statutory prayers, only scribes being taught to actually write themselves. Some Jews, who belonged to socially and economically upper strata, opted for the education and culture of the dominant majority (language/literature, rhetoric, philosophy) but not many of the rabbinic leaders seem to have done so.[16] Hasan-Rokem has stressed that the numerous rabbinic midrashim making various comparisons between Athens and Jerusalem should be seen as belonging to wisdom literature. [17]

Stemberger

We may now return to Stemberger and what he concludes about sages, scribes and seers in Rabbinic Judaism.[18] He eschews as extreme the two views that see, respectively, all rabbinic literature as belonging to the wisdom genre, or only the mishnaic tractate 'Abot as truly containing wisdom material. He prefers to concentrate on a large variety of genres and topics that are reminiscent of wisdom literature. These are made up of the philosophical content of the Mishnah, social and political wisdom relaying to the well-ordered management of society, misogynous statements, and the search for wisdom as the ultimate goal in life. Treatises that are specifically relevant here are the post-talmudic tractate Derek Ereṣ with its collections of rules for implementation in daily life and the early medieval Alphabet of Ben Sira.[19] An important point – especially from the viewpoint of this paper – is Stemberger's argument that 'Abot does indeed represent traditional rabbinic wisdom in artistic literary form, including reflections on life, but reached the height of its popularity only in the early Middle Ages, when it was incorporated into the prayer-book. Within the talmudic-midrashic corpora, there are elements of wisdom literature such as proverbs, numerical sayings, parables, and disputes with the wise of other nations, in addition to medicine, magic and dreams. These do not constitute a direct continuity, according to Stemberger, of the ancient Near Eastern wisdom tradition but there is undoubt-

16 Hezser, *Literacy*, pp. 94–109.
17 Hasan-Rokem, 'Folklore', p. 961.
18 Stemberger, 'Scribes', pp. 295–319.
19 On these texts, see Stemberger, *Introduction*, pp. 250–53 and 372–73.

edly a continuation of many aspects of wisdom culture that are to be found in rabbinic education, administration and scribal practices. Stemberger's summary is worthy of close note:[20]

> Wisdom literature in the rabbinic world is no longer what it used to be in biblical and Second Temple times. It is no longer a clearly distinguished separate literary genre with a well defined agenda. But many of its forms, traditions, and themes have been handed on and transformed in these centuries and would deserve a more profound study.

Rabbinic liturgy

Having established the necessary background to the Jewish liturgical developments of the first few Christian centuries, this paper may now proceed to an examination of some of the early rabbinic prayers, beginning with some remarks about a collection of blessings known as the 'morning benedictions' (ברכות השחר).[21] These blessings appear to have begun their lives as domestically-based expressions of thanks to God for His gift of some of the natural world within and around us and were only later incorporated, not without objection on the part of leading figures such as Maimonides, into the synagogal liturgy.[22] For the mishnaic teachers of the first two centuries they were the recommended way of beginning the day in a pious fashion.[23] Most of the blessings had – or were subsequently given – formal structures to begin and/or end them, making use of the standard benedictory formulas such as ברוך אתה ה' אלהינו מלך העולם ('You, our Eternal God, are the essence of praise, and the universal sovereign'), or only the first three of these Hebrew words. The textual history of each of these blessings, as well as the manner and order of their discrete use in each of the different Jewish liturgical rites, are complicated matters that cannot be discussed or pursued in the present context. For the purposes of this overview, they, and other passages from subsequent parts of the rabbinic prayers, will be treated under a number of headings.

---

20 Stemberger, 'Scribes', p. 319.

21 Elbogen, *Gottesdienst*, pp. 89–90, *Tefillah*, pp. 69–70, *Liturgy*, pp. 77–78.

22 Maimonides, *Mishneh Torah*, *Tefillah* 7.6–9; Engl. trans., pp. 105a–6a. 'This, however, is an erroneous practice which should not be followed.'

23 *b. Ber.*, 60b and *b. Menaḥ.*, 43b.

Status

Three of the blessings thank God for the status of the male reciting them.[24] He considers his role in life and is glad that he is not a non-Jew or a pagan. This blessing may of course be triggered by the sight of his circumcision. He also welcomes the fact that he is not a slave, inspired by the reality that he is free to rise in the morning as and when he wishes. According to some texts, it is not a slave that is the subject here but an ignoramus of one sort or another, or an animal. The third of these blessings appreciates masculinity. The one reciting it was clearly aware that women in the ancient world often had an unenviable lot and he, before he puts his clothes on, glances at himself and is pleased not to have to share that.[25] It seems to me that these three blessings may justifiably be defined as linked to the wisdom tradition. They represent reflections on the relative roles of various humans in the world at large, as well as in the Jewish world, and were indeed inspired by similar statements severally attributed to the Greek philosophers, Socrates and Plato.[26]

Activities

Another group of benedictions, recited before or after the three just noted, relate to early morning activities. One of them acknowledges how important it is to be able to distinguish day from night and, if we understand the Hebrew of Job 38:36 correctly, the gratitude is for the cockcrow that has apparently woken him, and for the beginning of the natural day. Another makes use of Ps 136:6 and thanks God for the creation of the earth on which he is standing, while a third refers to 'all human needs' and may well refer to bladder and bowel functions. In this connection, there is, separately recited when relevant, a benediction noting how wisely God has created the human body with all the necessary organs and admitting that, if any of those fail to function properly, there is a risk to one's life. The topics dealt with in most of the remainder are the reciter's gift of sight, ability to walk, and possession of clothing, including his hat and his belt. It is open to argument whether mention of these latter items may be related

---

24 For an early text and an English translation, see Hedegård, *Amram*, Hebrew section, p. 4, English section, pp. 9–10. For a recent bi-lingual edition, see Sacks, *Siddur*, pp. 26–27.

25 The three Hebrew endings of the benedictions are שלא עשאני עבד,שלא עשאני גוי, and שלא עשאני אשה. The term for the ignoramus used in some versions is בור.

26 For scholarly discussion, see Tabory, 'Benedictions', esp. pp. 115–20, and Kahn, *Blessings*, esp. pp. 9–12.

to wisdom literature. What seems to me to be clearer is that the references to the natural day, to the creation and to bodily functions are in the nature of descriptions and appreciations of the world around him that may owe more than a little to wisdom notions.

Soul

Rabbinic theology sees the onset of sleep as marking the transmission of control from the human to the divine. God takes care of the soul until it is time to restore it to its owner in the morning, unless of course the Creator has made other plans for it! On waking, the Jew therefore recites a blessing in which he admits that God has created his soul, planted it in him and preserved it there for the moment. But it will at a later date be taken from him and then restored in a future life. He is grateful to the Creator, in the meantime, for restoring his soul to his body. Perhaps this is all simply rabbinic theology. On the other hand, such notions of the soul were part of the innovative religious ideology of wisdom circles in the Second Temple period, as earlier described, and it is not outside the realms of possibility that the manner in which the miracles of sleep, waking and breathing are here being lauded owes something to the ideas of the *ḥakhamim* who preceded the rabbis.

Torah

The Talmud records three benedictions that are related to Torah and that should be recited each day before one begins one's studies of such teachings.[27] One of these conveys the idea that Jews are commanded by God to study Torah and another that the election of the people of Israel has been for the precise purpose of presenting them with the Torah. The third is lengthier and entreats God to ensure that the Jewish people who study Torah will find it so enjoyable that they will transmit it from generation to generation and that they will all become well acquainted with the essence of God's being, as well as learned in His Torah.[28] It seems to me that this third benediction reflects a concern with learning and teaching, with the joy of study, with continuity, and with the association of

27 *b.Ber.* 11b.
28 The three central phrases are לעסוק בדברי תורה, (ו)הערב...את דברי תורתך בפינו ובפי עמך בית ישראל, and אשר בחר בנו מכל העמים ונתן לנו את תורתו. See Hedegård, *Amram*, Hebrew section, p. 5, English section, p. 15, and Sacks, *Siddur*, p. 9.

Torah with closeness to God that was undoubtedly part of the Jewish wisdom traditions of earlier periods. It should also be noted that the second pre-*shema‘* benediction both morning and evening has two main themes, namely, the election of Israel and the matter of the Torah and the religious precepts. Studying the Torah is to be done day and night, and the prayer is that it will be truly understood. It is to be taught as well as learned, and it will bring the students closer to God's commands, as well as ensuring good results in life.[29] If these are not wisdom concepts, they are certainly educational ones.

Also on the subject of Torah, there is a passage that is recited after the *‘amidah* (and the Torah reading when that is done) and that was originally designed as a praise of Torah after its study. It is the second part of what is known as the sanctification of God's name associated with a study session (*qedusha de-sidra*), in accordance with the first reference to it (or to an earlier form of it) in the Talmud.[30] God is blessed for having created the worshippers for His glory, distinguished between loyal believers and the religiously misguided, and given them the authentic Torah and eternal life. This is followed by a prayer for Torah knowledge, love and fear of God and obedience to His wishes through sincere commitment, so that the birth and life of those offering the prayer should not prove to be pointless. The passage ends with a plea that the Jewish people should keep God's commands in this world and be granted the experience of all the blessed pleasures of the messianic age and the eternal life.[31]

Ben Sira 17:6–23 refers to the religious wisdom granted to His people, to its effect on their correct behaviour, to their fear of God and their prayers and how these bring Him glory. Mention is also made there of the eternity of His revealed commands and Israel's special role in this connection and its everlasting covenant with Him. Towards the end of the section, the author expresses a triumphant confidence that God will ultimately dole out the appropriate reward to those who deserve it.[32] If we see that Ben Sira passage as a praise of wisdom and Torah – more precisely, wisdom that is Torah – it is difficult not to appreciate the degree to which the later rabbinic praise of Torah expresses similar sentiments. Given that similarity, may we not identify this part of the *qedusha de-sidra* as a later form of wisdom literature?

29 See Hedegård, *Amram*, Hebrew section, pp. 20, 71, English section, pp. 50–51, 164, and Sacks, *Siddur*, pp. 97, 243. Central phrases are תן בלבנו להבין and ונשמח בדברי תורתך, with slight variations in the various rites.

30 *b. Soṭa*, 49a. See Elbogen, *Gottesdienst*, pp. 61–67, *Tefillah*, pp. 47–54, *Liturgy*, pp. 54–62.

31 See Hedegård, *Amram*, Hebrew section, pp. 55–56, English section, pp. 130–32, and Sacks, *Siddur*, pp. 172–75.

32 Segal, *Sefer*, pp. 103, 105–6; Skehan/di Lella, *Wisdom*, pp. 277, 282–83.

Shema' benedictions

In accordance with rabbinic regulations codified in the second century, the twice-daily recitation of the *shema'*, that is, the three paragraphs from Deut 6:4–9, 11:13–21 and Num 15:37–41, is preceded by two benedictions and followed by one in the morning and by two in the evening. It is these benedictions that must now receive some attention. The first one in the morning blesses God for having created light and darkness, as well as good and everything else, carefully omitting the reference to evil that occurs in the original verse in Isa 45:7.[33] He is praised for mercifully providing light for the world and those who dwell in it, and for renewing the wonders of the creation on a daily basis.[34] There are a number of texts in the various rites that expand on the theme of light, making specific mention of the sun and other celestial illumination and in some cases switching to the future mode and expressing a desire for the ultimate light over Zion that will bring Jewish redemption. The equivalent evening benediction expresses gratitude for the manner in which God in His wisdom brings about the necessary changes in the world that lead to the return of darkness, makes a distinction between the day and the night, and arranges for the stars to shine.[35] Again, some texts go on to offer special praise of God in ways more specifically related to Israel. I propose that what we have in these benedictions is the kind of praise of nature and of the order of the universe that is so familiar to us from many wisdom texts.

There are two other topics in the *shema'* benedictions that are of relevance to this discussion. The first, entitled *qedushah*, concerns the use of the trisagion from Isa 6:3 and the description of how the angelic hosts on high recite this sanctification of God's name at the same time as Israel does so here below.[36] Other verses that are at times recited in this same context are Ezek 3:12, Ps 146:10 and Isa 5:16, and the use of such a *qedushah* is included not only in the *shema'* benedictions but also in the repetition of the *'amidah*, and in the first part of the *qedushah de-sidra* to which reference has already been made above.[37] Although the *qedushah* is mentioned in the talmudic sources,[38] it is not clearly defined and its use before

33 The preferred (!) Hebrew is יוצר אור ובורא חושך עושה שלום ובורא את הכל.

34 See Hedegård, *Amram*, Hebrew section, p. 18, English section, pp. 46–47, and Sacks, *Siddur*, p. 91. A central phrase about the creation is מחדש בכל יום מעשה בראשית.

35 See Hedegård, *Amram*, Hebrew section, p. 71, English section, p. 163, and Sacks, *Siddur*, p. 243. One of a number of phrases about the creation is מסדר הכוכבים במשמרותיהם.

36 Elbogen, *Gottesdienst*, pp. 61–67, *Tefillah*, pp. 47–54, *Liturgy*, pp. 54–62.

37 See Hedegård, *Amram*, Hebrew section, pp. 18–19, 47, English section, pp. 47–49, 113–115, and Sacks, *Siddur*, pp. 92–95, 112–13, as well as n. 31 above.

38 *t. Ber.* 1.9, *y. Ber.* 5.3 (9c) and *b. Ber.* 21a.

the recitation of the morning *shema'* certainly remained a matter of controversy in the ninth century when the Babylonian rabbinic leadership felt constrained to impose it on what they regarded as recalcitrant Palestinian communities. Who first inspired these *qedushah* prayers and when? There is, as yet, no definitive response to these questions but circles with preferences for mystical and angelological themes and an intense interest in cosmic matters look like the most obvious candidates. Some of them were responsible for the composition of *hekhalot* literature that combined mysticism with visions of heaven, apocalyptic ideas and gnostic themes. [39] They owed more than a little to earlier wisdom literature, at least as it evolved in the late Second Temple period, especially in the texts preserved among the Dead Sea scrolls.[40] It is therefore again possible that what is here being encountered is additional evidence of wisdom elements in such late talmudic or post-talmudic Jewish prayers.

Exodus

The benediction that immediately follows the three paragraphs of the *shema'* in the morning as well as the evening is centred on the topic of the redemption from Egypt.[41] It is entitled the *ge'ulah* benediction in the Mishnah and is explained in texts from the Tosefta and the Palestinian Talmud that are probably not much later than the Mishnah itself. According to the divergent views of various rabbis, it should include mention of the Exodus from Egypt, or the sovereignty of God, or the smiting of the first-born and the dividing of the sea to enable the Israelites to cross towards the Promised Land. As often occurs in Jewish liturgy, the solution is not to decide between these different preferences but to include all the topics. In some versions, it is not only the Egyptian redemption that is included in this benediction but also the future and final redemption. [42] The halakhic and liturgical controversy about this need not delay us in the present context. Suffice it to say that, according to all views, it is clear that the exodus from Egypt has a central role in this part of the early rabbinic liturgy. Quite why is less clear. It will, however, be recalled that the Wisdom of Solomon devotes much space to this topic and to its interpretation so that it was clearly of central significance

39 Alexander, 'Prayer', pp. 43–64, esp. p. 60.
40 Chazon, *Qedushah*, pp. 7–17.
41 See Hedegård, *Amram*, Hebrew section, pp. 27–30, 71–72, English section, pp. 70–75, 164–65, and Sacks, *Siddur*, pp. 104–7, 246–51. See Elbogen, *Gottesdienst*, pp. 22–24, 101–2, *Tefillah*, pp. 17–18, 78, *Liturgy*, pp. 21–22, 87.
42 *t. Ber.* 2.1, *y. Ber.* 1.9 (3d). See also Blank, 'Grammar'.

to such Jewish wisdom circles. In that work, from the first or second pre-Christian century, a lengthy section deals with the history of Israel's redemption from Egypt, and God is praised for the delivery of His people. The lives of Jewish heroes before the Exodus are recounted and the overall message is that true wisdom is not that of the gentiles but only one that is linked to a knowledge of God. Such knowledge leads to piety and immortality. God rescues the righteous and punishes the wicked, always ensuring that perfect justice is meted out. The Egyptians are regarded as having erred in taking pride in an intellectuality quite at odds with the Jewish notion of wisdom and Torah.[43]

Passover Haggadah

Another important piece of rabbinic liturgy that is particularly relevant in this context is of course the *Passover Haggadah*. It is recited during a domestic ceremony (*seder leyl pesaḥ*) on the first evening of Passover in which questions are raised about the eating of the paschal lamb, matzah bread, and bitter vegetables, and about the associated rituals, and explanations are given about the historical and religious circumstances in which these customs arose. The story of the Exodus is related, with the addition of many midrashic comments, and clear guidance is given as to how properly to understand the whole ritual. The paradox about this liturgy is that it is at one and the same time one of the oldest pieces of rabbinic liturgy, as well as containing some of its youngest elements. It has had a dynamic existence for two millennia and it is not an easy matter to sort out which section was composed when, and for what purpose. It undoubtedly has intellectual, educational and religiously inspirational aspects. It may also constitute a polemical response to the military, cultural and philosophical challenge of the Hellenistic and Roman worlds, in that it expresses confidence in ultimate rescue by God and true freedom. As a result, attempts have been made to link it with the Greek symposia (social and cultural drinking parties of the intelligentsia) and to argue that it represented a Jewish religious way of mimicking or replacing such (apparently attractive) pagan, intellectual activities.[44] In this context, the question is whether such Jewish responses on the part of the Wisdom of Solomon and the Passover Haggadah are to be defined as representative of a special kind of wisdom literature that fused the philosophical ideas of the general

43 See Wisd 10:10 – 19.

44 All these topics are full discussed in the recent editions of Safrai/Safrai, *Haggadah*, and Tabory, *Haggadah*.

movement with the religious ideas of Judaism, or are simply responses to such a movement and no longer truly characteristic of the broader wisdom traditions of the Near East. Either way, the Jews who composed such accounts of the Exodus (either before or after the destruction of the Second Temple[45]) were making use of some of these traditions. In that case, we may again propose that the rabbis have, with their notions of the Exodus, inherited or adopted a wisdom theme that had already had considerable theological significance for at least some of their religious and intellectual predecessors.

'Amidah/Shemoneh 'Esreh

The prayer that is central to all statutory rabbinic prayers, morning, afternoon and evening, is the *'amidah.* Its weekday version is composed of nineteen (apparently earlier, eighteen, hence *shemoney 'esreh*) benedictions. The topics covered are the biblical patriarchs, resurrection, sanctity, knowledge, repentance, pardon, redemption, healing, plentiful produce, end of exile and persecution, restoration of autonomy, removal of apostasy, blessing of righteous and of converts, Jerusalem and the davidic dynasty (either one or two benedictions), successful prayer, cultic restoration, thanksgiving and peace.[46] The first and last three are also part of the sabbath and festival *'amidot* which have appropriate central benedictions that are less in number. The question to be asked here is which of these, or which parts of each of these, may conceivably contain wisdom content. The first candidate for attention is the blessing that thanks God for reviving the dead, presumably at some appropriate, future date.[47] In its various textual formats, according to rite and period, it describes God's various powers in setting things aright in the world, dealing with humanity's needs, and arranging the weather.[48] One of these powers consists of restoring the souls of those who have departed, but no detail is given of how or when this is to be achieved. It is possible that the original benediction related to all divine powers concerning

---

45 Safrai/Safrai, *Haggadah*, p. 13, suggests that this aspect of the ritual came after the destruction but such a view is by no means definitive.

46 All the benedictions of the *'amidah* are fully discussed in Elbogen, *Gottesdienst*, pp. 641–60, *Tefillah*, pp. 32–47, *Liturgy*, pp. 37–54; see also Ehrlich, *Weekday Amidah.*

47 See Hedegård, *Amram*, Hebrew section, pp. 34–35, English section, pp. 85–86, and Sacks, *Siddur*, pp. 110–11.

48 For a variety of texts from the Cairo Genizah, some of them copied as early as the tenth century, see Luger, *Amidah*, pp. 53–62, and Ehrlich, *Weekday Amidah*, pp. 43–61. See also the manuscript evidence cited in Finkelstein, 'Amidah'.

nature, and that the issue of resurrection was inserted to establish a theological point, that is to say, to polemicize against those who rejected such a notion. God as the force of nature, as well as nature as an element of order in the universe, are certainly ideas that are characteristic of the wisdom literature of the Second Temple period. More than that, some of those responsible for the transmission of that literature also took the opportunity of stressing the immortality of the soul. There may therefore be some wisdom links here.

There is also a blessing – the fourth in the daily office – that is wholly concerned with knowledge. It requests the gift of knowledge and understanding and only a small minority of the earliest texts include any reference to Torah.[49] On the other hand, most of them describe what they are requesting mainly by way of the Hebrew roots ידע and בין, with some (later?) texts adding words from the roots שכל and חכם. The theme would therefore appear to be the divine furnishment of intelligence and understanding. In addition, the passage added to this benediction on Saturday evening, when shabbat is terminating, alludes to the divine ability to draw distinctions between times of day, days of the week and, in some versions, different parts of the universe, while also noting more parochial Jewish religious distinctions, such as between sabbath and weekday, and between Jews and non-Jews.[50] The topic, then, is primarily the ability of the human mind to categorize and analyse, and the Palestinian Talmud explains the presence of the added passage marking the departure of sabbath in this particular blessing with the comment 'because where there is no intelligence, how can distinctions be made?'[51] The topic is not one that is exclusively of interest to purveyors of wisdom but nor is it one that absent from their deliberations. Weinfeld argues for a direct link between this benediction (and those mentioned above in connection with Torah study) and the earlier texts of the Dead Sea scrolls.[52]

Other blessings in the *'amidah* that may justifiably regarded as of more general humanitarian interest rather than of specific importance to rabbinic theology are those that deal with health, the conditions for good agricultural produce, and thanksgiving for life. The basic content of the first of these, which differs only minimally in the various versions, is a prayer for full recovery from all pains, ailments and distress. The second, which does, incidentally, have a large number of variants even in its earliest manuscript forms, focuses on appealing for the kind of weather and conditions that are suitable for

49 See Hedegård, *Amram*, Hebrew section, p. 35, English section, p. 87, and Sacks, *Siddur*, pp. 114–15.
50 See Luger, *Amidah*, pp. 73–80, Ehrlich, *Weekday Amidah*, pp. 77–88.
51 *y. Ber.* 5. (9b).
52 Weinfeld, *Liturgy*, pp. 179–93.

ensuring adequate produce in the fields and subsequent culinary satisfaction. In the third benediction, thanks are offered for the gift of continuing life, the souls that are the divine possession, and the many benefits continuously received.[53] God is of course being addressed, and is the subject of all these benedictions, but they do also imply a degree of reflection about the world, its order and harmony, and the nature of human life and fate that would have been familiar to those who subscribed to the philosophy of wisdom.

'Alenu

Although the *'alenu* prayer has, at least since the high Middle Ages, functioned as a concluding prayer, it began its Jewish liturgical life as part of the additional (*musaf*) *'amidah* for Rosh Ha-Shanah (New Year) no later than the first part of the third century when it is employed in that context by the leading Babylonian teacher, and champion of Jewish liturgical development, Rav (Rabbi Abba Arikha).[54] Since there are Genizah texts of the New Year prayers that probably date from as early as the tenth century, and perhaps reflect established Palestinian custom in earlier centuries, and that include both paragraphs of this prayer, it seems reasonable to consider the whole text in the context of the present analysis.[55] The prayer is mainly concerned with the power of God, and how it will one day be universally recognized. God is the master of all and the author of creation who rules over everything and everyone, and who has given the Jews a special role in promoting monotheism. He is the one who has formed the whole universe, including our earth, and His throne and power are in the highest celestial spheres. The worshipper looks forward to the day when idolatry and evil will give way to a universal belief in God's sovereignty, marked by the desire of all humanity to worship Him and to glorify His name. Then everyone will be subject to His reign, since kingship truly belongs to Him. Here, once more, we have elements of a universalist approach, an appreciation of the creation, and a vision of the ideal future.[56] Since the *hekhalot* literature contains an early version of the *'alenu*, it has been suggested that it is among the composers of such mystical material that we should look for its original inspiration. Given the incontrovertible fact that the *hekhalot* circles borrowed much of their

53 See Hedegård, *Amram*, Hebrew section, pp. 35–38, English section, pp. 89–98, and Sacks, *Siddur*, pp. 118–31.
54 Elbogen, *Gottesdienst*, pp. 80–81, *Tefillah*, pp. 63–64, *Liturgy*, pp. 71–672; Langer, 'Censorship', pp. 147–49.
55 Fleischer, *Eretz-Israel*, pp. 127, 239; Wieder, *Formation*, pp. 453–68.
56 See Davidson/Assaf/Joel, *Siddur RSG*, p. 221, and Sacks, *Maḥzor*, pp. 524–27.

ideology from wisdom notions, the *'alenu* of rabbinic prayer may also represent a remnant of such ancient traditions.[57]

Lectionaries

It is also interesting that so many Psalms with wisdom content found their way into rabbinic liturgy. This is not the place to expatiate on such a tendency, or to analyse it closely, simply to record an interesting piece of data. Of the twenty-seven Psalms listed by Dell as belonging to the wisdom genre, no less than eleven make an appearance, in at least one standard rabbinic liturgy, with one function or another.[58] It should also not be forgotten that the book of Qohelet, despite its cynicism, is part of the synagogal lectionary for the festival of Sukkot and that, perhaps less surprisingly, there is a custom to read the book of Job on the intensively sad fast-day of Tish'ah Be-Av, which marks the destruction of both Jerusalem temples.[59] And of course the mishnaic tractate *'Abot* is already attested as part of liturgy for the afternoon of the sabbath in ninth-century Babylonia.[60]

Conclusions

As the 'wise' of their people, the composers of rabbinic liturgy appreciated the wonders of nature, reflected on human life and the gift of a soul, and actively promoted the learning, teaching and transmission of Torah. For them, Torah was not only an intellectual exercise – although it was also assuredly that – but a way of understanding the world, approaching God and worshipping Him, and making sense of history. Using the power of their intellect, combined with their ideas about God, they speculated about the cosmos and hoped for an ideal future.

It will be recalled that, on the basis of his analysis of the talmudic and midrashic sources, Stemberger concluded that wisdom literature was no longer a separate genre for the rabbis but that they adopted and transmitted many of its traditions. I believe that the brief study now here completed supports and strengthens that conclusion and perhaps lays the foundation for further and more detailed analysis of the topic of what 'wisdom' meant to the rabbinic teachers.

---

57 Alexander, 'Prayer', pp. 60–61.
58 Compare Dell, 'Wisdom', p. 873 and Jakobovits, *Prayer Book*, p. 993.
59 Elbogen, *Gottesdienst*, p. 139, *Tefillah*, p. 105, *Liturgy*, pp. 117 and 151.
60 Kronholm, *Amram*, Hebrew text, p. 26, English translation, pp. 131–32.

Works cited

Alexander, P. S., 'Prayer in the Heikhalot literature', in Goetschel, R. (ed.), *Prière, Mystique et Judaïsme* (Paris: Presses Universitaires de France, 1987), pp. 43–64.

Amram ben Sheshna, *Seder R. Amram*, part I, ed. D. Hedegård (Lund: Lindstedts, 1951).

Amram ben Sheshna, *Seder R. Amram*, part II, ed. T. Kronholm (Lund: CWK Gleerup, 1974).

Blank, D. R., 'The curious theological grammar of '*ga'al yisra'el*'', in *The Experience of Jewish Liturgy: Studies Dedicated to Menahem Schmelzer*, ed. D. R. Blank (Leiden: Brill, 2010), pp. 9–21.

Boadt, L, 'Wisdom, Wisdom Literature', in *Eerdmans Dictionary of the Bible*, ed. D. N. Freedman (Grand Rapids: Eerdmans, 2000), pp. 1380–82.

Chazon, E. G., 'The *Qedushah* liturgy and its history in light of the Dead Sea Scrolls', in *From Qumran to Cairo: Studies in the History of Prayer*, ed. J. Tabory (Jerusalem: Orhot, 1999), pp. 7–17.

Crenshaw, J. L., *Old Testament Wisdom: An Introduction*, (Louisville: Westminster John Knox, 2010, 3rd edn.).

Davidson, I./Assaf, S./Joel, B. I. (eds.), *Siddur R. Saadja Gaon. Kitāb Ǵāmi' Aṣ-Ṣalawāt Wat-Tasābīh* (Jerusalem: Mekize Nirdamim, 1963 2nd edn.).

Declaissé-Walford, N., 'Wisdom in the Ancient Near East', in *The New Interpreter's Dictionary of the Bible*, ed. K. D. Sakenfeld, vol. 5 (Nashville: Abingdon, 2009), pp. 862–65.

Dell, K. J., 'Wisdom in the Old Testament', in *The New Interpreter's Dictionary of the Bible*, ed. K. D. Sakenfeld, vol. 5 (Nashville: Abingdon, 2009), pp. 869–75.

Ehrlich, U., *The Weekday Amidah in Geniza Prayer Books: Origins and Transmission* (Hebrew; Jerusalem: Yad Ben-Zvi Press, 2013).

Elbogen, I, *Der jüdische Gottesdienst in seiner geschichtlichen Entwicklung* (Frankfurt-am-Main: Kauffman, 1931; reprint, Hildesheim: Olms, 1962); Hebrew edition, *Ha-Tefillah Be-Yisra'el Be-Hitpatḥutah Ha-Hisṭorit*, eds. J. Heinemann/I. Adler/A. Negev/J. Petuchowski/H. Schirmann (Tel Aviv: Devir, 1972); English edition, *Jewish Liturgy: A Comprehensive History*, Eng. trans. and ed. by R. P. Scheindlin (Philadelphia: Jewish Publication Society, 1993).

Finkelstein, L., 'The Birkat Ha-Mazon', *Jewish Quarterly Review* NS 19 (1928–29), pp. 211–62.

Finkelstein, L., 'The development of the Amidah', *Jewish Quarterly Review* NS 16 (1925), pp. 1–43 and 127–71.

Fleischer, E., *Eretz-Israel Prayer and Prayer Rituals as Portrayed in the Geniza Documents* (Hebrew; Jerusalem: Magnes, 1998).

Gilbert, M., 'Wisdom literature', in *Jewish Writings of the Second Temple Period: Apocrypha, Pseudepigrapha, Qumran Sectarian Writings, Philo, Josephus*, ed. M. E. Stone (Assen: Van Gorcum, 1984), pp. 283–324.

Hasan-Rokem, G., 'Jewish folklore and ethnography', in *The Oxford Handbook of Jewish Studies*, ed. M. Goodman (Oxford: Oxford University, 2002), pp. 956–974.

Hedegård, see Amram.

Hezser, C., *Jewish Literacy in Roman Palestine* (Tübingen: Mohr Siebeck, 2001), pp. 94–109.

Idelsohn, A. Z., *Jewish Liturgy and its Development* (New York: Holt, Rinehart and Winston, 1932).

Jakobovits, Lord (I.) (ed.), *The Authorised Daily Prayer Book of the United Hebrew Congregations of the Commonwealth* (London: Singer's Prayer Book Publication Committee, 1990).

Kahn, Y., *The Three Blessings: Boundaries, Censorship and Identity in Jewish Liturgy* (Oxford: Oxford University Press, 2011).
Kampen, J., *Eerdmans Commentaries on the Dead Sea Scrolls: Wisdom Literature* (Grand Rapids, Mich.: Eerdmans, 2011).
Kohler, K., 'Wisdom', *The Jewish Encyclopedia*, vol. 12 (New York: Funk & Wagnalls, 1901–06), pp. 537–38.
Langer, R., 'The censorship of Aleinu in Ashkenaz and its aftermath', in *The Experience of Jewish Liturgy: Studies Dedicated to Menahem Schmelzer*, ed. D. R. Blank (Leiden: Brill, 2010), pp. 147–66.
Luger, Y., *The Weekday Amidah in the Cairo Genizah* (Hebrew; Jerusalem: Orhot, 2001).
Maimonides, Moses, *Mishneh Torah: The Book of Adoration*, ed. and Eng. trans. M. Hyamson, ed. C. M. Brecher (Jerusalem: Feldheim, 1981).
Petuchowski, J. J., *Understanding Jewish Prayer* (New York: Ktav, 1972).
Reiterer, F. V., 'The sociological significance of the scribe as the teacher of wisdom in Ben Sira', in *Scribes, Sages and Seers: The Sage in the Eastern Mediterranean World*, ed. L. G. Perdue (Göttingen: Vandenhoeck & Ruprecht, 2008), pp. 218–38.
Ringer, F., *The Decline of the German Mandarins: The German Academic Community, 1890–1933* (Cambridge, Mass.: Harvard University, 1969).
Sacks, J., *The Koren Siddur with Introduction, Translation and Commentary* (Jerusalem: Koren, 2009).
Safrai, S./Safrai Z., *Haggadah of the Sages: Introduction and Commentary* (Jerusalem: Carta, 2009).
Schechter, S., *Agadath Shir Hashirim, edited from a Parma MS, annotated and illustrated with parallel passages from numerous mss and early prints, with a postscript on the history of the work* (Cambridge: Deighton Bell, 1896).
Segal, M. H., *Sefer Ben Sira Ha-Shalem* (Jerusalem: Mosad Bialik, 1972, 2nd edn.).
Skehan, P. W./Di Lella, A. A., *The Wisdom of Ben Sira. A New Translation with Notes... Introduction and Commentary* (New York: Doubleday, 1987).
Stemberger, G., *Introduction to the Talmud and Midrash*, Engl. trans. M. Bockmuehl (Edinburgh: T & T Clark, 1996, 2nd edn.).
Stemberger, G., 'Scribes, sages and seers', in *Scribes, Sages and Seers: The Sage in the Eastern Mediterranean World*, ed. L. G. Perdue (Göttingen: Vandenhoeck & Ruprecht, 2008), pp. 295–319.
Tabory, J., 'The benedictions of self-identity and the changing status of women and of Orthodoxy', in *Kenishta: Studies of the Synagogue World*, ed. J. Tabory (Ramat-Gan: Bar-Ilan University, 2001), pp. 107–38.
Tabory, J., *JPS Commentary on the Haggadah: Historical Introduction, Translation, and Commentary* (Philadelphia, Jewish Publication Society, 2008).
Urbach, E. E., *The Sages. Their Concepts and Beliefs*, Eng. trans. I. Abrahams, 2 vols. (Jerusalem: Magnes, 1975).
Weinfeld, M., *Early Jewish Liturgy. From Psalms to the Prayers in Qumran and Rabbinic Literature* (Hebrew; Jerusalem: Magnes, 2004).
Wieder, N., *The Formation of Jewish Liturgy in the East and the West: A Collection of Essays*, 2 vols. (Hebrew; Jerusalem: Ben Zvi, 1998).

11 The Figure of David in Early Jewish Prayer

The purpose of this article is to examine those instances in which the figure of David is employed in the early Jewish liturgy; to assign them to their relevant historical and geographical contexts in the evolution of Rabbinic Judaism; to assess the degree to which there is any significant consistency of purpose in such occurrences; and to offer some suggestions as to the historical and theological factors that may have played a part in their adoption and textual development. The treatment will begin with the late biblical background and the ideas that are documented in the Second Temple period and in the talmudic-midrashic sources, before moving on to the geonic period (7th-11th centuries). Liturgical texts will be closely examined and testimony will be cited from the first generations of authoritative prayer-books, as well as from their later equivalents in the diverse and dispersed rites that emerged in the twelfth and thirteenth centuries.

Background

It is hardly surprising that the biblical character of David should have been chosen as the personality with which so many religious ideas were associated by Jews and Christians in the post-exilic, axial and early Christian centuries. Powerful king, heroic warrior, ruthless politician, subsequently identified as scion of an aristocratic dynasty and prime ancestor of a royal household, founder and patron of the Jerusalem cult, and 'sweet singer in Israel', he was at the same time clearly portrayed as a sinner who knew how to win repentance.

As recent research on the topic, especially by Kenneth Pomykala, has determined, the late books of the Hebrew Bible, the apocryphal and pseudepigraphical literature, the Qumran texts and the writings of Josephus by no means subscribe to the idea of a davidic messiah who will be restored to leadership and will usher in an ideal, and idealized, age. Until the late Persian period there is no one model of Israelite kingship, and the davidic dynasty is not always expressed in terms of the covenant or as an unconditional bestowal.

As far as Qumran is concerned, Lawrence Schiffman broadly defines the two notions of the messianic age as the 'restorative' and the 'utopian' and explains that they sometimes occur in the same text. In the case of the former, the davidic messiah will be the divine agent in defeating the enemies of Israel and restoring Jewish power. The latter concept includes a cataclysmic and utopian ideology of the future, opting for a priestly, religious leader and excluding a davidic messiah. The two notions appear to merge in the religious ideology of the early rabbis.

DOI 10.1515/9783110486704-012

Rabbinic theology

In the talmudic-midrashic sources, David is often imaginatively presented as an assiduous student of Torah with a circle of distinguished scholars and rabbinic judges around him. He is said to be concerned with the practice of the Torah precepts and with the assessment of Jewish religious teachings. He set outstanding examples, according to the aggadists, in the matter of repentance, prayer and praise of God, and he and Moses were the Jewish people's greatest heroes. On the other hand, there are passages that damn him for his sexual impropriety, for his inappropriate language before God, for slander and for his failure as a parent.[1] There is even one passage that reflects an awareness on the part of some third-century rabbinic teachers that questions might legitimately be raised about David's origins, given that he was descended from the religiously dubious relationships of Tamar and Judah and of Ruth and Boaz.[2]

Early rabbinic liturgy

Given that David plays such a significant role in the religious ideologies and traditional lore of Jews and Christians, he may surely be expected to make a cameo appearance in what is one of the most practical manifestations of Jewish spirituality. Alas, the matter is not so simple and some challenges may immediately be made to such a supposition.

First and foremost, we need to be alert to the fact that items that appear in such prayer-books, even if some mention is made of them in the talmudic literature, may not be identical with what had existed at that earlier period, and may sometimes refer to topics of a fairly different nature. For example the terms *hallel* and *pesuqey de-zimra* in earlier sources may not mean precisely what they do in the post-talmudic and medieval sources.[3]

As far as personalities and events are concerned, it has also to be taken into account that the liturgy of the talmudic period, like much of its practice and ideology, had little serious interest in, or mastery of, historical and chronological matters. If such figures as Moses and Ezra, who play such important roles in rabbinic thought, do not enjoy a similar status in the earliest talmudic prayers such as the *'amidah*, the *birkat ha-mazon* and the Passover *Haggadah*, are we likely to

1 *b. Ber.* 62b, *b. Yoma* 22b and *b. Soṭah* 35a; ExR 1.1.
2 *b. Yebam.* 76b–77a.
3 Compare *b. Pesaḥ.* 118a, *b. Ta'an.* 28b and *b. Šabb.* 118b.

find that King David surpasses them in such contexts? A first glance at early rabbinic prayer-books does in fact reveal numerous references to David, some of them in the daily prayers and others in more occasional contexts, both statutory and supplicatory.

References to David

1 Prefacing the Psalms

The earliest reference to a prayer entitled ברוך שאמר is found in a responsum by Naṭronai Gaon that cites it in the name of Moses b. Jacob Gaon who flourished in Sura early in the ninth century.[4] If, simply for ease of analysis but without any claim about 'originality', we reduce that benediction to the skeletal parts that are common to all the early versions and rites, it would begin with the usual six-word benedictory formula and read something like this, followed by my own translation:

> האל מהולל בפה עמו, משובח ומפואר בלשון כל חסידיו, ובשירי דוד עבדך נהללך ונזכיר שמך יחד חי העולמים. ברוך אתה יי מלך מהולל בתושבחות
>
> God is blessed, with praise mouthed by his people, with acclaim and adulation uttered by his devotees. We shall praise you with the songs of David your servant and shall recite the uniqueness and eternity of your fame. God is blessed, his majesty praised in poetic acclaim.

Reduced to its simplest religious message, this benediction begins and ends with a statement that God is worthy of the praise heaped upon him by the Jewish people and by its especially pious members. Unless the final Hebrew word תושבחות specifically alludes to the Psalms of David,[5] there is a separate reference at the centre of the blessing that independently makes such an allusion, a point already noted by Ze'ev Jawitz almost a century ago. In some texts the sentence ובשירי דוד עבדך נהללך ('we shall praise you with the songs of David your servant') is followed by the phrase בשבחות ובזמירות ('with acclaims and with hymns'), while in others the words are phrased in the singular with the pronominal suffix in the third person, namely, בשבחו ובזמ(י)רו ('with his acclaim and with his

4 Elbogen, *Gottesdienst*, pp. 82–84, *Ha-Tefillah*, pp. 64–66, *Liturgy*, pp. 73–74; Rappel, *Gates*, p. 74; Jacobson, *Nethiv*, 1.192–94.

5 This is discussed below in the section headed 'Definitions of הבוחר and תושבחות'.

hymn'), on occasion supplemented by the word בשירו 'his song').[6] The first formulation may be the remnant of a more general reference to praise, while the latter applies it to David and therefore makes it more specific.

Another variant, which adds nothing to the meaning but is relevant to the topic in hand, relates to the use of parallelism in the reference to David's praises of God. The relevant text reads:

> [ו]בשירי דויד עבדך נהללך... בשירות [וב]זמירות [ותשבחות] בן ישי עבדך נהללך
>
> 'We shall praise you with the songs of David your servant...and with the songs, hymns and acclaims of your servant the son of Jesse we shall praise you'.[7]

What we have then here is a benediction introducing a selection from the Psalms that may conceivably, in an early or variant form, have made only general reference to the praise of God and that later (or elsewhere) spelt out, sometimes briefly and at others more expansively, that it is the biblical book of Psalms authored by King David that provides the authoritative material for such liturgical praise.

2 Concluding the Psalms

The text, which begins ישתבח שמך לעד מלכנו ('May your name be acclaimed forever, our King'), describes God with a wealth of epithets, and declares that he is worthy of all manner of eternal praises.[8] All the common liturgical words are employed to delineate such praises but there appears to be no specific mention of David or of the Psalms in the body of the benediction. All this unusual degree of uniformity would appear to indicate that this benediction was created, or at least championed, by the Babylonian geonic authorities, whose power and influence ranged widely until the eleventh century and left their permanent mark on all subsequent rites.[9]

Although there are examples of émigré communities from the land of Israel including the ישתבח שמך benediction in their prayer-books, as reflected in the evidence from the Cairo Genizah, their texts again largely conform to the norm. What is more interesting for our purposes is the earlier, and apparently

6 As in Maimonides, p. 193, *Persian PB*, p. 36, Solomon 'of Sijilmasa', p. 9 and *Tiklal*, 1.16r, and cited as erroneous by Abudraham, p. 60; see Wieder, *Formation*, 2.507–8 and Reif, *Problems*, p. 222.

7 MS CUL, T-S 10H2.1.

8 *Siddur OHT*, 1.244–46.

9 Elbogen, *Gottesdienst*, p. 86, *Ha-Tefillah*, pp. 67–68, *Liturgy*, p. 76.

more original, Palestinian version of this benediction that occurs in a brief format, similar to ישתבח שמך in its function and content.

This short formula begins with the words יהללוך ה׳ אלהינו וכל מעשיך ('Let all those whom you have created praise you, Lord, our God'). and the overall message is of God being worthily praised. There are, however, two important respects in which it differs from ישתבח שמך. As far as the final words of the benediction are concerned, in their simplest form they describe God as the recipient of praise, either by way of the single participle המשובח ('acclaimed') or with the use of the phrase המהולל (ברוב) התושבחות ('praised with much acclaim'). Perhaps more arrestingly, the first phrase, which refers to the praise offered by those whom God has created, is paralleled by a second phrase which invites those devoted to God to bless his name על שירי דויד בן ישי עבדך, the first word of which could mean 'together with', or 'for', or 'beyond', or 'through', and the remainder of which clearly alludes to the 'songs of David, son of Jesse, your servant'.[10] This יהללוך passage has survived in the concluding paragraph of the selection of Pss 113–18 known as *hallel* and used on various major and minor festivals, including the domestic *seder* service held on the first night of Passover. In that formulation, there is a greater plethora of words describing the praise of God but, more to the point here, there is no mention whatsoever of David or his songs.[11]

There are both Babylonian and Palestinian texts of the נשמת prayer and in at least one of the former there is a reference to David towards the end of the broader poetic section that cites Pss 119:175 and 35:10 with the words: דויד עבדך אמר לפניך ('David your servant recited before you').[12] Such a simple form of citation with regard to specific Psalms verses is not an uncommon phenomenon in Jewish liturgy, especially in supplicatory prayers.[13]

Before the נשמת prayer finally merges into the concluding ישתבח שמך paragraph, where, as in the examples cited above, no mention is made of David and his book of Psalms, there are two other sections, the first beginning בפי ישרים ('in the mouth(s) of the upright') and making reference to the various groups that praise God, while the second commences with the word ובמקהלות ('and in the

---

10 Mann, 'Genizah fragments', p. 279 (CUL, Add.3160.3); see also CUL T-S H2.115 and CUL T-S H2.123.

11 *Siddur OHT*, 2.897–98.

12 Wieder, *Formation*, 1.23, Fleischer, *Yoẓer*, p. 353 and CUL T-S 8H23.9. A similar phraseology, namely, שאמר לפניך דוד בן ישי עבדך משיחך ('which David, son of Jesse, your servant and messiah, recited before you') is used in the Romaniote rite cited by Goldschmidt, *On Jewish Liturgy*, p. 134, at a later point in this prayer where the other rites have simply דוד בן ישי.

13 This is discussed below in the section headed 'In the *seliḥot*'.

congregations') and alludes to the human obligation to praise God. Some shorter versions of the latter paragraph move ahead into ישתבח שמך without any additional content[14] while others – and they ultimately became the norm – use a number of expressions of praise to describe that human obligation and add to these words the phrase על (כל) דברי זמירות שירות ותושבחות דוד בן ישי.[15] That phrase undoubtedly refers to 'the words of hymns, songs and acclaims of David, son of Jesse' but what is not clear is whether all these forms of praise are being used to describe the book of Psalms, or only the final term תושבחות. Equally problematic is the meaning of the word על which could again mean, as discussed above with regard to the paragraph beginning יהללוך, 'together with', or 'for', or 'beyond', or 'through'. As far as the concluding eulogy is concerned, once the prayer has reached ישתבח שמך it appears to revert to type and the complex phraseology, summarized above as a description of God 'as recipient of praise and thanks, who 'chooses melodious hymns' (הבוחר בשירי זמרה) and whose existence is eternal', is again employed. As in the case of the introductory benediction, some versions of the concluding benediction make no reference to David and it is not clear whether all the terms used to describe the praises of God allude to the Psalms. If על conveys the sense of 'together with' or 'beyond', the allusion would then be to other praises too.[16]

3 Giving thanks

A collection of verses begins with the words הודו לי' קראו בשמו ('Give thanks to God, call on his name') and is derived from 1 Chr 16:8–36 (with parallels in Pss 105:1–15, 23–33 (= 8–22), 96:34–36 (=23–33) and 106:1, 47 and 48 (= 34–36). This passage, whether as an interruption or as a preface, is not to be found in the prayer-books of Sa'adya or Amram, or in the early Genizah texts, and an objection to such additions is made by Judah ben Barzilai al-Bargeloni in the late eleventh or early twelfth centuries.[17] If we check its original biblical context we find that the verse that immediately precedes it specifically mentions King David and the meaning would appear to be that these verses are the prayer that he instructed Assaf and his brothers to recite or, as in the commentary of David Qimḥi in the Rabbinic Bible, these verses are what he himself said as he instructed them on their musical duties in the Temple.

14 CUL T-S 6H6.6 and T-S 8H23.9; see Fleischer, *Eretz-Israel*, pp. 244–47 and Wieder, *Formation*, 1.263–64.
15 CUL T-S H15.15, T-S H18.18, T-S H18.25, T-S Ar.36.15; see also T-S 8H19.3.
16 As in CUL T-S 6H6.6.
17 *Sefer Ha-'Ittim*, p. 249.

According to Seder 'Olam Rabba, which is a combination of talmudic and post-talmudic traditions in the context of a Jewish chronology, the first fifteen verses were recited in the Temple to accompany the offering of the daily sacrifice.[18] In sum, although the evidence for its recitation is very late, this passage has a direct biblical connection with David and is related to the Temple worship in an undated rabbinic tradition.

4 David's blessing

In all the early medieval standard rites, there is another set of interruptions after the end of the Psalms selection and before the recitation of the ישתבח שמך benediction.[19] In this instance, they neither parallel nor include Psalms verses but consist of 1 Chr 29:10 – 13, Neh 9:6 – 11 and Exod 14:30 – 15.19, with a few additional single verses to follow the Song at the Sea. The first verse begins ויברך דויד את ה' לעיני כל הקהל ויאמר דויד ברוך אתה ה ('David then blessed God in the sight of the whole community and said You, God, are blessed'). There is no reference to this in any talmudic passage and Naṭronai seems to have only ברוך שאמר, a Psalms selection and, possibly, ישתבח.[20] The earliest authoritative prayer-book in which an interpolation is to be found is that of Sa'adya Gaon which includes only the Chronicles passage.[21]

Fleischer discusses the ויברך דוד section and suggests that it represents a use of various passages at the end of the Psalms selection in the same way that they were employed at the end of the *'amidah*, according to the Eretz Israel rite. He also cites a text from an old halakhic collection emanating from the Holy Land noting that it should be said only with the required *minyan* of ten adult males, suggesting that a reason for this might have been because it includes the phrase לעיני כל הקהל ('in the sight of the whole community').[22]

What we have then just demonstrated is that there is a degree of textual and liturgical fluidity between the end of the Psalms and the ישתבח שמך benediction, that the addition of the Chronicles passage detailing David's benediction seems to have been among the early additions, and that there was an interest in mark-

18 *Seder 'Olam Rabbah*, ed. Weinstock, 2.229 – 30.
19 *Vitry*, 1.64 and *Etz Hayyim*, 1.77; Roqeaḥ, 1.194 and 202 and Solomon of Worms, p. 68; Solomon 'of Sijilmasa', p. 10, Judah ben Yaqar, p. 7 and Abudraham, p. 63; *Maḥzor Roma*; and the Romaniote rite as cited by Goldschmidt, *On Jewish Liturgy*, p. 127.
20 Ginzberg, *Geonica*, 2.116.
21 Davidson/Assaf/Joel, *Siddur RSG*, p. 33.
22 Fleischer, *Eretz-Israel*, pp. 90 – 92.

ing the end of the Psalms collection in a manner other than by the use of the ישתבח שמך benediction.

5 In the *'amidah*

As I have indicated elsewhere, the fourteenth benediction of the *'amidah*, on the topic of Jerusalem, varies in content in the earliest prayer-books and manuscripts witnesses. The simplest form (often beginning with the word רחם, 'show mercy') prays for God's merciful return to Jerusalem and its physical restoration while other versions make more complex references to the Jewish people, the worshippers, the city and the Temple. The nature of the restoration also takes different forms, ranging from nothing more than a speedy, historical event to detailed eschatological descriptions of joyful returns and permanent arrangements. The most significant and earliest variation between the most common Palestinian and Babylonian rites is of course the matter of the place to be accorded to the topic of the davidic dynasty. The former generally includes the topic in the Jerusalem benediction, sometimes with a specific reference to the messianic element, and one of the divine epithets in its concluding doxology may be 'God of David' (אלהי דוד). The Babylonian rite, which by the twelfth and thirteenth centuries had come to dominate many aspects of the Jewish liturgical practice, may also allude briefly to the davidic dynasty in this benediction but devotes the whole of the next one to the subject.[23] The earliest detailed text is the one cited in the Talmud Yerushalmi for individual use on the Fast of the Ninth of Av, marking the loss of Jerusalem and the Temple. If the text, as we have inherited it almost two millennia later, is sound, it had no mention at all of the davidic dynasty.[24]

In what thus became the fifteenth *'amidah* benediction in the numerous medieval rites, the entreaty is for the re-establishment of a powerful and successful davidic dynasty. According to some versions, such an entreaty is followed by a request for divine succour, that subject, and not the davidic dynasty itself, forming the core element of the eulogy.[25] When and why this division into two benedictions occurred is a controversial point. It appears to have taken place no earlier than late third-century Babylon.[26] It may conceivably also have been one of the practices in the land of Israel but is not reflected in the Talmud Yerushalmi,

---

23 Reif, *Problems*, pp. 131–35 and 153–55.

24 *y. Ber.* 4.3 (8a).

25 Luger, *Amidah*, pp. 159–65; Ehrlich, *Weekday Amidah*, pp. 201–6.

26 This assumes that we can rely on the originality and historical authenticity of a statement cited in the name of Rabba bar Shila in *b. Pesaḥ.* 117b.

much of the midrashic and piyyuṭic literature, or a proportion of the early Genizah fragments emanating from the Holy Land. Elbogen regards it as a sop to the davidic origins of the Exilarch in Babylon but Heinemann in his Hebrew edition of Elbogen argues against clear dating or definitive identification of the rationale.[27] There is even a controversial view that links the benediction with the theology of the Jewish-Christians.[28]

There are four other instances of David's appearance in the *'amidah* that deserve attention, the first of them occurring in the abbreviated form of the daily *'amidah* sanctioned for use by the talmudic authorities in special emergencies when there is insufficient time for the whole prayer. In that abbreviation, known as הביננו ('grant us understanding') after its opening word, the middle benedictions are each reduced in size to one phrase, and the reduction recorded in the Babylonian Talmud for the fifteenth benediction on the subject of the davidic dynasty reads ובצמיחת קרן לדוד עבדך ובעריכת נר לבן-ישי משיחך ('through a flourishing existence for David your servant and a bright future for the son of Jesse your Messiah'). It should, however, immediately be countered that the version that appears in the Talmud Yerushalmi has, at least in some textual versions, a reference to the rebuilding of Jerusalem but not to the davidic dynasty.[29]

In the *qedushah* benediction for New Year and the Day of Atonement, there is also a custom to include some paragraphs, each beginning with the word ובכן ('So therefore'), that refer to the joyous events that will accompany the establishment of the divine kingdom throughout the world. One of these looks forward to the restoration of happiness to the land of Israel and joy to the city of Jerusalem, as well as to the successful davidic dynasty, again described as צמיחת קרן לדוד עבדך ובעריכת נר לבן-ישי משיחך.[30] Here, too, however, it has to be acknowledged that the talmudic references to the *qedushah* prayer on New Year make no mention of these paragraphs and that they were apparently unknown to the Babylonian authorities of the geonic period, being introduced only later. Maimonides in the twelfth century mentions them as an optional custom.[31]

Another paragraph beginning ובכן also occurs in the longer form of the *qedushah* benediction that is recited on the same two festivals during the prayer leader's repetition of the *'amidah*. The whole phrase is ובכן יתקדש שמך and the

---

27 Elbogen, *Gottesdienst*, pp. 39–41, *Ha-Tefillah*, pp. 29–32, *Liturgy*, pp. 34–37.

28 Liebes, 'Mazmiaḥ', assessed by Luger, *Amidah*, pp. 162–64.

29 Baer, p. 108; *b. Ber.* 29a and *y. Ber.* 4.3 (8a).

30 Baer, pp. 384–86; Goldschmidt, *Maḥzor* 1.227.

31 *m. Roš. Haš.* 4.5; *t. Roš. Haš.* 4.5; *y. Roš. Haš.* 4.6 (59c); Maimonides, p. 209; Wieder, *Formation*, 1.53.

hope is expressed that God's holy name should be sanctified through Israel his people, Jerusalem his city, Zion his habitation, the davidic kingdom and the Temple (על ישראל עמך ועל ירושלים עירך ועל ציון משכן כבודך ועל מלכות בית דוד משיחך ועל מכונך והיכלך). Although some of the phraseology may belong to the early liturgical poetry, the whole paragraph with these various constituent parts is not attested until about the eleventh century. Even more significantly, there are textual variations in the liturgical manuscripts, so that there is sometimes no mention of the davidic dynasty.[32]

The fourth case concerns the יעלה ויבא prayer, inserted in the festival *'amidah* to mark the special status of the day in the matter of God's remembrance of Israel. The prayer (in its various forms) is for such remembrance to take account of the patriarchs, the people, the holy city of Jerusalem, the Temple site and, of special importance here, the davidic messiah (זכרון משיח בן דוד עבדך). Although Elbogen argues that its original context may have been in the remembrance verses (זכרונות) of the *musaf* service on New Year in the period of the first composition of liturgical poetry, the earliest textual witness to this prayer is in the post-talmudic tractate Soferim where only the opening words are mentioned.[33] The critical edition of the prayer-book of Sa'adya Gaon includes versions of the text for the New Month, as well as for Passover and New Year but there is no consistency about whether the davidic dynasty is mentioned, while the text recorded by Maimonides includes such a reference. This, and the absence of the topic in Palestinian Genizah versions, would perhaps indicate that the matter was not definitively resolved until well into the post-geonic period. [34]

On the basis of all this complicated evidence, it may be concluded that not all early rabbinic sources made a point of giving a central place to the davidic dynasty in the *'amidah* but that there was a broader tendency during the geonic period to pay more attention to it. This appears to have been accompanied by the development and adoption of more fanciful futuristic notions. The tendency strengthened further in the early medieval period.

---

32 Goldschmidt, *Maḥzor*, 1.224. The linguistic data is available from Ma'agarim, the Academy of Hebrew Language's project for a historical dictionary of Hebrew, to which I am indebted here and elsewhere in this article.

33 Elbogen, *Gottesdienst*, p. 57, *Ha-Tefillah*, p. 44, *Liturgy*, p. 51; *Soferim*, ed. Higger, pp. 327, 333.

34 Davidson/Assaf/Joel, *Siddur RSG*, pp. 103, 150, 223; Maimonides, pp. 200–201; Fleischer, *Eretz-Israel*, p. 96 and Wieder, *Formation*, 2.574; MSS CUL T-S 8H16.1 and T-S 10H4.1.

6 In the *hafṭarah* benedictions

The *'amidah* benediction just discussed has a close parallel in the third of the four benedictions recited after the prophetic reading in the synagogue on sabbaths, festivals and fasts. It constitutes an entreaty to God to bring about the messianic age with the attendant restoration of the davidic dynasty. The earliest reference to it occurs in a statement made in the name of the fourth-century teacher, Rabba bar Shila, to the effect that the concluding eulogy should be מצמיח קרן ישועה in the *'amidah* benediction and מגן דוד in the *hafṭarah* benediction.[35] Not unexpectedly, there is a late midrash that explains that this represents a kind of consolation prize to King David. Having invited a temptation to prove himself capable of withstanding it, and therefore to be worthy, like Abraham, of having a benediction named for him (מגן אברהם), he failed the test and had to be satisfied with a *hafṭarah* benediction – obviously an *ex post facto* explanation, given the time difference between the talmudic remark and the midrashic exegesis.[36]

What is intriguing about the textual history of this *hafṭarah* benediction is that there are two surviving versions, with a somewhat unusual distribution of occurrence among the standard rites. One version follows the *'amidah* benediction almost word for word, occurring in the prayer-book of Sa'adya Gaon as צמח דוד עתה תצמיח וקרנו תרום בישועתך ('Now make the offspring of David flourish and raise his head high by granting your succour').[37] The message here is simple, expressing a hope for the ultimate salvation as marked by the return of the davidic kingdom, and the language, while poetic and figurative, is as brief and as direct as many prophetic and psalmic verses. This version is followed, with minor variations, by Amram Gaon (with manuscript variation of course), Maimonides, Solomon b. Nathan 'of Sijilmasa' and the traditional Yemenite liturgy (*baladi*). It also occurs as one option in the liturgical commentary of Judah b. Yaqar, the teacher of Naḥmanides in Spain.[38] The concluding eulogy, as talmudically mandated for the *hafṭarah* benediction (and noted by Rabba bar Shila, as cited above), is מגן דוד, which lays emphasis on the specific davidic kingdom, rather than on the more general divine salvation.

The second version first appears in the post-talmudic tractate Soferim and begins:

---

35 As cited above in n. 49.

36 *Midrasch Tehillim*, f. 77v.

37 Davidson/Assaf/Joel, *Siddur RSG*, p. 367.

38 *SRAmram*, ed. Goldschmidt, p. 78 and ed. Kronholm, Hebrew section, p. 22; Maimonides, p. 216; Solomon 'of Sijilmasa', p. 208; *Tiklal*, 1.139v; Judah ben Yaqar, 1.109.

> שמחנו ה' אלהינו באליהו הנביא עבדך ובמלכות בית דוד משיחך במהרה יבא ויגל לבינו ועל כסאו לא ישב זר ולא ינחלו עוד אחרים את כבודו כי בשם קדשך נשבעת לו שלא תכבה נרו לעולם
>
> Bring us the joyful return of your servant Elijah the prophet, and of the royal house of David, your messiah. May he arrive swiftly and to our great joy. Let no imposter occupy his throne and may alien powers never again usurp his glory, for you pledged to him by your sacred name that his flame would never be extinguished.

Soferim also has an additional section calling on salvation for Judah and security for Israel, with another reference to the divine promise.[39] Here the language is more recognizably that of early rabbinic liturgy and the nature of the expected messianic developments is spelt out in more detail. There is also a powerful polemic against attempts on the part of some theological opponents to aggregate to their own faith the davidic and messianic concepts and an allusion to a divine promise recorded in Ps 132:10–13 that the davidic dynasty would be eternal.

This alternative version, without the appendage and with some minor textual tinkering, is to be found in the commentary of Judah b. Yaqar (as an alternative), in Abudraham, in *Maḥzor Vitry* and the *'Es Ḥayyim* of Jacob b. Judah of London, and generally in subsequent Romaniote, Ashkenazi, Sefardi and Italian prayer-books.[40] Another surprising piece of evidence is that, contrary to the talmudic ruling, the eulogy reads מצמיח קרן ישועה in the Soferim text. It has been suggested that an early phraseology in this conclusion to the benediction made reference to both salvation and the davidic kingdom.[41] In that case it was either itself an expansion to give central significance to both topics or was the original format that came to be abbreviated to take account of more contemporary religious sensitivities or historical realities. What is clear is that some texts stress the davidic kingdom while others opt for the broader notion of salvation.

7 In the Grace after Meals

Given its content, technical format and fairly prominent status in the tannaitic literature, this piece of the daily liturgy probably belongs to the earliest stages of Jewish liturgical development in the late Second Temple period and the

---

39 *Soferim*, ed. Higger, pp. 247–48.

40 Judah ben Yaqar, 1.109–10; Abudraham, p. 173; *Vitry*, 1.158; *Etz Ḥayyim*, 1.56; MSS CUL Add.541, f. 120v and Add.1204, f. 73v; Romaniote rite as cited by Goldschmidt, *On Jewish Liturgy*, p. 135; Luzzatto, *Maḥzor*, 1.107–8, Baer, p. 227, Gaster, *Book of Prayer*, 1.111, and *Kavvanat Ha-Lev Ha-Shalem*, *Daily Prayers*, p. 495.

41 Luger, *Amidah*, pp. 163–64; see also Ehrlich, *Weekday Amidah*, p. 205.

immediate post-destruction decades and is therefore deserving of close consideration in the present discussion. Bearing in mind the central concerns of early rabbinic theology, and the historical events that underlie some of them, it is not surprising to find that the themes of God the Provider, the divine gift of the land of Israel, and the special status of the city of Jerusalem are of major concern to the formulators of the post-prandial grace.[42] The topic of Jerusalem is the theme of the third section (and benediction) of the rabbinic grace and there are close parallels with the earliest and/or simplest formats of the Jerusalem benediction included in the *'amidah* and mentioned above.[43] Talmudic authority lays it down that one's obligation in respect of this prayer has not been met unless one has mentioned the davidic dynasty (בית דוד), giving the distinct impression (as in the view cited in the name of R. Ilai) that at least some circles might here have made reference to Jerusalem and the holy site without necessarily expanding on the davidic connection.[44]

Following the talmudic requirement just noted, all versions of the grace include at least a brief reference to the davidic dynasty and the form that this takes in the prayer-book of Sa'adya Gaon is in the sentence ומלכות בית דויד תחזיר למקומה בימינו ('Restore the royal house of David to its rightful place in our days').[45] Some prayer-books expand on the messianic theme arising out of the davidic connection (as in מלכות בית דוד משיחך; 'the royal house of David, your Messiah'), while others include the rebuilding of Jerusalem and the restoration of the Temple service.[46] In the Italian rite, the davidic theme becomes wholly messianic and eschatological with an expansion into the sentence ויבא אליהו הנביא ומשיח בן דוד עבדך במהרה בימינו ויביאו לנו שמועה טובה מארץ מרחק ('May Elijah the Prophet and the messianic offspring of David, your servant, arrive swiftly in our days and bring us good tidings from a faraway land'). Joy at the city's reconstruction, as well as independence, security and the secure supply of future sustenance, are among the subjects that occupy the attention of other formulators within the context of the Jerusalem benediction in its broader liturgical manifestations.[47] All in all, the davidic theme often hovers in the background and,

---

42 *b. Ber.* 48b; *y. Ber.* 7.1 (11a).
43 Heinemann, *Prayer*, pp. 288–91.
44 *b. Ber.* 48b–49a; *y. Ber.* 1.5 (3d).
45 Davidson/Assaf/Joel, *Siddur RSG*, p. 102.
46 Maimonides, p. 216; *Persian PB*, p. 213; Solomon 'of Sijilmasa', p. 120; *SRAmram*, p. 45; *Vitry*, 1.52; and *Etz Ḥayyim*, 1.167.
47 For details see Davidson/Assaf/Joel, *Siddur RSG*, pp. 151–52; Elbogen, *Gottesdienst*, pp. 132–40, *Ha-Tefillah*, pp. 100–105, *Liturgy*, pp. 111–17; Mann, 'Genizah fragments', pp. 325–32; Jacobson, *Nethiv*, 4.14–27; and Fleischer, *Eretz-Israel*, pp. 93–159.

when it is later expanded, it tends to stress the new and better world at the end of time, while the Jerusalem theme may move off into political, social and cultic, as well as messianic themes.

8 In the *qedushah*

Modern views on the origins of the *qedushah* recited at the repetition of the *'amidah* opt for its existence, in at least a simple format, with the verses from Isa 6:3 (קדוש קדוש קדוש) and Ezek 3:12 (ברוך כבוד ה') at its centre, perhaps soon followed by Ps 146:10 (ימלוך ה' לעולם) or Exod 15:18 (ה' ימלוך לעולם), from talmudic times. Although forms of joint human-angelic praise from pre-Christian times are already attested at Qumran, and the genre was apparently adopted and expanded among mystical circles in the land of Israel, there is no doubt that by the geonic period it had, perhaps not without considerable controversy, found more earnest champions for its adoption and broader use within the Babylonian centres and somehow come to enjoy less popularity in the homeland. Apparently during the late geonic period, various forms were composed and found places in the liturgy so that by the time that the standard rites were taking shape in about the twelfth century there was considerable variation about which version was to be used on which occasion.[48] The text that contains a reference to David is to be found in the paragraph that begins ממקומך מלכנו תופיע ('From your place, our King, make an appearance') and constitutes a response to the recitation of Ezek 3:12 and a preface to the recitation of Ps 146:10. In the prayer-books of Sa'adya Gaon, Amram Gaon, Maimonides, Solomon b. Nathan 'of Sijilmasa' and the Yemenite rite, it is to be used at the daily morning service, while in *Maḥzor Vitry* and the *'Eṣ Ḥayyim* of Jacob b. Judah of London it occurs specifically in the sabbath morning service and in the Romaniote rite in the sabbath *musaf.*[49] There are some rites, such as the Italian, in which it appears in neither.

The poetic phrase that occurs towards the end of that ממקומך paragraph alludes to the future kingdom of God, expressing the hope, as in the text of Sa'adya Gaon, ועינינו תראינה במלכות עוזך כאמור על ידי דויד משיח צדקך ימלוך ('may our eyes

48 Elbogen, *Gottesdienst*, pp. 61–67, *Ha-Tefillah*, pp. 47–54, *Liturgy*, pp. 54–62; Idelsohn, *Liturgy*, pp. 94–99; Jacobson, *Nethiv*, 1.233–35; Wieder, *Formation*, 1.361–67; Fleischer, *Qedusha*; and Chazon, 'Qedushah liturgy'.

49 Davidson/Assaf/Joel, *Siddur RSG*, pp. 38–39; *SRAmram*, ed. Goldschmidt, p. 32; ed. Hedegård, Hebrew section, p. 47; Maimonides, p. 202; Solomon 'of Sijilmasa', p. 19; *Tiklal*, pp. 43v–44r; *Vitry*, 1.156 and *Etz Ḥayyim*, 1.93; Romaniote rite as cited by Goldschmidt, *On Jewish Liturgy*, p. 136. See also *Persian PB*, p. 67.

behold your powerful kingdom, as it is said by David, your true messiah, God will reign'). Among the textual variants are במלכותך for במלכות עוזך; כדבר האמור for כאמור; the insertion of בשירי עוזך or בשירי קדשך after האמור; מפי דוד for על ידי דוד or על יד דוד; עבדך משיח צדקך for משיח צדקך. The role of David here is primarily as the composer of one particular Psalms verse and the kingdom that is mentioned is described as that of God and not that of the davidic dynasty. David is, however, also given his messianic title, the use of the word צדקך being similar to that of the word צדק in the *hafṭarah* benedictions with reference to the 'true prophets' (נביאי אמת וצדק).

9 In the *qiddush ha-levanah*

A passage in the Babylonian Talmud extols the virtues of those who bless God for the gift of the moon and records the text of the required benediction (perhaps Babylonian and not Palestinian) in which the consistency and reliability of the calendrical cycles in general and the phases of the moon in particular are acknowledged.[50] This text is substantially what is used by Sa'adya Gaon, with the concluding eulogy מחדש ראשי חדשים, and by Maimonides, the Persian rite and Solomon b. Nathan 'of Sijilmasa' with the concluding doxology מחדש חדשים.[51] The version of the benediction that appears in the geonic period in Soferim has some minor variations and the concluding doxology is מקדש ישראל וראשי חדשים, and not מחדש חדשים. It also records the additional use of three texts that bless God as the creator using four different epithets, that mention the impossibility of touching the moon and the hope that Israel's enemies will find it equally impossible to touch them, and that cite the verse from Exod 15:16 (תפל עליהם). There are also exclamations calling for good fortune and wishing the liturgical participants peace.[52] With some variation in order, and the two-word rather than the longer conclusion, this is essentially the format that occurs in the prayer-books of Amram Gaon, Yemenite *baladi*, and *Maḥzor Vitry*.[53]

All the remaining parts of this liturgy, whether in the form of Psalms, or special entreaties, or quotations from the relevant talmudic literature, would appear

---

50 *b. Sanh.* 42a, and note the simpler version ascribed there to the practice of the land of Israel.

51 Davidson/Assaf/Joel, *Siddur RSG*, p. 91; Maimonides, *Mishneh Torah*, *Sefer Ahavah*, *Hilkhot Berakhot* 10.16; *Persian PB*, pp. 209–10; Solomon 'of Sijilmasa', p. 126.

52 *Soferim*, ed. Higger, pp. 337–40.

53 *SRAmram*, ed. Goldschmidt, p. 90; *Tiklal*, pp. 158v–60r; *Vitry*, p. 183.

to have been added from about the thirteenth century onwards.[54] One of these additions specifically concerns us here and is generally recited after the texts that appear in Soferim and the sources that follow the version recorded in that tractate, as listed above. It is the sentence דוד מלך ישראל חי וקים ('David, King of Israel, is present and alive'). This originates in *b. Roš Haš.* 25a where it is reported that R. Judah asked R. Ḥiyya to declare the arrival of the new moon and to send him a message using these five words when this had been done. There the context is the declaration of the new moon, and not the blessing on seeing it more clearly a few days later. The use of the sentence about David appears to be linked to the verses in Ps 89:36–38 which promise that the davidic dynasty will be as stable as the sun and moon. Perhaps, therefore, a political point was being made as well as a religious one in the original context. In that case the introduction of the sentence into the liturgy for the appreciation of the moon may also have wished to link the two.

Given that the other additions are probably to be ascribed to the kabbalists, it would not be unreasonable to suggest a similar ascription here. The earliest source for it is Baḥya b. Asher, in his pentateuchal commentary on Gen 38:29, who is undoubtedly offering a kabbalistic interpretation.[55] As Scholem has explained, David is important to the mystics because he, with the three patriarchs, Abraham, Isaac and Jacob, constitute the four legs of the throne of the *merkavah*, or mystical chariot. David is the founder of the kingship of Israel, the מלכות, the last of the mystical Sefirot that represent the ten divine aspects and emanations, and the messiah receives a special emanation from the Sefirah מלכות. Also discussed by the kabbalists is the messianic soul of David, its possible migrations and its place in the gradual manifestation of the redemption.[56] In view of these links between the divine power, the cosmos, the moon and the messianic son of David, the use of the talmudic statement in this liturgical context must have represented a contribution to the ongoing development towards the ultimate redemption. Just as the redemption will see the return of the moon's pristine power, so will it bring the restoration of the original glory of the davidic dynasty.

---

54 For full text and useful summaries of the content, see Baer, pp. 337–39 and Jacobson, *Nethiv*, 3.336–48.

55 Baḥya, *Bi'ur*, ed. Chavel, 1.316–19.

56 Scholem, *Kabbalah*, pp. 111, 167 and 334.

10 In a daily supplication

The idea of reciting what were originally private supplications (תחנונים) after the *'amidah* goes back to the talmudic period but has developed extensively since then. Not only have many biblical passages, especially from Psalms, been added but the whole supplicatory act has been ritualized and, in common with so many other Jewish prayers, been changed from the personal to the communal. This continuous evolution has meant that the various rites, even as they became standardized in the high Middle Ages and did retain some common factors, tended to express themselves in different ways in this liturgical context. The choice, length, and order of the verses differed from community to community, as well as from rite to rite, and various customs were adopted with regard to the practice of the ritual.[57]

From about the late seventeenth century, the Ashkenazi communities introduced into one of the final sections of the supplicatory prayers the recitation of the verse from 2 Sam 24:14.[58] This verse begins ויאמר דוד אל גד and describes David's contrition after having angered God by conducting a census of the people. It is suitable for inclusion here primarily because of the subject matter and because of the use of the stem נפל 'fall' which recalls the Hebrew for supplication נפילת אפים 'falling on the face', which was the original physical act before it was altered to something more symbolic and less dramatic. Unless the kabbalists, who probably introduced this use of the verse, had something more mystical in mind, it seems that it is the context and not the specific reference to David that is relevant here.[59]

11 In the *seliḥot*

In the penitential prayers (סליחות) that are recited daily before New Year, as well as during the Ten Days of Repentance between New Year and the Day of Atonement, and on fast-days, a litany is often used which requests that God should answer the worshipper of today as he did those heroes of Jewish history who appealed to him in the past. The litany is repeated in connection with each of these heroes. The precise timing, choice of language, phraseology and historical coverage vary from age to

---

57 Elbogen, *Gottesdienst*, pp. 73–81, *Ha-Tefillah*, pp. 58–64, *Liturgy*, pp. 66–72; Idelsohn, *Liturgy*, pp. 110–13; Jacobson, *Nethiv*, 1.345–56.

58 Compare *Shabbethai*, 2.195 with Baer, p. 116 (where the reference to רמ"ע surely requires correction).

59 Even among the kabbalists, there appears to have been some controversy about the introduction of the verse; see the additional editorial notes with Hebrew pagination that follow Shabbethai's prayer-book text, *Shabbethai*, 2.כו.

age, and from rite to rite, but they are all based on the mishnaic passage that records the ceremony and liturgy that was apparently customary in the Jewish homeland some two thousand years ago. Examples of the liturgical formulation that is of special significance for this discussion are the following:

מי שענה לדוד ולשלמה בנו בירושלים הוא יעננו
ענית לדוד ושלמה בירושלם עננו
דעני לדוד ולשלמה בנו בירושלם ענינן

In each of these examples, God is being asked to answer the penitents, as he answered David and Solomon in Jerusalem.[60]

The prototype for this is in *m. Ta'anit* 2.2–4 which lays down the liturgy for the special first three and latter seven fasts decreed on the occasion of droughts, in which six benedictions are added to the usual eighteen of the *'amidah*. Having reported the custom to add six benedictions, the Mishnah later lists seven benedictions, the last of which is:

מי שענה את דוד ואת שלמה בנו בירושלים הוא יענה אתכם וישמע בקול צעקתכם היום הזה. בא"י המרחם על הארץ

May the One who answered David and Solomon his son in Jerusalem answer you and hear the sound of your cry on this day. You are blessed, God, merciful to the land.

A problem of interpretation arises because the seven listed here do not match the six enumerated earlier. What is more, the reference to David and Solomon should undoubtedly come before the one to Jonah since all the others are in chronological order. Tosefta does not assist us since it has no specific benedictions. Talmud Yerushalmi deals with the matter of the chronology by arguing that the concluding eulogy מרחם על הארץ ('merciful to the land') is a more appropriate (that is, less depressing) phrase with which to end the series of benedictions than the sixth one, העונה בעת צרה ('who responds in times of trouble').[61] Talmud Bavli argues that 'seventh' means 'the seventh of the longer benedictions' of the *'amidah* (*ge'ulah*) into which are incorporated the additions for the special fasts.[62] This means to say that the reference to six in the earlier mishnah alluded to the six *additional* benedictions. That mishnah did not count the *ge'ulah* benediction as one of them, while this one does. It is obviously tempting to explain the chronological and numerical discrepancies as arising out of a later addition of the

---

60 Goldschmidt, *Maḥzor* 2.55.
61 *y. Ta'an.* 2.9 (65d).
62 *b. Ta'an* 16b; see Malter, *Treatise*, pp. 208, 228–30.

davidic reference when there was a greater interest in stressing the importance of the davidic dynasty. This indeed was already suggested by Viktor Aptowitzer in 1927[63] and although Albeck rejects the suggestion, his argument against is somewhat weak and even circular. It amounts to saying that it could not have originally been six because, without the reference to David, it would then have been five, very much a begging of the question![64]

David's name is also used elsewhere in the *seliḥot* when references are made to verses in the Psalms that are particularly appropriate to the subjects of penitence and forgiveness. Sa'adya Gaon, for example, in his set of *seliḥot* for Yom Kippur uses the introductory phrase דוד משיח צדקך אמר לפניך ('David your true Messiah recited before you'), before then citing a concatenation of Psalms verses including 130:3, 65:4, 51:9, 103:3–5, 78:38, 19:13, often changing the singular to the plural, and interpolating among these some liturgical phrases.[65] In the *seliḥot* for the Ten Days of Repentance according to the Ashkenazi rite, David is dubbed משיח צדקך (without the name דוד) but in its *seliḥot* for Yom Kippur he is given the simpler nomenclature of דוד עבדך when citing the verse from Ps 19:13 (שגיאות מי יבין מנסתרות נקני).[66] There are also numerous other examples, such as in the Sefardi rite.[67] In liturgical terms, David is being employed not only as the author of the most suitable penitential poetry but also as one who is known as an expert in achieving forgiveness.

Definitions of הבוחר and תושבחות

It will be recalled that the concluding eulogy for the benediction recited after the morning selection of psalms included the phrase הבוחר בשירי זמרה and that its meaning and message did not appear to be unambiguously clear. What is required at this stage of our discussion is a survey of some similar rabbinic phrases and an assessment of what they are attempting to convey, which may conceivably clarify the linguistic significance of this occurrence and help us reach some broader conclusions about how it relates to the figure of David.

The stem בחר in the Hebrew Bible is already used to describe God's special relationship with Israel (whole and part), the royal dynasty, Jerusalem, the Temple, the priesthood and Abraham, the patriarch. All these have a special sta-

63 Aptowitzer, *Parteipolitik*, pp. 53–54.
64 Albeck, *Mishnah*, 2.492–93.
65 Davidson/Assaf/Joel, *Siddur RSG*, p. 308.
66 Rosenfeld, *Selichot*, p. 18; Goldschmidt, *Maḥzor*, 2.52.
67 Gaster, 2.4, 13–17; and *Kavvanat Ha-Lev, New Year*, pp. 46, 67, 70–71, 74.

tus and function.[68] At Qumran too, there are examples from pre-Christian times of the liturgical use of the phrase אשר בחר בנו.[69] The earliest liturgical use of the term הבוחר in rabbinic literature occurs in the Talmud Yerushalmi's description of the benedictions recited by the High Priest on Yom Kippur where the subjects of Israel, the Temple and the priesthood are joined by the Torah, all of them again enjoying an exceptional theological prestige.[70] Both the *qiddush* for sabbath and festivals and the talmudic benediction for studying Torah incorporate this theological notion of בחירה into various parts of their wording.[71] What appears to happen in the geonic period is that the term is employed in a number of eulogies in a special way that not only includes the institutions already enjoying the prestige just noted but applies it to others. In the earliest known form of the *hafṭarah* benedictions, it adds Moses and the Prophets to the Torah and Israel[72] and there are three other benedictions that are documented in Genizah manuscripts but did not survive in active liturgical use into the medieval period.

The first of these three precedes the recitation of the second chapter of Mishnah *Shabbat* (במה מדליקין) and reads:

> ב[ר]וך [אתה] יוי אלהינו מלך [ה]עולם אשר בחר בח[כמים] ותלמידיהם [ונת]ן להם תורה מהר סיני [על ידי] משה רבנו ו[צו]ה אתם לקרא בתורה במשנָה ב[ת]למוד בהלכה לקנות חיי שני עולמים. ובחר במשה רבנו מכל הנ[בי]אים ודבר עמו פנים בפנים שנ׳ פה אל פה אדבר בו וג׳ ואחריו בחר [ביהו]שע תלמידו ושב[עים] [ז]קנים וחכמים ותלמידיהם ו[צוה א]תם בשמירות [שב]ת ובהדלקת הנר שלשבת [במה] מדליקין וג׳
>
> You are praised, Lord, our God, universal king, for having chosen the scholars and their students, given them the Torah at Mount Sinai by the hands of Moses our teacher, and instructed them to study Torah, Mishnah, Talmud and Halakhah, in order to be granted life in both worlds. And for having chosen Moses out teacher above all the prophets and spoken to him face to face as the verse [Num 12:8] has it 'Mouth to mouth I would speak with him etc.', and then later having chosen Joshua his student and the seventy elders and the scholars and their students and having instructed them about sabbath observances and lighting the sabbath lamp: *With what may one kindle* etc.[73]

---

68 *TDOT*, 2.73–87. On the festival of *Sukkot*, David is also one of the *ushpizin* ('guests'), as well as occurring in the *hosha'anot* and the grace after meals; see Baer, pp. 381 and 561, but these are late usages.

69 E. g. 4Q503, 24 7 9 and 4Q508 4 2; see Baillet, *DJD* 7.111 and 180.

70 *y. Yoma* 7.1 (44b).

71 b. *Ber.* 11b and Davidson/Assaf/Joel, *Siddur RSG*, pp. 115 and 135. For some of the linguistic data used here and in connection with the word ת(ו)שבחות, I am again indebted to the Ma'agarim Project (see n. 55 above).

72 *Soferim*, ed. Higger, pp. 244–45.

73 CUL, T-S NS 299.150, first published by Wieder in *Sinai* 82 (1978), pp. 197–221 and reprinted in his *Formation*, 1.323–47. See also Reif, *Jewish Prayer Texts*, pp. 106–14.

This benediction is clearly being used to link the authority of Moses and the Pentateuch, through Joshua and the elders, with that of the rabbis and their pupils in the particular matter of their interpretation of the sabbath laws concerning fire. It uses the stem בחר for all of them in order to indicate that they all have this special status.

In a second example, the special status is granted to the books of the hagiographa so that their reading is accompanied by a similar benediction:

> ברוך אתה ה׳ אלהינו מלך העולם אשר בחר בכתבי הקדש טוב אתה ומטיב למדני חוקיך ברוך אתה ה׳ למדני חוקיך
>
> You are praised, Lord, our God, universal king, for having chosen the books of the hagiographa. You are the source of all goodness. Teach us your laws. You are praised, Lord, teach us your laws.[74]

The third example moves nearer to our current topic of interest and deals specifically with the recitation of David's book of Psalms:

> ב אתה י אלהנו מלך העולם אשר בחר בדוד עבדו ורצה בתהלתו ובשירי קדשו להללו לשבחו ולפארו על רוב גבורותיו כל הימים ב אתה י מצמיח ישועה שלימה קרובה לעמו ישראל מנחם ציון ובנה ירושלם
>
> You are praised, Lord, our God, universal king, for having chosen David as the divine servant, and having chosen his psalms and sacred hymns in order to praise, laud and glorify God's many outstanding acts on all occasions. You are praised, Lord, as the One who, as the comforter of Zion and the rebuilder of Jerusalem, will bring to his people Israel a speedy, complete and flourishing salvation.[75]

What emerges from the evidence just cited is that the stem בחר is being used as a technical term to describe a special status – one that carries authority, canonicity and the right to be recognized as such within a formal rabbinic benediction. It is extended from Moses and the Torah to the rabbinic teachers and their compositions. The question now to be answered is whether this has relevance for our understanding of the phrase הבוחר בשירי זמרה at the conclusion of a liturgical selection of psalmic literature. Given what has just been demonstrated, it seems perfectly reasonable to propose that such a selection is being accorded the authoritative status enjoyed by others institutions that God chooses (בוחר). The items of biblical literature being recited in the liturgy deserve to be recognized as liturgically institutionalized not so much, in this context, because they are

---

74 CUL Or.1080 3.52, cited by Fleischer, *Eretz-Israel*, p. 187, n. 141.

75 CUL T-S NS 155.1; see Wieder, *Formation*, 1.243–44, also citing similar benedictions for New Year in T-S H8.80, for Tabernacles in T-S NS 197.33 and for the sabbath in T-S NS 271.16. See also Reif, *Jewish Prayer Texts*, pp. 201–10.

from scripture, but because they have been sanctioned as such by rabbinic tradition. In addition, Adiel Kadari has recently argued that the notion of בחירה in the Torah benedictions not only includes an aspect of rabbinic theology but also reflects the inclusivist idea of according a special status to all those who are involved in the formal ritual of reading scripture. Perhaps this also applies to the lost benedictions just noted.[76]

As far as the word ת(ו)שבחות, and terms deriving from the same stem, are concerned, it was noted earlier that they occur either with or without the stems שיר and זמר, both within the body of the benediction and in its concluding eulogy. Since it is on a number of occasions not spelt out that such praises are specifically from David's book of Psalms, we are left with a number of possible interpretations. Either there was a hesitation about identifying the praises as exclusively from the Psalms, or a preference for stressing that they were chosen by rabbinic authority for this context. Another possibility is that there was a wish to leave open the possibility that such praises could also refer to other psalmic or hymnic materials not derived from the book of Psalms. In the morning *ge'ulah* benediction, for instance, the Song at the Sea (Exod 15) is identified as זמירות שירות ותושבחות and the stems also occur with reference to the *qedushah* recitation derived from Isaiah and Ezekiel.[77]

Summary of specific findings

We are now in a position to summarize what has been demonstrated by the textual evidence. The recitation of a selection of consecutive chapters from the book of Psalms is preceded and followed by specially composed benedictions (ברוך שאמר and ישתבח) that acknowledge God's worthiness of such praises. Depending on the versions, God may also be thanked for authorizing such praises, or specific reference may be made to the Psalms of David, but these elements are by no means ubiquitous. In the post-geonic period, a medley of verses (הודו) from Chronicles and Psalms is added either before or after the benediction introducing the consecutive collection of Psalms chapters. The medley's initial verses are presented in the original biblical context as those that David instructed Assaf and his brothers to recite. Another selection from Chronicles and Nehemiah, followed by the Song at the Sea, becomes common in the high Middle Ages but is

76 Kadari, 'Who Has Chosen Us', pp. 272–73.
77 Davidson/Assaf/Joel, *Siddur RSG*, p. 16, *SRAmram*, ed. Goldschmidt, p. 13; ed. Hedegård, Hebrew section, p. 19.

already adumbrated, at least in parts, in the earlier Genizah period. It begins with David's blessing of God (ויברך דוד) in 1 Chr 29:10 – 13. Between this selection and the original set of Psalms chapters there are a number of Psalms verses (ברוך ה' לעולם) that appear to function as a concluding quasi-benediction, more akin to the style of the Karaites than that of the Rabbanites.

From the *'amidah* and *hafṭarah* benedictions, as well as from the grace after meals, it emerges that while some versions of the Jerusalem benediction give a central place to the davidic kingdom, at times even with strong polemical (anti-Christian?) content, others are inclined to refer to the divine salvation in more general terms, or to develop around the prayer for the restoration of Jerusalem various political, social, cultic and messianic themes, some of them somewhat more fanciful than others. Although one of the *qedushah* versions of the repeated *'amidah* cites a Psalms verse in the name of David, it also gives him his messianic title. This method of introducing Psalms verses also occurs in a number of supplicatory and penitential prayers (תחינות and סליחות). One of the סליחות is based on a liturgical ceremony that was probably already of some age when reported in the Mishnah. It mentions David but there is some doubt about whether that mention dates from the prayer's earliest format or was added in the early talmudic period. It is clear from the benediction recited over the fully visible moon that from about the thirteenth century use is being made by the mystics of the special role of David, the Messiah, and the associated redemption, in the additions that they make to the benediction.

Issues underlying these variations

There is little question but that the whole history of rabbinic liturgy is permeated by a tension between the use of the language and content of scripture and objections to an extension of such a use that might deny or doubt the rabbinic role, and indeed right and obligation, to formulate substantial parts of its content. What the rabbis ultimately did was to employ many parts of scripture but within their own style and framework and sometimes with minor adjustments.[78] Although parts of the Hebrew Bible occupied significant and even central roles within the rabbinic liturgy, they tended to make their appearances within the theological, liturgical and linguistic restraints imposed by the authorities. The problem was that different authorities did not necessarily agree about the required extent of such restraints. If the situation could at all times be tense

78 See Reif, *Problems*, pp. 48 – 49, 68 – 69.

and problematic with regard to scripture in general, it became even more complicated in the geonic period in connection with the book of Psalms because of the theological controversy with the Karaites.

The rabbis saw themselves as duty-bound to add to the praise of God as recorded in scripture by way of new forms, expressions and contexts. For Sa'adya Gaon, the book of Psalms was pure scripture and therefore not daily liturgy. It was a divinely inspired moral and theological guide, and not a literary structure already prepared for liturgical use. The Karaites, on their part, argued that the Psalms were the most exalted form of prayer and the exclusive source for daily liturgy. They were a perfect prophetic or poetic product and therefore a mandatory ideal for human liturgical needs and purposes. This was proved by their literary features and their lack of historical context. They played down the idea of exclusive davidic authorship, pointing to many other authors within the book itself. They also pointed to what they regarded as the extensive rabbinic use of the Psalms as liturgy. The argument about the liturgical use of Psalms raged on between rabbinic and Karaite leaders from the tenth to the twelfth centuries.[79]

Another area of tension within the rabbinic tradition, and indeed between it and rival theologies, related to the nature of the redemption. Given the genuine ignorance of the theologians about when this great event of the future was destined to occur, and any sound information about its precise nature, there was a wide range of views about how it should be viewed. Would it be primarily social and political? Were the messianic and mystical elements to dominate? Was the rebuilt Temple to figure prominently in the arrangements? How did the figure of King David and his messianic role figure in the visions about the future? In what way should Jews respond to the messianic ideas of Christianity and was it appropriate to stress the personal rather than the national messiah in all its manifestations?[80]

From the early talmudic period, as Arnold Franklin has convincingly demonstrated, claims were made by both the exilarchs in Babylon and the patriarchs in the land of Israel that they were the descendants of King David. In the geonic period, the exilarchs expanded this claim with the support of detailed genealogies and even used seals relating their family to the 'lion of Judah'. They also adopted names and titles with davidic and biblical connections. In the Islamic world, there was admiration for the quranic Dāwūd and a paradigm, in the form of the prophet Muhammad's lineage, which Jewish leaders may have wished to follow. There is, however, also evidence that during the talmudic and

79 Simon, *Approaches*, pp. 59–144; Yahalom, 'Scriptural allusions', pp. 101–4.
80 See n. 4 above.

geonic periods not all rabbinic individuals and groups were wholly enthusiastic about such claims and their ramifications.[81]

There was also doubt, and adjustment from generation to generation, in the matter of the role of historical personalities and events within the rabbinic tradition. Early rabbinic liturgy had little interest in historical matters, as is clear from its attitude to Moses and its preference for midrashic exegesis rather than historical summary in the domestic service for the first night of Passover (*Seder Leyl Pesaḥ*). It has been argued that this ahistorical approach was more typical of the Babylonian rather than the Palestinian centres but certainly the situation changed in the post-talmudic period, as clearly demonstrable from the liturgical references to the origins of the festival of Ḥanukkah. In the geonic age there was more of a tendency to import biblical figures into the liturgy, as exemplary religious figures, or as trend setters in the matter of prayer and custom, while in the Middle Ages any mystical or messianic bent was championed by the kabbalists and often ultimately incorporated into the standard prayers.[82]

General conclusions

It will perhaps be useful in this final section to list what may be deduced from the evidence with regard to the figure of David in the rabbinic liturgy, not only thematically but also chronologically.

1. Already in the talmudic period, there was doubt about whether mentions of the final redemption should specifically relate to the davidic kingship, or remain broader in their coverage. It remains equivocal whether the choice was made on political, social or theological grounds and it may indeed be argued that more than one element played a part. The figure of David by no means occupies a central role in the skeletal rabbinic liturgy.
2. The use of scripture was undoubtedly expanded in the geonic age but there was some hesitation about clearly identifying the book of Psalms, as used in the prayers, as the composition of David, with some preference for seeing the selections as part of the approved rabbinic formulations. What is not clear is whether the hesitations about the attention to be given to David, the composer of biblical psalms, represent a negative response to the expanding role being given to David in the liturgy, or emanate from circles that had al-

81 Franklin, 'Exilarchal ties', pp. 92–93, 94–102, 102–10.
82 See the next chapter in this volume, on the matter of rabbinic notions of history.

ways felt uncomfortable with the specific matter of the Jewish liturgical use of the biblical psalms.

3. In the early Islamic period, and to a greater extent in the early medieval period, there seems to have been some expansions of the use of the davidic figure in the rabbinic liturgy, especially in matters relating to the ultimate political and spiritual redemption. At least part of the inspiration for this may have come from the efforts of the exilarchate and its supporters to promote and extend the idea of its davidic genealogy.
4. In the centuries straddling the late geonic and early medieval eras, David also came to be cited more simply as the psalm-writer, the messianic king, the specialist in doing penitence and achieving divine forgiveness, or the symbol of God's eternal promise to Israel about ultimate times. In these respects, aspects of the historical figure in a sense return to the fore. There is then here a broadening role for David.
5. From the thirteenth century, mystical ideas about David, the messianic soul, the emanation of מלכות, the cosmos, and the redemption, brought David a fresh liturgical role. There were features of such ideas that certainly had their precedents and manifestations in earlier times and circles but their major impact on the standard liturgy appears to have been a late medieval and early modern development. These ideas did not replace the earlier ones but were appended to them.

In the event that it is not yet clear enough from earlier research, such findings leave little room for doubt that the development of Jewish liturgical content and formulation was motivated by a number of factors. Scripture, history, spirituality, mysticism and eschatology, as well as the more mundane matters of language and literature on the one hand, and political and social considerations on the other, all played a part in forcing textual choices and adjustments. Even a simple name like David could carry very different connotations for specific periods and places. If the composers or worshippers in a new generation added the mention of religious status, dynasty, poems, or messianic role, they might well be understanding, expressing and transmitting a davidic dimension that ranged beyond, even greatly beyond, what had been familiar to their predecessors.

Works cited

Abudraham, D., *Sefer Abudraham Ha-Shalem*, ed. S. A. Wertheimer (Jerusalem: Usha, 1963).
Albeck, C. (ed.), *Shishah Sidrey Mishnah*, 6 vols. (Jerusalem–Tel Aviv: Bialik–Dvir, 1959).

Amram ben Sheshna, *Seder Rav 'Amram Ga'on*, ed. E. D. Goldschmidt (Jerusalem: Rav Kook, 1971); collated with *Seder R. Amram*, part I, ed. D. Hedegård (Lund: Lindstedts, 1951) and with *Seder R. Amram*, part II, ed. T. Kronholm (Lund: CWK Gleerup, 1974).

Aptowitzer, A., *Parteipolitik der Hasmonäerzeit im rabbinischen und pseudoepigraphischen Schrifttum* (Vienna: Kohut, 1927).

Baer, S., *Seder 'Avodat Yisra'el* (Rödelheim: Lehrberger, 1868).

Baḥya ben Asher, *Bi'ur al-Ha-Torah*, ed. C. B. Chavel, 3 vols. (Jerusalem: Rav Kook, 1966–68).

Baillet, M. (ed.), *Dead Sea Scrolls. 4Q. Qumran Grotte 4.3 (4Q482–4Q520)* (DJD 7, Oxford: Clarendon, 1982).

CUL = Cambridge University Library.

Chazon, E. G., 'The Qedushah liturgy and its history in light of the Dead Sea Scrolls', in *From Qumran to Cairo: Studies in the History of Prayer*, ed. J. Tabory (Jerusalem: Orhot, 1999), pp. 7–17.

Davidson, I., Assaf, S., Joel, B. I. (eds.), *Siddur R. Sa'adya Gaon. Kitāb Ǵāmi' Aṣ-Ṣalawāt Wat-Tasābīh* (Jerusalem: Mekize Nirdamim, 1963, 2nd edn.).

Ehrlich, U., *The Weekday Amidah in Geniza Prayer Books: Origins and Transmission* (Hebrew; Jerusalem: Yad Ben-Zvi Press, 2013).

Elbogen, I., *Der jüdische Gottesdienst in seiner geschichtlichen Entwicklung* (Frankfurt a. M.: Kaufmann, 1931; reprint, Hildesheim: Olms, 1962); Hebrew edition, *Ha-Tefillah Be-Yisra'el Be-Hitpatḥutah Ha-Hisṭorit*, eds. J. Heinemann, I. Adler, A. Negev, J. Petuchowski, H. Schirmann (Tel Aviv: Devir, 1972); English edition, *Jewish Liturgy: A Comprehensive History*, trans. and ed., R. P. Scheindlin (Philadelphia,: JPSA, 1993).

Eleazar of Worms, *Perushey Siddur Ha-Tefillah La-Roqeaḥ*, eds. M. Herschler and Y. A. Hershler, 2 vols. (Jerusalem: Hershler, 1992).

Etz Ḥayyim – see Jacob ben Judah Ḥazzan.

Finkelstein, L. (ed.), *Sifre on Deuteronomy* (New York: JTSA, 1969, 2nd edn.).

Fleischer, E., *Eretz-Israel Prayer and Prayer Rituals as Portrayed in the Geniza Documents* (Hebrew; Jerusalem: Magnes, 1998).

Fleischer, E., 'The Qedusha of the Amida (and other Qedushot): historical, liturgical and ideological aspects', *Tarbiz* 67 (1998), pp. 301–50.

Fleischer, E., *The Yozer. Its Emergence and Development* (Hebrew; Jerusalem: Magnes, 1984).

Franklin, A., 'Cultivating roots: the promotion of exilarchal ties to David in the Middle Ages', *AJS Review* 29.1 (2005), pp. 91–110.

Gaster, M. (ed.), *The Book of Prayer and Order of Service according to the Custom of the Spanish and Portuguese Jews*, 3 vols. (London: Frowde and OUP, 1901–6).

Ginzberg, L., *Geonica*, 2 vols. (New York: JTSA, 1909).

Ginzberg, L., *The Legends of the Jews*, 7 vols. (Philadelphia: JPSA, 1909–38).

Goldschmidt, E. D. (ed.), *Maḥzor Le-Yamim Ha-Nora'im Le-fi Minhagey Bney Ashkenaz*, 2 vols. (Koren–Leo Baeck Institute: Jerusalem–New York, 1970).

Goldschmidt, E. D., *On Jewish Liturgy: Essays on Prayer and Religious Poetry* (Hebrew; Jerusalem: Magnes, 1978).

Goldschmidt, E. D., 'The Oxford Ms. of Maimonides' Book of Prayer', in his collected articles *On Jewish Liturgy: Essays on Prayer and Religious Poetry* (Hebrew; Jerusalem: Magnes, 1978), pp. 187–216.

Halpern, B., 'David' in *Eerdmans Dictionary of the Bible*, eds. D. N. Freedman, A. C. Myers, A. B. Beck (Grand Rapids, Mich.: Eerdmans, 2000), pp. 318–22.

Heinemann, J., *Prayer in the Talmud: Forms and Patterns* (Studia Judaica 9; Berlin: de Gruyter, 1977).

Higger, M. (ed.), *Massekhet Soferim* (New York: Debe Rabbanan, 1937).

Idelsohn, A. Z., *Jewish Liturgy and its Development* (New York: Holt, Rinehart and Winston, 1932).

Jacob ben Judah Ḥazzan of London, *The Etz Ḥayyim*, ed. I. Brodie, 3 vols. (Jerusalem: Rav Kook, 1962–67).

Jacobson, B. S., *Nethiv Binah*, 5 vols. (Hebrew; Tel Aviv: Sinai, 1968–83).

Jawitz, W. (Z.), *Siddur 'Avodat Ha-Levavot* (Berlin: Itzkowski, 1922).

JPSA = Jewish Publication Society of America.

JTSA = Jewish Theological Seminary of America.

Judah ben Barzilai al-Bargeloni, *Sefer Ha-'Ittim*, ed. J. Schor (Berlin: Kaufmann for Mekize Nirdamim, 1903).

Judah ben Yaqar, *Perush Ha-Tefillot Ve-Ha-Berakhot*, ed. S. Yerushalmi, 2 vols. (Jerusalem: Me'orey Yisrael, 1968).

Kadari, A., 'Who Has Chosen Us: about the ritual significance of the blessings for Torah reading', in *Kenishta. Studies of the Synagogue World*, 3, ed. J. Tabory (Ramat Gan: Bar-Ilan University, 2007), pp. 257–73.

Kavvanat Ha-Lev Ha-Shalem Ke-Minhag Ha-Sefaradim Ve-'Edot Ha-Mizraḥ, ed. R. Doron (Petaḥ Tikvah: Shirah Ḥadashah, 2005).

Liebes, Y., 'Mazmiaḥ qeren yeshu'ah', in *Jerusalem Studies in Jewish Thought* 3 (1983–84), pp. 313–48 and 4 (1984–85), pp. 181–217 and 341–54.

Luger, Y., *The Weekday Amidah in the Cairo Genizah* (Hebrew; Jerusalem: Orhot, 2001).

Luzzatto, S. D. (ed.), *Maḥzor Kol Ha-Shanah Ke-fi Minhag Italiani*, 2 vols. (Livorno: Belforte, 1856).

Maḥzor Roma (Bologna, 1540).

Maimonides, 'The Oxford Ms. of Maimonides' Book of Prayer', ed. E. D. Goldschmidt, in his collected articles *On Jewish Liturgy: Essays on Prayer and Religious Poetry* (Hebrew; Jerusalem: Magnes 1978), pp. 187–216.

Malter, H. (ed.), *The Treatise Ta'anit of the Babylonian Talmud* (Philadelphia: JPSA, 1928).

Mann, J., 'Genizah fragments of the Palestinian order of service', *Hebrew Union College Annual* 2 (1925), pp. 269–338.

Midrasch Tehillim (Schocher Tob), ed. S. Buber (Vilna: Romm, 1891).

OUP = Oxford University Press.

The Persian Jewish Prayer Book. Facsimile of MS Adler ENA 23 in the Jewish Theological Seminary Library, ed. S. Tal (Jerusalem: Ben-Zvi, 1980).

Pomykala, K. E., *The Davidic Dynasty Tradition in Early Judaism: Its History and Significance for Messianism* (Atlanta, Ga.: Scholars Press, 1995).

Rappel, D., *Gates to the Jewish Liturgy*, eds. Y. and N. Rappel (Hebrew; Tel Aviv–Jerusalem: Yedioth Ahronot and Lipschitz Institute, 2001), pp. 72–87.

Reif, S. C., *Jewish Prayer Texts from the Cairo Genizah. A Selection of Manuscripts at Cambridge University Library, Introduced, Transcribed, Translated, and Annotated, with Images* (Cambridge Genizah Studies 7, Leiden: Brill, 2016).

Reif, S. C., *Problems with Prayers. Studies in the Textual History of Early Rabbinic Liturgy* (Studia Judaica 37, Berlin: de Gruyter, 2006).

Roqeaḥ – see Eleazar of Worms.

Rosenfeld, A. (ed.), *The Authorised Selichot for the Whole Year* (London: Labworth, 1969, 4th edn.).
Schiffman, L. H., *Reclaiming the Dead Sea Scrolls. The History of Judaism, the Background of Christianity, the Lost Library of Qumran* (Philadelphia: JPS, 1994), pp. 317–27.
Scholem, G., *Kabbalah* (Jerusalem and New York: Keter and Quadrant, 1974).
Seder 'Olam Rabbah Ha-Shalem, ed. M. Y. Weinstock, 3 vols. (Jerusalem: Torat Ḥesed, 1956–62).
Shabbethai Sofer, *Siddur Shabbethai Sofer*, ed. I. Satz, D. Yitschaki, 5 vols. (Hebrew; Baltimore: Ner Yisrael, 1987–2002).
Solomon ben Nathan 'of Sijilmasa', *Siddur Rabbenu Shelomo ben Nathan*, ed. S. Ḥaggai (Jerusalem: Ḥaggai, 1995).
Solomon of Worms, *Siddur Rabbenu Shelomo*, ed. M. Hershler (Jerusalem: Ḥemed, 1971).
Siddur 'Oṣar Ha-Tefillot, 2 vols. (Vilna: Romm, 1923).
Simḥah of Vitry, *Maḥzor Vitry*, ed. S. Hurwitz, 2 vols. (Nuremburg: Mekize Nirdamim, 1923, 2nd edn.).
Simon, U., *Four Approaches to the Book of Psalms from Saadiah Gaon to Abraham Ibn Ezra*, Eng. trans. L. J. Schramm (Albany, N. Y.: State University of New York, 1991).
Solomon, N., 'Messiah and messianism', in *Reader's Guide to Judaism*, ed. M. Terry (Chicago–London: Fitzroy Dearborn, 2000), pp. 406–7.
TDOT = *Theological Dictionary of the Old Testament* (Eng. trans.), essay on בחר by J. Bergman/H. Ringgren/H. Seebass in volume 2, revised edition (Grand Rapids, Mich: Eerdmans, 1999), pp. 73–87.
Tiklal – see Yaḥya ben Joseph.
Trèves, Naphtali Herz, *Perush Ha-Tefillah* (Thiengen: Eliezer and Joseph Trèves, 1560).
Urbach, E. E., *The Sages. Their Concepts and Beliefs*, Eng. trans. I. Abrahams, 2 vols. (Jerusalem: Magnes, 1975).
Vitry – see Simḥah of Vitry
Wieder, N., *The Formation of Jewish Liturgy in the East and the West: A Collection of Essays* 2 vols. (Hebrew; Jerusalem: Ben Zvi, 1998).
Yahalom, J., 'From the material to the scriptural: Scriptural allusions and their development in Judeo-Arabic liturgical poetry', in *Prayers that Cite Scripture*, ed. J. L. Kugel (Cambridge, Mass.: Harvard University Press, 2006), pp. 101–19.
Yaḥya ben Joseph ibn Ṣaliḥ (ed.), *Tiklal*, 3 vols. (Jerusalem: Joseph Ḥasid, 1894).

12 The Function of History in Early Rabbinic Liturgy

This chapter will assess the degree to which the mention of the past plays a part in the early rabbinic liturgy, and how this relates to the general notion of history to be found in earlier Hebrew literature. Prayers or parts of prayers that include historical elements will be discussed and an attempt will be made to identify their precise sense and purpose. The analysis will also deal with the question of whether what is relevant to the early rabbinic liturgy also holds good for its post-talmudic development.

Biblical Background

As with so many religious themes in early Rabbinic Judaism, their meaning and development can be little understood without reference back to the Hebrew Bible that constituted the authoritative source for all subsequent Jewish theologies. The precise definition and interpretation of the historical elements in the Hebrew Bible have long been the subject of debate and dispute but it is safe to say that there is broad agreement that many of the biblical writers ascribe to history or, if it is preferred, the events of the past, a central significance in their understanding of God and the divine relationship with Israel. As Yehezkel Kaufmann put it, both simply and unequivocally, 'The religion of the Bible is not set forth philosophically. It is urged on Israel on the basis of history; the basic attributes of Israel's God are historical.'[1] The degree of uniqueness that this concept enjoys in the Ancient Near East is also a point much debated but, again, it is difficult to gainsay the notion that while the interest of many other peoples was broadly chronographical, the Hebrew Bible often made use of history primarily for didactic and theological purposes.[2] Israel was more preoccupied with its past and with introspection than were the cultures of Mesopotamia and Egypt.[3] Even those who take issue with the idea of a uniquely Hebrew mode of memory acknowledge that the meaning of the Hebrew word *zakhor* greatly extends beyond the simple meaning of 'remember'.[4]

The Hebrews were often commanded to remember, and not to forget, and this kind of religious imperative is unique to Israel. In the words of Andrew Mayes, 'In

1 Kaufmann, *Religion*, p. 132.
2 Herr, 'History', pp. 129–42.
3 Schniedewind, *Eerdman*, p. 594.
4 Childs, *Memory.*

DOI 10.1515/9783110486704-013

that Israelite historians did not critically evaluate their sources their historiography may be pre-modern, but its classification as historiography is scarcely to be denied.'[5] It was not *all* facts that were to be remembered but those that specifically documented God's intervention and man's response since in this way human history could be interpreted as the revelation of God's will. Memory was a central element in ritual and recital, and the festivals manifestly had historical as well as religious and agricultural dimensions.[6] The biblical narrative revolves around the reality of everyday life rather than having its focus on the exclusively spiritual, yet the result is a coherent and organic presentation with its own sacred character. Thus, Israel's history was incorporated – even transformed – into its scripture. The whole process was maintained and nurtured by transmission, recitation and education. All this is convincingly argued by Yosef Hayim Yerushalmi who identifies the three essential elements of the whole exercise as meaning in history, memory of the past and the writing of history.[7]

While history is not merely chronographical in much of the Hebrew Bible, a different situation may be detected in the books that belong to the Wisdom tradition, a genre that does have its parallels in Ancient Near Eastern and Greek sources, and may not therefore match the dominant style of Israelite history.[8] Furthermore, in the late biblical period, the Greeks produced scholars who championed the writing of history both as records of facts and as lessons for the future, the Greek word *historia* carrying the basic meaning of 'investigation'.[9] The idea of writing this kind of history then acquired increasing significance in broader hellenistic circles, so that the Jewish literature of the Second Temple period, in Hebrew, Greek and Aramaic, reflects, in varying degrees, both the historical ideology of the Hebrew Bible and the Greek understanding of history. Epochs and areas were identified and divided and, probably under the influence of Indian, Persian and Greek ideas, universal history was linked to a cosmic system and the mythical fused with the historical.[10]

---

5 Carefully and convincingly argued by Mayes in *Biblical World*, 1.68.

6 An oft-cited example is the declaration associated with the offering of the first fruits in Deut 25:5–9.

7 Yerushalmi, *Zakhor*, pp. 5–16.

8 Useful summaries of the nature of biblical wisdom literature are by Whybray in *Dictionary*, pp. 726–29; Boadt in *Eerdman*, pp. 1380–82; and Dell in *Biblical World*, 1.119–23. See also chapter 10 in this volume.

9 On Greek historians, see the brief and useful summary, Luce, *Greek Historians*; on the meaning of the Greek word, see Liddell/Scott, *Lexicon*, p. 842.

10 See, for example, Hengel's remarks in *Judaism* 1.181–94.

Since the early rabbis were deeply influenced by many aspects of hellenistic culture, it is somewhat surprising to find that the historiographical method did not become central to their beliefs and practices. That this is so, is clearly evinced by the simple fact that rabbinic literature is either ignorant of, or uninterested in, the true chronology of the Persian period, reducing over two centuries of the Persian empire to a mere fifty-two years.[11] Given the biblical and hellenistic backgrounds to much of rabbinic learning, this apparent revolution in Jewish thinking requires some further description and explanation.

Rabbinic approach

Before assessing the nature of the rabbis' apparent indifference to history as such, it is necessary to point out that they were by no means unaware of the ramifications of the past in the present, so that records of the past, or references to it, were an important element in rabbinic traditions. It hardly requires stressing that they saw the source of later rabbinic *halakhah* in the earlier biblical precedent, even if they were conscious of the fact that it had sometimes to be modified or rejected, and they noted the disproportionate amount of history vis-à-vis *halakhah* in the Hebrew Bible. A commitment to the continuity of Jewish law was also an expression of the historical dimension in rabbinic literature, but that same literature displayed knowledge that the *halakhah* was different in earlier times and that it was necessary to know what it had been. The halakhist had to take account of current events, even if this required halakhic change, and the destruction of the Second Temple had undoubtedly precipitated adjustments in Jewish religious requirements.[12] All this having been said, and indeed discussed, the assessment of the past was a simple one in so far as its current standing was concerned. It stated that מה דהוה הוה 'what happened in the past is now in the past' and was no longer applicable.[13] In the words of Celia in *As You Like It* (Act III, scene 4), '*Was* is not *is*'.

With regard to the aggadic material, a common underlying assumption was that there was a continuous process of Torah transmission from Moses to the rabbinic teachers. This was in itself an interesting combination of the past and the present, but one which recognized that what was obvious to Akiva may

11 See, e.g., *Seder 'Olam Rabbah* 30 and *b. 'Abod. Zar.* 9a, as cited by Herr, 'History', p. 136.
12 Urbach, 'Halakhah', pp. 112–28.
13 *y. Kil.* 1.4 (27a) and *b. Pesaḥ.* 108a; see Urbach, 'Halakhah', p. 120.

have been incomprehensible to his mosaic forbear.[14] In its totality, aggadah is a critical interpretation of past events and personalities, and *midrash*, like *historia*, means 'investigation'. Although Seder 'Olam dealt primarily with a summary of biblical history, it is no more than a list of personalities and events while Megillat Ta'anit is in essence a ritual calendar. What is more, the rabbis generally offered evaluations of biblical heroes that ran contrary to the plain sense of scripture and were often very much at loggerheads with the accounts in the Hebrew Bible. Since they were very interested in the lessons to be derived from such heroes, they were sometimes loath to paint all characters as wholly black or white, preferring a shade of grey that allowed for repentance, while on other occasions they exaggerated the wickedness or goodness of a biblical personality. In essence, they were not writing or recording history as such but using past events and personalities to make current points.[15]

Rabbinic literature was not in the business of reconstructing biblical history, or even its own history, but was searching for the meaning of history for each generation. Anachronisms were no problem to them and, as Yerushalmi puts it, they 'seem to play with time as though with an accordion, expanding and collapsing it at will'.[16] Neither the future nor the past were worthy subjects of critical speculation. If the Jews achieved holiness by studying and observing the Torah, both Written and Oral, and did repentance, the messiah would come. Political uprisings were destined to end in disaster. In Yerushalmi's words, 'even the convolutions of the Hasmonean dynasty or the intrigues of the Herodians – Jewish history after all – revealed nothing relevant and were largely ignored'. The actual past was over, finished with, and different. The rabbis were indifferent to historiography and to the recovery of the *precise* details of the past for their own sake. For Yerushalmi, all this means that the rabbis had so totally absorbed the biblical interpretation of history that they saw no need to take the topic any further. So much for what appears to be the consensus on what is indicated about the matter of history in early rabbinic literature, as clarified by scholars such as E. E. Urbach, M. D. Herr and Yosef Hayim Yerushalmi.

Is it, then, true to say that for the rabbis historiography ceased, but belief in the meaning of history remained? For Jacob Neusner, even such an assessment paints too positive a picture of the rabbinic attitude to history. He takes issue with Yerushalmi's contention that the rabbis totally absorbed the biblical interpretation of history and argues for an absolute contrast between rabbinic and

---

14 The clearest example is of course the first chapter of *m. 'Abot*. See also the Akiva story in *b. Menaḥ*. 29b.

15 Herr, 'History', pp. 136–39.

16 Yerushalmi, *Zakhor*, p. 17.

biblical thought. For him, rabbinic literature from 200 to 600 C.E. totally rejected the Hebrew Bible's historical way of thinking and replaced it with a paradigmatic approach to time and events. In his words, 'The past takes place in the present. The present embodies the past.'[17]

Hebrew University scholar Daniel Schwartz does not always find himself in agreement with Jacob Neusner but in the case of the topic in hand, one would be hard pressed to place them in different camps.[18] For Schwartz, issues of time, place and change were, taken together, a *sine qua non* for the true notion of history, and talmudic-midrashic literature does not therefore qualify as historical. Even when there is an awareness of time and change in the matter of the practices of earlier generations, the assumption is that everything is Sinaitic and that change is merely the re-establishment of neglected custom.[19] The Talmud's position is that there is validity only in halakhic and not in historical argument and that whatever happened in the past is no longer relevant to current rulings since Israel's status stands outside the ordinary workings of time and place. This amounted to a total commitment to remove the Jewish collective presence from the theatre of historical reality and, according to Schwartz, such an outlook continued into the Middle Ages.

Liturgical style

We shall shortly return to this matter of the consensus concerning the interpretation of history in early rabbinic literature. Let us in the meantime turn to early rabbinic liturgy and assess the degree to which such a consensus also applies to that specific area of Jewish religious expression in the first Christian millennium. If we presuppose that the early rabbinic prayer-book is a reflection of the *Weltanschauung* of the rabbis whose ideas are the core of the Babylonian Talmud, it would not be surprising to find that its form and content take little or no account of history. As Alan Mintz expresses it, 'The major features of the prayerbook crystallized during the first two centuries of the Common Era', '...the prayerbook remains to this day essentially a document of the early rabbis' and 'the essence of the experience of the Siddur has always been a timeless one.'[20] According to such a view, the ritual and liturgical spheres became the areas in which Jewish memory functioned and

17 Neusner, *History*, esp. p. 3.
18 Schwartz, 'Alexandria', pp. 40–55. At the end of that article Schwartz calls Neusner to task for an alleged misinterpretation of the views of the late Menahem Stern.
19 He exemplifies this by reference to such expressions as בראשונה, חזרו והתקינו and באמת אמרו.
20 Mintz, 'Prayer', pp. 404 and 406.

there was no clear distinction between the past and the present. The authority for an idea or a custom was to be found in the halakhic or ritual context and its survival was dependent on the past, not because history was what controlled its future but because it was identified almost wholly with the present.

Evidence for such an interpretation of the role of the past in the early rabbinic liturgy is to be found in various prayers. The obvious starting point for a brief summary of their contents is the *'amidah*, the essential framework of which was built in the first two Christian centuries, even if it probably had precedents in the Second Temple period and certainly underwent considerable development in the late talmudic and post-talmudic periods. The first benediction is devoted to the subject of the biblical patriarchs and bears the name *'avot* ('fathers') or *magen* (shield [of Abraham]). It refers to God as the God of Abraham, Isaac and Jacob (אלהי אברהם, אלהי יצחק ואלהי יעקב) and in all the versions the three patriarchs are initially and specifically mentioned. The subject is God's power and the protection it provided for them.[21]

There is also then a mention (missing in some manuscripts) of either the future redemption (in the words ומביא גואל לבני בניהם 'who will bring a redeemer to their children's children', or ומביא גואל לזרעם אחריהם 'who will bring a redeemer to their progeny who follow them'), or a reference to current protection 'in every generation' מבטחנו בכל דור ודור.[22] The very existence of these two options indicates an awareness of the past, the present and the future in terms of God's relationship with Israel. Arthur Marmorstein indeed argued that the mention of the redeemer in the Babylonian version reflects the fact that the worshippers were not living in the homeland.[23] On the other hand, this may reflect post-talmudic rather than talmudic thought since the original benediction probably concluded at the reference to God as the Creator of heaven and earth, or of everything, in the expression קונה שמים וארץ or קונה הכל, the latter probably adopted later as reflecting an objection to the possibility that the reference may be to Abraham. [24] What emerges, therefore, is that the context is very much a theological and liturgical one and that the historical reference is wholly employed in the service of that context.

In an earlier study, I dealt with the eleventh benediction in the context of Jewish ideas of restoration and it will be useful in the present context to summarize the relevant conclusions.[25] The benediction in its earliest form must have commenced

---

21 See, for instance, Davidson/Assaf/Joel, *Siddur RSG*, p. 18. See also 3 Macc 6:2, as discussed by Corley, 'Review'.

22 Luger, *Amidah*, pp. 40–47; Ehrlich, *Weekday Amidah*, pp. 29–42.

23 Marmorstein, 'Shibolim', pp. 209–13.

24 Wieder, *Formation*, 1.65 and 1.82–87.

25 Reif, 'Restoration', pp. 282 (144) and 292–93 (153).

something like 'Restore our leaders as once they were and our counsellors as in earlier times' (השיבה שופטינו כבראשונה ויועצינו כבתחלה). What is being requested in this benediction is the restoration of some sort of pristine state in which correct judgements are made, as they once were, by those among the Jewish people with special responsibilities for these activities. Such judgements are then linked in the concluding eulogy with God's own qualities. Remarkably, there is no consensus among early or late commentators about what precisely the whole benediction wishes to see restored. Is it a fair system of theodicy, or the elementary punishment of the wicked? Are we looking forward to messianic judgement, or the integrity of law-courts? Could there be here a polemic against non-Jewish courts, or against the alleged misjudgements of apostates from Judaism, or sectarians? Unsurprisingly, the leading scholarly analysts of the benediction a few decades ago could not agree about the original, pristine period which is here being cited as the best precedent. Finkelstein thought he saw a reference to Rome while Ginzberg detected an anti-Sadducean *tendenz* here. For Elbogen, it simply was no longer possible to identify the circumstances that had once inspired the benediction. What better evidence could there be for the conclusion that the theological element in the liturgy had successfully ousted its historical equivalent?[26]

Equally of interest for this discussion is the benediction that joins the recitation of the *shema'* in the morning and the evening to the praying of the *'amidah*, namely the *ge'ulah* or redemption benediction.[27] This benediction begins with an affirmation of the truth of the *shema'* and moves on to the matter of God's special acts of redemption. In the talmudic discussions relating to its recitation, there are various views as to what should be included and among the suggestions are the exodus from Egypt, God's kingship, the slaying of the first-born and the crossing of the Red Sea. The morning version of this benediction is said to deal with the past redemption, and the evening version to focus on the future redemption. The subsequent stage in the history of this benediction sees (in addition to a little more detail of the Egyptian experience) an increasing degree of attention – controversial attention it may be added – being given to the future redemption. Even the two versions of the concluding eulogy, the Babylonian גאל ישראל ('who redeemed Israel') and the Palestinian (מלך) צור ישראל וגואלו ('(Royal) Rock of Israel and its Redeemer') reflect a tension between noting the past and stressing the future.[28]

---

26 Elbogen, *Gottesdienst*, pp. 32–35; *Ha-Tefillah*, pp. 24–26 and 39–40; *Liturgy*, pp. 28–30 and 45; Finkelstein, 'Amidah', pp. 14–15, 154–55; Ginzberg, *Palestinian Talmud*, 3.325–29.

27 Elbogen, *Gottesdienst* pp. 22–25, *Ha-Tefillah*, pp. 17–19, *Liturgy*, pp. 21–23.

28 *t. Ber.* 2.1 (ed. Zuckermandel, p. 3); y. *Ber.* 1.9 (3d). See also 3 Macc 6:2, as discussed by Corley, 'Review'.

The version of the *ge'ulah* benediction to be found in the domestic service for the first eve of Passover reflects a similar tension. The Mishnah legislates that all Jews are obliged to see themselves as having been personally rescued from Egypt and to offer praise to God who miraculously brought them 'from slavery to freedom, from sorrow to joy, from mourning to festivity, from darkness to great light, and from bondage to redemption' (הוציאנו מעבדות לחרות מיגון לשמחה ומאבל ליום טוב ומאפלה לאור גדול ומשעבוד לגאולה). For Rabbi Akiva, the past is not sufficient, nor perhaps deserving of the last word. He argues for an addition that entreats God 'to bring us peacefully to future such festivities, rejoicing in the rebuilding of Jerusalem and enjoying again the Temple service' (יגיענו למועדים ולרגלים אחרים הבאים לקראתנו לשלום שמחים בבנין עירך וששים בעבודתך).[29]

The exodus from Egypt has just been mentioned as having been accorded, during the second Christian century, an important place in the redemption benediction that joins the *shema'* and the *'amidah*, Rabbinic Judaism's two central liturgical expressions. The phrase זכר ליציאת מצרים 'in remembrance of the exodus from Egypt' was also used in early rabbinic liturgy to refer to the sabbath, as indeed was the parallel expression זכר למעשה בראשית 'in remembrance of the creation of the world', both on the basis of the reasons given for the sabbath in Exod 20:11 and in Deut 5:15. Elbogen dates the first of these expressions to the Hasmonean period: 'The notion of redemption became the focus of religious imagination, and longing for freedom not only from oppression and misfortune in this world, but also for messianic salvation, became an important impulse to religious development. The exodus from Egypt was the event that people of this [Hasmonean] period brought to mind gladly and often, and the redemption from slavery in Egypt became the symbol of redemption in general; its commemoration became an important component of daily prayer.'[30] It could just as convincingly be argued that the notion of redemption acquired a special poignancy and relevance during the Roman occupation of the second century. For our current purpose, what is significant is that such a historical reference was undoubtedly no more centred on the original event than its counterpart that dealt with the creation. In both instances, it is the spiritual, eschatological and consolational aspects that came to dominate and that ensured places in the regular liturgy.

---

29 *m. Pesaḥ.* 10.5–6.

30 Elbogen, *Gottesdienst*, p. 244, *Ha-Tefillah*, p. 185, *Liturgy*, p. 195. See also the *zikhronot* section of the New Year liturgy and the *ya'aleh ve-yavo* festival prayer discussed by Elbogen, *Gottesdienst*, pp. 57 and 141–44, *Ha-Tefillah*, pp. 44 and 106–9, *Liturgy*, pp. 51 and 118–21, and Neusner, *History*, p. 205, n. 18.

Again historical theory

With these few examples now firmly tucked into our belts, the time has come to return to the matter of the interpretation of history in early rabbinic literature. Is there any alternative view to that which sees the whole notion as totally distinct from the past as such, from chronology, and from the recording of events? A fairly recent article by Shlomo Fischer deserves some attention in this connection.[31] He acknowledges that the Babylonian Talmud is anxious to move away from non-textual matters and from historical realities and to concentrate on *halakhah* and on the dialectical method used to study and codify it. Babylonian Jewry, until about the end of the seventh century, found its highest expression of religiosity in a study of Torah through such an ahistorical approach. But Fischer draws a subtle distinction between the Babylonian approach of that period and what succeeded it in the geonic period from the eighth to the eleventh centuries. The latter geonic attitude to history was less negative and reflected a position that was also held earlier in the land of Israel, according to which the chronicling of history had a place in the religious framework.

The massive changes that occurred in the Babylonian centres after the rise of Islam and that led to greater political, judicial and educational authority and centralization, brought the real world back into the rabbinic academy. The Geonim strengthened the reliability of the chain of tradition by once again encouraging historical writing, and their interest in the unchanging truth of Torah led to historical consciousness and the conclusion of the earlier talmudic process.[32] A similar degree of reality had existed in the Jewish homeland in earlier times and accounts for the different style of the Yerushalmi or Palestinian Talmud. If we accept only that the Palestinian and Babylonian positions were not always identical and that the methods of the Babylonian Talmud may not have been universally applied in the rabbinic world at all periods, Fischer's suggestions may assist us in our analysis of the liturgical situation in early Rabbinic Judaism.

To assess the significance of Fischer's views precisely for that purpose, it will be necessary to say a little more about the place of history in the early medieval period and how this relates to Jewish liturgy. True as it is that serious historiography was not pursued until the later medieval and early modern periods, account nevertheless has to be taken of the such works as the *Seder Tanna'im Va-*

31 Fischer, 'Exit', pp. 56–70.

32 Fischer, 'Exit', p. 68: מסוף תקופת הסבוראים חדלו אפוא הגאונים לפתח את השקלא וטריא באופן חפשי אלא קיבעוהו, וחיזקו וטיפחו את אמינות שרשרת המסורת בכתיבה היסטורית כרוניקאית: ניתן לומר שהעניין של ההנהגה היהודית בבבל בתקופת הגאונים בתורה כ'אמת' בלתי משתנית הביא אותם לסוג של תודעה היסטורית ולידי חתימת התלמוד

Amora'im, the *Letter of Sherira Gaon*, *Yosippon*, *Sefer Ha-Kabbalah* and the *Scroll of Antiochus*[33] and of the impetus given to a greater interest in history by the Jewish scholars of early medieval Italy who enjoyed close links with the Holy Land. Indeed, one of the Cambridge Genizah texts of the *Scroll of Antiochus* for recitation in Aramaic on Ḥanukkah takes its interest in history further than the story itself by recording that it was copied in Isfahan in 1451 according to the Seleucid calendar and in 4900 *anno mundi.*[34] It may well be the case, as implied by Fischer, that such developments have their earliest origins in the Palestinian Jewish homeland and we would then expect some ramifications in the liturgical sphere.

Both Yerushalmi and Neusner express their awareness that much still remains to be done in relating history to liturgy and *vice versa*. In Yerushalmi's opinion, 'To fully probe the memory-banks available to medieval Jews nothing less would suffice than a thorough re-examination of the entire range of Jewish liturgy and ritual, so heavily charged with intricate associations to past and future, and indeed of the entire gamut of rabbinic law and custom as well.'[35] Neusner is equally cautious: 'The relationship of the Prayerbook, or Siddur, to the 'Rabbinic sages' recorded in the Mishnah and its exegetical literature, Tosefta and the two Talmuds, as already noted, simply is not settled. Clearly, sages legislated with respect to the liturgical documents and their contents: they took for granted the theology in them; they obviously said those prayers, even though there were other prayers they recognized as particular to their own setting and group (the master-disciple-circle and its prayers are so designated). But whether or not sages in particular composed the prayers assembled in the (much-later) Siddur, or whether they wrote some of them but not others, remains to be considered.'[36] Is it then possible to identify some evidence of a changing attitude to historical matters in the liturgy that is more obviously linked with the geonic period than with its earlier talmudic equivalent?

Historical liturgy

The Ḥanukkah liturgy, given that it is, with the exception of the main benediction on kindling the lights, substantially the product of the post-talmudic period, is an obvious candidate for attention. If Yerushalmi may be cited again, his re-

33 See the editions and studies cited in Stemberger, *Introduction*, pp. 6–7 and 331–32; Flussser, *Josippon*; Cohen, *Ha-Qabbalah*.
34 Reif, *Why Medieval Hebrew*, pp. 45–47.
35 Yerushalmi, *Zakhor*, p. 42.
36 Neusner, *History*, p. 205.

marks are a good starting point for our discussion. In his view, the rabbis 'ignored the battles of the Maccabees in favour of the cruse of oil that burned for eight days, but their recognition of this particular miracle should not be passed over lightly. Ḥanukkah alone, be it noted, was a post-biblical Jewish holiday, and the miracle, unlike others, did not have behind it the weight of biblical authority. The very acceptance of such a miracle was therefore a reaffirmation of faith in the continuing intervention of God in history. Indeed, we may well ponder the audacity with which the rabbis fixed the formal Ḥanukkah benediction as: Blessed be Thou O Lord our God...who has commanded us to kindle the Ḥanukkah light.'[37] Was this 'reaffirmation of faith in the continuing intervention of God in history' accompanied by a growing interest in presenting a record of the events that took the historical aspect a little further than had been customary among the talmudic teachers of Babylon? The text as recorded in the prayer-book of Sa'adya Gaon is:[38]

על הנסין והגבורות והתשועות והמלחמות והפדות והפרקן שעשיתה עמנו ועם אבותינו בימים ההם ובזמן הזה. בימי מתתיהו בן יוחנן כהן גדול חשמונאי ובניו כשעמדה מלכות יון על עמך לשכחם את תורתך ולהעבירם מחוקי רצונך. ואתה ברחמיך הרבים עמדתה להם בעת צרתם ורבתה את ריבם ודנתה את דינם ונקמת את נקמתם ומסרת גבורים ביד חלשים ורבים ביד מעטים וטמאים ביד טהורים ורשעים בכף צדיקים ומזידים בכף עושי תורה. ולך עשיתה שם גדול וקדוש ולעמך ישראל עשיתה תשועה גדולה ופרקן. ואחר כך נכנסו עמך לדביר ביתך ופנו את היכלך וטיהרו את מקדשך והדליקו נרות בחצרות קדשך. ועל כולם תתברך ותתרומם ומן אלנס מן יזיד פיה [ויש מוסיפים בו] וקבעו שמונת ימים הלל והודאה לשמך כשם שעשית נסין לראשונים כך תעשה לאחרונים ותושיענו בימים האילו כבימים ההם ועל כולם.

'(We thank you) for the miracles, the mighty deeds, the acts of salvation, the battles, the redemption and the rescue that you performed for us and for our forefathers in those days and at this time. In the days of Mattathias son of Johanan the High Priest, the Hasmonean, and his sons, when the kingdom of Greece arose against your people with the aim of making them forget your Torah and transgress your express instructions, you stood up for them in your manifold mercies in their time of trouble, pleaded their cause, represented their case, took revenge for them, handing the mighty into the power of the weak, the many into the power of the few, the impure into the power of the pure, the wicked into the power of the righteous and the insolent into the power of those who engage in Torah. You enhanced your great and holy reputation and brought about great salvation and rescue for your people Israel. Afterwards your people entered the shrine of your temple, cleansed your palace, purified your sanctuary and kindled lights in your holy courtyards. For all these things may you be blessed and exalted.' Some then add here 'They instituted eight days of praise and gratitude to your name. Just as your performed miracles for earlier generations, so do likewise for the later ones and save us these days as in those days, for all these things...'

---

37 Yerushalmi, *Zakhor*, p. 25.

38 Davidson/Assaf/Joel, *Siddur RSG*, p. 255.

The content of the above text may be analysed as follows:

a. Gratitude for the miracles, victories and rescues perpetrated by God for us and our fathers at this time in earlier days.
b. Historical note about how the Greeks tried to suppress Judaism in the time of the Hasmonean high priest, Mattathias, and his sons.
c. Poetic summary of how God acted for Israel in this crisis and brought victory to a small and weak group of pure, righteous and observant Jews over a powerful and numerous enemy, with its contaminated and evil practices.
d. How this brought rescue for Israel and publicized the greatness and holiness of God.
e. Another historical note about how the victorious Jews reconsecrated the Temple and kindled lights there.
f. An entreaty that miracles should be performed in the present and future just as they were in the past.

How then may we summarize developments in the geonic period with regard to this liturgical topic? It was apparently agreed that, while thanks were being offered to God in the *'amidah*, reference should also be made to the miraculous Hasmonean victory. This was expanded in three different ways. In one, the historical circumstances were simply chronicled while in another they were lyrically summarized. It may be the case that in the Sa'adyanic version we can detect a fusion of the historical and the poetic formulations, sections b. and e. representing the former and c. and d. the latter. A third style opted for a link with the present and the future and requested a repeat performance of divine intervention. This is no longer history but eschatology and was a particularly common characteristic of the liturgical rite of the land of Israel in the period under discussion. It is possible, as in many instances in the development of the prayer-book, that the ultimate response to the competitive existence of numerous options was to remove the element of controversy by including them all in the standard formulation. Interestingly, these liturgical references to the Ḥanukkah miracle include the kindling of lights in the Temple and rejoicing for eight days but make no specific mention of the oil that marvellously lasted for eight days. We may therefore conclude that the historical element has found its way into this geonic formulation in a way that would have been much less likely among the talmudic rabbis.

There is another text that appears to betray a concern for historical accuracy, or at least for theological accuracy relating to historical background. The second benediction of the grace after meals is devoted to the land of Israel and begins by thanking God for the inheritance of the land. The question is who actually inherited it? The phraseology הנחלתנו ארץ ('you have given us a land as an inheritance') presupposes that the worshipper is in the land of Israel, while the alternative הנחלת את אבותינו ('you gave our ancestors a land as an inheritance') is undoubtedly more suited to those praying in the diaspora. The former version is, however, still retained by Sa'adya and perhaps also by Maimonides (about whose preference there is some textual doubt) before later giving way more widely to the latter. Earlier Genizah fragments often begin the benediction with the phrase על ארצינו ועל נחלת אבותינו, perhaps an alternative Palestinian version and position for the phrase being discussed.[39] Are we perhaps entitled to see in this textual variation a growing interest in history?

Other liturgical texts

A number of other liturgical texts deserve mention but cannot be examined in detail in the present context. I shall therefore summarize them briefly:

i. Catenae of verses were used to preface the central liturgy and grew in range and extent as the medieval centuries passed.[40] They included passages from 1 Chr 16 and 29 and from Neh 9. Perhaps there is significance in the introduction of Neh 9:6–11 which is, after all, a historical summary. Elbogen sees it as an addition which was introduced to link the Chronicles passage and the Song at the Sea (Exod 15)[41] but was there also some impetus from those with a growing interest in including historical summaries of one sort or another in the prayer-book?
ii. The eighteenth benediction of the *'amidah*, on the topic of thanksgiving, has two interesting textual variants:על כל הטובות החסד והרחמים שגמלתנו ושעשיתה עמנו ועם אבותינו מלפנינו ('[We thank you] for all the good, love and mercy that you have bestowed upon us and that you have performed for us and for our fathers') and ועל נסיך שבכל יום עמנו ועל נפלאותיך שבכל עת ערב ובקר ('and for your miracles which are with us every day and your wonders which are present at all times, evening and morning'). The first text is clearly keen to link the thanks with the past while the second is exclusively about the present.[42]

39 Davidson/Assaf/Joel, *Siddur RSG*, p. 102 and Goldschmidt, 'Maimonides', p. 215. See also Finkelstein, 'Birkat Ha-Mazon', pp. 247–49 and Jacobson, *Nethiv Binah*, 3.57–59. Among Genizah fragments at Cambridge University Library that have the introductory phrase and/or the word הנחלתנו are T-S K8.7 (= Mann, 'Genizah fragments', no. 18), NS 154.95, 235.173 and 271.14, and AS 108.134.
40 For the whole subject of the Hebrew Bible's use in the liturgy, see Reif, 'Bible', pp. 1937–48.
41 Elbogen, *Gottesdienst*, p. 86, *Ha-Tefillah*, p. 67, *Liturgy*, pp. 75–76.
42 Luger, *Amidah*, p. 186; Ehrlich, *Weekday Amidah*, pp. 240–41.

iii. There is a special version of the *qiddush* recited at the domestic *seder* service on the first eve of Passover that perhaps originated in the land of Israel. Used in the geonic period, and preserved in the prayer-book of Sa'adya Gaon and in some Genizah documents, it has a most interesting poetic expansion. Instead of simply referring to God's choice of Israel and of the festive day, the prayer makes some detailed remarks about the historical emergence of the festival day, the events associated with it and the purpose of God's special deeds performed on it. In the rite that ultimately became the norm there is virtually no such 'historical' material.[43] The expansion reads:

...זכר ליציאת מצרים ויבחר בו ביום הזה מכל הימים ורצה בו ויקדשיהו מכל הזמנים להיות מהללים בו על פלאי מעשיו להיות מזכירים אותו בכל שנה ושנה להודיע כי בו הוציא את עבדיו מכור הברזל ואותנו מילט להודיע כי בו עשה יי אלהינו נקמות גדולות לאויביהם ושקע צריה ברבים להודיע כי בו קבלו מלכותו לעבדו בלבב שלם ובנפש חפיצה להודיע כי בו עשה יי אלהינו נסים וגבורות ונפלאות לבני ידידיו כי בנו בחרת...

'...IN REMEMBRANCE OF THE EXODUS FROM EGYPT; and he chose this very day of all days and favoured it and sanctified it above other times so that formal praise could be offered on it for his wonderful deeds and mention made of it every year. His intent was to indicate that on that day he brought his servants out of the iron furnace and rescued us; to indicate that on that day the Lord our God enacted powerful revenge against our enemies and publicly felled their foes; to indicate that on that day they accepted his kingship in order to serve him with a perfect mind and a willing spirit; to indicate that on that day the Lord our God performed miraculous, powerful and wonderful deeds for his dearest children. FOR YOU HAVE CHOSEN US...

Although one can classify this expansion as poetic, it nevertheless chooses a style and content that lays stress on the historical events. Perhaps, indeed, one of the areas in which historical material came to be more widely used in the late talmudic and early post-talmudic periods was precisely that of the *piyyuṭim* (liturgical poems). Did this constitute the development and indulgence of a new literary need or the reflection on an earlier tendency that had been somewhat suppressed?

iv. In the late geonic period some of the Genizah texts that record early versions of the *musaf* prayer for festivals contain elements that may be described as historical expansions:

חרדו בנים מפני הגבורה ולא יכלו לקבל את הדברות מזיו השכינה ששרת עליהם הרתיעו כולם ונתעלפו כולם ונפלו על פניהם ונפשותיהם יצאו מקול הדברות ענני הכבוד עמדו עליהם מניפים עליהם גשמי נדבות להחזיר נפשות וגופות חסידים ככ' בדב' קדש' גשם נדבות וג': כאחת השמיעו קטון וגדול כל אשר דבר יי נעשה ונשמע

43 See Davidson/Assaf/Joel, *Siddur RSG*, pp. 141–42, and Genizah fragment T-S H2.124 at Cambridge University Library.

'(Your) children were afraid of God's power and were unable to receive the [Ten] Commandments directly from the glory of the Shekhinah that you laid upon them. They were all startled and collapsed, falling down and passing out at the noise of the Commandments. The clouds of glory then moved over them and brought upon them waves of bountiful rain to restore to them pious souls and bodies, as it is written in your holy scripture [Ps 68:10] 'You released a bountiful rain'. At this all of them, young and old, announced 'We shall observe and obey' [Exod 24:7].' [44]

v. In the prayer-book of Sa'adya Gaon, the *'amidah* for *musaf* on festivals includes the text:

אלהינו ואלהי אבו' מפני חטאינו גלינו מארצנו ונתרחק מעל אדמתנו ואין אנו יכולין לעלות לראות להשתחות
לפניך בבית בחירתך בבית הגדול והקדוש אשר אתה שמך נקרא עליו מפני היד שנשתלחה במקדשך

Our God, and the God of our fathers, for our sins we have been exiled from our land and removed far from our territory so that we are unable to come up and appear before you at worship in your chosen abode, in the great and holy house to which your own name is attached, because of the power that has occupied your sanctuary.[45]

The expansion is undoubtedly poetic and midrashic but one is also surely entitled to see in it elements of the historical or narrative approach.

I hope that what I wrote about the above prayer in another context[46] may bear repetition in the current discussion: 'The basic themes common to the various versions of this benediction are the restoration of God's exclusive rulership over his people Israel and the demonstration of his power to the world at large; the joyous return of the Jewish exiles from various parts of the earth to Jerusalem and to the Temple; and the people's appearance and cultic participation at the Temple in accordance with the ancient pilgrim rite. The shorter version, such as that generally to be found in texts demonstrating allegiance to the Palestinian rite, adds to the future vision a universal acknowledgement of God's sovereignty supported by the use of part of a verse from Ps 103:19, as well as poetic embellishments of the manner in which the restoration will be experienced.[47] The additional material contained in the longer version, such as appears in the Sa'adyanic text, does broaden the theological treatment of the subject. The introductory section firmly blames the Jewish exile on the people's sins while

44 See Mann, 'Genizah fragments', in the section dealing with the New Year prayers, p. 330; Ginzberg, *Legends*, 3.95 and 6.39 (n. 210).
45 Davidson/Assaf/Joel, *Siddur RSG*, p. 151.
46 Reif, 'Restoration', pp. 297–98 (158).
47 Mann, 'Genizah fragments', pp. 325–32, and Fleischer, *Eretz-Israel*, pp. 93–159.

bewailing the occupation of the Temple area by other powers and predicates the restoration on the renewal of God's special relations with Israel.'[48]

Conclusion

In conclusion, it may well be true to say that much of the earliest rabbinic liturgy has little interest in historical matters. At the same time, texts have been cited that demonstrate that some elements of the historical did occur from time to time and that these certainly increased in number and significance in the immediate post-talmudic period. If Fischer is correct in his assessments of Jewish attitudes in the land of Israel in the first few centuries, it may well be the case that the origins of such elements are not to be sought exclusively in post-talmudic Babylonia but may also have had some existence in earlier Palestine. In that case, they would be relevant to scholarly understanding of what history meant to the Jews in the first few Christian centuries.

Works cited

Boadt, L., 'Wisdom, Wisdom Literature', in *Eerdman's Dictionary of the Bible*, eds. D. N. Freedman/A. C. Myers/A. B. Beck (Grand Rapids, Mich./Cambridge: Eeerdmans, 2000), pp. 1380–82.

Childs, B. S., *Memory and Tradition in Israel* (London: SCM Press, 1962).

Cohen, G. D. (ed.), *The Book of Tradition (Sefer Ha-Qabbalah) by Abraham ibn Daud* (Philadelphia: Jewish Publication Society, 1967).

Corley, J., 'The Review of history in Eleazar's prayer in 3 Macc 6:1–15', in *Deuterocanonical and Cognate Literature. Yearbook 2006. History and Identity. How Israel's Later Authors Viewed its Earlier History*, eds. N. Calduch-Benages and J. Liesen (Berlin: de Gruyter, 2006), pp. 201–29.

Davidson, I./Assaf, S./Joel, B. I. (eds.), *Siddur R. Sa'adya Gaon* (Jerusalem: Mekize Nirdamim, 1963, 2nd edn.).

Dell, K., 'Wisdom', in *The Biblical World*, ed. J. Barton, 2 vols. (London: Routledge, 2002), 1.107–28.

Elbogen, I., *Der jüdische Gottesdienst in seiner geschichtlichen Entwicklung* (Frankfurt-am-Main: Kaufmann, 1931; reprint, Hildesheim: Olms, 1962); Hebrew edition, התפילה בישראל בהתפתחותה ההיסטורית (eds. J. Heinemann/I. Adler/A. Negev/J. Petuchowski/H. Schirmann, Tel Aviv: Devir, 1972); English edition, *Jewish Liturgy: A*

48 Note also that in the special prayers for the fast-day of the Ninth of Av, the prayer for the restoration of Jerusalem begins as many others of its kind in the liturgy but continues with what I would call a 'poetic-historical' reference to the detailed ruination of the city; see Heinemann, *Prayer*, pp. 288–91 and Reif, 'Restoration', p. 299 (159).

Comprehensive History, Eng. trans. and ed. R. P. Scheindlin (Philadelphia/Jerusalem/New York: Jewish Publication Society, 1993).
Finkelstein, L., 'The Birkat Ha-Mazon', *Jewish Quarterly Review* NS 19 (1928–29), pp. 211–62.
Finkelstein, L., 'The development of the Amidah', *Jewish Quarterly Review* NS 16 (1925), pp. 1–43, 127–70.
Fischer, S., 'The exit of the Jews from history and the Talmud', in *Zionism and the Return to History: A Reappraisal*, eds. S. N. Eisenstadt/M. Lissak (Hebrew; Jerusalem: Yad Ben-Zvi Press, 1999), pp. 56–70.
Fleischer, E., *Eretz-Israel Prayer and Prayer Rituals as Portrayed in the Geniza Documents* (Hebrew; Jerusalem: Magnes, 1998).
Flussser, D. (ed.), *The Josippon [Josephus Gorionides]*, 2 vols. (Hebrew; Jerusalem: Bialik Institute, 1978–80).
Ginzberg, L., *A Commentary on the Palestinian Talmud*, 3 vols. (Hebrew; New York: Jewish Theological Seminary of America, 1941).
Ginzberg, L., *The Legends of the Jews*, 7 vols. (Philadelphia: Jewish Theological Seminary of America, 1909–38).
Goldschmidt, E. D., 'The Oxford Ms. of Maimonides' Book of Prayer', in *On Jewish Liturgy: Essays on Prayer and Religious Poetry* (Hebrew; Jerusalem: Magnes Press, 1978), pp. 187–216.
Heinemann, J., *Prayer in the Talmud: Forms and Patterns* (Berlin: de Gruyter, 1977).
Hengel, M., *Judaism and Hellenism*, 2 vols., Eng. trans. J. Bowden (London: SCM Press, 1974).
Herr, M. D., 'The conception of history among the sages', in the *Proceedings of the Sixth World Congress of Jewish Studies*, Division C, Volume 3 (Hebrew; Jerusalem: World Union of Jewish Studies, 1977), pp. 129–42.
Jacobson, B. S., *Nethiv Binah*, 5 vols. (Hebrew; Tel Aviv: Sinai, 1968–83).
Kaufmann, Y., *The Religion of Israel*, Eng. trans. M. Greenberg (London: Allen and Unwin, 1961).
Liddell, H. G./Scott, R., *A Greek-English Lexicon* (revised edition, Oxford: Oxford University Press, 1996).
Luce, T. J., *The Greek Historians* (London: Routledge, 1997).
Luger, Y., *The Weekday Amidah in the Cairo Genizah* (Hebrew; Jerusalem: Orhot, 2001).
Mann, J., 'Genizah fragments of the Palestinian order of service', *Hebrew Union College Annual* 2 (1925), pp. 269–338.
Marmorstein, A., '*Shibolim*' in *Dissertationes Hebraicae: Ve-Zot Li-Yehudah*, eds. S. Hevesi/B. Heller/M. Klein (Vienna: Union Press, 1926), pp. 209–13.
Mayes, A. D. H., 'Historiography in the Old Testament', in *The Biblical World*, ed. J. Barton, 2 vols. (London: Routledge, 2002), 1.65–87.
Mintz, A., 'Prayer and the prayerbook', in *Back to the Sources: Reading the Classic Jewish Texts*, ed. B. W. Holtz (New York: Summit Books, 1984), pp. 403–29.
Neusner, J., *The Idea of History in Rabbinic Judaism* (Leiden: Brill, 2004, 2nd edn.).
Reif, S. C., 'The Bible in Jewish liturgy', in *The Jewish Reading Bible*, eds. A. Berlin/M. Z. Brettler (Oxford/New York: Oxford University Press, 2004), pp. 1937–48.
Reif, S. C., 'Some notions of restoration in early rabbinic prayer', in *Restoration: Old Testament, Jewish and Christian Perspectives*, ed. J. M. Scott (Leiden: Brill, 2001), pp. 281–304; reprinted in Reif, *Problems with Prayers. Studies in the Textual History of Early Rabbinic Liturgy* (Berlin: de Gruyter, 2006), pp. 143–64.

Reif, S. C., *Why Medieval Hebrew Studies?* (Cambridge: Cambridge University Press, 2001).
Schniedewind, W., 'Historiography, Biblical', in *Eerdman's Dictionary of the Bible*, eds. D. N. Freedman/A. C. Myers/A. B. Beck (Grand Rapids, Mich.: Eerdmans, 2000), pp. 594–95.
Schwartz, D., 'From Alexandria to rabbinic literature to Zion: the Jews' departure from history and who it is [sic] who returns to it?', in *Zionism and the Return to History: A Reappraisal*, eds. S. N. Eisenstadt/M. Lissak (Hebrew; Jerusalem: Yad Ben-Zvi Press, 1999), pp. 40–55.
Stemberger, G., *Introduction to the Talmud and Midrash*, Eng. trans. M. Bockmuehl (Edinburgh: T. & T. Clark, 1996).
Urbach, E. E., 'Halakhah and history', in *Jews, Greeks and Christians: Religious Cultures in Late Antiquity: Essays in Honor of W. D. Davies*, eds. R. Hamerton-Kelly/R. Scroggs (Leiden: Brill, 1976), pp. 112–28.
Whybray, R. N., in *A Dictionary of Biblical Interpretation*, eds. R. J. Coggins/J. L. Houlden (London: SCM Press, 1990), pp. 726–29.
Wieder, N., *The Formation of Jewish Liturgy in the East and the West: A Collection of Essays*, 2 vols. (Hebrew; Jerusalem: Ben-Zvi Institute, 1998).
Yerushalmi, Y. H., *Zakhor: Jewish History and Memory* (Seattle: University of Washington Press, 1996, 2nd edn.).

13 Peace in Early Jewish Prayer

Although it is not my purpose in this chapter to deal with the notion of *shalom* (usually translated into English as 'peace') as it occurs in the Hebrew Bible, there are numerous reasons why a brief account of what is to be found in this connection in that source, as well as in the Jewish literature of the Second Temple period and the Qumran corpora, might be found useful. The primary reason is perhaps that one cannot deal with any topic in early rabbinic literature without first noting such precedents and thereby assessing the degree to which there is continuity and change between these two major Jewish sources.[1]

Hebrew Bible

Salutations that enquire after, and express a wish for, the well-being and happiness of the other are expressed by the use of the word *shalom*.[2] When God grants such a state, what is implied is a broad band of security and prosperity for the people and the land. Although the priestly blessing in Num 6:24–26 is given a cultic setting, the language in which it is couched goes no further than invoking the blessing that divine favour will grant its recipients precisely such security and prosperity. In more 'political' contexts, such as those described in Deuteronomy, the meaning may be the absence of war, but not necessarily so. It is sometimes used in a war situation to convey the senses of treaty, alliance, friendship and peaceful intent.[3] There is of course a direct, theological aspect when God is involved but the overall concept of peace very much relates to daily life and to a totality of well-being. Since the basic sense of the stem *šlm* has much to do with wholeness and completion, *shalom* may often best be translated as 'life at its most complete and whole'.

In the prophetic literature, spiritual as well as physical well-being is stressed. In addition to political and military security, a just environment, and a successful economy, Israel will enjoy *shalom* through its special relationship with the Creator.[4] God, who has created not only *shalom* but also its opposite

1 For a number of the references and some of the conclusions with regard to passages in the Hebrew Bible, I have made use of the helpful and extensive treatment of the entry by Stendebach, *TDOT*.

2 E.g. Gen 28:21, 43:23, Exod 18:7, Lev 26:6.

3 E.g. Deut 2:26, 20:10–11, 23:7.

4 E.g. Isa 26:1, 32:17, 54:10, 55:12, 60:17.

DOI 10.1515/9783110486704-014

רע (meaning 'total unpleasantness'), will in his steadfast love grant Israel the former for its loyalty and will dog the wicked with the latter. This ideal state of bliss will mark Israel's rescue from exile, oppression and suffering.[5] It will not come when the false prophets promise it in their futile expectations but will arrive at a later date and become a permanent fixture of Israelite life.[6]

As one would expect from the hagiographical and wisdom literature, *shalom* is used not only in reference to tranquillity, protection and longevity, but also to describe proper and admirable human conduct and the fine ordering of the world. In Job, a cosmic or celestial aspect is introduced when God is said to create *shalom* in the high places.[7] As Gerleman and Stendebach rightly claim, no sharp distinction occurs in Israelite and Judahite thought between the secular and the theological applications of the word *shalom*, any more than such a distinction is valid in any other area of religious thought and practice as recorded in the Hebrew Bible.[8] Although many proper names include elements that derive from the root *šlm*, it is not always clear whether they refer to the god Shalem, to the city of Jerusalem, or to the divine blessing itself, and they do not therefore provide us with any helpful evidence for an investigation of the meanings carried by the word *shalom*.[9]

Second Temple period

As far as the apocryphal literature is concerned, the senses of political peace, treaty, well-being, health and happiness recur, as does the notion of the divine gift of such bliss. There is, however, in addition, a reference in Wisdom of Solomon 3:3 to the souls of the just being 'at peace'.[10] The use there and elsewhere in apocryphal and pseudepigraphical texts of the Greek *eirene* undoubtedly reflects the Hebrew *shalom* and appears to cover the same semantic field. Such a field is again represented in the Dead Sea Scrolls where the mundane topics covered by the word *shalom* include health, welfare, protection, safety, success and happiness. In relation to fellow beings, honesty, harmony, tranquillity and treaty may also be described as *shalom*, while the same term may refer to divine bless-

---

5 E.g. Isa 45:7, 57:21, Jer 33:6–9, Hag 2:9.
6 E.g. Jer 6:14, Ezek 13:10, Mic 3:5.
7 E.g. Ps 34:15, 72:3, 85:11, 122:6–8, Prov 3:2, Job 25:2.
8 Stendebach, *TDOT*, p. 43; Gerleman, *TLOT*, 3.1347.
9 Stendebach, *TDOT*, pp. 44–46.
10 Stendebach, *TDOT*, pp. 46–48.

ing and a more long-lasting form of blessing.[11] In sum, the Jewish literature of the Second Temple period, in both Hebrew and Greek, demonstrates a stable and consistent use of the word *shalom*, with a few, but no more than few, novel developments in theological thought.

In Ben Yehuda's Dictionary the definitions of the word *shalom* are given as *Wohlbefinden* and *Heilsein* in German, *bien-être* and *bon état* in French, and 'well-being' and 'welfare' in English. A note added by the editor, N. H. Tur-Sinai, makes the point that these are the basic senses of the word in Hebrew, as in other Semitic languages, and that 'peace' meaning the absence of war is no more than one of its specific extensions.[12] That Dictionary also points to the occurrence of the phrase *šmʿt šlm* ('good news') in the Lachish letters of the early sixth century B.C.E.[13]

Rabbinic literature

What, then, are the notions of *shalom* found in early rabbinic literature? Perhaps the most dominant one relates to the overall well-being of humanity. That well-being may relate to physical health or safety at the individual level, or to marital harmony, including sexual satisfaction. Such safety may include protection, not only from other human beings, but also from evil spirits.[14] *Shalom* may also apply to the wider social ambit, where it is by no means simply the absence of war but is also the operation of a society based on humanity, truth and justice.[15] In such a society, politics, the law-courts, the executive, scholars and the army ensure that friction is kept to a minimum, while ethical behaviour makes life more tolerable for the under-privileged and handicapped. It is a Jewish religious duty always to maximize efforts to ensure that such *shalom* reigns in families, within one's community and in the wider world (both here and in heaven), particularly when there is a tendency to indulge more aggressive emotions.[16]

A favourite saying of the fourth-century Babylonian teacher Abbaye was that one was duty-bound to develop the most cordial relations (מרבה שלום; 'increase

11 E.g. 1QS 2.9, 4.7; 1QM 3.11, 17.7; CD 6.21; 1QH 10(=2).15, 15(=7).15, 19(=11).27, 21(=18).15 (=30).
12 Ben Yehuda, *Dictionary*, 14.7130.
13 Tur-Sinai, *Lachish Ostraca*, p. 26, for one of a number of examples.
14 *t. ʿAbod. Zar.* 1.17, *ʾAbot R. Nat.* A 28 and B 14 (ed. Schechter-Kister, pp. 85–86 and 33), *b. Ber.* 16b and 55b, *b. Šabb.* 152a, *Midr. Teh.* 92.5 (ed. Buber, p. 405), *Sifre Zuṭa*, ed. Horovitz, p. 247.
15 *m. ʿAbod. Zar.* 4.6, *m. ʾAbot* 1.18, *t. Taʿan.* 2.10, *y. Taʿan.* 4.2 (68a).
16 *m. Šeb.* 5.9, *m. ʾAbot* 1.12 and 2.7, *t. Peʾa* 4.21, *ʾAbot R. Nat.* A 12 and B 24 (ed. Schechter-Kister, pp. 48–50), *b. Ber.* 6a, *b. Giṭ.* 56a, *y. Ber.* 4.2 (7d).

peace'), not only with fellow Jews and family members, but with everyone else too, including the non-Jew in the street, thus ensuring popularity on earth and in heaven. Resh Laqish expressed the view that, where dishonesty exists between people, only the reproof of such behaviour can ultimately lead to peaceful relations.[17] The notion is also employed to describe a situation in which the natural world functions precisely as it should, and not as it sometimes does when catastrophes occur. When a Jew meets another Jew, or sometimes when he encounters a non-Jew, he is obligated to offer and receive peaceful greetings.[18]

There are also what one may justifiably dub the cosmic, celestial and theological aspects of *shalom*, as the early rabbinic teachers perceived it. God created *shalom* before creating the universe and, when he brought mankind into being, he chose to do so by way of one individual, Adam. His motivation for this was to encourage *shalom* by eliminating the justification for any claim that one person's ancestry was superior to that of any other.[19] He also generates *shalom* among his heavenly servants, among whom are the 'angels of peace', and it is said of Elijah that he will come one day and make peace in the world. Some Torah legislation is laid down in order to bring about *shalom* between God and the people of Israel, a state of affairs that was constantly promoted by Moses himself.[20]

In an early midrashic interpretation of the prohibition in Exod. 20:22 to use a sword in building the simple earthen altar, reference is made to the view of Rabban Yoḥanan ben Zakkai concerning the complete stones to be used in the altar prescribed in Deut 27:6. Because the stem of the word for 'complete' is the same at that used for the word *shalom* (in both cases *šlm*), the altar is seen as engendering *shalom* between Israel and God. The aggadic passage argues that, if stones that can neither see nor hear nor speak, but simply create such *shalom*, suffer no violence, 'how much more should it be the case that anyone who brings *shalom* between individuals, between man and wife, or between cities, peoples, kingdoms and families, deserves to be spared any form of adversity.'[21] *Shalom* is what the dead can best hope to be granted and is so central that there are circumstances in which idolatry may be overlooked if *shalom* is achieved. Sincerely motivated students of the Torah can bring about *shalom* in the

17 *b. Ber.* 17a, *Bereshit Rab.* 54.3 (ed. Theodor-Albeck, p. 578).
18 *m. Ber.* 2.1, *m. Giṭ.* 5.9, *m. Ḥag.* 2.6, *m. Soṭah* 10.2, *m. Sanh.* 11.9.
19 *'Abot R. Nat.* B 24 (ed. Schechter-Kister, p. 49), *m. Sanh.* 4.5.
20 *m. 'Ed.* 8.7, *t. Pe'a* 4.21, *t. 'Abod. Zar.* 1.17, *'Abot R. Nat.* A 12 (ed. Schechter-Kister, p. 51), *Masechet D. E. Perek Ha-Shalom* (ed. Sperber, p. 196); *b. Ber.* 16b and 55b, *Sifre Zuṭa* (ed. Horovitz, pp. 248–49), *Seder Eliyahu Rabba* 3 (ed. Friedmann, p. 17).
21 *t. B. Qam.* 7.7, *Mek R. Ish.* 11 (ed. Horovitz-Rabin, p. 244). See Urbach, *Sages*, 1.370–71.

world. *Shalom* can also be employed as a proper name for God, the Messiah, Israel and Jerusalem.[22]

In the anthology that he prepared with Claude Montefiore, and that was published almost eighty years ago, Herbert Loewe noted that the Jewish pursuit of 'peace' does not mean non-resistance. or viewing apathetically the slaughter of the innocent and helpless. One has a duty to defend the persecuted, and indeed oneself, since the object is to live by God's commands and not die by them. Loewe also made the point that the 'love of the Rabbis for peace, and the tremendous emphasis that they attached to it, can be seen...from the prominence assigned to peace in so many portions of the liturgy.'[23] Of the various passages that he undoubtedly had in mind, the most powerful is perhaps that in which one of the third century's most acclaimed homilists in the Holy Land, R. Joshua b. Levi, demonstrated the outstanding nature of the concept of *shalom* by pointing out that the major Jewish prayers all conclude with the mention of this notion.[24]

Rabbinic liturgy: i

We may now define such prayers and analyse the place occupied by *shalom* within each of them. Since we are here dealing with the early rabbinic prayers that were composed and transmitted during the first Christian millennium, we must, in the course of such definition and analysis, also take account of any relevant textual variants. Examples of these latter are to be found in the earliest prayer-books of the ninth and tenth centuries, are represented in the variations between the Babylonian and the Palestinian rites, and are richly documented in the manuscripts from the Cairo Genizah.[25]

Our first example concerns God as the supreme peacemaker, and has a biblical as well as a rabbinic context. Mention is already made in the Mishnah of the two benedictions that precede the recitation of the *shema'* passages in the morning service.[26] No text or subject is there specified but the Babylonian Talmud

---

22 *'Abot R. Nat.* B 39 and 48 (ed. Schechter-Kister, pp. 107 and 134), *Der. Er. Zuṭa* 9 (ed. Sperber, p. 53), *Masechet D. E. Perek Ha-Shalom* (ed. Sperber, pp. 198 – 200), *b. Nazir* 66b, *Siphre d'Be Rab*, p. 42 (ed. Horovitz, p. 46), *Sifre Deut* 199 (ed. Finkelstein, p. 237).

23 Montefiore and Loewe, *Anthology*, pp. 257–58; see also pp. 530 – 37 and 650 – 51.

24 *y. Ber.* 2.4 (5a), *Masechet D. E. Perek Ha-Shalom* (ed. Sperber, pp. 202– 3), *Wayyik. Rab.* 9.9 (ed. Margulies, 1.194).

25 On the importance of the Genizah source for Jewish liturgy, see Reif, *Genizah and Jewish Liturgy*, pp. 29 – 45.

26 *m. Ber.* 1.4.

later indicates that the first benediction offers thanks to God for the renewal of light after the dark of the night in the context of his overall management of nature, while the second expresses gratitude for his generous choice of Israel for the receipt of the Torah.[27] The earliest reference to the beginning of that first benediction is to be found in the Palestinian Talmud in a list of cautions about how properly to recite this section of the prayers, and the need to avoid any mistakes in text or pronunciation. It is apparently correct to begin with the first phrase from Isa 45:7 יוצר אור ובורא חושך ('who forms light and creates darkness') but not to alter the final word to נוגה. It may be surmised that that such an alteration was required by its proponents because a word with the meaning of 'light' is more appropriate to God than the negative connotation conveyed by the word חושך, meaning 'darkness'.[28]

This same issue is raised in the Babylonian Talmud which adds a comment about the change made, and accepted, in the liturgy from the biblical phrase עושה שלום ובורא את הרע ('who makes peace and creates evil') – which is the second part of the same Isaianic verse – to עושה שלום ובורא את הכל ('who makes peace and creates everything').[29] It seems unlikely that the Palestinian Talmud would have ignored such an obvious and startling amendment, had it already been the practice in the land of Israel in about the third century. What therefore seem feasible is that the Babylonians incorporated the second half of the biblical verse into their liturgy but at the same time made a drastic change from the original 'evil' to what they saw as a less dualistically inclined word, namely 'everything'. In that case, we have also to note that they extended the description of God from one that praised him for the creation of light to one that also noted his responsibility for *shalom* and for 'everything else'. This indicates that *shalom* was not being understood by these liturgical composers as the opposite of evil, and therefore as everything good, but in some considerably more restricted sense. If any expression is replete with theological significance for the extent of divine power it must surely be הכל and not שלום. Given the context of the creation of the morning light and the removal of the dark night that was always seen as unsafe, the liturgical sense, as distinct from the biblical sense, of the two divinely created entities mentioned here would be akin to 'safety/security and omnipotence' and not 'bliss and unpleasantness'.

Such controversy about the use of biblical verses in Jewish liturgy, including the extension of coverage from one topic to others, is not unusual. Both the Dead

---

27 *b. Ber.* 11b.
28 *y. Ber.* 2.4 (4d).
29 *b. Ber.* 11b.

Sea Scrolls and the early rabbinic liturgy attach other theological themes to the topic of God's gift of light. Weinfeld draws attention to 11QPs^{a} [=11Q5] and to 1QH, as well as to the rabbinic expansion of this benediction into a trisagion (*qedushah*), and I have myself dealt with the inconsistency regarding the inclusion of biblical verses in the early rabbinic liturgy, as documented in the earliest manuscript sources.[30] What emerges, then, in the case of this prayer is that *shalom* is being used in the senses of safety and security, that it occurs only in the introductory phraseology, and that it is by no means central to the benediction.

Rabbinic liturgy: ii

The second instance here to be considered is again to be found in a daily rabbinic prayer. The notion of *shalom* re-appears in the second benediction recited after the *shema'* in the evening. Once again, this benediction is prescribed in the Mishnah but without indication of its text or subject.[31] The Palestinian Talmud mentions its eulogy in the context of an aggadic interpretation of the phrase בנוי לתלפיות in Song 4:4 that refers it to the ruins (תל) of the city of Jerusalem, the rebuilding of which is on the lips (פיות) of the worshippers as they recite the grace after meals, the *shema'* and the *'amidah*. The text offered in the eulogy of this post-*shema'* benediction is פורס סוכת שלום עלינו ועל כל עמו ישראל ועל ירושלים, praising God as the one who 'spread his peaceful covering over us, over all his people Israel, and over Jerusalem.'[32]

The subject of this second benediction, as is implied in the Babylonian Talmud, is an extension of the first benediction.[33] The latter extols God for rescuing the Jewish people from Egypt, while the former takes this further and seeks divine protection from the dangers of the night. Given that the benediction originated when the *shema'* was still separate from the *'amidah*, and when the recitation of the evening *'amidah* (with its many specific requests) was not yet a religious requirement, it is not surprising that such a request for protection should merit a place in that liturgical context. The phrase סוכת שלום ('peaceful covering') undoubtedly bears the sense of a protective shield against the assailments of the night but it is given a more intense theological flavour by the use of such metaphorical language, the direct action attributed to God, and the appeal for the restoration of Judaism's holiest city. Although the passage just cited from

30 Weinfeld, *Early Jewish Liturgy*, pp. 167–78; Reif, *Problems*, pp. 71–92.
31 *m. Ber.* 2.4.
32 *y. Ber.* 4.5 (8c).
33 *b. Ber.* 4b.

the Palestinian Talmud records no more than the ten words quoted, there can be little doubt that the original eulogy added, as in other instances, the phrase מנחם ציון ובונה ירושלים ('Comforter of Zion and Rebuilder of Jerusalem'), thus clearly spelling out such an intensity. In the Palestinian rite as it developed from, say, the second century until the destruction of the community by the Crusaders at the end of the eleventh century, the metaphor of God's peaceful covering is retained in both text and eulogy, and continues to include the three elements just mentioned.[34] It is clear, however, that the essential prayer is for a peaceful night since the text begins with an appeal to God to see the worshippers securely to bed and to ensure that they rise again safely in the morning.

The earliest and most reliable version of the Babylonian rite – or, at least, one common form of it – appears to be that of Sa'adya Ga'on (882–942), and here the metaphor of God's peaceful covering is no longer central to the daily evening composition, only to its sabbath version.[35] There is one reference (if it is textually reliable) to being hidden 'in the shadow of the divine wings' but the remainder has given way to more prosaic language. The worshipper still makes the request that he should retire and awake 'in peace' (לשלום) but the prayer now specifies what should be ruled out by the presence of such peace. There should be no troubles, mishaps or night-time fears, and evil and satanic powers should be curtailed on all sides. The eulogy describes God, in a somewhat less poetic fashion, as the eternal protector of his people Israel (שומר את עמו ישראל לעד), and there is no mention of the restored Jerusalem of the future. Although the request for God to spread his protective covering (ופרוש עלינו סוכת שלומך), which apparently originated in the Palestinian rite, was adopted widely by later communities[36], the overall atmosphere of the prayer, as in so many other instances, remained true to the dominant Babylonian trend. We may therefore conclude that while there was in this case a tendency in the land of Israel to see the divine peace as something more than a rescue from life's nightly tribulations, the essential sense of the word *shalom* in the dominant liturgy was still more closely related to the 'well-being' of today than to any serious theological development of that concept with regard to the long-term future.

34 Mann, 'Genizah fragments', pp. 302–11; Fleischer, *Eretz-Israel*, p. 83; Wieder, *Formation*, 1.106–7.

35 *Siddur RSG*, pp. 27 and 11.

36 Examples are cited in *'Osar Ha-Tefillot*, 1.543–45.

Rabbinic liturgy: iii

For a third case relevant to our discussion, we must move from the *shema'* to the other primary component of rabbinic liturgy, namely, the *'amidah*, and consider the final benediction in that rich collection of praise, entreaty and thanksgiving. The nomenclature that is applied to this final section of the *'amidah* in the earliest rabbinic sources itself indicates controversy about the essential nature and function of the benediction since it is entitled both ברכת כוהנים and שים שלום.[37] This reflects the fact that the first half of the benediction contains the priestly blessing as it occurs in Num. 6:24–26 while the second is composed of a more standard rabbinic format with a request for *shalom* and a conclusion on that theme. Such a dual composition testifies to a liturgical transformation from the Jerusalem Temple to the context of early rabbinic prayer.

The priestly blessing itself as well as a blessing relating to the priests, had been a part of the Temple ritual, and the rabbis of the second century were faced with the dilemma of how to relate to priesthood and to Temple ritual in their reconstruction of Jewish religious life after the loss of the cultic centre, and indeed the Jewish political state, in 70 C.E. As with the Decalogue, the recitation of which had also been part of Temple procedures, they had to decide whether the new rabbinic context, which ultimately found its liturgical home in the synagogue, would incorporate, adjust or reject the established priestly custom. What they did was to incorporate the priestly blessing into the *'amidah*, not as an independent entity but as an introduction to a benediction on the theme of *shalom*, since the blessing does, after all, call down on Israel God's blessing of 'peace' and concludes with the word *shalom*. The strength of ancient authority was thus added to a novel composition, while the opportunity was taken of responding to the blessing with words and phrases that were characteristic of rabbinic religious thought.[38]

Uri Ehrlich has argued cogently that the two elements were capable of being successfully fused since they had a common phenomenological factor. If one regards the *'amidah* as an active discourse between the Jew and God, it is not difficult to see the nineteenth benediction – consisting as it does of peace and priestly blessing – as a necessary and integral part of the formal process of leave-taking. Such leave-taking between people is well-known from the Hebrew Bible and from an ancient Jewish tradition that is mentioned a few times in the Talmud, with specific guidance as to its formulation. The blessing of peace is central to forms of welcome

---

37 *m. Roš. Haš.* 4.5 and *m. Tamid* 5.1, *b. Meg.* 18a and *b. Soṭah* 39b.
38 Reif, *Problems*, pp. 93–105.

and departure, and occurs in the expressions used by the Levites to mark their departure from the Temple. It denotes the pleasure of the meeting and the well-wisher's commitment to the friendship. So, too, the priestly benediction, with its ancient pedigree and an early valedictory function, connotes God's response to Israel's praise with an assurance of his commitment and affection, while the changing of the priestly watches was marked by similar benedictions.

There is rabbinic disagreement as to the relative roles of God and the priests in the mediation of the blessing as well as a rabbinic determination to include it in the *'amidah* as part of the new liturgical composition. The sense of the benediction is therefore a request for the implementation of that 'peace' mediated in the priestly blessing. According to Ehrlich, the linguistic distinction of this final benediction from other requests in the *'amidah* proceeds from the fact that here we are not requesting national and political restoration (*pace* Finkelstein), but divine peace.[39]

Ehrlich may well be right about phenomenological compatibility of the two halves of this final benediction, and its definition as a request for divine peace. The problem that remains to be resolved is whether the nature of that divine peace may be ascertained from the text of the rabbinic benediction. Its resolution is complicated by the existence of a number of textual prototypes that form the basis for many of the rabbinic rites used in the post-talmudic and early medieval periods. At the same time, this very textual variety may itself provide the key to an understanding of the theological issues that faced those wishing to finalize the composition of the benediction and of the preferences they were expressing when they opted for one formulation over another. Without entering into all the technical details of the textual history of the benediction, it is possible to see some trends within each of the three basic formats that the benediction took on in its early existence. Such formats have been carefully defined by Yehezkel Luger and Uri Ehrlich in their studies of the Genizah texts of the *'amidah* and, although there is room for argument about the detail, the overall schemes that they adopt are sufficiently convincing for us to draw some general conclusions about the variety of ways in which the Jewish liturgical composers understood the gift of *shalom* here being solicited.[40]

If we turn first to the text that is the most common among the Cairo Genizah fragments, that is apparently the favoured (but by no means exclusive) version among the Babylonian authorities of the post-talmudic and pre-medieval periods, and that is also recorded by Maimonides, we find that this is the longest of the

39 Ehrlich, *Ha-Tefillah*, pp. 481–97 and *Weekday Amidah*, pp. 259–74.
40 Luger, *Amidah*, pp. 196–208; Ehrlich, *Weekday Amidah*, pp. 260–61.

three basic prototypes. It requests, for 'us and Israel your people' (עלינו ועל ישראל עמך), not only *shalom* but also good, blessing, favour, benevolence and compassion, and goes on to crave divine blessing 'from the light of God's countenance' for the whole Jewish people, 'all of us together' (כולנו כאחד). Such blessing, declares this formulation, has already ensured for Israel the gifts of Torah, life, love, benevolence, justice, compassion, blessing and *shalom*. The body of the benediction ends with an appeal for God to agree to bless his people Israel at all times and the eulogy praises God as the one who blesses his people Israel.[41]

Close analysis of this formulation highlights a number of points. Picking up from the word *shalom* with which the priestly blessing concludes, this form of the benediction adds a list of other items being requested, thereby indicating that *shalom* is being understood in its basic biblical sense of total well-being, including of course the absence of conflict. The central phraseology refers to the 'light of God's countenance' (מאור פניך) that occurs in the priestly blessing and asks for a renewal of this blessing, seeing it as the source of the special favour granted to Israel by God and made manifest in a variety of gifts at various points in its history. Again, *shalom* and blessing occurs with a list of other benefits received, implying that it refers to those times when Israel enjoyed a tranquil and privileged existence.

The message conveyed by the phrase 'all of us together' is perhaps that we have moved from an élitist arrangement, that sets the priests atop the hierarchy, to a more democratic set-up, where God is asked to offer his blessing to everyone, and no mention is made of any mediators. Having stated the request for a list of blessings and noted that this request has at times in the past been granted, the petitioner than makes a plea for such blessings, including *shalom*, to be available on a more permanent basis in the future. As the eulogy describes him, God is the one who can, as the priestly blessing indicates, provide *shalom* for his people Israel. He is therefore the one who can bring about all the other blessings that have just been listed and that apparently complement *shalom*.

The second textual format to be considered is not the only one used by the Palestinian Jews of the pre-Crusader period but certainly makes a regular appearance in remnants of their rite. Addressing God, it asks him to grant 'your *shalom*' (שים שלומך) to Israel, with some texts expanding Israel to include, for example, its people. The central portion, as in the first prototype, requests a blessing for us, and the benediction immediately concludes with a eulogy of God as 'creator of *shalom*' (עושה שלום). Although a democratic tendency is again revealed in some texts by the use of

[41] *SRAmram*, ed. Goldschmidt, p. 26: שים שלום טובה וברכה חסד ורחמים עלינו ועל [כל] ישראל עמך וברכנו [אבינו] כלנו [כאחד] באור פניך כי באור פניך נתת לנו ה' אלהינו תורת חיים אהבה וחסד צדקה ורחמים ושלום. וטוב בעיניך לברך את עמך ישראל. בא"י המברך את עמו ישראל בשלום. See Luger, *Amidah*, p. 198, Ehrlich, *Weekday Amidah*, p. 261, and Maimonides, ed. Goldschmidt, p. 200.

the phrase ‘all of us together’, there appears to be something a little different in the remainder of the religious message here conveyed.[42]

Ehrlich has recently published a slightly more unusual Genizah text of the Palestinian version of this benediction, housed at the Bodleian Library in the University of Oxford.[43] He is correct in noting that this version again makes a link with the priestly blessing, that it may be influenced by liturgical poetry, and that its eulogy (now textually defective) was originally מעון הברכות ועושה השלום. What is important for our purposes is that it is again God’s peace and his peaceful protection that is being requested for ‘us’.

In these prayers emanating from the Jewish homeland, then, *shalom* is not listed with any other benefit and is described, directly and simply, as belonging to God and as his creation. The benediction is therefore making a plea for a gift of whatever it was that the priests were requesting in their blessing, and defining it no more precisely than of divine origin and possession. It may therefore perhaps be surmised that the *shalom* here being requested is more closely related to the kind of *shalom* that occurs in those rabbinic passages concerned with the special relationships between God and Israel, between God and the heavenly retinue, and between God and the cosmos. That would make it less descriptive of a practical state of affairs and more of a spiritual notion, with an affinity to concepts of divine emanation such as became popular in Neoplatonic religious thought.

The third formulation of the final benediction in the *‘amidah* has today survived only in the Ashkenazi rite and is used only on those occasions when the priestly blessing itself is not recited, such as during the afternoon and evening services. Although its regular use is documented from about the twelfth century, it does occur in versions of *Seder Rav ‘Amram*, is attested in Genizah texts, has a parallel in early Sefardi custom for the fast of the Ninth of Av, and is mentioned in a geonic responsum.[44] All these factors, plus the brevity and simplicity of the

42 Luger, *Amidah*, p. 198, and Ehrlich, *Weekday Amidah*, p. 260: שים שלומך על ישראל עמך ועל עירך [ועל נחלתך] וברכנו כולנו כאחד. בא׳י עושה השלום. See Mann, ‘Genizah fragments’, pp. 307, 311.

43 U. Ehrlich, ‘*Tefillat*’, especially pp. 15–17, and *Weekday Amidah*, p. 260. MS Bodley Heb.d.55.33–34: ברכינו אלהינו ושמ[רנ]ו וחנינו ושלומך שים עלינו וסוכת שלומך פר[וס] [ע]לינו ברוך אתה יי מעון הברכו[ת] [ועושה השלום?].

[43] Elbogen, *Gottesdienst*, p. 520, *Ha-Tefillah*, p. 396, n. 56, *Liturgy*, p. 399, n. 56 (J. Heinemann’s additional notes); Luger, *Amidah*, p. 198; Ehrlich, *Weekday Amidah*, p. 261. The Hebrew text is: שלום רב על [כל] [ישראל] [עמך] תשים לעולם [ועד] כי אתה [הוא] [אל] [מלך] אדון [כל] השלום וטוב בעיניך לברך את עמך ישראל בכל עת [ובכל שעה בשלומך] בא׳י המברך את עמו ישראל בשלום. See Cambridge Genizah MSS: T-S H 5.135, T-S H 5.224, T-S NS 120.62, T-S NS 123.105, T-S NS 150.141, T-S AS 102.164. These texts have been noted by Uri Ehrlich in the context of a joint Genizah liturgical project of Ben-Gurion University of the Negev and Cambridge University Library that was run by him and by my Cambridge colleague, Dr Ben Outhwaite. I am grateful to them both for generously making this

text, convinced Heinemann that it was an ancient Palestinian text of the benediction, the eulogy for which originally read 'master of peace' (אדון השלום).[45] It begins with a request to God for 'ample *shalom*' (שלום רב) to be eternally granted to Israel/'your people' because God is the '(royal) master of all *shalom*' (מלך אדון לכל השלום) and concludes with an appeal for God to agree to bless his people Israel at all times with his *shalom*.

The wording of the eulogy (המברך את עמו ישראל בשלום) matches that of the first version described earlier. There is some discrepancy about this since the theme of the whole benediction is God's role as the supreme lord of *shalom* and this led to Heinemann's conclusion about the original form of the eulogy, and its having been changed to match the more standard form, with an accompanying change having to be made in the phrase immediately preceding the eulogy in order to lead naturally into it. Ehrlich rightly points to the additional Genizah evidence that calls into question the degree to which Heinemann's theories about the content and the original eulogy may be accepted. Wieder also senses that a change has been made but suggests that the original wording of the eulogy in Palestine was 'source of blessings and creator of *shalom*' (מעון הברכות ועושה השלום) and that this was widely abbreviated to 'creator of *shalom*' (עושה השלום) because of the well-known Babylonian halakhic objection to eulogies containing more than one theme.[46]

What then is the religious message of this version and how is *shalom* perceived by its composers? Since *shalom* has just been mentioned in the priestly blessing, God, who is its creator, is asked to grant it in abundance to his people Israel. The final appeal, whether an addendum or not, does not depart from this theme but stresses that *shalom* comes directly from God and prays for a constant supply to Israel. Since there is serious doubt about the originality of the wording of the eulogy, it should be brought into the equation only as evidence of how one form of early rabbinic understanding of *shalom* influenced another. Taking into account all these factors, it seems clear that the sense of *shalom* in this third formulation is virtually identical to the one that was above identified in the second textual version.

---

data available to me and to Dr Rebecca Jefferson and other colleagues in the Genizah Research Unit at the Library for important assistance with their decipherment.

45 Heinemann, *Jewish Liturgy*, p. 43.

46 Ehrlich, *Weekday Amidah*, p. 266, n. 40; Wieder, *Formation*, 1.103–7; Fleischer, *Eretz-Israel*, p. 34.

Rabbinic liturgy: iv

The fourth early rabbinic prayer of relevance to our discussion consists of only one verse and has a simple structure. Its first half makes use of the phrase in Job 25:2b, namely עושה שלום במרומיו ('the one who creates peace in his high places'), to describe God. It then adds to that biblical quotation the second phrase הוא יעשה שלום עלינו ועל כל (עמו) ישראל which constitutes an appeal to God to apply his heavenly skills to the earthly situation and bring *shalom* to the worshippers and all their co-religionists. Although it is brief, biblical in half of its source, and attached to the end of *qaddish*, to the appended supplication that follows the final *shalom* benediction of the *'amidah*, and to the end of the grace after meals, it has no direct relevance to the previous prayer formulations and is therefore entitled to be regarded as an independent prayer, albeit a very limited one, on the topic of *shalom*.[47]

The midrashim that refer to prayers ending in peace have in mind the prayers already discussed above and make no mention of the use of this brief liturgical formula.[48] This in itself indicates a late date but it should be acknowledged that it does appear in the prayer-book of Sa'adya Gaon at the end of the grace after meals and in Genizah fragments of the Palestinian rite in various contexts.[49] It is not our task here to analyse carefully the origins and development of the liturgical usage, but a feasible working hypothesis would be that prayer was in the process of being adopted in the geonic period between the seventh and tenth centuries. It is not clear whether it began at the end of the *'amidah* and was then attached to the end of the grace after meals, or vice versa. Alternatively, its presence in some Genizah fragments after a morning Torah benediction testifies to its use in a different context. The source of this addendum is understood by some scholars as a formal leave-taking, so that various suggestions have been made as to who is being greeted with *shalom* in this way, whether God, the angels, or one's fellow Jews.[50]

For the purposes of this brief study, the question is how the word *shalom* is being understood in this formulation. Since the composers chose to use a biblical phrase that refers to the divine creation of *shalom* in the celestial spheres, we may conclude that their intention was that their wording of the second half of

---

47 *'Osar Ha-Tefillot*, 1.165, 1.368 and 1.490. The simplest text, as found in *SRAmram*, ed. Goldschmidt, p. 39, is: עושה שלום במרומיו הוא (ברחמיו) יעשה שלום על (כל) ישראל

48 See n. 24 above.

49 Davidson/Assaf/Joel, *Siddur RSG*, p. 107; Mann, 'Genizah fragments', pp. 280, 293, 311; Cambridge University Library, MS Add.3162, f. 4r, ed. Reif, 'Tischdank', p. 15.

50 Zimmels, '*Ha-Ḥatimah*', pp. 49–55. See also Sperber's notes in *Masechet D. E.*, pp. 230–31.

the liturgical verse should express a plea for such a celestial peace to be granted to the worshippers and to the people of Israel as a whole. Indeed, in the context of the non-statutory phrases appended to the *'amidah* after the final benediction, the personal addition that was made by the fourth-century Babylonian teacher R. Safra constituted a similar plea. His entreaty was that God should bring *shalom* to both the heavenly and the earthly authorities.[51] Some of the medieval liturgical commentators stress that *shalom* carries the sense of a totality of all that is good, and that is why it is so deserving of a major place in the prayers.[52]

In that case, the essence of the invocation here being discussed is less related to greetings or leave-taking but more closely associated with the kind of atmosphere that we have already encountered in two liturgical contexts. Such an atmosphere was defined as of more exclusively spiritual a nature and the result of some form of divine emanation. It is consequently more likely to have originated in circles that were enthused by mystical considerations. They undoubtedly made mundane requests of God but also employed a rich variety of pietistic and even occult vocabulary and phraseology. This is not to say that such circles were opposed to the achievement of the religious ideal by halakhic discipline but to stress that their concept of prayers and benedictions understood these in terms of a broader cosmic theosophy. The *qaddish* and the *qedushah* were among prayers heavily influenced by such notions and it is now widely recognized that these latter made a major impact on rabbinic prayer in the post-talmudic period. The informal addenda recited at the end of the *'amidah* proper was one of the contexts into which they could, fairly uncontroversially, insert a brief composition such as *'oseh shalom.*[53]

Other liturgical contexts

There are a few other contexts in which *shalom* occurs in early rabbinic prayer. Psalms 29:11 is used in a similar way to *'oseh shalom* and may also have been motivated by the same mystical considerations. It is, however, difficult to assess this usage since it has no rabbinic formulation to provide any clues, and is

---

51 *b. Ber.* 17a.

52 Judah b. Yaqar, 1.77; Eleazar of Worms, 2.440; Abudraham, p. 68. See also Yaḥya b. Ṣaliḥ, 1.32 and 1.91.

53 For some of the background to the impact of mysticism on the early liturgy, see Dan, 'Emergence'; Fenton, *Treatise*; Schäfer, *Hekhalot*; Idel, *Perspectives*; Goetschel, *Prière*; Bar-Ilan, *Mysteries*; and Swartz, *Mystical Prayer.* See also Elbogen, as in n. 43 above; de Sola Pool, *Kaddish*, pp. 76–78; and Lehnardt, *Qaddish*, pp. 60–61.

simply the biblical Hebrew verse in its original wording. The prayer recited before undertaking a journey is also concerned with *shalom* but the context there is undoubtedly at one with the evening post-*shema‘* benediction in being concerned with physical safety; the sense is therefore clearly a mundane one. Shalom is briefly included in a number of other prayers such as *birkat ha-mazon*, *ya ‘aleh ve-yavo* and *birkat ha-ḥodesh* but in none of these instances is the theme of the broader context itself that of *shalom*.[54] The notion appears there merely as one of a list of *desiderata* such as health, longevity, rescue from persecution, and happiness.

Conclusions

In the Hebrew Bible, the notion of *shalom* is best understood as 'life at its most complete and whole' and it is also used to describe proper and admirable human conduct and the fine ordering of the world. The prophetic literature employs the term in alluding to the ideal state of bliss that will mark Israel's rescue from exile, oppression and suffering, while in Job a cosmic or celestial aspect is introduced when God is said to create *shalom* in the high places. The Jewish literature of the Second Temple period, in both Hebrew and Greek, demonstrates a stable and consistent use of the word *shalom*, with a few – but no more than a few – novel developments in theological thought that include more lasting forms of divine blessing and what is granted to the righteous after death.

For the early rabbis, there exists a religious duty always to maximize efforts to ensure that *shalom* reigns in families, within one's community and in the wider world, particularly when there is a tendency to indulge more aggressive emotions. This may be achieved by the correct ordering of society through the imposition and monitoring of ethical standards but does not necessarily require an intensive degree of pacifism. There are also what one might justifiably dub the cosmic, celestial and theological aspects of *shalom* as they occur in connection with God's relations with the angels, with creation, and with the Jewish people.

In the first rabbinic prayer analysed, *shalom* is being used in the senses of safety and security, and it occurs only in the introductory phraseology, and is by no means central to the benediction. The second prayer displays a tendency in the land of Israel to see the divine peace as something more than a rescue from life's nightly tribulations, but the essential sense of the word *shalom* in

54 *'Osar Ha-Tefillot*, pp. 736, 526–28, 487–89, 348 and 709.

the dominant liturgy is still more closely related to today's 'well-being'. There are three basic forms of the third prayer:

a. Having stated the request for a list of blessings and noted that this request has at times in the past been granted, the petitioner then makes a plea for such a list of blessings, including *shalom*, to be available on a more permanent basis in the future from God who is in control of such gifts.
b. *Shalom* being here requested is more closely related to the kind of *shalom* that occurs in those rabbinic passages concerned with the special relationships between God and Israel, between God and the heavenly retinue, and between God and the cosmos. That makes it less descriptive of a practical state of affairs and more of a spiritual notion.
c. the sense of *shalom* is virtually identical to the one that was above identified in the second textual version.

Having probably been incorporated into the statutory liturgy later than the other liturgical texts discussed, the fourth prayer belongs to a genre that is less concerned with mundane matters but more closely related to the theme of the spiritual connection between heaven and earth. The mentions of *shalom* in other texts are too limited to permit any close assessment but it may safely be suggested that the composer essentially had in mind notions of physical safety and daily comfort.

Works cited

Abudraham, D., *Sefer Abudraham Ha-Shalem*, ed. S. A. Wertheimer (Jerusalem: Usha, 1963).

Amram ben Sheshna, *Seder Rav 'Amram Ga'on*, ed. E. D. Goldschmidt (Jerusalem: Rav Kook, 1971).

Avoth de-Rabbi Nathan, ed. S. Schechter, reprinted with a prolegomenon by M. Kister (New York and Jerusalem: Jewish Theological Seminary of America, 1997).

Bar-Ilan, M., *The Mysteries of Jewish Prayer and Hekhalot* (Hebrew; Ramat-Gan: Bar-Ilan, 1987).

Ben Yehuda, E. E., *A Complete Dictionary of Ancient and Modern Hebrew* (Hebrew; Jerusalem, New York: Yoseloff, 1908–1959, 1960).

Dan, J., 'The emergence of mystical prayer', in *Studies in Jewish Mysticism*, eds. J. Dan and F. Talmage (Cambridge, Mass.: Association for Jewish Studies, 1982), pp. 85–120.

Davidson, I., Assaf, S., Joel, B. I. (eds.), *Siddur R. Sa'adya Gaon. Kitāb Ǵāmi' Aṣ-Ṣalawāt Wat-Tasābīh* (Jerusalem: Mekize Nirdamim, 1963, 2nd edn.).

Der. Er .= The Treatises Derek Erez: Masseket Derek Erez, Pirke Ben Azzai, Tosefta Derek Erez, ed. M. Higger (New York: DeBe Rabbanan, 1935).

De Sola Pool, D., *The Kaddish* (Leipzig: Drugulin, 1909).

Ehrlich, U., '*Ha-Tefillah ke-siaḥ u-fenomenologiya shel peridah*', in *Higayon L'Yona: New Aspects in the Study of Midrash, Aggadah and Piyut in Honor of Professor Yona*

Fraenkel, eds. J. Levinson, J. Elbaum and G. Hasan-Rokem (Hebrew; Jerusalem: Magnes, 2006), pp. 481–97.
Ehrlich, U., '*Tefillat shemoney 'esreh shelemah 'al piy minhag ereș yisra'el*', *Kobez 'Al Yad* 18 (28), 2005, pp. 1–17.
Ehrlich, U., *The Weekday Amidah in Geniza Prayer Books: Origins and Transmission* (Hebrew; Jerusalem: Yad Ben-Zvi Press, 2013).
Elbogen, I., *Der jüdische Gottesdienst in seiner geschichtlichen Entwicklung* (Frankfurt a. M.: Kaufmann, 1931; reprint, Hildesheim: Olms, 1962); Hebrew edition, *Ha-Tefillah Be-Yisra'el Be-Hitpatḥutah Ha-Hisṭorit*, eds. J. Heinemann, I. Adler, A. Negev, J. Petuchowski, H. Schirmann (Tel Aviv: Devir, 1972); English edition, *Jewish Liturgy: A Comprehensive History*, Eng. trans. and ed. R. P. Scheindlin (Philadelphia: Jewish Publication Society, 1993.
Eleazar b. Judah of Worms, *Pirushey Siddur HaTefilah LaRokeach; a Commentary on the Jewish Prayer Book*, ed. M. and Y. A. Hershler, 2 vols. (Jerusalem: Hershler, 1992).
Fenton, P. B., *Deux traités de mystique juive* (Lagrasse: Verdier, 1987).
Fenton, P. B., *The Treatise of the Pool* (London: Octagon, 1981).
Fleischer, E., *Eretz-Israel Prayer and Prayer Rituals as Portrayed in the Geniza Documents* (Hebrew; Jerusalem: Magnes, 1998).
Gerleman. G., 'Shalom', in *Theological Lexicon of the Old Testament*, eds. E. Jenni and C. Westermann, vol. 3, Eng. trans. M. E. Biddle (Peabody, Mass.: Hendrickson, 1997), pp. 1337–48.
Goetschel, R., (ed.), *Prière, Mystique et Judaïsme* (Paris: Presses Universitaires de France, 1987).
Goldschmidt, E. D., 'The Oxford Ms. of Maimonides' Book of Prayer', in his collected articles *On Jewish Liturgy: Essays on Prayer and Religious Poetry* (Hebrew; Jerusalem: Magnes, 1978), pp. 187–216.
Heinemann, J., *Studies in Jewish Liturgy*, ed. A. Shinan (Hebrew; Jerusalem: Magnes, 1981).
Idel, M., *Kabbalah: New Perspectives* (New Haven: Yale University Press, 1988).
Judah b. Yaqar, *Perush Ha-Tefillot Ve-Ha-Berakhot*, ed. S. Yerushalmi, 2 vols. (Jerusalem: Me'orey Yisrael, 1968).
Lehnardt, A., *Qaddish. Untersuchungen zur Entstehung und Rezeption eines rabbinischen Gebetes* (TSAJ 87; Tübingen: Mohr Siebeck, 2002).
Luger, Y., *The Weekday Amidah in the Cairo Genizah* (Hebrew; Jerusalem: Orhot, 2001).
Maimonides, 'The Oxford Ms. of Maimonides' Book of Prayer', ed. E. D. Goldschmidt, in his collected articles *On Jewish Liturgy: Essays on Prayer and Religious Poetry* (Hebrew; Jerusalem: Magnes 1978), pp. 187–216.
Mann, J., 'Genizah fragments of the Palestinian order of service', *Hebrew Union College Annual* 2 (1925), pp. 269–338.
Masechet Derech Eretz Zutta and Perek Ha-Shalom, third, expanded edition, by D. Sperber (Jerusalem, Ṣur 'Ot, 1994).
Mechilta d'Rabbi Ismael, ed. H. S. Horovitz and I. A. Rabin (Jerusalem: Shalem, 1997, 2nd edn.).
Midrash Bereshit Rabba, eds. J. Theodor and Ch. Albeck, 3 vols. (Jerusalem: Wahrmann, 1965, 2nd edn.).
Midrasch Tehillim (Schocher Tob), ed. S. Buber (Vilna: Romm, 1891).
Midrash Wayyikra Rabbah, ed. M. Margulies, 5 vols. (Jerusalem: Ministry of Education and Culture of Israel and American Academy of Jewish Research, 1953–60).

Montefiore, C. G., and Loewe, H., *A Rabbinic Anthology* (London: Macmillan, 1938).
'Osar Ha-Tefillot, ed. A. L. Gordon, 2 vols. (Vilna: Romm, 1923).
Reif, S. C., 'Ein Genisa-Fragment des Tischdank', in W. Homolka (ed.), *Liturgie als Theologie: Das Gebet als Zentrum im judischen Denken* (Berlin: Frank & Timme, 2005), pp. 11–29.
Reif, S. C., 'Genizah and Jewish liturgy: past achievements and a current project', *Medieval Encounters* 5 (1999), pp. 29–45.
Reif, S. C., *Problems with Prayers. Studies in the Textual History of Early Rabbinic Liturgy* (SJ 37, Berlin: de Gruyter, 2006).
Schäfer, P., *Geniza-fragmente zur Hekhalot Literatur* (Tübingen: Mohr, 1984).
Seder Eliyahu Rabba and Seder Eliyahu Zuta, ed. M. Friedmann (Jerusalem: Bamberger & Wahrman, 1960, 2nd edn.).
Sifre on Deuteronomy, ed. L. Finkelstein (New York: Jewish Theological Seminary of America, 1969, 2nd edn.).
Sifre Zuṭa, as included in *Siphre d'Be Rab*, ed. H. S. Horovitz, pp. 227–336.
Siphre d'Be Rab, ed. H. S. Horovitz, (Jerusalem: Wahrmann, 1966, 2nd edn.).
Stendebach, F. J., 'Shalom', in *Theological Dictionary of the Old Testament*, eds. G. J. Botterweck, H. Ringgren and H.-J. Fabry, vol. 15, Eng. trans. D. E. Green (Grand Rapids Mich.: Eerdmans, 2006), pp. 13–49.
Swartz, M. D., *Mystical Prayer in Ancient Judaism: An Analysis of Ma'aseh Merkavah* (Tübingen: Mohr Siebeck, 1992).
Tur-Sinai, N. H., *The Lachish Ostraca. Letters of the Time of Jeremiah*, revised and expanded edition, ed. S. Ahituv (Hebrew; Jerusalem: Bialik Institute and Israel Exploration Society, 1987).
Urbach, E. E., *The Sages. Their Concepts and Beliefs*, Eng. trans. I. Abrahams, 2 vols. (Jerusalem: Magnes, 1975).
Weinfeld, M., *Early Jewish Liturgy. From Psalms to the Prayers in Qumran and Rabbinic Literature* (Hebrew; Jerusalem: Magnes, 2004).
Wieder, N., *The Formation of Jewish Liturgy in the East and the West: A Collection of Essays*, 2 vols. (Hebrew; Jerusalem: Ben-Zvi Institute, 1998).
Yaḥya ben Joseph ibn Ṣaliḥ, *Tiklal*, 3 vols. (Jerusalem: Joseph Ḥasid, 1894).
Zimmels, Y., "*Al ha-ḥatimah be-shalom shel berakhot u-tefillot*', *Sinai* 20 (1947), pp. 49–55.

14 The *'Amidah* Benediction on Forgiveness: Links between its Theology and its Textual Evolution

In the volume in which this article originally appeared, other contributors dealt broadly with the nature of penitential prayer in Rabbinic Judaism, the manner in which it differs from its equivalent in the Second Temple period, and the forms which it took in early synagogal poetry (*piyyuṭim*), as well as in the later liturgies.[1] It therefore seemed to me that I should focus more sharply on one of the relevant benedictions in the *'amidah* and attempt to trace how it relates to earlier material, how its text evolved in the talmudic and post-talmudic (geonic) periods, and how it was understood by some of those involved in explicating its religious meaning and message. In order successfully to complete such an agenda, it proved necessary to deal with linguistic and literary matters, as well as theological ones, and to include in the discussion some remarks on how Jewish liturgical history through the ages is to be accurately reconstructed.

Jewish penitential prayer is of course not simply the performance of physical acts of mourning and worship, accompanied by exercises in self-effacement, contrition, historical reflection, and repentance, with a view to recreating oneself in a better religious image, although those are undoubtedly central parts of the spiritual intention.[2] Given that inadequate religious behaviour also disturbs the relationship between Israel and her God and reflects a degree of rebellion on the human side of the covenant, the object of such prayer is to request divine forgiveness so that, as it were, the slate may be wiped clean, and any damage made good. It is therefore hardly surprising that the fifth benediction of the *'amidah*, which requests God's assistance in bringing about the worshipper's sincere and far-ranging repentance, should immediately be followed by an entreaty for the assurance of God's forgiveness. The wish is for guidance to true *teshuvah* ('repentance') and the granting of divine *seliḥah* ('forgiveness'). It is the latter benediction – the sixth in the *'amidah* – that will here occupy our close attention.[3]

---

1 See, particularly, the articles of R. Sarason, R. Langer, R. Kimelman, and L. Leiber in *Seeking the Favor of God. Volume 3.*

2 See Werline, *Penitential Prayer*; Newman, *Praying*; and *Seeking the Favour of God: Volume 1*, eds. Boda, Falk and Werline.

3 For the standard modern editions and translations of the Ashkenazi and Sefardi versions of these benedictions, see Gaster, *Book of Prayer*, 1.32, and Singer, *Authorised Daily Prayer Book*, p. 46 (and many subsequent editions). Richard Sarason (p. 4 of the volume cited in n. 1 above) has astutely described this form of penitential rhetoric as 'a somewhat low-key appearance'.

DOI 10.1515/9783110486704-015

Starting point

But what is to be our starting point if we wish to examine how the text of this benediction is likely to have commenced its liturgical life, and the manner in which it evolved through the early centuries of rabbinic religious development? Various talmudic texts refer to the benediction but none of them record any more than its opening and (perhaps) closing words. This is a common phenomenon in the early history of rabbinic prayer; it effectively prevents us from assuming that what became the standard forms in the geonic period are already to be taken for granted in the tannaitic and amoraic eras that preceded it.[4] What we are forced to do is to look for the most reliable text in the geonic period and then postulate, on the basis of the biblical, Second Temple and talmudic evidence, what are likely to have been its earliest elements.

The consensus is that the evidence we have for the prayer-book of Sa'adya ben Joseph Gaon, head of the Babylonian rabbinic centre in Sura from 928 to 942, is at least a good reflection of the text that he originally composed, since the primary manuscript, as well as the many fragments from the Cairo Genizah, permit the reconstruction of a rather stable and consistent version. That it remains unclear to us whether that version is essentially from the communities of Egypt, the land of Israel or Iraq, makes difficulties for those attempting to trace the emergence and interrelationship of such rites, but does not adversely affect our present purpose.[5] As far as the prayer-book of Amram ben Sheshna Gaon is concerned, it was certainly written before that of Sa'adya but its text is undoubtedly less well preserved, having been seriously altered by the influences of later rites in the various communities where it was cited and used. In this case, it is not greatly different from the text of Sa'adya but the latter is decidedly more reliable.[6] Sa'adya's Hebrew text (followed by my own English translation) reads as follows[7]:

סלח לנו אבינו כי חטאנו ומחול לנו מלכנו כי פשענו ב א י חנון ומרבה לסלוח

4 See Reif, *Hebrew Prayer*, pp. 122–27.

5 The place of Sa'adya's prayer-book in the critical study of Jewish liturgy (especially in contrast to that of Amram ben Sheshna Gaon) is briefly but succinctly discussed in Reif, *Hebrew Prayer*, pp. 185–88 and in Brody, 'Liturgical use', pp. 63–66.

6 *SRAmram*, ed. Coronel, p. 8; ed. Frumkin, 1.242; ed. Hedegård, p. 35 (Hebrew), p. 88 (English); ed. Goldschmidt, pp. 24 and 95.

7 Davidson/Assaf/Joel, *Siddur RSG*, p. 18.

> Forgive us, our Father, that we have sinned, and pardon us, our King, that we have done wrong. You, Lord, are to be praised as the One who generously and consistently grants forgiveness

What is to be particularly noted in this text is that there are two requests for forgiveness, one addressing God as Israel's father and the other as her king, in a form of parallelism that is reminiscent of biblical Hebrew poetry; that the forgiveness is required in response to the inadequate religious behaviour of the worshipping community, represented by the 'we' and the 'us' of the entreaty; and that the concluding eulogy refers to God in a somewhat complex fashion. The language, structure and meaning of the benediction in this form must now be compared with the evidence from earlier periods.

Bible and Second Temple period

With regard to the notion of סליחה ('forgiveness') in the Hebrew Bible, the subject is almost invariably God and it is usually improper acts, often described by the Hebrew words חטא ('sin'), פשע ('transgression') and עון ('iniquity'), that are being forgiven, and only occasionally those who have perpetrated them.[8] It is presupposed that one of the divine attributes is a fundamental willingness to forgive and, even if punishment is not precluded, such an attribute is almost always exercised.[9] One of the purposes of the human approach to God is, as it were, to jog the divine memory by referring to God in terms of such an attribute and thereby to activate that tendency, with successful results for the one making the entreaty.[10] Only rarely is the verb used in the imperative form (סלח) as a direct address to God, and the norm is for the suppliant to supply some sort of justification, explanation or expansion of his request.[11] The stem tends not to occur in parallelisms, is used only once (Neh 9:17) in association with the epithet חנון, and appears with the *hiph'il* conjugation of the stem רבה only in Isa 55:7: כי ירבה לסלוח. The stem מחל is simply not biblical Hebrew, not being attested until early tannaitic literature.[12] As for the substantives אבינו and מלכנו, they are not

---

8 Exod 34:9, Jer 31:34, 33:8, 36:3, and 1 Kgs 8:50. There is an excellent summary of the uses of the stem in the Hebrew Bible by Hausmann, pp. 258–65. See also the distinct levels of evil presupposed by these terms, as explained in Gane, *Cult*, pp. 215–302.

9 Num 14:20, Ps 86:5, 103:3 and 130:4.

10 Isa 55:7, Neh 9:17 and Dan 9:9.

11 Num 14:19, 1 Kgs 8:50 and Amos 7:2.

12 Ben Yehuda, *Dictionary*, pp. 2911–12; Even-Shoshan, *Ha-Millon*, pp. 1295–96. I was able to check usage of the two stems by consulting 'Maagarim', the subscription online database of

linked with divine forgiveness, although the former is used metaphorically to describe Israel's relationship with God [13] There is no evidence of a standard or daily request for forgiveness, only of entreaties formulated on special occasions in accordance with the contemporary or local need or crisis.[14]

If we move into the apocryphal literature, there is a passage in Ben Sira that is particularly intriguing in this context. The Hebrew text (with my own English translation) reads as follows:

> אל תאמר חטאתי ומה יעשה לי מאומה כי אל ארך אפים הוא
> אל תאמר רחום יי וכל עונותי ימחה
> אל סליחה אל תבטח להוסיף עון על עון
> ואמרת רחמיו רבים לרוב עונותי יסלח
> כי רחמים ואף עמו ואל רשעים ינוח רגזו

> Do not say 'I have sinned but God will do nothing to me since he is divinely patient'. Do not say 'The Lord is merciful and will blot out all my iniquities.'
> Do not rely on such forgiveness and compound your iniquities,
> Saying 'His mercies are manifold and he will forgive all my iniquities.'
> For God can be angry as well as merciful and his wrath can alight upon the wicked.[15]

What is being suggested by this passage is that there was some anxiety on the part of Ben Sira, and the circles he represented, about taking it for granted that God would by his very nature always prove to be forgiving. This apparently militates against so many earlier passages in the Hebrew Bible that may legitimately be understood to be making such a presupposition. There are two other points to be made. In addition to the usual usage of the three words סליחה, חטא and עון, there is a use of the 'wiping away' metaphor for sin, already present in biblical Hebrew texts. God's kindness and generosity are also linked with the notion of forgiveness, as if to stress that it requires more than activation of one divine attribute for sin to be expunged from the record.[16]

The stress in some of the Qumran texts that deal with our topic is somewhat similar, indicating a strong belief that those who repent and who are in God's favour will be forgiven while the others will be punished. According to the 'Words of the

---

the Historical Dictionary of the Hebrew Language prepared at the Hebrew Language Academy in Jerusalem, for which I am deeply grateful.

13 As in Isa 63:16, 64:7 and 1 Chr 29:10.

14 Werline, *Penitential Prayer*, p. 195.

15 Sir 5:5–9 (Heb), 4–6 (Gk); see Lévi, *Ecclesiasticus*, p. 5; Segal, *Ben Sira*, p. 30; Skehan and di Lella, *Wisdom*, pp. 179 and 182.

16 Sir 16:14 (Heb), 16:11(Gk); Lévi, *Ecclesiasticus*, p. 25; Segal, *Ben Sira*, p. 96 and Skehan/di Lella, *Wisdom*, pp. 268–69 and 274. For the biblical Hebrew texts on 'wiping away' and 'removing', see Isa 43:25, Ps 51:3,11 (מחה) and 2 Sam 24:10 (העבר).

Luminaries' (4Q504), confession and supplication are part of that process of repentance. Although such a notion is undoubtedly present in the later rabbinic *taḥanun* (supplicatory) texts, Schiffman is correct in concluding that 'we cannot claim on this evidence that...[such texts] go back to Second Temple times'.[17] The extensive and generous nature of divine forgiveness is also a recurrent theme, sometimes expressed in the form of poetic parallelism, and generally flagged by such Hebrew expressions as נדבת לב, רוב טוב, גדול רחמים, המון רחמים, רוב רחמים, רוב סליחות/סליחה, and חסד.[18] One of the most characteristic of such verses is 1QH7(=15):30 which reads as follows (followed by my English translation):

> וכול בני אמיתכה תביא בסליחות לפניכה לטהרם מפשעיהם ברוב טובכה ובהמון ר[ח]מיכה להעמידם לפניכה לעולמי עד
>
> You will bring all your loyal followers before you for forgiveness, purifying them of their disobedience through your goodness and manifold mercies, and granting them audience with you for all time

Talmud

The next task is to take stock of the what may genuinely be learned from the talmudic literature about the forgiveness benediction, without becoming too involved in the wider issue of the origins and early development of the whole *'amidah*, a putative exercise that would take us greatly beyond our present remit. It is clear that between the second and fourth centuries the rabbis were still explaining and justifying the number and order of the benedictions in the *'amidah.*[19] Whether this was a dialectical exercise, or had the practical intent of adding to the authority of the ritual practice, remains open to debate.[20] What is clear is that there was already a benediction requesting divine forgiveness; that it was sixth in the order of the daily office; that it followed the benediction for repentance; that it commenced with the words סלח לנו ('forgive us'); and that it probably concluded with a description of God as

17 'Words of the Luminaries' VI 2–6, as cited by Schiffman, *Reclaiming*, p. 297; see also the reconstructed text of 4Q506.

18 See, for example, 1QS2:8, 1QH14:24, 1QH6:9, 1QH9:34, 1QH11:9, CD2:4, 4Q257 II 5, 4Q400 I 18 and 4Q427 7 II 16. I am grateful to the library of Tyndale House, Cambridge, and to Dr David Instone-Brewer, of its permanent academic staff, for kindly providing electronic access to Qumran material.

19 *y. Ber.* 2.4 (4d) and 4.3 (8a), MS Leiden 2.3 and 4.3, ed. J. Sussmann, cols 18 and 38.

20 *b. Meg.* 17b certainly has the flavour of a later piece of dialectic that links verses and topics in an *ex post facto* exegesis of the *'amidah*'s order.

מרבה לסלוח ('who consistently grants forgiveness').[21] It occurred, with repentance, within a group of benedictions that constituted entreaties for divine blessing on the most mundane and personal of daily requirements, such as intelligence, rescue, health, environment. It seems reasonable to suppose that they were included there to add a more spiritual dimension to such topics. Finkelstein argues that they are older than the more mundane items, but they may simply have come from an alternative, original context and been simultaneously joined with the others when the *'amidah* was composed.[22]

As far as the theology of forgiveness is concerned, the rabbis of course struggled with this, as all monotheists always have, trying to reconcile the notions of divine love and forgiveness, repentance, and fair recompense for human behaviour. They certainly adhere to the scriptural concept of the ubiquity and comprehensiveness of God's forgiving attribute, but they are, at the same time, aware of divergent approaches to the manner in which this attribute relates to other, equally central, theological ideas. Without ever losing their awareness of the complications, what the later talmudic rabbis appear to have done is to have given an increasing importance to the notion of repentance, arguing for its greater power than prayer, its relevance to all sin and its centrality especially during the ten days from Rosh Ha-Shanah (New Year) to Yom Kippur (Day of Atonement).[23] In the words of Ephraim Urbach, the 'Amoraim followed the doctrine of the Tannaim, and even enlarged the sphere and power of repentance, to the point of extravagance.'[24] Morris Joseph put it neatly and succinctly: 'The Divine forgiveness, then, is moral, spiritual. The sinner is not let off, in the schoolboy's sense of the expression, but is taken back to the arms of the loving Father'.[25]

Moving on to the language and literary style of the benediction, there is a distinct wariness on the part of the earlier rabbinic authorities about confusing written, received scripture with their own oral liturgy, as recently stressed by Shlomo Naeh.[26] This led them, wherever possible and practical, to prefer their own vocabulary, style and formulation, especially at the earliest period of rabbinic prayer. Gradually, however, it became more acceptable, and consequently more common, to adopt and adapt biblical models in a more direct fashion. Although Heinemann's form-critical approach tends to prefer synchronic to diachronic explanations, he does seem to imply that biblical versions of the

---

21 See y. *Roš. Haš.* 4.6 (59c), MS Leiden 4.5, ed. J. Sussmann, col. 678.
22 Finkelstein, 'Amidah', pp. 10–11, 18, 43 and 146–47.
23 Urbach, *Sages*, 1.462–471.
24 Urbach, *Sages*, 1.467.
25 Joseph, *Judaism*, p. 126.
26 Naeh, 'Biblical verses'.

rabbinic prayers are early. [27] Finkelstein had, however, already made the valid point that one can envisage rabbis changing their own forms to more biblical ones but it would have been highly controversial had they rejected a biblical formulation that was already part of their liturgical tradition in favour of their own composition.[28] Also to be taken into account is the rabbinic suspicion of any customs that were characteristic of such groups as that (or those?) of Qumran.[29]

There is also considerable doubt about whether the formulators of the earliest benedictions inserted into the body of an entreaty to God a variety of metaphorical, divine epithets in the vocative (such as 'king' and 'father' and 'master') that are no more than parenthetical to the whole theme. If they did address God vocatively and parenthetically, would it not have been via his more direct names such as and אלהים and אדני?[30] The inclusion of a justification for optimism, as it were, that says something like 'please grant us *x* because you are the generous provider of *x*' also smacks of later expansion, especially since it appears only in a small minority of the *'amidah* benedictions.

Post-talmudic developments

The point has also to be made that *seliḥot*, as they developed in the post-talmudic period, are not part of the statutory talmudic prayers. There are those early texts that were recited on public fast-days declared on the occasion of calamitous situations such as droughts, but these are not in the form that was later used.[31] That complex style evolved at the time of the early liturgical poems (*piyyuṭim*) and was used for a host of additional prayers attached to the central ones, or after the central ones, on fast-days and to mark the lead-up to the New Year and for a few days afterwards, especially on Yom Kippur.[32]

If we may turn again to Sa'adya's tenth-century text, it may reasonably be argued, on the basis of the considerations laid out above, that, some eight centuries earlier, perhaps in the decades immediately following the destruction of the Temple, the form of the benediction may have been considerably simpler.

---

27 Heinemann, *Prayer*, pp. 147–48; *Forms and Patterns*, pp. 234–36.
28 Finkelstein, 'Amidah', p. 10.
29 See Reif, *Problems*, pp. 74–76.
30 Finkelstein (see n. 28 above) argues in this way but then attempts a precise dating of each prayer that seems to go far beyond the available evidence.
31 *m. Ta'an.* 2.1.
32 On the early *seliḥot* poems, see Weinberger, *Jewish Hymnography*, pp. 27, 60–61, 79–80, and 125–30.

The parallelism, with its use of the stem מחל not documented as early as that period, may not yet have occurred and the vocative אבינו ('our father') may have been a development of the future.[33] The prototype that was used for incorporation into the *'amidah* may therefore have been no more than: סלח לנו כי חטאנו ברוך אתה ה' מרבה הסליחה.[34] This is not to say that such a prototype did not immediately take a variety of forms, simply that there was a popular version that was adopted by the rabbinic formulators. It is also not perfectly clear what is meant by the phrase כי חטאנו. If the dominant theological view was that Jews were, as mortals, bound to sin, and God's tendency was to forgive them, the sense would be 'forgive us in that we have sinned'. Alternatively, if the view was already moving towards stressing repentance, that would explain the presence of a benediction on that theme immediately before the one on forgiveness, and the meaning would rather be 'forgive us although we have sinned.'

Genizah

Unfortunately, as in so many other areas of Jewish history, there is little manuscript evidence to assist our inquiry between the second and ninth centuries. We are therefore required *faute de mieux* to look to the fragments from the Cairo Genizah to obtain some idea of the textual variations that were introduced from talmudic to geonic times.[35] It seems to me that the earliest forms of these may well have occurred as early as the late tannaitic period, but one should also take into account the view championed by Ezra Fleischer, and those who adhere to his preferred historical analysis, according to which many of these adjustments were the work of those who composed and recited the new genre of *piyyuṭim* in the late talmudic and subsequent periods.[36] Many of the relevant Genizah texts have been identified by Yehezkel Luger in his study of the *'amidah* and by Uri Ehrlich in the context of the joint Genizah liturgical project of Ben-Gurion University of the Negev and Cambridge University Library being run by him and by my Cambridge colleague, Dr Ben Outhwaite. They have kindly

---

33 See notes 12 and 13 above for the biblical Hebrew and lexicographical evidence.

34 Finkelstein, 'Amidah', p. 147, offers המרבה לסלוח for the final two words but I have omitted the definite article from the participle and made the word that it qualifies a substantive rather than an infinitive in order to match the concluding phrases of many of the other benedictions. See also the end of n. 40 below.

35 Fleischer, *Eretz-Israel*; Reif, *Jewish Archive*; and Schmelzer, 'The contribution of the Genizah'.

36 Fleischer, 'Obligatory Jewish prayer' followed by the exchange between him and myself in *Tarbiz* 60.

made them available to me. The fragments reveal some interesting textual developments *vis-à-vis* the text that is recorded by Sa'adya and that seems broadly to reflect the Babylonian rite.[37]

In some instances the words אבינו ('our father') and מלכנו ('our king') are omitted, replaced or written above the line, perhaps confirming the supposition that they were not part of any prototype.[38] Where there is pointing, the word מחל or ומחל ('pardon') still widely occurs with *ḥolem* and not *pataḥ*.[39] In the concluding eulogy, both המרבה and ומרבה occur, and חנון ('gracious') is not always present, supporting the hypothesis that the primitive form may have been מרבה לסלוח.[40] There are also alternative explanatory additions before that benediction, similar to those found in other *'amidah* benedictions and beginning כי, and presumably copied from there. Examples of such additions are כי מוחל וסולח אתה ('for you provide pardon and forgiveness')[41] and כי [אל] טוב וסלח אתה ('for you are [divinely] good and forgiving').[42] The additional biblical phrase ורב חסד לכל קוראיך is also attested.[43] A final word about the use of the word חנון and the possibility that it was theologically motivated and not simply a verbal whim. For a Jewish thinker anxious to stress that God's act of forgiveness is, as it were, above and beyond his divine duty, it would be natural to add a reference to his graciousness.[44]

37 Luger, *Amidah*, pp. 86–91; Ehrlich, *Weekday Amidah*, pp. 97–104.

38 See Cambridge University Library Genizah fragments (henceforth 'CUL'), T-S 8H10.22, T-S H8.90, T-S NS 150.37 and T-S NS 152.35; but, as Luger points out (*Amidah*; p. 87, n. 5), Weinfeld in *Tarbiz* 48 (1979), p. 187, n. 8, argues for the originality of אבינו. If he is correct, then its removal from some Genizah texts may reflect a hesitation to over-emphasize God's fatherhood since this was a central notion in Christian theology and anathema to dominant Islamic conceptions of God. On the historical development of the practice of addressing God as 'Father' in Jewish liturgy, see chapter 15 below.

39 For example, CUL, T-S NS 154.18. See the comments on Shabbethai and Baer cited towards the end of this paper.

40 CUL, T-S 8H9.12, T-S 8H11.3, T-S 10H1.2, T-S 8H10.22, and Jewish Theological Seminary (henceforth 'JTS'), Adler 2017, f. 9, all have ומרבה, while the alternative version המרבה occurs in CUL, T-S 8H10.6, T-S 8H24.5, T-S NS 154.120, T-S NS 230.96, T-S NS 278.151 and T-S AS 109.126. Interestingly, the word occurs with no prefix (מרבה) in CUL, T-S NS 195.77, while T-S 8H24.5 has no חנון in the concluding eulogy.

41 As in CUL, T-S 8H9.12.

42 CUL, T-S 8H10.6, T-S NS 154.18, T-S NS 157.193, T-S NS 159.112, T-S NS 230.19, T-S AS 108.57 and JTS Adler 2017, f. 9. The phrase occurs without the word אל in CUL, T-S NS 120.105.

43 CUL, T-S AS 109.126; the expansion derives from Ps 86:5.

44 See *Midrasch Tehillim* 29.2, p. 116b, for an early occurrence.

What is generally assumed to be closer to the rite as practised in pre-Crusader Palestine and imported by emigrants from there into Egypt ran along the following lines:[45]

> סלח לנו אבינו כי חטאנו לך מחה והעבר (על) פשעינו (מנגד עיניך) כי רבים רחמיך בא״י המרבה לסלוח
>
> Forgive us, our Father, that we have sinned against you. Remove totally out of your sight our wrongdoing, for your mercies are manifold. You, Lord, are to be praised as the One who consistently grants forgiveness

In order to explain the content of that version, a few variants require to be noted. The word לך is replaced by לפניך or omitted, suggesting that the verb חטאנו perhaps originally stood alone without such an indirect object, which may have been borrowed from such occurrences of the verb in the Hebrew Bible, or in liturgical poetry which was often composed under its influence.[46] The preposition על is inserted before the word פשעינו ('our wrongdoing'), as it occurs in the biblical Hebrew passage in Mic 7:18.[47] Indeed, this whole metaphor concerning the weight and removal of the wrongdoing is based on such biblical Hebrew passages as Ps 51:3, Lam 1:14, Mic 7:18 and Prov 19:11. The phrase מנגד עיניך ('out of your sight') also reflects an interest in adopting a biblical precedent, in this case a typically prophetic phrase, as in Isa 1:16, Jer 16:17, Amos 9:3 and Jonah 2:5. The fact that there are instances of its omission would support the supposition that it represents the expansion of a simpler text.[48] In this rite, the explanatory phrase כי רבים רחמיך ('for your mercies are manifold') is borrowed directly from Ps 119:156 (see also Dan 9:18). What we then have here, in sum, is an alternative form of parallel to the first phrase that demonstrates a greater and more literal tendency to 'biblicize'. At least one Genizah text, cited by Uri Ehrlich from

---

45 See Mann, 'Genizah fragments', p. 416. Luger, *Amidah*, p. 87, refers to this as נוסח ב, and Ehrlich, *Weekday Amidah*, p. 99, lists it as a rite of the land of Israel.

46 CUL, T-S K27.18 and T-S NS 196.107; Jud 10:10, Jer 14:20 and Dan 9:11,15; *Siddur RSG* (see n. 7 above), in a *seliḥah* for Yom Kippur, p. 316; and many *seliḥot*. Manuscripts of the 'Babylonian version' also have the word לך with either or both verbs in CUL, T-S 10H1.2 and T-S NS 235.172. The textual variations to be found with the word חטאנו in the Mekhilta's comments on Exod 15:25 support my supposition of liturgical variation during the late talmudic and geonic periods; see ed. Lauterbach, 2.93; eds. Horovitz/Rabin, p. 156; eds. Epstein/Melamed, p. 104. I am again indebted to the 'Maagarim' database for important linguistic data in this connection. See now also E. Fleischer's posthumously published edition of Cambridge Genizah fragment T-S 20.57 in his '*Megillah qedumah*'.

47 CUL, T-S K27.18.

48 CUL, T-S K27.18.

the Antonin Collection in St Petersburg, testifies to a conflation of these two alternatives and reads: סלח לנו אבינו כי חטאנו ומחול לנו מלכינו ומחה פשעינו מנגד עיניך.[49] There are other manuscripts that have an even more extensive conflation, namely, מחה והעבר פשעינו מנגד עיניך כי רבים רחמיך כי אל טוב וסלח אתה.[50] What is more, it is only the first phrase and the shorter version of the concluding benediction that all the versions have in common, again supporting our hypothesis about the prototype.

Medieval rites

It will instantly be recalled that some thousand years ago the explanatory note immediately before the concluding eulogy occurred most commonly as כי [אל] טוב וסלח אתה ('for you are [divinely] good and forgiving') in the Babylonian rite that was destined to dominate most of the later liturgical rites, although there is also manuscript testimony to the phrase כי מוחל וסולח אתה ('for you provide pardon and forgiveness'). With the exception of the addition of substantives such as מלך and epithets such as מטיב, the common Babylonian formula is recorded in the rites of Persia, Byzantine, Italy, Spain, North Africa, Yemen and France.[51] What is interesting is that the Ashkenazi (German) rite is the only one to adopt the alternative phrasing. It will contribute to this analysis of the religious ideas of the forgiveness benediction if an attempt is made to understand why this text was preferred by some liturgical commentators.

Once the parallel use of the stems סלח and מחל had become widespread, the next step was to treat the text as authoritative and to add to its theological exegesis. Just as in the biblical text, nothing was redundant, so it was assumed that the worshipper was not merely indulging in literary and aesthetic variation but making two distinct points.[52] It is well recognized that the Ashkenazi mystics of the twelfth and thirteenth centuries made a major impact on the overall content, precise wording and spiritual message of the daily prayers.[53] Recorded in the name of one of its leading figures, Eleazar ben Judah of Worms (c. 1165 – 1230; called the 'Roqeaḥ' after his

49 Ehrlich, 'Early version' p. 560, on MS Evr. III B 995. See also Tal, *Persian Jewish Prayer Book*, p. 82 (MS, fol. 42b).

50 CUL, T-S NS 278.247, T-S NS 150.37 and T-S AS 102.132.

51 All conveniently cited by Finkelstein, 'Amidah', p. 146; in *'Osar Ha-Tefillot*, pp. 163b–164a; and by Jacobson, *Nethiv Binah*, 1.278 – 79. See also Ehrlich, *Weekday Amidah*, p. 104.

52 Such developments are discussed in Reif, *Problems*, pp. 195 – 99.

53 See Dan, 'Mystical prayer'.

main ethical treatise), is an interesting view of the meanings of the two stems used in our benediction (followed by my English translation)[54]:

> סלח לנו אבינו כי חטאנו לא תיקנו אבינו כי אם בתשובה ובסלח וברכת כהנים, לפי שחייב האב ללמד לבנו לכך תיקנו השיבנו אבינו לתורתך, ברכינו אבינו כולנו כאחד באור פניך כי באור פניך נתת לנו ה' אלהינו תורת חיים, והאב סולח סרחון בנו [טור קטון], וישוב אל ה' וירחמיהו ואל אלהינו כי ירבה לסלוח [ישעיה נה:ז], וכתי' כרחם אב על בנים [תהלים קג:יג], לכך סלח לנו אבינו כי חטאנו זהו שוגג כמו וחטאה בשגגה [ויקרא ה:טו], מחל לנו מלכינו כי פשענו במזיד במרד. ואומרים סלח לנו אבינו כי חטאנו מחל לנו מלכינו, לפי שכתו' ואם אב אני איה כבודי ואם אדונים אני איה מוראי [מלאכי א:ו]
>
> *Forgive us, our Father, that we have sinned:* The composers of the *'amidah* benedictions included the word אבינו ('our father') only in the texts dealing with repentance, forgiveness and the priestly benediction. Since a father is obligated to instruct his son in Torah, they included a metaphorical reference to fatherhood in the phrases *Restore us to your Torah* and *bless us all as one...because you have gifted us your eternal Torah.* If the son is rebellious, the father naturally forgives him as is clear from Isa 55:7 and Ps 103:13. Therefore the sixth benediction includes the phrase *Forgive us, our Father, that we have sinned* which is a reference to the fact that we have sinned unintentionally (as in Lev 5:15) and the next phrase *Pardon us, our King, that we have done wrong* includes wilful and rebellious wrongdoing. The whole text is therefore used to remind us of God's claim on us as our Father, as stated in Mal 1:6, *If I am your father where is my respect, if I am your master where is my reverence?*

Here, as in so many other cases, these mystics protected their suggested text by counting the number of its words and immediately offering explanations of that number's significance and relevance. Those in the Ashkenazi communities appear to have preferred the phrase כי מוחל וסולח אתה just before the benedictory conclusion because they believed that if the two kinds of forgiveness need to be requested here, with their independent senses, so too is it appropriate to mention, in the same language, that God is the provider of both of these. This explanation of the two Hebrew stems also occurs in the liturgical commentaries of Judah ben Yaqar, the teacher of Naḥmanides in twelfth-century Spain; of David ben Joseph Abudraham in that same country two centuries later; and of Yaḥya ben Ṣaliḥ in Yemen in the nineteenth century, indicating its wide dissemination and popularity. But the liturgical rites of the communities in which these three teachers wrote were not textually influenced in the same way as those of the Ashkenazim.

Like his pupil, Judah ben Yaqar tends to be somewhat diffuse but the essence of what he writes tallies with the comments of Roqeaḥ, with the addition of two fresh remarks.[55] In the first, he explains that the stem מחל refers to a situation where the wounded party expects to be asked for forgiveness; if the

---

54 *Pirushey Siddur*, ed. Hershler, 1.333–34.
55 Judah ben Yaqar, *Perush*, 1.46.

offender admits his fault, he should be forgiven. As far as סלח is concerned, even if we have done wrong, the arrangement is that God will forgive us. In both cases כי has the sense of 'although'. He then links the notion of 'father' with one who seeks mercy, that is, undeserved good. Abudraham is much clearer and more succinct, stating that סליחה is what one may expect from a father when one has done wrong since a father is more likely to be automatically forgiving, while מחילה is what will be requested by one's equal or one's inferior who has in some way caused offence and cannot assume that he will be forgiven. He also stresses that כי can mean 'although' and not 'because', a theologically important point, as already suggested earlier in this paper.[56] Yaḥya makes similar points adding, very much along the lines of earlier comments by Judah ben Yaqar, that 'forgiveness and unintentional sin are linked here with the notion of fatherhood because even wilful wrongdoing is considered by a father as unintentional. The link between פשע and rulership is made because, to a ruler, even unintentional error may be regarded as wilful.'[57]

Conclusions

By way of conclusion – and indeed of contrast – it is interesting to note the comments made by three later Ashkenazi liturgical authorities on the forgiveness benediction. Writing in early seventeenth-century Poland, and adumbrating many aspects of the Haskalah approaches of two hundred years later, Shabbethai Sofer of Przemysl offered no comment whatsoever on the meaning of the text but concentrated entirely on the issue of pointing מחל with a *pataḥ* or a *ḥolem*. As elsewhere, and in common with a number of predecessors, he argues his case on the basis of the vocalization of standard biblical Hebrew, as it had become widespread in biblical codices, and cites Elijah Levita in support, characterizing those who opt for the rabbinic form as pseudo-grammarians (המראים את עצמם מדקדקים), and expressing surprise at Solomon Luria's preference for that form.[58] Seligmann Baer, in his liturgical text and commentary of 1868 makes a similar grammatical point, albeit in a somewhat more sophisticated and modern

56 *Sefer Abudraham*, p. 56; ed. Wertheimer, p. 98.

57 *Tiklal* of Yaḥya b. Joseph Ṣaliḥ, 1.44b–45a.

58 On Shabbethai Sofer (c. 1565 – 1635), see Reif, *Shabbethai Sofer*. For the reference in his commentary (MS, f. 36a), see סדור המדקדק הגדול בקי בכל חדרי התורה מה'ר שבתי סופר ב'ר יצחק מפרעמישלא תלמיד הלבוש, יוצא לאור ע'פ כ'י בית הדין בלונדון על ידי הרב יצחק סץ והרב דוד יצחקי, eds. Satz/Yitschaki, 1.143. On the slavish adoption of the biblical rather than the rabbinic forms, see Reif, *Shabbethai Sofer*, pp. 29 – 38.

fashion, but he does add a remark about the exclusive use made by the Ashkenazim of the phrase כי מוחל וסולח אתה. He contrasts this with the alternative phraseology which he dubs the original text (נוסחא העקרית), as indeed preserved even by the Ashkenazim in their *seliḥot* poems. He thus reflects the kind of German-Jewish scholarly attitude of his day that so often saw the Sefardi precedent as somehow superior to the Ashkenazi one.[59] Early in the twentieth century, Elbogen's classic study of the liturgy deals with textual variation in the rites, seeming to betray something of a *tendenz* towards the Palestinian rather than the Babylonian rite, perhaps identifying what were then newly discovered variants as somewhat parallel to the liturgical adjustments being proposed in his own day by the Jewish progressive movements. Be that as it may, he offers no comments on the theology of the benediction in its various textual forms.[60]

The nineteenth-century Orthodox rabbinic leader, Samson Raphael Hirsch, on the other hand, in his posthumously published commentary on the traditional rabbinic prayers, attempts a definition of the two terms סליחה and מחילה. The former is 'personal forgiveness granted so that the transgression that was committed may not permanently blight the relationship of the transgressor to the one against whom he has sinned'. The latter is 'objective pardon, the waiver of the punishment which the transgressor would have deserved'. Hirsch also stresses that repentance has to precede forgiveness, of either sort, and that this accounts for the order of these two benedictions.[61] There is an interest here in theology that seems distinctly absent in the comments of Shabbethai, Baer and Elbogen, but it is hardly novel. Almost a thousand years earlier, as should already be clear from previous comments in this study, similar remarks were being made and were leaving their impact on the structure of the liturgical text as well as on the meaning it was held to convey. The author of Eccl 1:9 – 10 cautioned us well about confidently defining instances of novelty. Today's worshipper, no less than contemporary students of liturgy, can do worse than to look back at the early sources.

Works cited

Abudraham, D., *Sefer Abudraham* (Warsaw: Schriftgisser, 1877); *Sefer Abudraham Ha-Shalem*, ed. S. A. Wertheimer (Jerusalem: Usha, 1963).

Amram ben Sheshna, *Seder Rav 'Amram*, ed. N. Coronel (Warsaw: Kelter, 1865); ed. A. L. Frumkin, 2 vols. (Jerusalem: Zuckerman, 1912); ed. D. Hedegård (Lund: Lindstedts, 1951); ed. E. D. Goldschmidt (Jerusalem: Rav Kook, 1971).

---

59 Baer, *'Avodat Yisra'el*, pp. 90 – 91.

60 Elbogen, *Gottesdienst*, pp. 47 – 48; *Tefillah*, Hebrew edition, p. 37; *Jewish Liturgy*, p. 42.

61 Hirsch, *Siddur*, pp. 136 – 37; compare Jacobson, *Nethiv Binah*, 1.314 – 15.

Baer, S., *Seder 'Avodat Yisra'el* (Rödelheim: Lehrberger, 1868).
Ben Yehuda, E., *A Complete Dictionary of Ancient and Modern Hebrew* (Hebrew; Jerusalem and New York: Yoseloff, 1908–1959, 1960).
Boda, M. J., Falk, D. K. and Werline, R. A. (eds.), *Seeking the Favor of God. Volume 1: The Origins of Penitential Prayer in Second Temple Judaism* (Atlanta: SBL, 2006).
Boda, M. J., Falk, D. K. and Werline, R. A. (eds.) *Seeking the Favor of God. Volume 3. The Impact of Penitential Prayer beyond the Second Tempe Judaism* (Atlanta: SBL, 2008).
Brody, R., 'Liturgical use of the Book of Psalms in the Geonic period', in *Prayers that Cite Scripture*, ed. J. L. Kugel (Cambridge, Mass.: Harvard University Press, 2006), pp. 61–81.
Dan, J., 'The emergence of mystical prayer', in *Studies in Jewish Mysticism*, eds. J. Dan and F. Talmage (Cambridge, Mass.: Association for Jewish Studies, 1982), pp. 85–120.
Davidson, I, Assaf, S. and Joel, B. I. (eds.), *Siddur Rav Se'adyah Ga'on: Kitāb Ǵāmi' aṣ-Ṣalawāt wat-Tasābīḥ*, (Jerusalem: Mekize Nirdamim, 1963, 2nd edn.).
Ehrlich, U., 'An early version of the *Gevurot, Kedushat Ha-Shem*, and *Da'at* blessings according to a new fragment of a Palestinian siddur', *Tarbiz* 73 (2004), pp. 555–84.
Ehrlich, U., *The Weekday Amidah in Cairo Genizah Prayerbooks. Roots and Transmission* (Hebrew; Jerusalem: Yad Ben-Zvi, 2013).
Elbogen, I., *Der jüdische Gottesdienst in seiner geschichtlichen Entwicklung* (Frankfurt-am-Main: Kauffman, 1931; reprint, Hildesheim: Olms, 1962); Hebrew edition, התפילה בישראל בהתפתחותה ההיסטורית (eds. J. Heinemann, I. Adler, A. Negev, J. Petuchowski and H. Schirmann, Tel Aviv: Devir, 1972); English edition, *Jewish Liturgy: A Comprehensive History* (Eng. trans. and ed. R. P. Scheindlin, Philadelphia, Jerusalem and New York: Jewish Publication Society, Jewish Theological Seminary, 1993).
Eleazar b. Judah of Worms, *Pirushey Siddur HaTefilah LaRokeach; a Commentary on the Jewish Prayer Book*, ed. M. and Y. A. Hershler, 2 vols. (Jerusalem: Hershler, 1992).
Even-Shoshan, A., *Ha-Millon He-Ḥadash* (Jerusalem: Kiryath Sepher, 1979).
Finkelstein, L., 'The development of the Amidah', *Jewish Quarterly Review* NS 16 (1925–26), pp. 1–43 and 127–70.
Fleischer, E., *Eretz-Israel Prayer and Prayer Rituals as Portrayed in the Geniza Documents* (Hebrew; Jerusalem: Magnes, 1988).
Fleischer, E., '*Megillah qedumah*', in *Higayon L'Yona: Studies in New Aspects in the Study of Midrash, Aggadah and Piyut in Honor of Professor Yona Fraenkel*, eds. J. Levinson, J. Elbaum and G. Hazan-Rokem (Hebrew; Jerusalem, 2006), pp. 529–49.
Fleischer, E., 'On the beginnings of obligatory Jewish prayer', *Tarbiz* 59 (1990), pp. 397–441 and *Tarbiz* 60 (1991), pp. 677–88.
Gane, R. E., *Cult and Character: Purification Offerings, Day of Atonment, and Theodicy* (Winona Lake, Ind.: Eisenbrauns, 2005).
Gaster, M., *The Book of Prayer and Order of Service according to the Custom of the Spanish and Portuguese Jews* (London: Frowde, 1901–6).
Hausmann, J., on סלח, in *Theological Dictionary of the Old Testament*, eds. G. J. Botterweck, H. Ringgren and H.-J. Fabry, vol. 10, Eng. trans. D. W. Stott (Grand Rapids, Mich. and Cambridge: Eeerdmans, 1999), pp. 258–65.
Heinemann, *Prayer in the Period of the Tanna'im and Amora'im: Its Nature and Its Patterns* (Hebrew; Jerusalem: Magnes, 1966, 2nd edn.); revised English edition, *Prayer in the Talmud: Forms and Patterns* (Berlin and New York: de Gruyter, 1977).

Hirsch, S. R., *The Hirsch Siddur. The Order of Prayers for the Whole Year*, Eng. trans. J. Breuer (Jerusalem and New York: Feldheim, 1969, from the original German of Frankfurt-am-Main: Kauffmann, 1895).
Jacobson, B. S., *Nethiv Binah*, 5 vols. (Tel Aviv: Sinai, 1968–83).
Joseph, M., *Judaism as Creed and Life* (London: Routledge & Kegan Paul, 1903).
Judah ben Yaqar, *Perush Ha-Tefillot Ve-Ha-Berakhot*, 2 vols. (Jerusalem: Me'orey Yisra'el, 1968–69).
Lévi, I., *The Hebrew text of the Book of Ecclesiasticus* (Leiden: Brill, 1969, 3rd edn.).
Luger, Y., *The Weekday Amidah in the Cairo Genizah* (Hebrew; Jerusalem: Orhot, 2001).
Mann, J., 'Genizah fragments of the Palestinian order of service', *Hebrew Union College Annual* 2 (1926), pp. 269–338.
Mekilta de-Rabbi Ishmael, ed. J. Z. Lauterbach, 3 vols. (Philadelphia: Jewish Publication Society, 1933–35); eds. H. S. Horovitz and I. A. Rabin (Frankfurt-am-Main: Kauffman, 1931).
Mekhilta D'Rabbi Šim'on b. Jochai, eds. J. N. Epstein and E. Z. Melamed (Jerusalem: Mekize Nirdamim, 1955).
Midrash Tehillim, ed. S. Buber (Vilna: Romm, 1891).
Naeh, S., 'The role of biblical verses in prayer according to the rabbinic tradition', in *Prayers that Cite Scripture*, ed. J. L. Kugel (Cambridge, Mass.: Harvard University Press, 2006), pp. 43–59.
Newman, J. H., *Praying by the Book: The Scripturalization of Prayer in Second Temple Judaism* (Atlanta: SBL, 1999).
'Osar Ha-Tefillot, 2 vols.(Vilna: Romm, 1923).
Reif, S. C., *A Jewish Archive from Old Cairo. The History of Cambridge University's Genizah Collection* (Richmond, Surrey: Curzon, 2000).
Reif, S. C., *Judaism and Hebrew Prayer* (Cambridge: Cambridge University Press, 1993).
Reif, S. C., *Problems with Prayers. Studies in the Textual History of Early Rabbinic Liturgy* (Berlin: de Gruyter, 2006).
Reif, S. C., *Shabbethai Sofer and his Prayer-book* (Cambridge: Cambridge University Press, 1979).
Schiffman, L. H., *Reclaiming the Dead Sea Scrolls. The History of Judaism, the Background of Christianity, the Lost Library of Qumran* (Philadelphia and Jerusalem: Jewish Publication Society, 1994).
Schmelzer, M., 'The contribution of the Genizah to the study of liturgy and poetry', *PAAJR* 63 [1997–2001] (2001), pp. 163–79.
Segal, M. H., *Sefer Ben Sira Ha-Shalem* (2nd revised edition, Jerusalem: Bialik, 1958).
Shabbethai Sofer, *Siddur*, eds. I. Satz and D. Yitschaki, 5 vols. (Hebrew; Baltimore: Ner Israel, 1987–2002).
Singer, S., *The Authorised Daily Prayer Book of the United Hebrew Congregations of the British Empire, with a New Translation* (London: Wertheimer, Lea, 1890).
Skehan, P. W. and. di Lella, A. A., *The Wisdom of Ben Sira: A New Translation with Notes, Introduction and Commentary* (New York: Doubleday, 1987).
Tal, S. (ed.), *The Persian Jewish Prayer Book* (Hebrew; Jerusalem: Ben Zvi, 1980).
Urbach, E. E., *The Sages. Their Concepts and Beliefs*, Eng. trans. Israel Abrahams, 2 vols. (Jerusalem: Magnes, 1975).
Weinberger, L. J., *Jewish Hymnography. A Literary History* (London and Portland, Oregon: Littman, 1998).

Weinfeld, M., 'The prayers for knowledge, repentance and forgiveness in the Eighteen Benedictions: Qumran parallels, biblical antecedents, and basic characteristics', *Tarbiz* 48 (1979), pp. 186–200.
Werline, R. A., *Penitential Prayer in Second Temple Judaism. The Development of a Religious Institution* (Atlanta: SBL, 1998).
Yaḥya b. Joseph Ṣaliḥ, *Tiklal*, 3 vols. (Jerusalem: Ḥasid, 1894).

15 The Fathership of God in Early Rabbinic Liturgy

Divine fatherhood in other religions

Since the families and genealogies of the gods have an important place in Egyptian mythology, 'father' is often used as a divine epithet. Several gods are known as the 'father of the gods' among them Atum, Re, Nun, Geb and Ptah, and sometimes as both father and mother. Similarly, in Mesopotamia, Anu, Enlil, Sin and Assur are called the 'father of the gods'. In the Ugaritic texts, Keret and Danel are mentioned as 'fathers' and Danel addresses El as 'Bull El, my Father'. El is the father of the sons of the gods, i.e. of the whole pantheon. The broad picture in the Ancient Near East reveals that kings and other leaders, as well as gods, were known as 'father', and names were constructed that referred to a particular god as father, with 'abu' or 'abi' as a theophorous element.[1]

Although the traditions of the ancient Indian faiths and those of the Classical world are perhaps less directly relevant to this analysis, they are certainly of comparative interest and may help to create an overall impression of the issues at stake here. As far as the Indian religions are concerned, addressing a god, or the supreme being ('God') as 'father' is liturgically unusual, though in the descriptions of, and even address to, the supreme being, this does occur from time to time. At the same time, in addressing or describing the supreme being in its form as (a) goddess it is extremely common to use 'mother' (*mata*, *ma*, *amba* etc.).[2] Within the Greek and Roman worlds, a standard phrase for Zeus in Homer is 'father of gods and men' and Jupiter is similarly addressed. Many gods are called 'father x' in Latin literary texts. The paternal metaphor is used in many other circumstances, but there is not much of a standard liturgy in which usages may be found that parallel the Ancient Near Eastern practices.[3]

Hebrew Bible

Moving on to the Hebrew Bible, we encounter many names with the theophorous element in the form of אבי ('father of' or 'my father'). Examples are Avidan,

1 Ringrren, *TDOT*, pp. 2–7.

2 Coburn, *Devi-mahatmya*. I owe this reference, and an explanation of the situation regarding the Indian religions, to my friend and colleague, Professor Julius Lipner.

3 Norden, *Agnostos Theos*. I owe this reference, and an explanation of the situation regarding the Greek and Roman religions, to my friend and colleague, Professor Simon Goldhill.

DOI 10.1515/9783110486704-016

Avinadav and Avishur. Yah is also incorporated into some names as the father of the child, as in Yoav and Aviyyahu. As often with names, these constructions are very ancient and need not tell us a great deal about the notion of God as father in the Hebrew Bible as a whole. The father simile occurs a great deal, with God being said to be like a father who has mercy on his children, pities them, cares for them, or takes delight in them. God is the father of the people, that is, the one who has given them their existence. Israel has rebelled against God as a child rebels against its father. The idea of God as the father of the king occurs more frequently than God as the father of the individual, but neither idea is what one could call a common concept. The overall impression is that the notion of God as father is merely figurative and by no means central to the theology of the Hebrew Bible. What is especially interesting is that God is only rarely *addressed directly* as father.[4]

Moreover, it is rare to find God addressed in prayer, entreaty or praise as '*my* father' or '*our* father'. Examples are to be found in the Ps 89:27–28 (הוא יקראני אבי אתה אלי וצור ישועתי, אף אני בכור אתנהו עליון למלכי ארץ),[5] Isa 63:16 (כי אתה אבינו), Isa 64:7 (ועתה ה' אבינו אתה אנחנו החמר ואתה יצרנו),[6] Jer 3:4 (הלא מעתה קראת לי אבי אלוף נערי אתה) and Jer 3:19 (ואמר אבי תקראי לי ומאחרי לא תשובי).[7] It should be noted that the Psalms passage describes the relationship between the king, not the people, and God, and the Jeremiah passages are complicated by the overall metaphor of Israel as the unfaithful wife. Only the Isaiah passages have the real flavour of liturgical entreaty. What is more, none of the verses is pre-exilic. The description of Elijah's ascent to heaven in 2 Kgs 2:12 (אבי אבי רכב ישראל ופרשיו) includes a reference to 'my father, my father' but this is widely taken, by commentators ancient and modern, to allude to Elijah as Elisha's 'master' or 'teacher', that is, his spiritual guide.[8] Although 1 Chr 29:10 is undoubtedly a liturgical context (ויאמר דויד ברוך אתה ה' אלהי ישראל אבינו מעולם ועד עולם), the word אבינו is certainly a reference to Jacob and not to God, as is clear from v. 18 and is presupposed in the Masoretic pointing.[9] That verse is effectively a good example of how אבינו ('our father') is used in the liturgical sphere to refer to ancestors, and not to God. Addressing God directly as one's father seems therefore to be less unusual in later prophetic (pietistic?) contexts but is not apparently a widespread liturgical notion *per se* when one takes into account how often God is addressed, and

---

4 Ringrren, *TDOT*, pp. 16–19.

5 Briggs, *Psalms*, pp. 260, 268; Kirkpatrick, *Psalms*, p. 538.

6 Watts, *Isaiah*, pp. 902–3, 906; Skinner, *Isaiah*, pp. 203, 207.

7 Bright, *Jeremiah*, p. 23; McKane, *Jeremiah*, pp. 61–62, 79; Streane, *Jeremiah*, pp. 22, 26.

8 See the medieval commentators on the verse, as printed in Cohen, *Mikra'ot Gedolot*, pp. 164–65. See also Montgomery, *Kings*, p. 354; Lumby, *II Kings*, p. 13.

9 Curtis and Madsen, *Chronicles*, pp. 305–6; Myers, *Chronicles*, pp. 195–96.

that it is not usually by way of the expressions אבי or אבינו ('my/our father'). Interestingly, and not unexpectedly, the Targum on the prophetic passages does not provide a literal translation of the expressions אבי or אבינו but paraphrases it in order to avoid what it obviously regards as an anthropomorphism.[10]

Was there then a reluctance to address God in prayer in this way because for many groups of Hebrews, Israelites and Jews, who were at various stages faced with the challenge of polytheistic notions, it still conjured up a concept of God that was too anthropomorphic for them to employ without feelings of theological guilt? Those that were less mystically inclined could accept the employment of the fatherhood metaphor but apparently drew the line at calling God 'Dad'! J. B. Segal has argued that the Jews wholly rejected the 'worship of the Nature goddess that was at the heart of Semitic polytheism'.[11] Perhaps, in a similar fashion, they were hesitant about addressing God as father, given the ubiquitous presence of divine royal couples, male and female, in many polytheistic faiths.

Apocryphal literature

Any attempt at finding a significant liturgical use of the expression אבי (or אבינו) in the Apocryphal literature is similarly doomed to failure. If statistics are anything to go by, it would appear that there is even less in these texts than there is in the Hebrew Bible. The kind of phrase that relates to God's fatherhood has again to do with the fact that he is creator of the world, the protector of mankind, and the one by whom humanity is chided when the need arises. There are, however, three references that are worthy of citation since they appear to continue the trend already found in some of the prophetic books. In Sira 51:10, the prayer of the author makes use of the expression 'you are my father', a form of which has already been encountered in Isaiah. Ben Sira is exalting God as his father and his powerful saviour (וארומם ה' אבי אתה כי אתה גבור ישעי), but God is not actually being addressed directly as 'my father' or 'our father'. Father Di Lella correctly states that God is 'often called 'Father' in the Old Testament' but does not define more closely the precise applications of the nomenclature, and what underlines each of them.[12] In Ben Sira 23:1, the Greek has 'God, my father', taking both terms as vocatives, in a short prayer addressed to God. Although Di Lella sees this as another example of petitioning God as one's

10 Sperber, *Aramaic*, pp. 125, 127; Stenning, *Targum*, pp. 211, 213.
11 Segal, *Women*, p. 134.
12 Segal, *Ben Sira*, pp. 352–55; Skehan and Di Lella, *Ben Sira*, p. 566.

father, the Hebrew has אל אבי and not אלי אבי and is therefore better translated as 'God of my father' (as in Gen 31:42).[13] Perhaps the Greek translator was more inclined to address God as his father than his Hebrew predecessor. At the beginning of Wisdom 14, the author berates those who make idols out of the same wood as the ships that are carrying them, and who expect the former to provide protection for the voyagers. He then goes on (v. 3), 'But it is your providence, O father, that guides, for you have provided a route even in the sea and a safe path in the waves.' Here, the vocative use is almost, if not wholly, liturgical.[14]

Dead Sea Scrolls

The Dead Sea Scrolls do not provide us with a situation that is significantly different from that of the Hebrew Bible. Once again the simile of the father and the child is used in a number of instances to describe the relationship between God and his people. He disciplines them, speaks to them, has mercy on them and protects them in a paternal fashion. In addition, he is the father of the 'scion of David who will arise with the interpreter of the Torah', and well as father of all the 'children of truth', i.e. the father of all committed members of the sect. There is one clear instance of God's being addressed as 'our father' in a liturgical context. It occurs in the Apocryphon of Joseph (4Q372) and is included in the prayer placed in the mouth of Joseph by the author, requesting divine assistance for himself during his period of sojourn among the gentiles. Joseph is stated to have cried out 'My father, my God, do not abandon me among the gentiles' which, in the original Hebrew, reads אבי ואלהי אל תעזבני ביד הגוים. But there is no general use of this term in the numerous liturgical texts recently published from the Dead Sea Scrolls.[15]

New Testament

Was there then reluctance on the part of the early forms of Rabbinic Judaism and Christianity to address God as father? Here we are faced with the problem of relating the text of the Lord's Prayer with its opening phrase of 'our father who is

13 Segal, *Ben Sira*, pp. 136–37; Skehan and Di Lella, *Ben Sira*, p. 322; Rahlfs, *Septuaginta*, p. 415.
14 Reider, *Wisdom*, pp. 167–68; Winston, *Wisdom*, pp. 255–56.
15 Schuller, 'Joseph', pp. 362–63, where she also refers to 4Q460 5 6; García Martínez, *Scrolls*, p. 225. I am grateful to Tyndale House Library, Cambridge, for providing access to its online version of the Scrolls, and to Dr David Instone–Brewer for his kind assistance in this connection.

in heaven' to the earliest phraseology of such rabbinic prayer-texts as the *shema'* benedictions and the *'amidah*. We need to assess the reliability of the relevant texts, attempt to establish their date as well as their context, and offer some conclusions as to what was novel, and what represented the continuation of earlier traditions. How valid is the view that the reference to God as 'our father' in the Lord's Prayer is a totally fresh means of address used by Jesus?[16] Or are we to adopt the idea that there is complete conformity between the Paternoster and the Jewish norms of prayer?[17]

Firstly to the New Testament passages. In Luke 11:2, God is addressed as 'father', perhaps reflecting the simple and common Aramaic term *'abba* (אבא) and the Greek Πάτερ, while in Matt 6:9 the form of address is 'our father in heaven', from which we may presuppose an original Hebrew of אבינו שבשמים or Aramaic אבונא דבשמיא (Greek: Πάτερ ἡμῶν ὁ ἐν τοῖς οὐρανοῖς).[18] Even if we assume the Lukan version to be the more original, we still have, at the very least, a liturgical piece that commences by calling God 'father' and that may conservatively be dated to the late decades of the first century and, even by the most sceptical assessment, not later than the first third of the second century.[19] There are certainly enough references to God as father within other New Testament passages to support the assumption that such a view of the Creator was thoroughly familiar to the earliest Christians, if not to Jesus himself.[20] What is more, there is another liturgical use recorded in Mark 14:36 where Jesus, in a personal petition, again addresses God as *'abba*.

Rabbinic liturgy

What of any parallels in early statutory, rabbinic liturgy? At first glance, they seem legion but the situation becomes more complicated as we consider them one by one. Throughout our analysis of these texts, it should not be forgotten that the early textual evidence is clear in one respect, namely, that the early

---

16 Jeremias, *Message*, pp. 9–30 and Kasper, 'Jesus', p. 235, as cited by Oesterreicher, 'Abba', in Petuchowski and Brocke, *Lord's Prayer*, p. 135.

17 De Sola Pool, *Kaddish*, p. 112, as cited by Heinemann, 'Background', in Petuchowski and Brocke, *Lord's Prayer*, p. 81.

18 Plummer, *Luke*, pp. 294–95; Fitzmyer, *Luke*, pp. 896–901; Allen, *Matthew*, p. 58; Albright and Mann, *Matthew*, pp. 75–76.

19 Vögtle, 'Prayer' in Petuchowski and Brocke, *Lord's Prayer*, p. 94.

20 Examples are Matt 11:27, 13:43, 26:34. Lachs, *Rabbinic Commentary*, p. 119, sees the source of this prayer in neither the *'amidah* nor the *qaddish* but among the brief prayers of Jewish individuals, but he does propose that the phrase 'our father' here is not an original usage.

textual evidence is unclear. One is therefore obliged either to follow traditional rabbinic exegetes, and assume that the talmudic mention of a liturgical text implies that the text in mind is that which was later spelt out in the post-talmudic period, or adopt a more historical and literary-critical view and presuppose that there may well have been an evolution in the form of the text in the course of these centuries that can only theoretically be reconstructed.[21]

Torah benediction before *shema'*

אבינו מלכנו ('our father, our king') occurs in the Torah benediction before the morning recitation of the *shema'*. The relevant passage in one of the oldest known text versions reads בעבור אבותינו שבטחו בך ותלמדנו חקי חיים כן תחננו אבינו אב הרחמן המרחם רחם עלינו ('For the sake of our fathers who trusted you and whom you taught instructions for life, do favour us, our father, the merciful father, who shows mercy, by being merciful to us').[22] This benediction commences by praising God for the intense love he has expressed for Israel. He is said to have rewarded the faith demonstrated by the people's founding fathers by teaching them Torah precepts that are life-giving. God is then entreated to grant in his mercy similar knowledge to contemporary Israel. In all the earliest textual versions, this latter entreaty addresses God as 'our father, the merciful father'.[23] The early medieval French rite expands 'our father' into 'our father, our king' and uses this phrase when dealing with the historical statement as well as the entreaty, while some of the texts broadly from the same period apply it only to the latter section.[24]

It seems reasonable to propose that this expansion is a later phenomenon, given that it is the divine love and mercy that are being acknowledged in connection with the gift of Torah. Both the Babylonian (Bavli) and the Palestinian (Yerushalmi) Talmud refer to this Torah benediction, and to its opening few words

---

21 Liturgical poetry is a singularly different genre from statutory prayer and provided fertile ground for penitential expansions. It deserves the kind of independent treatment that is beyond the scope of this brief, present analysis. With regard to the statutory prayers, I am grateful to my friend Rabbi Dr Jeffrey Cohen for some helpful comments and suggestions.

22 Davidson, Assaf and Joel, *Siddur RSG*, pp. 13–14. See also Genizah fragments CUL, T-S 6H3.1, Add.3160.6 and Add.3356. I am grateful to Professor Uri Ehrlich for his kindness in sharing with me data about Genizah fragments compiled in the context of the liturgy project he is directing at Ben-Gurion University of the Negev, Beersheba, Israel.

23 *SRAmram*, ed. Goldschmidt, p. 14; Goldschmidt, 'Maimonides', p. 196; and the references cited in the previous footnote.

24 Simḥa of Vitry, 1.65; Jacob ben Judah, 1.84.

that refer to God's special love.[25] There is no talmudic evidence about precisely what form the remainder of the text took in the early Christian centuries. On the basis of the theme of the generous gift of Torah, the parallels between the morning and evening benedictions, and the context that links Torah study and practice with the subsequent reading of the *shema'*, one may justifiably argue that the original rabbinic formulation of the second, or maybe even the late first, century mentioned God's love, and his gift of Torah.[26] It then went on to request divine support for the people of Israel in its response to this when it recites the *shema'*, and in its adherence to the theological principles underlying its recitation.

The use of the root רחם, usually translated 'to show mercy' (or its Hebrew semantic equivalents), is a common liturgical phenomenon in the earliest rabbinic prayers such as the *'amidah* and the grace after meals.[27] One is therefore perhaps justified in presupposing that the entreaty to God may have been headed by the imperative form רחם ('be merciful'), constituting a request to assist the worshippers in fulfilling these, their religious obligations. But it is not possible, on the basis of this benediction alone, to date in any definitive way the rabbinic liturgical use of the phrases relating to God's fatherhood (אבינו, אב הרחמן and אבינו מלכנו – 'our father', 'merciful father' and 'our father, our king'). One may say no more than that they appear (inconsistently) in all the early prayer-books and are therefore not later than the early post-talmudic period (sixth or seventh centuries).[28] The same conclusion applies to other occurrences of the phrase אבינו מלכנו, such as in the special penitential prayers (*taḥanun*) of the daily morning (*shaḥarit*) liturgy, in the service for fast-days, and in the additions made to the daily office during the ten days between Rosh Ha-Shanah and Yom Kippur, and in the *'amidah* for the *musaf* (additional) service on some of the festivals.[29]

---

25 *b. Ber.* 11b; *y. Ber.* 1.8 (3c).
26 Davidson, Assaf and Joel, *Siddur RSG*, pp. 13–14 and 26. The suggested simplicity of the basic form is supported by the early Genizah fragment on vellum, CUL NS J502, which has: אהבת עולם ישראל אהבתה וברית שלמך לנו יה קיימתה ב'י אוהב את ישראל.
27 Heinemann, *Tefilla*, pp. 48–51, *Prayer*, pp. 288–91.
28 See the editions and Genizah fragments cited in n. 22 above.
29 See (for example, but by no means exhaustively), Davidson, Assaf and Joel, *Siddur RSG*, p. 24; *SRAmram*, ed. Goldschmidt, pp. 38, 46, 57, 93, 126 and 138–39; Baer, pp. 109, 113–15 and 352; *Siddur 'Oṣar*, 1.384–88, 1.399, and 2.923.

Prayer for rain

There is, however, talmudic evidence for the use of the phrase אבינו מלכנו in another liturgical context, and this may be of assistance to us in our quest for origins and early development. The Talmud Bavli in tractate *Ta'anit* 25b reports an extra-mishnaic tannaitic tradition (*baraita*) relating to the matter of special petitionary prayers that were recited on the fast-days prescribed on occasions of serious drought. On one such occasion, the second-century *tanna* Rabbi Eliezer ben Hyrcanus decreed thirteen fast-days for the community but the project did not achieve its aim and the congregants pessimistically abandoned the project, leading him to declare that they had better prepare for their deaths. The congregants then wailed pitifully and that succeeded in bringing the required rain. In another instance, R. Eliezer himself led such prayers for rain and recited twenty-four prescribed benedictions, but the hoped-for meteorological response was not forthcoming. Rabbi Akiva took over from him and offered the simple prayer אבינו מלכנו רחם עלינו ('Our father, our king! Have mercy on us!') and the rains came at once. At which point, a heavenly voice explained that the success of R. Akiva was in no way indicative of his greater stature, but of his more intense humility.

As Malter's critical editions of this tractate makes clear, there are numerous textual variations after the initial phrase of אבינו מלכנו ('our father, our king'), each one including a different form of entreaty.[30] This is a common phenomenon in talmudic passages that report prayers and indicates that each generation of scribes felt the need to adjust the text in the light of its own liturgical experiences and usages. But does the occurrence of the phrase אבינו מלכנו in all the variants unequivocally permit us to assume that the *baraita* testifies to the liturgical use of the phrase around the time of the editing of the Mishnah or soon afterwards, say in the early part of the third Christian century? Interestingly, the parallel passage in the Yerushalmi reports more simply that R. Eliezer observed a fast but no rain came, while R. Akiva did the same and achieved instant success.[31] It makes no mention whatsoever of any text of R. Akiva's prayer and therefore provides no support for a second- or third-century dating of the liturgical phrase אבינו מלכנו.

30 Malter, *Ta'anit*, pp. 116–17 and *Treatise Ta'anit*, pp. 386–87. See also *b. Ta'an* 23b and Winston, *Wisdom*, pp. 255–56.
31 *y. Ta'an.* 3.4 (66cd): ר' ליעזר עבד תעני ולא איתנחת מיטרא. עבד ר' עקיבא תעני ונחת מיטרא.

Interpretation of the data

A number of important conclusions are possible on the basis of the two passages just cited. Firstly, the liturgical phrase אבינו מלכנו was either not in use until after the redaction of the Yerushalmi, that is, not before the early fourth century, or such penitential prayers were in use in some circles while being thought less appropriate in others. Secondly – and following from what was just stated about a theological disagreement – the two passages reflect a tension between those who saw efficacious prayer as the privilege of the pietistic, charismatic (and perhaps mystically inclined) few, and those who promoted the idea that statutory prayer on the part of the community, regular and formal as it had to be, was the way forward regardless of special cases and events. This interpretation is supported by an interpretative gloss placed on the story of R. Eliezer and R. Akiva in the Yerushalmi which, at least initially, tries to justify R. Eliezer's approach by arguing that God so much enjoys the attentions of such suppliants that he does not quickly respond to them!

The phrase under discussion, אבינו מלכנו, also provides a clue for our historical reconstruction. Referring to God as the worshipper's father implies a close, warm and intense relationship and one that presupposes not only discipline but also the kind indulgence, forgiveness and generosity, of which one can on occasion take advantage. Addressing God as one's king lays a different stress on the relationship. He is the creator, the power and the authority, and, as his subject, one is obliged to follow his instructions in order to achieve a favourable result for one's entreaties, and to maintain an approved status. If there were, during the second and third centuries, as I have argued elsewhere,[32] serious divergences in rabbinic circles on such matters of liturgical theology, it would make sense for these to have been resolved by the later Babylonian talmudic authorities, or even by earlier Palestinian authorities anxious to propose something of a compromise, by the adoption of a term to address God that incorporated both elements, namely, אבינו מלכנו ('Our father, our king').

What emerges then is that the term is likely to have been widely adopted by the fourth century but was conceivably employed in more restricted pietistic contexts at least two centuries earlier.[33] It should be added that the long list of entreaties headed by אבינו מלכנו ('Our father, our king') that was included in the prayers for special occasions of penitence such as fast-days and the period

32 Reif, *Hebrew Prayer*, pp. 103–8.

33 Vermes, *Jesus*, chapter 3, 'Jesus and charismatic Judaism', which appears with different pagination in each of the various editions. In the SCM edition of 2001, it is to be found on pp. 40–63.

covering the ten days between Rosh Ha-Shanah and Yom Kippur is associated by the traditional liturgical commentators with the story about R. Akiva, but cannot be presupposed to have existed in such a form simply on the basis of that aggadic source.[34] The composers of Hebrew liturgical poetry made extensive use of the phrase but the consensus about their date would place them in the late talmudic or early post-talmudic era.

It seems to me unlikely that the totality of Rabbinic Judaism made little use of the liturgical address 'our father' in the second century but then enthusiastically adopted it two centuries later, especially since by that time Christian notions of the fatherhood of God had become much more complex and certainly open to theological question by the rabbinic sages. What appears to me to be a more convincing scenario is that the views of some mystical/pietistic and/or charismatic groups within and around Rabbinic Judaism as to the fatherhood of God gradually became accepted as more normative and were amended to take account of the prejudices of the less mystically inclined rabbinic teachers. Such a theoretical reconstruction would explain the addition of the word מלכנו ('our king'), and why the phrase אבינו מלכנו was attributed to R. Akiva. It provided the prayer with a more respectable pedigree and therefore a sanction for its broader adoption. As Shamma Friedman has argued, the critical student of a talmudic passage, unlike his fundamentalist counterpart, can scrutinize a statement made in the name of R. Akiva 'in light of tannaitic parallels (Tosefta etc), *in light of Yerushalmi's interpretation* [my italics – SCR], in terms of the simple linguistic or grammatical meaning of his words, or even other categories yielding a historical meaning different from that assigned to it at the sugya's conclusion.'[35] It will be recalled that various items were ultimately incorporated into the rabbinic liturgy from *hekhalot* material that may have originated, in some form, in the talmudic period.[36]

Merciful father

When earlier discussing the Torah benediction that introduces the recitation of the *shema'* in the morning service, we had reason to make reference to the phrase אבינו האב הרחמן ('our father, the merciful father'). Where else in the early liturgy is the terminology האב הרחמן employed, and what assistance does this provide for us in our attempts to date its earliest occurrence in rabbinic prayer? The block of Psalms read

34 Goldschmidt, *SRAmram*, p. 138, ed. Warsaw, p. 45, with textual variations as to who instituted it: רבנן קמאי or רבנן or קמאי, 'our early rabbis', or 'our rabbis', or 'the early ones'.
35 Friedman, *Sugyot*, preface, p. v.
36 Schäfer, *Hidden God*, p. 8.

as a devotional preparation for the morning service proper is introduced and concluded with rabbinic benedictions. The introductory benediction, beginning with the usual six-word formula ('you are praised, our divine lord, the universal king') begins and ends with a statement that God is worthy of the praise heaped upon him by the Jewish people in general, and by its specially pious and devoted members in particular. Its concluding equivalent, which begins ישתבח שמך לעד מלכנו ('may your name be acclaimed forever, our king'), describes God with a plethora of epithets and declares that he is worthy of all manner of eternal praises. The earliest texts of both these benedictions, which are not recorded in the talmudic sources, appear to be well established by about the ninth century, and therefore apparently came into existence no later than about the seventh or eighth century.[37] What is significant for our discussion is that there are some versions of the introductory benediction in which there appear the additional words האב הרחמן, sometimes prefixed by האל ('God').[38] Their absence from other texts, as well from the concluding benediction, and the fact that the overall theme of praise is related in both benedictions to God's kingship, would indicate that the addition of these epithets represents a calculated extension of the thought to include God's merciful fatherhood.[39] Similarly, there are some texts of the *shema' qolenu* benediction in the *'amidah* that begin by addressing God as אב הרחמן.[40]

God is of course known as 'the merciful one' (usually by the employment of the Aramaic word רחמנא) in many earlier talmudic and midrashic sources but it needs to be recalled that what is being sought is not simply the nature of the divine attributes in rabbinic thought but liturgical addresses to God that refer to him directly as 'the merciful father'[41] It should be added, that, as in the case of the phrase אבינו מלכנו noted earlier, there are other (inconsistent) post-talmudic liturgical occurrences of the phrase אב הרחמן (or the variant אב הרחמים) such as in the special penitential prayers in the daily morning liturgy, in the additions made to the daily office during the ten days between Rosh Ha-Shanah and Yom Kippur, and in the *'amidah* for the *musaf* (additional) service on some of the festivals.[42]

---

37 See chapter 11 above, pp. 232–35.

38 Fleischer, *Eretz-Israel*, pp. 236, 246. See also early Genizah fragment CUL T-S 6H6.6 discussed in Reif, *Jewish Prayer Texts*, pp. 129–38.

39 See early Genizah fragments CUL T-S 8H9.1 and Add. 3160.5.

40 See Luger, *Amidah*, pp. 169–72, and Genizah fragments CUL T-S NS 121.37, 156.7, 278.51, AS 108.57 and Or.1081 2.76.

41 Ben Yehuda, *Dictionary*, p. 6543.

42 See (for example, but not exhaustively, and with textual variations) Davidson, Assaf, Joel, *Siddur RSG*, pp. 151, 220; Goldschmidt, *SRAmram*, p. 135; Baer, pp. 113, and 384; *Siddur 'Oṣar*, 1.396 and 2.1022. See also Tabory, 'Father of Mercy'.

Grace after meals

The grace after meals is undoubtedly one of the oldest of the rabbinic liturgies, regarded by the talmudic sages as being of biblical origin but also acknowledged by modern, historical scholarship as having some of its origins in pre-Christian days.[43] Perhaps, then, the occurrence in the grace after meals of a benediction that addresses God as האל אבינו מלכנו ('God, our father, our king') is indicative of early rabbinic use of liturgy that addresses God as 'Father'. Alas, here too the evidence cannot safely be interpreted in such a way. The phrase occurs in the fourth benediction which is undoubtedly later than the other three, according to both talmudic opinion and liturgical historians. Granted that it is already known as the הטוב והמטיב benediction (dealing with God as 'source and purveyor of goodness') in the second century, there is no evidence from that century or indeed from the whole talmudic period that indicates its precise wording. It has been convincingly suggested that in its earliest form it was a precise reflection of its name, simply a benediction that used the usual six-word formula of praise followed by nothing more than the phrase הטוב והמטיב.[44] That this may well have been the case is supported by the total lack of consistency about the wording that is encountered as late as the end of the first Christian millennium. Although the word אבינו ('our father') occurs in the middle of the third benediction in a list of epithets referring to God in some of the later rites, it does not occur in the earliest ones and may therefore be discounted from discussion in the present context.[45]

What is interestingly consistent in all these early textual variations is that אבינו ('our father') is always accompanied by מלכנו ('our king'), and that the epithet רחמן ('merciful one') is used – when it is used at all – separately from the word אבינו. We are instantly reminded of the situation that was earlier described with regard to the use of this phrase in other parts of the liturgy. There, we concluded that the early talmudic period may well have witnessed a deliberate linking of kingship and fatherhood in order to incorporate two competing theological tendencies. The same may then apply in the case of the fourth benediction of the grace after meals. It is also possible that the attachment of the name האל ('God') at the beginning of the list of epithets is intended, like the addition of the word מלכנו, to soften the effect of using the potentially anthropomorphic and overly intimate expression אבינו.

---

43 Finkelstein, 'Birkat Ha-Mazon'; and Schmidman, *Grace after Meals*.
44 Jacobson, *Nethiv*, 3.52–55 and 64–65.
45 Reif, *Problems*, p. 341.

Father in heaven

And so to the phrase אבינו שבשמים ('our father in heaven'), where we are in distinctly different territory. Describing God as a father who resides in the heavenly sphere – whatever precisely was envisioned by those who employed such a description – is already a common phenomenon in the tannaitic texts that date from the second century. It is, however, remarkable that the earliest references from that period generally refer to his, your, and their 'father in heaven', and not to our, or my, 'father in heaven'.[46] Where 'our father in heaven' does occur, it is not in a direct liturgical address to God.[47] As far as I am aware, the earliest use of the first person pronoun in a direct entreaty to God is found in the singular form rather than in the plural, namely, אבי שבשמים ('my father in heaven'), which occurs in Seder Eliyahu Rabba in a prayer that runs: אבי שבשמים, יהי שמך הגדול מבורך לעולם ולעולמי עולמים ('my father in heaven, may your great name be blessed eternally and to all eternity').[48] Although the body of the blessing about God's name undoubtedly goes back to the earliest rabbinic times,[49] if not to Second Temple times, the prefixing of the blessing with the phrase אבי שבשמים is another matter altogether.

The date of compilation currently being suggested for Seder Eliyahu Rabba is as late as the tenth century although it is generally acknowledged that the work contains rabbinic traditions of some centuries earlier.[50] In ascertaining how much earlier we should go back in the case of our phrase אבי שבשמים, we are assisted by the numerous occurrences of the form with the plural pronominal suffix אבינו שבשמים, either in liturgical or quasi-liturgical contexts, throughout the late talmudic and post-talmudic periods, say from the sixth to the tenth centuries.[51] The earliest of these occurrences include texts from the daily liturgy, as well as from the *hekhalot* literature, the mystical texts that are traced by Gershom

46 See, for example, *m. Yoma* 8.9; *m. 'Avot* 5.20; *m. Kil.* 9.8; *t. Ber.* 3.14 (variant).

47 See, for example, *m. Soṭah* 9.15 and y. *Ḥag.* 2.1 (77a).

48 *Seder Eliyahu Rabbah* 10.53. I am grateful to my friend, Professor Chaim Milikowsky, for kindly sharing with me his thoughts on the dating of this work.

49 On the uses and development of the Hebrew and Aramaic forms, see Lehnardt, *Qaddish*, pp. 81–103 and De Sola Pool, *Kaddish*, pp. 43–53.

50 Stemberger, *Introduction*, pp. 340–42.

51 See the *Attah hu* prayer after the morning benedictions, as in, for example, *SRAmram*, ed. Goldschmidt, pp. 6–7 and Baer, p. 46. I am grateful to the Ma'agarim Project of the Hebrew Language Academy and the Bar-Ilan Responsa Project for the location of many of the phrases to which I make references throughout this article, and to the Syndics of Cambridge University Library for kindly permitting access to, and citation of, its Genizah manuscripts here, and elsewhere in this volume.

Scholem to the talmudic period but have more recently been assigned a later date.[52] We may therefore safely state that our phrase in liturgical form came into the more standard rabbinic texts only in the late talmudic or early post-talmudic periods, while at the same time recognizing that it may well have been used that way in certain, more mystically inclined, circles at an earlier time.

Our father

Attention may now be paid to the simple form אבינו ('our father') and how it is used in early rabbinic liturgy. Here, its occurrence is entirely parenthetical within the prayer, the word being placed after an entreaty to God as a way of drawing the worshippers closer to the divine one they are entreating. Hence, in the prayer for forgiveness of the daily *'amidah*, the text reads סלח לנו אבינו כי חטאנו ('forgive us, our father, that we have sinned'). Since the *'amidah* prayer dates from the second century, may we date this usage of 'our father' to that period? Alas, the matter is again more complicated. In the ninth- or tenth-century Babylonian prayer-books, that phrase is followed by one that offers a parallel מחל לנו מלכנו כי פשענו ('pardon us, our king, that we have done wrong'), but this second idea is expressed in quite a different textual way in the contemporaneous Palestinian rite. We may therefore fairly justifiably assume that the parallel is a later addition. In that case, the use of אבינו ('our father') may also have been an addition made at the same time as the parallelism, with the object of balancing the reference to the fatherhood of God with a reference to his kingship. As Finkelstein has argued,[53] the original benediction may have read simply סלח לנו כי חטאנו ('forgive us that we have sinned'), which would make it more akin to many of the other benedictions, at least in their basic forms. Much the same may be said about the textual evolution of the prayer for repentance in the *'amidah*. In its Babylonian form, it begins השיבנו אבינו לתורתך ('bring us back, our father, to your Torah'), and there is then a parallel phrase וקרבנו מלכנו לעבודתך ('draw us near, our king, to your service'). Again, the Palestinian rite begins השיבנו ה' אליך ונשובה ('bring us back to you, God, and we shall return') and has no parallel, suggesting that the simplest form of the benediction was at one point no more than השיבנו אליך('bring us back to you').[54]

52 Schäfer, *Hidden*, p. 8.

53 Finkelstein, 'Amidah', pp. 146–47.

54 See chapter 14 above, pp. 303–8; Luger, *Amidah*, p. 82; Ehrlich, *Weekday Amidah*, p. 91.

The third of the nineteen benedictions that addresses God as אבינו ('our father') is the final one of the *'amidah* and deals with the subject of peace. Of the three basic forms, only one inserts the parenthetical אבינו after the request to God to 'bless us all' and it is reasonable to assume that the simplest form requested peace and blessing for Israel and ran along the lines of שים שלום וברך את עמך ישראל ('provide peace and bless your people Israel'). Support for such an overall theory about the later addition of אבינו comes from the textual evidence provided by the earliest texts from the Cairo Genizah, in some of which, dating from about the tenth century, the word אבינו ('our father') is still absent from the relevant phrases in all three benedictions. It may therefore be concluded that the inclusion of a paternal nomenclature when addressing God represented a trend towards stressing this aspect of his relationship with Israel within the liturgical framework. Such a trend had not yet become unequivocally standard even four centuries after the talmudic period but had been accepted in many circles, especially if it could be paralleled by a reference to the royal aspect of the divine character.[55]

Midrashim

It may at this stage be helpful to refer to two midrashim on the subject of God's fatherhood. In the first of these, based on Jer 3:19, God declares to Israel that he has not performed miracles and wonders for them with the intention of obtaining reward (simple obedience?) from them. His object was, rather, that they should see themselves as God's children, behave towards him with respect, and call him 'father'.[56] The second is on the topic of adoption and is an aggadic interpretation of Isa 64:7. Orphaned young children who are adopted call their adoptive parent 'father' but do not retain this appellation for the one who actually sired them originally. Similarly, Israel may choose to ignore their forefathers Abraham, Isaac and Jacob, and yet still feel entitled to address God as their father and to seek his direct assistance.[57] What both these passages appear to be arguing is that there has been some sort of shift in Jewish theology towards a relationship with God that stresses not only his power, authority and instructions but also his love, loyalty and care.

55 See chapter 13 above, pp. 285–89.
56 *Shemot Rabbah*, 32.5.
57 *Shemot Rabbah*, 46.5.

Conclusions

It remains only to draw together all the evidence and attempt some sort of overall assessment of the evolution of the notion of the divine father in early rabbinic liturgy, and how this reflected its ongoing struggle to establish a successful and competitive theology. The earliest rabbinic thought of the first three centuries is of course committed to the idea of the fatherhood of God in the same way as this appears in the biblical and apocryphal writings. Just as there was during those earlier periods a hesitancy about some aspects of this religious idea because of the manner in which it was expressed in the pagan religions, so the early rabbis were cautious about devoting themselves wholly and enthusiastically to conceiving of God as a paternal figure and to utilizing this conception in expressing themselves liturgically.

It would seem that by about the fourth century a liturgical use of the word אבינו ('our father') was establishing itself and that it was balanced by an accompanying reference to God as מלכנו ('our king'). An expanded use of the paternal image to include God as (ה)אב הרחמן or אב הרחמים ('merciful father') became more standard at the end of the talmudic and into the geonic (post-talmudic period) and was incorporated into many of the earliest prayer-books from the ninth and tenth centuries. Addressing God as אבינו שבשמים or אבי שבשמים ('our/my father in heaven') came from pietistic circles and followed a similar, chronological evolution. Heinemann sees all these expressions as originating in private prayer.[58] This may just be another way of characterizing what were special, penitential themes, but the interpretation preferred here is to associate such terminology with particular religious circles rather than only with individuals.

It would appear, then, that either within rabbinic circles themselves, or within the wider Jewish world including that of the early Jewish-Christians, there were mystical and ascetic tendencies that stressed a close, intense and warm Jewish relationship with God. The response to such tendencies, in what ultimately became the outlook represented in the standard talmudic-midrashic sources, was to adopt them gradually, at times with some degree of dilution. At the beginning, when the Christian notion of the Trinity was taking hold, there was perhaps a fear of drawing too close to fatherhood concepts. Once, by the fourth and fifth centuries, the two religions had gone their separate ways, Rabbinic Judaism was able to adopt a more relaxed view of the fatherhood concepts and to absorb them more centrally into various aspects of its liturgy. Some of the midrashim

---

58 Heinemann, *Tefillah*, p. 119; *Prayer*, p. 190.

that make reference to God's fatherhood of Israel are perhaps promoting, and even conceivably polemicizing on behalf of, such a theological trend.

It is not possible to give a definitive reply as to why some texts as late as the tenth century are still omitting the word אבינו from some common prayers. Is it a remnant of the early hesitancy to which allusion has just been made? Or is it a reaction by the Jews in the Islamic world to the powerful animosity expressed by what emerged as mainstream Islam to any representation of God by way of a father figure, perhaps because this was seen by the Muslims as part of the division (or unification?) of God into Father, Son and Holy Spirit that was championed by Christianity. There is insufficient evidence to reach a conclusive view on this but we can say that the evidence we have considered testifies to innovation and adaptation, as well as caution and reflection, on the part of those who formulated the rabbinic liturgy in the first millennium of its existence.

Works cited

Albright, W. F. and Mann, C. S. *The Anchor Bible. Matthew* (New York: Doubleday, 1971).

Allen, W. C., *A Critical and Exegetical Commentary on the Gospel according to S. Matthew* (Edinburgh: T & T Clark, 1907).

Amram ben Sheshna, *Seder Rav 'Amram Ga'on*, ed. N. Coronel (Warsaw: Kelter, 1865); ed. E. D. Goldschmidt (Jerusalem: Rav Kook, 1971); collated with *Seder R. Amram, part I*, ed. D. Hedegård (Lund: Lindstedts, 1951) and with *Seder R. Amram, part II*, ed. T. Kronholm (Lund: CWK Gleerup, 1974).

Baer, S., *Seder 'Avodat Yisra'el* (Rödelheim: Lehrberger, 1868).

Ben Yehuda, E. E., *A Complete Dictionary of Ancient and Modern Hebrew* (Hebrew; Jerusalem, New York: Yoseloff, 1908–1959, 1960).

Briggs, C. A. and E. G., *A Critical and Exegetical Commentary on the Book of Psalms*, vol. 2 (Edinburgh: T & T Clark, 1907).

Bright, J., *The Anchor Bible. Jeremiah* (New York: Doubleday, 1965).

Coburn, T. B., *Devi Mahatmya. The Crystallization of the Goddess Tradition* (Delhi: Motilal Banarsidass, 1984).

Cohen, M. (ed.), *Mikra'ot Gedolot 'Haketer'. Kings I & II* (Ramat-Gan: Bar-Ilan University Press, 1995).

Curtis, E. L., and Madsen, A. A., *A Critical and Exegetical Commentary on the Books of Chronicles* (Edinburgh: T & T Clark, 1910).

Davidson, I., Assaf, S., Joel, B. I. (eds.), *Siddur R. Sa'adya Gaon. Kitāb Ǵāmi' Aṣ-Ṣalawāt Wat-Tasābīh* (Jerusalem: Mekize Nirdamim, 1963, 2nd edn.).

De Sola Pool, D., *The Kaddish* (Leipzig: Drugulin, 1909).

Ehrlich, U., *The Weekday Amidah in Geniza Prayer Books: Origins and Transmission* (Hebrew; Jerusalem: Yad Ben-Zvi Press, 2013).

Finkelstein, L., 'The Birkat Ha-Mazon', *Jewish Quarterly Review*, NS 19 (1928–29), pp. 211–62.

Finkelstein, L., 'The development of the Amidah', *Jewish Quarterly Review* NS 16 (1925–26), pp. 1–43 and 127–70.
Fitzmyer, J. A., *The Anchor Bible. The Gospel according to Luke X-XXIV* (New York: Doubleday, 1985).
Fleischer, E., *Eretz-Israel Prayer and Prayer Rituals as Portrayed in the Geniza Documents* (Hebrew; Jerusalem: Magnes, 1998).
Friedman, S., *Five Sugyot from the Babylonian Talmud. Towards an Edition of the Talmud with Original Commentary* (Hebrew; Jerusalem: Society for the Interpretation of the Talmud, 2002).
García Martínez, F., *The Dead Sea Scrolls Translated. The Qumran Text in English*, Eng. trans. W. G. E. Watson (Leiden: Brill, 1994).
Goldschmidt, E. D., 'The Oxford Ms. of Maimonides' Book of Prayer', in his collected articles *On Jewish Liturgy: Essays on Prayer and Religious Poetry* (Hebrew; Jerusalem: Magnes, 1978), pp. 187–216.
Heinemann, J., 'The background of Jesus' prayer in the Jewish liturgical tradition', in Petuchowski and Brocke, *Lord's Prayer*, pp. 81–89.
Heinemann, J., *Prayer in the Talmud: Forms and Patterns* (Berlin: de Gruyter, 1977).
Heinemann, J., *Tefillah Bi-Tekufat Ha-Tanna'im Ve-Ha-Amora'im* (Jerusalem: Magnes, 1966).
Jacob ben Judah Ḥazzan of London, *The Etz Ḥayyim*, ed. I. Brodie, 3 vols. (Jerusalem: Rav Kook, 1962–67).
Jacobson, B. S., *Nethiv Binah*, 5 vols. (Hebrew; Tel Aviv: Sinai, 1968–83).
Jeremias, J., *The Central Message of the New Testament* (London: SCM Press, 1965).
Kasper, W., 'Jesus im Streit der Meinungen', *Theologie der Gegenwart* 16 (1973), pp. 233–41.
Kirkpatrick, A. F., *The Cambridge Bible for Schools and Colleges. The Book of Psalms: Books II and III: Psalms XLII-LXXXIX* (Cambridge: University Press, 1895).
Lachs, S. T., *A Rabbinic Commentary on the New Testament. The Gospels of Matthew, Mark and Luke* (Hoboken, NJ: Ktav, 1987).
Lehnardt, A., *Qaddish. Untersuchungen zur Entstehung und Rezeption eines rabbinischen Gebetes* (Tübingen: Mohr Siebeck, 2002).
Luger, Y., *The Weekday Amidah in the Cairo Genizah* (Hebrew; Jerusalem: Orhot, 2001).
Lumby, J. R., *The Cambridge Bible for Schools and Colleges. The First and Second Books of the Kings* (Cambridge: Cambridge University Press, 1897).
McKane, W., *A Critical and Exegetical Commentary on Jeremiah* (Edinburgh: T & T Clark, 1986).
Malter, H., *Massekheth Ta'anith Min Talmud Bavli* (New York: American Academy for Jewish Research, 1930).
Malter, H., *The Treatise Ta'anit of the Babylonian Talmud, critically edited and provided with a translation and notes* (Philadelphia: Jewish Publication Society of America, 1967).
Montgomery, J. A., *A Critical and Exegetical Commentary on the Book of Kings*, ed. H. S. Gehman (Edinburgh: T & T Clark, 1951).
Myers, J. M., *The Anchor Bible. 1 Chronicles* (New York: Doubleday, 1965).
Norden, E., *Agnostos Theos. Untersuchungen zur Formengeschichte religiöser Rede* (Stuttgart: Teubner, 1956, 4th edn.).
Oesterreicher, J. M., ''Abba, Father!'. On the humanity of Jesus', in Petuchowski and Brocke, *Lord's Prayer*, pp. 119–36.
'Oṣar Ha-Tefillot, ed. A. L. Gordon, 2 vols. (Vilna: Romm, 1923).

Petuchowski, J. J. and Brocke, M. (eds.), *The Lord's Prayer and Jewish Liturgy* (London: Burns & Oates, 1978).

Plummer, A., *A Critical and Exegetical Commentary to S. Luke* (Edinburgh: T & T Clark, 1896).

Rahlfs, A. (ed.), *Sepuaginta. Vol. II. Libri Poetici et Prophetici* (Stuttgart: Privilegierte Württembergische Bibelanstalt, 1935).

Reider, J., *The Book of Wisdom. An English Translation with Introduction and Commentary* (New York: Harper & Brothers, 1957).

Reif, S. C., *Jewish Prayer Texts from the Cairo Genizah. A Selection of Manuscripts at Cambridge University Library, Introduced, Transcribed, Translated, and Annotated, with Images* (Cambridge Genizah Studies 7; Leiden: Brill, 2016).

Reif, S. C., *Judaism and Hebrew Prayer. New Perspectives on Jewish Liturgical History* (Cambridge: Cambridge University Press, 1993).

Reif, S. C., *Problems with Prayers. Studies in the Textual History of Early Rabbinic Liturgy* (Berlin: de Gruyter, 2006).

Ringgren, H., entry אב in *Theological Dictionary of the Old Testament*, eds. G. J. Botterweck and H. Ringgren, vol. 1, Eng. trans. J. T. Willis (Grand Rapids, Mich.: Eerdmans, revised edition, 1977), pp. 1–19.

Schäfer, P., *The Hidden and Manifest God. Some Major Themes in Early Jewish Mysticism*, Eng. trans. A. Pomerance (Albany: State University of New York, 1992).

Schuller, E., '4Q372 1. A text about Joseph', in 'The Texts of Qumran and the History of the Community', *Revue de Qumran* 14/3, no. 55 (1990), pp. 349–76.

Seder Eliyahu Rabbah, ed. M. Friedmann (Ish-Shalom) (Warsaw: Achiasaf, 1904).

Segal, J. B., 'The Jewish attitude towards women', *Journal of Jewish Studies* 30 (1979), pp. 121–37.

Segal, M. H., *Sefer Ben Sira Ha-Shalem* (Jerusalem: Mosad Bialik, 1972, 2nd edn.).

Shmidman, A., *The Poetic Versions of the Grace after Meals from the Cairo Genizah: A Critical Edition* (Hebrew; doctoral dissertation, Ramat-Gan: Bar-Ilan University, 2009).

Siddur 'Oṣar Ha-Tefillot, ed. A. L. Gordon, 2 vols. (Vilna: Romm, 1923).

Simḥa of Vitry, *Maḥzor Vitry*, ed. S. Hurwitz, 2 vols. (Nuremburg: Mekize Nirdamim, 1923, 2nd edn.).

Skehan, P. W. and Di Lella, A. A., *The Wisdom of Ben Sira. A New Translation with Notes... Introduction and Commentary* (New York: Doubleday, 1987).

Skinner, J., *The Cambridge Bible for Schools and Colleges. The Book of the Prophet Isaiah, Chapter XL-LXVI* (Cambridge: Cambridge University Press, 1898).

Sperber, A. (ed.), *The Bible in Aramaic. Vol. III. The Latter Prophets according to Targum Jonathan* (Leiden: Brill, 1962).

Stemberger, G., *Introduction to the Talmud and Midrash*, Eng. trans. M. Bockmuehl (Edinburgh: T. & T. Clark, 1996, 2nd edn.).

Stenning, J. F., *The Targum of Isaiah* (Oxford: Clarendon, 1949).

Streane, A. W., *The Cambridge Bible for Schools and Colleges. The Book of the Prophet Jeremiah together with the Lamentations* (Cambridge: Cambridge University Press, 1913).

Tabory, J., 'Father of Mercy or Merciful Father? The influence of the Ari on the oriental Siddur' (Hebrew), in *Jewish Prayer. New Perspectives*, ed. U. Ehrlich (Goldstein-Goren Library of Jewish Thought 20; Beer Sheva: Ben-Gurion University of the Negev Press, 2016), pp. 375–98.

Vermes, G., *Jesus the Jew. A Historian's Reading of the Gospels* (London: SCM Press, 2001).

Vögtle, A., 'The Lord's Prayer: a prayer for Jews and Christians?', in Petuchowski and Brocke, *Lord's Prayer*, pp. 93 – 117.
Watts, J. D. W., *Word Biblical Commentary, vol. 25, Isaiah 34 – 66* (Nashville, Tn.: Nelson, 2005).
Winston, D., *The Anchor Bible. The Wisdom of Solomon* (New York: Routledge, 1979).

16 Some Divine Metaphors in Early Rabbinic Liturgy

Theological and linguistic background

Rabbinic Judaism in the first few centuries of its existence chose not to compile any form of systematic theology. It found ways of expressing its religious ideas in terms of the performance of hundreds of daily precepts (*halakhah*); the blending of the implicit Talmud, or 'Oral Teaching' (*torah shebe'al peh*), with explicit Torah, as transmitted in the written books of the Hebrew Bible (*torah shebikhtav*); the interpretation of Scripture in a variety of ways that supported its spiritual ideology (*midrash*); and the requirement for the recitation of daily prayers, mostly of a communal nature, by its adherents (*tefillah*). By contrast, Christianity, for its part, and Islam, in its wake, provided their thinking followers with authorized and well-constructed doctrine, taking up the example of the pre-Christian Jewish thinker Philo in Alexandria (20 BCE to 50 CE) and extending his ideas to take account of its own notions, as well as the challenges of the Greek and Roman world. Ultimately, of course, Rabbinic Judaism could remain unaffected neither by those Christian and Islamic developments, nor by the emergence of Jewish religious movements, such as Karaism, that questioned rabbinic concepts. By the tenth century, its spiritual leaders, especially in the Mesopotamian area, took up the challenge and began the process of systematizing their theology on the basis of the vast talmudic and midrashic corpus that had been amassed in the course of almost a whole millennium.[1]

That process reached its completion – indeed its apogee – in the brilliant work of Moses Maimonides (1038–1204). A Jewish religious refugee from Islamic Spain and Morocco, and from Crusader Palestine, he became the leading light of the rabbinic communities of the Islamic world in his own lifetime and later – inevitably not without controversy – of the Jewish centres in Europe too. As a committed philosopher, as well as a pious rabbinic Jew, he saw the need to combine talmudic and halakhic ideas and practice with the advanced thought of his day. He did this, as well as much else besides, by first writing a commentary (*Perush Ha-Mišnayot*) on the Mishnah, the second-century rabbinic code from the land of Israel, then compiling a complete guide (*Mišneh Torah*) to all aspects of Jewish religious law, and finally authoring a systematic philosophy of Judaism (*Moreh*

1 For aspects of the historical, theological and literary backgrounds, see Alexander, *Judaism*; Neusner, *Rabbinic Judaism*; Safrai, *Literature*; and Schafer, *History*.

DOI 10.1515/9783110486704-017

Nevukhim –'*Guide of the Perplexed*'). One of the problems that he faced was the tendency of some rabbinic teachings, especially in the midrashic and liturgical fields, to address God in colourful metaphors. For him as a critically minded thinker, this constituted theologically intolerable behaviour.[2]

Maimonides expresses his views on the topic in chapters 58–59 of his *Guide*.[3] Just as humanity can never really achieve a true and complete understanding of the universe, so it is beyond human ken to comprehend the essence of God. All that may be acknowledged is the existence of God. Anything said by way of positive descriptions concerning the attributes of God amounts to anthropomorphism. One is consequently forced, for want of any better human ability, to employ only negative attributes to describe God. Such expressions reflect the fact that God is unique – that is to say, totally distinct from all our human and worldly experiences. Maimonides rails against those preachers, mystics and liturgical poets who use all manner of human language to address and describe God as if he were a cherished personal acquaintance, and not the Supreme Being. This is, for him, nothing short of profanity and blasphemy. Ideally, prayer should rather be conducted in total silence, and by way of images of God that are philosophically acceptable. This would be the highest level of intense devotion. Given that this is beyond the capabilities of ordinary Jewish congregants, they should follow the terminology and formulation laid down by the rabbis and their predecessors from as early as the Second Temple period, and in no way expand or adjust it. The statutory prayers should be treated precisely as such, since they do not go beyond the limits of rational thought in their depiction of God and his nature.[4]

It occurred to me, in the context of the present scholarly interest in metaphors, that it might be interesting to see how rabbinic prayer in the first few centuries of its existence employed metaphors with regard to its description of God. Chaim Rabin, who was born in Gießen, Germany, in 1915 and studied at the Hebrew University of Jerusalem, as well as at the Universities of London and of Oxford, was Professor of Hebrew Language at the Hebrew University of Jerusalem from 1956 and died there in 1996.[5] He gave some attention to the language used by the rabbis in their liturgical compositions, and a number of his conclusions are of particular relevance to the current discussion. Rabin pointed out that the language of rabbinic liturgy was a specific kind of idiom within the larger context of Mishnaic Hebrew and was orally

---

2 For biographical details in addition to the standard reference works, see Goitein, 'Maimonides'.

3 See the edition of Pines, *Guide*, pp. 134–43.

4 On Maimonides with regard to Jewish prayer, see Blidstein, *Prayer*, Friedman, 'Prayer reforms', and Reif; 'Maimonides'. See also Benor, *Worship*, a reference I owe to my Cambridge colleague, Dr D. Davies.

5 *Enyclopaedia Judaica*, 13.1470–71.

transmitted in its early form. Its linguistic development, which was complex and extended over many centuries, involved a gradual process of literary improvement and linguistic selection, ultimately leading to a distinct written format.[6] In the light of such an assessment, which I have long regarded as valid and insightful, how did the liturgical traditions of Rabbinic Judaism treat metaphors for God? Did they make use of biblical and qumranic precedents when they referred to God in their prayers? Or was their policy to adapt rather than to adopt those? Can one distinguish any trends among the most common metaphors at various periods and, if so, how and why did these differ as time moved on? What kind of religious, literary and linguistic factors were at play in the utilization of such metaphors in the liturgy? For the course of our discussion, it will be necessary to bear in mind the differences between a metaphor and an epithet. A metaphor is a figure of speech that describes a subject by asserting that it is, on some point of comparison, the same as another otherwise unrelated object. For Richard Nordquist, it is an implied comparison between two unlike things that actually have something important in common. An epithet or byname is a descriptive term (word or phrase) accompanying, or occurring in place of, a name and having entered common usage. For Nordquist, it is a stated comparison (usually formed with 'like' or 'as') between two fundamentally dissimilar things that have certain qualities in common.[7]

Ben Sira

A good starting point – and one that may safely be dated before the end of the Second Temple period – is Sir 51:22–34. Here we encounter a psalm that follows the same model as Ps 136, in which the first half invites gratitude to God while the second half of each verse repeats the refrain כי לעולם חסדו 'for his devotion is eternal', that is, God's love for us will never cease. Where the Ben Sira text differs is in its provision in the first half of each of these verses of an alternative set of epithets for praising God to those that appear in Ps 136. They are worthy of close attention. Seven of them, in verses 23–29, describe God by one of the actions through which the people of Israel benefit from his attention. He is the protector, creator, redeemer, restorer of exiles, builder of Jerusalem, promoter of the davidic dynasty and supporter of the Zadokite priesthood. These are by the definition of Maimonides metaphorical expressions but, given that they relate more directly to

6 See two articles by Rabin, 'Qumran Hebrew', and 'Linguistic investigation'.
7 See Nordquist's definitions online at http://grammar.about.com/od/rhetoricstyle/a/20figures.htm.

what God does, rather than what he is, we may, for our purposes, define them as epithets rather than metaphors. The first expression invites gratitude for the God of praises (אל התשבחות) which presumably means, as the later rabbinic expression spells it out more clearly, 'God who is praised with poetic acclaim' (מהולל בתשבחות). That is again descriptive, albeit this time in the opposite direction, that is, not what God is doing for us but how we respond to him. The remaining three expressions are, however, undoubtedly metaphorical. They represent God as 'the shield of Abraham' (מגן אברהם), 'the rock of Isaac' (צור יצחק) and 'the champion of Jacob' (אביר יעקב). Whether we date this chapter of Ben Sira from the second century BCE, or regard it as an addition from a century later, it is undoubtedly early enough to be relevant to the analysis of the earliest rabbinic metaphors of about the second century C.E.[8]

Shield of Abraham

Indeed, the first two metaphors (מגן, 'shield', and צור, 'rock') have their origins and parallels in biblical and rabbinic formulations. First, the word מגן. There are fifteen instances in the Hebrew Bible of God being described as a מגן for those who trust in him, take refuge in him, or deserve his protection. These are, with the exception of one verse in Genesis and two in Proverbs, all located in the book of Psalms. There are suggestions, based on Semitic cognates, that the meaning is 'one who gives or grants', rather than 'shield', but that is not germane to our argument.[9] The phrase מגן אברהם, 'shield of Abraham', is not biblical but is clearly based on the divine promise to Abraham, enunciated in Gen 15:1, that God will be a shield (or supporter) to him. The first benediction of the *'amidah* prayer, the origins of which, in one form or another, are usually dated to the land of Israel no later than the second century, is concerned that God should recall the loyalty and piety of the three patriarchs, Abraham, Isaac and Jacob, presumably in order to reward their descendants accordingly.[10] It is briefly defined as ברכת האבות, that is, 'the benediction concerning the patriarchs'. But there is an interesting variation of the metaphor that occurs in the abbreviated *'amidah*

---

8 See Lévi, *Ecclesiasticus*, pp. 73–74; Segal, *Ben Sira Ha-Shalem*, pp. 355–57; and Skehan and Di Lella, *Wisdom of Ben Sira*, pp. 568–71.

9 See entry *magen* by Freedman, O'Connor and Ringgren in *TDOT*, 8.74–87, and Kessler, 'Shield'.

10 The earliest edition of the whole benediction according to the Babylonian rite is to be found in the prayer-book of Sa'adya, *Siddur RSG*, pp. 17–18, and the modern Ashkenazi text is based on Baer, *'Avodat Yisrael*, pp. 87–88. On the textual history of the benediction, and the Genizah variants, see Elbogen, *Liturgy*, pp. 38–39 and Ehrlich, *Weekday Amidah*, pp. 29–42.

used on Friday evening and in the phrase that occurs according to the rite of the land of Israel (as distinct from that of Babylonia).

In the first case, the benediction is cited not as מגן אברהם, 'shield of Abraham', but as מגן אבות, 'shield of patriarchs', and in the second the phrase used is מגננו ומגן אבותינו, 'our shield and the shield of our patriarchs'.[11] In the text that became standard in Babylonia, and was then widely accepted in the later Jewish world, the eulogy is universally recorded as מגן אברהם. It emerges that between the time of Ben Sira and the early rabbis, say about a century after the destruction of the Jerusalem Temple, there was some difference of opinion as to whether the emphasis in this benediction should be on Abraham, or on the patriarchs as a whole. According to Joseph Heinemann, following Heinrich Brody, there was a diachronic development from מגן אברהם to מגן אבות and then back to מגן אברהם.[12] It is of course also possible that the difference was a synchronic one and that different groups opted for different phraseology at the same time. It is interesting to speculate on the reason for the variation. Was it perhaps related to the argument between rabbinic Jews and early Jewish Christians as to whether the figure of Abraham was an idealized observer of Torah even before the Sinaitic revelation, or a typological example of intense faith in God. Passages in the talmudic-midrashic literature and the New Testament testify to such a theological clash.[13] In this first case (מגן אברהם, 'shield of Abraham'), the metaphor is pre-rabbinic but has been subject to some controversial adjustment. A later use of מגן was made in the benediction of thanksgiving that appears as the penultimate benediction in all *'amidot*. There God is described, among other epithets and metaphors, as מגן ישענו. We shall shortly return to this phrase.

Rock of Isaac

To revert to Ben Sira, Abraham's son Isaac is described there as צור יצחק, 'rock of Isaac'. The description of God as a rock goes back to the Hebrew Bible and may have been borrowed from surrounding peoples. Whether associated by way of a literary metonymy with the Jerusalem shrine, or not, the word is often employed in the book of Psalms to describe God's strength, stability and power. In some contexts, the usage goes beyond simple description and constitutes a title for God, as in Ps 18:3, with the parallel in 2 Sam 22:3. A repeated refrain is that

---

11 Schechter, 'Specimens', p. 656, Luger, *Amidah*, pp. 40 – 52, and Ehrlich, as cited in the previous footnote.

12 Heinemann, *Studies*, pp. 40 – 41, citing H. Brody, 'Besprechungen', p. 500.

13 On the figure of Abraham in early Judaism and early Christianity, see Levenson, *Inheriting Abraham*; Van Ruiten, *Abraham*; and Hunt, *Perspectives*.

there is no rock comparable to God the rock, and the word צור is used together with one or other of the expressions אל, גואל, ישועה, מגן, מושיע, מחסה, מנוס, מעוז, מעון, מפלט, מצודה, משגב, סלע, that is, with a number of words that describe God as saviour, protector, shelter and (again, but via a different word) rock.[14] Interestingly, I can find no trace of צור יצחק, 'rock of Isaac', in the Hebrew Bible, the Dead Sea Scrolls (where, interestingly, there appears to be no description of God by the use of the word צור at all), or the talmudic-midrashic literature. Isa 26:4 has צור עולמים and 2 Sam 23:3 has צור ישראל, 'Rock of Israel'. It is this latter metaphor for God that is picked up by early Jewish liturgy.

I say 'early Jewish liturgy' because צור ישראל occurs in a number of prayers that could go back to the second and third centuries. There is a benediction recited after the reading of the *shema'*, and before the *'amidah*, in the morning and in the evening, on the subject of God's redemption of Israel from bondage in Egypt. The standard eulogy widely used for this benediction in the early Middle Ages became ברוך אתה ה' גאל ישראל, 'You, Eternal one, are the essence of blessing, (who) redeemed Israel'. But this was under the powerful influence of the leading talmudic teachers of Babylonia. In the Jewish homeland the eulogy did not usually conclude with the two words גאל ישראל but with the longer phrase צור ישראל וגואלו 'Rock of Israel and its Redeemer'.[15] The difference between Babylon and Palestine in this respect is already recorded in two talmudic passages recording the traditions of the third and fourth centuries.[16]

The longer phrase did find its way into wider liturgical use, but in the early rabbinic period it was apparently used in the land of Israel specifically for the evening and morning benedictions just mentioned. The name ישראל is of course an alternative name for the patriarch Jacob and, while צור is not applied to Isaac, it does occur in connection with Jacob. The phrase צור יעקב occurs in the first section of the *ge'ulah* (redemption) benediction commencing אמת ויציב, 'true and stable', immediately following Num 15:37–41, which is the third of the three paragraphs of the *shema'* recited in the morning. It occurs with the phrase that was discussed earlier in this paper, namely, מגן ישענו. The next paragraph contains the further adaptation צור ישועתנו, 'Rock of our salvation'. There is no mention of such phrases in the talmudic period[17]) but they do occur in the prayer-book of Sa'adya ben Joseph Ha-Gaon (882–942), head of the Babylonian tal-

---

14 See the entry *ṣur* by Fabry in *TDOT*, 12.311–21.

15 Sa'adya, *Siddur RSG*, pp. 16, 27; Elbogen, *Liturgy*, p. 22: Mann, 'Genizah fragments', pp. 295, 303, Fleischer, *Eretz Israel*, p. 309n; Blank, 'Theological grammar', p. 13.

16 *b. Pesaḥ*. 117b.

17 *y. Ber.* 1.9 (3d).

mudic academy in Sura,[18] allowing us to speculate that these metaphors were added in the late talmudic or early post-talmudic period.

Also probably belonging to the late talmudic period is the phrase צור ישענו, 'Rock of our salvation'. This occurs in the rite of the land of Israel at a later point in the same *ge'ulah* benediction just discussed, both in the morning and the evening versions. Another use of the metaphor צור is the one that attaches it to the noun חיים, describing God as צור חיינו, 'Rock of our lives'. This appears in the benediction of thanksgiving that appears as the penultimate benediction in all *'amidot*, together with the phrase מגן ישענו. But what we have in this case appears to be an expansion of the thanksgiving benediction that took place after the tenth or eleventh century since it is absent from the pre-Crusader rites of the land of Israel, as well as from the prayer-book of Sa'adya Gaon.[19]

What may then be concluded about the use of the word צור as a divine metaphor in the present context? It seems incontrovertible that such a usage continued its existence from biblical into medieval times, without any objection or rejection. There were, however, equally incontrovertibly, some adjustments that were made in rabbinic liturgy in the course of the early Christian centuries. The metaphor was attached to Jacob instead of Isaac and this cries out for an explanation, albeit even a speculative one. Given that Jacob (= Israel), more than any of the other patriarchs, was the eponymous figure for the people of Israel, it is not surprising that the authors of liturgical compositions should wish to opt for that name, rather than Isaac. The preference in Babylonia for גאל ישראל rather than צור ישראל וגואלו seems to me to be more related to general liturgical policy than to theological doctrine. In that centre, unlike its counterpart in the Holy Land, the principle was that the concluding eulogy of a benediction should contain only one theme, and not range over two.[20] God should therefore be described either as a Rock or as a Redeemer, with the use of only one epithet (or metaphor) at a time! In addition, if we detect a tendency from, say, the fifth to the tenth centuries, to expand on linguistic forms and variations with צור, no less than with other expressions, it is reasonable to assume that this represents a move towards linguistic and literary embellishment. Given that the liturgical poems of the fifth and sixth centuries onwards were experts at this, such an expertise obviously left its mark on the statutory prayers, either because the former genre was highly approved, or because there were others who wished to deny the devil the privilege of having the best tunes.

---

18 Sa'adya, *Siddur RSG*, pp. 15–16.

19 Earliest occurrence is in *SRAmram*, as transmitted in post-geonic times, p. 26, and 'Maimonides', p. 201.

20 *b. Ber.* 49a.

Champion of Jacob

The third expression in the Ben Sira passage, אביר יעקב, now requires attention. The metaphor is used of God five times in the Hebrew Bible (Gen 49:24, Isa 49:26 and 60:16, Ps 132:2, 5; see also Isa 1:24 where ישראל occurs and not יעקב). The original meaning of the Semitic root has to do with 'power' and 'strength', and in the Ugaritic texts it is especially applied to an animal, probably an ox or a bull. The usage in the Hebrew Bible may well be based on ancient Canaanite terminology but, as with so many divine epithets and metaphors from that source, it gradually loses the 'bull-god' motif and becomes acceptable to the prophet and the psalmist, and indeed to Ben Sira.[21]

Although there are talmudic and midrashic passages that refer to the phrase as it occurs in Gen 49:24, they are generally not concerned to utilize it as a divine metaphor but rather as an indication that when Joseph wished to submit to the seductive charms of Potiphar's wife, an image of his father Jacob appeared to him and this immediately cooled his passion.[22] Such passages appear to take the word אביר as indicative of Jacob's power and not God's. It is in the liturgical poetry of the post-talmudic period that the phrase returns by way of colourful descriptions of God.[23] As far as the statutory prayers are concerned, the phrase אביר יעקב makes no appearance and in that respect appears to have suffered a somewhat different fate from מגן אברהם and צור יצחק, for each of which there was some degree of continuity, albeit in various sorts of adjusted forms.[24]

Are we in a position to explain this omission from the daily prayers? A clue to its understanding is to be found in the masoretic treatment of the word אביר. In the five cases already cited, the letter *bet* is vocalized without a *dageš* following a *ḥaṭaf pataḥ* while in all the other instances, such as 1 Sam 21:8 and Job 34:20, the word appears with a *dageš* in the *bet*, following a full *pataḥ*. It is clear that the Masoretes wished to make a clear distinction between the two uses of the word, for a bull and for God. Perhaps the rabbinic tradition of the first few Christian centuries was also not totally comfortable with the expression and found no place for the metaphor in its early liturgy. If that is true, it may then be necessary to date this particular masoretic tradition to the talmudic period. Be that as it may, אביר יעקב remained out of the liturgical repertoire for a number of centuries.

---

21 See entry *avir/abbir* by Kapelrud in *TDOT*, 1.42–44.
22 *y. Hor.* 2.4 (46d) and *Bereshit Rabbah* 87.7, ed. Theodor-Albeck, 3.1073.
23 For example, Fleischer, *Anonymus*, p. 118.
24 The phrase אביר יעקב is used, together with אלהי אברהם and פחד יצחק, in a poetic *seliḥah* used at the end of the evening service for Yom Kippur entitled עננו, but this is unlikely to date from earlier than the high Middle Ages; see Davidson, *Thesaurus* 3.285.

Shepherd of Israel

If God could on the one hand be a shield and a rock for Israel's protection, he could on the other also be a shepherd who looked after them. In his blessing of Joseph and his two sons (Gen 48:15), Jacob begins by mentioning that God, who was loyally followed by his father and grandfather, had acted as his shepherd (הרעה אותי) throughout his life. The Psalmist (Ps 23:1) famously refers to God as his shepherd (ה' רעי), and the poetic phrase in Gen 49:24 (משם רעה אבן ישראל), however textually problematic, appears to refer to God as both a rock and a shepherd. For our purposes, this is more categorically spelt out in Ps 80:2, in which God is asked to hearken to the needs of his flock. There God is addressed as רעה ישראל and the parallel makes it perfectly clear what is intended by offering נוהג כצאן יוסף, 'the one who guides the sheep of Joseph'. Perhaps the Tanḥuma midrash, which is essentially aggadic in content and probably dates from post-talmudic times, makes a good exegetical point by explaining that Joseph is here mentioned to remind us of the manner in which guided, as a shepherd, the people of Egypt during its periods of plenty and of famine.[25] The prophet Ezekiel draws distinctions between bad shepherds (Israel) and a good one (God) in the colourful description and rebuke contained in chapter 34.[26]

The verse from Gen 49:24 (משם רעה אבן ישראל), is cited in qumranic, talmudic and midrashic texts, but always in an exegetical context, rather than in any specifically liturgical sense.[27] Where, then, if at all, does rabbinic liturgy make use of the expression רועה ישראל? The earliest occurrence would appear to be in the fourth benediction of the grace recited after meals, the *birkat ha-mazon.*[28] The talmudic rabbis themselves argued that this benediction was of lesser status and had been added to the existing three, and there seems little doubt that the language and content point in this direction.[29] While these rabbis, however, explain the addition as a second-century development, there is no reason to assume that the whole first paragraph of the benediction, in which the phrase רועה ישראל is to be found, should be dated at that time. There is no textual evidence whatsoever during the talmudic period for anything more fixed than the two words הטוב והמטיב ('who is good and does good'), at the end of the usual six-word benedictory formula. In the post-talmudic period, there is so much

25 *Tanḥuma, Miqqeṣ* 7, p. 50b.
26 See entry *ra'ah/ro'eh* by Wallis in *TDOT*, 13.544–53.
27 As in 4Q254 7.3; *b. Soṭah* 36b; *Tanḥuma*, ed. Buber, *Terumah* 6, p. 46b and *Ki Tissa* 12, p. 56b, Eng. trans. Townsend, 2.132, 2.155.
28 Baer, *'Avodat*, p. 558.
29 *b. Ber.* 46a.

inconsistency about the wording that we are justified in assuming that it was only then that it was moving towards a text that could be fully accepted as authoritative. The paragraphs that follow this first paragraph (of which more anon) are undoubtedly of later pedigree since in the early Middle Ages they still took on very different shapes within each of the many rites.

There is, however, a passage in the Talmud Yerushalmi, paralleled in the Midrash Wa-Yiqra Rabbah, that does refer to the word רועה, though not to the phrase רועה ישראל.[30] A question is asked by Rabbi Ze'ira in the late third or early fourth century about praying for one's needs on the sabbath. If it is indeed forbidden, he inquires, how does one explain how some Jews make the plea רועינו פרנסינו, 'our shepherd, sustain us' in the grace for that day? The reply is that this is the way that the benediction is worded, although the midrashic text makes it clear that this is a text that only some use. It is consequently clear that the text at that time did not have רועה ישראל and what it did have was by no means concrete and authoritative. Indeed, the text of Sa'adya Gaon some five centuries later still does not have any reference to רועה or רועה ישראל.

It seems fair to raise the question whether there was any hesitancy about the use of this metaphor. Given that it is full of theological meaning, and says so much about the leadership, care, and guidance provided by a God who is close to his flock, did some rabbinic worshippers have some doubts about its liturgical suitability? It will be recalled that the image of the divine shepherd is one that figures centrally in early Christianity. The parable about the lost sheep in Luke 15:4–7 draws an obvious parallel between the shepherd's anxiety at the loss of one of the hundred in his flock, and his great joy at finding it, and the notion of God's deep concern for sinners, and the heavenly relief at the repentance of even a single one of those. Even more forcefully, John 10 has Jesus describing himself as the good shepherd, willing to lay down his life for his own sheep and even for the flocks of others, and thereby deserving the love of his heavenly Father. The passage goes on to report that the Jews who heard this were very disturbed and confused by the message. Could this possibly be the reason why it took some centuries for such a metaphor to be acceptable in the liturgy? By that time, the communities had each gone its own way and the issue was therefore less of a burning one. If this speculative suggestion has some validity, it might also be possible to suggest that the question that troubled Rabbi Ze'ira in fourth-century Palestine was not only to do with the observance of the shabbat but also had a hidden motivation. Could it be that he was somewhat troubled by the expression because he knew it

---

30 *y. Šabb.* 15.3 (15b); *Wa-Yiqra Rabbah* 34.16, ed. Margulies, 4.816.

still to be so central to the Christians who constituted a theological challenge to rabbinic Jews in the Roman Palestine of his day?

Abode of blessings

Mention was earlier made of the abbreviated *'amidah* used on Friday evening according to the rite of the land of Israel. If we may return to that prayer, there is another metaphor that is worthy of closer attention in the current discussion. In the context of the final three benedictions dealing, respectively, with the Temple service, thanksgiving and the blessing of peace, God is described as מעון הברכות.[31] This is not an easy phrase to translate but it would not be too inaccurate if we rendered it 'abode of all blessings'. The biblical Hebrew term מעון ranges over a wide variety of meanings, being used for the lair of an animal, for a place of refuge, for God's Temple, and for God himself. It is the last-mentioned usage that is of most distinct interest to the topic in hand. Examples in which it is difficult, to a greater or lesser extent, to disentangle the protective location from the protective divinity are to be found in Ps 71:3, 90:1, 91:9, and Deut 33:27.[32] There are among the Dead Sea Scrolls numerous references to God's dwelling place as מעון, but none of them may incontrovertibly be understood as a metaphor for God himself.[33] The same applies to Sir 50:4 (50:2). In a number of these cases, suggestions have been made about emending the text from מעון to מעוז.[34] Such an emendation could be construed as a flight from the reality of a daring divine metaphor that is expressed or implied. Be that as it may, there is more than a little justification for arguing that the Hebrew Bible is the source for מעון as a metaphor for God.

The rabbinic phrase מעון הברכות makes sense in the context noted above only if it is construed as a description of God, since the other expressions used adjacent to it are also epithets for God, such as אדון השלום ('Divine Peacemaker') and אל ההודאות ('Divine Recipient of Gratitude'). The standard eulogy used for the final benediction of the *'amidah* according to the rite of the land of Israel was indeed מעון הברכות ועושה השלום, 'abode of all blessings and creator of peace'. The reason for this was that there were two elements in the final benediction, one relating to the priestly benediction of Num 6:24–26 that had been used in the Temple, and the other relating to the longing for peace that could be

31 Heinemann, *Prayer*, pp. 98, 286; Fleischer, *Eretz*, pp. 34, 43, 73; Luger, *Amidah*, pp. 206–8; Ehrlich, *Weekday Amidah*, pp. 259–78.

32 See entry *ma'on* by Preuss in *TDOT*, 8.449–52.

33 As in 1QS 11.7 and 4Q491 11.15.

34 See Preuss (n. 32 above), pp. 451–52.

expressed, after the destruction of the Temple, without the necessary inclusion of priestly involvement. The tendency in Babylonia was towards handing over responsibility for the benediction to the cantor while the preference in the land of Israel was to retain priestly involvement. The Babylonian rite had two reasons for restricting the final eulogy to the theme of peace, without allusion to the special nature of the priestly blessing. Firstly, the Babylonians had their liturgical principle of allowing only one topic per eulogy. Secondly, they wished to stress the non-priestly aspect of the benediction.[35]

Either in the final period of Babylonian domination, around the eleventh century, or as the basic Babylonian rite was accepted around the Jewish world then and thereafter, those transmitting the prayers had lost the sense of, or perhaps a sympathy for, the ramifications of the expression מעון הברכות. Proof of the latter comes in the textual development that saw the rejection of the word מעון and its replacement with מֵעֵין. This latter vocalization is no longer from the absolute form מעון but is from the substantival עין, meaning 'the essential nature', with the prefixed preposition ,-מ meaning 'some essence of', that is, 'a kind of'.[36] Since we have no repetition of the *'amidah* even on Friday night, we substitute an essence of the *'amidah*, or an abstract of its benedictions, מעין הברכות. It is difficult to say what precisely precipitated this change but one possible reason is that מעון was by the time of the high Middle Ages being used widely in the liturgy for the Jerusalem Temple, perhaps under the influence of the liturgical poets who held literary and linguistic sway over the Jewish world from the sixth century onwards. In that case, the phrase מעון הברכות would have made little sense, or conveyed the wrong sense, to the worshippers. Metaphors are undoubtedly dependent for their survival on their users being able to make the necessary leap from the metaphor to the intended, and more literal subject.

Protection around us

It will be recalled that in Ps 62 and 2 Sam 22 there are examples of other words being used together with צור as metaphors for God. One of these is משגב, which occurs throughout the Hebrew Bible in the sense of 'protected place', 'high rock', 'stronghold', 'refuge'.[37] Not surprisingly, it was particularly popular as a divine

35 On this benediction, see Ehrlich, *Weekday Amidah*, pp. 259–74.

36 Recorded in this form in medieval manuscript versions of *SRAmram*; see ed. Goldschmidt, p. 64. See also Simḥa of Vitry, *Maḥzor Vitry*, 1.83, with a somewhat forced (twelfth-century?) explanation, attempting to justify the text מֵעֵין.

37 See entry *sagab/misgab* by H.Ringgren in *TDOT*, 14.34–36.

metaphor in the book of Psalms. There are also qumranic parallels to this usage.[38] Interestingly, there appears to be only one specific reference to the word משגב in the whole of the two Talmudim. It occurs in the Talmud Yerushalmi where a piece of liturgical advice is offered by the students of Rabbi Joḥanan, in the name of their third-century teacher in Galilee.[39] He had suggested that the Jewish worshipper should make constant use of the verse in Ps 46:8 (repeated in v. 12), in which the God of Jacob (Jacob meaning, of course, the people of Israel) is described as his משגב. Not unexpectedly, the verse therefore makes its way into many liturgical contexts; but that is strictly speaking a Biblical Hebrew usage and not an example of rabbinic liturgy. In what form does the word משגב occur in the prayers of the post-talmudic period?

The earliest recorded occurrence would appear to be in the tenth-century prayer-book of Sa'adya Gaon. In the pre-*shema*' benedictions of the morning prayers, God is described as אדון עזינו, 'Our Powerful Master', and צור משגבנו, 'Our Protected/Protective Rock'.[40] Both such usages may fairly be described as adaptations of Biblical Hebrew. There is another phrase containing the word משגב that appears to have been incorporated into the same section of the rabbinic liturgy in the next century or two. The phrase is משגב בעדינו, 'Stronghold Around Us'. If we are right that there is no example of this in earlier times, and that it later became a standard usage, is it possible to detect any special reason for the coinage and to see in it some sort of liturgical tendency?

The key to a possible answer to this question lies in the other phrases that are found together with משגב בעדינו within that standard usage in the early part of the first pre-*shema*' benediction of the morning service.[41] There are four and they are אדון עזינו, צור משגבנו (as cited and translated above), as well as מגן ישענו ('Our Shield of Salvation') and משגב בעדינו. There is clearly a linguistic and literary pattern, even a poetic style, to all of these, and their use together creates a lyrical framework for the liturgy. Probably under the influence of the hundreds of liturgical poems that had been composed in the previous few centuries, and had so often been imported into the various liturgical rites as the latter expanded and developed, the composers of the statutory liturgy felt the need to versify the prayers to an increasing degree. A way of doing this was to take the biblical and mishnaic precedents, modify them in some way, and create poetic patterns that were to their liking. It seems reasonable to suppose that משגב בעדינו is an example of such a development.

38 As in 1QH 17(=9).28.

39 *y. Ber.* 5.1 (8d).

40 Sa'adya, *Siddur RSG*, p. 36.

41 *SRAmram*, pp. 12–13, 'Maimonides', p. 195.

Divine place and holiness

A few words are now in order about two expressions that are very common in the mishnaic, talmudic and midrashic texts from the second to the sixth centuries. The first is המקום, meaning 'the place' but used as a metaphor for God with no obviously special sense, and the second is הקדוש ברוך הוא 'the Holy One, who is blessed' which was probably in its earlier form הקודש ברוך הוא 'the Holiness, who is blessed' (or 'the Holy Place, who is blessed'). Both המקום and הקודש may apply to the Temple as well as to God. As in the case of מעון that was discussed above, they represent an overlap between the place of God's most intense presence and the divinity itself. Arthur Marmorstein argued in 1927 that the former is the earlier of the two and that it gradually gave way to the latter.[42] This should obviously be assessed in the light of the manuscript evidence that we currently have before us and that is greatly improved and much more extensive than what was available to him at that time. The task is not one that can be undertaken in the present context. In any case, what is relevant here is the use of metaphors for God in prayer.

The early rabbinic texts that utilize both these expressions on a regular basis are, by and large, of a midrashic nature, the first praising God for what he has done for the world as a whole and for the Jewish people in particular, while the second teaches lessons about the power of God and the nature of his relationship with Israel from the patriarchal period, through the Sinaitic revelation and onwards throughout history.[43] Although the prayer-books of the medieval and later periods make use of these two expressions in special contexts, neither of them figures in any major way in the earliest liturgies, such as the basic forms of the benedictions surrounding the *shema'* or in the *'amidah*. The first occurs in a part of the Passover Haggadah which cites a midrash about the four types of child that a parent must educate on the matter of the significance of Passover. That midrash is no earlier than the fourth century and it may not have found a regular place in the Haggadah until a few centuries later since it is still absent in many Genizah texts.[44] The second expression, does, however, occur in one prayer that is undoubtedly ancient, the *'alenu*.

The *'alenu* was first used in the liturgy for Rosh Ha-Shanah, the New Year festival, in the third century, perhaps at the instigation of the leading talmudic figure Abba Arikha, commonly known as Rav (d. 247). Much later, in the high

---

42 Marmorstein, *Names*, pp. 92–93, 97.

43 See, for example, *m. Mid.* 5.4, *m. Yoma* 8.9, *m. Sanh.* 4.5, *b. Ber.* 40b.

44 Tabory, *Haggadah*, pp. 39–44; Safrai, *Haggadah*, pp. 106–9.

Middle Ages, it was adopted as a concluding prayer for all services, perhaps because of its association with Jewish martyrdom.[45] The content of the prayer is very different from most of the other statutory prayers. It is urges the worshippers to praise God for all his qualities and looks forward to a time when his sovereignty will be recognized the world over. God is not addressed and, consequently, it is not perhaps surprising that a term that is used here is not commonly or widely employed in the liturgy. What emerges from this brief description of these two expressions is that they do not seem to have been part of the expansion and development of liturgical metaphors for God that marked the transition from the talmudic to the post-talmudic and early medieval periods. Perhaps the close link between Holy Place and Holy One was being eroded as the rebuilding of the Jerusalem Temple became a more distant and less realistic prospect.

Female feelings?

While dealing with the ultimate, liturgical fate of expressions that are common in the talmudic literature, some brief attention should also be paid to the description of God as רחמנא in Aramaic, or its Hebrew equivalent הרחמן, 'the merciful one'.[46] The root not only has to do with being merciful but probably also relates to matters maternal and female since the word רחם carries the basic sense of 'womb' in Biblical Hebrew. The Aramaic form רחמנא is ubiquitous in the Babylonian Talmud and was obviously widely used by the rabbinic Jews of the third until the sixth centuries in their references to God. There are some popular and laical blessings that make use of the term but it is nowhere cited as an element in the statutory prayer. Where it makes a major appearance in such texts is in the grace recited after a meal. During the post-talmudic period there was an expansion of special requests made of God at the end of the grace, essentially in connection with the overall improvement of the Jewish worshipper's lot in the world. Each of these was introduced by the term הרחמן which was then followed by the specific wish. Because this development reached its peak only in the Middle Ages, these requests were not seen as essential to the grace and they therefore took on all sorts of different forms within the different rites of the widespread Jewish communities. I have argued elsewhere that the presence of the word הרחמן within the statutory prayers, other than the grace after meals, is to be dated no later than the end of the talmudic period, say,

45 Elbogen, *Liturgy*, pp. 71–72; Langer, "Aleinu', pp. 147–49.
46 Jastrow, *Dictionary*, p. 1468; Marmorstein, *Names*, pp. 101–2; Sokoloff, *Dictionary*, p. 522.

around the sixth or seventh centuries.[47] It is tempting to make a connection between the Islamic use of *al-raḥman al-raḥim* and the expanded use of הרחמן in the medieval Jewish liturgy but more evidence requires to be collected and assessed before we jump to such as conclusion.

Male parentage?

Our presentation would not be complete without making brief reference to conclusions reached in an earlier chapter, since the topic there was another divine metaphor used in the rabbinic liturgy, namely, God as father.[48] The earliest rabbinic thought of the first three centuries was of course committed to the idea of the fatherhood of God in the same way as this appears in the biblical and apocryphal writings, while at the same time revealing some hesitancy about aspects of the notion of God being directly addressed as a paternal figure. Such a figure was partially modified in the liturgy by the attachment, in some circles, of a royal epithet, as in the phrase אבינו מלכנו, 'our Father, our King' The more mystically inclined Jews made their own theological point by placing an increased stress on the compassion (such as female compassion?) of God. Those who kept on eye on what their Muslim counterparts said, and how they prayed, could not but notice the latter's abhorrence of the paternal metaphor as a liturgical expression. The obvious conclusion was that the historian can detect innovation and adaptation, as well as caution and reflection, on the part of those who formulated the rabbinic liturgy in the first millennium of its existence.

Tentative conclusions

If we may now return to the Ben Sira text that we cited early in this presentation, it will be recalled that there were three metaphors that gave us our lead for this overall treatment. There were also eight epithets that described God's activities. In this connection, it should be borne in mind that there are large numbers of such epithets in the rabbinic liturgy from its earliest period and throughout its existence. By their very nature, epithets are less likely to get worn out, to become redundant, and to attract amendment. They therefore constitute a different breed of liturgical expression from metaphors. What can be drawn from this analysis of

47 Reif, *Problems*, pp. 342–43.
48 See chapter 15 above.

metaphors may or may not be relevant to the study of epithets. To reach a conclusion on that question is a topic for another treatment.

But our present treatment does now require some tentative conclusions. They must by definition remain speculative since composers of liturgy, or those who amend, expand or contract it, do not share with us the precise reasons for their actions. They themselves may not even be fully aware of such reasons. But even if they are so aware, it suits their purpose much more to argue on other grounds. Theirs is the original or true meaning of the text; other versions are corrupt or misleading; what is being suggested improves concentration and devoutness; one of the people's great leaders made such a suggestion; and so on. As historians, our task is to try to see behind these protestations and uncover the contemporary motivations of each adjustment.

Our brief excursion into Jewish liturgical history has uncovered the *contre temps* between early rabbinic Jews and early Christians, perhaps even Jewish-Christians, when the two groups were still living in each other's theological pockets. As the two religious persuasions became more distinct, so it sometimes became necessary for each to identify ideas and practices that had become characteristic of the other and to abandon those. When Islam became the dominant faith of the Near East and much of the Mediterranean area, its impact on Judaism was massive and there is little doubt that linguistic and literary styles were duly affected. While there still existed, until the eleventh century, two powerful and influential Jewish communities, one based in Mesopotamia and the other in the land of Israel, both of which wished to influence the smaller and less well-established communities elsewhere, each took every opportunity of promoting its own religious agenda, with the former especially anxious to continue and promote the teachings of the Babylonian Talmud.

Of course, the nature of God, the role of Israel and the status of the patriarchs preoccupied the Jews at their prayers, no less than at their studies. Some may have been ambivalent about identifying God in terms of his Jerusalem Temple, while others simply lost a connection with the sense of an earlier phrase. Linguistic and literary embellishment of the statutory prayers was one of the responses to the colourful, intricate and allusive language championed by the liturgical poets. At the same time, there was almost always an awareness of, and an affection for the words and phrases that occurred in the Hebrew Bible, even if they were adjusted to the overall style of Mishnaic Hebrew. Given that there were changes in synagogal interests, priorities and preferences, it is only to be expected that these should have left their mark on what was recited by cantors and congregants within the Jewish house of worship. Metaphors are not simply metaphors; they are also some of the smaller building blocks for the construction of massive edifices of religious teachings and customs. Maimonides the philosopher was not too pleased about this but Maimonides the Rabbi undoubtedly accepted it.

Works cited

Alexander, P. S., *Textual Sources for the Study of Judaism* (Manchester: Manchester University Press, 1984).

Baer, S., *Seder 'Avodat Yisra'el* (Rödelheim: Lehrberger, 1868).

Benor, E., *Worship of the Heart: a Study in Maimonides' Philosophy of Religion* (Albany: SUNY Press, 1995).

Bereschit Rabba (=Bereshit Rabbah), eds. J. Theodor and Ch. Albeck, 3 vols. (Jerusalem: Wahrmann Books, 1965, 2nd edn.).

Blank, D. R., 'The curious theological grammar of *ga'al yisra'el*', in *The Experience of Jewish Liturgy. Studies Dedicated to Menahem Schmelzer*, ed. D. R. Blank (Leiden: Brill, 2011), pp. 9–21.

Blidstein, G. (Ya'akov), *Prayer in Maimonidean Halakha* (Hebrew; Beersheba: Ben-Gurion University of the Negev Press, 1994).

Brody, H., 'Besprechungen', reviewing Elbogen's *Studien zur Geschichte des jüdischen Gottesdienstes*, *MGWJ* 54th year (1910), issue 4, pp. 491–503.

Davidson, I., *Thesaurus of Mediaeval Hebrew Poetry*, 3 vols. (Hebrew; New York: Jewish Theological Seminary of America, 1930).

Ehrlich, U., *The Weekday Amidah in Cairo Genizah Prayerbooks. Roots and Transmission* (Hebrew; Jerusalem: Yad Ben-Zvi Press, 2013).

Elbogen, I., *Jewish Liturgy: A Comprehensive History*, Eng. trans. and ed. R. P. Scheindlin (Philadelphia, Jerusalem, and New York: Jewish Publication Society, 1993).

Fabry, H.-J., entry on *ṣur*, in *Theological Dictionary of the Old Testament*, vol. 12, Eng. trans. D. W. Stott (Grand Rapids, Mich., Cambridge: Eerdmans Publishing, 2003), pp. 311–21.

Fleischer, E., *Eretz-Israel Prayer and Prayer Rituals as Portrayed in the Geniza Documents* (Hebrew; Jerusalem: Magnes Press, 1988).

Fleischer, E. (ed.), *The Pizmonim of the Anonymus* (Hebrew; Jerusalem: Israel Academy of Sciences and Humanities, 1974).

Freedman, D. N., O'Connor, M. P., and Ringgren, H., entry on *magen*, in *Theological Dictionary of the Old Testament*, vol. 8, Eng. trans., D. W. Stott (Grand Rapids, Mich., Cambridge: Eerdmans Publishing, 1997), pp. 74–87.

Friedman, M. A., 'Abraham Maimuni's prayer reforms. Continuation or revision of his father's teachings?', in *Traditions of Maimonideanism*, ed. Carlos Fraenkel (Leiden: Brill, 2009), pp. 139–54.

Goitein, S. D., 'Moses Maimonides, man of action. A revision of the master's biography in light of the Geniza documents', in *Hommage à Georges Vajda*, eds. G. Nahon and C. Toutai (Louvain: Peeters, 1980), pp. 155–67.

Heinemann, J., *Prayer in the Talmud: Forms and Patterns*, translated and revised from the original Hebrew edition of 1966 (Studia Judaica 9, Berlin: de Gruyter, 1977).

Heinemann, J., *Studies in Jewish Liturgy*, ed. A. Shinan (Hebrew; Jerusalem: Magnes Press, 1981).

Hunt, S. A. (ed.), *Perspectives on our Father Abraham. Essays in Honor of Marvin R. Wilson* (Grand Rapids, Mich., Cambridge: Eerdmans Publishing, 2010).

Jastrow, M., *A Dictionary of the Targumim, the Talmud Babli and Yerushalmi, and the Midrashic Literature*, 2 vols. (New York, London: Luzac, Putnam's Sons, 1903).

Kapelrud, A. S., entry on *avir/abbir*, in *Theological Dictionary of the Old Testament*, vol. 1, Eng. trans. J. T. Willis (Grand Rapids, Mich., Cambridge: Eerdmans Publishing, 1997), pp. 42–44.

Kessler, M., 'The shield of Abraham?', *Vetus Testamentum* 14 (1964), pp. 494–97.

Langer, R., 'The censorship of Aleinu in Ashkenaz and its aftermath', in *The Experience of Jewish Liturgy. Studies Dedicated to Menahem Schmelzer*, ed. D. R. Blank (Leiden: Brill, 2010), pp. 147–66.

Levenson, J. D., *Inheriting Abraham. The Legacy of the Patriarch in Judaism, Christianity and Islam* (Princeton: Princeton University Press, 2012).

Lévi, I. (ed.), *The Hebrew text of the Book of Ecclesiasticus* (Leiden: Brill, 1904, facsimile edition, 1969).

Luger, Y., *The Weekday Amidah in the Cairo Genizah* (Hebrew; Jerusalem: Orhot, 2001).

Maimonides, Moses, *The Guide of the Perplexed*, Eng. trans. S. Pines, intro. L. Strauss (Chicago: University of Chicago Press, 1963).

Maimonides, Moses, 'The Oxford Manuscript of Maimonides' Book of Prayer', in E. D. Goldschmidt, *On Jewish Liturgy: Essays on Prayer and Religious Poetry* (Hebrew; Jerusalem: Magnes Press, 1978), pp. 187–216.

Mann, J., 'Genizah fragments of the Palestinian order of service', *Hebrew Union College Annual* 2 (1926), pp. 269–338.

Marmorstein, A., *The Old Rabbinic Doctrine of God. 1. The Names and Attributes of God* (London: Oxford University Press/Humphrey Milford, 1927).

Neusner, J., *Rabbinic Judaism: The Theological System* (Leiden: Brill, 2002).

Preuss, H. D., entry on *ma'on*, in *Theological Dictionary of the Old Testament*, vol. 8, Eng. trans. D. W. Stott (Grand Rapids, Mich., Cambridge: Eerdmans Publishing, 1997), pp. 449–52.

Rabin, C., 'The historical background of Qumran Hebrew', in *Scripta Hierosolymitana* 4 (Jerusalem: Magnes Press, 1965), pp. 144–61.

Rabin, C., 'The linguistic investigation of the language of Jewish prayer' (Hebrew), in *Studies in Aggadah, Targum and Jewish Liturgy in Memory of Joseph Heinemann*, eds. J. J. Petuchowski and E. Fleischer (Jerusalem and Cincinnati: Magnes Press, Hebrew Union College Press, 1981), Hebrew section, pp. 163–71.

Reif, S. C., 'Maimonides on the prayers', in his *Problems with Prayers* (Berlin: de Gruyter, 2006), pp. 207–28.

Reif, S. C., *Problems with Prayers. Studies in the Textual History of Early Rabbinic Liturgy* (Berlin: de Gruyter, 2006).

Ringgren, H., entry on *sagab/misgab*, in *Theological Dictionary of the Old Testament*, vol. 14, Eng. trans. D. W. Stott (Grand Rapids, Mich., Cambridge: Eerdmans Publishing, 2004), pp. 34–36.

Sa'adya ben Joseph, *Siddur Rav Se'adyah Ga'on: Kitāb Ǵāmi' aṣ-Ṣalawāt wat-Tasābīḥ*, eds. I. Davidson, S. Assaf, and B. I. Joel (Jerusalem: Mekiẓei Nirdamim, 1963, 2nd edn.).

Safrai, S. & Z. (eds.), *Haggadah of the Sages. Introduction and Commentary* (Jerusalem: Carta, 2009).

Safrai, S. *et al.* (eds.), *The Literature of the Sages*, in two parts (Assen/Maastricht, Philadelphia: Van Gorcum/Fortress, 1987, 2006).
Schafer, P., *The History of the Jews in the Greco-Roman World. The Jews of Palestine from Alexander the Great to the Arab Conquest*, revised edition (London: Routledge, 2003).
Schechter, S., 'Genizah specimens', *Jewish Quarterly Review* 10 (1898), pp. 654–59.
Segal, M. H., *Sefer Ben Sira Ha-Shalem* (Jerusalem: Bialik Institute, 1972, 2nd edn.).
Simḥa of Vitry, *Maḥzor Vitry*, ed. S. Hurwitz, 2 vols. (Nuremburg: Mekize Nirdamim, 1923, 2nd edn.).
Skehan, P. W., and Di Lella, A. A., *The Wisdom of Ben Sira* (Anchor Bible 39, New York: Doubleday, 1987).
Sokoloff, M., *A Dictionary of Jewish Palestinian Aramaic of the Byzantine Period* (Ramat-Gan: Bar Ilan University Press, 1990).
Tabory, J., *JPS Commentary on the Haggadah. Historical Introduction, Translation, and Commentary* (Philadelphia: Jewish Publication Society, 2008).
Tanḥuma, ed. Ḥanokh Zundel (Warsaw: Munk, 1879).
Tanchuma (= Tanḥuma), ed. S. Buber, 2 vols. (Vilna: Romm, 1885); Eng. trans. in 3 volumes, J. T. Townsend, *Midrash Tanhuma* (Hoboken, N. J.: Ktav, 1989–2003).
Van Ruiten, J. T. A. G. M., *Abraham in the Book of Jubilees. The Rewriting of Genesis 11:26–25:10 in the Book of Jubilees 11:14–23:8* (JSJSup 161, Leiden: Brill, 2012).
Wa-Yiqra Rabbah (= Wayyikra Rabbah), ed. M. Margulies, 5 vols. (Jerusalem: American Academy for Jewish Research, 1953–60).
Wallis, G., entry on *ra'ah/ro'eh*, in *Theological Dictionary of the Old Testament*, vol. 13, Eng. trans. D. E. Green (Grand Rapids, Mich., Cambridge: Eerdmans Publishing, 2004), pp. 544–53

Index of Names

Abbaye, the amora 280
Abraham Ibn Ezra 44, 66, 76–79, 82, 88–91, 98–101, 112–13, 116–21, 123, 125–27, 130, 132, 134, 136–37, 139–40, 155, 157–58, 166, 173, 185–86, 189, 191–92
Abraham the Patriarch 59, 60, 67, 69, 83, 95–96, 117, 174, 176, 241, 246, 249, 265, 328, 337–38
Abrabanel, I. 45, 135n
Abraham ben Nathan 155
Abudraham, David 242, 308–9
Adler, C. 16, 21–22
Akiva ben Joseph 170–72, 262–63, 267, 321–323
Albeck, Ch. 249
Amram ben Sheshna 154–55, 236, 241, 244–45, 289, 298
Aptowitzer, A. 249

Baer, S. 305n, 309–10, 337n
Baḥya ben Asher 246
Baker, C. 90n
Barton, J. 34–35
Beentjes, P. C. 26
Bekhor Shor, Joseph ben Isaac 115, 117n–118n, 123n–124n, 127n–128n, 130n, 134n, 140
Ben-Horin, M. 15n
Benor, E. 335n
Ben-Sasson, M. 27–28
Ben-Shammai, H. 29n
Bentwich, N. 15, 25
Ben Yehuda, E. 182, 198, 280
Berlin, A. 74n, 161
Berlin, N. T.Y. 46
Bernhard, L. 210n
Bewer, J. A. 188
Blachman, E. 50
Blenkinsopp, J. 188
Boadt, L. 212
Bodner, K. 103–4
Bomberg, D. 75n
Braude, W. G. 151n
Briggs, C. A. 145–46, 188, 192
Briggs, E. G. 145–46, 188, 192
Brock, S. 52
Brody, H. 338
Brody, R. 77n, 298n
Brown, F. 145
Buber, S. 167
Büchler, A. 23–24, 30
Budd, P. J. 136
Burkitt, F. C. 24n
Burns, R. 13

Caquot, A. 165n
Carr, E. H. 10–11
Cashdan, E. 150n
Cassuto, U. (M. D.) 83n–84n, 86n–92n, 94n–96n, 98n, 102n
Charles, R. H. 24–25
Chavel, C. B. 117n
Chazon, E. G. 13n
Cheyne, T. K. 188
Childs, B. S. 83n–84n, 86n–88n, 91n–93n, 95n–97n, 101n
Clements, R. 35n
Clines, D. J. A. 74n, 183
Cohen, J. M. 379n
Cohen, M. 27–28
Cooper, B. 53n
Crenshaw, J. L. 212–13
Curtis, E. L. 188, 190

Davidson, A. B. 190
Davies, D. 64, 335n
Davies, G. 35n
Davies, P. R. 30n
Declaissé-Walford, N. 212–13
De Lagarde, P. 38n
Dell, K. J. 213, 228
Di Lella, A. A. 316
Dillmann, A. 190
Dinah and her brothers 168
Driver, S. R. 3, 83n–84n, 86n–88n, 90–94n, 96n–98n, 145
Duhm, B. 188

Ehrlich, A. B. 46, 135, 190
Ehrlich, U. 286–87, 289–90, 304, 306, 319n
Eisenstein., J. D. 174
Elbogen, I. 211, 239–40, 266–67, 272, 310
Eleazar of Worms 307–8
Eli at Shiloh 168
Eliezer ben Hyrcanus 170, 172, 321
Elijah the Prophet 242–43, 281, 315
Elijah ben Solomon 46
Elmslie, W. A. L. 188, 190
Emerton, J. A. 2, 144, 162
Ephrem, Syriac Father 61
Epstein, I. 24n
Erder, Y. 29n
Even-Shoshan, A. 183
Ezra, grandson of Avtolos 149

Feinberg, G. 169n
Finkelstein, L. 211, 225n, 266, 287, 302–3, 304n, 327
Firkovich, A. 27–28
Fischer, S. 268–69, 275
Fishbane, M. 54
Fleischer, E. 154, 211, 237, 304, 306n
Ford, D. 35n
Franklin, A. 254
Friedlaender, I. 18
Friedman, S. 323
Füglister, N. 210n

Gane, R. E. 299n
Gerleman, G. 279
Gibson, M. D. 12
Gidney, W. T. 24n
Gilbert, M. 213
Ginzberg, E. 19
Ginzberg, L. 19–20, 22–24, 27, 55n, 266
Goldhill, S. 314n
Goldin, J. 150n
Goldschmidt, E. D. 235n
Goller, I. 53n
Gordon, R. P. 2, 180, 193
Gray, G. B. 136
Greenberg, M. 190
Greenstein, E. L. 37
Grossman. A. 78n
Grunberger, M. 17n

Ḥagga, the amora 149
Ḥaggai in Tiberias 152
Haran, M. 28–29, 35n
Hart, H. 165
Hartom, E. S. 187–88, 191
Hasan-Rokem, G. 217
Hausmann, J. 299n
Ḥayyuj, Judah 182
Heinemann, J. 239, 289n, 290, 302, 329, 338
Hengel, M. 261n
Herr, M. D. 263
Hezekiah ben Manoaḥ (Ḥizzequni) 66–67, 76, 79–80, 93–95, 98, 100–1, 113–18, 120–23, 125–30, 134–37, 140
Hezser, C. 216–17
Hillel 170
Hirsch, S. R. 46, 310
Ḥiwi al-Balkhi 42
Ḥiyya, the tanna 246
Hooker, M. 35n
Howard, D. M. 147
Hyatt, J. P. 82n–84n, 86n–88n, 90n–92n, 94n, 96n–97n

Ibn Janaḥ, Jonah 130, 166, 181–82
Idelsohn, A. Z. 211
Ilai, the amora 243
Instone-Brewer, D. 301n, 317n
Isaac the Patriarch 63–64, 67, 95–96, 176, 246, 265, 328, 337–40

Jacob, B. 46, 83n–84n, 86n–88n, 91n–92n, 94n, 96n–98n
Jacob ben Judah Ḥazzan 242, 244
Jacob the Patriarch 55, 57, 59–60, 63–64, 67, 96, 117, 173, 175, 246, 265, 315, 328, 337, 339–42, 346
Jacob of Serugh, Syriac Father 58, 61, 64
Japhet, S. 78n
Jawitz, W. (Z.) 233
Jefferson, R. 290n
Jenkinson, F. 22
Jerome 41

Jeshuah ben Judah 89n
Jesus of Nazareth 7, 36, 318, 343
Johanan ben Napaḥa 64, 346
Joseph, son of the Patriarch Jacob 55, 57, 63, 116–17, 132–33, 137, 140, 173, 317, 341–42
Joseph, M. 302
Josephus Flavius 40, 55, 90n, 231
Joshua 109–10, 116–17, 123, 125, 137, 140, 205, 250–51
Joshua ben Ḥananya 172
Joshua ben Levi 282
Joshua Ibn Shuaib 64
Judah and Tamar 50–70, 232
Judah ben Barzilai al-Bargeloni 236
Judah Ha-Nasi 246
Judah ben Yaqar 241–42, 308–9

Kadari, A. 252
Kampen, J. 214–15
Kasher, M. 59n, 62n, 64n
Katz, J. 2, 10
Kaufmann, Y. 260
Kessler, E. 50
Kirkpatrick, A. F. 145–46
Kohler, K. 17, 23, 212

Lachs, S. T. 318n
Leibowitz, N. 83n–84n, 87n, 91n, 93n, 96n–97n, 136
Levenson, J. D. 38, 47n
Levi, son of Jacob 28, 69, 117, 137, 140, 168
Levi ben Gershom 189
Levine, B. A. 137, 187
Levita, E. 309
Levy, B. B. 47n
Lewis, A. S. 12
Lewis Carroll 196
Lipner, J. 314n
Lockshin, M. I. 78n
Loeb, J. 22
Loewe, H. 282
Loewe, R. J. 38
Luger, Y. 287, 304, 305n–306n
Luzzatto, S. D. 46

Macintosh, A. A. 2, 74n, 165–66, 177
McNeile, A. H. 135
Madsen, A. A. 188, 190
Maimonides, M. 7, 79, 154–55, 218, 239–41, 245, 272, 287, 334–46, 350–51
Malter, H. 18–19, 321
Margoliouth, D. S. 24–25
Margoliouth, G. 13, 23–24
Marmorstein, A. 265, 347–48
Marx, A. 18–19
Mayes, A. D. H. 260–61
Meir, the tanna 189
Meir Leibush ben Yeḥiel Michal 46
Meir ben Samuel 78
Menaḥem Ibn Saruq 86, 88, 99
Menaḥem ben Shelomo 173
Menaḥem ben Solomon Me'iri 159, 193
Mendelssohn, M. 45
Menn, E. M. 54
Milgrom, J. 137, 142
Milikowsky, C. 326n
Mintz, A. 264
Montefiore, C. G. 282
Moore, G. F. 23–24
Morag, S. 2, 73
Moses in Egypt 76, 81–102
Moses in Sinai 64, 109–37, 149, 152–53, 168–71, 176, 192, 250
Moses ben Jacob Gaon 233
Moses ben Naḥman (Ramban, Naḥmanides) 44, 67, 79, 91–93, 99, 101, 113–15, 120–21, 124, 128–29, 132–33, 135–37, 140–41, 186
Mowinckel, S. 147
Myers, J. M. 190

Naeh, S. 302
Naṭronai ben Hilai 42, 154, 233, 237
Neubauer, A. 24, 64n
Neusner, J. 263–64
Nöldeke, T. 18
Nordquist, R. 336
Noth, M. 83n, 87n–88n, 91n, 94n–95n, 97n, 136

Og, king of Bashan 174
Origen 41
Outhwaite, B. 289n, 304

Pass, H. L. 15–16
Petuchowski, J. J. 211
Philo of Alexandria 40, 90n, 334
Plato 219
Plummer, A. 145
Polliack, M. 42, 89n
Pomykala, K. E. 231
Propp, W. H. C. 104, 190
Provan, I. W. 35n

Qimḥi, D. 44–45, 158–60, 173, 181–82, 193, 236
Qimḥi, J. 44–45
Qimḥi, M. 44–45
Qirqisani, Jacob 21

Rabba bar Shila 238n, 241
Rabin, Ch. 335–36
Rav (Abba Arikha) 170, 227, 347
Ray, J. 90n
Reif, S. C. 34n, 165, 211, 298n
Reifmann, J. 151n
Reiterer, F. V. 210–14
Resh Laqish 64, 281
Reuchlin, J. 45, 80
Ringgren, H. 184, 188, 191, 193, 199
Rosenbaum, M. 78n
Rosin, D. 88n

Sa'adya ben Joseph 43, 76–77, 82–84, 100, 117, 119–20, 122, 124, 128, 132–33, 135, 138, 154, 236–37, 240–41, 243–45, 249, 254, 270–74, 285, 291, 298, 303–5, 337n, 339–40, 343, 346
Safra, the amora 292
Samuel ben Ḥofni 43
Samuel ben Meir (Rashbam) 44, 66, 76, 78, 86–88, 93n, 98–101, 112, 116, 118, 121, 123, 130, 134–37, 139
Samuel ben Naḥman 94n, 149, 170
Sarason, R. 297n
Sarna, J. D. 15n
Sarna, N. M. 146–47, 190
Sayce, A. H. 90n
Schechter, S. 2, 10–30
Schiffman, L. H. 29–30, 231, 301
Scholem, G. 246, 326–27
Schwartz, D. 264
Segal, J. B. 316
Segal, M. H. 23, 47n, 202
Sforno, Obadiah 45, 67, 76, 80, 95–100, 102, 114–17, 119–22, 126–29, 131, 133, 135–37, 141
Shabbethai Sofer of Przemysl 309–10
Shachter, J. F. 79n, 185
Shammai 170
Shivtiel, A. 173n
Silbermann, A. M. 78n
Silver, A. M. 66n, 79n, 158n
Simeon ben Gamaliel 193
Simeon the Righteous 197
Simḥah of Vitry 154, 345n
Simon, U. 74n, 79n
Skinner, J. 188
Smith, J. M. P. 188
Socrates 219
Solomon ben Isaac (Rashi) 44, 57–58, 66–67, 76–78, 84–86, 92, 98–101, 103–4, 111–12, 114, 116–17, 118–19, 121–22, 124–38, 154, 157–58, 191–93
Solomon 'of Sijilmasa' 241, 244–45
Sperber, A. 168n
Sperling, S. D. 47n
Stein, S. 210n
Steiner, R. 74n
Steinsalz, A. 149n
Stemberger, G. 51n, 167n, 212, 217–18, 228
Stendebach, F. J. 278n, 279
Stern, M. 264n
Stillman, Y. 28
Stone, M. 13n
Strickman, H. N. 66n, 79n

Tabory, J. 219n, 224n
Taylor, C. 12, 14, 21, 22n
Thomas, D. W. 165
Timotheus, the Patriarch 29
Titus, the general 176
Touitou, E. 78n

Tropper, A. 197
Tur-Sinai, N. H. 280

Urbach, E. E. 215–16, 263, 302

Ward, W. H. 188
Weinfeld, M. 226, 284, 305n
Wellhausen, J. 37
Wieder, N. 155, 210n, 290

Yaḥya ben Joseph Ṣaliḥ 308–9
Yerushalmi, Y. H. 261, 263, 269–70
Yoḥanan ben Zakkai 281

Zechariah Ha-Rofeh 59n
Ze'ira, the amora 343
Zohary, M. 82n

Index of Sources

1. Hebrew Bible

Genesis
1:9 160
2:16 198
6:4 134–35
14:14 125
15:1 337
15:13 95
17:5 117n
17:15 117n
21:16–17 99
28:21 278n
29:27 202
30:26 203
31 168
31:42 317
32:10 64
32:28 117n
37:1–2 78
37:2 116, 132–33
37:10 173
37:32 63
38 50–70
38:6 61n–62n
38:17 63n
38:24 60n
38:29 246
38:30 63n
41:45 116, 117n
48:15 342
49:24 341–42

Exodus
3:14 78n
3:17 112
4:21 192
7:7 96
11:10 192
13:3 204
13:5 205
14:30–15:19 237
15 149, 151, 252, 272
15:10 149
15:16 245
15:18 150, 244
15:25 306n
18:7 278n
20:11 267
20:20 189
20:22 281
21:1 87n
22–23 185
23:24 185, 188
23:33 189
24:7 274
24:13 116
31:16 207
32:17 116
33:11 116
34:6 152
34:9 299n
40:35 87n

Leviticus
1:1 87n
5:15 308
15:2 186
15:19 186
17:7 185
18:3 185, 189–90
18:26 185
21:7 171
26:6 278n

Numbers
1:5–17 112–13
4:26 200
6:24–26 278
7:5 200
10:35 149
11:2 176
11:28 116
12:8 250

13 103
13:3 112
13:32 120
14:19 299n
14:20 299n
14:36 132
14:37 114n, 133
14:45 131
15:13 39n
15:37–41 222, 339
15:39 112
16:28 192
20:8 64
25:1–15 168
26:59 125
34 122
34:7 122
34:17–28 113
34:23 116

Deuteronomy
1:23 115n
1:29 130–31
1:36 122–23
2:26 278n
5:15 267
6:4–9 222
6:22 191
7:19 191
8:7 120
8:9 121
9:2 128
11:3 191
11:13 198
11:13–21 222
12:3 189
12:30 189
14:22 172
14:24 123
20:10–11 278n
23:7 278n
23:18 186
25:5–9 261n
27:6 281
28:29 167
33:27 344

Joshua
7 63
8:19 123
14:15 124
15:13–15 124
17:1 116
18:5 118
21:12 123
22:27 205

Judges
1:20 122
4:11 87
5:7 120
10:10 306n
13:8 99

1 Samuel
1:4–5 88
1:23–24 99
2:11 92
3:13 168
6:12 149
17:4 132
17:8 131
21:8 341
26:15 115

2 Samuel
4:2 113
8:18 90n
12:16 99
19:19 201
21:20 132
22 345
22:3 338
23:3 339
24:10 300
24:14 247

1 Kings
2:2 112, 115
8:50 299n
9:9 204
14:24 186

2 Kings
2:12 315
2:19 120
14:23–29 170
24:17 117n

Isaiah
1:16 306
1:24 341
5:16 222
6:3 222, 244
12:4 149
26:1 278
26:4 339
32:17 278n
33:20 123
40:22 134
42:18 158
43:25 300n
44:8 146
45:7 222, 279, 283
45:21 146
48:3 146
48:5 146
48:7–8 146
49:26 341
51:9 146
52:7 146, 159
54:10 278n
55:7 299, 308
55:12 278n
57:21 279n
59 151
60:16 341
60:17 278n
63 151
63:16 300n, 315
64:7 315, 328
66:7 65n
66:18 188

Jeremiah
1:5 151
3:4 315
3:19 315, 328
6:14 279n
9:22 216
10:6–7 151
10:8 216
14:20 306n
16:17 306
23:35 92
29:27 173
31:34 299n
33:6–9 279n
33:8 299n
36:3 299n
48:7 181
51 151

Ezekiel
3:12 222, 244
4:2 119n
6:6 190
13:10 279n
16:26 186
20:5–10 101
23:20 186
28:4 181
37:16 116n

Hosea
12:8 59

Amos
6:10 130
7:2 299n
7:10–17 170n
9:3 306

Jonah
2:5 306

Micah
1:15 57
2:13 63, 65
3:5 279n
6:16 188
7:18 306

Habakkuk
3:2 93

Haggai
2:9 279n
2:12 186

Zechariah
2:17 130

Psalms
2:1 167
3:2 167
8:7 112
9:6 174
10:16 150
16:3 149
18:3 338
19:13 249
29:11 151n, 292
33:1 159
34:15 279n
35:10 235
46:8 346
51:3 306
51:9 146, 249
51:11 300n
62 345
65:4 249
68:31 173
71:3 344
72:3 279n
78:38 249
80:2 342
80:17 173
85:11 279n
86:5 299n, 305n
89:27–28 315
89:36–38 246
90–92 147
90–100 149, 153
90:1 149
91:9 344
92 153–55, 159
92–93 153–55
93 144–62
93–100 147
93:1 149–51, 153
93:2 149
93:4 149
93:5 149, 152
94 147
94:1 152
96:34–36 236
96–100 146
98:1 149
99:1 149
101:5 57
103:3 299n
103:3–5 249
103:13 308
103:19 274
103:23 202
104:7 176
104 (103):23 202
105:1–15 236
105:23–33 236
106:1 236
106:13 192
106:33–40 187
106:47 236
106:48 236
107:21–22 192
111:6 192
113–18 235
119:21 175
119:156 306
119:175 235
122:6–8 279n
130:3 249
130:4 299n
132:2 341
132:5 341
132:10–13 242
136 336
136:6 219
146:10 222

Proverbs
3:2 279n
10:18 133
19:11 306

Job
14:18 134
25:2 279n, 291
34:20 341

34:34 132
38:36 219

Song
1:10 159
4:4 284
7:10 132

Ruth
1:1 123

Ecclesiastes
1:9–10 310
2:1 100
7:5 168, 173

Lamentations
1:14 306

Esther
8 151

Daniel
1:7 116n
7 174
7:9 151
9:9 299
9:11 306n
9:15 306n
9:18 306

Ezra
6:18 204
7:19 201
8:20 204

Nehemiah
8:9 117n
9 272

1 Chronicles
6:33 202
9:13 202
16 272
16:8–36 236
23:28 190
26:30 201
28:21 201
29 272
29:10–13 237, 253

2 Chronicles
4:6 190
11:15 188
13:8–9 188
17:4 188

2. Apocrypha/Pseudepigrapha, New Testament and Dead Sea Scrolls

Ben Sira
5:5–9 300n
6:19 203
6:24–29 210
7:15 203
16:14 300n
17:6–23 221
23:1 316
36:6–22 214
50:4 344
50:28/19 202
51:10 336
51:22–34 336

3 Maccabees
4:14 205
6:2 265–66

Testaments of the Twelve Patriarchs 16, 20, 28, 54, 64n, 200

Wisdom of Solomon
3:3 279

10:10–19 224n
14:1–3 317

Book of Eldad the Danite 90

Book of Enoch 20

Book of Jubilees 20

Book of Zerubbabel 90

Chronicles of Moses 90

Matthew
6:9 318

Mark
14:36 318

Luke
11:2 318
15:4–7 343

CD 2.4 301n
CD 6.21 280n
CD 10.19 199
CD 14.16 199
CD 20.7 199

1QH 284
1QH 6.9 301n
1QH 7 301
1QH 9.18 199
1QH 9.34 301n
1QH 10(=2).15 280n
1QH 10.38 200
1QH 11.9 301n
1QH 14.24 301n
1QH 15(=7).15 280n
1QH 17(=9).28 346n
1QH 19(=11).27 280n
1QH 21(=18).15 (=30) 280n
1QM 2.9 199
1QM 3.11 280n
1QM 13.5 199
1QM 17.7 280n
1QpHab 10.11 199
1QS 2.8 301n
1QS 2.9 280n
1QS 4.7 280n
1QS 4.9 199
1QS 11.7 344n
1QSa 1.19 199

4Q215 2 ii 8 200
4Q254 7 3 342n
4Q257 II 5 301n
4Q372 1 317
4Q400 I 18 301n
4Q408 3/3a 9 300
4Q427 7 II 16 301n
4Q460 5 6 317n
4Q491 11 15 344n
4Q503 24 7 9 250n
4Q504 301
4Q506 301n
4Q508 4 2 250n
4Q511 18 ii 6 199
4Q511 63 iii 3 199
4Q511 63–64 ii 4 199
4Q521 2 ii 3 200
4QPs[b] 148

11QPs[a] 284

3. Talmud, Midrash, Rabbinica

Mishna & Tosefta

m. Berakhot
1.4 282n
2.1 281n
2.4 284n

m. Kil'ayim
9.8 326n

m. Šebi'it
2.5 207
5.9 280n

m. Pesaḥim
10.5–6 267n

m. Yoma
7.1 197
8.9 326n

m. Roš Haššanah
4.5 239n

m. Ta'anit
2.1 303n
2.2–4 248

m. Megillah
4.10 56n

m. Ḥagigah
2.6 281n

m. Soṭa
9.15 326n
10.2 281n

m. Giṭṭin
5.9 281n

m. Sanhedrin
4.5 281n
7.6 207
11.9 281n

m. 'Eduyot
8.7 281n

m. 'Abodah Zarah
4.6 280n

m. Abot
1.2 197
1.12 280n
1.17 193n
1.18 280n
2.7 280n
5.20 326n

m. Ḥullin
9.2 207

m. Tamid
5.1 286n
7.4 148

m. Middot
5.4 347n

t. Berakhot
1.9 222n
2.1 223n, 266n
3.14 326n

t. Pe'ah
4.21 280n

t. Ta'anit
2.10 280n

t. Roš Haššanah
4.5 239n

t. Soṭah
9.3 59n

t. Baba Qamma
7.7 281n

t. 'Abodah Zarah
1.17 281n

Yerushalmi Talmud

y. Berakhot
1.5 (4) (3d) 173n, 243n
1.8 (3c) 320n
1.9 (3d) 223n, 266n, 339n
2.4 (4d) 283n, 301n
2.4 (5a) 282n
4.2 (7d) 280n
4.3 (8a) 238n–39n
4.5 (8c) 284n

5 (9b) 226n
5.1 (8d) 346n
5.3 (9c) 222n
7.1 (11a) 243n

y. Kil'ayim
1.4 (27a) 262n

y. Šabbat
15.3 (15b) 343n

y. Yoma
7.1 (44b) 250n

y. Roš Haššanah
4.6 (59c) 239n

y. Ta'anit
2.9 (65d) 248n
3.4 (66cd) 321n
4.2 (68a) 280n

y. Ḥagigah
2.1 (77a) 326n

y. Soṭah
1.4 (16d) 60n
1.8 (17a) 59n

y. Sanhedrin
4.8[7] (22b) 64n

y. Horayot
2.4 (46d) 341n

Babylonian Talmud

b. Berakhot
4b 284n
6a 280n
11b 220n, 250n, 283n, 320n
16b 280n – 81n
17a 281n, 292n
21a 222n
29a 239n
40b 347n
43b 60n
46a 342n
48b 243n
48b – 49a 243n
49a 340n
55b 280n – 81n
60b 218n
62b 232n

b. Šabbat
31a 170n
67a 189a
89a 127n
118b 232n
152a 280n

b. Pesaḥim
50a 59n
108a 262n
117b 238n, 329n
118a 232n
118b 174n

b. Yoma
22b 232n
67b 133

b. Beṣah
15b 149

b. Roš Haššanah
25a 246
31a 146, 148, 153

b. Ta'anit
16b 248n
23b 321n
25b 321
28b 232n
29a 126, 136

b. Megillah
10b 57n, 60n
13a 95n
14a 61n
17b 301n
18a 286n
25b 56n

b. Mo'ed Qaṭan
28a 173n

b. Ḥagigah
12a 176n

b. Yebamot
34b 62n
59a 56n
64b 58n
76b-77a 232n

b. Ketubot
67b 60n

b. Nedarim
39b 149, 151

b. Nazir
23b 60n
66b 282n

b. Soṭah
7b 58n
10ab 59n
10b 59n–60n, 63n, 65n
11b 115n
12ab 82n
34b 113n, 115, 116n, 122n–23n, 125n, 130n, 134
35a 114, 126–27, 130n-131n, 133, 134n, 232n
36b 342n
39b 286n
49a 221n

b. Giṭṭin
56a 280n

b. Baba Qamma
92a 58n
109b 207

b. Baba Meṣi'a
59a 60n
59b 172n

b. Baba Batra
15a 121n

b. Sanhedrin
42a 245n
61b 189n
64a 189n
68a 170n
102a 64n
111b 149, 152

b. 'Abodah Zarah
9a 262n
24b 149

b. Horayot
13a 190

b. Makkot
11b 58n
23b 65n

b. Menaḥot
29b 263n
43b 218n
53a 149

b. Niddah
13a 62n
28a 56n
45a 172n
61a 133

Avot de R. Nathan 18n, 150, 169–71
Derekh 'Ereṣ 281n–82n, 291n
Derekh 'Ereṣ Zuṭa 282n
Kallah 62n, 150, 151n
Soferim 150, 153, 174n, 240–42, 245–46, 250n

Aggadat Bereshit 174n
Aggadat Shir Hashirim 18n
Leqaḥ Ṭov 82–100
Megillat Ta'anit 263
Mekhilta de R. Yishma'el 59n, 306n
Mekhilta de R. Shim'on b. Yohai 59n, 306n

Midrash Aggadah 173, 176n
Midrash Avkir 94n, 96n
Midrash Bereshit Rabbati 175n–76n
Midrash Ha-Gadol 57–65
Midrash Ha-Ḥefeṣ 59n, 62n
Midrash Rabbah 39n, 54, 59n, 82n, 113n–14n, 129n, 169n, 170, 173, 176
Midrash Shemuel 168–69
Midrash Tehillim 149–51
Midrash Zuṭa 169
Pesiqta Rabbati 168–76
Pesiqta de Rav Kahana 172–75
Pirqei de-Rabbi Eliezer 55, 168
Qohelet Zuṭa 169n
Seder Eliyahu Rabba and Seder Eliyahu Zuṭa 170n, 281n
Seder 'Olam Rabbah 237, 262n
Sekhel Ṭov 173
Sifra 186, 189n
Sifrei 169, 170n, 198, 207, 282n
Sifrei Zuṭa 280n–81n
Tanḥuma 82–100, 112–13, 114n, 117n–18n, 125–126n, 127, 130n, 134n, 167, 168n, 171n, 172, 175n, 176, 342
Tanḥuma Buber 92n, 112n-114n, 117n–18n, 123n, 125n–26n, 130n, 134n, 167, 172n, 175n, 342n
Targum 16, 54, 59n, 60n, 62n, 65n, 75, 120, 128, 140, 181, 187, 316
Yalquṭ Shim'oni 64n, 82–100, 168, 169n–70n, 172–73, 175n–76n

Letter of Sherira Gaon 269
Mishneh Torah 218n, 245n
Scroll of Antiochus 269
Sefer Ha-Kabbalah 269
Seder Tanna'im Va-Amora'im 268–69
Sefer Yosippon 269

4. Manuscripts cited

Bodleian Library, Oxford
Opp. 187 64n
Heb.d.55.33–34 289n

Cambridge University Library
T-S 16.311 14n, 17
T-S 16.359–367 17
T-S 20.57 306n
T-S 6H3.1 319n
T-S 6H6.6 236n, 324n
T-S 8H9.1 324n
T-S 8H9.12 305n
T-S 8H10.6 305n
T-S 8H10.22 305n
T-S 8H11.3 305n
T-S 8H16.1 240n
T-S 8H19.3 236n
T-S 8H23.9 235n–36n
T-S 8H24.5 305n
T-S 10H1.2 305n–6n
T-S 10H2.1 234n
T-S 10H4.1 240n
T-S 10K6 14n, 17, 22n
T-S F2(1).122 150n
T-S H2.115 235n
T-S H2.123 235n
T-S H2.124 273n
T-S H5.135 289n
T-S H5.224 289n
T-S H8.80 251n
T-S H8.90 305n
T-S H15.15 236n
T-S H18.18 236n
T-S H18.25 236n
T-S K8.7 272n
T-S K27.18 306n
T-S Ar.36.15 236n
T-S Misc.35 1–57 17n
T-S NS 120.62 289n
T-S NS 120.105 305n
T-S NS 121.37 324n
T-S NS 123.105 289n
T-S NS 150.37 305n, 307n
T-S NS 150.141 289n
T-S NS 152.35 305n
T-S NS 154.18 305n

T-S NS 154.95 272n
T-S NS 154.120 305n
T-S NS 155.1 251n
T-S NS 156.7 324n
T-S NS 157.193 305n
T-S NS 159.112 305n
T-S NS 195.77 305n
T-S NS 196.107 306n
T-S NS 197.33 250n
T-S NS 230.19 305n
T-S NS 230.96 305n
T-S NS 235.172 306n
T-S NS 235.173 272n
T-S NS 271.14 272n
T-S NS 271.16 250n
T-S NS 278.51 324n
T-S NS 278.151 305n
T-S NS 278.247 307n
T-S NS 299.150 250n
T-S NS J502 320n
T-S NS 102.132 307n
T-S AS 102.164 289n
T-S AS 108.57 305n, 324n
T-S AS 108.134 272n
T-S AS 109.126 305n
Add.3160.3 235n
Add.3160.5 324n
Add.3160.6 319n
Add.3356 319n
Add.6463.7061 22n
Add.6463.7072 22n
Or.1081 2.76 324n

Jewish Theological Seminary, New York

Adler 2017, f. 9 305n

Russian National Library

MS Evr. III B 995 307n

Index of subjects, rites and prayers

academy, yeshivah, bet midrash 39, 41–42, 88, 268
afterlife 214
aggada, *see* midrash, *derash* and aggada
'alenu 227–28, 347
'amidah 6, 206, 221–22, 225–27, 232, 237–42, 247–48, 253, 265, 267, 271–72, 274, 284, 286–92
anger, vengeance 67, 97, 152, 165, 172, 176–77, 184, 247, 270, 273
Ancient Near East 5, 124, 146, 186, 212–13, 217, 260–61, 314
angels, spirits, demons 6, 58, 65, 99, 169, 171, 174–75, 185, 215, 222–23, 244, 280–81, 285, 291, 293
anthropomorphism 7, 42, 77, 91, 96, 316, 325, 335
anti-Semitism, enemies of Israel 37, 38n, 152, 174
apocalypse 215, 223
Apocrypha and Pseudepigrapha 15, 20, 24, 27–30, 50, 90, 196, 214, 231, 279, 300, 316–17, 329, 349
'aqedah 176
Arabic 18–19, 43, 77, 82, 90, 166
Aramaic 16, 43, 56, 85, 128, 151, 168–70, 187, 198, 201, 261, 269, 318, 324, 326n, 348
archaeology 47
'arvit (evening prayer) 153–55, 222–26, 266, 272, 284–85, 289, 293, 320, 338–39, 341n, 344
asher baḥar 220n, 250–51
Ashkenaz/Ashkenazi rite 154, 242, 247, 249, 289, 297n, 307–10, 337n
Assyria 159
astrology 97n
attah hu 326n
'avodah 4–5, 196–208

Babylonia/Babylonian rite 41–42, 76–77, 151–52, 154–55, 167, 206, 223, 227–28, 234–35, 238–39, 244, 254–55, 265–66, 268, 270, 275, 282–85, 287, 290, 305–7, 310, 322, 327, 337–40, 345
Bar-Ilan University Responsa Project 167n, 326n
benedictions/blessings 6, 63, 218–22, 225–27, 233, 237–39, 241–45, 246–53, 266, 278–79, 280, 282, 286–90, 292–94, 297, 301–5, 308–10, 318, 320–21, 324, 326–28, 338–39, 342, 344–48
Ben-Gurion University of the Negev 289n, 304, 319n
Ben Sira 12, 25
Berlin 18
Bethel Theological Seminary 147
bet midrash, *see* academy, yeshivah, bet midrash
Bible/Bible study 1–7, 20, 26, 34–46, 50, 55, 60–61, 63–64, 69, 73–78, 98, 100, 102, 108, 132, 134, 138–40, 144–48, 150–51, 153, 156, 159, 161–62, 165–69, 176–77, 180, 186–87, 196, 208, 213–14, 231, 249, 253, 260–64, 278–79, 283–84, 286, 291, 293, 299–300, 305–6, 314–17, 334, 337–39, 341, 344–45, 350
Biblical Hebrew 2, 40, 43, 73, 139, 145–46, 165, 180–81, 193, 198–99, 208, 293, 299–300, 304n, 306, 309, 344, 346, 348
biblical verses 28, 40–41, 75, 78–79, 84, 92, 98–102, 111–35, 140, 144, 147–48, 150–51, 153–54, 159–60, 167, 169, 181, 184–88, 196, 235–37, 241, 247, 249, 252–53, 272, 283–84
'biblicisors' 306
birkat ha-ḥodesh (blessing of new month) 293
birth and pregnancy 53, 56, 62, 65, 69n, 76, 81, 85, 87n, 89, 92–95, 98–99, 135, 221
bodily functions 219–20
Brandeis University 146
Britain/British 11

British Museum 13, 23, 155
burial, *see* death, mourning, burial
Byzantium/Byzantine 51, 307

Cairo (Fustat) 1, 2, 4, 10–12, 14, 17, 26–30, 225n, 234, 282, 287, 298, 304, 328
calligraphy, *see* paleography/calligraphy/handwriting
calumny 57, 85, 111, 116, 133, 136, 141, 204
Cambridge 2–3, 12, 14, 16–17, 21–22, 25, 35, 37, 51, 145, 165–66, 180, 269, 301, 317n, 335n
Cambridge University Library 11, 14n–15n, 150, 272, 289n, 304, 305n, 326n
Cambridge University Press 16, 145
Canaanites 52–53, 55, 57, 59, 62, 65, 67, 110, 126, 131, 141, 187–90, 341
cantor, *see ḥazzan/cantor*
celestial spheres, *see* heaven, Gan 'Eden, celestial spheres
censor 173n, 216n
censure, *see* moral rebuke, guidance, censure
charity, kindness 98, 184, 197, 202, 215, 300, 322
child/ren 64–65, 67, 81–83, 85, 88, 89n, 92–93, 96n, 97–99, 101, 167–68, 171, 173, 187, 265, 315, 317, 328, 347
Christianity 3–4, 7, 12, 15–16, 23–24, 34–42, 44–47, 50, 52, 56, 61, 64, 67, 69–70, 73–74, 79–80, 102, 138, 144, 147, 156–57, 159–60, 174, 210, 216, 231–32, 239, 253–54, 305n, 317–18, 323, 329–30, 335, 338, 343–44, 350
chronology 44, 46, 52, 66, 79, 96n, 101, 139–40, 232, 237, 248, 262, 268, 329
circumcision 98, 219
Classical world 5, 42, 145, 314
Columbia University 17
codices, manuscripts 10–30, 63, 75, 117, 153–55, 167, 168n, 225–26, 238, 240–41, 250, 265, 282, 284, 298, 306n, 307, 309, 326n, 345n, 347
commands, *see miṣvot*, commands, precepts
conversion, intermarriage 15, 24, 36, 55, 59, 68–69, 92, 100, 225
creation/cosmology 5–6, 145–53, 158, 160–61, 175, 193, 212, 214–16, 219–22, 227–28, 245–46, 256, 259, 267, 281, 283, 289, 293–94, 336, 316, 318, 322, 336
Crusades 51, 153, 285, 334
curse 100, 173–77
custom, *see halakhah*, custom

Damascus Document 10–30
Davidic dynasty 5–6, 54, 56, 59, 62, 69, 188, 225, 231–56, 317, 337
death, mourning, burial 53, 55, 60–61, 84n, 93–95, 98n, 100–2, 132, 114, 169–70, 173, 177, 212, 267, 297, 321
Decalogue (Ten Commandments) 274, 286
demons, *see* angels, spirits, demons
Dosithean 16–17, 21, 23, 29–30
dreams 173, 212, 217
Dropsie College, Philadelphia 18, 146

Eastern Europe 46
Edomites 174–75
education 5, 38–39, 45, 51, 90, 145, 210, 214, 217–18, 221, 224, 261, 268, 347
Egypt/Egyptian rite 23, 25–27, 40, 76, 81–85, 88–91, 93, 95, 97–98, 100–2, 109, 113, 117, 123–24, 140, 151, 154, 176, 185–87, 191, 204, 223–24, 260, 266–67, 273, 284, 298, 306, 314, 339, 342
election of Israel 220–21, 273, 283
eschatology, end-time, messiah 5, 17, 36, 41, 54, 56, 61, 63–65, 67, 69, 145, 149, 151, 157, 159–60, 167, 215, 238, 243, 256, 267, 271, 200, 221, 231, 235n, 238–46, 249, 253–56, 263, 266–67, 282
Essenes 30
eternity 58, 61, 155, 158, 221, 326
ethical inadequacy, wrongdoing 6–7, 41, 57, 126, 151–52, 159, 174, 192, 214, 227, 271, 280, 283, 293, 299, 306, 308–9, 327
Europe/European rites 35, 38, 43–45, 47, 157, 210, 334
eulogy 236, 238, 241–42, 245, 248–50, 252, 266, 284–85, 288–90, 299, 305, 307, 338–40, 344–45
evil spirits, *see* angels, spirits, demons

exilarch 239, 254–56
Exodus from Egypt 95, 214, 223–25, 266–67, 273

Falasha 20, 29
festivals, fasts 41, 147, 154–55, 225, 228, 235, 238–41, 247–48, 250, 255, 261, 267n, 273–75, 289, 303, 320–22, 324, 347
Firkovich Collection 27–28
forgiveness 6–7, 58, 68, 114, 249, 256, 297–310, 322, 327
France/French rite 43, 77–79, 156, 189, 307
Franco-Germany 3, 44, 77, 88, 154, 157
Friday and Friday eve 148, 153–54, 170, 338, 344–45

Gan 'Eden, *see* heaven, Gan 'Eden, celestial spheres
Genizah 1, 2, 4, 10–30, 133, 144, 150n, 153–54, 225n, 227, 234, 236, 240, 250, 253, 269, 272–74, 282, 287, 289–91, 298, 304–6, 319n–20n, 324n, 326n, 328, 337n, 347
gentiles, *see* non-Jews, gentiles, nations, heathens
geography, *see* science, geography, medicine
Geonim 268
Germany 7, 10, 20, 27, 45–46, 52, 78, 146, 196, 310, 335
ge'ulah, *see* redemption *(ge'ulah)*
God
– anger/displeasure 52, 92, 247, 300
– assistance 101, 297, 328
– as Creator 148, 160, 184, 219–20, 227, 265, 278–79, 281, 283–84, 289–90, 293–94, 336
– eternity of 146–47, 150, 155, 158–61, 233, 236
– as Father and King 7, 299, 305n, 308, 314–330
– fear of 213–14, 221
– forgiveness 6, 297–310
– inspiration 92, 153, 157–58
– instructions 109–14, 192, 220–21, 282
– justice/punishment/reward 93, 152, 171, 174, 176, 184, 192, 213, 221–22, 224, 300
– kingship/sovereignty 145–48, 151, 157, 159–60, 223, 227, 244–45, 266, 274, 324
– knowledge, wisdom 82, 84, 91, 96, 212–13, 222
– love of Israel (Jacob) 6, 38, 58, 68–69, 93n, 141–42, 240, 243, 249, 256, 260, 265, 273, 275, 281, 286–89, 293–94, 297, 300, 317, 320, 324, 336
– mercy/patience 6, 93, 152–53, 238, 319–20, 324, 348–49
– metaphors for 7, 150–51, 157, 234, 285, 303, 314–30
– name 100, 116, 221–22, 240, 282, 326
– plan and promise 54, 64, 66, 69, 85, 90, 92, 94, 101, 109–14, 132, 160, 169–70, 175, 184, 198, 261, 267, 270–71, 284
– power 131, 146–47, 149, 151, 157–61, 175–76, 192, 225–27, 265, 273–74
– praise, love, service 152, 192–93, 198–204, 208, 218–19, 221–22, 224–25, 227–28, 232–37, 245, 252–54, 271, 319, 336, 347–48
– protection 220, 285, 289, 336–39
– throne of glory 145, 149, 151, 159, 171,
grace after meals *(birkat ha-mazon)* 207, 242–44, 250n, 253, 271, 284, 291, 320, 325, 342–43, 348
grammar and lexicography 4, 7, 37, 43–44, 46, 73–74, 77, 79–80, 93, 138, 142, 159, 161, 166–67, 181–84, 191, 193, 304n, 309
Greek 3–5, 22n, 36, 42, 54, 90, 138, 151, 192, 196–206, 208, 214, 217, 219, 224, 261, 271, 279–80, 293, 314, 316–18, 334
guidance, *see* moral rebuke, guidance, censure

hafṭarah 241–42, 245, 250, 253
halakhah, custom 8, 12, 30, 38, 40, 51, 56, 77, 89n, 116–17, 150, 153–55, 207, 161, 169, 172, 186, 223–24, 227–28, 237, 239, 247–48, 250, 255, 262, 264–65, 268–70, 286, 289–90, 292, 303, 324, 334, 350

hallel 232, 235
handwriting, *see* paleography/calligraphy/handwriting
Ḥanukkah 255, 269–71
Harvard University 23
Haskalah 309
ḥazzan/cantor 345, 350
health/healing 119–20, 141, 192, 225–26, 279–80, 293, 302
heathen, *see* non-Jews, gentiles, nations, heathens
heaven, Gan ʻEden, celestial spheres 6–7, 25, 55, 58, 96, 130, 133, 147, 149, 151, 158, 160, 170–71, 175, 198, 216, 222–23, 227, 279–81, 289, 291–94, 315, 318, 326, 329, 343
heavenly voice, *see* Holy Spirit, heavenly voice
Hebrew/hebraica/hebraists 3–5, 11–16, 23–27, 36–37, 39, 43, 45–47, 55–56, 62–63, 73–74, 77, 80–82, 88, 94, 96, 100, 135, 138–39, 142, 147, 149–50, 166–67, 169, 175, 181–83, 187, 190, 193, 200, 203, 206, 208, 216, 218–19, 222n, 226, 233, 247, 260–61, 279–80, 293, 299–301, 308, 320, 326n, 335, 344, 348, 350
Hebrew Language Academy 167n, 216n, 240n, 300n, 326n
Hebrew Union College 17, 23, 50
Hebrew University of Jerusalem 23, 47n, 264, 335
Hekhalot 223, 227, 323, 326
Hellenism 40, 50, 54, 90n–91n, 208, 214, 224, 261–62
heresy/heretics 28, 146
Hildesheimer Rabbinical Seminary 18
historiography 5, 10–11, 38, 80, 232–33, 260–75, 349–50
hodu 236, 252
Holy Land, *see* Israel/Palestine/Holy Land/Zion and its rite
Holy Spirit, heavenly voice 59, 61, 64, 321, 330
home (domestic) rituals 205, 218, 224, 235, 255, 267, 273
homiletics 41, 51, 138, 149–53, 174, 216, 282
hoshʻanot 250n
hymns 233–36, 251–52

idolatry 85, 94, 100n, 101, 170, 175, 185, 187–89, 207, 227, 281
immorality 58, 62, 67, 83n, 168, 185–87
India 261, 314
Islam/Muslim 3, 7, 16, 18, 29, 40, 42–44, 51, 76, 155–56, 210, 254, 256, 268, 305n, 330, 334, 349–50
Israel Museum 11n
Israel(ite)/Palestine/Holy Land, Zion and its rite 5, 29, 36–37, 41, 47, 51, 55, 57–58, 60, 63, 65, 68, 82, 84–86, 92, 94–95, 100–2, 109–10, 112–14, 116–18, 121, 123–24, 126, 131–33, 138–39, 141, 145–47, 151–55, 161, 167–68, 174–77, 180, 185–89, 191–93, 204, 206, 212–14, 220–24, 227, 231, 234–35, 237–40, 242–46, 248–51, 254–256, 260–61, 264–66, 268–69, 271–75, 278–79, 281–94, 306, 310, 315–16, 319–20, 322, 327–28, 330, 334, 336–40, 342–47, 350
Italy/Italian rite 3, 45–46, 52, 76, 78, 80, 242–44, 269, 307

Jerusalem/Zion and its restoration 5, 12, 74, 79, 103n, 117, 145, 152, 159–60, 176, 186, 190, 197, 206–7, 214, 217, 222, 225, 228, 231, 238–40, 243–44, 248–49, 251, 253, 267, 274, 275n, 279, 282, 284–86, 336, 338, 345, 348, 350
Jewish-Christians 7, 239, 329, 338, 350
Jewish Chronicle 14
Jewish Publication Society 146
Jewish Theological Seminary 12n, 14, 17, 305n
Jews' College 23, 146
Judaeo–Arabic 75
Judaism 15, 23, 24–25, 27, 42, 46, 79, 92, 147, 165, 170, 208, 210–11, 225, 266, 271, 284, 334, 338, 350

kabbalah, pietism, mysticism 5–6, 8, 41, 44, 76, 79, 92–93, 223, 227, 244, 246–47, 253–56, 292, 307–8, 315–16, 322–23, 326–27, 329, 335, 349
Karaites 29
kindness, *see* charity, kindness
King James Version 45, 77

labour, work 182–84, 190, 198–204, 206–8, 213
leave-taking 286, 291–92
lectionaries 5, 41, 56, 228
leprosy 85, 101
levirate marriage 52, 56, 59
Levites 150, 190, 192, 201–2, 204, 287
Library of Congress 17n
liturgy, worship 1, 4–7, 39, 41, 144–50, 153–56, 161, 172, 188–91, 197–201, 204–8, 210–12, 218, 223–24, 227–28, 231–35, 237–51, 253–56, 260, 264–75, 282–94, 297–99, 302–10, 314–30, 334–50
Loeb Classical Library 22

Maccabees/Hasmoneans 263, 267, 270–71
magen avot 338
magic, superstition, miracles 11, 83, 85, 89n, 95, 98, 113, 126, 138, 160, 172, 176, 189, 191–93, 212, 216–17, 220, 267, 279–73, 328
Manicheans 29
manuscripts, *see* codices, manuscripts
marriage 52–53, 55–57, 59–60, 65–69, 81, 84–85, 89, 92, 94–95, 101–2, 171, 186, 280
martyrdom, *see* persecution, suffering, martyrdom
Masoretes 42, 45, 88, 108, 315, 341
medicine, *see* science, geography, medicine
memory 26, 82, 260–61, 264, 267, 269, 299
Mesopotamia 147, 260, 314, 334, 350
messiah, *see* eschatology, end-time, messiah
metaphors, figures of speech 7, 86, 121, 124, 140–42, 148, 152–53, 157–59, 161, 284–85, 300, 303, 306, 308, 314–16, 334–51
Midian(ites) 81, 85–86, 90–91, 94, 96, 101–2, 168
midrash, derash and aggada 4, 7, 38, 41, 44, 51–52, 54–69, 74, 76–87, 89–95, 98n, 100–103, 123, 138–39, 149, 151–53, 156, 167–69, 171–77, 186, 189, 193, 198, 215–17, 224, 231–32, 239, 241, 255, 262–63, 274, 281, 284, 291, 328–29, 334–35, 338–39, 341–43, 347
Middle Ages/medieval 1, 3, 4, 6–7, 16, 18–19, 30, 37, 43, 45, 50, 54, 58, 65, 67, 73–76, 80–81, 95, 98, 102–4, 108, 110–11, 137–38, 141–42, 144, 153–56, 161–62, 167, 177, 181–82, 184, 187, 193, 217, 227, 232, 237–38, 240, 247, 250, 252, 255–56, 264, 268–69, 272, 287, 292, 307, 315n, 319, 339–40, 341n, 343, 345, 347–49
mi-meqomekha 244
minḥa (afternoon service) 225, 228, 289
minyan (quorum) 237
miracles, *see* magic, superstition, miracles
Mishnaic Hebrew, *see* Rabbinic (Mishnaic) and post-biblical Hebrew
miṣvot, commands, precepts 40, 110–12, 198, 201, 220–21, 232, 260, 270, 274, 282, 319, 334
moral rebuke, guidance, censure 36, 54, 60, 83, 90, 97, 165, 167–73, 175, 177, 213, 254, 302
morning prayers 153–55, 218–23, 225, 244, 249, 252, 266, 272, 282–83, 285, 291, 319–20, 323–24, 326n, 339–40, 346
Morocco 334
mourning, *see* death, mourning, burial
musaf (additional service) 227, 240, 244, 273–74, 320, 324
mysticism, *see* kabbalah/pietism/mysticism

names 43, 55, 62–63, 67, 69, 77, 82, 87n, 89n, 92, 100, 110–12, 115n, 116, 123, 125, 127, 137, 139, 140–41, 254, 279, 303, 314–15
nations, *see* non-Jews, gentiles, nations, heathens
New Moon (Rosh Ḥodesh) 245–46

New Testament 35–38, 91n, 156, 317–18, 338
New Year (Rosh Ha-Shanah) 147, 227, 239–40, 247, 251n, 267n, 274n, 302–3, 320, 323–24, 347
New York 12n, 14, 17–18, 21–22, 145
nishmat 235
non-Jews, gentiles, nations, heathens 5, 18, 25, 45, 64–65, 68–77, 79, 96n, 129, 145, 152, 157, 161, 166–67, 187, 189, 216–17, 219, 224, 226, 266, 281, 317
North Africa 77–78, 154, 307

offerings, *see* sacrifices/offerings
Oral Torah 40, 46, 217, 334
Orion Institute 12
Orthodox Judaism 7, 23, 46, 310
Oxford 11–12, 24–25, 63–64, 142, 145, 289, 335

paleography/calligraphy/handwriting 24n, 26
Palestine, *see* Israel/Palestine/Holy Land/Zion and its rite
Passover (Pesaḥ) 224, 235, 240, 255, 267, 273, 347
Passover Haggadah 224–25, 232, 347
Patriarchs 16, 20, 225, 240, 246, 254, 265, 337–38, 340, 350
peace 6, 184, 225, 245, 278–94, 328, 344–45
penitence, *see* repentance/penitence
persecution, suffering, martyrdom 54, 94, 97, 101–2, 212, 225, 279, 293, 348
Persia/Persian rite 42, 154, 170, 213–14, 231, 245, 261–62, 307
peshaṭ 41, 43–44, 46, 65–66, 79, 86–87, 94–95, 102, 156
pesher 40
pesuqey de-zimra 232
Pharisaism 19–23, 29
Philistines 95, 152
philosophy and rationalism 4, 7, 18–19, 36, 38, 43–46, 74, 76–80, 84, 88–92, 94, 98, 140, 156–57, 173, 160, 189, 217, 219, 224, 227, 239, 260, 334–35, 351
pietism, *see* kabbalah, pietism, mysticism
piyyuṭ/poetry 4, 7, 149, 154, 169, 177, 182, 192, 213–14, 233, 235, 239–41, 244, 249, 254, 256, 271, 273–74, 275n, 289, 297, 299, 301, 303–4, 306, 310, 319n, 323, 335, 337, 340–42, 345–46, 350
Poland 27, 309
prayer 5–8, 58, 93, 102, 116–17, 149–50, 154–55, 158, 172, 198–200, 206, 210–28, 231–56, 260–75, 278–94, 297–310, 314–30, 334–351
prayer-book 5, 154, 217, 231–34, 236–38, 240–45, 264, 269–70, 274, 282, 291, 298, 320, 327, 329, 339–40, 346–47
precepts, *see miṣvot*, commands, precepts
priesthood 29, 57, 60, 67, 69–70, 85, 90n, 91, 168, 170–71, 190, 192, 200–4, 213–14, 231, 249–250, 270–71, 286–89, 336, 345
priestly benediction 6, 278, 286–90, 308, 344–45
Progressive Judaism 310
prophecy 17, 20, 41, 46, 56–57, 60–61, 65, 68–69, 84–85, 91–92, 96n, 125n, 145, 151, 157, 159–60, 168, 170, 188, 213–14, 241–43, 245, 250, 254, 278–79, 293, 306, 315–16, 341–42
Protestantism 36–37, 39, 47
Provence/Provençal rite 3, 43–44, 154, 156, 158–59, 181, 193
Psalms readings 6, 41, 148, 150, 144–62, 228, 233–38, 249–56, 323–24

qaddish 291–92, 318n
qedushah 222–23, 239, 244–45, 252–53, 284, 292
qedushah de-sidra 221–22
qiddush 250, 273
qiddush levanah 245–46
Qumran/Judean/Dead Sea Scrolls 4–5, 13, 25, 28–30, 38, 40, 50, 183–84, 196, 199–200, 206, 208, 214–15, 223, 226, 231, 244, 250, 278–79, 300–1, 303, 317, 336, 339, 342, 346

Rabbinic (Mishnaic) and post-biblical Hebrew 24, 75, 96, 335, 350
Rabbinic Judaism 19–20, 24, 29, 40, 42–43, 212, 217, 231, 260, 267–68, 297, 317, 322n, 323, 329, 334, 336
rain 274, 321
Red Sea 130, 176, 266
redemption (*ge'ulah*) 6, 54, 65, 86, 93, 222–25, 246, 248, 252–56, 265–67, 336, 339–40
Reform Judaism 17, 23
Reformation 3, 36, 138
religious ideas/theology 3–7, 11–13, 15, 18–20, 28–29, 35–39, 41, 47, 50–52, 56, 77, 79–80, 84, 92, 102–3, 141, 151, 155–56, 160, 196–97, 208, 210–12, 220, 225–26, 231–32, 239, 242–43, 250, 252–55, 260, 265–66, 269, 271, 274, 278–81, 283–85, 287, 292–93, 297–310, 315–16, 320, 322–23, 325, 328–30, 334–36, 338, 340, 343–44, 349–50
remembrance, remebrance verses 240, 267, 273
Renaissance 3, 45, 80
repentance/penitence 6, 54, 58, 68, 101–2, 114, 141, 149, 151, 225, 231, 247–49, 253, 256, 263, 297, 300–2, 304, 308, 310, 319–20, 322, 324, 327, 329, 343
responsa 233, 289
restoration, *see* Jerusalem/Zion, and its restoration
resurrection 225–26
Romaniote rite 154, 235n, 237n, 242, 244
Rome/Roman rite 3, 5, 51, 80, 138, 174, 176, 224, 266–67, 314, 334

Sabbath 41, 148, 153–55, 170, 225–26, 228, 241, 244, 250–51, 267, 285, 343
sacrifices/offerings 150, 183–84, 190–91, 199, 205, 207, 237, 261
Sadducees 21, 23, 29–30, 266
salvation 241–42, 251, 253, 267, 270, 339–40, 346
Samaritans 16–17, 20–21, 23, 29, 42
Sanhedrin 63
Satan 171, 175–76, 285
science, geography, medicine 44–45, 79, 96, 119, 139, 158, 160, 212, 217
Second Temple period 4, 6–7, 16, 23–24, 29, 50–52, 196, 200, 211–14, 218, 220, 223, 226, 231, 242, 261, 265, 278–80, 293, 297–301, 326, 335–36
sects/sectarians 13–23, 27, 29–30, 62, 77, 214, 266, 317
Sefardi/Spain 3, 43–44, 76–79, 154–57, 181, 185, 207, 241–42, 249, 289, 297n, 307–8, 310, 334
Sefirot 246
seliḥot 247, 253
Semitics 43, 47, 86n, 102, 165, 199, 210, 280, 316, 337, 341
Septuagint (=LXX) 4, 40, 84n, 87n, 145–46, 148, 184, 187, 191, 200–6, 208
sexual relations 53, 57, 60–62, 64–65, 68–69, 86, 89, 168, 183, 185–87, 232, 280
shaḥarit (morning service) 153–55, 218–23, 225, 244, 249, 252, 266, 272, 282–83, 285, 291, 319–20, 323–24, 326n, 339–40, 346
Shekhinah (Divine Presence) 86, 274
shema' and its benedictions 221–23, 266–67, 282, 284, 286, 293, 318–20, 323, 339, 346–47
sin 6–7, 17, 53, 56, 68, 110, 112–14, 131, 133, 184, 231, 274, 299–300, 302, 304, 306, 308, 310, 327, 343
sleep 220
Society of Biblical Literature 17
Song at the Sea (Exodus 15) 237, 252, 272
soul 169–70, 198, 214, 220, 225–28, 246, 256, 274, 279
spirits, *see* angels, spirits, demons
St John's College, Cambridge 9, 12, 165
St Petersburg 307
suffering, *see* persecution, suffering, martyrdom
Sukkot (Tabernacles) 228, 250n, 251n
superstition, *see* magic, superstition, miracles
supplications 233, 235, 247, 253, 291, 301

synagogue 12, 27–28, 39, 41, 56, 68, 144, 152–53, 161, 169, 217–18, 228, 241, 286, 297, 350
Syriac Fathers 52, 61

taḥanun 301, 320
Talmud 3–7, 19–20, 23, 28, 38, 41–42, 56, 58–61, 76, 79, 98–99, 123, 133–34, 138–39, 146, 148–53, 159, 167–74, 177, 189–90, 206, 215–17, 220–23, 226, 228, 231–32, 237–48, 250, 253–55, 260, 264–66, 268–71, 273, 275, 282–87, 292, 297–98, 301–4, 306n, 319–29, 334, 338–43, 346–48, 350
Targum 16, 41, 54, 68, 75, 120, 128, 138, 140, 168n, 169, 181, 187, 316
teacher/ing 1, 10, 18–19, 30, 35–37, 44–45, 51, 54, 58, 67–68, 73, 78, 80, 93, 114n, 149, 152–53, 160, 169–70, 172, 197, 206, 213–15, 217–18, 220, 227–28, 232, 241, 251, 262, 270, 280–81, 292, 308, 315, 319, 323, 334–35, 339, 346–47, 350
tefillin 170
Temple, shrine 17, 23, 30, 64, 91, 145–46, 148–53, 158–61, 176, 190–91, 197–98, 204–7, 214, 225, 228, 236–38, 240, 243, 249–50, 254, 262, 267, 270–71, 274–75, 286–87, 303, 338, 344–45, 347–48, 350
Ten Days of Repentance 247, 249
Tetragrammaton/divine name, *see* also God, name 54, 78, 85, 89, 100
theology, *see* religious ideas/theology
Times 14
Tish'ah BeAv (Ninth of Av) 228, 238, 275n, 289
Toledo 155
Torah reading/Torah study 5, 39, 79, 197–98, 220–21, 226, 232, 250, 268, 281
Torah revelation 38, 40, 46, 64, 68, 145, 171, 217, 228, 250, 262, 268, 283, 319–20, 334, 338
Torah scroll 150
Tyre 63, 159
Tyndale House, Cambridge 301n, 317n

Ugarit 147, 314, 341
Union Theological Seminary 145
United States 14, 17, 47
University of Cambridge 3, 9, 12, 21, 25, 35n, 50, 145, 165
University of Glasgow 165, 180
University of Michigan 147
ushpizin 250n
u-ve-khen 239
uve-maqhalot 235

vengeance, *see* anger/vengeance
virginity 62, 67, 69, 86n, 186

warfare, military matters 54, 79, 113, 118–19, 137, 139–41, 158–59, 167, 184, 200, 203, 216, 224, 278, 280
water(s) 64, 83, 85, 89, 91, 93, 96, 120, 133, 141, 152–53, 159, 175
wine 54, 121, 172
wisdom 5, 91n, 191, 210–28, 261, 279
Wissenchaft des Judentums 1, 46, 210
Wissenschaftsgeschichte 3, 11
women, females and girls 52, 54, 57, 61–62, 64–65, 66–67, 69, 81, 85–87, 86n, 90, 93–94, 96, 97n, 168, 171, 186, 219, 316, 348–49
Woolf Institute 50
work, *see* labour, work
World Congress of Jewish Studies 74
worship, *see* liturgy, worship
wrongdoing, *see* ethical inadequacy, wrongdoing

ya'aleh ve-yavo 240, 267n
yehalelukha 235–36
Yemen/Yemenite rite 241, 244–45, 307–8
yeshivah, *see* academy, yeshivah, bet midrash
Yiddish 10, 13
yishtabaḥ 234–38, 252, 324
Yom Kippur (Day of Atonement) 249–50, 302–3, 306n, 320, 323–24, 341n

Zadokite Document 10–30
Zadokites 17n, 21, 23, 29–30
Zion, *see* Jerusalem/Zion and its restoration

www.ingramcontent.com/pod-product-compliance
Lightning Source LLC
Chambersburg PA
CBHW032134250426
43661CB00077B/1818
9783110636765